The Book of Koheleth,

Commonly called Ecclesiastes

Considered in relation to modern criticism, and
to the doctrines of modern pessimism, with
a critical and grammatical commentary
and a revised translation

Charles H. H. Wright

Alpha Editions

This edition published in 2020

ISBN : 9789354005596

Design and Setting By
Alpha Editions
email - alphaedis@gmail.com

As per information held with us this book is in Public Domain.
This book is a reproduction of an important historical work. Alpha Editions uses the best technology to reproduce historical work in the same manner it was first published to preserve its original nature. Any marks or number seen are left intentionally to preserve its true form.

THE
BOOK OF KOHELETH,

COMMONLY CALLED ECCLESIASTES,

*CONSIDERED IN RELATION TO MODERN CRITICISM, AND
TO THE DOCTRINES OF MODERN PESSIMISM, WITH
A CRITICAL AND GRAMMATICAL COMMENTARY
AND A REVISED TRANSLATION.*

The Donnellan Lectures for 1880-1.

BY THE REV.
CHARLES HENRY HAMILTON WRIGHT, D.D.,
*of Trinity College, Dublin; M.A. of Exeter College, Oxford;
Ph.D. of the University of Leipzig; Incumbent of St. Mary's, Belfast.*

London:
HODDER AND STOUGHTON,
27, PATERNOSTER ROW.
MDCCCLXXXIII.

In Memoriam

OF MY BELOVED PARENTS,

EDWARD WRIGHT, LL.D., BARRISTER-AT-LAW,

OF FLORAVILLE, EGLINTON ROAD, DUBLIN,

AND

CHARLOTTE WRIGHT, HIS WIFE,

WHO ENTERED INTO "THE SAINTS' EVERLASTING REST,"

ON NOVEMBER 1ST, AND MARCH 30TH, 1881, RESPECTIVELY,

AND WHO BOTH TOOK A DEEP INTEREST

IN THESE

DONNELLAN LECTURES.

INTRODUCTION.

THE greater part of the following work consists of the Donnellan Lectures delivered from the pulpit of Trinity College, Dublin, in 1880-1. In a course of lectures, restricted to six in number, it was impossible to do more than allude to several questions which are here more fully discussed. Most of the second chapter, and considerable portions of other chapters were not included in the Donnellan Lectures, and the larger part of that on "the Song of Koheleth," was delivered as a lecture in the Law School of the University of Cambridge, in April, 1882. The publication of Prof. Robertson Smith's Lectures in 1881, on *The Old Testament in the Jewish Church*, and of M. Ernest Renan's work on Ecclesiastes early in 1882, necessitated considerable alterations and additions being made to this work. As in my Bampton Lectures at Oxford, so in the Donnellan Lectures, I did not consider it advisable to throw my dissertations into the shape of ordinary pulpit discourses. Such a form would have fettered the treatment of the subject, and have been entirely unsuited to the object I had in view. That some critics should have blamed this exercise of freedom is only what might have been expected, but I have seen no reason to regret the course taken. Hence the following chapters exhibit few traces of having been delivered as University sermons.

The work will, I believe, be perfectly intelligible to the ordinary English reader, and does not, save in a very few places, require for its comprehension any acquaintance with Hebrew. The grammatical and critical commentary is, of course, mainly designed for the use of students of Hebrew and theology. But an intelligent reader of the English Bible will find, even there, much of which he can avail himself with almost as much ease as the observations in a purely English commentary, if he be not deterred from its perusal by the necessity of having to pass over the critical and grammatical remarks. The grammatical and critical commentary, which ought to be studied in connexion with the translation of the Book of Koheleth on pp. 283-304, will be considered by some too copious, and yet there are defects in it, which could have been amended, had it not been necessary to curtail the work as much as possible. I trust that, even as it is, it may be useful to those engaged in Biblical researches, and may help in some measure to raise the tone of Hebrew scholarship in this country.

I have not attempted to conceal the obligations which I have been under to scholars of almost every school of thought. I have freely availed myself of their writings, and have striven to do full justice to the opinions of those from whom I have felt constrained to differ. For myself, I firmly adhere to the doctrine which I have always held, namely, that the Holy Scriptures contain a Divine revelation, and that God has of old time spoken unto men "by divers portions and in divers manners" (Heb. i. 1) through the writers whose books compose the Old and New Testament (see p. 200). I deeply regret the want of scholarship too often exhibited in this country on the part of many, who, however, hold much which I believe to be true; and I deplore the suspicion with which all higher Biblical researches are regarded in many quarters where they ought to be most warmly welcomed and prized. It is not, I confess, without some feelings of regret that I have felt myself constrained, by the evidence adduced by modern critics, to abandon the traditional view of the Solomonic authorship of the Book of Ecclesiastes. But I do not consider the canonical character of the book, or its Divine inspiration, to be at all affected by the abandonment of a theory at variance with the linguistic features of the book, as well as with internal evidence, and with the statements of its epilogue, when rightly understood. In the investigation of many questions connected with the Sacred Volume the Christian theologian will act wisely to hold aloof from the adoption of those popular theories of inspiration which only fetter and encumber him, when seeking to defend "the truth once delivered to the saints." The cautious remarks on this point of the Rev. Professor Charteris of Edinburgh (a theologian whose orthodoxy is above suspicion) in his recent popular volume on *The New Testament Scriptures: their Claims, History, and Authority* (London, 1882), are worthy of the attention of those who falsely imagine that the truth of Scripture depends upon the acceptance of some special theory of inspiration.

In the brief, but thoughtful and suggestive, commentary of Mr. Tyler on the Book of Ecclesiastes (Williams & Norgate, 1874), an attempt has been made to prove that the author of the book was acquainted with the writings of the Greek philosophers. Notwithstanding some interesting and curious coincidences of thought, most of which will be found noted in the course of our work, I cannot but concur in the opinion arrived at by scholars, differing so widely in opinion as Delitzsch and Renan, that no real trace of Greek influence can be pointed out. Zirkel's former attempt to discover Græcisms in the Book of Ecclesiastes has been admitted to have been a failure even by Graetz, though the latter scholar has endeavoured to show that a few of the instances adduced by Zirkel are genuine. Plumptre has, however, exhibited a disposition to adopt partially at least the view advocated by Tyler. And, if I am not mistaken, the theory of the close connexion of the Book of Ecclesiastes with Greek thought is likely shortly to be presented in a more developed form by an able Continental scholar. We shall wait to see what new arguments will be adduced by that writer. But the intimation I have received on this point has made me indisposed prematurely to re-open a discussion, which for the present may be considered as closed.

In the sixth and seventh chapters I have ventured to contrast the teachings of the Book of Koheleth, which are unquestionably in some aspects pessimistic, with the conclusions arrived at by the writers of the modern school of Philosophic Pessimism. Notwithstanding the raciness and brilliancy which characterize the writings of Schopenhauer and von Hartmann, I cannot but regard the appearance of such a school of philosophy as not only one of the most remarkable, but also one of the saddest phenomena of the present age. The doctrines of Modern Pessimism are certain soon to attract in England more notice than they have yet received. For two of the most important writings of that school, Schopenhauer's *Welt als Wille und Vorstellung*, and von Hartmann's *Philosophie des Unbewussten*, will shortly appear in an English translation in the Philosophical Library series of Messrs. Trübner & Co. The vigour of style of those authors, and the novelty and boldness of their conclusions, are certain to awaken as much discussion in this country as they have called forth in Germany. It is moreover a sad fact, admitted by advocates of that philosophy, that the disregard shown by Schopenhauer and von Hartmann for what some persons are pleased to speak of merely as "the conventionalities of society,"—and the plain-spoken manner in which matters are discussed, of which the Apostle was constrained to remark, "it is a shame even to speak of those things which are done of them in secret" (Eph. v. 12),— have attracted a vast number of readers who do not generally

Introduction.

trouble themselves with philosophical speculations. In a work of this kind, it would have been quite out of place to enter into any formal refutation of that philosophy. My object has been mainly to point out, from these and other writings of the philosophers referred to, the conclusions at which they have arrived, conclusions destructive not only of faith, but of morality,—to show the source from whence some of their principles have been derived, and to contrast them with the teaching of the sacred Jewish philosopher, whom Schopenhauer and other writers of his school vainly claim as a precursor.

It may be well, however, to call attention not only to the important works published in England on this subject by Mr. Sully and Dr. M. M. Kalisch (of which considerable use has been made in the following pages), but also to refer to a work, little known on this side of the Atlantic, by Professor Bowen, of Harvard College, Cambridge, United States, namely, *Modern Philosophy, from Descartes to Schopenhauer and Hartmann* (3rd edit., New York, 1877), in which Modern Pessimism is treated from a philosophical and Christian point of view. Of more importance, however, is the vigorous and able essay, recently published by Professor Barlow of Trinity College, Dublin, entitled *The Ultimatum of Pessimism: an Ethical Study* (London: Kegan Paul, Trench & Co., 1882). Though written from a purely philosophic standpoint, this work deserves the attention of theologians, and cannot fail to interest even the general reader. The quiet manner in which Mr. Barlow's *reductio ad absurdum* of some of von Hartmann's speculations is conducted is worthy of all commendation. Mr. Barlow's book was published too late to permit of its being made use of in the present work. It must be noted that it is difficult to define what Pessimism really means. The term is generally employed throughout the following work in the sense in which it is used by Schopenhauer, although the further development of Pessimism as represented in the writings of von Hartmann has been duly noted. I observe that Mr. Barlow has drawn attention to the argument in favour of Pessimism against Christianity arising from the exaggerations of theologians on questions concerning which little has been revealed in sacred Scripture. See his remarks on p. 24 of his essay, and compare our note on p. 179. Illogical and unscientific, when thoroughly examined into, as many of the conclusions of the Pessimist philosophers may be, I cannot but believe that their philosophy is but the natural outcome of atheism. There are, indeed, few halting places on the terrible road which begins with the denial of the existence of the Eternal,—too often because men do not like to retain God in their knowledge (Rom. i. 28), and long to cast away from them the bands and cords of religion (Ps. ii. 3),—and that "reprobate mind" which generally leads men to do those "things which are not fitting" (Rom. i. 28), and finally conducts them to the precipice over which they not unfrequently hurl themselves by suicide.

The literature which has been evoked in Germany on this subject is far too extensive to be mentioned here. Some of these works will be found referred to in the following pages. It may be useful to call attention to the thoughtful work of Professor Gass of Heidelberg, entitled, *Optimismus und Pessimismus: der Gang der christlichen Welt- und Lebensansicht* (Berlin, 1876).

In the treatment of this important subject,—superficially though it has been handled by me,—I have to acknowledge my obligations to my friend Pastor Dr. Hermann Ferdinand von Criegern, of the S. Thomaskirche, Leipzig, an able scholar as well as an earnest and eloquent pastor, whose lately published work on *Johann Comenius als Theolog* (Leipzig, 1881), will, it is to be hoped, not be his last contribution to theological literature.

Introduction. xiii

It was originally my intention to have affixed to the work a sketch of the extensive literature in connexion with the Book of Koheleth. But inasmuch as, notwithstanding all my efforts to compress this volume into smaller compass, it has grown unduly large, I must reserve the carrying out of this project for some other opportunity. I have given up the idea for the present with less reluctance on account of the valuable historical sketch of the exegesis of the book, both Jewish and Christian, given by Dr. Ginsburg in his *Historical and Critical Commentary*, published in 1861. The list of works on Ecclesiastes compiled by Dr. Ginsburg has been considerably added to by Delitzsch, in the Einleitung to his *Commentary*, which is, in my opinion, the ablest and most instructive which has yet appeared on this portion of the Old Testament. Zöckler has made important additions to the catalogue in his contribution to Lange's *Bibelwerk*, and it has in turn been considerably added to in the American edition of Zöckler's work by the late Prof. Tayler Lewis, which appears in the series of Lange's *Commentary*, published not only in America, but also by Messrs. T. & T. Clark, of Edinburgh.

I shall therefore content myself with mentioning the commentaries chiefly used in the execution of this work, observing only that many others have been occasionally consulted by me in the library of Trinity College, Dublin. Owing to the pressure of other public duties, I have not had the opportunity of prosecuting my researches as widely as I would have desired. It is, however, scarcely necessary to make any apology for passing over without special mention most of the popular Commentaries of the Bible in general use in this country. True exegesis must be built upon a thorough grammatical and critical examination of the original text, a point generally neglected in those commentaries. The main object of my work, moreover, was to exhibit the results arrived at by modern criticism, and it would have been impossible in any reasonable compass to have noted either the mistakes or the excellencies of such writers as Bishop Reynolds, Matthew Henry, and Thomas Scott; or of the more recent popular expositions of Ecclesiastes, such as those of Hamilton, Wardlaw, and Buchanan. This work does not profess to be an exhaustive treatise on the subject. Some commentators of considerable eminence I have been obliged to quote at second-hand, and consequently their works are not included in the subjoined list.

Arnheim, H., Transl. in the German Version of the Old Testament, by Zunz, Arnheim, Fürst and Sachs, 8th edit. (Berlin, 1864). *Bauer, Ch. F.*, Erläuterter Grundtext vom Prediger Salomo, etc. (Leipzig, 1732). *Bernstein, H. G.*, Quæstiones nonnullæ Kohelethanæ (Vratislav, 1854). *Bloch, J. S.*, Ursprung und Entstehungszeit des Buches Kohelet (Bamberg, 1872); Studien zur Geschichte der Samml. der alt-heb. Lit. (Leipzig, 1875). *Bleek, Fried.*, Einleitung in das Alte Test., 2te Aufl. (Berlin, 1865), and 4te Aufl. by Wellhausen (Berlin, 1878). *Boehl, Ed.*, De Aramaismis Libri Koheleth (Erlang., 1860). *Bunsen, C. C. J.*, Vollständiges Bibelwerk (Leipzig, 1858-69). *Bridges, Rev. Charles, M.A.*, Exposition of the Book of Ecclesiastes (London, 1860). *Böttcher, Fried.*, Proben alttest. Schrifterklärung (Leipzig, 1833); Exeg.-kritische Aehrenlese zum alten Test. (Leipzig, 1849); Neue exeg.-kritische Aehrenlese zum A.T. (Leipzig, 1863, 1864); De Inferis rebusque post mortem futuris (Dresden, 1846). *Critici Sacri* (Frankf., 1695). *Bullock, Rev. W. T., M.A.*, Comm. and Critical Notes on Ecclesiastes, in the Speaker's Commentary (London, 1878). *Cox, Samuel, D.D.*, The Quest of the Chief Good; Expository Lectures on the Book of Ecclesiastes with a New Translation: A Commentary for Laymen (London, n.d., but published in 1867). *Dathe, J. A.*, Job, Prov., Eccl., and Cant., Latine versi notisque illust. (Halle, 1789). *Dale, Rev. T. P., M.A.*, A Commentary on Ecclesiastes (Lond. and Camb., 1873). *Davidson, Dr. S.*, Introduction to the Old Test. (Lond., 1862, 1863). *Derenbourg, J.*, Notes détachées sur l'Ecclésiaste, 1880, see note 1, p. 190. *Delitzsch, Prof. Dr. Franz*, see *General Index*. *Elster, Ernst*, Commentar über den Prediger Salomo (Göttingen, 1855). *von Essen, Ludwig*, Der Prediger Salomos (Schaffhausen, 1856). *Ewald, Prof. H.*, see *General Index*. *Fürst, Prof. J.*, Der Kanon des alt. Test. nach den Ueberlieferungen in Talmud u. Midrasch (Leipzig, 1868), see *General Index*. *Given, Prof. Dr.*, Truth of Scripture in connection with Revelation, etc. (Edinb., 1881). *Ginsburg, Dr. C. D.*, Coheleth, commonly called the Book of Ecclesiastes, with comm., hist. and crit. (London, 1861). *Graetz, Dr. H.*, Kohélet oder der Salomonische Prediger übersetzt und kritisch erläutert (Leipzig, 1871); Monatsschrift für Gesch. u. Wissenschaft des Judenthums. *Geiger, Dr. Abraham*, Urschrift u. Uebersetzungen der Bibel (Breslau, 1857); Jüdische Zeitschrift (Breslau, 1862-1875). *Hengstenberg, Dr. E. W.*, Comm. on Ecclesiastes, Engl. Transl. by D. W. Simon (Edinb. 1860). *Hävernick, H. A. C.*, Einleitung in das alt. Test., 2te Aufl. by Keil (Frankf., 1854). *Hahn, Dr. Heinr. Aug.*, Commentar über das Predigerbuch Salomos (Leipzig, 1860). *Heiligstedt, Aug.*, Comm. gramm., hist. crit. in Eccles. (1848), in Maurer's Comm. in Vet. Test. *Herzfeld, Dr. L.*, Coheleth übersetzt u. erläutert (Braunschweig, 1838). *Hitzig, Dr. Ferd.*, Der Prediger Salomos erklärt; in the Kurzgef. exeget. Handb. z. A. T. (Leipzig, 1847). *Hoelemann, Prof. Dr.*, Bibelstudien. This work I have only quoted second-hand. I have, however, used his Exeget. Adversarien in the *Sächsisches Kirchen- u. Schulblatt* for 1882. *Janichs, Dr. G.*, Animadversiones Criticæ in vers. Syriacam Peschitt. Libb. Koheleth et Ruth (Vratisl., 1871). *Johnston, Rev. David*, A Treatise on the Authorship of Ecclesiastes (Macmillan & Co., 1880), issued anonymously, see p. 114. *Kaiser, Dr. G. P. C. K.*

Introduction.

Koheleth, das Collectivum der Davidischen Könige in Jerusalem (Erlangen, 1823). *Kalisch, Dr. M. M.*, Path and Goal : A Discussion on the Elements of Civilisation and the Conditions of Happiness [with a translation of the Book of Ecclesiastes] (London, 1880). *Kleinert, Dr. P.*, Der Prediger Salomo, Uebersetzung, sprachliche Bemerkungen u. Erörterungen zum Verständniss (Berlin, 1864). *Knobel, August*, Commentar über das Buch Koheleth (Leipzig, 1836). *Leathes*, Prof. Stanley, see n. on p. 114. *Lewis, Prof. Tayler* (see under *Zöckler*). *Luther, Martin*, German Version of the Bible; Exeg. Opera Latina cura Irmischer et Schmidt, vol. xxi. (Erlang., 1858), Ecclesiastes cum annotat. *Meyer, J. H.*, Comm. Exegetica in Koh. xi. 1–6 (Heilbronn, 1803). *Perowne, J. J. S., Dean of Peterborough*, Articles in "The Expositor" for 1879. *Plumptre, E. H., Dean of Wells*, Ecclesiastes, or the Preacher, with Notes and Introduction (Cambridge, 1881), see p. 133. *Poli, Matthæi*, Synopsis Criticorum (London, 1699–1674). *Preston, Theodore*, Ecclesiastes, Hebrew Text and a Latin Version, with original Notes philol. and exeget. and a Transl. of the Comm. of Mendelssohn (London, 1845). *Renan, Ernest*, L'Ecclésiaste traduit de l'Hébreu avec une Étude sur l'age et le caractère du livre (Paris, 1882). *Rosenmüller, E. F. C.*, Scholia in Vet. Test., Koheleth and Cant. (Lipsiæ, 1830). *Schäfer, Dr. Bernhard*, Neue Untersuchungen über das Buch Koheleth (Freiburg in Breisgau, 1870). *Stähelin, J. J.*, Specielle Einleitung in die kanon. Bücher des A.T. (Elberfeld, 1862). *Strack, Prof. H. L.*, Einleitung in das A.T., in the Handbuch der theolog. Wissenschaften (Nördlingen, 1882). See *General Index*. *Taylor, Dr. C.*, The Dirge of Coheleth in Eccl. xii., discussed and literally interpreted (London, 1874). See *General Index*. *Tyler, Thomas, M.A.*, Some New Evidence as to the Date of Ecclesiastes (London, 1872); Ecclesiastes : A Contribution to its Interpretation, with Introd., Exeget.

Introduction. xvii

Analysis and Transl., with Notes (Lond., 1874). *Umbreit, F. W. C.*, Koheleth's des weisen Königs Seelenkampf, oder philos. Betrachtungen über das höchste Gut (Gotha, 1818); Coheleth Scepticus de summo bono : Comment. philos.-critica (Gottingæ, 1820). *Vaihinger, J. G.*, Der Prediger und das Hohelied (Stuttgart, 1848). *Wordsworth, Bishop*, Holy Bible in the Auth. Version with Notes and Introd.: Proverbs, Ecclesiastes, and Song of Solomon (Lond., 1872). *Wardlaw, Ralph, D.D.*, Lectures on the Book of Ecclesiastes (Edin., 1821). *Winzer, J. F.*, Comm. de Koh. xi. 9—xii. 7. Three parts (Leipzig, 1818, 1819). *Young, Rev. Loyal, D.D.*, A Commentary on the Book of Ecclesiastes (Philadelphia, 1865). *Zirkel, G.*, Untersuchungen über den Prediger nebst kritischen und philolog. Bemerkungen (Würzburg, 1792). *Zöckler, Prof. Otto*, Das Hohelied u. der Prediger, theologisch-homiletisch bearbeitet in Lange's Bibelwerk (Bielefeld and Leipzig, 1868); American edition, with annotations, dissertations, etc., by Prof. Tayler Lewis, LL.D., of Schenectady, N.Y. (Edin., 1872).

The General Index will show the books which have been consulted on questions affecting the text, and on other subjects. It is only here necessary to observe that, alongside of Field's splendid edition of *Origen's Hexapla* (Oxon. 1875), which has been used for the Greek versions, I have used Nestle's (E.) *Vet. Test. Græc. Codd. Vat. et Sin. cum textu recepto collati*, Lee's edition of the *Syriac Peschitto*, and for the Targum, Walton's *Polyglott*, along with de Lagarde's edition of the same (*Hagiographa Chaldaice*, Lipsiæ, 1873).

On questions of Hebrew Grammar I have uniformly referred to the last and most valuable edition of *Gesenius's Heb. Grammatik*, the 23rd "vielfach verbesserte u. vermehrte Auflage," edited by Kautzsch (Leipzig, 1881), though in almost all cases the references can be verified in the earlier editions. It has been necessary occasionally to refer to

Introduction.

Gesenius's *Lehrgebäude der Heb. Sprache* (1817). Side by side with Kautzsch's edition of Gesenius (noted as *Ges.-Kautzsch*), references have been given to Kalisch's *Hebrew Grammar* (London, 1862, 1863),—the sections numbered with Arabic numerals refer to the first vol., those in Roman numerals to the second,—and also to Ewald's *Ausführl. Lehrbuch*, 8th edit. (Göttingen, 1870). English students have now the inestimable advantage of possessing an excellent translation of the more important part of Ewald's great work in the edition of *Ewald's Syntax of the Hebrew Language of the Old Test.*, translated from the 8th German edition, by James Kennedy, B.D. (Edinb., T. & T. Clark, 1879), to which reference can be made without difficulty. I have also used Olshausen's *Lehrbuch der Heb. Sprache* (Braunschweig, 1861), Philippi's sagacious work on the *Wesen und Ursprung des Stat. Constructus in Hebräischen* (Weimar, 1871), and more especially Driver's (S. R., now Regius Professor of Hebrew at Oxford) most instructive *Treatise on the Use of the Tenses in Hebrew*, 2nd edit., 1881. I would gladly have made much more frequent reference to these works had space permitted, and if grammatical commentaries were more popular in England. But it is to be feared that such notes as are here appended, while they increase the bulk of the volume, may considerably lessen its sale. Böttcher's *Ausführl. Lehrbuch*, edited by Mühlau (Leipzig, 1866, 1868), has necessarily often been referred to, as well as the two most recent works on Hebrew grammar, namely, Stade's (Professor Bernhard, of the University of Giessen) *Lehrbuch der Heb. Grammatik*, Erster Theil (Leipzig, 1879), and Prof. Dr. Friedrich E. König's *Historischkritisches Lehrgebäude der Heb. Sprache*, Erste Hälfte (Leipzig, 1881), both original works well worthy of careful study.

For the Babylonian Talmud I have generally used the very convenient edition of the same in 25 quarto vols. recently completed in Warsaw (Sussman u. Wolf Jabez), the pagination of which coincides with the earlier editions. For the Jerusalem Talmud I have employed the folio edition issued in Krotoschin in 1865. The text of the Midrash Rabboth has been cited from the Warsaw edition printed by Goldman in 1867. I need scarcely say that I have availed myself of the valuable work of Dr. Aug. Wünsche, *Bibliotheca Rabbinica: Eine Sammlung alter Midraschim zum ersten Male in Deutsche übertragen*, a work which, though defective in some particulars, is not to be judged as a whole by the portion on the Midrash Koheleth, which is its weakest part, and which no doubt will be greatly improved when a second edition is called for.

I have to apologise for the want of uniformity in the transliteration of Hebrew words and proper names in my work. It has partly arisen from the fact that I had not the advantage of being able to revise the work as a whole before sending it to press. The duties of my clerical profession,—largely increased by the present state of things in Ireland,—which have entailed upon me weekly often five or six sermons or addresses, besides the work of pastoral visitation in a very large and populous town district, the building of large schools connected with my parish, opened only a month ago; all these, and many other duties also, involving incessant interruptions, have rendered it exceedingly difficult to execute a work of this kind, requiring such constant care. Possibly at some future time I may have an opportunity of devoting my main energies to Old Testament studies. Meanwhile, under circumstances of considerable difficulty, I have endeavoured in this, as in my previous commentaries, to help forward the important work of Old Testament criticism which has been for a long time sadly neglected in our country.

With regard to the translation given on pp. 280–304 of

this work, it may be well here to observe that a few notes have been added in thin brackets. It has been my endeavour there to give the results of modern criticism. In reply to the charge, often recklessly preferred, of "needlessly departing" from our Authorized Version, I would refer to p. ix. of the preface of my Bampton Lectures. In every attempt to translate faithfully the work of an ancient author the ruggedness of the original must occasionally reflect itself in the translation. The headings assigned to the various sections of the Book of Koheleth will, it is hoped, be useful; while a general synopsis of the subjects touched on by the Sacred Writer can be obtained from the "contents" on pp. xxii. xxiii. The explanation of several technical words employed in this work may be obtained by the help of the Index.

I have in conclusion to acknowledge my warmest thanks to my dear friend, Professor Dr. Franz Delitzsch of the University of Leipzig, for most kindly revising the proof-sheets of this work while passing through the press. Several valuable remarks of his have been embodied in the notes. I have also to acknowledge with grateful thanks the readiness with which Professor Dr. H. L. Strack of the University of Berlin undertook the same kind service, and the important help I have in many places received from him. The responsibility of the work is, however, solely and entirely my own. Professor Dr. William Wright, of Cambridge, has kindly given me the benefit of his opinion on many points, though unable to undertake as a whole the revision of the proof-sheets. Mr. R. L. Bensly of Caius and Gonville College, Cambridge, has afforded me much assistance in the correction of the proofs, as has also Rev. T. J. Corr, M.A., Ex-S.T.C.D., Curate of the Magdalen Church, Belfast.

ANTRIM ROAD, BELFAST,
Feb. 20th, 1883.

CONTENTS.

CHAPTER I.
THE ADMISSION OF THE BOOK OF KOHELETH INTO THE CANON OF THE JEWISH CHURCH 3

CHAPTER II.
THE BOOK OF KOHELETH AND THE BOOK OF JESUS THE SON OF SIRACH 31

CHAPTER III.
THE BOOK OF WISDOM AND THE BOOK OF KOHELETH . 55

CHAPTER IV.
THE AUTHORSHIP OF THE BOOK OF KOHELETH . . . 79

CHAPTER V.
THE AUTHORSHIP OF THE BOOK OF KOHELETH (*continued*) . 109

CHAPTER VI.
THE PESSIMISM OF THE BOOK OF KOHELETH AND THAT OF SCHOPENHAUER AND VON HARTMANN . . . 141

Supplementary Note on Buddhism . . 182

CHAPTER VII.
THE PESSIMISM OF THE BOOK OF KOHELETH, ESPECIALLY IN RELATION TO A FUTURE STATE AND THE CHARACTER OF WOMEN, CONTRASTED WITH MODERN PESSIMISM 187

CHAPTER VIII.
THE CLOSING SECTION OF THE BOOK OF KOHELETH—THE DAYS OF LIFE AND THE DAYS OF DEATH . . . 217

THE BOOK OF KOHELETH: A NEW TRANSLATION, ARRANGED IN SECTIONS, WITH A CRITICAL AND GRAMMATICAL COMMENTARY:—

 Preliminary Note on the title Koheleth 279
 The Jewish Division of the Book 282

THE NEW TRANSLATION 283–304

 § 1. The absolute vanity of everything earthly—Earthly phenomena like a circle with no real progress . 283
 § 2. Koheleth's first discovery—The vanity of wisdom . 284
 § 3. Koheleth's second discovery—The vanity of pleasure and riches 284
 § 4. Koheleth's third discovery—
  (*a*) The vanity of wisdom, since the end of the wise man and the fool is alike . . . 285
  (*b*) Riches, though obtained by much toil, are vanity 286
  (*c*) The conditions necessary for cheerful enjoyment 287
 § 5. The short-sightedness and powerlessness of men before God, the Disposer and Arranger of all things 287
 § 6. The unrighteous actions of men when left to themselves—Men compared to the beasts that perish . 288
 § 7. The misery common to man—
  (*a*) The oppression of man by his fellow . . 289
  (*b*) The rivalry and useless toil of man . . 289
 § 8. The disadvantages of a man being alone by himself, and the benefit of companionship . . . 290
 § 9. The vanity of popular enthusiasm for a new monarch 290
 § 10. Vanity in religion—Divine worship, and vows . 291
 § 11. The vanity of riches (*a*) in a state under despotic rule; (*b*) riches are little advantage in themselves, and (*c*) are gathered for others . . . 291
 § 12. The ultimatum—The vanity of possessing riches without enjoying them 292
 § 13. The insatiability of desire 293
 § 14. Human powerlessness and short-sightedness with respect to destiny 293
 § 15. Proverbs concerning things to be preferred by man . 294

		PAGE
§ 16.	Patience and wisdom the best preservatives in the time of oppression and adversity	294
§ 17.	The importance of keeping "the middle mean," and the practical advantages of wisdom . . .	295
§ 18.	The snare by which men are generally caught—The wicked woman	295
§ 19.	The benefit of wisdom in days of oppression—The wise man will be obedient and patient, knowing that there is a God who judgeth the earth . .	296
§ 20.	Man knows not the work of God, but is in all things conditioned by a higher power than his own, which permits the same things to happen to all alike	297
§ 21.	The fate that awaits all, the state of the dead—Men ought therefore to enjoy life, while working for their daily bread—The uncertainties of life, and the certainty of death in an unexpected time .	298
§ 22.	The poor wise man, and the benefits of wisdom .	299
§ 23.	The usefulness of wisdom and the danger of folly, shown by various proverbs	299
§ 24.	The fool noted for his useless talk and aimless toil	300
§ 25.	The misery of a land cursed with a foolish king, and the necessity of prudence in the subjects of such a monarch	301
§ 26.	The wisdom of beneficence—The future belongs to God, but man ought to labour and enjoy life while he can	301
§ 27.	The Song of Koheleth—The Days of Life and the Days of Death	302
§ 28.	The Epilogue	303

GRAMMATICAL AND CRITICAL COMMENTARY . . 305–448

APPENDIX :—

Excursus I. The statements of the Talmud with respect to the Old Testament Canon in general, and specially in reference to the Hagiographa 451

§ 1. The Tradition as to the Canon 451
§ 2. The Threefold Division of the Jewish Scriptures . 458
§ 3. The Aboth of R. Nathan 465
§ 4. The Book of Ben Sira 467
§ 5. The Book of Koheleth 469

		PAGE
Excursus II. On the Talmudic statement that "the Holy Scriptures defile the hands"	. . . .	470
Excursus III. "The Men of the Great Synagogue"	. .	475
Excursus IV. § 1. Grammatical peculiarities of the Book of Koheleth	. . . .	488
§ 2. Glossary of Hebrew words, phrases, and forms peculiar to the Book of Koheleth	. . . .	490
INDEX OF TEXTS ILLUSTRATED	. . . . .	501
GENERAL INDEX	. . . .	506

ERRATA.

Page.
- 51. Line 7 from bottom, add a comma before "cod. B."
- 58. Line 7 of note read ῆ.
- 83. Line 10 from bottom read "synonym for wisdom."
- 94. Last line read "fact!" for "fact ï."
- 131. Line 18 add a comma after "godliness."
- 134. Line 9 delete comma after "soon."
- 137. Line 15 from bottom read "taught" for "thought."
- 318. Line 16 read "Isa." for "Jer."
- 345. Line 13 from bottom read اَلْفَاظُ مُتَرَادِفَةٌ and נִרְדָּפִים
- 348. Line 7 from top remove comma before "instances."
- 356. Line 9 from bottom read "*whose head he is.*"
- 367. Line 9. ,, read "12" in place of "13."
- ,, Line 8 ,, read "Nah. for "Neh."
- 368. Line 5 add "13" at beginning of line.
- 388. Line 14 read צְדָקָה
- 426. Line 5 read "Sirach (xii. 13)."

ADDENDA.

- 41. Notice additional remarks on Sirach xii. 13, on p. 426.
- 56. Line 1 of notes, add: See a paper by Prof. J. E. B. Mayor, upon the history of the phrase "the four cardinal virtues," in the Transactions of the Cambridge Philological Society, vol. i. p. 96.
- 343. On chap. iii. 11, notice additional remark on p. 437.

CHAPTER I.

THE ADMISSION OF THE BOOK OF KOHELETH INTO THE CANON OF THE JEWISH CHURCH.

CHAPTER I.

The tradition of the Talmud, 3—Hezekiah and his religious reforms, 3—His college of scribes, 4—Succeeded by the men of the Great Synagogue, 5—Their work with respect to the Canon, 5—Views of Kuenen and Robertson Smith as to the legendary character of that tradition, 6—Summary of their leading arguments, 7—Arguments in favour of its historical truth, 8—The testimonies of the Talmud, 9—The early difficulties felt with regard to the Book of Ecclesiastes, 12—These difficulties, according to tradition, solved by the men of the Great Synagogue, 11, 13—The later contests with respect to Ecclesiastes between the schools of Hillel and Shammai, 14—The book admitted into the Canon previous to that controversy, 15—Explanation of the point in dispute, 16—"The Holy Scriptures defile the hands," 16—The canonicity of the Book of Ecclesiastes, 18—The Herodian theory of Professor Graetz, 19—The Book of Ecclesiastes quoted as canonical in the interview between Herod the Great and Ben Būta, 19—And in the discussion respecting the Messianic age between Gamaliel and his disciple, 22 ff.—Probabilities in favour of that disciple having been St. Paul, 22, 24, note—The Book of Ecclesiastes prior to the Herodian era, 24—The Antilegomena of the Old and New Testament Canons, 26.

THE BOOK OF KOHELETH,

IN RELATION TO MODERN CRITICISM AND MODERN PESSIMISM.

CHAPTER I.

THE ADMISSION OF THE BOOK OF KOHELETH INTO THE CANON OF THE JEWISH CHURCH.

"MOSES received the law from Sinai, and delivered it to Joshua, and Joshua to the elders, and the elders to the prophets, and the prophets to the men of the Great Synagogue." Such are the opening words of the remarkable treatise of the Talmud, entitled Massecheth Aboth, "the Sayings of the Fathers," often termed Pirke Aboth, or "the Chapters of the Fathers." The Prophets and the men of the Great Synagogue were, according to the Talmudic tradition, important links in the line of succession, not only of the Law, but also of the other Sacred Writings of the Jews.

In the latter days of the Jewish monarchy, Hezekiah was remarkable for the extent and boldness of his religious reforms. He restored the true religion of Jahaveh, the precepts and ritual of which had been disregarded in the dark days of Ahaz, and suppressed the open practice of idolatry throughout the land. But while he brake down the carved and molten images erected in every place, and according to the Jewish tradition [1] destroyed the books of sorcery and incantations then current among the people, he also manifested the utmost concern in all matters connected with the preservation of the Sacred Writings of the nation. For this purpose, as may be inferred from Proverbs xxv. 1, he organized a special company of learned men interested in the study of that ancient literature. They busied themselves in collecting from all sides the Sacred Writings then extant, and in multiplying copies of those books. Under their superintendence a considerable number of the proverbs of Solomon, not previously included in the Book of Proverbs, were rescued from oblivion and added to the original collection. On account of such labours Hezekiah has been justly styled by a great modern critic and expositor, "the Pisistratus of Israelitish Literature." [2]

This important company, or College of Scribes, entitled in the Proverbs, "the men of Hezekiah king of Judah" (inasmuch as the society was originally founded by that monarch), continued to exist as a Jewish institution for several centuries. It may have lasted, under some form or other, down to and during the period of the exile. According to the Talmud,

---

[1] According to the traditions mentioned in Berach. 10 b, and Pesach. 56 a, Hezekiah "hid a Book of Remedies" (גנז ספר רפואות), or, according to the Jer. Sanhedr. I. 18 d, "a Table of Remedies" (טבלה של רפואות), in order that the people might seek to God in sickness for recovery, and not look to the physicians (2 Chron. xvi. 12). The old remedies for disease probably consisted in great part of incantations. Vid. Gideon Brecher, *Das Transcendentales, Magie u. magische Heilarten im Talmud*, Wien, 1850; D. Joel, *Der Aberglaube und die Stellung des Judenthums zu demselben*, 1 Heft, Breslau, 1881. Dukes, in the introduction to his *Rabb. Blumenlese*, however, notes that the remarks of Ben Sira in honour of physicians (in Sirach xxxviii. 1 ff) were intended to counteract the prejudice against the use of medicines, probably based on a mistaken view of Exodus xv. 26. Ben Sira, however, also urges on the sick at the same time the duty of prayer (Sirach xxxviii. 9, 10). The recommendation of St. James (v. 14, 15), which urges prayer combined with the use of the best known remedies (such as the anointing with oil, Luke xi. 34) seems directly or indirectly to have been based on the maxim of Ben Sira; see chap. ii. p. 49.

[2] See Delitzsch's *Comm. über das Salomonische Spruchbuch*, in loco.

"Hezekiah and his college wrote Isaiah, Proverbs, Song of Songs and Koheleth" (Baba Bathra, 15 a).[1] This statement is not to be regarded as a stupid anachronism. The fact that Hezekiah died previous to Isaiah was not forgotten, and the word "wrote" was probably used in the sense of "copied out and edited." For the College of Hezekiah continued in existence for centuries after the death of that monarch. "The men of Hezekiah" appear to have employed themselves in editing correct copies of the Sacred Writings, and while doing so to have occasionally, as in the case of the Book of Proverbs, added new matter to the old.[2] It is highly probable that this body decided from time to time what books were to be regarded as of Divine authority. Fürst estimates the period of its activity as extending from B.C. 724, when Hezekiah ascended the throne of Judah, to B.C. 444, when Nehemiah became governor of Judæa. "The men of Hezekiah" no doubt included in their number some of the "former prophets" (Zech. i. 4) and others known afterwards as "the latter prophets." Hence that company may, perhaps, be referred to in the passage quoted from the Treatise Aboth, under the general term of "the Prophets."

According to the tradition referred to, "the men of the Great Synagogue" in later days discharged the functions performed in earlier times by "the men of Hezekiah." The establishment of the Great Synagogue is generally ascribed to Ezra. The accounts given of its origin and acts cannot, indeed, in all points be relied on as historically correct. Part of the work said to have been accomplished by the members of this body is thus described by Rashi: "The men

---

[1] See Excursus on the Talmud and the Old Testament Canon.

[2] Ewald considers it probable that nine Psalms contained in the first book of the Psalms (Ps. i–xli.), namely, Psalms vi., xiii., xv., xx., xxi., xxiii., xxvii., xxx., xli., may have been out of a collection arranged by Hezekiah. See Ewald's *Gesch.*, vol. iii. p. 654 [vol. iv. p. 198 of the English translation by J. Estlin Carpenter], etc.; Fürst's *Bibl. Lit.*, vol. ii. p. 369.

of the Great Synagogue, namely, Haggai, Zechariah and Malachi, seeing that Ezekiel and Daniel had died during the Babylonian Exile, and that the books of the twelve minor Prophets, as also the history of Esther, were of small size, wrote out these anew from the books of the exile and formed the twelve into one book, in order that the single books might not be lost on account of their small size, and thus Esther and the four other books, Ruth, Koheleth, Song of Songs, and Lamentations, were united together. But they did so because they knew that after them the prophetic spirit would depart from Israel." See his Comm. on Baba Bathra, 15 a.

Kuenen has, indeed, ably maintained that the whole story of "the men of the Great Synagogue," and of their work in reference to the Canon of the Old Testament, is a legend utterly devoid of any real historical truth.[1] Professor Robertson Smith has adopted the same view, and regards Kuenen's arguments as conclusive. It has, in his opinion, "been proved in the clearest manner that the origin of the legend of the Great Synagogue is derived from the account given in Nehemiah viii. ix. of the great convocation which met at Jerusalem and subscribed the covenant to observe the Law. It was, therefore, a meeting and not a permanent authority. It met once for all, and everything that is told about it, except what we read in Nehemiah, is pure fable of the later Jews."[2]

Such a conclusion is, however, not justified by the facts of the case. It is true indeed that much of that which tradition asserts to have been performed by "the men of the Great Synagogue" proves, when carefully examined into, to be merely a repetition with legendary accompaniments of

---

[1] A. Kuenen, *Over de Mannen der Groote Synagoge.—Verslagen en Mededeelingen der Koninklijke Akademie van Wetenschappen.* Afdeeling Letterkunde. Tweede Reeks. Zesde Deel. Tweede Stuk. 1876.

[2] See his work on *The Old Testament in the Jewish Church*, pp. 156-7, and his note, pp. 408-9.

facts recorded in the Books of Ezra and Nehemiah, which occurred in connexion with the great assembly of the Jews at Jerusalem after the Return from Babylon. But this is just what might have been expected. Ezra, Nehemiah and the prophets of that day are constantly spoken of as belonging to "the men of the Great Synagogue." Hence it is natural that what was done by Ezra and his fellows, or performed in consequence of their directions, should be spoken of in later times as performed by "the men of the Great Synagogue." It does not, therefore, surprise us to find that even the acts and sayings of the chief men of the families who returned from Babylon should be referred to as acts and decrees of "the men of the Great Synagogue." Many things ascribed to the latter body turn out on investigation to have actually occurred in the great assembly of the Jewish people recorded in the Book of Nehemiah. But this fact in itself is not sufficient to justify the assertion that all that is said respecting the existence of such a governing body in the Jewish Church of that age ought to be set aside as entirely legendary. The silence of the Apocryphal books, as well as of Josephus and Philo, with respect to "the men of the Great Synagogue," is neither strange nor remarkable. It is well known that the Jewish annals from the death of Nehemiah (circa B.C. 415) down to B.C. 175 are almost a complete blank. The writers of the Apocryphal books had no occasion at all to refer to the acts of "the men of the Great Synagogue," and Josephus appears to have been almost totally devoid of information with respect to the Jewish annals during the period referred to. That writer has, indeed, been clever enough to prevent this gap in his history from being perceived by ordinary readers. Although he may have been fully aware of the existence of such a body as "the men of the Great Synagogue," and may have often heard of the difficulties which that body felt with respect to certain books of the Canon, such facts were scarcely those which Josephus would have cared to record in his *Antiquities* when he had no further incidents to adduce which bore on the history of the period in question. In writing against Apion, Josephus had every reason to pass over such facts in silence. His silence, too, is not so inexcusable; as the facts known to us, while not really opposed to the conclusions at which he arrived, would readily have placed convenient weapons in the hands of an unscrupulous antagonist.

It must not be forgotten that the earliest references to the existence of such a body, namely, those in the Treatise Aboth, are entirely free from those legendary accretions of later days on which Krochmal and Kuenen rely in support of their hypothesis. The last man of distinction who, according to tradition, was a member of that body previous to its final dissolution, lived at least two centuries prior to the Christian era.

Many of the acts of "the men of the Great Synagogue" referred to in the Talmuds cannot, indeed, in the exact form in which they are there related, be regarded as historically true. The very numbers mentioned in connexion with that body (85 at one time and 120 at another) are curious transformations of the narrative of Nehemiah. The formulæ of prayer said to have been drawn up by them, and the epithets which they are said to have directed to be made use of in addressing the Almighty, are but echoes of the self-same narrative; while other works ascribed to them, such as the well-known "corrections of the scribes" in certain passages of the Sacred Writings (the תִּקּוּן סֹפְרִים [1]), are generally acknowledged to have been the work of the "scribes" of a much later era.

But, though we are not prepared to endorse as indubitable

---

[1] See my *Bampton Lectures on Zechariah and his Prophecies*, critical note on Zech. ii. 12, p. 541.

facts of history many of the statements made in reference to the Old Testament canon and its authoritative settlement in the days of Ezra, it is going too far in historical scepticism to call in question the existence of "the men of the Great Synagogue" at, or shortly after, the Restoration. There was a grave necessity for the creation of some such body then in connexion with the Jewish Church, a body whose special business it should be to collect together and preserve the Sacred Writings of the nation, to decide in cases of doubt what books were to be regarded as authoritative in matters of faith and ritual as having been composed in "the spirit of prophecy," and to investigate any difficulties which might be raised concerning their interpretation.

Although, according to the common tradition, Ezra, Nehemiah, and the prophets of that period, namely, Haggai and Zechariah, along with Malachi (who, however, prophesied somewhat later), belonged themselves to "the men of the Great Synagogue," "the men of the Great Synagogue" are in other places spoken of as a body who were the successors of the prophets Haggai, Zechariah and Malachi. The idea of Elias Levita that the whole period of "the men of the Great Synagogue" did not last more than forty years is utterly groundless. [1]

The name of Simon the Just is mentioned in the Treatise Aboth as one of the last of "the men of the Great Synagogue." [2] This statement is not to be interpreted as if it signified that Simon was one of the last survivors of the band

---

[1] See Ginsburg's edition of *Levita's Massoreth ha-Massoreth*, p. 108, and Ginsburg's note there.

[2] "Simon the Righteous (or the Just), was of the remnants of the Great Synagogue. He used to say, on three things the world stands : on the Law (the Thorah), and on the worship [or 'on prayer'], and on the bestowal of kindnesses." See Taylor's (Rev. Dr., Master of St. John's College, Camb.) notes in his excellent edition of the *Sayings of the Jewish Fathers*, p. 26, and compare Romans ix. 4. See Excursus No. 3—"On the Men of the Great Synagogue," at the end of this volume.

of men who co-operated with Ezra in the restoration of the Jewish Church, after the return from Babylon. Its meaning is rather that Simon was one of the last members of that Synagogue, which appears to have been finally dissolved prior to the era of the Maccabees, or about that time, in some way or other not mentioned in extant annals or traditions. Simon is in other parts of the Talmud identified with Jaddua the high priest, who, according to Josephus, went forth with his fellow-priests in solemn procession to meet Alexander the Great, when that conqueror, after having taken Tyre, marched against Jerusalem.[1] He is with greater probability regarded as high priest during the reign of Ptolemy Lagus from B.C. 298 to 287. Herzfeld and Holtzmann have maintained that "Simon the Just" is rather to be identified with Simon II., who was high priest from B.C. 226 to B.C. 198 or 196.[2] No very conclusive arguments can be adduced on either side of this question.

The Treatise Aboth thus pithily describes in its opening verse the work of "the men of the Great Synagogue." "They said three things: be deliberate in judgment; and raise up many disciples; and make a fence to the Thorah" (the Law of Moses). In other words, the business of the men of the Great Synagogue was to define, to teach, and to develop the Law. The last clause has been well explained by Taylor as follows: They were "to surround the Law with a margin of casuistry, to evolve the principles which underlay its words, to develop and apply its decrees, accommodating them to the varied requirements of the time."[3]

---

[1] See my *Bampton Lectures*, pp. 224 ff

[2] See Taylor's *Sayings of the Jewish Fathers*, note on Simon the Just on p. 26. See also Chap. II. p. 36.

[3] Taylor's *Sayings of the Jewish Fathers*, p. 125. It is, however, not certain that this is really the true sense of the saying in Aboth i. 1. Under the term "the Law," not merely the Books of Moses but also the other books of the Holy Scriptures were sometimes comprehended, and Bloch, in his *Studien zur Geschichte d. Sammlung der altheb. Literatur*, p. 56, maintains that the sense of making a

Their Deliberateness in Judgment.

An illustration of the sense and application of the first of these "three words," namely, "be deliberate in judgment," is afforded in the Aboth of Rabbi Nathan. "The men of Hezekiah" are there adduced as an example of persons who were deliberate in judgment, in that they, after careful investigation, added to the original Book of Proverbs as composed by Solomon many proverbs which they considered to have been uttered by that king. A spirit of the opposite kind was, according to it, displayed by those in the Jewish Church who denied the authenticity of the Book of Proverbs, the Song of Songs, and Koheleth, "because they spoke proverbs," and also because "they were not of the Kethubim," the third great division of the Hebrew Scriptures, known as the Hagiographa. On such grounds certain persons "stood up and declared those books apocryphal, until 'the men of the Great Synagogue' came and interpreted them."[1]

The difficulties felt with respect to the first admission of the books in question into the sacred Canon, or their continued retention in that Canon, were, if one can judge from the statements of later days, of a rather singular character. Some of the maxims contained in the Book of Proverbs which relate to the ordinary matters of human life, appeared too homely to have been the subjects of Divine inspiration, and the existence in the same collection of proverbs apparently of a contradictory character increased the perplexity.[2] One of the passages in the Song of Songs which in the eyes of the early critics presented peculiar difficulties, is the beautiful description of the charms of nature as incentives

---

fence to the Law was to separate the books which were of Divine origin from those which had merely a human source. See on the nomenclature of the books of Holy Scriptures in the Talmud, our Excursus No. 1.

[1] Aboth R. N. 69 a, 69 b. See Excursus No. 1.

[2] The passages mentioned in the Aboth of R. Nathan as having presented difficulties are Prov. vii. 7, 10-20 ; Song of Songs vii. 11, 12 ; Koh. xi. 9 ; Song of Songs vii. 10. Other passages are cited in Sabbath 30 b. The latter are those referred to above.

to love (chap. vii. 12–14), a passage which causes no difficulty whatever to a modern theologian.

The objections brought forward against the Book of Koheleth or Ecclesiastes were of a graver character. They were founded on the apparent contradictions met with in the book itself, the alleged opposition between some of its statements and others in the Psalms of David, and the countenance given in parts of the work to heretical opinions.

The following were adduced as specimens of the contradictions referred to. Koheleth affirms at one time that "sorrow is better than laughter" (chap. vii. 3), while at another he actually commends merriment.[1] He represents Solomon as in one place praising joy (chap. viii. 15), and exclaiming on another occasion, "to joy, I said, what doeth it?" (chap. ii. 2) In chapter iv. 2 Solomon praises "the dead which are already dead," but in chapter ix. 4 he affirms that "a living dog is better than a dead lion." Hence the Talmudic writer feels himself driven to exclaim, "O Solomon, where is thy wisdom, where thine intelligence? Is it not enough that many of thy words contradict the statements of David thy father, unless they also contradict one another?"

Another class of difficulties arose from the apparently erroneous opinions propounded in parts of the book. The Midrash on Koheleth (xi. 9), states that "Rabbi Samuel bar R. Isaac said: The wise (men) sought to declare the Book of Koheleth apocryphal because they found in it expressions which inclined to heresy. They said for instance, Is this all the wisdom of Solomon when he says, *Rejoice O young man in thy youth?* [Although] Moses says, *and go not after your own heart* (Num. xv. 39) Solomon says, *and walk after*

---

[1] The objection in this case is based on a misunderstanding of chap. ii. 2. See Excursus on the Talmud and Old Testament Canon. On the contests mentioned in the Talmud with respect to various books of the Old Testament, see Prof. H. L. Strack's article on the *Kanon des alten Test.* in Herzog-Plitt, *Real-Encyclopädie f. protest. Theologie u. Kirche*, 2te Aufl. Band viii. 1880, pp. 429, 430.

The Solution of these Difficulties.

the ways of thy heart. When the rein is let loose there is no judgment nor judge. But inasmuch as he says also, *but know that for all these things God will bring thee into judgment,* they said, Solomon has spoken well."[1]

These and other difficulties were, however, finally adjusted by comparing carefully the passages objected to with others which explain or modify their meaning. The closing verses of the book (xii. 12–14) were considered perfectly satisfactory, inasmuch as a belief in the existence of a future state is there clearly expressed, and the doctrine of a final retribution in another world is there distinctly taught.

The genuineness of the epilogue, or the closing verses of Koheleth, which, according to the traditions preserved in the Talmud and Midrash, finally satisfied the "wise men" who investigated these subjects, has, indeed, been often called in question by modern critics. It can, however, be satisfactorily maintained on critical grounds. But a more important question to be considered is the period at which this controversy actually took place.

Taking it here for granted that the Book of Koheleth was received into the Canon of Scripture before the Christian era, these discussions could not have taken place in the earlier days of "the men of the Great Synagogue." Such a controversy could not have occurred in the days of Ezra or Nehemiah. The very expression made use of, namely, "to declare apocryphal," implies the existence of a literature that was "apocryphal" alongside of literature which, for want of a better term, must be designated as "sacred." The Book of Koheleth must have been recognised by a large number as belonging to the latter class before any controversy at all could have arisen on the subject. Fürst maintains that the objections brought forward against the book arose from

---

[1] Midrash Koheleth on chap. xi. 9. See Excursus No. 1.

the supposed countenance given by its teachings to the heresies propounded by the Sadducees. Consequently, as the Sadducees only came into notice after the Maccabean wars, that scholar considers that "the wise men" referred to were not "the men of the Great Synagogue," but the Teachers of the Law, or Tannaim, who lived in the century immediately preceding the Christian era.

Inasmuch, however, as the difficulties already detailed have been felt more or less by Biblical students in all ages, it is probable that the tradition preserved in the Aboth of R. Nathan (see p. 11), may be historically correct, and these, or similar objections may have been discussed and answered by "the men of the Great Synagogue" in the latter days of the existence of that body. The form, however, in which the objections have been cast in the Rabbinical writings is certainly derived from later times. But, as other evidence can be adduced to prove that the Book of Koheleth was recognised as part and parcel of the Canon previous to the century preceding the Christian era, we incline to maintain the essential trustworthiness of the tradition referred to.[1]

It has been often stated that much difference of opinion prevailed on the question of the canonicity of the Book of Ecclesiastes between the rival Jewish schools of Hillel and Shammai. The controversy on this point is said not to have been finally closed until the Synod of Jamnia, A.D. 90, when the Book of Koheleth or Ecclesiastes was acknowledged as one of the canonical books of the Jewish Church. Dr. Samuel Davidson, in his *Introduction to the Old Testament*, regards these statements as admitted historical facts, and they have recently been ably defended by Professor Graetz,

---

[1] The controversy referred to is not to be regarded as identical with that which certainly took place at a much later era between the rival schools of Hillel and Shammai, see next page, and Excursus No. 2.

on whose authority they have obtained unquestioned acceptance in many quarters.

The facts of the case are as follows. In the Talmudic treatise entitled Yadaim mention is made of a difference between the schools of Hillel and Shammai as to whether the Book of Koheleth was or was not included in the dictum "the Holy Scriptures defile the hands." The school of Hillel maintained the affirmative of this proposition, while that of Shammai upheld the negative. When the question was put to the vote in B.C. 65, the school of Shammai was found to be in the majority. Some twenty-five years later a similar controversy agitated these schools. On the latter occasion the dispute affected not only the Book of Koheleth, but also the Song of Songs, which is not said to have been alluded to in the earlier discussion. The strife was brought finally to an end at a second Synod of Jamnia (A.D. 118), remarkable for the deposition from the patriarchal chair of Gamaliel II., the renowned grandson of the great Gamaliel. Seventy-two doctors of the law took part in that assembly, and its decision was that both Koheleth and the Song of Songs " defile the hands."

Graetz has maintained that this controversy was about the reception of the Song of Songs and Koheleth into the Canon. But the very opposite is the fact. The decisions arrived at prove rather that the books in question had been admitted into the Canon at an earlier period. The point of dispute was not, whether these particular books were to be admitted for the first time into the Canon, but rather, whether, though acknowledged to be canonical, they ought to be regarded as inferior to the other books of Scripture. For, even long after the general acceptance of certain books as canonical, objections were occasionally brought against their Divine inspiration. Thus Simeon ben Manasseh, who was a contemporary of the editor of the Mishna, maintained that the Book of Koheleth ought not to be regarded as holy, its contents being not the result of Divine inspiration, but the outcome of Solomon's natural wisdom.[1]

It is necessary here to explain the meaning of the strange phrase used in this controversy, namely, that the Holy Scriptures "defile the hands." It has often been pointed out by J. S. Bloch, Levy, and others that the reverence with which the Holy Scriptures were regarded by the Jews, led to the destruction of valuable manuscripts of the Sacred Books. For the people often deposited copies of the Holy Scriptures in the place where they kept bread and other things designed for the use of the priests. The bread and other things designed for the holy offerings were holy, and the Scriptures were also holy, and hence they imagined that both ought to be kept in one and the same place. Manuscripts preserved in such localities were not unfrequently injured, and sometimes utterly destroyed, by the attacks of mice and rats. This profanation of the Sacred Writings occasioned no little scandal, and often involved serious pecuniary loss, books being peculiarly valuable in that early age. To put an end to such a state of things, and to prevent its recurrence at any future period, a solemn ordinance was made, whereby the bread and other things touched by the Holy Scriptures were declared ceremonially "unclean," and consequently unfit to be presented to the priests as heave-offerings. The result of this regulation seems to have been most beneficial. The Sacred Writings were no longer kept in larders, where they were exposed to peculiar dangers, but were henceforward preserved in more fitting depositaries.

Bloch has clearly shown, by a quotation from another Talmudic tract, that the regulation "the Holy Scriptures defile the hands," though applicable only to certain canonical books, had no real bearing upon the canonicity of any book.

[1] See Excursus No. 1—"On the Talmud and the Old Testament Canon."

Not connected with the question of Canonicity. 17

For it is expressly stated in the Talmud that the said regulation did not apply to the copy of the Pentateuch used by the high-priest in the temple. It is evident that it would be absurd to interpret such a statement to mean that that copy of the Pentateuch was to be viewed as uncanonical. The reason of its special exemption from the regulation was because serious inconvenience might otherwise occur, and the copy used by the high-priest was not exposed to the same danger of profanation as copies of the Holy Scriptures in private houses.[1]

Moreover, in Megillah 7 a mention is made of Samuel having asserted that the Book of Esther was inspired by the Holy Spirit, although he is reported at the same time to have affirmed that the Book of Esther did not "defile the hands," or, in other words, did not properly come under the ceremonial regulation referred to.[2] That ordinance appears to have been designed at first to apply only to those sacred books which were in most common use among the people, and to have been by degrees extended to others. There was no need, however, to apply the directions to a work which was read only once a year, like the Book of Esther, or even to the Book of Koheleth, which was not in such common use as the others. The Samuel referred to, who lived nearly a century and a half after the Synod of Jamnia, could not possibly have impugned the canonicity of the Book of Esther, inasmuch as he himself distinctly asserted its inspiration; but he did dispute the propriety of applying to that particular book the regulation agreed to by the Synod of Jamnia.

Bloch (p. 142) gives a passage from the commentary of Maimonides on the Mishna (Megillah 7 a), in which he ex-

[1] כל הספרים מטמאין את הידים חוץ מספר העזרה, "all the books (of the Sacred Scriptures) defile the hands except the book belonging to the temple." Kelim xv. 6. See Excursus No. 2, "On the Talmudic statement that the Holy Scriptures defile the hands."

[2] See Excursus, as before.

C

presses himself to the same effect, namely, "and already thou knowest that the Holy Writings defile the hands, and that they differ with respect to Koheleth, whether it is in this particular one of the Holy Writings,"[1] that is, the Jewish doctors differed not as to whether that book actually belonged to the canonical Scriptures or no, but whether it came under that special regulation.

Bloch refers also to the dispute mentioned in the Talmud, between R. Joshua and Rabbi Eleazar ben Hyrkanus. The latter teacher belonged to the school of Shammai, and lived not long after the destruction of Jerusalem. He was the pupil of Rabban Jochanan ben Zaccai, and the preceptor of R. Akiba. Both these Rabbis seem to have taken a part in the Synod of Jamnia. The subject of controversy on the occasion was the special sins which are punished by the early death of one's children. In the course of discussion, Rabbi Joshua affirmed that only the total neglect of the Law was thus punished by God, and cited Hosea iv. 6 in support of his view. Rabbi Eleazar on the contrary maintained that sins committed with respect to vows would *per se* be visited with such a punishment. He cited in defence of his opinion Koh. v. 5, with the formula "as it is written," explaining the words "thy flesh" in that passage to mean children.[2] As a disciple of the school of Shammai, he would scarcely have done this, had that school denied the canonical character of the Book of Koheleth.

Professor Robertson Smith is, therefore, incorrect in following Graetz so far as to assert that the Book of Ecclesiastes and the Song of Solomon "were still controverted up to the very end of the first Christian century,"[3] and in quoting in defence of that opinion the contest between the rival

[1] וכבר ידעת שכתבי קדוש מטמאין את הידים ונחלקו בקהלת אם הוא מכתבי קודש לענין זה.

[2] See Excursus No. 1.

[3] *The Old Testament in the Jewish Church*, p. 172.

The Story of Herod and Ben Būta.

schools of Shammai and Hillel. That controversy was not on the question of the canonicity of those books. Whatever difficulties may have been occasioned by some of the statements of the Book of Koheleth, that book was accepted as canonical, and its teachings regarded as authoritative, long previous to the time assigned by Graetz for its reception into the sacred canon, *i.e.*, prior to the reign of Herod the Great, who, according to that critic, is the monarch pourtrayed in the book under the name of Koheleth.

That the Book of Koheleth was looked upon as Holy Scripture even in the days of Herod the Great is evident from the following narrative, related in the pages of the Talmud (Baba Bathra, 4 *a*), of which we subjoin a somewhat free translation, accompanied by a few introductory remarks and explanations:—

In the early part of his reign Herod put to death the members of the Jewish Sanhedrin, partly in revenge for the insult done to him of having been once tried for his life before that body (*Joseph. Antiq.*, xiv. 9, 4), and partly because he feared their influence among the people. He, however, spared Sameas (identified by some with Shimeon the son of Shatach, by others, with Shemaiah, both mentioned in Aboth i. 9-11), "on account of his righteousness," and also, as we learn from other sources, Baba ben Būta, a distinguished follower of the school of Shammai. The latter was, however, by the orders of Herod deprived of sight. Some time after, Herod desired to know whether that Rabbi was hostile to him on account of the loss of his eyesight, or grateful because his life had been spared. Herod used often to go about disguised in the garb of a private citizen, in order to ascertain the feelings of the Jews towards himself and his government (*Joseph. Antiq.*, xv. 10, 4). He accordingly visited Ben Būta in disguise, and complained bitterly to him of the tyrannical yoke to which the Jews were subjected. "See master," said the subtle monarch, "what this wretched slave is doing." "And what can I do to him?" was the reply of the Jew. "Curse him, master," rejoined his visitor. "Curse not the king, no, not in thy thought," said Ben Būta, quoting the words of Koheleth (x. 20). "But he is no king," urged the stranger. "And if he were only a rich man," replied the Rabbi, "it is also written, 'curse not the rich in thy bed-chamber,'" citing the concluding words of the same passage (x. 20): "yea, if he were only a ruler, it is written, 'Curse not the ruler of thy people'" (Exod. xxii. 27, E.V. ver. 28). "True," rejoined the crafty inquirer, "if he acts according to the practice (religious customs) of thy people, but that fellow does not act according to the practice of thy people." "I am afraid of him," exclaimed Ben Būta. "There is no one here," urged the king, "to go and tell it to him, for I and thou are here alone." "It is written," rejoined Ben Būta, quoting again from the same passage in the Book of Koheleth, "the birds of the heaven shall carry the voice, and that which hath wings shall tell the matter." "I am he," exclaimed Herod, struck with admiration at the caution of the Rabbi, " and if I had known that the Rabbis were so prudent, I should not have put them to death. But now, what reparation can I make?" "Let him," answered Ben Būta, "who has extinguished the light of the world,—for it is written, 'the commandment is a lamp and the Law a light' (Prov. vi. 23),—go and busy himself about the light of the world [that is, let him rebuild the temple], for it is written, 'and all nations shall flow unto it' (Isa. ii. 2)."

Herod hesitated for a little, and pleaded as an excuse the peculiar position in which he stood to the Roman power. He consented, however, at last after due consideration to do so, in order to win over the Jewish Rabbis to his side.[1]

[1] Bloch also observes (*Ursprung u. Entstehungszeit d. Koheleth*, p. 143) that on the occasion of another controversy between two teachers of the law respecting

Although this narrative may at first sight strike one as somewhat legendary, it appears on a closer examination worthy of credence. The conduct of Herod in the story corresponds with other facts recorded by Josephus. In later times, as Bloch observes, the Jews were wont frequently to discuss the question whether Ben Būta was justified in having given Herod this advice, but no one ever called in question the truth of the narrative.

If the story be true, it is a proof that the Book of Koheleth was cited in the days of Herod the Great as of co-ordinate authority with the Law of Moses; and even if its historical truth be questioned, it is clear from the foregoing and from other passages that the compilers of the Talmud had not the faintest conception that the Book of Koheleth sprang into existence in the days of Herod the Great.

Bloch has called attention to another narrative of the Talmud which in some respects is even more interesting, and which is found in Shabbath, 30 b. We think it well to give the passage at more length than Bloch has done in his interesting treatise. Gamaliel, the grandson of the celebrated Hillel, and, like his grandfather, President of the Jewish Sanhedrin, flourished about A.D. 44.[1] He is remarkable

the shape of the world and the movements of the sun, which those Rabbis naturally thought could be most certainly proved from expressions of the Holy Scriptures, Koheleth i. 5 was the verse round which the whole discussion turned. See Baba Bathra, 25 b, compare also Erub. 40 b, Mishn. Succ. ii. 5, Chag. i. 2. Nor are these the only instances which could be cited of cases in which even the most ancient and renowned Jewish divines referred to the Book of Ecclesiastes as canonical Scripture. See Excursus, No. 1.

[1] Gamaliel died about eighteen years before the destruction of the temple. There is a Christian legend that he became a secret convert to Christianity. A grave of St. Gamaliel is pointed out at Pisa. His father is mentioned in Shabb. 15 a as having had the name of Simeon. Nothing more is known of him. In Aboth i. 16 a saying of Gamaliel is preserved: "Make to thyself a master, and be quit of doubt; and tithe not much by estimation." Leusden (as quoted by Strack in his handy edition of *Die Sprüche der Väter mit kurzer Einl., Anmerk., und einem Wortregister*: Leipzig, Reuther, 1882) explains the last clause: "Ne dato sæpius decimas ex conjectura, vel minus dando vel plus. Si minus dederis, avarus judi-

among other things as having been the teacher of the Apostle Paul (Acts xxii. 3), and as having given the notable advice to the Jewish council, when Peter and the other apostles were brought before that august assembly, "Refrain from these men, and let them alone: for if this counsel or this work be of men, it will be overthrown; but if it is of God, ye will not be able to overthrow them; lest haply ye be found even to be fighting against God" (Acts v. 38, 39).

Though Gamaliel gave such advice to the Sanhedrin, he soon found that it was impossible to ignore altogether the remarkable progress of the Christian Church. He appears to have set himself to oppose the spread of Christian ideas among Jewish students, by arguing that the statements in the prophets concerning the Messiah and the dispensation to be brought in by him were totally different from those advanced by the new school which acknowledged Jesus of Nazareth to be the Messiah sent from God. In pursuing this line of argument, he laid great stress upon the literal interpretation of the prophecies, which, if it had been maintained in all cases, would have been fatal to the new views so widely disseminated among the people.

The following narrative occurs in the Talmud (Shabbath, 30 b). We have introduced explanatory remarks into our translation in order to show more clearly the drift of the argument. Bloch considers, but the matter is incapable of positive proof, that the anonymous disciple of Gamaliel, contemptuously referred to as "that disciple," was none other than Gamaliel's most celebrated pupil, the great Apostle Paul.[1]

---

caberis et peccabis; plus dando vel prodigus habeberis vel hypocrita." Taylor explains the whole saying: "Let duties be defined as far as possible by rule; let doubts be resolved by authority; leave as little scope as possible for personal bias and the temptations of self-interest."

[1] It is, however, quite possible. But the expression אותו תלמיד, on which Bloch seems to lay stress, is so often used in an indefinite manner in the Talmud, that

Rabban Gamaliel was sitting one day explaining to his disciples, that in the Messianic age it would come to pass that the curse pronounced in Paradise on woman would be removed, and that a woman would be able to bear a child every day. In proof of this he quoted the words of Jeremiah xxxi. 8 : "She travails and brings forth at once." That disciple, laughing at this, said, "Rabbi it is written 'there is nothing new under the sun'" (Koh. i. 9). Gamaliel said to him, "Come, and I will show you instances, even in this world" (or in this dispensation). He went out and showed his opponent hens which lay eggs every day. By this example Gamaliel sought to prove that there was nothing absolutely novel in the opinion propounded, for that something analogous might be observed even in the present dispensation. Another day the Rabbi was sitting and explaining to his pupils that in the new dispensation the trees would bear fruit every day, in accordance with the prophecy of Ezekiel (xvii. 23), "and it shall bring forth boughs and bear fruit," that is even as a tree shall produce boughs every day, so it shall likewise bear fruit. That disciple, laughing at this, said, "Rabbi, it is written, 'there is no new thing under the sun.'" Gamaliel quickly replied, "Come, and I will show instances in this world," (or in this dispensation). He went out and pointed out to him the caperberry which bears fruit and leaves at all seasons of the year. Again, as Gamaliel was sitting and teaching his disciples that the land of Israel in the Messianic age would produce cakes and clothes of the finest wool, for it is written "there shall

it can scarcely be pressed. It is remarkable, however, that a Rabbi like Bloch should take this view. Though the narrative in the Talmud intends to represent Gamaliel as the victor in the controversy, one can easily see how hardly he was pushed, and the judgment of modern readers, we fancy, will be in favour of the disciple rather than of the great master. Bloch's opinion on this point is quoted with approbation by David Cohen (Kahana) in his Rabb. Hebrew Commentary on Koheleth, printed in Wilna, L. L. Maz, 1881. See more in the note on p. 25.

The Importance of Gamaliel's Argument.

be an abundance of corn[1] in the earth" (Ps. lxxii. 16); that disciple, laughing, said, "Rabbi, and it is also written 'there is nothing new under the sun,'" (Koh. i. 9). Gamaliel replied, "Come, and I will show thee instances of what I mean even in this dispensation." He went out and showed him cakes, mushrooms and funguses (which spring up rapidly, and are round like cakes of bread), and clothes of Milesian wool, and the fine bark which surrounds the soft twigs of the date-palm.[2]

Gamaliel thus seems to have endeavoured to prove that it was quite possible that the predictions of the prophets might be literally fulfilled without anything taking place which could not be more or less paralleled by processes which are even now observable in nature. We have, indeed, no sympathy with the views of the great Rabbi on this head, though they show a great deal of ingenuity; but his arguments may be profitably commended to the attention of those would-be expositors of prophecy in the present day, who so constantly exhibit a longing after the marvellous and after so-called literal interpretations of Scripture.

The importance of this story, which is narrated in the Talmud as one of several practical illustrations of the precept, "answer a fool according to his folly, lest he be wise in his own conceit" (Prov. xxvi. 5),[3] is, so far as our present

---

[1] There is a connexion falsely assumed here between פֶּסַח בַּר (in Ps. lxxii. 16), and the word פַּס which occurs in the phrase כְּתֹנֶת פַּסִּים (Gen. xxxvii. 3, 23; 2 Sam. xiii. 18, 19). The Talmud assumes that פַּס had a plural פִּסּוֹת; compare Kimchi in his Dictionary. Of course there is no real connexion between the words.

[2] It is difficult to comprehend the full meaning of this passage. The true reading of the last sentence seems to be גלוסקאות כמיהין ופטריות וכלי מילת נברא בר קורא, instead of ואכלי מילת. See *Rabbinowicz*, Band vii., in loco.

[3] Immediately following this narrative there occurs the story illustrative of the patience of Hillel, quoted by Delitzsch in his valuable tract, *Jesus und Hillel, mit Rücksicht auf Renan und Geiger, verglichen von Franz Delitzsch* (3te Aufl. Erlangen, 1879). The anecdote is also quoted by F. W. Farrar, in his *Life of Christ*, vol. ii. Appendix. See also Strack's article on *Hillel* in Herzog-Plitt's

purposes are concerned, that it tends strongly to disprove the novel theory that the Book of Ecclesiastes was a production of the Herodian age. Had this been the case, Gamaliel need not have given himself any trouble to refute, by far-fetched illustrations, his refractory disciple, inasmuch as the entire force of the latter's argument rested on the assumption of the canonicity of the Book of Koheleth.[1]

Real-Encyclopädie, 2te Aufl. Band vi. 1880, where he points out the incorrectness of the wild assertions of Geiger and others as to our Lord's teaching being founded on that of Hillel.

[1] These stories of the Talmud, though probably embellished by later additions, may be justly regarded as resting in the main on a real historical basis. They often preserve valuable incidents concerning individuals as well as much that is illustrative of the life and manners of very early days.—In his *Studien zur Geschichte der Sammlung der altheb. Literatur*, p. 154 ff. Bloch defends the narrative given above at greater length than in his *Ursprung und Entstehungszeit des Kohelet*. He considers that it is an historical fragment of undoubted antiquity. The style in which it is composed differs materially from that of the treatise in which it is embedded, and certain peculiar forms of expression in the narrative are indicative of a high antiquity. In his later work Bloch maintains even more clearly than in his earlier, that Gamaliel was controverting the idea that the Messianic prophecies were accomplished in the person of Jesus of Nazareth. That distinguished Jewish Rabbi argued that a Redeemer could not have atoned for the sins of the world, and have left in full force the penalty pronounced in Paradise upon man for his disobedience. Not only the guilt of sin, but the effects of sin were, according to him, to be done away with in the Messianic days. In that era in place of the "great pain and peril of childbirth," which was the curse pronounced on the weaker sex, women would bring forth children without pain and without long expectation ; fruitful trees would take the place of the thorns and briers ; and man, in place of being forced to "eat bread in the sweat of his face," would have his food provided by the bounteous earth ready for use. Such were the views propounded by Gamaliel. Christianity had not realized such expectations, and consequently, according to him, Jesus was not the Messiah. Hard pressed by his obstinate pupil, who urged again and again that all such ideas were contrary to the written word in Eccl. i. 4, Gamaliel maintained that there was no opposition whatever between his views and the teaching of the Book of Ecclesiastes, inasmuch as even a superficial examination of nature showed that the fulfilment of his expectations would require nothing absolutely new ; for although the world has, in consequence of man's sin, been thrown into confusion, facts of a similar character can be actually pointed out even under the present constitution of nature.

Bloch still maintains that the pupil who so pertinaciously opposed the great Jewish master was in all probability the Apostle Paul. In defence of this view he argues : (1) That that disciple must have been a well-known individual. The expressions used concerning him indicate that he must have been one

It is not surprising that peculiar difficulties should have been felt even at that early day to exist with respect to certain books of the Old Testament, though long recognised as forming part and parcel of the sacred Canon, nor that attempts should have been made to exclude them from the Canon. These difficulties seem, however, to have been at that time fairly examined and discussed again and again by men versed in Sacred Scripture. No attempt appears to have been then made to stifle discussion on such points by any *a priori* theory of inspiration. Some of the learned Jewish Rabbis had no doubt higher views of "inspiration" than others of their class. But no dogmatic utterance on the question of inspiration was promulgated by the Jewish Church. The precedent is worthy of imitation by all Christian Churches. The Canon of Old Testament Scripture, like the Canon of the New, had, as Delitzsch has justly observed, also its antilegomena. Certain books in the Old Testament Canon, long after that canon had been closed, were from time to time objected to, not only by the assailants, but also by many avowed defenders of revelation. These books were opposed because their contents were regarded as "militating against the truth of revelation and the

who had achieved a certain fame and popularity. (2) That he was no stranger to the Pharisees, but one who belonged to their school, although opposed to many of their views and disposed to ridicule the same. He was evidently one who was not loved by them, as is shown by the suppression of his name. The name of Jesus is in a similar manner suppressed in the Talmud, though there is much there spoken against him. "Recollections of a painful character," were, notes Bloch, "connected with the name" of the anonymous disciple, "which the Talmud, according to its usual custom, did not wish to revive." (3) The pupil in question was himself a disciple of Gamaliel. (4) The answer of Gamaliel contains a vigorous onslaught on Christianity, and his style of argument shows that the discussion affected him not a little. His opponent was one who held very different views concerning the Messianic dispensation. "In a word," says this distinguished Jewish writer of the present day, "we have brought before us in the narrative of the Talmud, a very well known disputant on the side of Christianity, well acquainted with the Rabbinical mode of argumentation, therefore, no other than the fiery and zealous Apostle Paul."

spiritual character of revealed religion." Those difficulties were, however, after careful examination shown to be capable of a fair explanation, and both the scholars who attacked the books referred to, and the Doctors of the Law who defended them, jointly agreed, after full and repeated discussion, to recognise their Divine authority and to maintain their canonicity.

CHAPTER II.

THE BOOK OF KOHELETH AND THE BOOK OF JESUS THE SON OF SIRACH.

CHAPTER II.

Testimony borne to the Book of Ecclesiastes by the Book of Jesus the Son of Sirach, 31—The author of the latter work, 31—Ecclesiasticus translated from a Hebrew original, 32—Fragments extant in Hebrew and Chaldee, 32—Its use of the LXX. translation, 33, 38—The first note of time in the prologue, namely, "Euergetes the king," 34—The second note of time, the eulogium on Simon the high-priest, 36—The two high-priests of the name of Simon, 36—No decisive conclusion possible, 38—Ben Sira's reference to the Canon, 39—Graetz's attempt to invalidate this testimony, 40—Use made by Ben Sira of the Book of Koheleth, 41—Ben Sira's additions to old proverbs, 46, 48 note.—References in the Talmud to Ben Sira's work, 46, 47—Sometimes referred to as if canonical, 47—Explanation of that fact, 48—New Testament allusions to Ben Sira, 48, 41—His work that of a Palestinian Jew, 48—The LXX. version of the Book of Koheleth, 49—Its peculiarities, 50, 51—Traces of the influence of Aquila on the present LXX. text, 50—Origen a witness to the existence of a LXX. translation of Ecclesiastes, 50—The importance of this fact in relation to the theory of Graetz, 51.

CHAPTER II.

THE BOOK OF KOHELETH AND THE BOOK OF JESUS THE SON OF SIRACH.

THE silence of the New Testament and of the early Fathers of the Church with respect to the Book of Koheleth is, as Graetz fully admits, no argument in favour of the late date of this book. That scholar, however, maintains that this silence proves that a dislike to the book prevailed in the Christian Church as well as in the Jewish Synagogue. Inasmuch, however, as he has brought forward no evidence in support of this latter dictum, it may be passed over without any formal discussion.

Satisfactory evidence, however, is afforded of the existence of the Book of Koheleth at least two, if not three centuries before the Christian era. That evidence is contained in the Book of Wisdom of Jesus the Son of Sirach, more commonly known by the title of Ecclesiasticus, a title the meaning of which is still a subject of dispute. The full name of the writer of that remarkable book of proverbs and wise sayings appears to have been Joshua ben Sira ben Eliezer,[1] or Ben Sira (בן סירא) as he is called by the Rabbinical writers. We shall speak of him under the latter designation.

The reference to the Jewish Scriptures in the prologue of Ecclesiasticus, when viewed in connexion with the statements

---

[1] The fact of his grandfather's name being Eliezer rests only upon the reading of the Alex. and other MSS. in chap. l. 27, where that name is inserted before the word Ἱεροσολυμίτης. But the authority for this reading is doubtful. See *Fritzsche* in the *Kurzgef. exeget. Handb. zu den Apokryph.*

on the subject found in the literature of a later period, goes far to prove that the Book of Koheleth had been admitted into the Canon long before the time of Ben Sira's grandfather. The Greek text of the Wisdom of Jesus the Son of Sirach is avowedly a translation from a Hebrew original. More than forty verses of that Hebrew original have fortunately been preserved in the Babylonian or Jerusalem Talmuds; a few are also to be found in other early Rabbinical writings. Some sayings ascribed to Ben Sira are extant only in Chaldee, others in both Hebrew and Chaldee. By far the greater number of the verses extant in Hebrew and cited by Delitzsch (in his *Geschichte der jüdischen Poesie*), or inserted in the larger collection of Ben Sira's Hebrew and Chaldee proverbs (in Dukes' *Rabbinische Blumenlese*), may be easily identified with passages which occur in the Greek version.[1]

Though there is reason to doubt the genuineness of all these sayings of Ben Sira, most of the Hebrew proverbs ascribed to him, and not a few of those in Chaldee, must be regarded as genuine. The Greek version executed by Ben Sira was by no means a simple translation, but rather a working-up of the old materials left by his grandfather, with a considerable number of new aphorisms.

The Book of Ecclesiasticus is supposed by Dr. Pusey and others to have been composed as early as the latter part of the third century before Christ. The majority of the critics of the present day consider, however, that it cannot be assigned to an earlier date than the second century before Christ. For the earliest date assigned by tradition to the

---

[1] The following are the verses extant in Hebrew: chaps. iii. 21; vi. 6; vii. 10; ix. 8, 9; ix. 10; xi. 1; xii. 4, 5; xiii. 15 (xxvii. 9); xiii. 25; xiv. 11, 17; xviii. 23; xxv. 3, 4; xxv. 17; xxvi. 1, 3; xxviii. 12 (14); xxx. 22, 23; xxxiii. 20, 24; xxxvii. 17; xxxviii. 1; xxxviii. 4, 8; xl. 30; xlii. 9, 10. Some of these, however, assume a somewhat different form in the Hebrew from that in which they appear in the Greek.

Greek translation of the Jewish Scriptures, commonly known as the LXX. version, is the reign of Ptolemy Philadelphus (B.C. 283–247). Reference is made in the prologue of Ben Sira's work to a translation of the Jewish Scriptures into Greek as then in existence, and the allusion is of such a nature as to leave the impression on the reader's mind that it was even at that period no recent innovation. The proverbs of Ben Sira, moreover, afford evidence not to be gainsayed of an intimate acquaintance on the part of the editor with the LXX. translation,[1] and that fact has been regarded by some as inconsistent with the hypothesis of the early composition of the work.

It must, however, be remembered that the earliest date assigned to Ben Sira's Greek edition of his grandfather's work is B.C. 237–211; and if the correct explanation of the title commonly given to the Greek translation, namely, the version of the LXX., be that that translation,—though it afterwards fell into disfavour,[2]—received the formal sanction of the Jewish Sanhedrin of the day (for no one, of course, credits the story told by Aristeas of the seventy translators), it is quite possible for Ben Sira to have made use of it even so early as B.C. 237–211.

The account given by Ben Sira in his prologue with regard

---

[1] Fritzsche (*Einleitung*, p. xxii.) compares in proof of this, chap. ii. 2 with the LXX. version of Deut. xxxii. 36; chap. xx. 29 with Deut. xvi. 19; chap. xxxvi. 29 with Gen. ii. 18; chap. xliv. 16, 17, 19, 21 with Gen. v. 24, vi. 9, xvii. 4, xxii. 18; chap. xlv. 12 with Exod. xxviii. 36; chap. xlix. 7 with Jer. i. 10, and notes that in chap. xlv. it is plain from a comparison of the references there made to the Book of Exodus that the LXX. translation of the passages in question formed the model which Ben Sira followed. As examples of this he adduces words or phrases, such as περισκελῆ, ἔργον ποικιλτοῦ, λογεῖον κρίσεως. Moreover, certain phraseology had been introduced into popular use from the Greek translation which preceded Ben Sira, and the mode of writing Hebrew names in Greek had become fixed, so that even errors were perpetuated without any attempt to alter them. Bissell also, in his excellent work on the *Apocrypha of the O. T.*, gives additional instances. See his introd. to Eccles. p. 277.

[2] See note, p. 38.

34 Two Kings of Egypt surnamed Euergetes.

to the time when he visited Egypt is unfortunately obscure. His words may be interpreted to mean that he visited Egypt when he was thirty-eight years of age, "when Euergetes was king." But they have been also interpreted to mean that he visited Egypt in the thirty-eighth year of the reign of Euergetes. If the latter translation could be proved to be correct, the actual date of the book could be approximately ascertained. Able scholars, however, differ as to the correct translation of the clause, and very confident assertions have been made on both sides of the question.[1] Two of the monarchs of Egypt bore the title of Euergetes, or Benefactor. The first was Ptolemy III., who was justly designated a benefactor of the people. He reigned from B.C. 247 to 222, and during his reign Egypt was prosperous and flourishing. The second monarch known by that title was Ptolemy VII., nicknamed Physcon, or the Fat, who was noted for his immorality and cruelty. He assumed the title of Euergetes, misnomer

---

[1] The Greek phrase in the prologue ἐν γὰρ τῷ ὀγδόῳ καὶ τριακοστῷ ἔτει ἐπὶ τοῦ Εὐεργέτου βασιλέως is obscurely rendered in the A.V. "for in the eight and thirtieth year coming into Egypt when Euergetes was king." Fritzsche translates: " coming into Egypt in the eight and thirtieth year of king Euergetes." Professor Westcott of Cambridge, in his article on *Ecclesiasticus* in Smith's *Dictionary of the Bible*, remarks in a note that "it is strange that any doubt should have been raised about the meaning of the words, which *can* only be, that the translator 'in his thirty-eighth year came to Egypt during the reign of Euergetes'; though it is impossible now to give any explanation of the specification of his age. The translations of Eichhorn and several others, 'in the thirty-eighth year of the reign of Euergetes,' is absolutely at variance with the grammatical structure of the sentence." Many instances, however, of this very same construction actually occur in the LXX. translation of Haggai and Zechariah, *e.g.*, ἐν τῷ δευτέρῳ ἔτει ἐπὶ Δαρείου (בשנת שתים לדריוש), Hagg. i. 1, ii. 1; Zech. i. 7, vii. 1, etc., and it is quite possible that one so thoroughly acquainted with the LXX. translation as Ben Sira was, would imitate its renderings, even if Dr. Pusey (*Daniel the Prophet*, pp. 301, 302, and note) be correct in maintaining that the rendering of the passages in Haggai and Zechariah "is no natural translation, not the way in which a Hebrew would think in Greek, and so not a Hellenistic idiom, but a mere rendering of one man." Dr. Pusey refers to 1 Macc. xiii. 42, xiv. 27, to prove that the idiom implies a concurrent date, but the examples referred to tell quite in the opposite direction. Bissell well remarks: "The grammatical point of Westcott, upon which Winer [*De utriusque Siracidæ ætate* (Erlangen, 1832); and *Bibl.*

What is meant by the Thirty-eighth Year. 35

though it was, with the royal diadem in B.C. 170. Though he did not obtain real possession of the throne of Egypt until the death of his brother Ptolemy VI., or Philometor, in B.C. 146, he yet termed that year the twenty-fifth of his reign, thus dating his reign back from the year in which he had first assumed the royal title.[1] Hence Ben Sira might well speak of the thirty-eighth year of Euergetes II., although that monarch's actual reign over Egypt did not extend to more than twenty-nine years. In face of the fact that Ptolemy VII. actually assumed the title of Euergetes, we can attach little importance to the argument of Dr. Pusey, that a pious Jew would not have referred to a blood-stained monarch like Physcon by the title of Euergetes. It would probably have been dangerous for Ben Sira to have applied any other title to the then reigning monarch. It must not be forgotten that the expressions used in his prayer at the close of his book, prove that he himself was once in imminent

---

Realwörterbuch, ed. v.] also insists is not proved. Winer says, if the thirty-eighth year of the reign of Euergetes were meant, the Greek would not have been ἐπὶ τῷ ὀγδοῷ etc., but ἐν . . . ἔτει τῷ ἐπὶ τοῦ Εὐεργέτου. But the passages from the LXX. cited by Stanley [*Jewish Church*, vol. iii. p. 266, namely, those mentioned above, with the two passages from 1 Macc.], and others adduced by Abbot in his note in the American edition of *Smith's Bible Dictionary*, have a direct bearing on the question; and, if allowed the full weight that belongs to them in a grammatical point of view, they approach the binding force of a rule. Hence the opinion that Euergetes I., who reigned but twenty five years (B.C. 247–222), is not meant, but that Euergetes II., Physcon, is meant, who reigned jointly with his brother twenty-five years (B.C. 170–145) and alone twenty-nine years (B.C. 145–116), must be accepted as probable."

[1] This strange fact is proved beyond dispute. Fritzsche refers in proof of it to Lepsius' *Königsbuch der alt. Aegypter*, 1858, Synopt. Taf. p. 9, and quotes the following passage from Porphyrius (in Euseb. Chron. ed. Aucher, vol. i. p. 240): μετακληθεὶς ἐκ Κυρήνης ὁ Εὐεργέτης καὶ βασιλεὺς ἀναγορευθεὶς τὰ ἔτη αὐτοῦ ἀναγράφει, ἀφ' οὗ πρῶτον βασιλεὺς ἐνομίσθη, ὡς δοκεῖν μετὰ τὴν τοῦ ἀδελφοῦ τελευτὴν ἄρξαντα αὐτὸν ἔτεσιν εἴκοσι πέντε ἀνατιθέναι ἑαυτῷ τέσσαρα καὶ πεντήκοντα. Τὸ γὰρ τριακοστὸν ἕκτον Φιλομήτορος δέον προσαγορεύεσθαι τῆς τούτου βασιλείας, πρῶτος αὐτὸς εἰκοστὸν πέμπτον προσέταξε γράφεσθαι, καὶ οὕτως ἀμφοτέρων μὲν ἑξήκοντα τέσσαρα, τοῦ μὲν Φιλομήτορος λέ, τὰ δὲ ὑπολειπόμενα τοῦ Εὐεργέτου. Ἡ δὲ ὑποδιαίρεσις ἐν τοῖς κατὰ μέρος ποιεῖ πλάνην.

peril on account of some accusations preferred against him before the king of Egypt (chap. li. 2-12).

Hence the note of time given in the prologue to the book does not afford as much assistance as might have been expected on the question of the date of its composition. It, however, proves clearly that the book cannot have been translated much later than B.C. 120, and that the date of Ben Sira's grandfather cannot be assigned to a later period than B.C. 170.

The second note of time found in the work, namely, the poetical eulogium on Simon the son of Onias the high priest (chap. l. 1-21), is somewhat more decisive. The language, indeed, of that glorious eulogy suggests the idea that the writer is there speaking from personal recollections. Too much reliance, however, cannot be placed on this argument, for it is of course possible that the writer took his description from some poet of an earlier date, or from the reminiscences of his grandfather. If there were two monarchs of Egypt who bore the title of Euergetes, there were also two remarkable high priests named "Simon the son of Onias." The first of these was Simon the Just, spoken of in the Talmud as one of the last of "the men of the Great Synagogue" (see p. 9). He probably lived in the earlier days of the Grecian domination (B.C. 299-287). The second was Simon II., who was high priest from B.C. 266-198. Scarcely any historical incidents of the life of the latter are recorded, although he appears to have been held in reputation among the Jews. The legend concerning him given in 3 Maccabees ii. 1-24 proves this. According to it, when Ptolemy Philopator was about to profane the sanctuary at Jerusalem, he was, at Simon's earnest prayer, suddenly stricken down, and had to be dragged out half-dead from the temple which he had just entered. The narrative of 3 Maccabees has, no doubt, little claim to be regarded as

The Character of Simon II.

historical fact, but it proves at least that the hero of such a story must have been popularly regarded as a man of sanctity. Bissell, indeed, asserts that Josephus does not give a single favourable feature in his delineation of Simon II.'s character, but on the contrary describes him as siding with the sons of Tobias, "who were violent supporters of Hellenism as opposed to the strict interpretation and practice of the Mosaic law" (*Antiq.*, xii. 4, § 11). But this statement is scarcely correct. Josephus nowhere gives any delineation of the character of Simon II. In the passage referred to, he simply states that when the elder sons of Joseph, the distinguished farmer of the taxes of Syria,—whom Josephus speaks of, as "a good and magnanimous man," ἀνὴρ ἀγαθὸς καὶ μεγαλόφρων, *Antiq.*, xii. 4, § 10,—broke out into open hostility against Hyrcanus their half-brother, Simon the high priest sided with them because he was nearer of kin to them than to Hyrcanus.

It is, however, worthy of note that Schürer, one of the most eminent modern scholars who have investigated the subject, asserts (*Neutest. Zeitgeschichte*, p. 453) that there is no doubt that Simon the Just was the high priest Simon I. Fritzsche argues that Ben Sira must necessarily refer to Simon II., because he speaks of "the house" as having been repaired again in his days and of the temple as having been fortified (chap. l. 1-4). Tradition is silent on this point, and this silence of history is, according to him, in favour of Simon II. But as Bissell well notes, the silence of history tells as much against Simon II. as against Simon I. He argues also that history is not wholly silent. "In his wars with Demetrius, Ptolemy I. Soter found it necessary at one time to leave his possessions in Cœle-Syria and Phœnicia, and, in doing so, in order to give his opponent no advantage on account of the fortified places which they contained, he caused such fortifications to be destroyed. This we know to have been true of

Acco, Joppa, Gaza, and Samaria, and there is good reason for supposing that it was true of Jerusalem also. Here, then, would be found the needed occasion for Simon I. to repair the house again and fortify the temple."

If, however, Simon I. be the high priest alluded to in the eulogy of Ben Sira, it is possible that, after all, the interpretation of the doubtful expression in the prologue defended by Dr. Pusey and by not a few German scholars may be correct, and that the book was composed in the reign of Euergetes I. The use of the LXX. translation is by no means a certain proof that Ben Sira's translation of his grandfather's work must have been so late as B.C. 120. The book of Ben Sira, as it lies before us, is unquestionably the production of a Palestinian Jew, and the translation of the LXX., though, as noted before (p. 33), held at first in high esteem, was afterwards looked upon as a national calamity, when the results of the Hellenic influence on Jewish national life became fully apparent.[1] A Palestinian Jew, though he might write in Greek for the benefit of his Greek-speaking countrymen, and for others also, would scarcely, so shortly after the revolt against the Grecian supremacy, allude, in the way Ben Sira

---

[1] The manner in which the LXX. translation of the Pentateuch is spoken of in the Babylonian Talmud (*Megilla*, 9 a), where reference is made to the legend of the seventy translators, and to King Ptolemy's command to translate the Law, is highly favourable. The number seventy-two, which occurs in the text of the Talmud, is a mistake (See Müller, *Sopherim*, p. 13). Even certain differences of reading between the LXX. and the Hebrew text are spoken of as made by Divine suggestion. A similar spirit pervades the parallel place in the Jerus. Talmud, though no mention is made of several points in the legend. See Frankel, *Vorstudien zu der Sept.*, pp. 25 ff. But the Masechet Sopherim, i. § 8, which speaks of only five translators,—one probably for each book of the Pentateuch,—breathes a different spirit. There the day in which the Greek translation was completed is spoken of as a day of misfortune to Israel, like that in which the golden calf was made at Horeb. The latter view, according to the opinion of Dr. Joel Müller, *Masechet Sopherim* (Leipzig, 1878), p. 12, dates from the times of war and conflict with the Greeks, when war was also waged against the language of the foe. See also Biesenthal's remarks in his *Trostschreiben des Apostels Paulus an die Hebräer* (Leipzig, 1878), pp. 60 ff.

has done, to a translation which had caused so much offence. An Alexandrian Jew would, of course, have no difficulty in this matter.

All such arguments are, however, not only inconclusive but specially liable to be fallacious, and hence we are disposed to accept, provisionally at least, the general conclusion arrived at by modern scholars, namely, that Ben Sira's work was executed about B.C. 120; the date of his grandfather, according to this, cannot have been later than B.C. 170. If then evidence can be adduced to show that the original author, or his translator, was acquainted with the Book of Koheleth, the latter work must have been in existence at least two centuries before the Christian era. And, if it can be shown that Ben Sira speaks of a canon of Scripture, and no proof can be adduced that that canon received additions at a later period, the conclusion is rendered more certain that the Book of Koheleth formed part of the Jewish Scriptures prior to the Maccabean era.

In the prologue to his work Ben Sira refers to the triple division of the Jewish Scriptures not only as well-known to himself, but also as in use in the days of his grandfather Jesus. Short as that prologue is, it contains no less than three distinct references to this fact. It begins with the clause: "Whereas many and great things have been delivered to us by the Law and the Prophets, and by others who have followed after them." Next Ben Sira remarks, "My grandfather Jesus, having given himself up more and more to the reading of the Law and the Prophets and the other Books of our fathers, and having obtained sufficient experience in those, was drawn on to write something himself." And finally he observes that not only his own translation of his grandfather's work, "but even the Law itself and the Prophecies and the remainder of the books, have no small difference when recited in their own language," in which last clause distinct reference is made to the Greek translation of the Scriptures.

These allusions to the Jewish Scriptures as forming one great whole sub-divided into three parts, the Law, the Prophets, and the Writings, are just as clear as our Lord's allusion to the same fact in Luke xxiv. 44. Such references are not, indeed, sufficient evidence to prove that all the books included in the third division of the Jewish Scriptures in later times were actually contained in the canon as it existed in the days of Ben Sira. Nor do they altogether exclude the possibility that the Canon of Scripture in that early day may have contained some books which at a later date were not permitted to retain their place in it.

But, in order to render such hypotheses at all probable, evidence must first be adduced to prove that new books were actually added to the number of the Sacred Writings subsequently to the time of Ben Sira, or at least that the canon was altered in some way or other. No such evidence, however, has yet been discovered. Considerable controversy, no doubt, arose at a later period on the question whether certain books ought not to be excluded from the number of the Sacred Scriptures, the argument put forward for such exclusion being that they did not bear the impress of Divine inspiration. But the fact of such discussions having taken place actually proves that the special books objected to were regarded as "canonical" at that time.[1]

Graetz admits that the prologue to Ben Sira's work proves that the "Canon" of the Prophets was already closed. But he maintains that its language indicates plainly enough that the third division of the Scriptures was not then regarded as completed; inasmuch as that division, designated in later times by the name of "the Writings" (כתובים), or Hagiographa, had then no special name. It is sufficient

---

[1] See pp. 15 ff, and Excursus No. 2.

here to observe in reply, that the order and arrangement of the Sacred Books were not always the same. Such books as Ruth and Lamentations, etc., which in later times were placed in the Hagiographa, are said, though this is doubtful,[1] to have been in earlier days classed among the Prophetical Writings. The third division of the Sacred Writings received no fixed appellation for centuries later, a fact abundantly proved by the references to that division in 2 Maccabees, in the New Testament, in the writings of Josephus, and even in the traditions of the Talmuds.[2]

In addition to the general testimony borne in the prologue to the Jewish Canon as a whole, the work of Ben Sira contains not a few passages which show beyond all reasonable doubt that the writer was well acquainted with the Book of Koheleth. It may indeed be affirmed that it is as easy to maintain that the author of the Book of Koheleth borrowed ideas from the Book of Ben Sira. But the latter work is confessedly the work of a compiler, while the Book of Koheleth is, as is generally acknowledged, "marked by an almost exceptional originality" (*Plumptre*).

An examination of a few of the aphorisms found in the Book of Ecclesiasticus will be sufficient to show that Ben Sira in many passages imitated Koheleth.

Little importance must, indeed, be attached to resemblances such as that which exists between aphorisms like, "Who will pity a charmer that is bitten by a serpent" (Sir. xii. 13), and "Surely the serpent will bite without enchantment" (Koh. x. 11). But the expression used in Sir. xiii. 25, "The heart of man changeth his countenance," is certainly akin to that in Koh. viii. 1, "A man's wisdom makes his face to shine, and the coarseness of his face shall be changed." The

---

[1] See Strack on the *Kanon des alt. Test.* in Herzog-Plitt's *Real-Encyclopädie*, p. 433.

[2] See Excursus No. 1—On the Talmud and the Old Test. Canon.

two passages appear even more nearly related when compared, as is possible in this case, in the original Hebrew. The question asked in Sir. xix. 16, in reference to the undue notice often taken of careless or angry expressions: "There is one that slippeth in his speech, but not from his heart; and who is he that hath not offended with his tongue?" may well be compared with the remark of Koheleth, "There is not a just man upon earth that doeth good and sinneth not;" which observation, it must not be forgotten, is immediately followed by the precept, "take no heed unto all words that are spoken, for oftentimes also thine own heart knoweth that thou thyself hast cursed others" (Koh. vii. 20–22). St. James seems to refer to the aphorism of Ben Sira in a remark which he makes to the same effect, namely, "in many things we all offend," or "stumble," in words (James iii. 2).[1]

Ben Sira observes (xx. 6, 7) that "There is one that keeps silence, knowing there is a time" (καιρός) i.c. for silence. "A wise man will keep silence until the time (ἕως καιροῦ); but the braggart and the fool passes over a time" (καιρόν). These are observations evidently founded on the teaching of Koh. iii. 7, who speaks of a "time to keep silence and a time to speak" (καιρὸς τοῦ σιγᾶν καὶ καιρὸς τοῦ λαλεῖν— LXX.). On the fool and his propensity for talking Ben Sira also says, "The lips of talkers will be telling such things as pertain not unto them; but the words of such as have understanding are weighed in the balance" (xxi. 25, 26). Compare with this Koheleth's sayings (x. 2, 3), "A wise man's heart is at his right hand; but a fool's heart at his left; yea also, when he that is a fool walketh by the way, his wisdom faileth him, and he saith to every man that he is a fool;" and (verses 12, 13) "The words of a wise man's mouth are

---

[1] It is worthy of notice that the Epistles of the two "brethren" of our Lord, James and Jude, are full of references to current Jewish traditions, and to writings not canonical.

gracious, but the lips of a fool will swallow up himself. The beginning of the words of his mouth is foolishness; and the end of his talk is mischievous madness."

In Sir. xxvii. 26 we read, "Whoso diggeth a pit shall fall therein; and he that setteth a trap shall be taken therein." This is nearly identical with Koh. x. 8, " He that diggeth a pit shall fall into it; and, whoso breaketh a hedge, a serpent shall bite him." But, forasmuch as the same thought is found in Prov. xxvi. 27, "Whoso diggeth a pit shall fall therein; and he that rolleth a stone, it shall return upon him" (also in Ps. vii. 15), we cannot consider such passages as conclusive proofs of an acquaintance on the part of Ben Sira with the Book of Koheleth. A number of other passages may be accounted for by the fact that parallels are to be found in other books of Scripture, such as the Proverbs, Psalms and Prophets. Hence we do not adduce such texts as Sir. ix. 3; xi. 17; xvii. 28; xxxiii. 13, etc.

The maxim "Make not much babbling (or rather "repeat not thy words ") when thou prayest " (Sir. vii. 14),—an injunction which is also given by our Lord in a somewhat modified form in His Sermon on the Mount (Matt. vi. 7),—is most probably founded on the directions given by Koheleth (chap. v. 1, in A.V. chap. v. 2) with respect to prayer, "let thy words be few." Similarly, the warning of Ben Sira with respect to vows is so evidently based on Koh. v. 3, that it is impossible to believe that the two passages can be independent of one another. " Let nothing," says Ben Sira, " hinder thee to pay thy vow in due time, and defer not till death to be justified (by the performance then of vows made long before). Before thou prayest (rather, "before thou vowest," for the original Hebrew of this maxim, which is fortunately preserved, proves that the latter is the correct interpretation of the Greek phrase [1]) prepare thyself (Heb. " thy vows "), and be

[1] Sir. xviii. 23. The verse preceding is, "Let nothing hinder thee to pay thy

not as a man that tempts the Lord." Similarly, the saying of Ben Sira (xxi. 12), "There is a wisdom which multiplieth bitterness," strongly reminds us of Koheleth's statement (i. 18), "In much wisdom is much grief, and he that increaseth knowledge increaseth sorrow."

Who will not at once perceive in the aphorism of Ben Sira (xiv. 18) "One cometh to an end and another is born," a repetition in other words of Koh. i. 4, "One generation cometh and another goeth"? In Sir. xvi. 30, "And they (the living) shall return into it (the earth) again," there is a reappearance of the thought expressed by Koheleth (iii. 20), "All are of the dust, and all turn to dust again," although both passages are, of course, founded on Gen. iii. 19. A more distinct reference to Koheleth, however, is to be found in Sir. xl. 11, "All things that are of the earth shall turn to the earth again, and that which is of the waters doth return into the sea," which certainly reminds us of the remark of Koheleth, used, however, in another connexion: "all the rivers run into the sea." Sir. xiii. 22, 23, and x. 23, may be profitably compared with Koh. ix. 14-16; and the warning against a presumptuous continuance in sin because God does not immediately punish the sinner, which is given in Sir. v. 5-7, seems, though the words are dissimilar, to be a reminiscence of Koh. viii. 11-13. The latter passage appears also to have been in the mind of Ben Sira when he wrote (i. 13), "Whoso feareth the Lord, it shall be well with him at the last." The directions given in Sir. xiv. 14 ff. not to refrain from enjoying a day of festivity, and to do so because death will soon deprive men of all such enjoyments, must unquestionably be regarded as

vow in due time;" or, as Bissell better renders it, "be not hindered from paying a vow (εὐχήν) in due time," "and defer not until death to be justified" by the due performance thereof; verse 23 is rendered in the Auth. Version, "before thou prayest prepare thyself." The Greek is πρὶν εὔξασθαι ἑτοίμασον σεαυτόν, which is explained by the Hebrew בְּטֶרֶם תִּדּוֹר הָכִין נְדָרֶיךָ, "before thou vowest, prepare thy vows," i.e., see that thou hast the power and readiness to fulfil the same. See Dukes' *Rabb. Blumenlese*, p. 70, and Fritzsche's note on the passage.

Ben Sira's imitations of Koheleth.

based on the teaching of Koheleth (v. 18 ff; vi. 1 ff, etc.). The like may also be affirmed of Sir. xl. 1, which is akin in some respects to Koh. i. 3, 5.

Nor is this all. Mr. Tyler has admirably pointed out the intimate connexion which exists between the several clauses of Sir. xxxiii. 13-15 and those of Koh. vii. 13-15. The remark about the potter's clay in the former passage is no doubt derived from Isaiah, but in every other clause of the passage of Ben Sira, when examined in the original, there appears such a remarkable correspondence with the verses in Koheleth that it cannot be regarded as fortuitous. Similarity of phraseology between the two books often occurs when we least expect it, and even in the original of single expressions such as Sir. xxxiii. 11, "in much knowledge" (ἐν πλήθει ἐπιστήμης) we often come across imitations of the Hebrew Koheleth. (Compare ברב הכמה, Eccl. i. 18).

Casual readers of the two books may be struck by the allusion made by Koheleth to princes walking on foot and servants riding on horses (ix. 15), and the similarity between it and Ben Sira's remark that "many kings have sat down upon the ground, and one that was never thought of hath worn the crown" (xi. 5). But far more noteworthy is the close resemblance between Ben Sira's aphorism (xiii. 26), "The finding out of parables is a wearisome labour of the mind," and the observation of Koheleth (xii. 12), "Of making many books there is no end, and much study is a weariness of the flesh." It has also been thought that Sir. xviii. 6 is founded on the expressions used in Koh. vii. 13; xi. 5. The connexion is more plain between Ben Sira's proverb (xxvi. 23), "A wicked woman is given as a portion to a wicked man; but a godly woman is given to him that feareth the Lord," and the remark of Koheleth on the evil woman (vii. 26), concerning whom he says, "whoso pleaseth God shall escape from her, but the sinner shall be taken by her." Equally significant is the likeness between the aphorism of Ben Sira (xxxiv. 7), "Dreams have deceived many, and they have failed that put their trust in them," and the saying of Koheleth (v. 7), "In the multitude of dreams and many words there are also divers vanities; but fear thou God." The praise of agricultural pursuits in Sir. vii. 15, is also remarkable, and may be an imitation of the second clause of Koh. v. 8.

We are tempted to append to this enumeration of passages, proving that Ben Sira was well acquainted with the work of Koheleth and borrowed thoughts from it, a remarkable quotation from the latter among the proverbs in Chaldee ascribed to Ben Sira. "Cast (lit. strew) thy bread upon the face of the water and on the dry land, and thou shalt find it in the end of days." The reader need not be told that this aphorism is quoted from Koh. xi. 1, with the addition of the words "and on the dry land." It is this latter that marks the aphorism in this form as probably a genuine saying of Ben Sira. For that sage was fond of tacking on new endings to old proverbs. One of the Hebrew proverbs several times ascribed to him in the Talmud is, "All the days of the afflicted (poor) are evil, (and) also their nights," the first portion of the saying being a quotation from Prov. xv. 15. The same peculiarity may be observed in many passages found in the Greek Sirach, as for instance chap. xv. 19, the first part of which is a quotation from Ps. xxxiii. 18; and chap. xvi. 16, where a similar addition is made to Gen. i. 4.[1]

Many interesting questions present themselves with respect to the Book of Ecclesiasticus which cannot here be fully discussed. Though the Talmud cites Ben Sira's sayings with approval, it prohibits his book to be read in public; persons being permitted to read it in private as they might read ordinary letters. It classes the work with "the extraneous

[1] See note 2, on p. 48.

Ben Sira sometimes quoted as Canonical. 47

books," and R. Akiba declared that the man who reads such profane works "has no portion in the world to come" (Jer. Talmud, Sanhedrin, chap. x. 28 a).[1] Delitzsch considers (*Gesch. der jüd. Poesie*, p. 20) that the unfavourable judgments of the Babylonian teachers relate only to the Chaldee Targum, or version, of the book, and not to its Hebrew original. The Hebrew original was, however, driven out of the field by the Chaldee version, which, though abounding in interpolations, was more accessible to the people. Earlier Jewish authorities of repute strangely speak of Ben Sira's work as if it were canonical, notwithstanding that the prologue distinctly speaks of it as making no claim to "canonicity." Among those persons who speak of it as "canonical," the name of Simon ben Shatach (B.C. 90) stands pre-eminent. He was esteemed as one of the Jewish "fathers," and a saying of his is given in the Treatise Aboth (i. 10). A remarkable instance of a similar fact occurs in Baba Kamma (92 b), where the proverb is quoted "a bad palm-tree wanders about and goes along with lazy, or barren, trees," and Rabbah bar-Mare observes that "this matter is written in the Law, repeated in the Prophets, reiterated a third time in the Kethubim (the writings, or Hagiographa), and handed down in the traditions, and again in the Barajtha. Written in the Law, as it is written [Gen. xxix. 9] '*and Esau went to Ishmael;*' repeated in the Prophets, as it is written [Judges xi. 3], '*and there were gathered to Jephthah vain men, and they were with him;*' and reiterated a third time in the Kethubim (the writings), as it is written, '*every bird dwells by its kind, and the son of man by one who is akin to him.*'" The last passage is a saying of Ben Sira, found in chap. xiii. 15; xxvii. 9. These facts give an appearance of plausibility to the opinion advanced by Professor Graetz, namely, that the Book of Ben

---
[1] See Excursus No. 1.

Sira and other Hebrew writings may have been at one time admitted into the Jewish Canon, though eliminated from it at a later age. This is, however, scarcely probable, and the evidence adduced in favour of the opinion is not sufficient to justify such a theory.[1] The true explanation of the difficulty seems to be, as Strack has pointed out, that Rabbah bar-Mare quoted from memory as usual, and forgot that the passage adduced by him as a proof text was not to be found in the Kethubim, from which he had intended to have quoted an appropriate text.[2]

Graetz refers, indeed, further to the statement of the

[1] See Excursus No. 1.

[2] The passages adduced to prove that the Book of Ben Sira was at one time or other regarded as canonical are as follows :—The first instance is a passage quoted in the Babyl. Talmud (*Berach.* 48 *a*), with the formula דכתיב, "as it is written," and quoted in the Jer. Talmud (*Berach.* vii. 11 *b*), in the Midr. Bereshith § 91, and in the Midr. Koh. vii. 12, with the formula בסיפרא דבן סירא כתיב. The citation which immediately after follows is in the Jer. Talmud and Midrash, סלסליה ותרוממך ובין נגידים תושיבך ; the first two words are the beginning of Prov. iv. 8, "exalt her and she shall promote thee," to which Ben Sira added, "and she shall set thee between princes." See my remarks, on p. 46. In the Babyl. Talmud the latter clause does not occur, but Prov. iv. 8 is quoted entire, so that the quotation there is wholly from canonical Scripture ; and that instance is not *ad rem*. It may be noted that this proverb of Ben Sira does not occur in the Book of Ecclesiasticus. The nearest approach to it is perhaps chap. xv. 5. The second case is Erub. 65 *a*, where Chija bar Ashi is adduced quoting the remark of Rab, "he who is not of a calm understanding should not pray." It is added " according to that which is written (משום שנאמר בצר אל יורה), in excitement let him not pray." The corresponding passage in Ecclesiasticus is supposed to be chap. vii. 10, μὴ ὀλιγοψυχήσῃς ἐν τῇ προσευχῇ σου, "*be not faint-hearted in thy prayer*" (Comp. Luke xviii. 1). The identity of the proverbs is disputed by several scholars. Strack, in his article in the *Kanon des alt. Test.* before referred to, considers that in this instance, as in the third example which is fully quoted above in our text, there was a direct intention on the part of the teacher in question to give a quotation from canonical Scripture, but that by a slip of memory in both cases the passage cited was from Ben Sira, the mistake arising from his book being for the most part written in the phraseology of the Sacred Writings. No Jewish authority ever speaks of the Book of Ben Sira as belonging to the Canon ; on the contrary, the reverse is expressly stated. It is worthy of note that John Bunyan similarly relates, in his *Grace Abounding*, § 65, that he was for a long time comforted by a passage which he thought was from canonical Scripture, and was perplexed at last on discovering that the passage was from the Book of Ecclesiasticus, namely, chap. ii. 10.

New Testament allusions to Sirach.

Barajtha (to be found in Yadaim iii. fol. 141 a) in which, commenting on the books which do not "defile the hands" (see p. 15) the remark is made that "the Book of Ben Sira and all the books which were written from that time onwards (מכאן ואילך) do not defile the hands," or, in simple language, are not canonical. But Graetz's view of this passage, namely, that it refers, not to the period later than the age of Ben Sira, but rather to that after the Synod of Jamnia (which Synod is alluded to in the text of the Mishna) or even to a later period, is not likely to meet with the approval of scholars.[1]

Broad and liberal in its tone, the work of Ben Sira, though its Greek translation was executed in Alexandria, is a genuine product of the Old Testament dispensation, and in the main reflects the opinions of a Palestinian Jew. Not a few passages of the New Testament seem to show an acquaintance with its sayings, though they are nowhere quoted as Scripture.[2] The Epistle of St. James, peculiarly Palestinian as it is in its tone, exhibits perhaps the most distinct traces of its influence. Even the exhortations of

---

[1] The words of the Toseft. Yadaim are, according to the edition of Zuckermandel, p. 683, הגליונים וספרי המינין אין מטמאות את הידים ספרי בן סירא וכל הספרים שנכתבו מכאן ואילך אינן מטמאין את הידים: "the gospels (הגליונים for הָאֱוַונְגְלִיוֹנִים) and the books of the heretics do not defile the hands, the Book of Ben Sira, and all the books which were written from that time onwards, do not defile the hands."

[2] The only distinct reference to Ben Sira in the New Testament is that in James i. 19, the phrase used there, ἔστω δὲ πᾶς ἄνθρωπος ταχὺς εἰς τὸ ἀκοῦσαι, being based on, though not a quotation of, Sirach v. 11, γίνου ταχὺς ἐν ἀκροάσει σου. The thought contained in the latter clause of James i. 19, βραδὺς εἰς τὸ λαλῆσαι, is akin to Sirach iv. 29, μὴ γίνου τραχὺς ἐν γλώσσῃ σου, but is far nearer that of Koheleth v. 1. See also our remarks on James iii. 2, p. 42. The direction in James v. 14-15 shows traces of an acquaintance with Ben Sira's remarks on prayer and medicine. See note on p. 4. St. Paul in Rom. ix. 20, 21 may have had Sirach xxxiii. 13 in his mind, though his illustration of the potter is more akin to Isa. xlv. 9; lxiv. 8; or Jer. xviii. 6. Other supposed references, such as that to Sirach ii. 15 in John xiv. 23, to Sirach xi. 18, 19 in Luke xii. 19, and to Sirach xv. 15 in Matt. xix. 17, are fallacious, and arise from the fact that "similarity of topics led to similar modes of expression." (See Davidson's *Introduction to the O. T.*, vol. iii. p. 421.)

that epistle, directing men in the case of sickness to make use, along with earnest prayer, of the best remedies which human skill could suggest, may be traced to the influence of the Jewish sage of an earlier period. For Dukes has satisfactorily shown that the praise and commendation of physicians to be found in the book of Ben Sira (xxxviii. 1-15) are not to be regarded as a proof that Ben Sira exercised that profession himself, but on the contrary that his exhortation "to honour a physician" and his medicines, "for the Lord hath created him" and them, was levelled at the spirit of fatalism which was beginning to leaven the minds of the Palestinian Jews. The Book of Ben Sira, we would only note in conclusion of this subject, must have been composed at a considerably earlier date than the "Book of the Wisdom of Solomon," and prior to that outburst of sensual scepticism which led to the production of the latter work by a writer, who with all his failings was inspired with a spirit more akin to the New Testament dispensation.

The existence of the Book of Ecclesiastes in the Canon of the LXX. is opposed to the novel hypothesis of its composition so late as the time of Herod the Great. There are no doubt many points with respect to the LXX. which are as yet very imperfectly understood, and the Greek translation of Ecclesiastes, which forms now part and parcel of that version, presents some very striking peculiarities which require more investigation than has yet been bestowed upon them. The phraseology used in the LXX. version of that book is in some particulars strongly redolent of the translation of Aquila, and Graetz has maintained that it is really the second and improved edition of Aquila. But if the version incorporated into the LXX. translation be that of Aquila, then that portion of the LXX. text cannot be ascribed to an earlier date than A.D. 120 or 125.

One of the most remarkable peculiarities of Aquila's

Traces of Aquila in the present Text. 51

version is his rendering by the Greek σύν the Hebrew particle (את) which distinguishes in certain cases the accusative. This phenomenon appears in the translation of the Book of Koheleth. But it is to be observed that the rendering is by no means uniform. Graetz remarks that twenty-one cases occur in the book in which the Hebrew particle is not thus rendered. He explains this fact by supposing, first, that the particle in question did not occur so often in the Hebrew text which Aquila used, as in that which formed the basis of the Masoretic recension; and by supposing, secondly, that the Greek copyists may have in many cases, either from accident or deliberation, omitted the same. Prof. Graetz has, however, not given an accurate statement of the facts of the case. There are more than seventy instances in the book in which the Hebrew particle is found in our present text; and in less than half does the favourite rendering of Aquila occur in the Greek text of the Septuagint.[1] Whilst, therefore, it is tolerably certain that the Greek translation of the Book of Ecclesiastes found in the LXX. version in the form in which it has been handed down to us, has incorporated not a few

---

[1] את is rendered by σύν in chap. ii. 17, iii. 10, iii. 17 *bis*, iv. 3 (את־המעשה, σὺν πᾶν τὸ ποίημα, the reading of the Greek differing here from the Hebrew text). So also in vii. 14, as a prep. with dative, vii. 26, vii. 29, viii. 8 (את הרוח), viii. 15, viii. 17, ix. 15 (את־האיש), xi. 7, xii. 9, *i.e.*, 14 times. So also את when followed by כל is rendered by σύν in composition with πᾶς *e.g.* chap. i. 14 σύμπαντα, ii. 18, iii. 11 *bis*; in this verse in the second instance codex B., but not A. or S., inserts "all" which is omitted in our Hebrew text, σύμπαντα τὸν αἰῶνα, את־העלם. So in chap. iv. 1 (not in S.); in chap. iv. 2, B. (not A. or S.) inserts "*all*," which is omitted in the Hebrew text, σύμπαντας τοὺς τεθνηκότας, את המתים; in chap. iv. 4 *bis*, iv. 15, vii. 15, viii. 9, viii. 17, ix. 1 *bis* (the clause, however, in which this occurs, forms part of viii. 17 in the Greek) ix. 11 cod. B. alone has σύμπασιν αὐτοῖς, את־כלם; xi. 5, xii. 14, *i.e.* 17 times. In all 14+17 = 31 times.

את is not rendered by σύν in chap. i. 13, ii. 3, ii. 10, ii. 12, ii. 20, ii. 24, iii. 11 (את־המעשה), iii. 15, iv. 3 (את אשר־ערן), iv. 5 *bis*, iv. 8, iv. 10, v. 3 (σὺ οὖν ὅσα ἐὰν εὔξῃ ἀπόδος), nor in v. 5, in three instances, את פיך, את בשרך, את מעשה. In chap. v. 6 for the Heb. ירא האלהים את, the Greek has ὅτι σὺ τὸν Θεὸν φοβοῦ. So also the את is not rendered by σύν in chap. v. 19, vii. 7. vii. 13 *bis*, vii. 18

52 A LXX. Translation independent of Aquila.

of the renderings of Aquila, it is unlikely that it was itself the work of that translator.

Dale has noted the care taken in the LXX. text to preserve the order of the Hebrew words. "In Ecclesiastes this order is so strict that, with hardly an exception, it would be possible to print the Greek text as it stands as an interlinear translation."

But the fact that Origen actually made use of another Greek translation of the Book of Koheleth which he cites as that of Aquila,—alongside of the Greek translation of Koheleth, which is given as that of the LXX.—proves very clearly that, although the present text of the LXX. is probably a composite one and may actually contain many of the renderings of Aquila, a Greek translation of Ecclesiastes was in existence in the days of Origen, which was recognised as forming an integral part of the well-known LXX. translation. Something similar may have occurred in regard to the version of Ecclesiastes like that which happened to that of the Book of Daniel, in which the translation of Theodotion has for many centuries taken the place of the LXX. The fact that Origen made use of a version of the book known as that of the LXX., as also that the present Greek one cannot in its entirety be regarded as that of Aquila, is a proof that the Book of Ecclesiastes itself must have been in existence for a considerable time previous to the execution of the LXX. translation of the Hebrew Scriptures, or, in other words, at an earlier period than the work of Ben Sira.

---

bis (את ידך and את כלם), in vii. 21, viii. 8. את בעליו, rendered τὸν παρ' αὐτῆς; nor in viii. 9, (את לבי), viii. 16 *bis*, ix. 7, ix. 12, ix. 15 (את העיר), x. 19 (את הכל), x. 20, xi. 5 ('ה המעשה את), xi. 6, xi. 8, xii. 1, xii. 13 *bis*, or in all 40 times.

This matter, as well as other points of a kindred nature, needs more critical examination than it has yet received. Aquila has no συν for את in Gen. vi. 3, ix. 22, 23, xxii. 2. xxvii. 15 ; Exod. xxiv. 10, and possibly in other passages.

CHAPTER III.

THE BOOK OF WISDOM AND THE BOOK OF KOHELETH.

CHAPTER III.

Leaning of the Book of Wisdom towards Greek philosophy, 55—Composed before the time of Philo, 56—Probably in reign of Physcon, 57—Viewed as inspired by several of the Fathers, 57—Not the production of a Christian Jew, 58—Written under the name of Solomon, 60—Strange denial of this fact, 60—The author not guilty of imposture, 61—His object in assuming the mask of Solomon, 61—Forgeries of Jewish writers in later times, 62—Favourable conception of the character of Solomon, 64—Difficulties of belief referred to in Book of Koheleth, 65—Object of the writer of that book, 66—Different state of thought in the later days of the Greek rule, 67—The free-thinkers of Alexandria, 67—Their appeal to the Book of Koheleth, 68—The writer of the Book of Wisdom opposes their views, 70—Apparent contradictions to the Book of Ecclesiastes, 70—Value of the Book of Wisdom, 72—Supplied a gap in the creed of the Jewish Church, 73—Allusions to its phraseology in the New Testament, 74—Wisdom a guide to immortality, 75—The description of the righteous man in the Book of Wisdom, 75—That book a preparation for the revelation of Christ, 76.

CHAPTER III.

THE BOOK OF WISDOM AND THE BOOK OF KOHELETH.

WE cannot enter further upon the consideration of the various questions connected with the date and authorship of the Book of Koheleth without considering at some length the peculiar relation which exists between it and the Book of Wisdom.

The latter work, generally known by the title prefixed to it in the LXX. version, namely, "The Wisdom of Solomon," must have been composed at a date subsequent to the completion of the celebrated Greek translation of the Jewish Scriptures. This is evident from the use made of that version.[1] The writer of Wisdom exhibits a deep and ardent faith in the leading doctrines of the Jewish creed, but at the same time shows that he has an acquaintance with, and a sympathy for, some of the characteristic tenets of the Greek philosophers. Thus, for instance, he has borrowed from the Platonic school the mention made of the four cardinal virtues, namely, temperance, prudence, righteousness, and manliness.[2] His doctrine about "shapeless matter" (ὕλη

---

[1] For instance, in chap. xv. 10, the author quotes from the LXX. translation of Isaiah xliv. 20, the phrase σποδὸς ἡ καρδία αὐτοῦ, though that is not a correct rendering of the Hebrew. In chap. ii. 12, the phrase put into the mouth of the free-thinkers concerning the righteous man, ὅτι δύσχρηστος ἡμῖν ἐστί, is taken from the LXX. translation of Isaiah iii. 10. Moreover, as Grimm notes, the sense in which ἐτάξειν is used in chap. vi. 7 is derived from the usage of the LXX., and in chap. xvi. 22, and xix. 21, there is a reference to the LXX. translation of Exodus xvi. 14, and specially to that of Numbers xi. 7.

[2] Chap. viii. 7, καὶ εἰ δικαιοσύνην ἀγαπᾷ τις, οἱ πόνοι ταύτης εἰσὶν ἀρεταί. σωφροσύνην γὰρ καὶ φρόνησιν ἐκδιδάσκει, δικαιοσύνην καὶ ἀνδρείαν. These are the

ἄμορφος, chap. xi. 17) the pre-existence of the soul, and sundry other matters is derived from the same source. Such a combination of Jewish faith and Greek philosophy was a marked characteristic of the Jews in Alexandria from the third century before Christ, but cannot be traced to an earlier period.

On the other hand the Book of Wisdom must have been written long before the age of Philo. It cannot have been composed after the Roman conquest, as Holtzmann considers possible, for its teaching on the chief points discussed is far from being identical with that of Philo. The Divine wisdom, though a central subject throughout, is nowhere regarded as a personified being like the Logos of the Alexandrian philosopher. Many Platonic doctrines which occupy an important place in Philo's system are sought for in vain in the Book of Wisdom. Opinions, which in Philo's writings assume the form of fundamental dogmas, appear in the Book of Wisdom only in a rudimentary form. In other words, the Book of Wisdom presents us with a far earlier stage of philosophic thought than the works of Philo. The two authors must have been separated from one another by a considerable interval of time.[1]

For these and other reasons it is most probable that the work was composed about a century, or a century and a half, before the Christian era. It was evidently written at a time when the Jews resident in Egypt had to suffer considerable persecution at the hands of their heathen neighbours. During the reign of the earlier Ptolemies the Jews were well

---

four cardinal virtues known to Greek ethics. In 4 Macc. v. 22, 23, εὐσέβεια takes the place of φρόνησις, but in 4 Macc. i. 18, the list is identical to that given in the Book of Wisdom. See Grimm on this passage, and Deane's note in his recent excellent commentary on the book (Oxford, Clarendon Press, 1881). See also Grimm on the passage in 4th Macc. in his Comm., pp. 300–1.

[1] See Deane's Prolegomena, p. 33; Grimm, *Einleitung*, p. 22; and Bissell, *Introduction to Book of Wisdom*, p. 226.

treated in Egypt. They were, however, much persecuted during the reign of Physcon (B.C. 145–117) and his successors. These persecutions called forth the reflections in the closing chapters, in which the writer enlarges on the origin and folly of idolatry, and the punishment of idolaters. His remarks were designed to comfort and support his countrymen amid the severe trials they had to suffer under Egyptian misrule. The original language of the book was Greek, not Hebrew or Aramaic, a fact which even a cursory examination is sufficient to prove.[1]

The writer was evidently a Jew resident in Alexandria, and his book contains several striking indications of its having been composed amid the scenes daily witnessed in that great maritime city.

It is scarcely necessary, in the face of such facts, to do more than allude to the opinion held by several of the Christian Fathers, such as Clement of Alexandria, Hippolytus and Tertullian, namely, that the Book of Wisdom was written by Solomon. No modern scholar of repute defends such a theory. But it is worthy of note that some of the Fathers, such as Origen, Eusebius, and Augustine, who doubted or denied the Solomonic authorship of the work, maintained withal its Divine inspiration.[2]

[1] No doubt a Hebrew colouring, as Grimm observes, pervades the first ten chapters in the parallelism which imitates the Psalms, Job and Proverbs, and in certain Hebraisms which occur in that portion. But the genuine Greek character of the book is seen in the richness of its vocabulary and the number of the synonymes employed, especially adjectives, in the technical expressions of the Platonic and Stoic philosophers, and in the numerous examples of compound words and expressions, as well as in the frequent play upon Greek words, and such figures of speech as paronomasia, onomatopœia, oxymora, etc. See Grimm, *Einleitung*, pp. 5–7; Bissell, p. 224.

[2] Thus Origen *Cont. Cels.* iii. 72, cites it as ὡς ὁ θεῖος λόγος ὁρίζεται : Eusebius *Præp. Evang.*, i. 11 (Tom. i. p. 66, ed. Gaisford) says κατὰ τὸ παρ' ἡμῖν λόγιον τὸ φάσκον· ἀρχὴ πορνείας ἐπίνοια εἰδώλων (Wisdom xiv. 12) &c. Augustine (*De prædest. sanct.* i. 11) says, "quæ cum ita sint, non debuit repudiari sententia libri Sapientiæ, qui meruit in ecclesia tam longa annositate recitari et ab omnibus Christianis . . . cum veneratione divinæ auctoritatis audiri . . . etiam temporibus

It has sometimes been maintained that the Book of Wisdom was the production of a Christian Jew. But this hypothesis has been conclusively disproved by Grimm. The speculations of Plumptre rest upon no real basis.[1] Some of the sayings which occur in the book sound indeed like echoes of sentiments found in New Testament writings. But all

proximi apostolorum egregii tractatores, . . . eum testem adhibentes nihil se adhibere nisi divinum testimonium crediderunt." It must, however, here be noted that the Book of Wisdom mentioned in Melito's letter, found in Eusebius *His. Eccl.* iv. 26, in which a list of the books of the Old Testament Canon is given (the Book of Esther being, however, omitted), is not the Apocryphal book, but only another title of the Proverbs of Solomon. The words of Melito are Ψαλμῶν Δαβίδ, Σολομῶνος Παροιμίαι, ἡ καὶ Σοφία, Ἐκκλησιαστής, Ἆισμα ᾀσμάτων, Ἰώβ. It can be clearly proved that some of the Christian Fathers called the Proverbs Πανάρετος Σοφία; and traces of the same usage are extant even among early Rabbinical writers. See Delitzsch, *Das Salomon. Spruchbuch*, Einl. p. 31. Grimm, *Einl. in Weisheit*, p. 36.

[1] Noack (in his *Ursprung des Christenth.*, Leipz. 1837, vol. i. p. 222) was the first to suggest the idea that Apollos was the author of the Book of Wisdom. The theory has been further developed and ably defended by Professor (now Dean) Plumptre in two articles on the *Writings of Apollos*, which appeared in the first vol. of *The Expositor*, edited by the Rev. S. Cox (Hodder and Stoughton, 1878). Plumptre partially reproduces some of his arguments in his Introd. to his work on Ecclesiastes, pp. 67 ff. He maintains that the Book of Wisdom was written by Apollos before his conversion to Christianity, and the Epistle to the Hebrews after that event. His whole argument is based on the admitted fact that certain phraseology peculiar to the Alexandrian school of Judaism occurs in the Book of Wisdom and reappears in the Epistle to the Hebrews. This, however, proves nothing more than that the writer of the latter book was well acquainted with the former. Deane well observes: "To any unprejudiced mind the contrast between the two is most marked; the difference of style is too great to be reasonably attributed to different phases of the same intellect. There is nothing in Wisdom like the continuous interweaving of the Old Testament Scriptures which is found in the Epistle; there is no exhibition in the Epistle of the acquaintance with Pagan learning which is so prominent a feature of the earlier work. The resemblance in language may be paralleled from Philo, and might be equally well used to support his claim to the authorship of either. For those who hold the Pauline origin of the Epistle to the Hebrews, no other argument is needed to discredit this theory; for those who leave the question about the Epistle doubtful, it is enough to say that the date of Apollos does not coincide with what we have shown to be the probable date of our book, that we know absolutely nothing of that Apostle's writings, that the verbal similarities are capable of another explanation, and that the scope and object of the two writings are wholly different." See also Grimm's able remarks on the supposed Christian origin of the book, in his *Einleitung*, p. 25.

such sayings can easily be accounted for, as the author of the Book of Wisdom and the writers of the New Testament drew their inspiration in this respect from a common source, namely, the Scriptures of the Old Testament. Ewald is certainly correct when he asserts that not even a single verse of the Book of Wisdom is derived from any Christian source. The doctrine of the immortality of the soul propounded in the Book of Wisdom is very different indeed from the doctrine of the resurrection of the dead taught by the writers of the New Testament. The author's dogma of the pre-existence of the soul was certainly not derived from an Apostolic source. The beautiful description of the righteous man (in chap. ii. 12–20), though regarded by many of the early Christian writers as a prophecy of Christ, and curiously corresponding in some of its details with the facts of gospel history, can be proved, on a closer examination, to have no such meaning.[1]

---

[1] The chief grounds on which it is maintained that this passage is intended as a description of Christ, prophetical or otherwise, are the statements "he calleth himself the child of the Lord" (ver. 13), and "he makes his boast that God is his father" (ver. 16) when compared with John v. 18, xix. 7. Compare also ver. 18 with Matt. xxvii. 40, 43. The statement also " he professeth to have the knowledge of God" (ver. 13) is strikingly parallel with those in John vii. 16, xv. 15; Matt. xi. 27. The shameful death of ver. 20, corresponds with the death on the cross, and the references of ver. 21 may be compared with John xii. 40, 1 Cor. ii. 8. But Grimm well remarks against this interpretation : (1) that δίκαιος, *the righteous* man is clearly a collective. This is plain from the interchange of the plural δίκαιοι (chap. iii. 1 ff) with the sing. δίκαιος (chap. iv. 7 ff). The δίκαιοι in chap. iii. 1 ff are identical with the δίκαιος of chap. ii. (2) The relation of the pious to the worldly and godless is the same at all times. Hence it is not strange that a description of the ideal righteous one should find its counterpart in Christ. (3) The similarity of the circumstances fully explains the similarity of many expressions in this chapter of the Book of Wisdom with certain found in the speeches of the Jews against our Lord. Several of the expressions are borrowed from Psalm xxii. If the description be regarded as having proceeded from the pen of a Christian writer, Grimm fairly argues that two points are incomprehensible : (1) That the author should have brought forward as the opponents of Jesus materialists and frivolous sensualists in place of hypocritical and self-righteous Pharisees who blindly adhered to the Mosaic law and the Jewish tradition. Noack's attempt to make out that the Sadducees are here described is most unsuccessful. (2) There

The writer of the Book of Wisdom put forward his views under the mask of Solomon. This fact has indeed been very strangely called in question by the Rev. David Johnston, the author of a recent *Treatise on the Authorship of Ecclesiastes*.[1] That gentleman asserts that " the allegation that the Book of Wisdom personates Solomon is scarcely borne out by the contents of the book." He adds, " In Ecclesiastes Solomon is specified as the author and autobiographer every whit as distinctly and definitely as if he were actually named; whereas he is neither named nor specified in the Book of Wisdom. It is indeed true that much which is said in the seventh chapter would suit Solomon, especially where the writer says, verse 7, 'Wherefore I prayed, and understanding was given me: I called *upon God*, and the spirit of wisdom came to me.'[2] Yet this is just such language as a Hellenistic admirer and imitator of Solomon might honestly use, without any desire or attempt to pass off his Greek treatise in the praise of wisdom as a production of the Hebrew monarch."

From such a statement—which, as it occurs in a work exhibiting a certain amount of scholarship, cannot be passed over in silence—it is evident that the writer of the *Treatise on the Authorship of Ecclesiastes* never read through the Book of Wisdom. One of the most striking peculiarities of the book is, that, although it abounds in allusions to the patriarchs and other heroes of the Old Testament, no proper name of person, town, country, or river, is ever mentioned.[3] It is true, therefore, that the name of Solomon does not

---

is not in all the description of the Book of Wisdom the slightest hint afforded of the atoning power of the sufferings and death of the righteous man pourtrayed by the author.

[1] See chap. iv. pp. 85 ff. and chap. v. p. 114.

[2] This verse is given by Mr. Johnston in the original Greek. We have taken the liberty of quoting it above in English.

[3] The mention of the Red Sea in chap. xix. 7 is the only apparent exception to this usage throughout the book, and it cannot be regarded as a real exception.

occur in the book. But it is no less certain that the author writes in the name and under the character of Solomon. Solomon's royal birth (chap. vii. 4, 5; ix. 12), his prayer for wisdom (chap. vii. 7, 8; ix. 4-12), his desire for that gift in his early days (chap. viii. 2) in order that he might be fitted to act as king over Israel (chap. viii. 10, 11, 14, 16; ix. 4-12; compare 1 Kings iii. 7, 8 ff), for which position his youth and inexperience would have otherwise rendered him unfit —all these facts, and more also, are distinctly referred to by the writer as his own personal experiences. In proof of this it is only necessary to quote the words of the prayer in chap. ix. 7, 8. "Thou hast chosen me to be a king of thy people, and a judge of thy sons and daughters: thou hast commanded me to build a temple upon thy holy mount, and an altar in the city wherein thou dwellest, a resemblance of the holy tabernacle, which thou hast prepared from the beginning."

It is not, however, right to accuse the author of the Book of Wisdom as guilty of forgery, or of "deceit and falsehood," because he chose to put forward his work under the name of the great monarch of Israel. Whatever may have been the misconceptions of later days in consequence of this assumption of a fictitious character, no person in the author's day and generation could have been ignorant that the mask of Solomon was put on only for a special purpose. The fact of the author having composed and published his book in Greek would of itself have been sufficient to prove that the work was not by the great king of Israel, and the frequent references to philosophic opinions current in Alexandria at the writer's day made it still more apparent.

The reasons which induced the author to put forth his views under the name of Solomon appear to have been as follows: The Jewish free-thinkers in the great Egyptian capital had dared not only as individuals to put in practice the ungodly maxim, "Let us eat and drink for to-morrow we die" (1 Cor. xv. 32), but had even ventured to defend their scepticism, and to apologise for their sensuality, by appealing to the authority of the wisest of men, and to his experience as recorded in the Book of Koheleth. It was to manifest their impiety, and to confute their folly, that the writer of the Book of Wisdom sought under the name of Solomon to point out the teachings of true wisdom, and to demonstrate that what these would-be wise men termed "wisdom," was, to use the Apostolic language of a later day, a wisdom which "cometh not down "from above," but "earthly, sensual," and—the last epithet applied by St. James to similar aberrations may also be added, namely,—"demoniacal" (James iii. 15).

The Book of Wisdom has, therefore, in some respects been correctly described as an Anti-Ecclesiastes. Its author does not venture to condemn the canonical Book of Ecclesiastes, but he again and again distinctly refers to that book, and unhesitatingly condemns false views of life and false principles of morality apparently enunciated under the sanction of a great name.[1]

In assuming, therefore, the name and stand-point of Solomon, and in stepping forward in that character to do battle for the cause of God and of religion, the writer of the Book of Wisdom acted more nobly than other Jewish writers in Alexandria, who at a later period laid themselves fairly open to the charge of "deceit and falsehood" by attempts, which seem to have been for a time successful, to introduce Jewish opinions, and even Old Testament prophecies, into the productions of heathen authors. Hence the oracles of the Sibylls were found to give utterance to Jewish sentiments.

---

[1] This lecture was delivered before the University of Dublin, Nov 28th., 1880. Plumptre, in his Introd. to his work on Ecclesiastes, published in 1881, has partly taken up the same ground, though he adheres to his theory as to the authorship of the Book of Wisdom, noticed in note on p. 58.

"The voice was Jacob's voice," although the form in which the teaching was presented was of Gentile origin. The evil practice once introduced soon became popular among a class of writers not deficient in a certain kind of literary ability, and Jewish ideas and Jewish principles were instilled into the minds of Gentile students under the apparent authority of ancient heathen poets, such as Linus and Orpheus.[1]

But, although forgeries such as those referred to, originally devised in the interests of religion, must be unhesitatingly condemned by all real lovers of truth and righteousness, it must not for one moment be supposed that the author of the Book of Wisdom, in assuming the mask of Solomon, has exposed himself to the same righteous condemnation. He wrote under the full conviction that the views advocated in his work were the conclusions of Divine wisdom, and he ventured to publish his opinions in the intellectual capital of the heathen world as in reality echoes of that wisdom which had been bestowed upon Solomon from above.

Grimm has well remarked that David was ever regarded as the great hero and religious poet of the nation of Israel. Psalms written by unknown writers at various times of Jewish history were without scruple ascribed to "the Sweet Singer of Israel," who had himself composed so many hymns. Solomon, on the other hand, was looked upon as the impersonation of wisdom; and, inasmuch as he was renowned both for the number and variety of his own proverbs, and as a collector of the wise sayings of others, the majority of the moral maxims and proverbs which passed current among the Israelites were ascribed to him. Justly celebrated in sacred history as the wisest of mankind, and as having had the largest practical experience as well as the highest intellectual knowledge, is it to be wondered at that moral writers, whose great object was to point out the teachings of the highest

[1] See Dähne's *Jüdisch.-Alexandr. Religions-Philosophie*, vol. i. pp. 81 ff.

wisdom, should have been led to represent its utterances as proceeding from the lips of Solomon?

One of the peculiarities of the Book of Wisdom is the favourable light in which the author throughout regards the character of Solomon. The contrast which exists in this point between the apocryphal Wisdom of Solomon and the canonical Book of Koheleth is remarkable, and may be adduced as a proof of the composition of the latter book at a far earlier period than that of the former. The Book of Koheleth does not scruple to refer to Solomon's polygamy in uncomplimentary terms, while the writer of the Book of Wisdom has gone so far on the other side as, without any allusion whatever to Solomon's gross misconduct in this particular, to put exhortations to chastity and purity into the mouth of that king. The silence of the Book of Wisdom with respect to the sensuality of the great monarch is highly significant. For in later times Jewish authorities, quoted with approbation in the Talmud, ventured not only to palliate but actually to explain away all the crimes which David and Solomon committed. These writers even dared to maintain, in face of the statements contained in the First Book of Kings, that Solomon was really innocent of the sin of idolatry.[1]

[1] In the Talmud Babli, Shabb. 56 b, Rabbi Samuel bar Nachmani states that Rabbi Jonathan said that "he who says Solomon committed sin makes a mistake." Compare Delitzsch, *Rohling's Talmudjude beleuchtet*, 7te Ausg. pp. 93 ff., where more will be found about Rabbi Jonathan and his attempts to exculpate Solomon, etc. Another authority quoted there attempts to prove that Solomon did not actually erect temples to the false gods of his wives, but merely had the intention of doing so. In the Jerusalem Talmud, Sanhed., chap. ii. fol. 20 b, Rabbi Jose is reputed to have maintained that Solomon loved his strange wives in order to win them under the Law, and to bring them under the wings of the Shekinah. The same idea is propounded in the Midrash on the Song of Songs on chap. i. 1, where many authorities are cited in its favour. The same Midrash in an earlier place endeavours to explain away the fact that Solomon spent thirteen years in building his own palace, while he spent only seven years in the erection of the temple, by maintaining that Solomon's palace was not more splendid than the temple, but that the work of building the former was prosecuted in a less energetic manner.

If we possessed no other account of his career than that given in the Book of Wisdom, we should naturally conclude that Solomon, not only at the commencement of his reign, but throughout his whole life, was a bright example both of intellectual wisdom and of moral purity. It must here in fairness be observed that the writer of the Book of Chronicles also makes no allusion to Solomon's grievous transgressions. In the latter case, however, it would be rash to assign a cause for the omission of all mention of that king's apostasy, for the Books of the Chronicles exhibit numerous other omissions which cannot with safety be ascribed to any particular causes known to us.

The form of scepticism presented in the Book of Koheleth, if it can with any propriety be designated by such an appellation, was that found among persons not only outwardly reckoned among "the faithful," but really believers. Those whom he addressed may perhaps be described as believers walking in darkness, and crying out amid the gloom for "light, more light." They were, like the Psalmist of old, pained within them because the ungodly were in such prosperity (Ps. lxxiii.), and because little or no distinction seemed to be made in the arrangements of Divine providence in this world between the just and the unjust. The secrets of the life to come had not yet been clearly revealed. The stone had not been rolled away from the grave by the resurrection of Jesus Christ from the dead. The earnest remonstrance, which even the prophet Jeremiah was constrained to give utterance to, may be considered as expressing the thoughts of many a heart. "Righteous art thou, O Lord, when I plead with thee; yet let me talk with thee of thy judgments: wherefore doth the way of the wicked prosper? Wherefore are all they happy that deal very treacherously?" The deep mystery of the sufferings of the godly in this life had even at an earlier period formed the subject of the Book of Job. But the difficulty still remained. It was deeply felt in the days in which Koheleth poured forth his bitter complaints. For, if that writer lived after the return from captivity, it was only natural that he and his fellow-believers should have felt perplexed at the fact that, notwithstanding the restoration of Israel to their own land, days of prosperity had not dawned upon the chosen people. Some of his fellows had gone over to the ranks of the sceptics; a still larger number, perhaps, were "murmurers" against the dispensations of Providence. Hope deferred had made many hearts sick. It was verily a time when some divinely inspired teacher was needed to strengthen and confirm the faithful in Israel.

Though sympathising deeply with the difficulties in which such persons were placed, Koheleth, the philosophic prophet or preacher, urged upon the "murmurers" the duty of contentment. That there was darkness around their path he did not venture to deny; but there was also, he argued, much to console them amid that darkness, and no man ought sullenly to refuse to enjoy the good things God has provided for him even in this life. If the question "Wherefore doth the way of the wicked prosper?" could not be answered, not even by a prophet in Israel—for the day for manifesting that "mystery," and for revealing that secret had not yet come— those who believed in God should at least learn to receive with thankfulness the common gifts freely bestowed upon mankind; and, by enjoying the blessings which they actually possessed, to make the best use of the short span of existence appointed to man on earth (Koh. iii. 13; v. 18).

Such was at least one of the objects for which the Book of Koheleth was written. But the difficulties expressed in that book in regard to God's dealings with man did not diminish in number, as the dreary ages rolled on during which the Gentile power continued more or less heavily to oppress the once-favoured Israel. The charm of Greek literature began to be appreciated after the days of the Maccabean heroes, the once-detested Greek philosophy made its way into Jewish schools, and Greek manners began to corrupt the simplicity of the Jewish national life. In place of the "murmurers" who existed in the days of Koheleth, a race of "blasphemers" sprang up in the days of the writer of the Book of Wisdom. The Jewish free-thinkers of Alexandria dared to defend their obnoxious tenets by arguments derived from the Book of Koheleth itself. They boldly propounded materialistic opinions, they denied a future state of existence, and even went so far as to persecute those who opposed their pernicious views. These daring spirits advocated the full enjoyment of all the pleasures of sense, and defended their actions and principles on the plea that Solomon, the very impersonation of wisdom, had declared himself on their side; for he had demonstrated human life to be but vanity, and had advised men to enjoy earthly pleasures, while time remained for such enjoyment.

It need not, therefore, surprise us if some of the statements put forth by the writer of the Book of Wisdom appear to be almost direct contradictions of those found in the Book of Ecclesiastes. The young scoffers of Alexandria had based their arguments upon certain positions taken up in the latter book. The writer of the Book of Wisdom denies many of the statements of Koheleth, that is, as interpreted by the adversaries of true religion. The verbal similarities which exist between the expressions of the adversaries of religion and morality as set forth in the second chapter of the Book of Wisdom, and the expressions which actually occur in the Book of Koheleth, are most remarkable.

Thus, the materialistic free-thinkers of that day are described as asserting that life is short and troublesome (λυπηρός), Wisdom ii. 1, in conformity with the statement in Koheleth: "All his days are sorrows and his travail grief" (Koh. ii. 23; so also v. 16, 17). They laid stress upon the fact that there is no deliverance from death (Wisdom ii. 2, 3, 5), a fact repeatedly alluded to by the Preacher (Koh. viii. 8; iii. 2, 18, 21) as one of those particulars which tend to lower man to the level of the brute creation. These materialists further asserted that men were born accidentally, by chance ($αὐτοσχεδίως$),[1] echoing, though in different phraseology, the thought which occurs several times in Koheleth, "the children of men are a chance" (Koh. iii. 19), "time and accident happen to them all" (Koh. ix. 11). It is of small advantage, said they, to seek to leave a good name behind us, "for our name shall in time be forgotten, and no one will remember our works" (Wisdom ii. 4). Compare this with the statements of Koheleth, "there is no remembrance of former things, neither shall there be a remembrance of things that are to come" (Koh. i. 11), "the fool and the wise man shall be alike forgotten (Koh. ii. 16), for "the memory of the dead is forgotten" (Koh. ix. 5). Life, these Jewish Alexandrians asserted truly, is a shadow (Wisdom ii. 5, comp. v. 9), a comparison also taken from

---

[1] $αὐτοσχεδίως$ is explained by Schleusner to mean, "casu, sine Dei consilio et providentia." The rendering of the Vulgate is incorrect, *ex nihilo*. Deane renders it "at all adventure," and explains it as meaning "off-hand, at hap-hazard." For this English rendering he refers to the marginal rendering of Lev. xxvi. 21, and Shakespeare, *Comedy of Errors*, ii. 2. A manuscript glossary on the book quoted by Schleusner explains it as ἐκ τοῦ παρατυχόντος, ταχέως, ἐκ τοῦ παραυτίκα παραχρῆμα, αὐτόματα. Hesych. explains αὐτοσχεδίως by αὐτομάτως. Grimm gives our translation "durch Zufall," and notes that the sentence contains an allusion to the Epicurean doctrine according to which all appearances of nature owe their origin to chance; and refers to Ritter, *Gesch. d. Philosophie*, vol. iii. p. 395. He also quotes *Lactant. Instt.*, ii. 1, 2, "homines . . ne se, ut quidam philosophi faciunt, tantopere despiciant, neve se infirmos et *supervacuos* et *frustra* omnino *natos* putent, quae opinio plerosque ad vitia compellit," and also *Cic. Tusc.* i. 49, "Non *temere* nec *fortuito* sati et creati sumus, sed profecto fuit vis quaedam, quae consuleret generi humano; nec id gigneret aut aleret, quod, quum exanclavisset omnes labores, tum incideret in mortis malum sempiternum; portum potius paratum nobis et perfugium putemus."

Koheleth (Koh. vi. 12; viii. 13). Hence, argued they, men ought to seek to compensate themselves for the sad circumstances under which they are placed by giving themselves up as far as possible, without any unnecessary restraint, to a life of pleasure.

There is a similarity between Koheleth's advice to make use of the innocent joys of life (Koh. ix. 7-9),[1] and the exhortation of the free-thinkers in the Book of Wisdom, to enjoy the pleasures of sin in their season.

> " Go, eat with joy thy bread,
> And drink with joyful heart thy wine,
> For long ago God hath approved thy works.
> At all times let thy garments be white!
> And let not oil on thy head be wanting!
> Enjoy life with a wife whom thou lovest,
> All the days of thy life of vanity
> Which he hath given to thee under the sun,
>   All the days of thy vanity,
> For this is thy portion in life
> And in thy toil with which thou toilest under the sun."

Should this advice of Koheleth appear somewhat Epicurean, its real character will be better seen by contrasting it with the exhortation of the ungodly depicted in the Book of Wisdom; that exhortation being evidently the interpretation or misinterpretation put upon the words of Koheleth by the sensualists of Alexandria.

> " Come therefore and let us enjoy the good things present [2]
> And let us eagerly make use of the world [3] as long as we are young.

---

[1] Koheleth nowhere gives any encouragement to a life of dissipation, though he frequently urges on men the use of the natural pleasures presented to them in this life. See Koh. iii. 12, 22; v. 17, 18 (E.V. v. 18, 19); viii. 15; xi. 19, and our remarks on the latter verse in chap. viii.

[2] The phrase τῶν ὄντων ἀγαθῶν means actual good things in opposition to such ideal blessings as piety, virtue and wisdom, and things which are in existence at the present time and not merely expected in a future state of being.

[3] So Grimm translates the clause καὶ χρησώμεθα τῇ κτίσει ὡς νεότητι σπουδαίως. Deane renders "let us use the creatures like as in youth," but we prefer Grimm's

> With costly wine and unguents let us fill ourselves,
> And let no flower of spring pass by us,
> Let us crown ourselves with buds of roses before they wither,
> [Let there be no mead though which our luxury does not pass,][1]
> Let not one of us be without a share of our wantonness,
> Everywhere let us leave behind us signs of our joyousness,[2]
> For this is our portion, and this our lot."
> Wisdom ii. 6-10.

It can scarcely escape notice, that the last words of this passage re-echo an expression which occurs several times in the Book of Ecclesiastes (ii. 10; iii. 22; v. 18; ix. 9).

Strange it is in face of such clear proofs (even if no others could be adduced), that Hitzig, who sought to prove that Koheleth was a book of a later age than the Book of Wisdom, should have ventured to assert that "for many reasons"—reasons be it observed which the learned critic has nowhere given in detail—the reference to Koheleth in this passage of the Book of Wisdom is "in the highest degree improbable."[3]

Such are a few of the more striking of those passages in the Book of Wisdom which were evidently directed against a one-sided and too-literal interpretation of the language of the Book of Ecclesiastes.[4] The stern condemnation of the

---

rendering, which is also adopted by Bissell. τῇ κτίσει, *the creation* is used in the sense of *created* things, the world, as in Rom. viii. 19, 20; Heb. iv. 13. On the readings of the passage, see Grimm and Bissell.

[1] This addition is found in the Vulgate, "nullum pratum sit quod non pertranseat luxuria nostra." It is accepted as genuine by Grimm and Bissell, and Deane remarks, "it is true that nothing to correspond with this clause is found in any existing Greek MS., but a clause parallel to the first half of the verse is required, if we regard the careful balancing of periods exhibited in the rest of the paragraph."

[2] Or joyfulness, ἀγερωχίας. Deane observes, "this word in classical Greek means insolence, haughtiness. Here, *unrestrained voluptuousness*, insolentia In luxurie vitæque mollitie conspicua, *Wahl. Clav.* Comp. 2 Macc. ix. 7; 3 Macc. ii. 3."

[3] Hitzig, *Der Prediger Salomo's*, p. 121 in the *Kurzgef. exeget. Handb. zum A.T.*

[4] Dean Plumptre has in his Introduction to his *Comm. on Ecclesiastes*, pp. 71 ff, given other examples, with some of which we are unable to coincide. See our comm. on Koh. ix. 9, and our remarks in chap. viii. on Koh. xi. 9. But the following in-

Koheleth and the Book of Wisdom.

young free-thinkers of Alexandria which follows the passage already cited was perhaps the more scathing, as it was represented to come from the lips of Solomon, whom they falsely quoted as having given judgment on their side.

There are, moreover, other passages in which the writer of this apocryphal book was not at all backward to express his opinion in language which savours of the spirit of contradiction to the Book of Koheleth, although it may be maintained that there is no more real contradiction between the apparently opposing statements when compared with one another, than actually exists between several passages of the Book of Ecclesiastes itself.

Thus, if Koheleth affirms (ix. 2) "all things come to all alike, one chance happens to the righteous and the wicked, to the good, and to the clean and unclean," the writer of the Book of Wisdom maintains "the souls of the righteous are in the hand of God, and no torment shall touch them. In the eyes of the unwise they seemed to die, and their departure is reckoned a misfortune, and their going from us destruction, but they are in peace" (Wisdom iii. 2, 3). In contrast with the ungodly, who are likened to dust blown away before the wind, to fine frost driven away by the whirlwind, to smoke dispersed by the storm, "the righteous" are said by him to "live for ever," "and their reward is with the Lord, and the care of them is with the Most High" (Wisdom v. 14, 15).

Koheleth asserts (i. 18) "In much wisdom is much grief,

---

stances may here be quoted:—" to the ever-recurring complaint that all things are 'vanity and feeding upon wind,' (Eccles. i. 14, 17; ii. 26, *et al.*) he [the author of the Book of Wisdom] opposes the teaching that 'murmuring is unprofitable' (Wisd. i. 11). The thought that death was better than life, to be desired as an everlasting sleep (Eccl. vi. 4, 5), [we dispute the correctness of this interpretation, see our comm.], he meets with the warning, 'seek not death in the error of your life' (Wisd. i. 12); and ventures even on the assertion that 'God made not death,' that it was an Enemy that had done this, that life and not death was contemplated in the Divine purpose as the end of man (Wisd. i. 13). It was only the ungodly who counted death their friend (Wisd. i. 16)."

and he that increaseth knowledge increaseth sorrow"; but the writer of the apocryphal book says of wisdom, "conversation with her hath no bitterness, and to live with her hath no sorrow, but mirth and joy" (viii. 16). Solomon, in the Book of Koheleth, complains that wisdom does not bring bread to the wise, that riches do not fall to the lot of the understanding, nor favour to the knowing (ix. 11); while, in the Book of Wisdom, he is described as saying, through wisdom "I shall have honour ($\delta \acute{o} \xi a \nu$) among the multitudes, and veneration ($\tau \iota \mu \acute{\eta} \nu$), though young, among the elders" (viii. 10). According to the Book of Ecclesiastes, there is no remembrance after death of the wise man any more than of the fool (ii. 16); in the Book of Wisdom, Solomon asserts "I shall have by her (wisdom) immortality, and I shall leave an everlasting remembrance to those after me" (viii. 13).

It is unnecessary to do more than mention the remarkable contrast before alluded to between the retrospect of Solomon's career given in Ecclesiastes i. and ii. and that presented in Wisdom vii.–ix. In the former the great monarch is represented as seeking to obtain satisfaction not only by following after noble ends, but also by following on every side after sensual pleasures, and to be from first to last dissatisfied with the result of his endeavours. Throughout the latter Solomon is described as an ardent seeker after wisdom, and a veil is drawn over the dark traits of his character.

The Book of Wisdom was a valuable contribution to theological literature at the time in which it appeared. The noble ideas expressed in it concerning the Divine Being, its frequent mention of love and charity, were peculiarly important. The writer manifests throughout a sympathy for man as man, and he exhibits also a firm belief in the Divine mission of Israel, although that people is not once mentioned by name in his book. The clear enunciation of the doctrine of a life beyond the grave, of future rewards and punishments, and of the immortality of the righteous, though the doctrine of the "resurrection" was hidden from his eyes, tends to invest the book with a special interest.[1] In its grasp of these verities the work occupies a higher standpoint than the Book of Ecclesiastes. It does not ignore the fact that "there are righteous who perish by their righteousness, and there are evil men who protract their lives by their wickedness" (Koh. vii. 15). But, in the light of the doctrine of future retribution, so prominently taught on its pages, the recognition of such a difficulty does not cast that heavy pall of gloom over the spirit which oppresses us in perusing the pages of the Book of Koheleth. Nor does the writer of the Book of Wisdom forget to emphasise the truth that the punishment of the ungodly is not always reserved for another world, and that God's anger frequently breaks out against the wicked even on this side of the grave (iii. 11 ff., iv. 3-6, etc). This truth is exhibited in the closing chapters, where an account—disfigured indeed in many places by needless and occasionally even absurd exaggerations—is given of the plagues poured upon the land of Egypt in the days of Moses, and of the marvellous exemption vouchsafed on that occasion to the people of Israel.

The Book of Wisdom, therefore, supplied an important gap in the creed of the Jewish Church. It guarded many a Greek-speaking Jew from errors, which either were directly founded on a narrow and over-literal interpretation of the Book of Koheleth, or indirectly drew a portion of their support therefrom. It brought into fuller light certain important doctrines, which in the Book of Ecclesiastes are discoverable only in the germ. In respect to the doctrine of the resurrection, the Book of Wisdom has fallen short of the

---

[1] On this subject compare Dr. Aug. Wünsche, *Die Vorstellungen vom Zustande nach dem Tode nach Apokryphen, Talmud, und Kirchenvätern*, in the Jahrbücher für protest. Theologie, Band vi. 1880, pp. 355-383 and 495-523.

standard reached in the Book of Daniel. But it retains throughout a firm grasp of "the hope full of immortality." Many of the peculiar terms and phrases employed in it, such as "Holy Spirit," "only begotten," "fatherhood of God," "philanthropy," and "love," reappear in a higher sense in the New Testament. As Deane notes, "allusions to its phraseology are frequent in St. Paul's Epistles. That noble passage in the fifth chapter of Wisdom seems to be the groundwork of the grand description of the Christian's armour in Ephesians (vi. 13-17), 'He shall take to Him His jealousy for complete armour' λήψεται πανοπλίαν: 'take unto you the whole armour of God,' ἀναλάβετε τὴν πανοπλίαν τοῦ Θεοῦ. 'He shall put on righteousness as a breastplate,' ἐνδύσεται θώρακα δικαιοσύνην: 'Having on the breastplate of righteousness,' ἐνδυσάμενοι τὸν θώρακα τῆς δικαιοσύνης. 'And true judgment instead of a helmet. He shall take holiness for an invincible shield'; 'above all taking the shield of faith . . . and take the helmet of salvation.' The passage too about the potter in Romans ix. is an echo of a similar sentiment in Wisdom xv." The language of Hebrews i. 3 is partially identical with that of Wisdom vii. 26; and many other instances are cited by Deane and others.[1] Of course, the use of the phraseology found in the Book of Wisdom is far from being equivalent to direct quotations from that book. These occur nowhere in the New Testament Scriptures. But in these and many other particulars the Book of Wisdom may well be viewed as a bright harbinger of the more glorious gospel revealed by our Lord and His apostles. If the Book of Koheleth must be regarded in some respects as the last piercing cry of the Old Testament dispensation for "light, light," the Book of Wisdom not merely re-echoes that cry, but partly answers it, marred

[1] See Deane's Prolegomena to his edition of the Book of Wisdom, chap. v. pp. 35 ff.

though the work be, in some places, by the inspirations of the Greek philosophy. Only one great Teacher, the Son of Man and Son of God, the Light and the Life of men, was able to shed a new and a true light upon the dark problems touched upon in the Book of Ecclesiastes. In His blessed light may we see light!

Throughout the apocryphal work, "wisdom" is commended as the true guide to a blissful immortality, and the conditions are laid down under which alone man can obtain possession of that Divine gift (chaps. i.–iv.). The Divine character of wisdom, and its mode of operation in enlightening the intellect and directing the life of man, are described in the second section, which closes with Solomon's prayer for wisdom (chaps. vi.–ix.). The beneficial result of wisdom in early Israelitish history is described in what appears at least at first sight to be a continuation of that prayer, which is so protracted as at last to become unnatural and tedious (chaps. x.–xix.). Some places in that description are occasionally obscure, owing to the artificial plan of the writer, which is consistently maintained throughout, of omitting all mention of proper names. The writer speaks of all men under the designation of the godly and ungodly, although he relates the histories of Adam, Enoch, Noah, Abraham, Lot, Jacob, Joseph, Moses, Israel in Egypt, and many incidents in the life of Solomon.

It was but natural that the Christian Fathers should regard the beautiful description of the righteous man in chap. ii. 12–20, as a prophecy of the life and sufferings, the death and exaltation of the only-begotten Son of God. When that passage, however, is submitted to a closer examination, it is manifest that the writer is there speaking of the righteous as a class, and not of any single individual.[1] But the picture there presented of the righteous man bold in his

---

[1] See note, on p. 59.

reproof of sin in every form, even when cherished in the hidden recesses of the soul, of his sufferings on account of his testimony against evil, and of his being put to death by his foes, must recall vividly to our minds the Righteous Martyr in whom the writer's ideal was more than realized. The ideal of the Book of Wisdom is a grand one, though the passage cannot be compared for beauty or force with the still grander prophecy of Isaiah liii., where the Righteous Servant of Jahaveh is represented as atoning by his sufferings, not for his own sins, but for the sins of the people.

The Book of Koheleth, in its exhibition of the darkness of the old dispensation, and the Book of Wisdom in its anticipations of New Testament light, were both preparations for the better revelation of Jesus Christ. We may safely endorse the beautiful remarks of Ewald concerning the Book of Wisdom: "but for such books there are many things which it would be difficult to comprehend in a Paul, a John and their contemporaries. In the nervous energy of his proverbial style, and in the depth of his representation we have a premonition of John, and in his conception of heathenism a preparation for Paul, like a warm rustle of the spring ere its time is fully come.[1]

[1] Ewald, *Hist.*, p. 484, vol. v. (Engl. Ed.), *Gesch. des Volkes Isr.*, Band iv. 3te Ausg. 1864, p. 632.

CHAPTER IV.

THE AUTHORSHIP OF THE BOOK OF KOHELETH.

CHAPTER IV.

Summary of preceding chapters, 79—The authorship of the Book of Koheleth, 80—Earliest doubts as to its Solomonic authorship, 80—Traces of hesitation even in early times, 81—Koheleth a title of Solomon, 82—The name not chosen to conceal the writer, 83—Meaning of the title, 84—Solomon a preacher, 85—The name no evidence of authorship, 85—Mr. Johnston's argument on this point, 86—Reasons assigned by Bloch for the use of the name, 87—Significance of phrase, "King in Jerusalem," 88—Attempts to explain it away, 89—Solomon redivivus, 90—Legend of Talmud, 91—Meaning "I was king," 91—Other attempts to explain the perfect tense, 92—The predecessors of Solomon, 94—Historical accuracy not aimed at, 95—Attempt of early translators to evade the force of the passage, 95—The Masoretic reading of the passage, 96—The epilogue of the work, 97—Opinions of Krochmal and Fürst, 97—Of Graetz, 98—Bloch's modification of Krochmal's view, 99—The view of M. Renan, 100—Koheleth and the Koheleth, 101—The three points of the epilogue, 100—Disavowal of Solomonic authorship, 102—Views of Ewald and Delitzsch as to epilogue, 102—"Masters of collections," 103—The words of the wise, 103—The inspiration of the Sacred Writings affirmed by the writer, 104—The warning how to learn, 105—The announcement of a coming judgment, 106.

CHAPTER IV.

THE AUTHORSHIP OF THE BOOK OF KOHELETH.

IN our first chapter we endeavoured to show that it is probable that the Book of Koheleth or Ecclesiastes was admitted into the Jewish Canon by "the men of the Great Synagogue," who flourished between B.C. 444 and B.C. 196. The fact of disputes having taken place on the question of the canonicity of the book between the rival schools of Hillel and Shammai, some thirty or forty years before the Christian era, is quite consistent with the theory that long prior to that date it was regarded as one of the books of Sacred Scripture. We also pointed out that Graetz's theory of the composition of the work in the days of Herod the Great is untenable, being contrary to the following facts. (1) That the Book of the Wisdom of Jesus the Son of Sirach, or Ben Sira, written in Palestine, in Hebrew or Aramaic, at latest about B.C. 180, contains many passages which show an intimate acquaintance with the Book of Koheleth. (2) That the Greek work entitled The Wisdom of Solomon, composed in Egypt about B.C. 150, was designed specially to counteract the false opinions propounded by the Jewish sensualists of Alexandria, and professedly based by them on statements which occur in the Book of Ecclesiastes. (3) That a translation of the Book of Koheleth formed part and parcel of the LXX. version of the Jewish Scriptures, and that, therefore, the book must have been in existence prior to the second century before Christ. And (4) lastly, that the Talmud contains direct proofs that the

Book of Koheleth was actually quoted as Sacred Scripture, on a par with the Law of Moses, in the days of Herod the Great, and even by the great Jewish teachers who flourished before that period, and consequently must have been looked upon as canonical long prior to that era.

In discussing the question (treated of in our last chapter) of the relation which subsists between the Book of Koheleth and the Book of Wisdom, we pointed out that the writer of the latter did not scruple to put forth his work, which contained profitable doctrine most necessary for the time at which it appeared, under the name of Solomon; but that in so doing the author had not the slightest idea of committing any fraud whatever, but simply sought to assert in the strongest manner possible that the views he advocated, in direct opposition to the Jewish sensualist school of Alexandria, were in full accordance with the utterances of that heavenly wisdom which had been bestowed upon the great Solomon.

We come now to consider more particularly the question of the authorship of the Book of Koheleth. It must be conceded at the very outset that no distinct evidence can be adduced of any doubts having been expressed as to the Solomonic authorship of the book earlier than the period of the Reformation. Nay more, if our theory respecting the object and aim of the Book of the Wisdom of Solomon be correct, a further concession must be made, namely, that the Book of Koheleth, known to the Alexandrian Jews through the medium of the Greek translation of the LXX., was regarded by them at that early period as a veritable production of the great monarch of Israel. This, however, is no more than might be expected under the circumstances of the case in that uncritical age, especially if it be borne in mind that the book was not generally studied by the Alexandrian Jews in its original language. But the fact remains that Luther, in his *Table Talk*, was the first who ventured distinctly to deny the Solomonic authorship of the work; and the great Dutch scholar, Hugo Grotius, more than a century later, was the first who ventured to assign critical arguments (not, it must be acknowledged, of the most cogent character) in support of that novel opinion.[1]

But, although the judgment of antiquity in favour of the Solomonic authorship of Ecclesiastes, as far as we possess distinct evidence, appears to have been unanimous, it is to be noted that certain sayings handed down in the Midrashim exhibit traces of hesitation on this very point. Again and again one encounters in these early commentaries (which, in spite of Dean Plumptre's unfavourable opinion,[2] are by no means to be despised as worthless) the distinct assertion that "while Solomon taught the Law the Holy Spirit descended upon him, and he composed the three books, Proverbs, Song of Songs, and Koheleth."[3] In the same place Solomon is represented as one who in his lifetime had experience of three worlds, having been "a king, a private person, and again a king;" or, as it is otherwise expressed, having been in succession "a wise man, a fool, and again wise."[4] Such sayings are probably based upon the legend preserved in the Targum, according to which Solomon, after he had provoked God to anger by his foreign marriages, was driven from his throne, and went through the towns and cities of Israel as a preacher, everywhere lamenting his own folly,

---

[1] See Luther's *Werke*, Erlangen Ausg. vol. lxii. p. 128. He affirmed the same opinion in the preface to his German translation of the work in 1524; but in his Latin Comm., issued in 1532, he has adopted the traditional view. See his Exeg. Operi Lat. vol. xxi. ed. Irmischer & Schmidt, 1858.

[2] One will often find that what seems to be childish has a deeper signification than at first sight appears. The trivialities, or as Dean Plumptre calls them, "the insanities," of the old Jewish expositors can be paralleled by similar quotations from the Patristic writers, and even from the works of commentators of later date who ought to have been better instructed.

[3] *Midrash Shir ha-shirim*, i. 1.

[4] See p. 76.

and reproving sin, crying out, "I am Koheleth, whose name was formerly called Solomon, who was king over Israel in Jerusalem."[1] This legend, which in later times assumed yet stranger forms, does not appear to have been originally intended to set forth an historical fact, but rather to be an allegory, illustrating the truth that the career of Solomon was a remarkable example on the one hand of the glory and honour attained by pursuing the path of wisdom, and on the other of the ruin and disgrace which result from following the way of folly. For, inasmuch as the story of that great monarch's transgression and fall is replete with lessons of wisdom, Solomon, "though dead yet speaketh," and utters in the Book of Koheleth lessons and words of wisdom, whether the book be an actual production of Solomon's pen, or the work of another author, who adduces that king as the most remarkable example of the vanity of all earthly things.

There have not, indeed, been wanting scholars who have had the hardiness to deny that the name of Koheleth was intended as a designation of Solomon.[2] A similar assertion, just as groundless, has been made with respect to the Book of Wisdom (see p. 60). Neither the one statement nor the other can for a moment be defended unless by persons either ignorant of facts or fond of paradoxes.

The record of the acts of Koheleth, the son of David, set forth in chap. ii., and the description given there of his wisdom, prove beyond all reasonable doubt that no other person can be meant by the name Koheleth than the world-renowned Solomon.

---

[1] See p. 91.
[2] Nachman Krochmal, in his *More Neboche ha-zeman* (*i.e.* Director errantium nostræ ætatis), published after the author's death by L. (Leopold) Zunz (Lemberg, 1851), as cited by Delitzsch, maintained that the name Koheleth was the designation of some descendant of David, who acted probably as governor of Jerusalem in the times of the Persian domination; and hence the expression used in chap. i. 12, "Koheleth, the son of David, who was king in Jerusalem."

There are, however, passages to be found in the Book of Koheleth itself in which the author lifts up his visor in such a manner as to show the intelligent reader that the character and name of Solomon were simply assumed, not for any purpose of deception, nor as "a pious fraud," but by a perfectly allowable literary device.

Hengstenberg, indeed, has gone too far when he asserts that the name of Koheleth was affixed to the work to indicate that it was not intended to be regarded as Solomon's. For, argues Hengstenberg, the proper name of Solomon is prefixed to all his genuine writings. But the induction of particulars is too small to permit of any such conclusion being arrived at with safety. The use of the name Koheleth in itself is of no real significance in deciding the disputed question of the authorship of the work.

The name Koheleth could not possibly have been made use of for the purpose of concealment. For, if Solomon had been really the writer, no assumption of a fictitious name could for one moment have rendered the authorship uncertain, as his acts and wisdom are so plainly spoken of in the first two chapters of the book. On the other hand, if that monarch is referred to merely as the highest impersonation of wisdom, he would have been more fitly brought forward in that character under the world-renowned name of Solomon, which in process of time became a synonym of wisdom itself. Even were the assumption of a Solomonic authorship to be regarded as a "pious fraud," one can scarcely understand what object a writer could have had in view in designating Solomon by a title not by any means easy of comprehension, instead of referring to him by the ordinary name by which that great king of Israel was universally known.

This is not the place in which to give a sketch of the various interpretations proposed for the title Koheleth, by which Solomon is uniformly characterised in this book of Scripture, and in no other.[1] The matter cannot, however, here be altogether passed over in silence. The word Koheleth (קֹהֶלֶת) is, by no means so enigmatical as Renan has asserted it to be. It is properly speaking a second form of the feminine of the active participle of the first conjugation of the verb kahal (קָהַל), used, however, in a neuter signification. Nouns of this particular form are often applied to individuals without regard to gender, to indicate that such persons are to a high degree possessors of the special form of activity expressed by the verb. Hence Koheleth signifies "a *preacher*" without any reference to the gender of the individual; and the term has been thus explained by the LXX., the Vulg., and the earliest expositors, as well as by our A.V. The use of nouns of that form as proper names of men belongs probably to a late stage of the Hebrew language.[2] In the present case the feminine has been supposed by Ewald, Hitzig, Ginsburg and others, to indicate Solomon as the personification of wisdom. This explanation is not, however, justified by the contents of the book. The writer nowhere brings forward Wisdom addressing men as in the Book of Proverbs. Solomon is not depicted in the Book of Ecclesiastes, as in the Book of Proverbs, in the character of a teacher who regards his readers as "children," "sons," or pupils. The single instance of this usage in the Book of Ecclesiastes (xii. 12) is only an apparent but not a real exception. In the character of personified wisdom Solomon could not have spoken of himself as having gotten more wisdom than all before him in Jerusalem, or be described as relating how his heart had great experience of wisdom (chap. i. 16–18), or how he had applied his heart to discover by means of wisdom certain things (chap. vii. 23).

The verb (קהל) from whence the name Koheleth is derived,

[1] See our Crit. Comm.   [2] See our Crit. Comm.

signifies *to call, to call together*, for the purposes of assembling. The noun signifies a "speaker" or "preacher" before an assembly convened for religious purposes, rather than a "convener" or "assembler." The historical fact which gave rise to the name was most likely that spoken of in 1 Kings viii. 55-61, where the historian records that Solomon gathered all Israel together (1 Kings viii. 1, comp. verse 65) for the consecration of the temple. On that occasion Solomon preached, as Delitzsch has rightly observed, to the people indirectly in the remarkable prayer which he then poured forth, and directly when he afterwards blessed them and exhorted them to continue faithful to the Lord God of Israel (1 Kings viii. 55-61).

Although the discourse delivered by Solomon before that great assembly in Jerusalem was probably the special reason which led the author of the book before us to designate Solomon by the peculiar name of Koheleth, it is to be observed that no other allusion whatever is made in the book to that "crowning period" in that king's history. In the Book of Koheleth Solomon is not represented as one who preached to assembled Israel at a great crisis in the nation's history; nor, indeed, is he introduced as addressing specially the Israelitish nation. He is represented rather as a preacher teaching mankind in general lessons drawn from his own personal experience, which led him to the mortifying conclusion that "all is but vanity and vexation of spirit." Hence the name Koheleth so far from being, as Mr. Johnston considers it, "intrinsic evidence of Solomon's authorship," is quite the reverse.[1] Solomon once "preached" to the people. Then he was "a wise man," "a rich man," and "a king." In the Book of Koheleth he speaks as "a poor man," who once indeed had been rich, but for whom riches no longer had any

---

[1] *A Treatise on the Authorship of Ecclesiastes.* Macmillan & Co., 1880. p. 119. See our remarks on p. 114.

charms. Though endued with the gift of wisdom above all who preceded him, he narrates how he had acted like a fool, and had thus learned the vanity and vexation even of earthly wisdom. He speaks, indeed, as "a wise man," but as one who had learned wisdom by experience, and had "come to himself," after having been first guilty of extreme folly. He speaks, too, no longer as "a king," but as one who had sat upon the throne in days gone by, and now sought to rule his fellow-men only by pointing out to them the lessons which he had learned by experience. The remark of Rabbi Judan and Rabbi Onyah, already quoted from the Midrash, is more profound than it appears at first sight to be. Solomon was "a king, a private person, and a king—a wise man, a fool, and a wise man—a rich man, a poor man, and a rich man." Rabbi Judan quotes in proof of this the words of Koheleth: "all have I seen in the days of my vanity," (chap. vii. 15), and observes, "a man reflects on his punishment (אונקי דידיה = τὴν ἀνάγκην αὐτοῦ) only in the hour of his enlargement." Rabbi Onyah cites as his proof simply the text: "I, Koheleth, was king over Jerusalem"[1] (chap. i. 12).

It is strange that Mr. Johnston did not perceive that the instances he has given (in p. 336 of his *Treatise*) cannot possibly be regarded as evidence in favour of the Solomonic authorship. He calls attention to the fact that "in contrasting a poor and wise child with an old and foolish king, Koheleth represents the child as standing up in the king's stead, adding: 'there is no end of all the people'" (chap. iv. 16). This statement, Mr. Johnston maintains, coincides remarkably with the expressions used by Solomon in his prayer at Gibeon in reference to the vast numbers of the people over whom that monarch was called to reign (1 Kings iii. 7, 8), and also with the narrative of 1 Kings, in which the crowds are spoken of who hailed with acclamations his

[1] See p. 90.

accession to the throne. This critic regards it as "a peculiarly interesting circumstance" that the only other place in which mention is made of the "people" (עם) in the Book of Ecclesiastes is in chap. xii. 9, "and moreover, because Koheleth was wise, he still taught the people knowledge." From an array of such statements Mr. Johnston seeks to derive an argument in favour of the Solomonic authorship of the book. But he seems to forget that even if it be granted that there is a connexion between the two passages, all that can possibly be proved from such trifling coincidences is, that the writer of the Book of Ecclesiastes was well acquainted with the incidents of Solomon's life which are recorded in the Sacred Writings, and that his book contains allusions to those incidents.

Bloch, in his able defence of the Solomonic authorship of Ecclesiastes, seeks to account in another manner for Solomon's styling himself by a different name than that by which he designated himself as the author of the Book of Proverbs and the Song of Songs. He maintains that it was becoming that the writer of the Book of Ecclesiastes should assume a name different from that by which he was ordinarily known. The glorious name of Solomon would have presented too glaring a contrast to the character of Koheleth. It would have been unsuitable to have prefixed to such a book the proud name of Solomon, the wisest among men, the prince of peace, the king of Israel, who ruled over a territory larger than that governed by his warlike sire, and vastly greater than that of any of his successors. For the Book of Ecclesiastes pronounces all his might, majesty, and wisdom to be but vanity. Hence, according to Bloch, in the Book of Koheleth Solomon sought as far as possible to assume the place of a private individual, who, though he had been a king, wished to be regarded in the light of an ordinary man addressing his fellow-mortals. Solomon had had full experience of the bitterness of life; and, in consequence of the extensive knowledge of men and things which he possessed, might well be justified in regarding his own experience as typical of that of mankind in general. If, therefore, in the course of his philosophical lamentations he speaks of himself as a king, and as a wise man, it is only to prove that he was thoroughly acquainted with the matters of which he treats. For he knew better than any other man the vanity of all earthly things.

The reason assigned by Bloeh for the use of the name Koheleth is ingenious. But, if it were well-founded, it would afford a strong argument against the Solomonic authorship of the book. Such considerations might have great weight in the eyes of a writer of a later date than Solomon, but it would scarcely have had any in the case of Solomon himself. It is highly probable that the real reason why Solomon is termed in the book by the name of Koheleth is that he is represented throughout as one who, not only by his teaching, but in a greater degree by the incidents of his individual career, demonstrated the vanity of all human efforts to attain real satisfaction. The experience of a Solomon proves distinctly that the certainty of death on the one hand, and the uncertainty attending all human efforts on the other, must necessarily cast a dark shadow over the path even of the most favourably situated, and of the wisest of mankind. If such persons are forced to exclaim, "all is vanity," much more must ordinary mortals be driven to the same conclusion.

Koheleth is represented as "king in Jerusalem" (chap. i. 1), and "king over Israel in Jerusalem" (chap. 1. 12). The phrase "king in Jerusalem" occurs nowhere else in the Sacred Writings. The phrase "reigned in Jerusalem" occurs often. It is used of David when his reign in Jerusalem is spoken of in contrast to his reign at Hebron (2 Sam. v. 5;

1 Kings ii. 10). It is used also in reference to Solomon, in 1 Kings xi. 42, where it is said "he reigned in Jerusalem over all Israel." The historian uses the same phrase of Rehoboam (1 Kings xiv. 21), of Abijam (1 Kings xv. 2), of Asa (1 Kings xv. 10), and others. In the case of the kings of Judah the phrase is applied by way of contrast, either expressed or implied, to the kings of Israel who reigned in Tirzah, or in Samaria. Hence Eichhorn and others naturally consider that its occurrence in the book of Koheleth points to a time subsequent to the schism between the kingdoms of Israel and Judah. When Preston lays stress on the fact that Solomon was "the *only* 'king over Israel in Jerusalem'" —for David held his court both in Hebron and in Jerusalem—and when he maintains that the statement of chap. i. 1 ought to be regarded as "an undesigned evidence" in favour of the hypothesis of the Solomonic authorship of the work, he is strangely unmindful of the fact that, however suitably such a phrase might have been used after the time of Solomon in referring back to events which occurred in the reign of that monarch, it could not have been used by that king himself in any such signification. Solomon is naturally spoken of as "king of Israel" (2 Kings xxiii. 13 ; Neh. xiii. 26). Bullock tries to account for the mention of the city of Jerusalem in chap. i. 1 on the ground that that city was "the scene of Solomon's peculiar work for many years," and "the place which he had made the chief monument of his grandeur." But this explanation is not satisfactory, especially when one calls to mind the number of other cities mentioned by the writer of 1 Kings (chap. ix.), which were built by Solomon in various parts of the land of Israel.

It may fairly be argued that the phrase "king in Jerusalem" could not have been used by Solomon without some reference expressed or implied to Jerusalem as the seat of the theocracy. Bloch has endeavoured to interpret the phrase in the disputed passage as having such a reference. But the interpretation is scarcely defensible. For the nation of Israel is not mentioned at all in the book, much less spoken of as God's peculiar people. No allusion is made throughout the work to "the Gentiles," or to the position of Jerusalem as the centre of the religious worship of Israel. Even the great theocratic name of Jahaveh does not once occur in the work. In this last particular the Book of Koheleth presents a striking contrast to the Book of Proverbs.

Consequently—although the expression "reigned in Jerusalem" is a common one, and is very suitably used by historians like the writers of the Books of Samuel, the Kings, and the Chronicles—the fact that the title "king in Jerusalem" occurs only in the Book of Koheleth must be regarded, not indeed as affording positive proof against the theory of its Solomonic authorship, but as a piece of evidence which, as far as it goes, tells in favour of the conclusion that the writer of that book lived at a time when Israel had ceased to be looked upon as an independent nation, and when Jerusalem was no longer a royal residence.

Delitzsch, in common with the ablest modern critics, not only regards the phrase "king over Jerusalem" as evidence against the Solomonic authorship of the book, but also maintains that the use of the perfect tense (הייתי) in the same sentence (chap. i. 12) is strongly in favour of this conclusion. In the statement "I Koheleth was king over Israel in Jerusalem," Solomon does not speak of himself as a reigning monarch, but rather as one who had in past times exercised regal authority. The remark of Vaihinger cannot easily be set aside, namely, that the past "was" indicates a writer of later date who adduces Solomon as speaking from his grave; that scholar, moreover, observes that the very expression proves that the author of the book had no intention to make use of any deception in representing Solomon as thus addressing mankind. Delitzsch calls attention to the fact that a Talmudic legend, probably connected with that already mentioned (p. 81), is based on this very expression, and that the legend exhibits a correct grammatical comprehension of the force and signification of the tense employed. The legend referred to relates that Solomon was driven from his throne on account of his sins and follies, and that his throne was for a season occupied by an angel who assumed the features and appearance of the great monarch, while the latter was forced to wander about through the land of Israel, begging his bread from synagogue to synagogue, and from school to school, and crying out all the while, "I Koheleth was king over Israel in Jerusalem." The dethroned monarch, according to the story, in the course of his sorrowful wanderings, was often beaten with a stick on account of his apparently insane pretensions to regal dignity, and was fed upon beans. In the bitterness of his soul he was wont ever and anon to exclaim, "This is my portion of all my labour" (chap. ii. 10).[1]

Delitzsch maintains that it is mere self-deception to endeavour to persuade oneself that Solomon (who was king for forty years without any interruption of his sovereignty, and whose reign only terminated with his death), could, in giving a retrospect of his life in advanced years, have written, "I Koheleth was king over Israel." He might, indeed, have used the phrase in the sense of "I Koheleth became," or "have become, and still am king over Israel." But that sense is inadmissible in chap. i. 12 on account of the perfect tenses which follow, which are all used in a past signification. Had the writer intended to express the

[1] Compare Longfellow's *Tales of a Wayside Inn*, in which he depicts in a similar condition Robert, King of Sicily.

present tense, "I Koheleth am king," in contrast to the past tenses which follow, he would have made use of a different construction. The verb cannot, in the context in which it occurs, be grammatically translated "I Koheleth am king," nor can it be explained to signify, "I have been king and am still so."[1]

Bloch and, still more recently, Bullock (in the *Speaker's Commentary*) have attempted to explain the perfect tense in Ecclesiastes i. 12, by adducing the story of Louis XIV. of France, who, after the unsuccessful war of the Spanish succession, was often wont to cry out: "when I was yet a king." In giving utterance to such an expression, the French monarch compared his condition of powerlessness with his former power and might. No such comparison between the past and the present can have been intended by Solomon in the simple narrative of chap. i. 12.[2] For, although he is represented in this book as taking a retrospect of his life, and as arriving at the conclusion that all his might, glory, and wisdom were but vanity and vexation of spirit, he is nowhere depicted as comparing the sad present with the glorious past, nor as looking back with regret upon days of enjoyment which had passed away for ever. Such a comparison would have been foreign to the purpose of the book, though it might be required in order to justify the interpretation sought to be put upon the terms of chap. i. 12.[3]

---

[1] As Dr. Given, Professor of Hebrew, Magee Coll., Londonderry, maintains in his *Truth of Scripture in connection with Revelation, Inspiration, and the Canon*. T. & T. Clark, 1881. He appeals to Exod. ii. 22, but see note on next page.

[2] The dying words of the Roman Emperor Septimius Severus (A.D. 193-211), *omnia fui et nihil expedit*, "I have been all and it profits me nothing" might, indeed, be suitably quoted in illustration of the meaning of Koheleth. But the second part of the sentence of the Roman Emperor expresses that very comparison between the past and the present of his individual life, the contrast between the state of glory he had attained and the dark future immediately before him, which is required in any interpretation of the words before us in order to make them suitable to Solomon.

[3] Passages like Gen. xxxii. 10 (11) or Psalm lxxxviii. 5 (4), have no bearing

Mr. Johnston has attempted to put another sense on the words, and argues that they may signify "that Koheleth (whether he was or was not king when he wrote the Book of Ecclesiastes) was king at the time when he did what he details throughout the treatise" (*Treatise on Authorship of Ecclesiastes*, p. 162). The suggestion is ingenious but improbable. Had Solomon been the writer, he would have added some such qualifying clause as "for many years" in verse 12, or, omitting that verse entirely, would have commenced verse 13 with: "I Koheleth gave my heart to seek, etc." Mr. Johnston is far from being able to justify his statement that the perfect in the passage in question, in place of being "adverse to the Solomonic authorship of Ecclesiastes," is "strongly confirmatory" of that theory; and the passages adduced by him in support of this statement entirely fail to prove his conclusion.

But the passage just discussed is not the only one which presents a difficulty in the way of accepting the traditional view of the authorship of the work. There are several expressions found in other passages which equally conflict with the supposed Solomonic authorship. Thus, in chap. i. 16, Solomon is represented as recording his experience in the

whatever upon the interpretation of the text. For הייתי in those passages is evidently used in the sense of "*I am become*"—"*I am*." Such presents are the results of the historical past. Nor can the perfect in Exod. ii. 22. גֵּר הָיִיתִי בְּאֶרֶץ נָכְרִיָּה be regarded as a fitting parallel. The perfect there is not equivalent to the Latin *fui*, but is rather *factus sum*; or, still better, is equivalent to the Greek perfect which denotes an action completed in the past, whose consequences last up to the time of the speaker. Hence Exod ii. 22 is best rendered, "I am (lit. have become) a stranger in a strange land." (See *Driver's Heb. Tenses*, § 8). In the passage (Prov. iv. 3) quoted by Mr. Johnston (p. 165 of his *Treatise on the Authorship of Ecclesiastes*), the reference is solely to the past; while in Eccl. vii. 19 the perfect in the second clause is conditioned by the imperfect in the preceding, and consequently is rightly translated by the English present tense. Those passages, therefore, are not *ad rem*. The passage in the Song of Songs viii. 10, quoted by Mr. Johnston, is not an appropriate parallel, while the perfect tenses in 1 Kings x. 6; 1 Kings xi. 11; 2 Chron. i. 11, are used in a strictly past signification.

94 *Phrase opposed to Solomonic Authorship.*

following terms: "I communed with my heart, saying, Behold I have attained great and ever increasing wisdom over all who were before me over Jerusalem." As that monarch had in reality but one predecessor who ruled over Israel in Jerusalem, namely, his father David, the passage is naturally considered to have been written at a time when the writer could look back to a long line of Jewish kings who had ruled in the sacred capital. The last clause of the verse is, as Delitzsch has noted, singularly like that met with so frequently in the inscriptions of the Assyrian monarchs, namely, "the kings who were my predecessors." Hengstenberg, Bloch, and others have indeed maintained that the reference is to the ancient Canaanitish kings who reigned over Jerusalem previous to the Israelitish conquest of the country, such as Melchizedek in the days of Abraham (Gen. xv.), and Adonizedek in those of Joshua (Josh. x.). The phrase, those "who were before me over (על) Jerusalem," evidently refers to kings who ruled over that city.[1] Prof. Taylor Lewis, the American commentator, has ventured to characterize such a conclusion as "entirely gratuitous." He maintains that the verse may refer to "any men of note and wealth together with David and Saul, or the writer may well have had in view old princes in Jerusalem, away back to the days

---

[1] It is curious that Bullock, in his Introduction to Ecclesiastes in the *Speaker's Commentary*, could write (p. 623); "the limitation of the word 'all' to kings is a pure assumption which nothing in the context justifies. The writer compares himself with all who in former times, in Jerusalem, possessed wisdom or riches, possessions which are certainly not confined to kings." The same expositor, however, in his note in chap. i. 16 says, that "the reference is probably to the line of Canaanitish kings who lived in Jerusalem before David took it, of whom the names of Melchizedek (Gen. xiv. 18); Adonizedek (Josh. x. 1), and Araunah (2 Sam. xxiv. 23), are known to us; or it may be to Solomon's contemporaries of his own country (1 Kings iv. 31), and of other countries who visited him (1 Kings iv. 34 and x. 24)." He mentions, at the end of the note, the fact which upsets completely his former argument, namely, that "the preposition 'in' Jerusalem should be translated 'over'"! And yet he refers back to his Introduction, p. 623, where no notice is taken of this important fact !

of Melchizedek."[1] Such assertions only show how far prepossessions in favour of a certain view may lead the mind away from the simple truth.

The sacred historian speaks of Solomon's wealth and wisdom as greater than those of the kings of other nations (1 Kings iii. 12; x. 23, 24). His wisdom is said to have exceeded that of the children of the East country, and the wisdom of Egypt (1 Kings iv. 30, 31). But such statements are very different from that in Ecclesiastes i. 16, namely, that it was greater than the wisdom of the rulers over Jerusalem who were before him. An allusion to the old Canaanitish kings who had lived centuries before Solomon would have been here singularly incongruous; nor were any of them, as far as we know, specially renowned for wisdom. It is far easier to suppose that the passage contains an anachronism of little importance, and not caused by any ignorance on the part of the writer of the well-known facts of Israelitish history, as Hitzig arbitrarily supposes. It was not necessary that the writer of the Book of Koheleth, in bringing forward a *Solomon redivivus* recounting to mankind the lessons derived from his experience, should study historical accuracy in such unimportant points of detail. On the contrary, such trifling inaccuracies make it tolerably plain that the writer desired his readers to understand that he had assumed the rôle of Solomon only for a special purpose, and that his work was not to be regarded either as an historical treatise, or as an actual production of Solomon's pen.

The early translators appear to have been quite aware of the difficulty of explaining the statement in question as Solomonic. They, therefore, had recourse to the device of slightly modifying the text to suit their views. Thus the Targum has translated the passage: "Behold I have increased

---

[1] See in his note 1 on p. 42 of the English and American edition of *Lange's Commentary*.

and multiplied wisdom above all the wise men which were before me in Jerusalem,"[1] evidently referring to the four Israelitish sages, Ethan and Heman and Calcol and Darda, mentioned in 1 Kings iv. 31. The reading "in Jerusalem," although apparently supported by the LXX., Syr., and Vulg., and found in not a few Hebrew MSS. (as well as adopted by our Authorised Translation), must unquestionably be viewed as a conjectural emendation of the original text. It is specially mentioned by the Masorites; and, notwithstanding their general belief in the Solomonic authorship, such a reading of the text is distinctly condemned as erroneous.[2] The Masoretic reading "over Jerusalem" could never have found its way into the Hebrew text in preference to the easier, and far more comprehensible, reading "in Jerusalem," had it not been genuine.

In spite, then, of all the efforts of commentators to evade the fact, we cannot but regard this as one of several indications given by the author himself, that his work was not really intended to be regarded as a production of the great Israelitish monarch, although written in his name.

The only other instance which we shall here adduce occurs in the epilogue of the work, which begins with verse 9 of chap. xii., the Book of Koheleth itself properly ending with the eighth verse of that chapter.

A sketch of the various interpretations proposed for the last six verses of the book will be found in the commentary. We must, however, here notice briefly the view put forward by Krochmal in 1851, and adopted with slight modifications by several other Jewish scholars, such as Fürst in his work on the Canon of the Old Testament (1868), and Graetz in his Commentary on Koheleth (1871).

According to Krochmal, the verses in question were added

---

[1] אֲנָא הָא אַסְגֵּיתִי וְאוֹסְפִית חוּכְמְתָא עַל כָּל חַכִּימַיָּא דִּי הֲווֹ קֳדָמַי בִּירוּשְׁלֵם.
[2] See Levita's *Massoreth ha-Massoreth*, edited by Ginsburg, p. 228.

Opinions of Krochmal and Fürst. 97

at the final settlement of the Canon at the Synod at Jamnia, A.D. 90, and were designed to serve not merely as a conclusion to the Book of Koheleth, but as a fitting close to the end of the third and last division of the Jewish Scriptures, commonly known as the Hagiographa. Krochmal considers Koheleth to have been the last book in that division, although no proof of this can be adduced except his interpretation of the epilogue of that work. He interprets the clause "the words of the wise are as goads," in verse 11 to refer to the authors of the several books contained in the third division. By the בַּעֲלֵי אֲסֻפּוֹת the "lords of assemblies," he considers the members of the Jewish Sanhedrin to be signified, who are likened to firmly fixed nails which cannot be moved. Why the members of the Jewish council should thus be referred to in the epilogue, and what is meant by their being thus termed, is hard to divine. The modification of this translation given by Fürst, namely, "the words of the wise are like goads, and like pegs driven in by the men of the assembly" is ungrammatical; because, as Delitzsch observes, "the accusative after the passive participle can express any nearer definition, but cannot, like the genitive, express the effective cause." It must be observed, too, in passing, that for the same reason our English Version "as nails fastened by the masters of assemblies" must also be abandoned, although formerly given by a scholar like Lightfoot, and recently adopted and commented on by Bullock in the *Speaker's Commentary*. The translation of Fürst being thus inadmissible, it is unnecessary to discuss his interpretation of the second clause, namely, that the books of the Hagiographa are signified by "the pegs firmly driven in," or, finally admitted into the Canon by the men of the Assembly.

The rendering given by Graetz requires several alterations to be introduced into the Hebrew text which are not sanctioned

H

by the authority of the MSS. or of the ancient versions (see our comm.). He translates: "Words of the wise are as ox-goads and like pegs planted in. The members of the Assembly have handed them down from one shepherd." Graetz, after Krochmal, considers "the words of the wise" to signify the writings of the Hagiographa, which were, according to him, not considered, like the Pentateuch, to be the outcome of direct revelation from God, nor to be books, like the writings of the Prophets, which could be indirectly traced up to the same source, but works written by various authors, who, though not prophets, were "wise men." The last clause, therefore, he considers to be an endorsement of the Book of Koheleth as a book approved of by the men of the Assembly as being the production of a truly wise man, or "shepherd."

Fürst explains the clause "they (the writings of the wise) are delivered from one shepherd," to mean that the books referred to were to be regarded as really proceeding from God, who is meant by the "Shepherd." But Graetz regards that sentence as "obscure," because God is termed only in poetry "the Shepherd of Israel," while the passage cannot possibly refer to Moses; although the latter is the interpretation given in the Targum and the Midrash.[1]

[1] The Targum paraphrases the verse thus: "Words of wise men are like to goads and to sharp-pointed instruments which are sharp to teach wisdom to those deficient in knowledge, as a goad teaches the ox; and the Rabbis of the Sanhedrin, the masters of the Halachas and the Midrashim which were given by means of Moses the prophet, who himself fed the people of the house of Israel in the wilderness with manna and with precious food." The Midrash Koheleth takes the word אֲסֻפּוֹת in the sense of "*assemblies*." It quotes in its explanation the saying of God to Moses in Deut. vi. 6, "these words which I command thee this day," which "words" it considers were partly handed down by tradition to the men of the Sanhedrin. In proof of this the saying of God in Num. xi. 16 is adduced, "gather unto me seventy men," and the remark is made that the words are not to be regarded as if they came from the mouth of the Sanhedrin, but as heard "from the mouth of Moses, because it is written 'they are given from one shepherd,' that is Moses; and not as if one heard it from the mouth of Moses but from the mouth of the Holy One, blessed be He! as it is written 'from one Shepherd,' and there is no shepherd except the Holy One, blessed be He! As it is written 'Give ear, O Shepherd of Israel.'" Ps. lxxx. 1.

Opinions of Bloch and Renan.

Bloch (in his *Studien*, p. 139 ff) has adopted another modification of Krochmal's view. He maintains that the epilogue consisting of ch. xii. 9–14 is an addition appended to the book not at a much earlier date than the Synod of Jamnia, namely, by the collectors of the third and last division of the Jewish Canon centuries before the Christian era. These, "the men of the Great Synagogue," are the בַּעֲלֵי אֲסֻפּוֹת, "the masters of assemblies," the descendants in office and position of "the chief of the fathers" mentioned in Nehemiah viii. 13. They inserted the Book of Koheleth in the last collection of the Holy Scriptures because they regarded it as a production of Solomon's pen, but they interpolated passages here and there in the original work. For, when the canon was finally closed, no book found admission into that collection which was supposed to have been written later than the period which terminated with the death of Artaxerxes Longimanus (B.C. 425). It did not lie within the compass of Bloch's later work to give any detailed explanation of the several clauses of the epilogue of Koheleth, so that we cannot be certain how far he agrees in the other details with the explanations of Krochmal, Fürst, or Graetz. But, if the epilogue really referred to the closing of the third part of the Jewish Canon, it is strange that the early expositions should have never spoken of that fact; and it is remarkable that no evidence whatever can be discovered, even in Talmudic sources, of a period in which the Book of Koheleth stood at the end of the third division of the O.T., which, according to this theory, is its true and proper place. The fact of the epilogue being found in the version of the LXX., and in all the other ancient versions, is opposed to Krochmal's ideas.

Renan in his recent work on Ecclesiastes has adopted the views of Krochmal and Graetz with respect to the composition of the epilogue. The work of Professor Graetz, which has found few admirers in Germany, is regarded by the

French savant as one of the most important contributions to the study of Ecclesiastes, while the far more profound work of Professor Franz Delitzsch is passed over by him in utter silence. The latter scholar has satisfactorily proved that the style and language of the epilogue is marked by the same peculiarities which characterise the other parts of the book. The language of the Book of Koheleth is akin to that of the Books of the Chronicles. Its idiom approximates in some respects to that of the Mishna, although the Hebrew is of a decidedly more ancient type. Several of its expressions are regarded by the Talmudists as obscure, and are commented on by them in such a manner as to prove that the words made use of were antiquated at the time when the Talmuds were composed. The language of the epilogue is identical with that of the body of the work. This fact tells strongly against a theory founded on no real basis of evidence.

The Book of Koheleth considered apart from the epilogue begins and ends with almost the same words: "Vanity of vanities, saith Koheleth, the whole is vanity." A noteworthy modification of this clause occurs, however, in the refrain at the end of the book. The name Koheleth is there found with the article affixed, "the Koheleth." Proper names in Hebrew, when special reference is made to their meaning, sometimes take the article. This appears to be the case in the epilogue, where a contrast seems to be drawn between the ideal Koheleth or Solomon, who is represented as the speaker throughout, and the actual Koheleth who ventures at the close of his work to say a few words concerning himself and his book.

The epilogue intimates that the author felt it necessary to say something in conclusion (1) about himself and the manner in which he had composed his book, (2) about the importance of the sacred writings in general and of his own book in particular, and (3) concerning the ultimate conclusion at which he arrived. The remarks of the writer on each of these three heads occupy in each case only two lines. The terseness and brevity of the author cause considerable difficulty in attempting to comprehend exactly his meaning.

In verse 9 the mask hitherto worn by the writer is cast aside, and he ceases to speak in the name of "the Koheleth" the son of David, but now addresses the reader in his own person. The change is denoted by the use of the title "Koheleth" without the article in verse 9 in close proximity to, and in striking contrast with "the Koheleth," with the article in verse 8. The writer thus proceeds: "And, moreover," that is, what remains to be said now at the close of the book is, that Koheleth, the actual preacher and author of the work, "was a wise man," not an actual king or a ruler in Israel, as was "the Koheleth," or Solomon. Still speaking of himself in the third person the author continues: "Further," that is, over and above being gifted with wisdom, "he (Koheleth) taught the people knowledge, and (in doing so) pondered over (lit. weighed) and investigated, arranged many proverbs." Inasmuch as he was himself a wise man, though not so wise as the great Koheleth of Israelitish history, the writer states further that he, too, had sought to make use of his wisdom by instructing the people of his own generation, and was wont to teach, like his great model the wise Solomon, by means of proverbs, well pondered over, carefully investigated and duly arranged for the special object in view. In drawing up original proverbs, or in collecting together such sententious sayings from various sources, "Koheleth sought to discover words of pleasantness, and that which was written in uprightness, words of truth." That is, the writer of the Book of Koheleth had adopted the plan of teaching by means of proverbs, because he found that they were peculiarly attractive to the popular taste. But he took great care to make use only of such "sayings of the wise" as were written with an honest and good intention, and were in reality "words of truth."

Language such as this could scarcely have been written by the actual Solomon of history.

The next verse of the epilogue (verse 11) speaks more generally concerning "words of the wise," and indirectly asserts the importance of the Book of Koheleth. This verse unquestionably presents considerable difficulties to the expositor. Its great difficulty lies in the use of the expression בַּעֲלֵי אֲסֻפּוֹת. The first word of the phrase signifies "lords," or "masters," but usage forbids it to be explained in the sense of "leaders" or "editors," as some have sought to interpret it. It is quite possible to expound the phrase as referring to the members of the Jewish Sanhedrin, or even in the sense of "members of academies," if such interpretations could be shown to convey any appropriate meaning, and were agreeable to the context. Despairing of being able to extract any satisfactory sense by such forced explanations, Ewald, Delitzsch, and other eminent scholars have been led to maintain that the phrase is a designation of the proverbs to which reference is made in the previous verse. Ewald translates the clause, "and like driven nails the well-compacted [sayings] given by one shepherd." That is, proverbs delivered not as isolated maxims, but well-compacted and well-arranged in their connection one with another "by one shepherd," or teacher of a congregation, are like nails well driven in. Delitzsch considers the expression to be a designation of the words of the wise as forming "collections" standing together in order and rank, which, like nails driven in, secured against separation, and standing on one common ground, are both a help to the memory on the one hand, and to a correct comprehension of their meaning on the other.[1]

The objection to this interpretation is, that although the

[1] For other interpretations of the clause see our Crit. Comm.

second word in the phrase, viz., אֲסֻפּוֹת, is a term which can be applied to "collections" of things or of sayings, as well as to "assemblies" of persons,[1] the first, (בַעַל) is always used of persons, except in cases where things are personified.[2] Such a personification does not appear natural here. We prefer, therefore, to understand the phrase in the sense of "persons skilled in collections," or well acquainted with collections of wise sayings, namely, with books in which such sayings are "intelligently grouped together" and compacted into one whole. Compare the well-known expressions בַּעֲלֵי מִקְרָא, "*masters of Scripture*," meaning, persons well versed in Sacred Scripture, בַּעַל מִשְׁנָה "*a master of the Mishna*," or one well versed therein ; בַּעֲלֵי כְשָׁפִים, "*masters of incantations*," or persons skilled in their use.

Our explanation of the verse is as follows : "Words of wise men are like the goads," for, as oxen are driven forward and guided by the goad into the path in which they should go, so are men impelled onward, and preserved in the right way by the "sayings of the wise." "And like nails firmly driven in (the noun does not signify *tent-pegs* or *stakes*) are those well versed in collections (of such sayings)—they (the collections themselves) are given from one Shepherd." Disciples thoroughly versed in "the sayings of the wise," and who not only "hear" the words of wisdom, but "do" what wisdom enjoins—for this is plainly the meaning of the writer—"are like nails firmly driven into" some wall, which cannot be easily pulled out. Such are, to use New Testament language,

---

[1] The Jerusalem Talmud, Sanhedr. x. 28 *a*, takes the word in the last signification. Its words are : "There are no אסופות except the Sanhedrin, according as it is written, *gather to me seventy men of the elders of Israel* [Num. xi. 16]. Another interpretation is that the בעלי אסופות [*the masters of the assemblies*] are the words which are spoken in the assembly" (אסיפה). See Excursus No. 4, Glossary, *s.v.*

[2] Delitzsch regards the proverbs or maxims as here personified, and compares the expression שָׁלִישִׁים (Prov. xxii. 20) *excellent men, princes*, used there of such aphroisms. Compare נְגִידִים, Prov. viii. 6.

no longer like "children tossed to and fro, and carried about with every wind of doctrine, by the sleight of men, in craftiness, after the wiles of error" (Eph. iv. 14). They are rather "like nails firmly riveted" which cannot be removed from the ground or place into which they are fastened.

The author evidently regarded his own book as belonging to the category of such collections of the sayings of the wise. Many of the proverbs in it were borrowed from other wise men, not a few being probably aphorisms of Solomon borne by tradition down the stream of time. The value and importance of such "collections" of the "sayings of the wise" as Koheleth speaks of, arise from their having a common origin, being alike the outcome of Divine inspiration. "They are given from one Shepherd," who is above, and from whom cometh "every good gift and every perfect boon" (Jas. i. 17). That great Shepherd of men imparts the ability to utter words which have power to impel men onward in the path of rectitude, and to preserve them from falling away into sin. The Books of the Old Testament in general, inclusive of the Book of Koheleth, are profitable for teaching, both in the way of conviction and correction, and are fitted to train up believers "in righteousness" (2 Tim. iii. 16). The "words of the wise" contained in the Book of Koheleth, whether sayings of Solomon himself, or attributed to him by a lawful literary device, "are given from the one Shepherd," who not only leads Israel as a flock, but also directs all those who put their trust in Him.

Words such as these of the epilogue cannot have proceeded from Solomon. They are only intelligible when explained, as Delitzsch has interpreted them, as containing "an important apologetic hint," indicating that the collection of the sayings of the wise in the Book of Koheleth, though not proceeding from the pen of Solomon, was, as well as the well-known Book of Proverbs (which is in the main a collection of that monarch's sayings), justly entitled to take rank as a book written under Divine inspiration.

"Moreover," adds Koheleth, who, here in the epilogue (though not in his book), addresses himself to an individual disciple, "My son, be warned," be on your guard against error in this matter.[1] "Of making many books there is no end, and much study is a weariness of the flesh." In the pursuit after wisdom the learner's true motto ought to be "*multum non multa*" (*Plinii Ep.*, viii. 9). A real knowledge of a little is better than a superficial acquaintance with many branches of human learning. Let the disciple deeply persuaded of the sad truth of the fact that "vanity of vanities, all is vanity," amid all the vanities of this present life be guided by the "words of the wise," especially by the words of those holy men upon whose shoulders the mantle of inspiration was cast by the great Shepherd of the flock of man. "For the end of the matter, when all is heard (which can be adduced by the wisest of mankind) is, fear God and keep His commandments —for this ought every man to do." This is the duty of the high and of the lowly, of the king and of the subject, of the rich and of the poor, of the learned and of the unlearned, of the man whose faith is so strong, that it can remove mountains, and of him whose faith is so feeble that he stumbles over every stone which may lie in his path. For there is a judgment which awaits man in a future state of existence. God shall not merely judge the nations—a doctrine often taught in Old Testament literature—and execute judgment on the ungodly by punishments meted out in this world, but He shall also judge all men. In that great judgment the inequalities of the present shall be duly adjusted, and its enigma fully solved.

---

[1] The expression for "moreover" in this verse is somewhat different from that in verse 9, and either signifies, as Ewald understands it, that what follows is to be looked upon as the result of what had been already said; or better, perhaps, as Delitzsch, "what still remains to be mentioned is" that which follows.

"God shall bring every work into a judgment (which shall pass) upon all that is concealed, whether good or whether evil."

This revelation of a coming judgment, in which every individual man is to be rewarded according to his deserts, is, perhaps, the most striking truth contained in the whole Book of Koheleth. In this particular Ecclesiastes is in advance of the other writings of the Old Testament. It was not even granted to a Daniel to understand this truth fully. He was permitted to speak of the resurrection of "many of those who sleep in the dust of the earth" in Messianic days, and to announce that some should then "awake to everlasting life" and others "to shame and everlasting contempt." Nowhere else in the Old Testament is it plainly revealed that in the judgment day every secret thing shall be made manifest, and that "each of us shall give an account of himself to God" (Rom. xiv. 12).

The announcement of this new doctrine at the close of this strange Book of Koheleth was the breaking forth, amid the darkness, of the dawn of a better and fuller revelation. It forms a precious link in the chain of the Old Testament preparations for the New. The revelation of Messianic days has shed a clearer light upon our path. Jesus Christ hath, indeed, brought immortality to light by His Gospel. He hath overcome death, and doubt too, and opened the gate of everlasting life to all them that believe on His name.

CHAPTER V.

THE AUTHORSHIP OF THE BOOK OF KOHELETH.

CHAPTER V.

The denial of the Solomonic authorship does not detract from the authority of the Book of Ecclesiastes, 109—No new facts of Solomon's life contained in the book, 110—Charge of forgery unjust, 111—The practice of Greek and Roman historians, 111—The Emperor Claudius' speech, 111—The Sacred Writers availed themselves of similar freedom, 112—Rev. David Johnston's work on Ecclesiastes, 114—Endorsed by Prof. Leathes, 114—His argument in favour of the common authorship of the Books of Proverbs and Ecclesiastes, 114—Reply to this argument, 115—The Writer of Koheleth uses Solomonic expressions, 116—Renan's former opinion as to the date of the book, 117—The linguistic features of the book, 118—Why Solomon is introduced by the writer as spokesman, 118—Dr. Pusey's unfair charge against the scholars who deny the Solomonic authorship, 119—Bloch's attempt, and the earlier attempt of Renan, to assign the phenomena of the book to copyists, 121—Peculiarities of grammar, 121—The picture of life given by Koheleth, 122—Oppression and tyranny during the days of Solomon, 122—Legend of the Midrash as to the stages of Solomon's fall, 123—The complaints of oppression in the book opposed to the Traditional view, 124—The book no penitential confession, 124—M. Renan's new work on Ecclesiastes, 125—His ideas as to Canticles and Ecclesiastes, 126—Maintains the modern date of the book, 126—Denies its Solomonic authorship, 127—His suggestions as to the name Koheleth, 127—His portrait of the author, 129—That portrait a caricature, 129—Renan maintains the writer to be a mere man of the world, 130—A type of the modern Jew, 132—Dean Plumptre's ideal biography of the writer, 133—His early life, 133—Crossed in love, 134—Turns philosopher, 134—Returns to his early faith, 135—Comments on this view, 135—Probable date of Koheleth, 136—The last of the Hebrew Prophets, 136—The work a preparation for Christ, 137.

CHAPTER V.

THE AUTHORSHIP OF THE BOOK OF KOHELETH.

IN our last chapter, on a survey of one portion of the evidence presented by statements which occur in the Book of Koheleth itself, we saw that it was highly probable that the real author of that work was not the great king of Israel, although the writer thought fit to put his own reflections on the vanity of human life into the mouth of Solomon. No more suitable person could have been adduced as a preacher of such sermon on the vanity of all earthly things than a monarch universally regarded as the wisest of men, and one who had fully experienced in his own case the unsatisfying character of all earthly joys.

A recent defender of the Solomonic authorship has ventured to affirm that "the impeachment of the traditional authorship of Deuteronomy and Ecclesiastes detracts from their trustworthiness, by representing as literary fictions what those ancient writings themselves represent as historic facts. Hence the interests at stake in discussing the authorship of Ecclesiastes or of Deuteronomy are vastly more momentous than any interests affected by discussing the authorship of anonymous writings like the Epistle to the Hebrews."[1] This critic further asserts that "the Book of Ecclesiastes claims Solomon as its author, precisely as Deuteronomy claims Moses, and the Pauline Epistles claim the Apostle Paul; and it is not easy to conceive how, if such indications

---

[1] *Treatise on the Authorship of Ecclesiastes.* (Macmillan & Co.) p. 11.

of authorship as are contained in Ecclesiastes are not literally true, any averment of authorship found elsewhere in the Scriptures can be accepted as trustworthy; or how, if the Scriptures ought not to be believed in such a plain matter of fact as the authorship claimed in them, they can deserve to be trusted in other details purporting to be simple statements of historical and doctrinal facts." [1]

The authorship of the Book of Deuteronomy cannot be discussed here. But the assertion just referred to, so far as the Book of Ecclesiastes is concerned, is completely unjustifiable. The authority and trustworthiness of the Book of Ecclesiastes are not imperilled by the denial of its Solomonic authorship. No "historical fact" whatever is thereby necessarily resolved into a mere "literary fiction." It is highly improper for any defender of the authority of Sacred Scripture to assert that the Book of Ecclesiastes is open to the charge of "deceit and falsehood," and that its doctrinal statements must be received with suspicion, if the superscription of the book (ch. i. 1) is viewed, not as expressing an historical truth, but as a literary device.

The general character and value of the Book of Koheleth are in no wise affected by a denial of the traditional opinion. The experience of Koheleth may have been truly and really the experience of Solomon, although not a single sentence in the book proceeded actually from the pen of the latter. It is remarkable that this so-called "autobiography" does not mention a single fact connected with Solomon's life which might not easily have been derived from the narrative set forth in the First Book of Kings. This could scarcely have been the case had Solomon been the writer. Nay more, the most important acts of his reign are passed over in silence. Not one word is said concerning the building of the temple, not a single allusion is made throughout the book to that

---

[1] *Treatise on the Authorship of Ecclesiastes.* (Macmillan & Co.) p. 11.

sin of idolatry whereby he provoked Jahaveh to anger, nor to the adversaries who were raised up to chastise him on account of that transgression, and whose actions embittered his last years.

It would be unjust to regard the Book of Wisdom, though professedly written by Solomon (see p. 60), in the light of an imposition or a forgery. The charge of forgery would be preferred against the Book of Koheleth with still greater injustice. It has always been considered perfectly justifiable for an author, in accordance with the indications found in history, to pourtray in prose or in verse the feelings and sentiments of distinguished persons on remarkable occasions. As instances of such a practice, Delitzsch pertinently cites the speeches of distinguished commanders and statesmen which are to be found in the works of the great Greek and Roman historians. Some of those orations rest no doubt upon a positive historical basis. But in the majority of instances the individual historian has himself worked up the material afforded to him, and the speeches to be found in his pages exhibit the same style and linguistic peculiarities which characterise the other parts of his work. The Emperor Claudius delivered in A.D. 48 a remarkable oration in favour of the full privileges of Roman citizenship being granted to the communities of Gallia Comata, or Gaul proper, and of the Æduan senators being permitted to present themselves as candidates for civic honours at Rome. This has been duly recorded by Tacitus (*Annal.*, xi. 24). But the form in which it appears on the pages of the Roman historian is very different from that which it assumes on the bronze tablets discovered in Lyons in A.D. 1528, and still preserved in the Museum of that city.[1] The tablets repre-

[1] The tablets in question are beautifully cut and are as legible now as when first engraved. The inscription is given in full in *Gruteri Inscriptiones Antiquæ totius orbis Romani*, p. DII. The tablets themselves, which are duly regarded as a monument of great national interest, are kept in the Palais des Arts, Lyons.

sent the speech as it was originally published by the Imperial command. But the Roman historian, in relating the emperor's oration in a form suited to his Annals, and in giving it a more elegant form than it assumes on the Bronze Tablets, had not the slightest intention of imposing on the credulity of his readers, nor has any scholar ventured to accuse him as guilty in this particular of "deceit and falsehood."[1]

Instances can also be given in which the sacred writers of the Old, and even of the New Testament Scriptures, have not hesitated to avail themselves of a similar literary freedom. The pen of the historian himself, as Delitzsch observes, is distinctly perceptible in the greater part of the prophetic addresses recorded in the Books of Kings and Chronicles. Caspari, an eminent scholar, and one of the most earnest defenders of the truths of Revelation, notices that several of the discourses in the Chronicles, when compared with those in the Books of the Kings, are distinguished by a noteworthy peculiarity of style, specially characteristic of the writers of the former books.[2] The sacred historians

---

[1] Delitzsch, in his important article, in *Luthardt's Zeitschrift für kirchliche Wissenschaft u. kirchl. Leben*, Heft vi. 1882, on "the Decalogue in Exodus and Deuteronomy," adduces other instances. Cicero's third oration against Cataline (*Cat.* iii. 2) contains the letter of Lentulus to Catiline, which is also communicated by Sallust in his *Bellum Catilinarium* (cap. xliv.). The substance of the letter has been given by both, but the form which it assumes varies considerably in the two narratives. Delitzsch points out that the differences in accounts of the Decalogue in Exod. xx. and Deut. v. are owing to the same cause.

[2] Caspari, in his treatise *Ueber den Syrisch-Ephraimitischen Krieg*, pp. 52 ff, adduces certain proofs to show that the writer of the Chronicles did not invent the speeches which appear in his history, but that he worked them up in a free manner from the original sources, clothing them in a form peculiar to himself and his time. A comparison of the discourses common to the Chronicles and the Kings shows that the editor of the Book of Chronicles has on the whole faithfully reproduced his original, but still has altered it in several places; and he has dealt in the same manner with the original of those speeches which are not found in the Books of the Kings. Compare, for example, 2 Kings xviii. 22 and Isaiah xxxvi. 7, with 2 Chronicles xxxii. 12. There is, moreover, a very striking similarity between the most of the speeches which occur in the Books of the

sometimes incorporate records into their narratives substantially in the form in which they were originally composed. But it is more usual for such authors to reproduce in their own style those poems and speeches which were suited to the object in view.

That the sacred writers did not consider themselves debarred from making use of the liberty ordinarily accorded to other historians is plain from a candid examination of their productions. The Psalter itself, notes Delitzsch, "contains not a few Psalms entitled לדוד (" *of David*"), which were not composed by David himself, but by unknown poets who transferred themselves in thought into David's place, situation, and feelings." Delitzsch considers Psalm cxliv. to be an instance of such usage. That Psalm, according to his opinion, was founded on the expressions used by David in his celebrated combat with Goliath (1 Sam. xvii. 47). This fact is also recognised by the LXX., who add to the simple superscription " of David," which occurs in the Hebrew Psalter, an explanatory clause, πρὸς τὸν Γολιάδ, "*concerning Goliath.*" Still more noteworthy is the fact that the writer of the Chronicles (1 Chr. xvi.), when he attempts to give an idea of the songs of praise sung on the occasion of the removal of the ark from the house of Obed-edom to the tabernacle which David pitched for it in Jerusalem, actually puts into the mouth of David the first and the last two verses of Psalm cvi.; although that psalm, as has been admitted by the most orthodox critics (as for example, Dean Perowne), must have been composed after the date of the Exile.[1]

Other instances might be adduced. These are, however,

Chronicles, which proves that the author considered himself at liberty to make a free use of the material which he had at hand, and did not consider himself bound in all cases to give the *ipsissima verba*.

[1] It is also worthy of note that passages from Psalms xcvi. and cv. are also quoted in the same song of praise, although these Psalms were evidently written in post-exilian times, and refer to the period of the captivity.

sufficient for our present purpose. Such points have been passed over in silence by the recent defender of the traditional theory of the Solomonic authorship of Ecclesiastes; whose work, as it is the most elaborate, though not the most scholarly, which has lately appeared on that side, cannot be left altogether unnoticed. It has been highly praised and its arguments have been pronounced conclusive by Professor Stanley Leathes of London.[1] Hence it requires more than a mere passing reference. Though issued anonymously, we are permitted to state that the writer is Rev. David Johnston of Herray, Scotland.

This critic has attempted, by an elaborate induction of "identical words" and "coincidences" in style and phraseology, to demonstrate that the Book of Proverbs and the Book of Ecclesiastes have one and the same author. The references to "kings" and "rulers," the frequent mention of "the eyes" in proverbial sentences, the occurrence of the same words in both books, such as the nouns signifying "street," "delight," "orchard," "slothfulness," "fool," "wisdom," "riches," "wealth," the frequent use of the common adjectives meaning "good," "better than," etc., have all been carefully registered, tabulated, and counted up, and the results are triumphantly paraded as undesigned evidences of a cumulative character in proof of the traditional view. The isolated instance of the expression "my son" in the epilogue has not been forgotten. The strength or weakness of this line of argument can be as well appreciated by the English student as by the Hebrew scholar. Professor Stanley Leathes in his review has incautiously observed that "the force of this evidence, so far as it goes, seems to be irresistible." These critics seem to forget that the argument on which they rely proves too much. By the same line of argument the

[1] In the *Christian Church* (London: Hodder and Stoughton), numbers for February, March, April, 1881.

Book of Wisdom and the Book of Ecclesiasticus, or Ben Sira, although extant only in Greek,[1] may with equal reason be ascribed to Solomon. For, if the English student will, with the aid of Cruden's Concordance to the A.V. translation of the Apocrypha, count up the number of times the majority of such words as are referred to by Mr. Johnston occur in the Books of Wisdom and of Ben Sira, and then compare the whole with the Book of Proverbs, he will obtain results of a similar character to those noticed by the Scotch critic. Nor have we to go far to discover the reason of this phenomenon. It is simply because the Book of Koheleth (or Ecclesiastes), the Book of Wisdom, and the Book of Ben Sira (or Ecclesiasticus), abound in "proverbs," more or less directly modelled after the pattern of the sententious sayings contained in the ancient Solomonic Book of Proverbs.

An attempt has been made by Mr. Johnston to derive an argument in favour of the Solomonic authorship of the Book, from the occurrence in it of a few expressions also found in several prayers of Solomon recorded by the writers of the Books of Kings and Chronicles. It will be readily admitted that there are some phrases common to the three books, namely "the heart of the sons of men," "there is no man who sinneth not," etc.[2] All, however, that such "correspondences" can be fairly considered to prove is, that the writer of

---

[1] The Greek text of Ben Sira is, as has been already noticed, a translation from a Hebrew original. See p. 32.

[2] Mr. Johnston, in p. 115 of his *Treatise*, seems to regard it as a significant fact that the temple is called in ch. iv. 17 (English Version, ch. v. 1) by the name of "house," inasmuch as Solomon uses that term of the temple no less than sixteen times in 1 Kings viii. It is not, however, certain, though it is, perhaps, probable, that the temple is alluded to in the passage in question. But as has already been noticed, in an "autobiography" of any kind whatever, Solomon could scarcely have avoided making some allusion to the building of the temple, which was the grand event of his reign. No such allusion, however, can be pointed out in the Book of Ecclesiastes. That the phraseology of Solomon should have been imitated by a later writer, writing under his name, is only what we might have expected.

Ecclesiastes was acquainted with the records of Solomon's sayings and acts as given by the sacred historians, a fact which no critic has ever called in question.[1]

For it was only natural that the writer of the Book of Koheleth in representing Solomon as setting forth his views upon the vanity of human affairs, arrived at after long and extensive experience, should occasionally employ words and expressions used also by Solomon. The wonder is, not that there are some words and phrases in the book drawn from such a source, but that there are so few. The "linguistic features" of the book, however, are decidedly not Solomonic. The author may, indeed, have availed himself in some places of certain genuine sayings and proverbs of Solomon handed down by oral tradition. But to what extent he has done so, it is, of course, now quite impossible to ascertain.

Renan's remarks in reference to the Song of Songs have been of late frequently quoted by English writers, as if they afforded a conclusive answer to all the objections against the traditional view of the authorship of Ecclesiastes derived from its linguistic characteristics. In speaking of the Song of Songs, Renan observes that the critics of Gesenius' school have occupied themselves too exclusively with grammatical and philological considerations, and have been too prone neglect historical and literary considerations in deciding questions concerning the authorship of particular books.[2] There is, no doubt, much truth in this remark, but it has no real bearing upon the question before us. There is a very marked distinction observable between the language of the Song of Songs and that of Ecclesiastes; and distinguished

---

[1] It ought to be noted in justice to Mr. Johnston that he has himself perceived the difficulty of urging such points as evidence on the question of authorship. He attaches, however, great importance to the occurrence of "certain words or phrases strikingly confirmatory of the Solomonic authorship," such as those noticed above.

[2] Renan, *Le Cantique*, pp. 90, 108. See Johnston's *Treatise*, p. 38.

critics like Delitzsch, while upholding the Solomonic authorship of the former poem, have felt themselves compelled to deny that Solomon was the writer of the latter work.

The grounds, on which Renan in his *History of the Shemitic Languages*[1] affirmed that the Book of Koheleth ought to be regarded as a work of the Solomonic period of Hebrew literature, are not such as are likely to commend themselves to critics with any belief whatever in the Divine inspiration of the Book of Ecclesiastes. It is dangerous in such a question to seek for an ally amongst writers of the school to which M. Renan belongs. In his work on *The Antichrist*, that critic speaks of Ecclesiastes as the only charming book that has ever been written by a Jew.[2] He praises it, however, not so much for its literary charms as for its scepticism. A work full of such daring sceptical opinions could not, he there maintained, have originated in the post-exilian period, when a severely Rabbinical type of Judaism held sway. Hence he argued

[1] "Ce dernier criterium [les nombreux aramaïsmes], toutefois, ne doit pas être employé sans quelques précautions, lorsqu'il s'agit de déterminer l'âge des différents écrits de la littérature hébraïque. Nous avons déjà dit que les plus anciens fragments de la poésie des Hébreux présentent des aramaïsmes. Trois ouvrages du plus grand caractère, le Livre de Job, le Kohéleth et le Cantique des Cantiques, offrent la contradiction singulière d'une pensée vraiment antique et d'un style qui appartient aux plus basses époques. Ces livres décèlent une inspiration vive et une liberté d'esprit presque incompatibles avec les idées étroites et les habitudes d'imitation servile qui règnent chez les Juifs depuis la captivité. Je croirai difficilement, pour ma part, qu'un poëme philosophique comme celui de Job, une idylle aussi passionnée que le Cantique des Cantiques, une œuvre d'un scepticisme aussi hardi que le Kohéleth, aient pu être composés à une époque de décadence intellectuelle, où l'on voit déjà percer les petitesses de l'ésprit rabbinique. Avec leur ton dégagé et nullement sacerdotal, leur sagesse toute profane, leur oubli de Jéhovah, ces ouvrages sont, à mes yeux, des produits de l'époque de Salomon, moment si libre et si brillant dans l'histoire du génie hébreu. Peut-être n'en possédons-nous qu'une rédaction moderne, où le style primitif aura été altéré."—Renan, *Histoire des Langues Sémitiques*, livre ii. chap. 1, pp. 130-1.

[2] "Nous essayerons de nous figurer Paul, en ces derniers jours, arrivant à reconnaitre qu'il a usé sa vie pour un rêve, repudiant tous les prophètes sacrés pour un écrit qu'il n'avait guère lu jusque-là, l'Ecclesiaste, livre charmant, le seul livre aimable qui ait été composé par un juif."—Renan, *l'Antechrist* p. 101. Troisième edit. Paris, M. Lévy Frères, 1873.

that the book was most probably a work of Solomon's, which had, however, undergone considerable revision by some later hand. To this supposed reviser Renan considered the linguistic peculiarities of the work to be mainly due. This theory, however, has found few supporters, and has been now abandoned by M. Renan himself, whose matured views on the authorship and character of the work will be shortly considered.

The internal evidence afforded by many passages of the Book of Koheleth itself is against the traditional view. The epilogue affirms the non-Solomonic authorship of the work. So far from the author having left himself open to the charge of being guilty of a "pious fraud," by writing under the mask of Solomon, he is not slow to inform his readers that that king was not the real author of the composition. Solomon is introduced as the speaker throughout the work in the same way as Cicero in his treatises "On Old Age" and on "Friendship," selects Cato the elder as the exponent of his views, or as Plato in his Dialogues brings forward Socrates.[1] Similarly, in the literature of the Old Testament, the writer of the Book of Job introduces into his magnificent dialogue that patriarch and his friends as speakers.

The linguistic features which characterise the Book of Koheleth are incompatible with the theory that Solomon was its author. Objections may, indeed, be made with an apparent show of reason to some of the examples cited by Delitzsch in his glossary of linguistic peculiarities. That list contains nearly one hundred words and forms occurring in the Book

---

[1] M. Renan has well remarked in his recent work on Ecclesiastes to the same effect: "L'auteur n'est donc pas plus un faussaire que Platon ne l'est dans *le Parménide* ou dans *le Timée*. Voulant nous donner un morceau de philosophie éléate, Platon choisit Parménide ; voulant nous donner un morceau de philosophie pythagoricienne, il choisit Timée, et il leur met dans la bouche des discours conformes aux doctrines de leur école. Ainsi fait notre auteur ; Solomon n'est pour lui qu'un prête-nom pour des idées qu'il trouve appropriées au type légendaire [?] de l'ancien roi de Jerusalem."—*L'Ecclésiaste*, p. 7.

of Koheleth characteristic of an era of the Hebrew language far later than that of Solomon. But objections to points of detail do not afford a sufficient answer to such an induction of particulars. The conclusiveness of the argument does not depend upon the decisive character of any one or two instances separately considered, but on the cumulative force of all such instances taken together.[1] Some of these words or forms occur only in books of the Old Testament composed at an era later than that of Solomon; while others, which do not occur in the whole range of Biblical literature save in this single book, are words or phrases of common use in the Hebrew of the Mishna.[2]

The attempts hitherto made to meet this philological difficulty have been unsuccessful. Boehl's pamphlet on the Aramaisms of the book is, perhaps, the best treatise on that point which has appeared in defence of the traditional view. The Roman Catholic theologians, von Essen and Schäfer, have argued with much ability on the same side. But their arguments are unsatisfactory. Dr. Pusey's observations on the same subject in his *Lectures on Daniel the Prophet* (third edit. p. 327), though quoted by Bullock as conclusive, do not fairly represent the state of the case. Dr. Pusey's re-

[1] In enumerating the instances of words common to the Books of Proverbs, Canticles and Ecclesiastes as items which "collectively establish identity of authorship," Mr. Johnston has endeavoured to make use of this argument in his favour. See his treatise, p. 66, and note our observations on p. 114.

[2] Mr. Johnston has unfortunately confined himself to the use of the English translation of Prof. Delitzsch's Commentary on Canticles and Ecclesiastes, issued by Messrs. T. & T. Clark of Edinburgh, in 1877. I freely acknowledge the services Messrs. Clark have rendered to the public by their valuable translation of the works of many of the great German Divines. But the translation in question has been executed in a most slovenly manner. It not only omits many passages of the original German, but incorrectly translates it in many places; and it is partly owing to this fact that Mr. Johnston has fallen into several serious mistakes. The translation of the glossary appended by Delitzsch to his work is peculiarly faulty in the English edition. Hence I have deemed it necessary to append to the present work, in Excursus No. 4, a glossary which is based to a considerable extent on that of Delitzsch.

marks are, moreover, based on the uncharitable assumption, that the scholars who have expressed opinions opposed to the traditional view have been influenced by a personal dislike of "the doctrine of future judgment and retribution according to our works," set forth in the book. This assumption, indeed, is abundantly disproved by the fact that Hengstenberg, Delitzsch, Zöckler and others, whose orthodoxy is beyond suspicion, have felt themselves constrained to accept the verdict of modern criticism. Scarcely a scholar of eminence now ventures to dispute this verdict. Notwithstanding the assertions of Dr. Pusey and Professor Taylor Lewis of Schenectady, it is impossible to account for the linguistic characteristics of Koheleth on the principle that its peculiar phraseology is necessitated by its subject matter. Bloch's treatise, short as it is, is on the whole the ablest work written in defence of the traditional opinion. But even that scholar has found it necessary to admit the fact that the work abounds in Aramaisms.[1] His words are: "It is a truth, that

---

[1] Prof. Given, in his work on the *Truth of Scripture*, referred to in note 1, p. 92, has sought to account for the Aramaisms of the book by the following extraordinary statements. He maintains (pp. 197-8) that Solomon "by such an accommodation and approximation to the dialect" of the eastern peoples which were under his sway, "would occupy a vantage ground in securing their attention to the great subjects, ethical and religious, discussed in this book. He would thus place himself in full accord with their sympathies, enlist their affections, and make his most effective appeals to both head and heart. The Book of Ecclesiastes would thus be a great missionary manifesto to the heathen inhabitants of those lands. Amid all the perplexities that embarrass human life, and all the dissatisfaction attendant on human pursuits, it would acquaint them with the living God as the true source and centre of all real happiness. It is no small confirmation of this view that God is not presented under the designation of Jehovah, the name by which he was known in his covenant relation to Israel, but as *Elohim*, the God of all the nations and peoples that call upon His name." If the above had been written by one who was only a popular preacher, it might be passed over in silence, but Dr. Given is a Professor of Hebrew, and ought to know better. The linguistic features of Koheleth are not such as to render the book useful in the way suggested. Though the Hebrew is more modern than the age of Solomon, it is very far from being Aramaic. The Aramaisms found in the work are indications of date, but could not have been designedly made use of by the writer in order to render his book popular among Aramaic-speaking peoples. It is

no one can ever get rid of who has a feeling for linguistic peculiarities, that this book has throughout an Aramaic colouring " (p. 124). Bloch seeks to reconcile this fact with the hypothesis of the Solomonic authorship by assuming, not unlike M. Renan in his former work, that such late words and forms are owing to copyists who introduced considerable interpolations into the work of Solomon. For, while that scholar defends the unity of the work as a whole, he maintains that words and passages have been added to it in later times. The epilogue he views as such an interpolation, though not by any means the only one to be found in the book.[1] Such views appear to us arbitrary, while they are utterly unsupported by any evidence whatever.

In Excursus, No. 4, certain peculiarities of grammar will be found noticed in detail, conducting to the same conclusion at which modern criticism has arrived. The most characteristic of these are certain verbal inflexions and the unfrequent use of several forms of mood of the verb which are of common occurrence in the more ancient language. The very fact that only three instances occur in the entire book of the use of the imperfect with strong vav (the so-called "vav conversive," or "vav consecutive"), while instances of the perfect with simple vav abound, is in itself strongly characteristic of a late date of Hebrew literature. The very opposite usage would have been expected in a work of the Solomonic age. Mr. Johnston has bravely, but in vain, sought to account for these phenomena, as well as for the

absurd to speak of Ecclesiastes as a "missionary manifesto." A book which contains no allusion whatever to idolatry could never have been designed for missionary purposes; for which, for many other reasons, it is manifestly unsuited. Nor can the book have been designed primarily to teach that God is "the true source and centre of all real happiness." Such statements only do harm to the cause they are intended to advance.

[1] Bloch considers chap. xi. 9 *b* as another such interpolation. Luzzatto has propounded similar views in reference to chap. xii. 1, 7. See *Bloch*, p. 127.

peculiar use of the personal pronouns, and of the relative, on principles favourable to the traditional view.

Knobel and other critics have maintained that the dark picture of human life presented in the pages of Ecclesiastes is inconsistent with the theory that the book was written by Solomon. Such gloomy views do not harmonize at all with the description of the Solomonic age given by the writer of 1 Kings, where the people are spoken of as eating, drinking, and making merry (1 Kings iv. 20), and his reign is depicted as a time in which Judah and Israel "dwelt safely, every man under his vine and under his fig-tree, from Dan even to Beer-sheba, all the days of Solomon" (1 Kings iv. 25).

It is, no doubt, quite true that there was a dark side to the bright picture of peace and prosperity. Even in the lifetime of Solomon there were not a few premonitory symptoms of that great national schism which occurred in the days of his successor. The magnificence and luxury of his court and the enormous works which he carried on in all parts of his kingdom entailed a heavy burden on his subjects.[1] The forced labour which was required in order to effect such results was peculiarly irksome to a people accustomed to greater liberty, and the taxation necessary to pay for such gigantic operations could not under any circumstances have been long borne by the Israelites. There must have been no doubt considerable oppression, especially in remote parts of the kingdom, and the heavy taxation was one of the chief causes of the great rebellion which broke out immediately after Solomon's death, and led to the establishment of the independent kingdom of Israel.

This state of things, even in the reign of that monarch, was in all probability considerably aggravated by the number of

[1] It is strange that the Books of the Kings and Chronicles give only scanty notices of the real history of the time of Solomon, while they contain detailed accounts of the events which occurred in the reign of David.

foreign wives which he had, who exercised no little influence for ill over the mind of the king. The erection of temples and shrines to the foreign gods which they worshipped gave, no doubt, deep offence, not merely to the priests and the prophets, but also to large numbers of the people. The existence of a royal harem has ever been a fertile source of evil in every country which is cursed by such an institution. In Solomon's later years it must have resulted in much oppression, and in the perversion of justice throughout the land. For it is only natural to suppose that the government must by degrees have fallen into the hands of his concubines and their favourites. The legend of the Midrash, based though it be on a misinterpretation of several passages, is not far from the truth when it states that Solomon fell from the height of his glory by several successive stages. He was first the mighty ruler of a vast empire, but that empire was so diminished that he was king only over Israel (Prov. i. 1); and afterwards his kingdom was further reduced so that he reigned only over Jerusalem (Koh. i. 12). Finally he was acknowledged as king only over his own house, and there had not rule even over his own bed, but was in constant dread of evil spirits.[1]

The statements which occur in the Book of Ecclesiastes concerning the oppression of the people by those in authority, and the lament of the writer that the past was better than the present (vii. 10), are supposed by some to be the natural reflections of Solomon as he pondered over the state of his kingdom in the closing years of his life.[2] The Midrash Kohe-

[1] *Midrash Shir-ha-shirim*, i. 1 and iii. 8.
[2] It is strange that Professor Taylor Lewis, in his edition of Zöckler's Commentary in the American edition of Lange's *Bibelwerk* p. 28, could write that the Book of Ecclesiastes "is just such a series of meditations as the history of that monarch would lead us to ascribe to him in his old age, after his experience of the vanity of life in its best earthly estate, and that repentance for his misuse of God's gifts, in serving his own pleasure, which would seem most natural to his condition." What verse of the book can be honestly considered as breathing the language of repentance?

leth (chap. i. 12) represents Solomon as there exclaiming as he looked back upon the glories of the earlier part of his reign: "I was, when I was, but now I am no more." But the complaints against unrighteous government found in the Book of Ecclesiastes are evidently penned by one who had himself writhed under such injustice, and cannot with any propriety be regarded as proceeding from the ruler who could have put a stop to such tyranny and wrong. The remark of Jahn (*Einleitung*, ii. p. 849) must commend itself to every thoughtful student. "Solomon," observes that critic, "could scarcely complain so bitterly concerning oppressions, the unrighteous acts of judges, and the elevation of fools and slaves to high honours, to the neglect of the rich and the noble, unless he had wished to write a satire on himself." Had he been desirous of writing a penitential confession of his own shortcomings and misdoings he must have expressed himself in a very different strain. In such a case the language of the book would have been more akin to that of David in the fifty-first Psalm, and the book would have contained some allusion to the sin of idolatry into which he fell, possibly through a desire to prove his large-hearted liberality and to conciliate his foreign wives.

Bloch gives an ingenious, if not satisfactory answer to this last objection. He maintains that in a book like Koheleth —which consists of a series of sorrowful reflections upon the deficiencies of human life, lamentations over the discordances of nature and spirit, and painful declarations concerning the unsatisfying character of all earthly things, and the nothingness of all happiness—a condemnation of idolatry would have been altogether out of place (p. 58).

We have only glanced at a few points of the evidence derivable from an examination of the contents of the book itself. The more deeply the matter is investigated the stronger does the internal evidence against the Solomonic authorship appear. Though much may indeed be urged in support of the view that the misery and oppression of Israel in the latter days of king Solomon were grievous, the details of the tyranny and violence given in the Book of Ecclesiastes do not suit that period, while they vividly represent the state of affairs at the time when the Jews groaned under the yoke of their Persian and Grecian oppressors. The doctrine concerning submission to unjust decrees and the absolute authority of the prince was of prime importance under the circumstances of that trying period.

All such considerations, indeed, would not be decisive, if positive proof could be brought forward in favour of the Solomonic authorship. But such evidence is not forthcoming. That tradition should have all but unanimously ascribed the composition of the work to Solomon is exactly what might have been expected from the fact that the book was written in the name of that monarch, and represents him throughout as the speaker.

The English defenders of the traditional view of the authorship of the Book of Ecclesiastes, inclusive of Mr. Johnston (industrious though he has proved himself to be), have in our opinion passed over without fair examination the real arguments against that theory, although long since presented in a convenient form at the close of Ginsburg's valuable introduction to his *Historical and Critical Commentary* on the book.

In the present state of critical opinion with regard to the Book of Ecclesiastes, it is unnecessary to combat the old arguments (long since refuted) against the unity of the book. But it is quite possible that the work may contain here and there fragments of earlier writings or poems, as Renan and others are disposed to maintain. The arguments in favour of the genuineness of the epilogue have been already briefly noticed.

M. Renan's recent "Study" on Ecclesiastes, has not

thrown that light upon the age and the character of the book which might have been expected from a scholar of his celebrity. The Song of Songs and the Book of Koheleth are in his view, a few "profane pages" which by some curious accident have found their way into that "strange and admirable" volume which is termed the Bible. These two books were, according to Renan (who in this particular has adopted the views of Graetz), first introduced into the Jewish Canon at the Synod of Jamnia (see p. 15). But the Jewish doctors understood neither the one book nor the other, for, had they done so, they would not have inserted such compositions in the collection of Sacred Writings. It was their stupidity that made them "able to make out of a dialogue of love a book of edification, and out of a sceptical book a book of sacred philosophy." For the Canticles and Koheleth are just "like a love-ditty and a little essay of Voltaire which have gone astray among the folios of a theological library."[1]

On the question of the antiquity of the Book of Ecclesiastes, Renan has widely departed from his former views (see p. 117), inasmuch as he now maintains that Ecclesiastes must be "certainly reckoned among the more modern books of the Hebrew literature," and that its very language proves it to be a modern work. For, although the language is but slightly tinged with Aramaisms, Koheleth is of all the Biblical books the one "most akin to the Talmud." He notes, however, at the same time that some have attempted to prove that the author's work exhibits traces of the influence of the Greek philosophy. "Nothing is less certain. Everything absolutely explains itself in this book by the logical development of Jewish thought. The author is very probably of a later date than Epicurus; it seems indeed that he did not receive a Greek education. His style is in the first place, Shemitic. In all his language there is not a Greek word, not a charac-

[1] Renan, *l'Ecclésiaste*, pp. 1, 67, 41.

His conjecture as to the term Koheleth.

teristic Hellenism. On the other hand he is far from pushing so far as Epicurus the radical negation of Providence, and the principle of the indifference of the gods in regard to human affairs."[1]

The author of the Book of Ecclesiastes, according to M. Renan, never intended his work to be regarded as a production of Solomon. It must not by any means be classed among the apocryphal writings of later days, whose authors, in order to secure a more wide acceptance of their opinions, endeavoured to palm off their works as productions of well-known personages of ancient times. The statements made in the epilogue to Ecclesiastes are, in M. Renan's opinion, decisive against the theory of the Solomonic authorship of that work.

While fully admitting the fact that Koheleth is used as a sort of "symbolical name" for Solomon, M. Renan expresses himself dissatisfied with the explanations of that name hitherto suggested by scholars. He considers it probable that the letters which form that word (K,h,l,t) may have been the initials of words, which initials were formed into a proper name,[2] as in the Middle Ages the great Jewish scholar Maimonides received the appellation of Rambam, a name composed of the initial consonants of his own name and title (Rabbi Moses ben Maimon); or as Rabbi Solomon Isaac (R. Shelomo Yiẓḥaki) was similarly known by the designation of Rashi.[3] M. Renan considers the words whose

---

[1] See *l'Ecclésiaste* pp. 52, 53, and 63.

[2] Professor Strack has informed me that De Lagarde has attempted to discover in the beginning of Psalm xxv. 22 a reference to the proper name פְּדַהְאֵל, Num. xxxiv. 28, and similarly in the opening words of Psalm xxxiv. 23 an allusion to the ordinary proper name פְּדָיָה, Pedaiah. But no such references to proper names can be proved to exist in the Bible.

[3] M. Renan refers also to the mystic alphabet known as the *Athbash*, wherein the first letter of the Hebrew alphabet was expressed by the last, the second letter by the penultimate and so forth, א being substituted for ת and ב for ש and *vice versa*. Jeremiah is supposed to have made use of this device when he designated

initials were thus united in the *nom de plume* of Koheleth are now unknown, so that his suggestion has cast no light whatever upon the supposed difficulty. It may prove fruitful in opening a door to fanciful interpretations on the part of ingenious scholars. There is not, however, the slightest foundation on which one might fairly base such a conjecture. For the name Koheleth can be so easily explained (vid. p. 84), that there is no real ground to consider it as an enigma yet unsolved.

Though M. Renan considers the title of the book enigmatical, he regards its object as plain and simple. The book he observes, has been generally considered as one of the most obscure in the Bible. Theologians for dogmatical purposes have endeavoured to darken its real significance. Its general import and character are perfectly clear, though there are a few difficulties to be found here and there. The author teaches that "all is vanity," for the world presents a series of phenomena which constantly recur, and there is no progress to be observed anywhere. "The past has been like the present, the present is like that which is to come. The present is bad, the past has not been better, and the future will not be preferable. Every attempt to ameliorate human affairs is chimerical." "Crime is undoubtedly a folly, but wisdom and piety are not recompensed. The villain is honoured as the virtuous ought to be. The virtuous man is overwhelmed with misfortunes which ought by right to fall upon the villain." Society is quite out of course, kings are egotistical and bad, judges are unjust, the people ungrateful. What then is the only practical wisdom? One should, if

Babylon (בָּבֶל) by Sheshach (שֵׁשַׁךְ), Jer. xxv. 26; and the Casdim (כַּשְׂדִּים), or *Chaldæans*, are possibly referred to by the words לֵב קָמָי (rendered in our A.V. by "*in the midst of them that rise up against me*") in Jer. li. 1. But these instances of *Athbash* cannot be relied on with certainty. For, as Prof. Friedrich Delitzsch has pointed out in his very able work *Wo lag das Paradies?* (Leipzig 1881) p. 215, *Shêsh-ku* appears to have been originally a designation of one part of Babylon. The second instance of this usage referred to is also open to doubt.

His attempted portrait of the Writer. 129

possible, quietly endeavour to enjoy the fortune which may be acquired by toil, and to live happily with a wife whom he has loved when young. One should seek to avoid excesses of every kind. It is vain to imagine that by any efforts of our own we shall be able to triumph over destiny. But it is dangerous to abandon oneself to folly, for sensuality is always punished; the man who is very rich is weighed down by anxiety; but it is well, on the other hand, to avoid poverty, for the poor man is despised. In order to live a quiet life one must not run counter to the prejudices of the world, must not fight against them, or seek to reform mankind. The wise man will be a practical philosopher; seeking to follow the just mean, he will be "without zeal, without mysticism." The writer of the Book of Koheleth, whose views M. Renan thus summarises, was "a worthy man, devoid of prejudices, good and generous at bottom, but discouraged by the baseness of the time and the sad conditions of human life." "He would willingly be a hero, but, verily, God rewards heroism so little, that one asks oneself if it is not going against His intentions to take up things in that manner."

Such is the "charming" portrait of the writer of the Book of Ecclesiastes as delineated by the pen of the French writer. A more selfish, mean-spirited and contemptible character could scarcely be described, one more dead to all the loftier aspirations of humanity, or more regardless of its bitter sorrows, provided only he might be able himself quietly to enjoy a moderate fortune! The portrait which M. Renan has painted is not a real likeness; it is a caricature.

Koheleth was, indeed, according to him, no atheist. He believed in the existence of a God who occasionally interposed in the affairs of the world. But the God of his creed was one who was too great to concern Himself deeply with human actions in general. God occasionally punishes men for their crimes. Hence it is a matter only of simple

K

prudence to abstain from crimes of a gross character. For in certain well-defined cases punishment for sin is a sort of natural law. The principles on which God acts are utterly incomprehensible to man. The religion which Koheleth, as explained by M. Renan, inculcates is a religion without zeal, without love, "without excess." Devotees are the most unbearable blockheads. "The impious man is a fool; he defies God, he exposes himself to the most terrible danger, but the pietist is a simpleton who wearies God with his prayers, and displeases Him while he imagines that he honours Him."

Renan's views of the various passages in the book in which reference is made to the state of the dead will be noticed elsewhere. Koheleth was (according to his conception of his character) not a man who like the patriarch Job would burst forth into indignant complaint against the Most High. He was of a more phlegmatic disposition. "It is so useless" to trouble oneself about such matters. He had learned to take things more quietly. He had no hopes of a coming Messiah, no belief in a resurrection of the dead, no pride in the history of his own people. He had no patriotism. His idea was, that his bodily frame would be dissolved at death, and then he would exist no more. Why then should he give himself any unnecessary trouble? Others might fancy, with the prophets of old, that at a future period there would be a reign of justice on the earth. Not so our enlightened and " charming" writer. He believed that the day of Jahaveh would never come. God would never leave heaven to reign on earth. For himself, Koheleth only desired to live in peace, to enjoy the fortune he had honestly obtained. He knew old age was coming on, and that death would inevitably follow, but he would wait quietly until it came, and meanwhile amuse himself with describing it in witty phraseology. "The fine and voluptuous temperament of our author shows us that he had many an inward sweetness wherewith to console himself for his pessimist philosophy. Like all the pessimists of talent he loved life; the idea of suicide, which at one time crossed the mind of Job [Job vii. 15; but qu.?] in view of the abuses of the world, did not for a moment enter into his thoughts (*l'Ecclésiaste*, p. 40).

The chief interest which the Book of Ecclesiastes, according to this critic, possesses, is, that it is the only book which presents us with a picture of an intellectual and moral position which must have been that of a large number of the Jews. The book is a rarity. It contains the only pages of *sang-froid* to be found in the gloomy volume of the Scriptures. The author was a man of the world, he was not a pious man or a theologian. One might almost imagine he had never known the *Thorah*, and if he had read "the prophets, those furious tribunes of justice," he had imbibed very little of their spirit. He did not believe in the victory of godliness for the world would never be better than it is. The Sadducees, who did not believe in angels or spirits or in a resurrection, those followers of Boethus, who were almost synonymous with the Epicureans, "all that rich aristocracy of the priests of Jerusalem who lived of the Temple, and whose religious coolness irritated so strongly Jesus and the founders of Christianity, were in reality the intellectual brethren of our author."[1] As M. Renan observes in another place: "the author was perhaps some great grandfather of Annas or of Caiaphas, of the aristocratic priests who with so light a heart condemned Jesus."

The bad taste which directed these last remarks needs no comment on our part. But such, according to M. Renan, was

---

[1] *L'Ecclésiaste*, pp. 50, 62. M. Renan observes, "the true commentary on Koheleth is to be found in Books xii. and xiii. of the *Antiquities* of Josephus, that tissue of crimes and of baseness, which especially about 200 B.C. and a little earlier than that time, made up the history of Palestine." P. 59.

the author who has bequeathed to posterity one of the most charming books of antiquity (*l'Ecclésiaste*, p. 85)!

What pleases M. Renan especially in the Book of Koheleth is the personality of the author. "No one was ever more natural or more simple. His egoism is so frankly avowed that it ceases to shock us. He certainly was an amiable man. I would have had a thousand times more confidence in him than in all the Ḥasidim [1] of his contemporaries. The good nature of the sceptic is the most solid of all; it rests upon a profound feeling of the supreme truth, *Nil expedit*." It is in consequence of this that Koheleth is a book so profoundly modern. The pessimism of our day finds there its finest expression. The author appears like a resigned Schopenhauer, very superior to that one whom a bad stroke of fortune forced to live at German *tables d'hôte*."[2] "One loves to picture him to oneself as an exquisite man and one of polished manners, as an ancestor of some rich Jew of Paris gone astray in Judæa in the time of Jesus and the Maccabees." In fact, the best representative one can have of the author of Ecclesiastes is "the modern Jew," as he appears in some of the great commercial cities of Europe. From Koheleth to Heinrich Heine, there is, according to Renan, only a step. When one compares him with the prophets of Israel one has some difficulty to understand how the same race could have produced characters so essentially different.

Such is the description of Koheleth presented to us by the French savant. M. Renan's eminence as a scholar renders it impossible to pass his work over in silence. He has unquestionably seized upon, and painted in striking colours, some of the more salient features of the book, but

---

[1] The Ḥasidim, or *the pious*, "puritans," were the party of the orthodox Jews whose fiery zeal is spoken of in the First Book of the Maccabees. Our English version has transcribed the word there by "Assideans."

[2] In M. Renan's article in the *Revue des Deux Mondes* for Feb., 1882, he speaks of "les brasseries allemandes," the *German beer-houses*.

he has altogether failed to comprehend its deeper meaning. As an article, M. Renan's essay may be deemed brilliant; but, judged as a contribution towards the understanding of the book, his "Study" is of little value, and must be characterized as flippant.

It may be interesting to notice here an attempt more reverent, though scarcely more successful, on the part of an English scholar to solve the mystery which enwraps the writer of Ecclesiastes. Dissatisfied with the efforts of former commentators, Professor, now Dean, Plumptre, first tentatively in his article in *Smith's Biblical Dictionary*, then in the pages of the *Expositor* for 1880, and still later in his edition of *Ecclesiastes with Notes* (1881), has struck out for himself a new and ingenious line of interpretation.

He regards the book as of the nature of an autobiographical confession, in some places distinctly, in others unconsciously revealing itself beneath the veil assumed by the author.

According to Dean Plumptre, Koheleth lived in Judæa about B.C. 220; not far from the city of Jerusalem, the road to which was often traversed by him. He was trained up as a child in the school attached to the synagogue of his native village, at a time when religion had become in general merely an empty form. In that synagogue school the boy learned to regard with reverence and affection the memory of the wise king, Solomon. His parents were wealthy, though the boy was from early years trained up to agriculture. Koheleth's mother was unfortunately one who left her son "no memory of a true pattern of womanhood for him to reverence and love." The young man was not long before he saw through the emptiness and hypocrisy of the religion current in his day, marked as it was with long-winded prayers, easily made and soon forgotten vows, and a superstitious regard for dreams. He by and by travelled into other lands, and in the course of his wanderings settled in Alexandria. There he lived for a considerable time under the yoke of a despotic government. He observed the oppression of the masses, and the artifices adopted by men who aspired to power and place. His wealth led him to indulge in all kinds of sensual pleasure and permitted him to gratify a taste for luxury and magnificence. In his wildest excesses his wisdom preserved him from utter ruin. He however, soon, learned to question the reality of a life beyond the grave, in which in earlier days he had been a believer.

During his stay in Alexandria, Koheleth met with one who proved in very deed to be a true friend, "one among a thousand." This friendship kept him in his darkest hours from abandoning himself to despair. For he had also a bitter experience of another kind. He imbibed a passionate affection for a beautiful woman whose utter baseness he discovered barely in time to escape from her net. Hence his strong denunciation of the female sex in the pages of his work. To solace himself for his bitter disappointment, Koheleth turned to the contemplation of art, and afterwards to the study of Greek philosophy. He was peculiarly drawn towards the philosophical schools of the Epicureans and the Stoics. The natural science and physiology of the former attracted a mind eager for knowledge. In chaps. xi. and xii. of his book he exhibits more than an ordinary acquaintance with the anatomy and construction of the human frame. But in both these schools of philosophy, while he found something to attract, he found still more to repel. They could not solve the mystery of human life. The old faith of the Jew revived at last in a purer form within his heart, and experience had taught him lessons of wisdom. His course of life for a while was more cheerful than before, and he came forward as a debater in the philosophic schools. But, like many others, Koheleth had to pay the penalty of his former life of dissipation, and premature old age weakened his frame. After a long and painful illness he had time to reflect on the past, and became a firm believer in a personal God and a personal immortality. In old age he learned to wait for death with calm trustfulness in the God who was above, and the thought of returning to his Maker supported him in the contemplation of the tomb. "It was in this stage of mental and spiritual growth, of strength growing out of weakness, that he was led to become a writer, and to put on record the results of his experience. He still thought in the language of his fatherland, and therefore in that language he wrote 'the Book of Ecclesiastes.'"

Thus does the learned Professor construct an interesting novel from indications supposed to be given in the course of our author's reflections. But what may not be constructed out of the most unlikely material by a similar display of ingenuity? If one is at liberty first to disconnect sentences from their natural position, and then to piece them together again, chipping off inconvenient corners, and filling up the gaps with imaginary details, what kind of a tesselated mosaic may not be formed? Such patchwork can scarcely be regarded as the honest result of sober criticism. For, whatever may have been the position in life of our author, if Solomon was to be brought forward by him in his book as the spokesman of his sentiments, the wealth, riches, and magnificent works of that monarch had of necessity to be mentioned. Nay more, as it was impossible to avoid making some reference under the circumstances to Solomon's enormous harem, the remark of the writer on the female sex (chap. vii. 28), especially in the connexion in which it stands, utterly loses the significance with which Professor Plumptre seeks to invest it.

But we must of necessity draw our remarks to a close.

We have in previous chapters pointed out that the Book of Ben Sira and the Book of Wisdom presuppose the existence of the Book of Ecclesiastes. We may thus conclude with tolerable certainty that the work itself could not have been composed later than B.C. 250. But if, as we have seen reason to believe, "the men of the Great Synagogue" were those who admitted the work into the Canon, it must have been written some time between B.C. 444 and 328. The internal evidence makes it likely that it was towards the close of this period that the author lived. The simple reason why no more definite date can be assigned is, as mentioned elsewhere, that Jewish history is almost a blank from the death of Nehemiah (about B.C. 415) down to the accession of Antiochus Epiphanes in B.C. 175. The annals of the Persian empire, too, are very deficient from the death of Xerxes in B.C. 465 down to the appearance of Alexander the Great on the stage of history. But, ere the Persian empire was finally broken up, Koheleth, who in some respects may be considered as the last of the Hebrew prophets, had appeared, and his work had been recognised by the ecclesiastical leaders of the Jewish nation as worthy to be inserted among their sacred writings, as bearing on its brow, however difficult some of its statements may be to us to comprehend, the unmistakable impress of Divine inspiration.

In speaking of Koheleth as the last of the Hebrew prophets of the Old Testament, we, of course, use that term not in the signification attached to it in the popular mind, but in the proper sense of the Hebrew word, namely, one who announces the Divine will. There are, indeed, in the Book of Ecclesiastes no passages which can in any proper sense be termed Messianic—though Hahn has attempted to point out some such.[1] The Messianic expectations of the Jewish

---

[1] For instance, chap. iv. 13 ff. and chap. v. 7, 8. But his interpretation of these passages cannot be sustained. See our Crit. Comm.

people seem in Koheleth's days to have been at the lowest point. It was not his mission to revive those waning hopes. The appointed time for that had not yet fully come. The age In which he lived was one of restlessness of thought, and of that kind which often precedes an age of action, of that general uneasiness of feeling which is a premonitory symptom of some coming storm. There were daring spirits who, perplexed with mysteries they could not comprehend, were inclined to cast aside altogether the yoke of religion; and others, who, sullenly dissatisfied with their earthly lot, were disinclined to make the best use of the good things within their grasp, and disposed at the same time to dash impatiently aside as vain and deceptive the solace presented by the thought of a life beyond the grave. The restlessness of the age was fully shared in by Koheleth, and he does not scruple to express in the boldest terms his feeling of the vanity of life. He was far, however, from abandoning himself to utter sadness or despair. He thought that it was man's duty to enjoy the gifts of God, to fear God, and keep His commandments. Heine has somewhere styled the book "the Song of Scepticism," but, as Delitzsch observes, it would be more correctly termed "the Song of the Fear of God." Throughout his work Koheleth holds fast his faith in the eternal. He never loses himself in the abyss of atheism. His belief in God, in a judgment to come, in the final victory of goodness, comes forth ever and anon distinct and clear.

The book was, as already observed, in many ways a preparation for the Gospel of Jesus Christ. It pointed out man's sin and helplessness, the vanity of his best estate and the darkness that enwrapped the tomb. In contrast with its teachings the surpassing glory of the New Testament revelation is more clearly seen, for the latter tells of One who has abolished death and brought life and immortality to light by His Gospel. Much of the advice given in the Book of

Koheleth indeed might be summed up in Apostolic aphorisms, such as: "See that ye walk circumspectly, not as fools, but as wise, redeeming the time because the days are evil." "Rejoice in the Lord, and again I say, rejoice." It is not granted to man as such to know the secrets of the life that is to come: the keys of that unseen world and of death are in the hands of the Crucified and Risen Redeemer. But Koheleth saw into the mystery, as far as it was possible under the circumstances in which he was placed; and his conclusion on this point is well expressed in chap. viii. 12: "I know surely that it shall be well with them that fear God."

CHAPTER VI.

THE PESSIMISM OF THE BOOK OF KOHELETH AND THAT OF SCHOPENHAUER AND VON HARTMANN.

CHAPTER VI.

The unique character of Book of Koheleth, 141—The work pervaded by a pessimistic tone, 141—The meaning of the phrase "under the sun," 142—The uniformity of nature depressing, 143—The unsatisfactory character of the search after wisdom, 145—Solomon as a philosophical investigator, 145—Advantages of wisdom in common life, 147—Vanity of riches, 148—Corruption of magistrates and rulers, 149—Koheleth's commendation of the day of man's death, 150—The cause for such a commendation, 151—Pessimists before Schopenhauer, 152—Schopenhauer and von Hartmann, 152—Natural temperament of Schopenhauer, 153—Sully on "unreasoned pessimism," 153—Principles of Schopenhauer's philosophy, 155—von Hartmann on "unconscious will," 155—"Will" identified with "desire," 157—"The will to live" a curse, 158—Koheleth claimed by the Pessimists, 158—Venetianer's description of the results of Pessimism, 159—von Hartmann's three stages of illusion, 159—Schopenhauer's abuse of the Jews, 160—Pessimist doctrines conduct to asceticism and suicide, 161—Schopenhauer's attempt to deny this, his extraordinary views, 162—Taubert's reference to suicide, 163—Taubert on Koheleth, 164—The doctrines of Koheleth opposed to those of modern Pessimists, 164—Pessimism and the socialistic movement, 165—Inconsistencies of Pessimist philosophers, 166—The natural results of Pessimism, 167—Schopenhauer's explanation of the passion of love, 168—Results of such teaching, 169—Polygamy and monogamy, 170—Schopenhauer's apology for sodomy, 170—Rapid progress of Pessimism, 171—Pessimism and modern science, 171—Points of truth in Pessimism, 171—Resemblance to Buddhism, 172—Inferiority to Buddhism as a moral system, 173—The Buddhist doctrine of Nirvāna, 173, 182—Buddhism selfish in its aims, 175—Charge of selfishness brought against Christianity, 176—Christianity and Pessimism, 177—Optimistic and pessimistic features of Christianity, 179—Selfishness of the new Philosophy, 181—Practical failure of Buddhism, 182.

CHAPTER VI.

THE PESSIMISM OF THE BOOK OF KOHELETH AND THAT OF SCHOPENHAUER AND VON HARTMANN.

THE Book of Koheleth is unique in the whole range of Biblical literature. There is no other book among all the Sacred Writings with which it can properly be compared. If, in the prominence it assigns to "wisdom," and in the use it makes of aphorisms, it has certain features in common with the Book of Proverbs, the general structure and design of the two are entirely dissimilar. Few works can be at all fairly judged by isolated passages considered apart from their context, and none have been more unfairly treated in this respect than the Book of Ecclesiastes. It is not at all surprising, therefore, to find that its writer has often been regarded as a sceptic, not only in the good sense of the term, that is, as a bold and impartial seeker after truth, but in its more objectionable signification. Nor is it, perhaps, strange that it should have been appealed to by several writers belonging to the school of Modern Pessimism as a work which, though received into the Old Testament Canon, sets forth substantially several of the most startling tenets of that new philosophy.

It is, indeed, undeniable that the Book of Ecclesiastes is pervaded by a kind of gloom, and distinguished by a pessimistic tone peculiar to itself. Inasmuch, too, as this harmonised with the feelings of Schopenhauer, the founder of the school of philosophy to which reference has been made, its writer has been designated by him as "the genial, philosophical Koheleth."[1]

The book opens and closes (for the epilogue may here be left out of consideration) with the words: "Vanity of vanities, saith Koheleth, all is vanity." The clause "all is vanity," occurs also in other passages (chaps. i. 14; ii. 11; iii. 19; xi. 8; and, slightly modified, in chap. xi. 8). The phrase "this also is vanity" is even more frequent.[2] As the writer noted how man obtains no certain benefit on earth in return for all his toil and trouble, and as one phase after another of the vanity of human life passed successively in review before his mind, he uttered again and again the same piercing cry, "all is vanity and a striving after wind."

An American commentator maintains that the key to the meaning of the writer lies in the oft-recurring expression "under the sun," in which there is a mental contrast intended to be drawn between the rewards of toil expended on the things of time, and "the rewards of another world." According to this commentator the book was designed to answer the question: "What advantage is there in this life irrespective of another? What advantage has this life without another life?" The treatise is thus regarded as an argument, "for a God, for immortality, and for future rewards."[3]

Very little consideration is required in order to show that such an interpretation is not warranted by the contents of the work. The most cursory examination of the numerous passages in which the phrase "under the sun" occurs, is quite sufficient to prove that our author never intended to

---

[1] Or, "the Jewish but so philosophical Koheleth," Schopenhauer, *Welt als Wille u. Vorstellung*, Band iii. p. 731. See also Venetianer, *Schopenhauer als Scholastiker*, p. 273.

[2] So in chaps. i. 15, 19, 21, 23; ii. 26; iv. 4, 8, 16; v. 10; vi. 2, 9; vii. 6; viii. 10, 14.

[3] *A Commentary on the Book of Ecclesiastes by the Rev. Loyal Young, D.D.*, with Introductory Notices by the Rev. Prof. McGill, D.D., Princeton, and Rev. Prof. Jacobus, D.D. Philadelphia: Presbyterian Board of Education, 1865.

contrast the state of things "under the sun," with those things which belong to "another or a future life."[1]

There is some truth in the remark of Schopenhauer, that a man cannot fully understand the second verse of Koheleth until he has reached the age of seventy. It is then that the feeling of the vanity of all earthly things is experienced in its keenness. There are, however, circumstances which may cause the vanity and melancholy of earthly existence to come home at any age with a crushing power to a human soul, especially if it has not learned to seek consolation from above.

The impressions made upon men's minds by the things of nature depend in a great measure upon the state of mind of the beholder. A melancholy spirit naturally sees everything through a distorted medium. "Optimism and pessimism," as a philosopher of the present day observes, "have their deepest psychological roots in differences of sensibility," though he carefully adds that "these are not the only internal factors. Other mental influences co-operate to turn the judgment in this or that direction."[2] Though man, as at present organised, is dependent in a great measure on his bodily organs and conditioned by them, there are other forces which must also be taken into account; and intellectual, moral and spiritual influences have no unimportant part to play in the formation of the opinions of an individual.

The writer of the Book of Ecclesiastes represents Solomon in his opening verses as offended by the uniformity everywhere exhibited in nature. In doing so, he shows an accurate knowledge of human character. Solomon in his old age, "sated and weary," had, to use the language of Cox, "large experience of life, had tried its ambitions, its lusts, its plea-

---

[1] See our Crit. Comm. on chap. i. 3.
[2] Sully, *Pessimism: A History and a Criticism.* H. S. King & Co., London, 1877.

sures; he had tested every promise of good which it held forth and found them all lies; he had drunk of every stream and found no pure living water that could slake his thirst. And men such as he, sated but not satisfied, jaded with voluptuous delights, and without the peace of faith, commonly look out upon the world with haggard eyes."[1] Hence the tone in which in the opening prologue the author expresses himself: "Generation goes and generation comes, and the earth stands for ever." The sun rises and sets the same as ever, the winds continue to blow in their perpetual circuits, the rivers run into the sea. All the things of nature are in a state of ceaseless activity, human language cannot express this constant coming and going; which, however, produces only the same effects as ever; "there is nothing new under the sun." This restlessness of nature on the one hand, and the uniformity of its action on the other, were felt by the writer to be depressing, especially when he reflected that he himself also was rapidly passing away from the everlasting earth, trodden by so many men before him, and which so many generations of men would tread after he was gone, each generation destined in its turn to be alike forgotten.

Urged forward by such considerations, and inspired with special wisdom from above, Koheleth set himself diligently to discover that thing which man ought to strive for on earth. What is there "under the sun" which can afford real satisfaction to the heart of man, and what man ought to regard as beyond his powers? With this special object in view, Koheleth sought to make use of the wisdom he possessed in order to take a survey, not so much of the phenomena of nature (which are only glanced at in the prologue), as of the actions of men. He desired to note carefully all that was

[1] *The Quest of the Chief Good: Expository Lectures on the Book Ecclesiastes*, with a New Translation, by Samuel Cox, D.D. A Commentary for Laymen: London, Arthur Miall.

done "under the sun," and to ascertain, if possible, that which was best for the sons of men. He, however, states in the outset the conclusion at which he ultimately arrived, namely, that the investigation itself was an evil toil, inasmuch as it could lead to no definite result, "for all is vanity and a striving after wind." In his case, the inquiry only brought into clearer light the various evils connected with man's lot, while it showed his inability to remove them : "the crooked cannot be made straight." For many of the sorrows of life can be traced up to a higher source than man. "Who can make that straight which God hath made crooked?" (chap. vii. 13). Hence the search after wisdom brought no satisfaction to Koheleth. He discovered that man was shut in on all sides, and confined within barriers which could not be passed. The highest conclusion to which human wisdom and knowledge can attain is to understand that one knows nothing yet as he ought to know (1 Cor. viii. 2). Still more unsatisfactory Koheleth discovered the attempt to attain "the highest good" by means of what is usually termed pleasure. The endeavours of Solomon to obtain satisfaction in this way are described as the writer's personal experience. He gives a vivid sketch of the eagerness with which that monarch pursued after all kinds of enjoyments.

Solomon is depicted in this part of the work in the character of a philosophical investigator, who, by the possession of more than ordinary wisdom, was preserved from ultimate ruin, although he indulged for a time in the keenest pursuit of those things which could gratify his desires. His wisdom enabled him to maintain such a control over his passions that he was not swallowed up in the abyss of sensuality never to rise again, as is the case with the majority of those who venture on such a dangerous course.[1] As

[1] In Professor Mozley's *Sermons, Parochial and Occasional* (Rivingtons, 1879),

Delitzsch observes: "There are drinkers who know how to regulate their drinking so that they do not end in the madness of intemperance; and there are habitual voluptuaries who so far understand how to control themselves as not become roués altogether ruined in body." Though Solomon possessed this great advantage over others, yet, when at the close of his life of "pleasure" he reviewed one by one the various "delights" in which he had so freely indulged, and contemplated the works of grandeur erected to gratify his purer tastes, he was constrained to confess that "all was but vanity and a striving after the wind, and there was no profit under the sun" (ii. 13).

Thus Solomon learned by experience the inability of wisdom on the one hand, and of folly on the other, to secure happiness or satisfaction. But though alike incompetent to

there is a remarkable discourse on this subject, entitled "Wisdom and Folly tested by experience." Speaking of this section of Ecclesiastes, Mozley observes that for a discerning person deliberately to set about a course of folly and madness in order to discover the evil effects of such a course, is something in the highest degree superfluous. There are two ways of arriving at the knowledge of the truth respecting the importance and benefit of holiness and goodness, either by the experience of that which is good or by the experience of that which is bad. Mozley contrasts the knowledge of the advantages of a good life gained by experience with the knowledge of the disadvantages of an evil life obtained in a similar manner. The conviction of sin in persons recovered from a course of transgression is no doubt deep and acute. But the great use of wisdom is to lead men to *act* uprightly, and the wisdom that comes after action comes too late. In both cases a moral conviction is gained, but in the case in which it has been obtained by the practice of ill, the conviction comes not in time to prevent the evil, but merely to acquaint one with it. Sin itself produces an effect upon the soul which does not cease when the course of sinning is past. The conviction of a man who does not yield to immorality is the result of his faith. He goes through life with the belief that a course of sin must end in misery. There is no similar exercise of faith in the case of the man who seeks first to discover by his personal experience the effects of sin. In the former case there is a gain in moral discipline which is wanting in the latter. In answer to the crude objection that the man who has actually proved the effects of sin is the only one who can speak with authority on the subject, Mozley observes that such a person may indeed speak with authority, but his advice is always open to the retort from the person whom he seeks to dissuade from a path of sin, You have learned your wisdom from experience, and I desire to follow the same course.

procure "the highest good," Koheleth affirms the vast superiority of wisdom over folly. Speaking still under the mask of the Israelitish king, Koheleth carefully guards against any misrepresentation of his real sentiments on this important point, and points out the advantages of wisdom in a few terse sentences. Who could venture to speak on such a subject with greater authority than Solomon? "For what is the man that is to come after the king, whom they made" king "long ago" (chap. ii. 12) amid the acclamations of the multitude (1 Kings i. 39, 40, comp. 1 Kings v. 1; 1 Chron. xxix. 22)? Surely a wise man like Solomon with his experience could point out the superiority of wisdom better than any other teacher that might come after him (chap. ii. 12). The excellency of wisdom is distinctly taught by that monarch in the Book of Proverbs, and consequently Koheleth was fully justified in expressing the views of the ideal Solomon in the following terms: "I saw that the superiority of wisdom over folly is like the superiority of light over darkness. The wise man has his eyes in his head, and the fool walketh in darkness" (ii. 13).

Koheleth points out the advantage which the possession of wisdom gives to man even in the ordinary affairs of daily life. "Wisdom strengthens a wise man more than ten powerful men which are in the city" (vii. 20). For there is no just man on the earth who doeth good and sinneth not. The most righteous are liable to fall into faults of some sort or other, but wisdom may deliver the truly upright from the evil results of such offences. Mindful, however, of his own natural tendency to evil and of his liability to fall, the wise man ought to pass over the minor offences of others, and take little notice of the angry speeches or curses uttered in moments of bitterness by persons in subordinate positions (chap. vii. 20, 21). Wisdom thus will often protect a man amid dangers which would swallow up a fool. It will teach him how to conduct himself in the presence of Oriental despots, it will instruct him how to moderate his speech and temper his manners. It will teach him to obey the king on account of the oath of allegiance which he has taken, while it will lead him to be patient in days of oppression, and to wait for the coming day of vengeance in which God will punish transgressors (chap. viii. 1 ff).

The story related in chap. ix. 13-15 of the little city besieged by the mighty king and delivered by the wisdom of a poor wise man may be adduced as an illustration of this truth. For wisdom, though despised in days of prosperity, when proclaimed by the lips of a poor wise man, has often been found in the day of adversity superior to all earthly power and might (chap. ix. 16).

Notwithstanding the essential superiority of the wise man over the fool, their ultimate lot in this world is identical. Wisdom may preserve a wise man from many dangers, but, sooner or later, he, too, must succumb to the common lot. "One chance happens to all" (chap. ii. 14). Death strikes down the wise man in the exercise of his wisdom, and the fool while intent on his folly. Both are swept away by that mighty torrent (Ps. xc. 5), and their memory is alike forgotten (Koh. ii. 16). The bitter lament of David over Abner (2 Sam. iii. 33) has ever and anon been repeated over the wise man's grave, "How dieth the wise man like the fool!" (chap. ii. 16).

It was under the pressure of such thoughts that Koheleth was driven to exclaim: "Then I hated life, for evil to me appeared the work which was done under the sun, for the whole is vanity and a striving after wind" (chap. ii. 17).

Similar were his reflections as he contemplated the vanity of riches which, though amassed by constant toil, must at last be left to others (chap. ii. 18-23, comp. v. 9 ff). Men are seldom disquieted in the day of prosperity (chap. v. 19) by reflections on the uncertainty of life, or on the possibility of a reverse of fortune. But it not unfrequently happens that riches are kept and guarded, only at last to be a source of greater grief to him who has amassed them, when he sees them borne away from his grasp by some terrible wave of misfortune. A man who has brought up his children in prosperity and with reasonable expectations of enjoying a life of affluence, is sometimes by a change of circumstances left with nothing in his hands, and though once wealthy is consigned at last to a poor man's grave. This, too, Koheleth notes as one of the worst evils of life that "as a man comes naked into the world so must he depart naked out of it again" (chap. v. 12-15). The final conclusion of Koheleth as to the unprofitableness of riches to procure man's highest good may well be summed up in Apostolic language: "They that desire to be rich ($βουλόμενοι\ πλουτεῖν$) fall into a temptation, and a snare, and many foolish and hurtful lusts (desires) such as drown men in destruction and perdition" (1 Tim. vi. 9, 10).

Reflections such as these naturally predisposed Koheleth to take a pessimistic view of life. The peculiar evils prevalent in his own day made the misery of life appear still more bitter in his eyes. It is difficult in any age to point out what man should strive for on earth, and this difficulty was in Koheleth's day aggravated materially by many circumstances. The careful student will note how often Koheleth wanders off from other subjects to make some reference to the galling despotism then rampant, and the terrible evils with which it was accompanied. Although he enjoined on his readers the duty of obeying those in authority, "for conscience sake," he was not unmindful of the frightful oppression which marked the government of the day. Not only did the lower magistrates tyrannise over the people, but they who were higher in office watched in turn for an opportunity to oppress their subordinates. Such was the case from the lowest officials up to the persons who stood highest in authority and power. Alongside of the satraps, the chief rulers under the Crown in the Persian Empire, there were other dignitaries in some respects "higher than they." Such an official was the Royal Secretary, designated "the King's Eye" and "Ear;" such were the royal inspectors.[1] These were often ready, sometimes under the influence of a wretched inmate of the royal harem, to pounce down like vultures on an unlucky satrap and gorge themselves with his plunder (chap. v. 7, comp. chap. x. 4-7, 16 ff). Under such a system, which was eating at that time like a cancer into the very heart of the Persian empire, a man of wisdom, though he might by the exercise of prudence and understanding escape personal danger, would often be compelled to behold human sorrows which he could not alleviate.

Koheleth thus relates his own observations on this point:—"And again I saw all the oppressions which occur under the sun, and behold the tear of the oppressed, and they have no comforter, and from the hand of those who are oppressing them violence, and they have no comforter" (chap. iv. 1). It was at such moments that Koheleth felt, to use the words of a pessimist philosopher, "the torment of existence," and was driven to exclaim that "he who increaseth knowledge increaseth also sorrow"[2] The thought amid such scenes forced itself upon his mind, what ends and objects were to be attained by the endurance of such misery? It was then that he regarded the state of "the dead that were already dead long ago" to be preferable to that of the living, and thought that the lot of those was to be envied who had never been born, and who had not

[1] Prof. George Rawlinson's *Ancient Monarchies*, vol. iii. pp. 423 ff. Xenophon, *Cyropædia*, lib. viii. 2, 10.

[2] Vide Moritz Venetianer, *Schopenhauer als Scholastiker*; Eine Kritik der Schopenhauer'schen Philosophie mit Rücksicht auf die gesammte Kantische Neoscholastik (Berlin: Carl Duncker, 1873), p. 275.

beheld "the evil that was done under the sun" (chap. iv. 2, 3). The toil and moil of life, and the constant efforts of men to overtop and surpass their fellows seemed to him but "vanity and striving after the wind."

Koheleth was in a similar frame of mind when he wrote "better is a name than good ointment and the day of (one's) death than the day of his birth" (chap. vii. 1). The first expression shows how deeply the desire was implanted in the writer's soul that his name should be kept in remembrance. The connexion in which the aphorism concerning "the day of one's death" occurs shows its meaning to be that expressed later, namely, "better is the end of a matter than its beginning" (chap. vii. 8). When "a man is born into the world" no one can tell "what manner of child it shall be." But, when the day of death has brought the individual's career to a close, a true estimate can be formed of the happiness of his life as a whole. The remark of Solon in reply to the inquiry of Crœsus, that "no man is to be counted happy until he has closed his life happily" (*Herod.*, i. 32), partly illustrates these aphorisms of Koheleth. Under the Old Dispensation, in times of terrible affliction such as that which darkened the life of Job, it was natural to bemoan the day of one's birth (Job iii. 3 ff, x. 18, 19), or even to give utterance to similar expressions in days of dire national distress and individual persecution, as in the case of Jeremiah (Jer. xx. 14-18). But to argue, with Venetianer, from such lamentations that the pessimism of Job and Koheleth is in accordance with that of Schopenhauer, is to assign to the expressions of these Old Testament writers a meaning never for a moment contemplated by them.

For what is the teaching of the modern school of Pessimism as to the life of man? This school of philosophy, as represented by Schopenhauer and others, it should be noted in the outset, is avowedly atheistic in its creed, though in the shape it has assumed in the writings of von Hartmann it exhibits somewhat of a Pantheistic tendency. It is in many respects one of the most extraordinary phenomena of the present age. Men have existed in all ages predisposed to melancholy and inclined to look upon life as dark and gloomy. This "unreasoned pessimism," as it has been well termed by Mr. Sully,[1] has assumed many forms. Some of the finest outpourings of poetry have been the outbursts of the feeling of melancholy which often seizes upon the human heart. The optimism of Leibnitz,[2] eagerly embraced both by the Deist philosophers and the Christian theologians of the eighteenth century, produced a reaction in an opposite direction among philosophic thinkers, a reaction strongly aided by the writings of David Hume. Several of the leading poets of the succeeding age, such as Byron and Shelley in England, and Heine and others in Germany, were deeply imbued with a dislike of the then prevalent optimism, and their poems often complain of the misery of human life. Some of them went further, and even Herder in some of his poems expressed sentiments not very different from those lately propounded.[3] Pessimism, however, may be considered to have been first elevated to the position of a philosophic creed by the writings of Schopenhauer and von Hartmann.[4]

[1] Sully's *Pessimism: a History and a Criticism* (London: H. S. King & Co., 1877), chap. ii.

[2] See Venetianer's remarks on Leibnitz, in his *Schopenhauer als Scholastiker*, p. 281, and still better, Sully's observations on the Theodicy of Leibnitz, in his *Pessimism*, chap. iii.

[3] As for instance in his poem entitled "Das Ich."

[4] A. Taubert, in her work *Der Pessimismus und seine Gegner* (Berlin: Duncker, 1873), remarks (p. 10) that the term "pessimism" is not well chosen, as it might express the idea that the present world was the worst that could be conceived. The term, however, she regards as correct so far as it conveys the idea that the non-existence of the universe is to be preferred to its existence. She observes that the more suitable expression would be that proposed by Knauer, namely, *Malismus*, or, as Haym has proposed, *Miserabilismus*. For these terms permit one to hold the opinion that, in spite of its badness, the world as it exists is the best of all possible worlds, while the word "pessimism" conveys a much stronger idea. On Taubert, see note 2 on p. 158.

It is highly probable that the natural temperament of Arthur Schopenhauer, the real founder of the modern school of Pessimism,[1] had not a little to do with the philosophic tenets he ventured to propound. The genesis of philosophic pessimism is a matter which we cannot here more than allude to. We have to deal with it as a fact, the existence of which is one of the most remarkable phenomena of the day. It is, however, worthy of mention that Schopenhauer's sanity has been seriously called in question.[2]

"Unreasoned pessimism" is, as Sully has well observed, in many cases but the natural outburst of a carping, fault-

[1] In his work *Zur Geschichte und Begründung des Pessimismus* (Berlin, 1880) von Hartmann maintains that, although Schopenhauer was the first philosopher who set forth Pessimism as a definite philosophy, the real author of that philosophy was Kant, though the term Pessimism does not occur in his writings. That Kant was the real Father of Pessimism is a startling statement, the truth of which cannot be here discussed. E. von Hartmann naturally seeks to roll away from the philosophy, of which he himself is now the most conspicuous advocate (but which is presented in some respects in a more objectionable form in his writings), the reproach of deriving its beginning and strength from the melancholy temper of its first advocate. Hence his efforts to trace its origin to one who was admittedly the greatest philosopher of his day.

[2] See the remarkable tract, *Doctor Arthur Schopenhauer vom medicinischen Standpunkte betrachtet*, von Carl von Seidlitz. Dorpat, 1872. Gwinner, his ablest and latest biographer, speaks of him as one who from childhood was always disposed to believe that some terrible misfortune was about to happen to him. He admits that his hero's intense anxiety often bordered on madness. As a young man he was tortured constantly with the idea that he had all sorts of diseases. When a student he once fancied he was dying of consumption. He fled from Naples through a nervous dread of the smallpox, and from Berlin on account of the cholera. For many years he was miserable, owing to his fear of a criminal process. He was greatly deficient in personal courage, and was in a constant state of alarm in 1813, fearing lest he should be forced into the army. If he was awoke by any noise at night he would rush out of his bed armed with a dagger and pistols, which he always kept loaded. He was more than inclined to be a regular misanthrope, although sometimes desirous not to be regarded as such, but simply as one who despised mankind in general. In his old age he seemed to look upon any contact with men as a contamination and a defilement, and maintained that the wisest man is he who in the whole course of his life has the least intercourse with his fellows. He regarded the vast majority of mankind as either knaves or fools. See *Schopenhauer's Leben*, von Wilhelm Gwinner, 2te umgearbeitete u. vielfach vermehrte Auflage der Schrift "Arthur Schopenhauer aus persönlichem Umgange dargestelt." Leipzig: F. A. Brockhaus, 1878.

finding disposition. Many take pleasure in finding fault with all around them, and in thus seeking to exhibit their own real or fancied superiority. "By how much, one wonders, would the amount of human criticism be diminished, if one no longer derived from the process any agreeable feelings of intellectual elevation." "Pessimism flatters a man by presenting him with a portrait of himself in which he appears as another 'Prometheus vinctus,' suffering tortures from the hand of the cruel Zeus-pater, the World-all, which begot and holds us, yet bearing up and resisting in proud defiance. . . . Pessimism enables its adherent to pose as some wronged and suffering divinity, to the admiration of himself at least, if not of spectators around him,"[1] an admiration not less real though it is generally disavowed. Many persons have adopted the creed of modern Pessimism, not because they have made for themselves any deep study of its principles, and still less any careful study of the arguments in favour of Christianity, but simply because of the novelty and temporary popularity which that system has attained in some quarters, and because, like other atheistic theories, it is unquestionably upheld by some writers of ability and renown.

Schopenhauer claims to start from the standpoint of idealism as expounded in the writings of Kant. He denounces the three great leaders of philosophic thought in Germany who succeeded that philosopher, and further developed his principles—namely, Fichte, Schelling, and Hegel, as "the three German sophists." The writings of Hegel especially are the subjects of his fiercest denunciations. He characterises them as full of such monstrous combinations of words, as to have destroyed in many persons all faculty of

---

[1] Sully's *Pessimism*, pp. 423, 424. Kalisch observes in his *Path and Goal*, p. 437, that Nihilism or Pessimism is for many "a practical canon adopted because they find it congenial to their nature, and grasped with increased tenacity because they hear it praised and supported by men of ability and fame."

thinking, and made them consider "hollow empty phrases" as real thoughts, and look on "transparent sophisms" as lofty wisdom.

The world, according to Schopenhauer's conception, consists of "will and representation" (Wille und Vorstellung). The external world of appearance exists only for the percipient mind. But, underlying the outer veil of phenomena there is something real, namely, "will," which is the ultimate cause of all existence. This "will," however, is "unconscious." It has no object or aim in its action. It exists outside all time, and is "one and indivisible," although it manifests itself in numberless individual appearances. How such "unconscious will" could, in the course of things, ever attain to consciousness is a problem of metaphysics which need not here be discussed. One is, indeed, often tempted to ask whether the language of condemnation so unsparingly applied by Schopenhauer to the philosophy of Hegel is not as applicable to the mystical principles of his own philosophy? It is not, indeed, strange that the man who invented such a philosophy should propound it as the highest wisdom, little as it is deserving of that title. But it is strange that it should have captivated the imagination of other able critics. It has been presented in a more developed form in the work of Dr. Eduard von Hartmann, namely, *Die Philosophie des Unbewussten*, and defended in other productions of his pen, especially in his *Phänomenologie des sittl. Bewusstseins*. It is hard to form any intelligible conception of the fundamental principle of a philosophical system which asserts the existence of an "unconscious Absolute," one of whose modes of manifestation is consciousness. "An Unconscious which performs acts of the will by which, as by sorcery, it is at any moment able to destroy matter and to call it again into existence? An Unconscious which is a *spirit*, serving as 'the common bond of the world, and as the principle of unity pervading its plan of creation'? An Unconscious that not only possesses 'reason and intelligence,' but is endowed with a clear-sighted wisdom infinitely superior to any conceivable consciousness?"[1]

It is out of our province to seek to give more than a sketch of this philosophical school. It is the use its leading advocates have made of the Book of Koheleth which renders it necessary to notice the wide difference between the pessimism of that book and that inculcated by the school of modern Pessimism. But, in order to understand the fundamental difference between the two, it is necessary to understand the leading ideas on which the new philosophy is founded.

An "unconscious will" is almost a contradiction in terms. Volition cannot exist without some object towards which that volition or desire is directed, or without some mental representation of that which is desired. Schopenhauer maintains that "will" may exist without intellect; because the lower we descend in the scale of creation the less intellect is perceptible, while "will" is as strongly marked as ever; and von Hartmann maintains that unconscious objects and aims are traceable throughout the whole course of nature. Sully, however, observes rightly that there is a radical distinction to be drawn between actions which are merely instinctive, and actions which proceed from volition. He argues that it is false to regard will or volition as including all emotional phenomena. The very idea of "will" presupposes some instinctive impulse, which exists prior to any exercise of volition, as well as some imagination of the act to be willed or not willed as one likely to be followed by some pleasure or pain. It is this imagination which ultimately excites the exercise of volition, although in the analysis of higher volitions other elements come into play.[2]

[1] See the sketch of Pessimism in Dr. M. M. Kalisch's interesting work, *Path and Goal: A Discussion on the Elements of Civilization and the Conditions of Happiness.* London : Longmans, Green & Co., 1880, p. 427.
[2] See Sully's *Pessimism*, pp. 207, 209, 211.

The philosophy of Schopenhauer and von Hartmann has for its fundamental basis this tenet of an "unconscious will." Is this, as Sully thinks, the reappearance in another form of the old hypothesis of a "substantial will," long since cast into the philosophical lumber-room as utterly incapable of proof? All human knowledge is necessarily phenomenal. Man cannot rise above the law of his being and grasp in thought that entity or substance which underlies phenomena. The pretence of having attained to such a knowledge will in every case, when investigated, be found to rest upon a *petitio principii*.

"Will" regarded by these philosophers as the cause of all existence is identified by them with "desire." It thus necessarily implies want on the one hand and a longing to appease that want on the other. Hence they maintain that it more or less distinctly involves the idea of suffering. It may, however, be seriously questioned whether "desire" of itself pre-supposes in all cases suffering, while on the other hand the correctness of the identification of "will" with "desire" is more than doubtful. Schopenhauer may be wrong in asserting that pleasure is in all cases preceded by "desire", or in other words, is absolutely inseparable from pain. Eduard von Hartmann has acknowledged that the conclusion is not justified by facts. For there are often pleasures, as Sully justly observes, which are wholly unexpected, and, therefore, not preceded by any volition whatever, while there are pains which are in like manner entirely independent of "will." In order to uphold the theory that pleasure and pain are nothing else than the satisfaction or non-satisfaction of "will," von Hartmann has recourse to his hypothesis of the Unconscious, and maintains that, in all cases "where we cannot find in consciousness any state of volition underlying our pleasures and pains, this substratum exists as unconscious will."[1]

---

[1] See Sully's *Pessimism*, pp. 200 ff.

158 Schopenhauer on the misery of Existence.

Inasmuch as Schopenhauer affirms that existence itself is the consequence of "will," or, of "the will to live," and every act of will is attended by more or less suffering, the exercise of will is looked upon as the real cause of all the misery of life. The non-existence of the world is to be preferred to its existence. The world is cursed with four great evils, birth, disease, old age, and death. "Existence is only a punishment," and the feeling of misery which often accompanies it is "repentance" for the great crime of having come into being by yielding to the "will to live."[1] Happiness is unattainable in this world, while a future state of existence is pronounced a mere delusion. And, even if there were another life, the pessimist asserts that there could be no real happiness in it. For life implies "will;" and the existence of "will," inasmuch as "the will" must ever meet with some hindrances to the attainment of its desires, is incompatible with happiness.[2]

In arriving at such conclusions, the pessimist writers assert that they are only carrying out to their natural consequences the doctrines taught in the Books of Job and Koheleth. In both these books (as we have seen, p. 151) the day of birth is spoken of as a day of sorrow. The circumstances under which the sacred writers gave utterance to such expressions ought indeed to have been sufficient to restrain our would-be modern philosophers from bringing them forward in favour of their doctrine of the absolute misery of all existence.[3]

The following is a description of the results arrived at by

---

[1] *Schopenhauer's sämmtliche Werke*, vol. iii. p. 666 (*Die Welt als Wille und Vorstellung*).

[2] See Taubert's *Pessimismus u. seine Gegner*, Kap. ix. pp. 85 ff. "A. Taubert," whom Sully in his *Pessimism*, pp. 108, 109, has mistaken for an author belonging to the sterner sex, was the name under which Dr. Eduard von Hartmann's first wife wrote in defence of the philosophy of which her husband is so conspicuous an advocate.

[3] Dean Swift's practice of bemoaning, or affecting to bemoan, the day of his birth does not deserve to be more than alluded to here.

this new philosophy as drawn by no unfriendly pen. "To live signifies to have wants, signifies suffering. Living implies having a body with the iron law of preserving and protecting it against a thousand dangers and pains. Then there is the preservation of the family, all which brings every day new sorrows and demands, calling for the exercise of all the powers, though with the full conviction, however, that we must at last lose the game, and that one is steering steadily towards death. If a man casts off all other burdens, he becomes a burden to himself. When cares vanish, man is consumed by ennui, and the greatest efforts have to be made to kill time. . . . These and similar meditations are the everlasting theme of Schopenhauer. Eduard von Hartmann has reduced these ideas to a system and carried them out still further in his three stages of illusion, (1) illusion especially as to the expectation of happiness here, (2) illusion as to the expectation of individual happiness in another world, (3) illusion as to the expectation of happiness as ultimately to be attained by the world's progress. All is illusion ; for the more knowledge, the more suffering." Such is the interpretation the pessimist puts upon the statement of Koheleth i. 18, "he that increaseth knowledge increaseth sorrow."[1] Schopenhauer has, however, curiously enough maintained that Pessimism may be made the means of benefiting mankind. "Everything is miserable, everything entreats for pity, be pitiful. Think not that thou hast before thee a wicked stupid creature, but think upon the suffering necessarily belonging to it, Virtue, indeed, according to Schopenhauer, can by no means be taught, but that does not hinder him from teaching it as forcibly as any one else. . . . No one down to Schopenhauer has known how to make such an idea (that of universal misery) the principle of a metaphysic of morals, which can also be supported by the finest psychological investigations."[2]

[1] See Venetianer, *Schopenhauer als Scholastiker*, p. 275. [2] *Venetianer*, pp. 281, 282.

Such is Venetianer's estimate of the results achieved by the Pessimist philosophy. He has, however, severely criticised his master for the intolerable pride and conceit which he everywhere exhibits, a pride which characterises other writers of the Pessimist school. Schopenhauer has been soundly rated by his disciple for his "barbarous ignorance" and gross attacks upon the Jewish religion as an utter "abomination," for his shameless misrepresentations of its principles, and for his bigotry against the Jewish race in general, to which Venetianer himself belongs. He points out, however, with considerable truth, that, although Schopenhauer may abuse and revile Jews and Judaism, not a little of his metaphysics may ultimately be traced up to Jewish sources.[1]

[1] Venetianer maintains that much of what Schopenhauer says about the unity of will harmonises with what Maimonides teaches about the unity of God. He notes also that a distinguished Jewish poet and philosopher, Salomo Ibn Gabirol, who died in A.D. 1070, conceived God chiefly as "will," an opinion which was followed by Duns Scotus, one of the most eminent of the scholastic doctors of the fourteenth century. As a philosopher, Ibn Gabirol was known by the name of Avicebron or Avicembrol in the Latin of the middle ages. On Ibn Gabirol's doctrine on this point Dr. David Asher's pamphlet (*Arthur Schopenhauer: Neues von ihm und über*, Berlin 1871) may be consulted with profit. Schopenhauer, in a letter to Dr. Asher, in 1857, speaks of Ibn Gabirol as follows: "Gabirol may be regarded as my forerunner inasmuch as he teaches that the will is, performs, and makes all in all, but there also his entire wisdom is at an end, because he teaches it only thus *in abstracto*, and repeats it a thousand times. In relation to me he is like a glow-worm which gives light by night in a thick mist compared with the sun."—See Gwinner, *Schopenhauer's Leben*, p. 584. The pride exhibited in these remarks is characteristic of Schopenhauer. Venetianer notes that Schopenhauer, though an opponent of faith, has not been able to emancipate himself from his traditional inclinations, and that his idea that ethics are closely connected with metaphysics when examined into is almost equivalent to the statement that morality depends upon faith in God. It is well, however, to be cautious against making a mistake on such points. Similarity of expression may cover radical differences of thought. The language of Trinitarianism has been often used to express ideas which are essentially pantheistic. Schopenhauer's ethics are far from corresponding with the doctrines of Christianity. It must not be forgotten that that philosopher declared that Christianity was quite possible, provided only that the "Jewish dogma" on which the gospels are based be abandoned, namely, that man is created by God, when the truth is that man is in reality only the product of his own will, *i.e.*, is in fact his own creator! See Kalisch's *Path and Goal*, pp. 430-432; Schopenhauer, *Welt als Wille u. Vorstellung*, Werke, vol. i. pp. 477-483.

Life is regarded by Schopenhauer as necessarily involving suffering. Man and animated nature are preyed upon by a burning thirst or desire which can never be quenched. Human life oscillates like a pendulum ever between the two points, of pain on the one hand and of ennui on the other.[1] Hence true freedom can only be effected by the "denial of the will to live." The fourth book of Schopenhauer's remarkable treatise is devoted to this subject. Existence is an evil which, according to his idea, can only be destroyed, as it has been created, by will. The goal which the pessimists set before them as the great object to be kept steadily in view is to lose all self-consciousness, and to be swallowed up in the great nothing out of which man rose. This doctrine, as taught by Schopenhauer, conducts first to asceticism,[2] and ultimately to suicide.

Schopenhauer admits the validity of the first conclusion, and consequently recommends celibacy and asceticism as "a denial of the will to live." He maintains, however, that his tenets do not lead to suicide. The denial of "the will to live," according to him, implies a denial of the pleasures of life, and not merely of its sufferings; and it is an inability

---

[1] Schopenhauer's *Welt als Wille und Vorstellung*. Werke, vol. i. pp. 366 ff, 418, and *Parerga*, ii. § 173.

[2] In his *Phænomenologie* (pp. 688 ff.), von Hartmann criticises the asceticism recommended by Schopenhauer and Mailänder. He refers to the practices of the Skopzecs of Russia, but without approving of them, and notices the still more objectionable recommendations in another direction, tending to the same end, namely, the lessening of the human race, which have been put forward unblushingly as a new "gospel of nature," by English writers whose names need not here be mentioned. It is too much the habit to trace all that is evil in practice, and unsound in theology, to continental sources; and hence the following remarks of von Hartmann may not be without instruction to those in England who are disposed to think "more highly than they ought to think" of the nation to which they belong:—"It is a remarkable irony of history that this weapon should have been forged by Manchester Bourgeois-Liberalism for the social democracy; for it is the land of Bentham and of Mill, from which this new 'gospel' comes to us, that appears to be essentially a medical outrider of the Ricardo-Malthusian Overpopulation theory."—*Phænom. sittl. Bewussteins*, p. 691.

to bear up against the inconveniences of life which drives an individual to suicide. "The true pessimist" is anxious not only to get rid of existence for himself, but is actuated still more by a desire to benefit his species. Hence he ought to live in order to point out to others the misery of life, and to induce them by his example voluntarily to deny the "will to live," and thus hasten the time when the whole species shall reach the Paradise of Nirvâna.[1]

Hence these philosophers have asserted that sufferings of every kind are useful inasmuch as they drive men to feel the weariness and misery of life, and events of the contrary character are hurtful because they make men love that which is so evil. One of the speakers in Kalisch's ingenious book *Path and Goal* (p. 424) points out pithily what results from such extraordinary premises: "Plainly this, that we can show to our fellow-man no greater love and affection than by inflicting upon him every possible torture and anguish, since we thereby bring him nearer to his true salvation, whereas it is fiendish malice and cruelty to show him any kindness, to help him out of difficulties, or to protect him against injustice and ignominy, since we thereby lure him away from the blessed path of deliverance which leads through trials, and thus make him miss the true object of existence.[2]

However theoretically opposed Schopenhauer's philosophy may be to suicide, and however much his followers have tried to avoid the accusation that the doctrines of Pessimism tend

---

[1] See on Nirvâna the notes on pp. 173, 175, 182.

[2] In his *Phænomenologie des sittlichen Bewusstseins*, pp. 42-46, von Hartmann has some striking criticisms on these notions of Schopenhauer. He points out that Pessimism in the form advocated by Schopenhauer is essentially selfish in its aims. It is selfish for a man to seek to escape from life and leave others to go on in the same "mad dance of fools which common life is." One ought, according to von Hartmann, to be perfectly indifferent to life or death, to the idea of our existence being prolonged indefinitely or terminated. The latter idea is in some aspects akin to the doctrine of the Yoga taught in the second chapter of the Bhagavad-Gîtâ.

to that result, suicide cannot but be regarded as a logical outcome of such doctrines. It must be borne in mind that pessimists are not opposed to suicide on any principles of morality. Every real basis of morality is destroyed by their system. If life be hateful and its burden unendurable, and if death lands us in the everlasting rest of nothingness (for we need not here discuss the possibility of some continuity of existence when consciousness has ceased), then the conclusion of the song is logical "the sooner 'tis over the sooner to sleep." Why should an individual continue to live a life of martyrdom and useless striving when the end of all is that nothing, into which ascetics and voluptuaries shall alike descend? Why not, as speedily as possible step behind the veil into the rest of unconsciousness? For even the miseries of those who remain still on earth, whose sufferings the individual might by living perhaps help to alleviate, only tend to make them more willing to seek the same blissful goal.

Taubert sneers at the man who regards life without pleasure as unendurable, at him who must needs whine over his sorrows. It may be a question for such a man to consider "whether existence for him at least is preferable to non-existence." She observes, however, that the choice, though a bad one, is open to every one; and she intimates tolerably plainly that many persons have made a much worse choice.[1]

This last-named writer has, also, the hardiness to maintain that the Pessimism which characterises the Books of Job and

[1] Taubert *Der Pessimismus und seine Gegner*, p. 128. Suicide in the present day is in many places almost an epidemic. Its frequency in Germany, especially in Saxony and the adjacent countries, has evoked a small literature. But it is not only in Germany that this fact is arousing attention. If it cannot be distinctly traced to the prevalence of the pessimist philosophy, it may without doubt be attributed in a great measure to that disbelief in a personal God, one of the results of which is this very philosophy. Men are beginning to practise that which they believe. It may be well that the natural fruits of atheism and ungodliness have thus terribly manifested themselves.

Koheleth, and the Prophecies and Lamentations of Jeremiah, is not essentially different from that of Schopenhauer. This fact she considers of great importance, because the writings of the Bible still exercise an influence over many minds. She terms chap. i.-iii. and chap. iv. 1-4 of the Book of Koheleth "a Catechism of Pessimism," and recommends these chapters to be read by every person not thoroughly acquainted with their contents.[1] But in these very chapters Koheleth expresses a firm belief in a personal God who, in His own time (for to everything there is a time and a season), will judge the righteous and the wicked. Koheleth also affirms the existence of a life beyond the grave;[2] and his faith in God and eternity, taken together with the belief in the reality of sin which pervades his entire book, is enough to show the essential difference which exists between his pessimism and the doctrines of the modern Pessimistic school.

If the doctrines of modern Pessimism be indeed true, then, as the writer just referred to grants,[3] the happiest persons on earth are those who (as long as no special misfortune occurs to them individually) live without troubling themselves with any speculations on such subjects, unconcerned with the misery of the universe in general, and untroubled with reflections on the difficulties it presents. If Taubert affirms that such a life is degrading to humanity, and is like that of the cattle in the pasturage, what matters it if men are little better than the beasts, and are destined to return to nothingness as they? If such be the ultimate goal of humanity, it is only wanton cruelty to seek to disturb men's present ideas respecting a future life, which at least hold forth to the more deserving sweet hopes of a better and more glorious life

---

[1] Taubert, *Der Pessimismus und seine Gegner*, p. 75.

[2] See our remarks in chap. vii. on Koheleth's views as to a future state of existence.

[3] See *Taubert*, p. 24. Compare $\dot{\epsilon}\nu\ \tau\hat{\varphi}\ \phi\rho o\nu\epsilon\hat{\iota}\nu\ \gamma\grave{\alpha}\rho\ \mu\eta\delta\grave{\epsilon}\nu\ \ddot{\eta}\delta\iota\sigma\tau o\varsigma\ \beta\acute{\iota}o\varsigma$. Sophocles' *Ajax*, 550. The opposite sentiment is expressed in Sophocles' *Antigone*, 1328.

beyond this earthly existence. It is well to be able to dream of something pleasant, even if it were but a dream!

Taubert lays stress upon the fact commonly observed, that the higher men advance in the scale of civilization the greater are their wants. Lassalle (in his *Arbeiterlesebuch*, p. 32) has maintained that the virtue suitable to the national economy of the present day is "to have the greatest possible wants, and to satisfy them in an honourable and proper manner." The working classes, though their condition is far better than in former days, are for the most part permeated with a feeling of discontent. Taubert regards this state of affairs as one of hope, for the more widely spread is the recognition on the part of the masses of the misery of their condition, the more easily will they be induced to adopt the principles of Pessimism unconsciously developing themselves in all socialistic movements. These principles are "the impossibility of human happiness" on the one hand, and "the wretchedness of existence" on the other. Taubert regards the adoption of Pessimism as a step towards the healing of all social evils, inasmuch as then men would recognise that misery is inseparable from being itself.[1] Such language might well be interpreted as that of bitter scorn. To attempt to soothe the woes of humanity by teaching the doctrines of Pessimism would be like seeking to quench raging flames by pouring oil upon them, or attempting to mollify wounds by rubbing salt into them. The Pessimist propaganda may well be compared to the "mad man" of the Book of Proverbs, who casts in every direction "firebrands, arrows and death" (Prov. xxvi. 18).

It is utterly impossible that the Pessimist philosophy, with its doctrine of the abnegation of the will to live, should gain any large number of adherents prepared to carry out its principles to their logical end. The asceticism of the Jewish

[1] See Taubert's *Pessimismus und seine Gegner*, p. 105, and pp. 114, 115 ff.

Essenes, and of the Christian hermits, was called forth by nobler principles, and directed to loftier ends. The world is not likely to see an outburst of a similar enthusiasm on the part of atheists desirous of hurrying on the human race to their imaginary goal of non-consciousness. Men are, moreover, often better than the creeds to which they profess to give their assent, and generally too wise to carry out absurd principles in practice to their legitimate conclusions. The lives of the Pessimist philosophers and writers of the present day have not yet exhibited any marked difference from those of others of the human species.[1] They have not yet shown themselves indifferent to the love of fame, to the attractions of the fair sex, or to the other "illusory pleasures" of life. They have not been as consistent as was the Cynic of antiquity. A filthy Diogenes in his earthenware tub (according to the popular legend) would not now attract many adherents. The spread

---

[1] Schopenhauer, though strongly inclined to misanthropy (see n. 2, p. 153), was keenly susceptible to all adverse criticism of his writings, and to matters affecting his reputation. He endeavoured in early life to obtain distinction as a University Professor, and failed. His denunciation in after life of all University Professors and of "Katheder-philosophie" (*Parerga und Paralipomena, Werke,* vol. v. p. 151 ff) was not a little influenced by his own failure. His great work, too, *Die Welt als Wille und Vorstellung,* was, notwithstanding the vigour of its style and the novelty of its opinions, for many years an utter failure (see *Sully's Pessimism,* p. 78 ff). Misogynist, too, as he became in later life, he was at least once guilty of writing a love-poem, and, when he was a Docent in the University of Berlin, thought seriously of marriage. His dread of the necessary cares and trouble of married life, however, led him to abandon his intention. The troubles of married life he describes characteristically as "endlose Ausgaben, Kindersorgen, Widerspenstigkeit, Eigensinn, Alt-und-garstigwerden nach wenigen Jahren, Betrügen, Hörneraufsetzen, Grillen, hysterische Anfälle, Liebhaber, und Hölle und Teufel" (*Gwinner's Leben,* p. 335). It was thus his melancholy forebodings rather than his philosophical opinions which restrained him from marrying. He was, however, not without exhibiting at times a susceptibility to the power of female charms, and was wont to confess, with Lord Byron, that he found it hard to fall out with women, and easy to fall out with men (*Gwinner's Leben,* p. 527). Luthardt (*Moderne Weltanschauungen,* p. 188), alluding to the phenomenon noticed above, very appropriately refers to the scoff of Voltaire, that, however pessimistically men may often express themselves, they usually try to live as optimistically as possible, and seldom prove insensible to the pleasures of venison and champagne.

of the principles of the Pessimist philosophy, and its adoption by numbers as their intellectual creed, are certain to lead to results different from those contemplated by its founders. Pessimism will not make men more self-denying (strange if it did !), or induce them to make (as Taubert imagines) the alleviation of suffering in all forms the object and aim of their fleeting existence. It will not lead them to make the smallest distinction possible between themselves and others, between the "*me*" and the "*not me*," and finally to become wholly engrossed with thoughts of how to benefit mankind.[1] But it will lead many to cast aside all belief in the existence of a God, of a future life, and of a time of retribution. It will break down many a barrier that restrained men as "with bit and bridle" (Ps. xxxii. 9) from a course of sin and folly. And, inasmuch as life is not only brief but uncertain, such a philosophy will impel men to seek to make the best use of their time (as far as is consistent with prudence) by enjoying the pleasures of sin for their little season.[2] Like other atheistic philosophies, it will lead to the same conclusions as those at which the Astronomer Poet of Persia arrived :

"But if in vain, down on the stubborn floor
Of earth, and up to Heav'n's unopening door,

---

[1] Vid. Schopenhauer's *Welt als Wille und Vorstellung. Werke* (herausg. von Dr. J. Frauenstädt), vol. iii. pp. 581-2. See also our remarks on *Taubert*, p. 165.

[2] Sully has endeavoured to combat this idea in his *Pessimism*, p. 318 ff. But he is driven almost to concede the point in his note on p. 319. However the highly trained philosopher may act, the adoption of an atheistic creed must lead the multitude to seek after sensual gratifications, and ultimately drive them into the most terrible excesses. Even Renan has clearly perceived this. Hence he writes (*Étude sur l'Ecclésiaste*, p. 88) : "In his greatest follies Koheleth does not forget the judgment of God. Let us do as he does. In the midst of the absolutely fleeting character of things let us maintain the eternal.! Without that we shall not be free nor easy in discussing it. The morrow of the day when men believe no more in God, the largest number of victims will be the atheists. One never philosophises more at ease than when he knows that his philosophy will not be carried out to its consequences. Ring, ye bells, entirely at your ease; the more you ring, the more I will permit myself to say that your voice does not mean anything definite. If I believed that I could silence you, ah ! it is then that I would be timid and prudent."

> You gaze TO-DAY while You are You—how then
> TO-MORROW, You, when shall be You no more?
>
> "Waste not your Hour, nor in the vain pursuit
> Of This and That endeavour and dispute;
> Better be jocund with the fruitful grape
> Than sadden after none, or bitter, Fruit.
>
> "YESTERDAY *this* day's madness did prepare;
> To-morrow's Silence, Triumph, or Despair:
> Drink! for you know not whence you came, nor why:
> Drink! for you know not why you go, nor where."

This is the old conclusion at which the Jewish sensualists of Alexandria arrived, and which is combated so vigorously in the Book of Wisdom. This is the practical outcome of the fool's philosophy so pithily characterised by the Psalmist (Ps. xiv. liii.), and glanced at by the Apostle of the Gentiles: "Let us eat and drink, for to-morrow we die" (1 Cor. xv. 32). This is the real logical result of all atheistic or agnostic theories of philosophy, however the devisers and founders of new systems may attempt to deny it.

The explanation given of the passion of love forms one of the strangest dogmas of the Pessimist philosophy. It is highly conducive to immorality, and the more hateful and degrading inasmuch as the conclusions arrived at are dignified with the name of "science." It is only possible to allude briefly to this subject. Though Schopenhauer was an idealist in his philosophical principles, he expresses on this point views closely akin to those of the materialistic philosophers of the present day. Schopenhauer maintains that the feeling of affection with which two young persons who are "in love" regard each other is but the working of "the will of the species" seeking an objectification of its nature in a new individual. He maintains, no doubt, that there is no con-

---

[1] Omar Khayyam, stanzas liii. liv. lxxiv. See the *Rubáiyát of Omar Khayyám and the Salámán and 'Absál of Jámí, rendered into English verse.* London: Bernard Quaritch, 1879.

Evil results of such teachings. 169

sciousness of this "will" present to the mind of the lovers But, if it be borne in mind that this philosophy recognises nothing which in a Jewish or Christian sense can be properly termed "sin," and that its "ethics" such as they are, are based not upon moral grounds but upon metaphysical arguments, the practical danger to morality can easily be conceived when all "love" is traced up to the "genius of species" represented anthropomorphically as plotting certain results. The longings of the "lover" and the pains of love are described as "the sighs of the spirit of species," and Schopenhauer informs us that that "genius in carrying out his purposes despises all human arrangements, such as marriage contracts and vows, and blows away like chaff all considerations which oppose the aim and object he has in view. Honour, duty, fidelity, yield to him alone, after they have withstood every other temptation, even the threat of death."[1]

It may be argued that this is only a scientific statement, and no incentive is thereby given to immorality. But it must be noted that Schopenhauer does not stop here. The preservation of a woman's honour he traces only to a feminine *esprit de corps*, while he observes that the *esprit de corps* of men on such points is different from that of women.[2] Eduard

---

[1] See Schopenhauer in chap. 44 of his *Welt als Wille u. Vorstellung*, entitled "Metaphysik der Geschlechtsliebe." On page 629 he says: "Dieses Forschen und Prüfen [mit welchem zwei junge Leute verschiedenen Geschlechts einander betrachten] ist die Meditation des Genius der Gattung über das durch sie beide mögliche Individuum und die Kombination seiner Eigenschaften. . . . Dergestalt also meditirt in allen, die zeugungsfähig sind, der Genius der Gattung das kommende Geschlecht. Die Beschaffenheit desselben ist das grosse Werk womit Cupido, unablässig thätig, spekulirend und sinnend, beschäftigt ist." See also p. 632, and p. 633: "Ihm allein weichen daher Ehre, Pflicht und Treue, nachdem sie jeder andern Versuchung, nebst der Drohung des Todes, widerstanden haben." And on p. 634 he says that the Genius der Gattung "seine, endlosen Generationen angehörenden Zwecke verfolgend solche Menschensatzungen und Bedenken wie Spreu wegbläst." See also Sully's *Pessimism*, p. 60 ff., and v. Hartmann's *Philosophie des Unbewussten*, 3te. Aufl., Berlin, 1871, on "Das Unbewusste in der geschlechtlichen Liebe."

[2] Schopenhauer, *Parerga u. Paralipomena*, p. 387 ff. Werke, vol. 5.

von Hartmann also observes that the natural instinct of men is in favour of polygamy, and that of women in favour of monogamy, hence, where men exercise exclusive rule, polygamy is lawful; but where, owing to a higher civilization, men have conceded to women a more honourable position, monogamy alone is recognised as legal, though the law to this effect is not practically observed by men in any quarter of the world.[1]

The acceptance of such a philosophy must of necessity lead many of its followers with "no fear of God before their eyes" (Ps. xxxvi. 1) to follow their so-called "instincts," whenever they can do so without inconvenience to themselves. "Nature," observes Schopenhauer, "only knows the physical not the moral, hence there is a decided antagonism between it and morality."[2] And if there be no God over all, whose laws we, as His creatures, are bound to obey, we cannot blame men for acting like "children of nature." Venetianer, pessimist though he is, has pointed out some terrible conclusions which result from Schopenhauer's theories.[3] But there are still lower "depths of Satan," when the vilest of all human crimes, that referred to by St. Paul in the Epistle to the Romans (i. 27), is apologised for as an attempt of nature to prevent the depravation of the species.[4] Such a

---

[1] E. v. Hartmann's *Philosophie des Unbewussten*, p. 201. See our remarks on p. 210. Note, however, that monogamy prevails among Hindus.

[2] Morality itself is described by von Hartmann as only a middle step between the unrestrained affirmation of the will to live and its negation, it is merely a palliative, whilst the latter is the radical cure. See his *Phænomenologie des sittl. Bewussts.*, p. 42.

[3] See Venetianer, *Schopenhauer als Scholastiker*, pp. 264-270.

[4] See Schopenhauer's Appendix to his chapter on the "Metaphysik der Geschlechtsliebe," in his *Welt als Wille u. Vorstellung*, p. 650. He says: "Demnach griff die in Folge ihrer eigenen Gesetze in die Enge getriebene Natur, mittelst Verkehrung des Instinkts, zu einem Nothbehelf, einem Stratagem, ja man möchte sagen, sie bauete sich eine Eselsbrücke, um, wie oben dargelegt, von zweien Uebeln dem grösseren zu entgehen. Sie hat nämlich den wichtigen Zweck im Auge, unglücklichen Zeugungen vorzubeugen, welche allmälig die ganze Species depraviren könnten, und da ist sie, wie wir gesehen haben nicht skrupulös in der Wahl der Mittel. Der Geist, in welchem sie hier verfährt, ist derselbe

philosophy, despite the efforts to trick it out with all the adornments which a vigorous and racy style can bestow, can only justly be described in the language of the Apostle as "earthly, sensual, demoniacal" (James iii. 15).

The rapid progress of Pessimism makes it impossible to ignore its existence. Its popularity in Germany at the present time is owing partly to circumstances connected with the political and social life of that country, partly also to the vigorous style of its first apostle, as well as to the fact that Schopenhauer and von Hartmann have addressed themselves not only to the students of philosophy but to the ordinary class of readers. Unverified as are many of the doctrines of "scientific pessimism," and palpably erroneous as are some of its scientific statements, its doctrines have been defended with no little parade of an acquaintance with modern science in all departments. The *Philosophy of the Unconscious* by von Hartmann is avowedly constructed upon the latest results of biology. It is satisfactory, therefore, to observe that an eminent biologist like Professor Oscar Schmidt has pronounced that philosopher mistaken in his interpretation of biological phenomena, and has pointed out numerous errors into which he has fallen.[1]

We are not forgetful of the fact that Pessimism has certain points of truth; and there is something to admire, while there is, perhaps, more to condemn in the writings referred to. It does not come within the limits of our subject to notice the better features of this philosophy. Its appearance at the present time may be regarded in some aspects as seasonable,

in welchem sie wie oben, Kapitel 27, angeführt die Wespen antreibt, ihre Jungen zu erstechen [He refers to Kirby and Spence's *Entomology*, vol. i. p. 374] : denn in beiden Fallen greift sie zum Schlimmen, um Schlimmern zu entgehen ; sie führt den Geschlechtstrieb irre, um seine verderblichsten Folgen zu vereiteln."

[1] *Die naturwissenschaftlichen Grundlagen der Philosophie des Unbewussten*, von Oscar Schmidt, Professor der Zoologie und vergleichenden Anatomie in Strassburg. Leipzig: F. A. Brockhaus, 1877. See also a sketch of the conclusions arrived at by this scholar in Sully's *Pessimism*, pp. 201-5.

for its tendency is not only to prevent men from being satisfied with that superficial optimism which has long borne sway, but also to keep them from too quickly imbibing the more novel doctrines of the new philosophy of "Meliorism," which, though adopted by Sully and other able English writers, rest in our opinion upon no very firm philosophical basis, though for a season Meliorism may also subserve a useful purpose. Pessimism, to whatever extravagant lengths it may logically conduct its adherents, is one of the natural outcomes of a materialism which denies the existence of a God, and of an agnosticism which regards the existence of the Divine Being as outside and beyond all human knowledge. It is well in some respects that the choice should lie between the acceptance of Christianity on the one hand, and of Pessimism on the other. Pessimism has unquestionably made considerable progress in philosophical circles, and has spread itself even more widely among the middle classes. It already counts adherents in England and America, and its tenets continually turn up in unexpected quarters. It is, therefore, no proof of wisdom to seek to ignore its existence or to refuse to take notice of the approaching danger.

The doctrines of this modern school, the reader cannot fail to have observed, bear a close resemblance to the principles of Buddhism. But, although Buddhism teaches that existence is an evil which the wise man will seek to get rid of, that system does not so directly lead to immorality and suicide as the doctrines of Schopenhauer and von Hartmann, if carried out to their logical consequences. For Buddhism maintains that there is a life after death, and a transmigration of souls in the case of the wicked, and of those who are deficient in virtue.[1] There is, according to Buddhism, some-

---

[1] Schopenhauer actually exhibits some leaning in this direction. He remarks in his *Welt als Wille und Vorstellung* that there is some relation between the number of births and deaths. He notes that in the fourteenth century after the

thing which the wicked may well fear, and something which the upright may desire to attain. The Buddhist dreads to be involved in an indefinite rotation of births, followed in each case by decay and death. The object of his desire is not merely to escape from life in one form, but from existence in any shape whatever, and to reach, as speedily as possible, his haven of rest and "city of peace," the Nirvâna where desire is totally extinct. Nirvâna is not, indeed, philosophically speaking, identical with annihilation, but it is a suspension from all exercise of thought and will, and has been described as "a perfect and unutterable tranquillity, for ever imperturbable, including exemption from all pain and uneasiness, and deliverance from the terrible law of transmigration."[1]

great mortality caused by the Black Death in the Old World a very great increase of births took place with a large proportion of twins. In proof of this he refers to *Schnurrer's Chronik der Seuchen*, 1825, and observes that Caspar confirms the principle that the number of births and deaths in every place rises and falls proportionately. See his *Werke*, vol. iii. p. 577. In connexion with the strange inclination towards Buddhism exhibited by this philosopher, it may be worth while quoting here an anecdote told by his biographer Gwinner (*Leben*, p. 547). He says that in a corner of Schopenhauer's room, upon a marble slab, stood a gilded statuette of Buddha. When Schopenhauer got the statuette from Paris in 1856, after removing the black polish with which it was covered, he stood contemplating it with satisfaction in the presence of his Roman Catholic servant (who had erected for herself in her own room a small altar richly adorned with artificial flowers). The latter, however, soon burst out into coarse laughter, saying, "he sits there just like a tailor." Schopenhauer was seriously offended at her remark and observed, "she is a rude person to speak thus of the Victoriously-Perfected One! Have I ever abused her Lord God?" Such an expression might have been reasonably expected from the lips of a Buddhist, scarcely from those of a philosopher.

[1] Kalisch, in *Path and Goal*, pp. 447-8. It is difficult to ascertain exactly what is meant by Nirvâna. Spence Hardy observes that the notices of Nirvâna in the sacred books are few, not by any means so frequent as we should have supposed from the importance of the subject in the system of Buddhism. He maintains that "that which is void, that has no existence, no continuance, neither birth nor death, that is subject to neither cause nor effect, and that possesses none of the essentialities of being, must be the cessation of existence, nihilism, or non-entity."—*Legends and Theories of the Buddhists*, p. 174. On the other hand Rhys Davids, who is perhaps even a greater authority, maintains that it is "the extinction of that sinful grasping condition of mind and heart, which

Buddhism and Pessimism.

The misery of human life is the starting-point of Buddhism as well as of Pessimism. The former has assumed the dogma as a fact; the latter seeks to demonstrate its truth by a variety of arguments.[1] Buddhism, as it has been well

would otherwise, according to the great mystery of Karma, be the cause of renewed individual existence." It is evidently then a cessation of individual existence though it may imply "ideas of intellectual energy," and if not actual annihilation, leads to it. "Death, utter death, with no life to follow is then a result of, but it is not Nirvâna." See Rhys David's *Buddhism: being a Sketch of the Life and Teachings of Gautama, the Buddha.* London: S. P. C. K. 1880.

Professor Beal's remarks on the subject are also worthy of notice here. He says:—

"It appears that the idea of annihilation as the one equivalent of Nirvâna must be confined (if at all) to one period only in the history of the system, and that period one during which scholastic refinement sought to explain or define that which is, in its very nature, incapable of definition, viz., the condition of the Infinite; for, all along, Buddhism assumes that the same condition awaits the 'emancipated soul' as is enjoyed by the Supreme Mind, and hence the constant reference to the state of the soul that has gone across (paramêtâ) to that shore where there is no 'birth or death.' This state, because it admits of no positive definition, is described *viâ remotionis, i.e.* by stripping from it every conceivable imperfection, and the process is carried to such an extent by the subtle logic of the schools that at length nothing is left for the mind to lay hold of, and this is the annihilation spoken of. But in the earliest and latest schools there is a different complexion given to the idea of Nirvâna. In the first period the thought seems to have been simply confined to a state of rest—rest or escape from all possible sorrow; and at this state, without attempting to describe or define it, Buddha directed his followers to aim. In the latest school, the idea of Nirvâna was 'restoration to the true condition of Being.' It would be tedious to bring proofs of this, for many of the latest works or Sûtras consist of the one idea, that there is but one Nature, to which all other Natures must in the end return; and this 'return' or 'ultimate union' is the perfection of the one nature of Buddha."—*Beal (Samuel), A Catena of Buddhist Scriptures from the Chinese.* London: Trübner, 1871. See note 2, next page, and the supplementary note at the end of this chapter (p. 182) on Dr. Oldenberg's recent work.

[1] Sully has pointed out that the empirical proofs adduced by von Hartmann in favour of Pessimism are unsatisfactory. Many of the statements of von Hartmann respecting the illusory character of human progress are founded on arbitrary assumptions. For instance, he asserts that the amount of immorality is to be regarded as a constant quantity; that diseases increase in a greater ratio than the remedies; that industrial progress has achieved nothing positive for the happiness of mankind; that the sense of misery arising from the fierce uncontrolled passions of savage races "is equalled by the sum of misery arising from the prudentially restrained but still active immoral tendencies of civilized society." Sully notes that a general theory of pleasure and pain is still far from complete,

observed, builds "not on conscience but on man's craving for happiness, and its ultimate end is not to free man from inward evil, but to emancipate him from misery, that is, from existence."[1] Hence, notwithstanding all its pretensions, it is, as popularly understood, essentially selfish in its aims; for, although it inculcates brotherly love and sympathy, it urges men to practise these virtues with the view only of personal advantage, namely, with the direct object of reaching the perfect calm of unconsciousness. The truth of this charge has no doubt been called in question, and probably with some amount of truth. For it is argued that the Buddhist in striving toward this object is impelled also by the belief, that he is helping to lessen the aggregate sum of human misery, and aiding on the progress of the universe to its goal of non-existence.[2]

and that it is impossible to estimate scientifically the relative value of different kinds of pleasure. He maintains that happiness is a balance of pleasure, and, though happiness is unattainable here, when thought of as an unbroken state of delicious excitement, yet it is to a very considerable extent attainable as an object of human pursuit. Sully admits that "the view of the present life as an opportunity of laying the foundations of our eternal well-being, or of helping to secure this immeasurable good for the souls of our fellow-men, has no doubt, its unique value as a stimulus to human effort." He observes also that "if men are to abandon all hope of a future life the loss in point of cheering and sustaining influence will be a vast one, and one not to be made good, so far as I can see, by any new idea of services to collective humanity;" and yet he remarks sadly in the next paragraph that "it is one thing to see the limits of an object, another to deny it its proper magnitude. After all, this earthly life *may be* our sole portion, and it is well not to dismiss it from view too scornfully."—*Pessimism : A History and a Criticism*, p. 250 ff., p. 303 ff. and p. 317. We maintain that it is only a one-sided induction that can lead to any such miserable conclusion. Some valuable remarks on Sully's standpoint will be found in Professor Flint's *Anti-Theistic Theories, being the Baird Lectures for* 1877 (Edin. and Lond. ; Blackwood & Sons, 1880).

[1] Dods' *Mohammed, Buddha and Christ*, 1878, p. 169. Kalisch has well contrasted Christianity and Buddhism in his *Path and Goal*, pp. 456-7.

[2] So Rhys Davids in *Contemporary Review*, 1877, but see Dods' remarks on p. 171 of his book. The former scholar observes, in his excellent sketch of Buddhism referred to in our previous note : "the true Buddhist saint does not mar the purity of his self-denial by lusting after a positive happiness, which he himself shall enjoy hereafter. His consciousness will cease to feel, but his virtue will live and

The same charge of selfishness may, indeed, with some show of justice, even be brought against Christianity. All creeds must begin with the individual, and hence are more or less open to the charge of egoism. Starting from the standpoint presented by Judaism, that "all have sinned and come short of the glory of God," Christianity makes known first to individuals a salvation designed and procured by God's fatherly love for all men, and insists on the necessity of "holiness without which no man can see the Lord" (Heb. xii. 14). It presses upon its followers the duty of doing good unto all men, and exhorts them to work for the salvation of the whole human race, taking as their noblest motive, "the love of Christ constraineth us" (2 Cor. v. 14). But it does not ignore the great fact that the love of self is implanted in our very nature, although it warns men against the sin of "selfishness," and seeks, by the principle of love, to transform the love which begins with self into the love of God.[1]

work out its full effect in the decrease of the sum of the misery of sentient beings." Rhys David notes in continuation: "Most forms of Paganism past and present teach men to seek for some sort of happiness here. Most other forms of belief say that this is folly, but the faithful and the holy shall find happiness hereafter in a better world beyond. Buddhism maintains that the one hope is as hollow as the other; that the consciousness of self is a delusion; that the organized being, sentient existence, since it is not infinite, is bound up inextricably with ignorance, and therefore with sin, and therefore with sorrow. 'Drop then this petty foolish longing for personal happiness,' Buddhism would say! 'Here it comes of ignorance, and leads to sin, which leads to sorrow; and there the conditions of existence are the same, and each new birth will leave you ignorant and finite still. There is nothing eternal; the very kosmos itself is passing away; nothing is, everything becomes; and all that you see and feel, bodily or mentally, of yourself will pass away like everything else; there will only remain the accumulated result of all your actions, words, and thoughts. Be pure, then, and kind, not lazy in thought. Be awake, shake off your delusions, and enter resolutely on the 'Path' which will lead you away from these restless tossing waves of the ocean of life,—the Path to the Joy and Rest of the Nirvâna of Wisdom and Goodness and Peace!'"—*Buddhism,* pp. 104-5.

[1] See also remarks in chap. viii. on Koh. xi. 2. In Row's remarkable work, *The Jesus of the Evangelists* (2nd ed. London: Fred. Norgate, 1880), the necessity of appealing to an enlightened self-love as a motive for human action is well pointed

Christianity is pessimistic in so far as it recognises that "the world is out of course" on account of sin, and that "the world" as it is "lies under the power of the Evil One" (1 John v. 19). This is also the doctrine of the Old Testament. For Judaism, notwithstanding Schopenhauer's assertions to the contrary, has also a pessimistic side. Judaism and Christianity both recognise the fact that "the whole creation groaneth and travaileth in pain together until now" (Rom. viii. 22). The doctrine that "all things work together for good to those that love God" (Rom. viii. 28) was taught even in the Old Testament, and the Book of Job was written with the distinct object of pointing out that afflictions and sorrows are not always to be regarded as marks of the Divine displeasure, but are often permitted in order to purify the righteous, and to test their integrity. Inasmuch as pain and misery exist in this world, Christians are taught by their great Master not to endeavour to go out of the world, but continuing in the same to seek to be preserved from the evil that abounds in it (John xvii. 15), while working for the good of others. They are not called upon to become ascetics, though "bodily exercise is profitable for a little," but to "exercise" themselves rather "unto godliness" (1 Tim. iv. 7, 8), bearing in mind, whether they eat or drink or whatever they do, to do all to the glory of God (1 Cor. x. 31).

A Christian, though convinced with the Psalmist that "the

out. Bishop Butler, long ago, in his great work on *The Analogy of Religion*, chap. v., has satisfactorily discussed the same subject in answer to the objections adduced by the Deists of his day. Row derives an important argument in defence of the historical character of the Jesus of the Evangelists from the fact that, although the Evangelists depict our Lord Himself as a moral teacher acting on a morality absolutely unselfish, they have narrated how He was wont to appeal to the hopes and fears of His disciples in order to incite them to action. In so doing, the Evangelists have ever "preserved the clearest distinction between the morality of the Master and that which is possible for the disciple" in a manner utterly impossible to conceive, if the Evangelists be regarded as a body of credulous men spontaneously elaborating myths.

earth is full of the goodness of Jahaveh" (Ps. xxxiii. 5),—and constrained at times, in contemplation of the glories of created nature[1] (Ps. lxv., civ., cxlv.), to sing and make melody with his heart unto God (Eph. v. 19)—may, when viewing the life of man from another standpoint, consistently express himself in a different strain. Thus the Christian poet Quarles, though he firmly believed in a life of glory beyond the grave, has used language quite as pessimistic as that of Koheleth :—

> " E'en so this little world of living clay,
> The pride of nature, glorified by art,
> Whom earth adores, and all her hosts obey,
> Allied to Heaven by his diviner part,
>   Triumphs awhile, then droops, and then decays,
>   And, worn by age, death cancels all his days.
>
> " Thus man that's born of woman can remain
> But a short time: his days are full of sorrow;
> His life's a penance, and his death's a pain,
> Springs like a flower to-day, and fades to-morrow;
>   His breath's a bubble, and his day's a span,
>   'Tis glorious misery to be born a man!"[2]

Christianity, however, no less than Judaism has its optimistic side. It declares emphatically the blessedness of existence by its doctrines of the Fatherhood of God, of a life of happiness beyond the grave, and of a resurrection to everlasting glory. If the New Testament Scriptures teach the doctrine of the destruction of the ungodly, they teach also that God is "the Saviour of all men, specially of them that believe" (1 Tim. iv. 10). If Christ speaks of His people as "a little flock" to whom it is "the Father's good pleasure to give the

---

[1] It must not be forgotten that Schopenhauer had also an eye for the beautiful. He says in his *Welt als Wille und Vorstellung* (p. 667), on this point: "Inzwischen heisst ein Optimist nicht die Augen öffnen und hineinsehen in die Welt, wie sie so schön sei, ein Sonnenschein, mit ihren Bergen, Thälern, Strömen, Pflanzen, Thieren, u.s.w.—Aber ist denn die Welt ein Gückkasten? Zu sehen sind diese Dinge freilich schön; aber sie zu sein ist ganz Anderes."

[2] *Quarles' Hieroglyphics of the Life of Man*, No. 15.

kingdom" (Luke xii. 32), His words, most true when spoken, are not to be understood as referring to the Church in all ages, nor to be interpreted in such a manner as to contradict the glorious vision beheld by John in Patmos, of those "who came out of great tribulation," a "great multitude which no man could number, out of every nation and of tribes and peoples and tongues" (Rev. vii. 9). Christian theologians have often, by their narrow-minded interpretation of Scripture, put weapons into the hands of the assailants of their holy religion. Christianity must not, however, be held responsible for the mistakes of its disciples, and we may hope and believe that in the great day of Jesus Christ there will be manifested, in a far grander manner than it is now possible to conceive, a blessed harmony between the perfect justice and the everlasting love of the Eternal.[1]

Christianity is a religion suited for man in his present state. It teaches distinctly that, notwithstanding all the ruin wrought by sin, it is possible to live to Christ on earth, and that the life in Christ even here is a state of happiness. "To me," writes the Apostle, "to live is Christ, and to die is gain" (Phil. i. 21). It looks forward, too, with hope to an era when "the creation itself shall be delivered from the bondage of corruption into the liberty of the glory of the children of God" (Rom. viii. 21). Thus it has an optimistic as well as a pessimistic side; and its optimistic features, it is willingly conceded, though enlarged and ennobled, are derived, more or less distinctly, from the Old Testament revelation.[2]

[1] The use Taubert (pp. 90–96) has made of the exaggerations which Christian theologians have fallen into in depicting the everlasting consciousness and torture of the ungodly in a future state on the one hand, and setting forth the doctrine of the predestination of a special few to everlasting happiness on the other, ought to make those who hold evangelical doctrine careful not to exaggerate the statements of Holy Scripture.

[2] It may be well to quote here the words of Prof. Dr. Luthardt, in his chapter on Pessimism in *Die modernen Weltanschauungen* (Leipzig, 1880), pp. 189, 190.

When the pessimist philosopher shall have shown some evidences of love to the human race such as that which has led missionaries of the cross to labour in foreign lands amid difficulties and privations for the benefit of the most degraded and savage races; when the system they have propounded shall have exhibited some such power to raise and improve mankind, it will be time enough to sing pæans over the approaching downfall of Christianity and to taunt Christianity with its selfishness.[1] While professing to be unselfish, this newborn philosophy is convicted at the very outset of

"Pessimism is the doctrine of hopelessness and despair. . . . Christianity is the announcement of a hope which lifts man out of his impotence into a new joyousness of life. The pessimist gives up the battle for lost before it is begun; it is all vanity. The Christian goes forward into the battle of life with the certainty of victory. 'This is the victory that overcometh the world, even our faith' (1 John v. 4). Pessimism and Christianity are the two great contrasts. They are, indeed, not unfrequently said to be closely related. Christianity is pessimistic, because it declares the earth to be a vale of sorrow. Yes! they are related, as contrasts are related. Both proclaim the misery of earth, and the inability of one's own will. But, while Pessimism pleases itself with the thought, and makes pain a subject of pride; Christianity makes use of the fact to point the look upwards to those 'hills from whence cometh our help' (Psalm cxxi. 1). With the former, the preaching of the misery of life is a subject of vain-glory; with the latter, it is a matter of humility. . . . Both speak of the impotence of man, but Christianity understands and says with the Apostle, 'When I am weak then am I strong'; for it is God's strength which is powerful in our weakness" [2 Cor. xii. 9, 10].

[1] It is absurd and unphilosophical for persons to sneer at missions, who have never honestly investigated the results attained by the missionary efforts of the Churches of the Reformation in modern days. The wonderful triumphs exhibited in Madagascar, where within very recent times the Protestant converts bravely endured for many years a terrible persecution; the success of the Wesleyan missions in Fiji, borne witness to by the highest authorities; the marvellous results of mission work in Sierra Leone and its neighbourhood, where there exists a large native Church supporting its own pastors and carrying on Christian work on its own behalf among the heathen in "the regions beyond"; the Christianization of New Zealand (borne witness to even by Charles Darwin); of the Sandwich Islands; the progress of the native church in Tinnevelly and Travancore; the evangelization of Metlahkatlah in North-West America,—these and many other instances of success which have resulted from modern missionary work accomplished by various sections of the Church of Christ can here be only alluded to. The heroism exhibited by many a martyr in Madagascar and even in China, the devotion of such men as Krapf and Livingstone, are proofs of the inner life and unselfishness of true Christianity.

the charge it brings against other systems. On what grounds but such as are essentially selfish, are men urged to seek the great "Nothing," which is so loudly extolled as the wished-for goal of humanity? Is it not in order to get rid of the misery and striving of life, and to obtain rest from all thinking, willing, and working? It is to the credit of von Hartmann that he has detected this defect in the original theory of Schopenhauer, but he has only disentangled himself from one difficulty to entangle himself the more deeply in absurdities worse than those enunciated in Buddhism.[1]

Buddhism, notwithstanding its lofty pretensions, and its remarkable philosophy, has proved a practical failure. However noble some of its principles, it has been a curse and not a blessing in all lands wherever its system has taken root. Its ascetics, like those of other countries and other faiths, have not, as might have been anticipated, been able to conquer the tendencies of nature. It has sought not to regulate but to overcome nature, and nature has overcome it.

"Naturam expellas furca, tamen usque recurret."
Hor. Epist., i. 10, 24.

Its monasteries and abodes of contemplation have proved frightful sources of corruption and sensuality. "That which is born of the flesh is flesh" (John iii. 6). Its religion, however spiritual in theory, has developed among other things the monstrosity of praying by machinery: and prayer wheels and prayer mills are the practical outcome of its teaching.[2] It is the "old, old story," "men professing to be

[1] See Kalisch, *Path and Goal*, pp. 428-9, and the notes appended at the end of his volume.
[2] Lieut. Col. Prejevalsky writes: "All lamas must be celibates, an abnormal state, which gives rise to every kind of immorality. . . . Lamaism is the most frightful curse of the country, because it attracts the best part of the male population, preys like a parasite upon the remainder, and, by its unbounded influence, deprives the people of the power of rising from the depths of ignorance into

wise have become fools" (Rom. i. 22). Are the results of European Buddhism, as modern Pessimism may well be termed, likely to be more beneficial?

which they are plunged."—*Mongolia, the Tangat Country and the Solitude of Northern Tibet*, by Lieut. Col. N. Prejevalsky of the Russian Staff Corps, translated by E. D. Morgan. London: 1876. 2 vols. vol. i. p. 80. Wilson also says: "Captain Harcourt, late Assistant Commissioner for the three British Provinces of Kúlú, Lahaul and Spiti, alleges that there are at times scenes of gross debauchery in the monasteries, a state of things which can be believed when lamas and nuns are living promiscuously together."—(Wilson's *Abode of Snow*, p. 245). The same writer has a whole chapter on Tibetan polyandry, or the polygyny, as he prefers to call it, which is prevalent in Tibet, namely, the custom for the same woman to be acknowledged and supported as the wife in common of several men. Wilson, indeed, observes that C. F. Köppen in his work on *Die Lamaische Hierarchie und Kirche* maintains that the religion of the country is not responsible for this enormous monstrosity, but thinks it existed before the introduction of Buddhism, and has arisen from the desire to set some bounds to the increase of the population. He refers to Cæsar, *De Bello Gallico*, v. 14, and to the Mahabhârata and Ramâyana where instances of a similar custom are referred to. Sir E. Tennant also speaks of its prevalence in the interior of Ceylon. But Wilson observes that all such cases are not to be compared with "the regular, extensive, and solidified system of Tibetan polyandry."—See Andrew Wilson's *Abode of Snow. Observations on a Journey from Chinese Tibet to the Indian Caucasus*. Edinburgh and London: Blackwood & Sons, 1875.

SUPPLEMENTARY NOTE ON BUDDHISM.

The most recent, as well as perhaps the most careful and elaborate work on Buddhism is that by Dr. Hermann Oldenberg, entitled *Buddha, sein Leben, seine Lehre, seine Gemeinde* (Wilhelm Hertz, Berlin, 1881). The author has pointed out in this treatise the original teachings of Buddha himself. A translation into English of the work of Dr. Oldenberg has been recently executed in an able manner by William Hoey, D.Lit., of the Bengal Civil Service (London: Williams & Norgate, 1882).

Oldenberg has discussed the following interesting points, namely, the growth of Indian thought previous to the time of Buddha, and its pessimistic tendencies, as well as the monasticism to which it gave rise. For monasticism was necessarily the outer form of life by which the professors of a pessimistic faith sought to attain their desired goal, the Nirvâna. Dr. Oldenberg expounds the four cardinal tenets of Buddha, viz.:—(1) the suffering of all being; (2) the origin of suffering; (3) the extinction of suffering; (4) the path to the extinction of suffering; and analyses the causal nexus of being, the theory of the will to live as the cause of being, and points out the weakness of that theory. The metaphysical hypothesis of the five constituent elements of our being is carefully discussed with special reference to the question of metempsychosis and annihilation, and the meaning of Nirvâna is clearly expounded. He points out, as Rhys Davids has also done, that the Nirvâna is the state which follows the extinction of the desire to live, and that it is attainable during life. But what follows on the death of a saint who has attained this state? The logical reply which suggests itself to most minds on the premises stated by Buddha is "the Nothing." But Oldenburg shows that in the early and primitive Buddhist Church the answer always given was, "this hath the Exalted One (Buddha) not revealed." In connexion with the tendency of Schopenhauer towards asceticism, it is well to note that the first great commandment laid on the Buddhist professor is, as stated by Oldenberg, "ein ordinirter Mönch darf nicht geschlechtlichen Verkehr pflegen," u. s. w., p. 358. We forbear to quote the conclusion of the commandment, which points out the terrible sins, into the commission of which such unnatural and vain attempts to overcome nature have often driven the sons of men.

Dr. William Hoey has kindly supplied me with the following remarks on the matters alluded to above:—

"The first of the cardinal tenets of Buddha's doctrine is a wail over the impermanence of everything earthly. Birth, old age, sickness, death, union with the unloved, separation from the loved, the clinging to earthly things, these all are suffering. The second tenet is the origin of suffering, and here we touch the kernel of Buddhism, and are face to face with the great difficulty of the origin of being, for being is suffering. The terms are equivalent in Buddhist thought. 'The thirst for being leads from birth to birth, together with lust and desire, which finds gratification here and there; the thirst for pleasure, the thirst for power:' this is the origin of suffering. The third tenet is the 'sacred truth of the extinction of suffering,' which is said to be accomplished by the extinction of the thirst for being, the annihilation of desire. Buddha evidently felt that there was something needed as an explanation and as a support of these two tenets, and hence he propounded the 'causal nexus of being.' It is not possible to quote the formula here *in extenso* [vid. pp. 223-252 of Dr. Hoey's translation], or to enter into the metaphysical analysis of our being, but suffice it to say that the ultimate origin of our being is 'ignorance,' the non-possession of that knowledge which is comprised in the four sacred tenets or truths. 'The ultimate root of all suffering is the delusion which conceals from man the true being, and the true value of the system of the universe. Being is suffering; but ignorance totally deceives us as to this suffering; it causes us to see instead of suffering a phantom of happiness and pleasure. From ignorance come 'conformations,' a term used to translate the technical Buddhist word '*Sankhâra*,' and 'from conformations comes consciousness;' and it is consciousness which, entering the womb at conception, assumes some material form. This brings us to the Buddhist idea of *Kamma* [*Kamma* is the Pâli form of the Sansk. *Karma*] or moral retribution. Whatever a man is is the result of former action, and hence his present state of being involves that some other unit of being occupied his place at a former time, and acted through ignorance so as to necessitate a re-birth. The cutting off of re-birth can only be attained by the attainment of knowledge, *i.e.* of the four cardinal truths, and the extinction of ignorance and desire,—the extinction of all clinging to the earthly. To express this clinging a figurative word is used, and the underlying figure is that of flame. A flame feeds on wood or other fuel, and not only devours it but also goes out on the air, seeking other fuel. This is the state of our being; it is a continuous process of burning. The wise man does not supply the fuel to the flame of desire. He extinguishes desire (for being) and all thirst. His state is that of 'Nirvâna.' The ignorant man, on the other hand, supplies fuel to the flame, and the flame of existence presses on in transmigration to further stages of being. The cessation of clinging to being may begin at any moment, and from that moment Nirvâna begins.

"The fourth tenet of Buddhism is the path to the extinction of suffering, and is a rule of life leading to pure habits of thought and action. The scope of Buddhist ethics is very different from that of the Christian. Buddhism does not recognise the will of a supreme lawgiver, or the principle of the good of others as a rule to regulate conduct. The Buddhist practises any course of good action solely because it is the best policy, not because it is right.

"To the Buddhist, 'soul,' as we understand it, is unknown. The identity of a soul, or the continuity of consciousness in transmigration is not a Buddhist tenet. The continuity of being, or of Kamma (the inner form of life), is all the Buddhist propounds. The usual illustration is that of a lamp, where the flame is continuous, but not identical at all hours of the night.

"The Buddhist analyses our being thus: corporeal form, sensations, perceptions, conformations [p. 245, et passim, Dr. Hoey's translation], and consciousness. Each of these ceases to exist at death. Does this cessation of earthly existence imply a total cessation of being? This is the vexata quæstio of Buddhist metaphysics, and a clear discussion of the matter is given in Oldenberg's work [Transl. pp. 267-285]. On this point 'Buddha has revealed nothing.' Buddha did not deem it advisable to dwell on what might be hereafter, but only on the suffering of life, its cause, and the path to its extinction by the extinction of desire. Everywhere the cry is suffering, and the problem which Buddha desired to solve was the extinction of suffering, not the penetration of that which lies beyond death."

CHAPTER VII.

THE PESSIMISM OF THE BOOK OF KOHELETH, ESPECIALLY IN RELATION TO A FUTURE STATE AND THE CHARACTER OF WOMEN, CONTRASTED WITH MODERN PESSIMISM.

CHAPTER VII.

Koheleth's belief in a God, 187—God directs all the events of human life, 187—And makes all beautiful in its season, 188—The vanity of philosophizing, 189—All the working out of a Divine plan, 189—Koheleth's tendency to fatalism kept in check by his creed, 190—Does death put an end to the difference between men and brutes? 191—The spirit of man and that of beast, 191—The interrogative rendering of the passage (chap. iii. 19), 192—The interrogative rendering not suggestive of doubt, 192—The expression "upwards and downwards," 193—Aphorism in the Book of Proverbs, 193—No contradiction in the words of Koheleth, 193—The idea of eternity implanted in man, 193—Different rendering of the passage, 195—The "world" or "eternity," 195—Man's thoughts grasp after eternity, 196—Koheleth's idea of a future state obscure, 197—Cheerless and gloomy, 198—Anecdote of the Talmud respecting the dead as knowing nothing, 198—Other attempts to explain, 199—Koheleth's idea of the dead as unconscious, 199—But destined to be awakened, 200—Imperfections of knowledge permitted, 200—The difference between Koheleth's pessimism and that of modern days, 201—The grave an eternal home, 201—Practical lessons learned by Koheleth, 202—His description of the evil woman, 202—Agreement with the Book of Proverbs, 202—Degradation of women under Persian rule, 202—"One in a thousand," 203—Koheleth's opinion of men in general, 204—Proverbs relative to woman, 204—Principle on which proverbs are framed, 205—Contradictory proverbs, 205—Jewish proverbs respecting women, 205—Koheleth no woman-hater, 206—Low views of women held by Pessimists, 207—Opinions of Schopenhauer and von Hartmann, 207—One-sided evidence, 208—Schopenhauer on women's intellectual powers, 208—von Hartmann's view of the want of rectitude in women, 209—The Pessimists on female education, 210—Schopenhauer's approval of the position of women in the East, 210—von Hartmann on the advantage of female society, 211—Venetianer's critique of Schopenhauer's views as unphilosophical, 212—Monogamy and polygamy, 212—Schopenhauer's praise of Mormons, 212—Degradation of the female an outcome of atheism, 213—Woman a help-meet for man, 214.

CHAPTER VII.

THE PESSIMISM OF THE BOOK OF KOHELETH, ESPECIALLY IN RELATION TO A FUTURE STATE AND THE CHARACTER OF WOMEN, CONTRASTED WITH MODERN PESSIMISM.

IN our preceding chapter we have given a sketch, necessarily imperfect in many particulars from its brevity, of some of the leading doctrines of modern Pessimism, and of that remarkable Oriental philosophy to which the system of Schopenhauer and von Hartmann owes so many of its leading features. We have now to notice more in detail the pessimistic view of human life, and of its anxieties and sorrows as set forth in the pages of the wise Koheleth.

However constrained by the facts which came under his own observation to take a pessimistic view of life as a whole, and however boldly he ventures to give utterance to his sentiments on this head, Koheleth everywhere expresses an unshaken belief in the existence of a God, who is not conceived of as withdrawn from connexion with the world, but as presiding over that world, which was originally called into being by the exercise of His Divine power and will.

God, according to Koheleth, makes a distinction even in His mundane arrangements between the sinner and the righteous. Koheleth was not blind, however, to the numerous exceptions in violation of this general rule which are to be met with. Man is under the government of a power above and beyond him, without whose permission he cannot even enjoy life. All events on earth are directed by God, who has appointed a season for everything and a time for every purpose under heaven. Birth and death, planting and uprooting, slaying and healing, take place according to the Divine arrangements. There are seasons appointed for pulling down and for building up, times for weeping and for laughter, days for mourning and for dancing. The times and occasions for each of what are termed the ordinary events of human life are all ordered by this superhuman power. It overrules also the extraordinary occurrences which happen in human history. Times of war and peace, though apparently brought about by the exercise of man's free action (which is not denied), are still under the control of the Most High.

Man, however, has no profit in all his labour, for he has no certain power to regulate his own destiny. His utmost efforts may result in failure. All is a sore labour which God hath given to the sons of men to plague themselves withal. It is remarkable that even here, when the discontent of Koheleth seemed to be reaching a climax, his faith was able to pierce some way through the dark clouds, and he appears to have caught a glimpse of the grandeur and sublimity of the Divine actions, notwithstanding the mystery in which they were enwrapped. For Koheleth added, "all this, however, God hath so designed as to be even beautiful in its season." Rashi gives a striking interpretation of this saying: "At a good season to reward good works is beautiful, and at an evil season to punish evil works is becoming."[1]

The powerlessness of man, and his shortsightedness with regard to his fate are set forth in other passages. All things are conditioned by a higher power. The actions of the wise

---

[1] Rashi's commentary on chap. iii. 11 is as follows: בעת הטובה יפה הוא לבוא
תשלום שכר מעשה הטוב ובעת הרעה ראויה היא לתשלום מעשה הרע:
Hengstenberg observes on this that even "things which in and for themselves are evil must occur in such a connexion that they further the good purposes of God. Only at such a fit season are they beautiful, and then they form an indispensable link in the chain of this world's events."

and the righteous are "in the hand of God." "Man knoweth not love or hatred, all lies before them" (chap. ix. 1 ff.). In other words, there are events connected with man's own being, circumstances which will happen in an individual's history, which will necessarily call forth his love or hatred; but all such things are concealed in a futurity impenetrable to the sons of men. Events of all kinds lie before us; that which will actually occur is known to God. All things seem, indeed, to a casual observer, to be governed by chance, and the heart of man is full of evil. Madness is in men's hearts during their lives, and then they pass onward—"to the dead." Men may talk much concerning the dealings of God, but the multiplication of words on such a subject is vain, fools prate often about things too high for them (chap. x. 12–14); "who can dispute with Him that is stronger than he?" Hence men, conscious of their own ignorance and weakness, should fear God and submit to His decrees. For no man knows what is really good for him, what position it is best for him to occupy, or how to conduct himself properly under difficult circumstances—while as to the future, whether it is near or far off, he understands nothing (chap. vi. 10–12).

Thus Koheleth forcibly points out the vanity of all that philosophising which man is naturally prone to engage in. He was, however, very far from abandoning himself to atheistic conclusions. Though unable to explain the difficulties which beset life, he was able at least to rest on the thought that everything occurs according to the working out of a Divine plan. He had, indeed, himself laboured to get practical wisdom, and having attained that object, he applied himself to examine into the toil which man has to undergo on the earth. The result of his search was to ascertain clearly that man could not find out the work of God which was done under the sun (chap. viii. 16–17). "The distinguishing characteristic of the wise," as Delitzsch has well observed, "is not so much the actual possession of wisdom as the striving after it. The wise man strives after knowledge, but the highest problems remain for him unsolved, and his ideal of knowledge is unrealized."

If a tendency to fatalism is exhibited in certain passages of this book, it is kept in check by the firm hold which the religious creed of Koheleth had upon his mind. As a distinguished Jewish critic, Derenbourg, writes: "The idea of a just God had penetrated too profoundly into the heart of Koheleth not to restrain his disappointed and discontented spirit. It is this that gives the peculiar charm to his little book; it is scepticism tempered and limited by the impassable barrier which that dogma, which was the base and centre of Judaism, opposed to it."[1]

It is interesting to note that Koheleth expresses his belief in the existence of fixed laws in nature. This is the real meaning of a passage, frequently and yet strangely adduced as a proof-text in support of the idea that the final destiny of man is irrevocably fixed at death. We refer, of course, to chap. xi. 3: "If the clouds are full of rain, they empty themselves on the earth, and if a tree fall toward the north or the south, in the place where the tree falleth there it shall lie." Koheleth, as the context of the passage shows, refers to the fact that men know not what misfortunes may take place on earth, many calamities which fall upon individuals being the result of laws beyond human control.[2] We ought, therefore, in all cases to remember that such contingencies may happen, though we ought not to permit the possibility of such accidents to make us inactive. The wise man will have boldness and courage to act in the same way as if confident that success would attend his efforts, although fully

---

[1] Notes détachées sur l'Ecclésiaste in the *Revue des Études Juives*, No. 2, Oct.-Dec., 1880. Paris: 17, Rue St. Georges.
[2] See our remarks in chap. viii. p. 229.

conscious that the future depends upon a higher power and will than his own.

The darkest feature in the Book of Koheleth is the uncertainty which the writer seemed to feel as to the doctrine of a future state of existence, and the cheerless view he expresses concerning the state of the dead. In chap. iii. 19 ff. Koheleth speaks as if he regarded man and beast as merely the creatures of chance, the actions of men being often dependent upon accidental circumstances, and man and beast alike being subject to the inexorable law of death. The language used by him on this subject is indeed so general in its terms, that he has often been charged with believing that death finally puts an end to all distinction between man and the brute creation. Koheleth contemplates the matter, however, solely from the standpoint of the present life. He makes no allusion to the explanation which the Book of Genesis gives of the entrance of death into the world, although he uses the language of that book. Nor does he speak of any distinction to be made after death between the righteous and the wicked, though it is almost certain from his phraseology that Ps. xlix. 14, 15 was in his mind, where that truth is plainly stated. In the passage in chap. iii. Koheleth thinks only of the earth under the aspect of a vast burial-place for successive generations. "All go to one place, all are from the dust, and all return to the dust" (chap. iii. 20).

Different translations have been proposed for the verse which follows. Our Authorised Version renders it: "Who knoweth the spirit of man that goeth upward and the spirit of the beast that goeth downward to the earth?" This version has found a few defenders in modern times (such as Hengstenberg, Hahn, Prof. Tayler Lewis, and others). It must be admitted that the Masorites intended their vocalization of the text to give that turn to the passage in order to avoid the appearance of scepticism (vid. crit. comm.). But the ancient translators with one consent recognise the fact that the interrogative particle, and not the article, is the true reading in both clauses. The most eminent scholars (such as Knobel, Ewald, and Delitzsch) agree substantially in translating the passage: "Who knows with respect to the spirit of the sons of men whether it goes upward, and with respect to the spirit of the beast, whether it descends downward to the earth?" This translation is condemned by Bullock as a rendering which is "neither necessary nor suitable." But he is plainly mistaken. Apart from purely critical reasons, the rendering of our A. V. does not suit the context, which would require a question of a very different kind, and the analogy of the two other passages in the book (chap. ii. 19; vi. 12), in which the expression "who knoweth" is used, is in favour of the opinion that the phrases which follow are really interrogative.

A similar question is found in the celebrated poem of Lucretius (i. 113),[1] but the answer there designed to be given to it is negative. The very manner in which Koheleth puts the interrogation shows that no infidel "sneer" was intended by him. Although forced to regard the translation of our A.V. as incorrect, we maintain that the interrogative clauses do not convey the insinuation that there is no difference between man and beast. On the contrary these interrogative clauses suggest, if they do not actually assert, the very opposite. Hence it is not surprising to find that the writer at the end of his book avows his real belief as to the future of man, and affirms that, although at death "the dust shall return to the earth as it was," *i.e.* from whence it was originally taken (Gen. iii. 19; Ps. civ. 29), "the spirit shall return unto God who gave it" (Koh. xii. 7).

---

[1] His words are :
"Ignoratur enim, quæ sit natura animai,
Nata sit, an contra nascentibus insinuetur?
An simul intereat nobiscum morte diremta?"

The expressions "upwards and downwards." 193

In the passage under consideration (chap. iii. 21) reference is made to an aphorism in the Book of Proverbs (xv. 24) in which the peculiar expressions "upwards" and "downwards" occur, which are found only in these two passages of Sacred Scripture. The aphorism in the Book of Proverbs is rendered in our A. V. "the way of life is above to the wise that he may depart from hell beneath." Its meaning, however, is rather: "to the wise man is the way of life upwards," *i.e.* the wise man goes the way of life which leads upwards, "in order that he may depart from Sheol (Hades) downwards." In other words, the wise man proceeds on the way of life which leads one upwards, with the distinct object before him of escaping from that path which leads to Sheol and ends there. Believers under the Old Testament dispensation were able at times to contemplate their ultimate deliverance from that Sheol into which, however, they believed even the righteous had to descend at death (Ps. xlix. 14; A. V. ver. 15). Sheol, or Hades, was regarded by them, even in the case of the godly, as a gloomy place of rest, and not as a place of felicity. In the passage in the Book of Proverbs the term Sheol begins, as Delitzsch has noted, to lose its general signification of a place in which all the dead are gathered together without any distinction being made between the good and the evil, and to assume a more definite signification as the place of punishment of the ungodly. The term "Hades" is possibly used in this latter sense in the end of the Book of the Revelation (xx. 14), comp. Matt. vii. 13, 14.

If this aphorism in the Book of Proverbs, and the statements of Ps. xlix. 14 (to both of which passages reference seems here to be made), be borne in mind, it is tolerably plain that there is no contradiction between the sentiments expressed by Koheleth in chap. iii. 21, and those given utterance to at the close of his book. Koheleth was not ignorant

O

of the doctrine of a future life, still less did he deny the truth of that doctrine. If it be remembered what the teaching of the book is respecting the punishment of all transgressors at a time and season appointed by God—a doctrine taught not merely in the epilogue, but in other parts of the book— it cannot but appear most unnatural to explain the return of the spirit to God (chap. xii. 7) as signifying a mere yielding back to God the vital breath of life which He has bestowed on man.[1]

For Koheleth on several occasions calls attention to the fact that God does not always execute judgment on men in this world according to their deserts. He affirms that God deals with men after this fashion in order to sift them, and to make them feel that, when left to themselves, they are naturally like the beasts (chap. iii. 18), and conduct themselves like wild beasts in the deeds of violence and oppression so often committed by them against one another. One reason why God has permitted such a state of things to exist for a season is, in order that the character and disposition of individual men may in all cases be made manifest by the scope thus afforded to every one for free action; and that the real distinction between the righteous and the wicked may at last become apparent to all. Though Koheleth, therefore, asks how man can arrive at any definite conclusion even on a question of such great importance as whether there is really any difference between the final destination of the spirit of man and of beast, it by no means necessarily follows that he was himself in doubt as to the doctrine of a future life. The longing after "eternity," described in this very context as implanted in the heart of man (chap. iii. 11), leads necessarily to a belief in the existence of a life beyond the

[1] Böttcher, *De Inferis*, § 473, has sought to explain away chap. xii. 7 in this manner. But the way in which the future judgment is spoken of in chap. iii. 17, viii. 10-15, and chap. xi. 9, proves that the writer did not refer merely to a judgment to be inflicted on transgressors in the present world.

grave, even though the reality of such a life cannot be satisfactorily demonstrated by the deductions of human reason. Man cannot by his own powers discover "that which shall be after him" (chap. iii. 21), inasmuch as all such knowledge has been denied to him. But the very fact of their ignorance in such matters ought, Koheleth argues, to lead men to enjoy all they lawfully can in this present life, ever remembering to "fear God and keep His commandments," because there is a judgment after death.

The statement that "eternity" is naturally implanted in the heart of man (chap. iii. 11) is one of the most profound sayings contained in this interesting book—"God hath made everything beautiful in its season, also eternity hath He placed in his heart, although man cannot find out the work which God hath done from the beginning to the end." The word rendered here "eternity" is that translated "world" in our A. V. The text, according to the latter translation, has often been explained to teach that man is a little world (microcosm) reflecting the greater world (macrocosm) in the midst of which he is placed. His mind, to use Lord Bacon's paraphrase, is like a mirror "capable of (reflecting) the image of the universe, and desirous to receive it, as the eye to receive the light." The "world" has been explained by others to mean "the love of the world" so natural to the heart of man, which in some aspects may be regarded as almost identical with that "love of life," that "will to live" (Wille zum Leben), so fiercely and so unnaturally denounced by Schopenhauer and his school. But, however true in itself it may be that man is "a little world," and that the love of the world or of life is natural to him, such is not the meaning of Koheleth. The Hebrew word used by him, עולם, is indeed found in the signification of "world" in later Hebrew, and possibly it may (though of this there is no proof) have been thus used in the popular Hebrew spoken in the days of Koheleth. But no other example of its use in that signification has been discovered in the entire range of Biblical literature.[1] On the other hand, the very same word occurs several times in the Book of Koheleth in the sense of "eternity,"[2] and in no other signification. These considerations, apart entirely from any argument fairly derivable from the unsuitability of such a rendering to the context—a point as to which there is considerable difference of opinion—are, in our judgment, decisive against the rendering of the A. V., backed up though that translation unquestionably is by the authority of the LXX., Aquila, the Vulg., Jerome and many modern scholars, such as Knobel and Ewald.

The passage (chap. iii. 11) has been well interpreted by Delitzsch. God has assigned to each man his appointed place, and has thus made him fully conscious that he is a being bounded by certain limitations which cannot be passed. God has also implanted in man's heart impulses and desires which are not satisfied with the things of time, but grasp at eternity. Man would fain burst the trammels which restrain him, but, in his discontent with the temporal, he consoles himself with the thought of something which lies beyond it. "That which is transient gives him no hold, it carries him away like a rushing stream, and compels him to save himself by seizing hold of the eternal." But Koheleth notes that man's powers fail whenever he attempts to comprehend the works and doings of God; and, notwithstanding that "eternity" is thus implanted "in his heart," it is practical

---

[1] It may, however, be well to note that Rashi, Grotius, Tarnov., Heidenheim, etc., have translated the expression הֲלִיכוֹת עוֹלָם לוֹ, in Habb. iii. 6, by "*itinera seculi ei*," "*omnia quæ in mundo sunt*, ipsi subsunt." But such a rendering is now defended by no critic, and is, moreover directly opposed by the fact that in the same verse the phrase גִּבְעוֹת עוֹלָם occurs, in which the word in question is used in the ordinary signification.

[2] It is, however, to be noted that the use of the word "eternity" in the sense in which here alone it can be taken, *i.e.* in the signification of *the idea of eternity*, must in any case be regarded as unique.

wisdom to content himself with that which is seen, and can be attained here on earth.

That Koheleth, at the very moment when the gloom of unbelief seemed to be settling down upon his soul, should thus give expression to the conviction that there is something grander and more noble than "things temporal," reminds us forcibly of the case of Job, whose faith in the advent at some distant day of One who was to be his Avenger and Redeemer, burst forth suddenly, like a bright gleam of sunshine, at the very time when the tempest of suffering and temptation seemed well-nigh about to overwhelm his soul (Job xix. 23-27).

The belief of Koheleth, however, in a future life was far too shadowy to lead him to "seek the things that are above" instead of "the things that are upon the earth" (Col. iii. 1, 2). For this end the fuller light of the New Testament dispensation was imperatively needed. His knowledge of the life beyond the present state of existence had all the imperfections which belonged to the Old Testament dispensation. A heavy stone then lay over man's sepulchre, and the time for it to be rolled away had not yet fully come.

The statements of Koheleth respecting the state of the dead show clearly that he had not those cheering views with respect to the blessedness of the pious dead, which can alone irradiate the darkness of the tomb. He was among those "who through fear of death were all their lifetime subject to bondage" (Heb. ii. 15). A living dog was in his eyes better than a dead lion (chap. ix. 4). "For the living," he adds almost sarcastically, "know that they shall die, but the dead know not anything, and have no further reward (that is, on earth), for their memory is forgotten" (chap. ix. 5, 6). The recollection of their deeds soon passes away; new generations spring up who trouble themselves but little about the actions of their forefathers. Love, hatred and envy exist for the dead no more. All such affections and strivings, at least so far as the persons and things of earth are concerned, are at an end. Those who have passed into another state of existence have no further concern with that which is done here on earth. Hahn adds: "In eternity they take no part any more in that which is done under the sun. Why therefore should any one on earth seek to obtain anything by the help of the dead?" This latter thought, however, does not occur in the Book of Ecclesiastes, and cannot well be interpolated here.

The description of the state of the dead presented in this passage is, it must be admitted, dark and cheerless. The account of the shadowy existence of the dead in Hades as set forth in Job and even in some of the Psalms is gloomy enough. But the view of Koheleth surpasses all others in gloominess. The Targumist has felt this, and, therefore, has ventured to explain the text as speaking of the state of the wicked. This interpretation is also given in the Midrash, which relates the following anecdote in explanation of the passage:—

"Rabbi Chiyya the elder (or the great) and Rabbi Jonathan were walking before the bier of Rabbi Simeon ben Jose ben Lakunya, when the tallith (or prayer-mantle) of Rabbi Jonathan hung down upon the coffin. 'Lift up thy tallith,' my son, said Rabbi Chiyya to him, 'that they (the departed) say not, "to-morrow (even) they are coming down to us, and (yet) they despise us."' 'Rabbi,' said Rabbi Jonathan to him, 'is it not written *the dead know not anything.*' 'My son,' said he to him, 'thou knowest well the letter, but not the interpretation; *the living know,* they are the just, for even after their death they are termed *living;* and the *dead they do not know,* they are the wicked, for even during their life they are termed *dead.*' 'And how is it proved that the just are called living even when they are dead?' 'Because it is written (Num.

xxxii. 10), *to the land which I have sworn to Abraham, Isaac, and Jacob, saying,* etc. He said not *to the fathers* but *to Abraham, to Isaac, and to Jacob.*[1] He said to Moses, *Go and say to them, The oath which I have sworn to them I have fulfilled,* as it is written *to thy seed I will give it.* And the wicked are termed *dead,* as it is written (Ezek. xviii. 32), *I have no pleasure in the death of him that dieth* (or, the dead). Does a dead man then die? But these are the wicked because in their life they are called *dead.*' He (Rabbi Jonathan) said to him, 'Blessed be thou for teaching me the interpretation,' and he kissed him upon the head."

This explanation, though ingenious, is not satisfactory. Nor are the attempts which have been made by many Christian interpreters to evade the meaning of the passage more so: such as, for instance, by explaining the words as those of an atheistic objector; or supposing that the writer speaks of a conflict between the voice of the flesh and that of the spirit. The same gloomy view of the state of the dead is found in several passages of the Book of Ben Sira, though brighter and more consoling views of the future are throughout characteristic of the Book of Wisdom. The happy and cheerful pictures of the state of the righteous after death presented in the latter work far surpass anything to be found in the Book of Koheleth.

But, if the passage in chap. ix. 5, 6, be taken in its most literal signification, it does not, when viewed in connexion with the distinct utterances of Koheleth with respect to the final judgment of the righteous and the wicked, conduct us to the miserable conclusions at which modern Pessimism has arrived. If Koheleth affirms that the dead know not love, hatred or envy, or in other words imagines that the consciousness of the dead in another world is but dim and

[1] It is interesting to note the resemblance of this argument to that employed by our Lord in His controversy with the Sadducees, as related Matt. xxii. 31, 32, etc.

shadowy, he maintains at the same time that "God will bring every secret thing into judgment" in "His own time and season." Consequently the dead, even though regarded by him as existing in a semi-conscious state in Hades, are supposed to be still in existence, and destined at some future period to be awakened out of this dreary slumber, and rewarded according to the merit or demerit of their actions on earth. Koheleth does not, it is true, speak of this awakening out of sleep, still less does he allude to the resurrection of the body. His book is mainly occupied with the search after man's highest good on earth, and it is only incidentally that he refers at all to the state of the dead. Too great stress must not, therefore, be laid upon the fact of the writer's silence with respect to points on which we would fain have understood his views. Koheleth teaches that there will be a personal judgment for every man, a judgment which will take place at some future period, beyond man's present state of existence. This doctrine of a personal judgment for all men without exception is a point on which the writer of this strange though fascinating book exhibits a knowledge surpassing that of all the other writers of the Old Testament. It has been well termed "the breaking forth of the dawn of a new revelation" (*Kleinert*). A day when all men shall be judged according to their works, a day of personal and individual retribution, requires as its necessary condition a conscious existence after death, though at a time and season appointed by God.

It must, as Delitzsch has well remarked, be admitted that there were imperfections of knowledge which made it impossible for Koheleth to rise above a certain sense of Pessimism. It was, indeed, "in divers portions" ($\pi o \lambda v \mu \epsilon \rho \hat{\omega}_{S}$) as well as "in divers manners" ($\pi o \lambda v \tau \rho \acute{o} \pi \omega_{S}$), Heb. i. 1, that God made known the mystery of His doings to the holy men of old, the men who spake from God (2 Pet. i. 21). And, though the revelations of the New Testament on this point far transcend those of the Old, a veil is still to a great extent drawn over the future state, which man would fain lift, but cannot. But the Pessimism which was permitted to cloud the soul of Koheleth was different from that taught by the miserable school of modern atheists. Koheleth never lost sight of his faith in a personal God, of a belief in a judgment to come, or even in a future state of existence, dark and cheerless in some respects though his conceptions of the latter may have been. He exhorted his fellow-men to live righteously, soberly, and circumspectly. In spite of his pessimistic views of life, he advised them cheerfully to enjoy the present, and not be unduly anxious for the future. If he spoke of the grave as man's "everlasting house" (chap. xii. 5), a phrase rendered with questionable fidelity in our Authorised Version by his "long home" (notwithstanding Bullock's attempt to defend that rendering), it must not be forgotten that he also speaks of the earth as abiding for eternity (chap. i. 4) without the smallest intention for a moment of denying the fact of its creation in time by God. A similar designation of the grave was in use not only among the Egyptians and the Assyrians, and in later times the Romans, but also among the Jews at a period not much later than that of Koheleth (see Tobit iii. 6), and may, therefore, have been in existence in his days. The phrase was used by him as harmlessly as it was by the Jews themselves, who, long after the doctrine of the resurrection had become a definite article of their creed, were wont to call their cemeteries by that designation.

The limited nature of man's knowledge is nowhere more distinctly taught by Koheleth than in chap. vii. 23. He points out there that, after his utmost endeavours to obtain wisdom with the view of solving the perplexing questions connected with mankind, their actions, and their relation to God, he found all such knowledge to be far beyond mortal ken. "For that which is," that which exists, or "the world of things in its essence and with its causes" (*Delitzsch*) "is far off," far removed from the sight of man, "and it is deep, deep, who can discover it?" (chap. vii. 23.)

While busied with searching after wisdom, Koheleth learned more than one practical lesson of utility as to the actions of the sons of men. In his endeavours to sift things to the bottom he learned to comprehend that wickedness was folly, that foolishness was madness (chap. vii. 25); that men who lived in the pursuit of folly were "beside themselves," and were mad. One great source of madness and folly to the sons of men he thus introduces : "And I found more bitter than death the woman who is like snares [hunting nets], and like nets is her heart, her hands (the voluptuous arms with which she seizes her prey) are like fetters, he who is good before God will be saved from her."

The expressions used by Koheleth in this passage show that he did not intend to condemn promiscuously the whole female sex. The language accords substantially with the description given in the Book of Proverbs of the strange and wicked woman, who is a snare to the "simple" and "foolish" among men, and who ultimately "descends with her house (all that appertains to her) to death, and her paths (the tracks of her chariot-wheels) are towards the shades" (Prov. ii. 18)."[1]

The verses that follow, indeed, show that Koheleth had a low opinion of the women of his day in general. Nor need the expression of this opinion cause any astonishment. Degraded as women have ever been more or less in the Eastern world, they were, perhaps, peculiarly so at the time of the Persian rule. Shut up for the most part in strict seclusion, isolated from general society, and yet liable to be

---

[1] Prov. v. 3 ff. ; vi. 24 ff. ; vii. 6 ff. compare especially verse 23, also xxii. 14 ; xxiii. 27, 28.

ordered in violation of their feelings of propriety to display themselves in public to men heated with wine (Esther i. 10, 11); at times tyrannised over in private, and crushed in heart and feeling; often treated as the mere toys and playthings of men—no wonder that women should have been deficient in virtue and goodness. The Book of Esther gives a terrible picture of the state of the female world, and shows us also that the evil example of those in high position had a pernicious effect upon the morals of the Jewish people, although Jewish women were not subjected to all the disabilities under which the Persians suffered. Under such circumstances it is not to be wondered at, that Koheleth, after having depicted the danger arising from the thoroughly licentious woman, should proceed to express himself more generally: "See! this have I found, saith Koheleth, adding one to one (one case to another) to find out the account (or, reckoning), what still (on and on, up to the present) my soul hath sought, and I have not found; one man out of a thousand I have found, but a woman among all those I have not found" (chap. vii. 27, 28). Among a thousand men who came under his observation, Koheleth discovered only one to come up to the ideal of what a man ought to be; while among an equal number of women he did not find one who attained to his ideal of the proper perfection of female character..

The expression "one of a thousand" is borrowed, like sundry other phrases in the Book of Koheleth, from the Book of Job, where it occurs twice (Job ix. 3; xxxiii. 23). It is scarcely necessary to observe that it is not used in either of the passages in that book, or in that in the Book of Koheleth, in reference to the Messiah. The phrase recurs in the Book of Ben Sira (Ecclesiasticus), chap. vi. 6, "Let many persons be friendly with thee, but let thy counsellors be one of a thousand," or, as the aphorism is worded in the Hebrew fragment, "Many will greet thee; reveal thy secret only to one of a thousand."[1] There is, therefore, no necessity to suppose that the author makes any reference to the number of women in Solomon's harem (1 Kings xi. 3), though it is quite possible that, writing as he did from the standpoint of Solomon, that fact was present to his mind.

Koheleth's opinion of mankind in general is by no means flattering. There is abundant proof afforded in his book that he regarded man as "very far gone from original righteousness," and "of his own nature inclined to evil." In the statement that follows the passage just quoted, the writer endorses the main points of the story told in the Book of Genesis about man's fall and his present sinful condition. For he observes: "Only this, see! I have found, that God made man (the whole human race, including both male and female) upright, but they (men in general) have sought out many calculations," devices, or inventions, whereby to gratify their inclinations towards that which is evil (chap. vii. 29).

If such was his opinion of the human race in general, it is not surprising that he expresses himself in even less complimentary terms when he speaks specially of women. In almost every country proverbs are in current use in which women are alluded to more or less contemptuously. Men in every age have been wont thus to vent their spleen on the other sex. The remark of the lion in the fable must however be borne in mind: "If there were sculptors on our side you would have seen more men conquered by lions than lions by men."[2] There are, however, it must not be forgotten, among most nations maxims in existence which speak of women in terms of praise. In proverbs all facts are expressed in

---

[1] See Dukes, *Rabbinische Blumenlese*, p. 81. This passage of Ben Sira is several times quoted in the Talmud, Sanhedrin 100 *b*, Jebamoth 63 *b*, etc.; in the former place the words of Micah vii. 5 are added, "keep the doors of thy mouth from her that lieth in thy bosom." See on Ben Sira, chap. ii.

[2] *Fabulæ Æsopiæ coll.* ex recogn. Halmii, No. 63 *b*. The fable as usually quoted in England speaks of painters, not of sculptors.

general terms, and no notice is taken of exceptions, however numerous they may be. Such exceptions, however, in their turn are formed into aphorisms of a different type. Instances of this usage occur frequently in the Book of Proverbs, where unfavourable judgments expressed in general terms in one place are practically modified in another by the admission of sentiments of an opposite nature. The intelligent reader is in all such cases left to decide for himself as to the cases in which the one or the other saying is really applicable. Sometimes in the Book of Proverbs the two apparently opposite aphorisms occur side by side, *e.g.* "Answer not a fool according to his folly, lest thou also be like unto him. Answer a fool according to his folly, lest he be wise in his own conceit." Prov. xxvi. 4, 5.

There are many Rabbinical proverbs which speak severely of the female sex, such as, "It is better to follow a lion than a woman." "He who follows the counsel of his wife falls into hell." "If an ass can go up a ladder, then knowledge may be found among women."[1] But, side by side with proverbs of this kind, many sayings of the very opposite character can be adduced, such as, "Honour your wives that you may become rich." "Is thy wife of small stature, bend down to her, and whisper to her," *i.e.* do nothing without her opinion.[2] "God hath given to the woman more intelligence than to the man." "He who is without a wife is without luck (Gen. ii. 18), without help (*id.*), without joy (Deut. xiv. 26), without a blessing (Ezek. xliv. 30), without atonement (Lev. xvi. 6), without peace (1 Sam. xxv. 26), and without life (Koh. ix. 9)."[3]

[1] See Buxtorf's *Florilegium Heb.* p. 122. אַחֲרֵי הָאֲרִי וְלֹא אַחֲרֵי הָאִשָּׁה אַחֲרֵי ע"א: Similarly in p. 210. כֹּל הַהוֹלֵךְ בַּעֲצַת אִשְׁתּוֹ נוֹפֵל בְּגֵיהִנָּם הָאִשָּׁה וְלֹא אַחֲרֵי ע"א: So also in p. 211. אִם יַעֲלֶה הַחֲמוֹר בְּסוּלָּם תִּמָּצֵא דַעַת בַּנָּשִׁים.

[2] Dukes, *Rabbinische Blumenlese*, p. 124. Compare also the essay of J. Stern, *Die Frau im Talmud*, Zürich, 1879.

[3] So says the Midrash Rabba, Gen. ii. 18. Par. 18. ד"א בשם ר' יוסי בן זמרא אמר.

Hence a single aphorism is by no means sufficient to show that Koheleth was a hater of the female sex. On the contrary, there is sufficient evidence in his book to prove that he adhered firmly on this point to the teaching of the Mosaic law, which sets forth plainly that woman was designed to be a "help meet" for man.[1] Despite the corruption of the period at which he wrote, he plainly recognised the truth that there were even then in existence women worthy of a man's honour and love. Thus, in urging the duty of making a cheerful use of present mercies granted from the hand of God, the writer says: "Enjoy life with a wife whom thou lovest all the days of the life of thy vanity, which He (God) hath given to thee under the sun" (chap. ix. 9).

Koheleth has, moreover, given a description (chap. iv.) of the aimless troubles and vexations of the single man, and he alludes to the miserly habits of life which such a one is apt to contract. His remarks on this point prove, though no direct mention of woman is made in the passage, that the writer had a full perception of the advantages of married life. For he observes that the man "who is one without a second, without son or brother," as he contemplates his severe labour and endless striving after riches, may well ask

---

תני ר׳ יעקב כל שאין לו אשה. ניתן בה בינה יותר מן האיש. So also in Par. 17. שרוי בלא טובה. בלא עזר. בלא שמחה. בלא ברכה. בלא כפרה: בלא טובה. לא טוב היות האדם לבדו. בלא עזר. אעשה לו עזר כנגדו. בלא שמחה שנא׳ (דברים י״ד) ושמחת אתה וביתך בלא כפרא. (ויקרא ט״ז) וכפר בעדו ובעד ביתו. בלא ברכה. (יחזקאל מ״ד) להניח ברבה אל ביתך. ר׳ סימון בשם ריב״ל אמר. אף בלא שלום. שנא׳ (שמואל א׳ כ״ה) ואתה שלום וביתך שלום. ר׳ יהושע דסכנין בשם ר׳ לוי אמר. אף בלא חיים. שנאמר (קהלת ט׳) ראה חיים עם אשה אשר אהבת.

[1] The Midrash says אם זכה עזר ואם לאו מנגדו "when a man is good his wife is a help to him, but if not she corresponds to him," or perhaps better, "she is an opposition to him," *i.e.* stands in his way and contends with him. The clause is explained by the commentator, אם יזכה תהיה לו לעזר ואם לא יזכה בנגדו Wünsche translates the second clause "she is to him like a thorn," and he notes בנגדו like בנגיר as a thorn."

himself the question, "For whom am I toiling and depriving my soul of good?" (chap. iv. 8.)

From this brief review of Koheleth's sentiments concerning woman (so far as they can be gathered from the scanty allusions in his book to the subject), we turn to notice the opinions on this point propounded by the chief writers of the Pessimist school. These philosophers have no sympathy whatever with the views so energetically propounded and urged in many quarters at the present day respecting so-called "women's rights." On the contrary they are disposed to look upon woman at the best as only the "moral parasite of man."[1] If the advocates of "women's rights" have gone too far in one direction, the defenders of the novel school of thought have on the other hand propounded views which lead directly towards the degradation of the female sex and the demoralization of humanity.

Schopenhauer has a low opinion of women both intellectually and morally. Women, from a deficiency in their powers of reasoning and reflection, are, according to him, predisposed to cunning. E. von Hartmann remarks that "it is quite natural for the female sex to be more inclined to lying and cunning than the male, inasmuch as it is the weak sex, and cunning is the natural weapon of the weak. Moreover, women in their daily occupations have more to do with women than men have, and, consequently, more frequently have to carry on war with lying and cunning, which of itself induces them to use similar weapons."[2] Hence, according to Schopenhauer, women as naturally make use of deceit and lying in fighting their battles, as a lion does of its teeth and claws, or a bull of its horns. The sex is in his opinion so disposed to lying that it is impossible to find a really truthful and ingenuous woman. He regards

---

[1] E. von Hartmann, *Phænomenologie des sittlichen Bewusstseins*, p. 526.
[2] *Ibid.*, p. 348.

the character of women in general as a compound of falsehood, faithlessness, treachery and ingratitude, and asserts that women are more inclined to commit perjury than men.

It is unquestionable that a certain amount of evidence may be adduced in support of all these charges against the female sex. But it must not be forgotten that such charges may be retorted, and men may with equal justice be accused of similar baseness. The depravity of the entire human race is a doctrine which no believer in the Divine revelation will for a moment seek to call in question. But the railing of sex against sex, of men against women, or of women against men, is altogether unphilosophical. All such assertions, whether made on one side or the other, are utterly incapable of real proof. And, if it could be clearly shown that women are more depraved than men, or, as von Hartmann maintains, that the notions of morality held by women are lower than those of the other sex, it would by no means follow that this was a natural result of the physical constitution of woman, seeing that other reasons might be assigned for such a state of things. Notwithstanding, therefore, the arguments by which Schopenhauer and von Hartmann have sought to uphold their opinion, we regard all such representations as gross caricatures.

Schopenhauer's description of women's intellectual powers is equally unflattering. He would thoroughly endorse the Turkish proverb: "Long hair, little brains." Women have no real and true sense or susceptibility for music, poetry, or the plastic arts. They often indeed pretend to have such tastes, but the pretence is only made for the purpose of coquetry. A portion of this description of women has been borrowed by Schopenhauer from Rousseau. Schopenhauer complains especially of the way in which women keep on talking to one another in the theatres, and suggests that the Apostolic direction, "let the women keep silence in the churches" (1 Cor. xiv. 34), in order to be rendered suitable to the present day, ought to be altered into "let a woman keep silence in the theatre." He denies that women have ever produced anything great or original in the fine arts. There may, he cautiously admits, possibly be a few exceptions to this general rule; but, as a class, women are "the most thorough-going and incurable Philistines."

Nor is von Hartmann, albeit that he has twice entered into the bonds of matrimony, a whit more complimentary to the female sex. He, as well as Schopenhauer, maintains that women are grossly wanting in the sense of rectitude and righteousness; that, out of love for a particular person, they will readily act with the grossest injustice to a competitor; that they are naturally inclined to commit acts of dishonesty, and are in many cases only restrained by the fear of detection; that they have an instinctive leaning towards lying and falsification, and cling thereto the more readily as they have often no idea of the criminal character of the alteration of a word or a date. In proof of this he adduces the fact that one-fourth of the " service-books " of the female servants in Berlin contain gross falsifications. Where women have influence, nepotism prevails, and, consequently, in public life and in the State unrighteousness extends exactly so far as the influence of the female sex reaches. Nor is there, in his opinion, much hope of a gradual improvement of the female character in the course of generations, because mothers usually have the management of the education of their daughters entirely in their own hands, and daughters cannot in general be removed away from their mothers' influence without still greater disadvantages. "Their deficiency in a proper moral firmness, their weakness in moral reason, and, above all, their want of the sense of rectitude" form the most powerful arguments "against every female-emancipation swindle, and especially against the female sex being allowed actively to participate in political life."[1]

Most sensible persons will, indeed, agree with von Hartmann in advising that women should be kept as far as possible from all contact with the rough battle of life; and many justly maintain that the education of women, even of the highest kind, ought to be such as is adapted to the special requirements and peculiar position of their sex. If, however, the advocates of the higher education of women have been injudicious in the claims they have often put forward, it is not a little remarkable that those European apostles of a semi-Oriental philosophy, who depreciate the female sex for its want of intelligence and comprehension, should so strongly urge that particular care ought to be taken not to make women too intelligent. These modern preachers of "the rights of man" express as strong opinions against "the higher education of women" as the most bigoted ultramontane priests might be expected to give utterance to, through fear of their craft being in danger, inasmuch as a higher education might weaken their hold over the female sex. This advice savours somewhat of a sort of male "trades-unionism," which, for its own selfish purposes, seeks to emblazon upon its banner the old Jewish proverb, "No other wisdom becomes a woman than the knowledge of the spindle."[2] We do not forget that von Hartmann recommends the enlargement of women's education in another direction, which motives of propriety forbid us here to particularize.[3]

According to Schopenhauer, the position which women occupy in the East is in many respects more befitting the sex than that which is conceded to women in Europe and

[1] E. von Hartmann's *Phænomenologie des sittl. Bewusstseins*, p. 520 ff.
[2] Dukes' *Rabbinische Blumenlese*, p. 100.
[3] E. von Hartmann's *Phænomenologie des sittl. Bewusstseins*, p. 697 ff.

America. The deference paid to the fair sex in the West is, in his opinion, altogether unnatural. Woman ought not to be the object of man's respect and veneration; nor ought she to be permitted to assume the position universally granted to her in civilized countries. The real European lady was a special object of Schopenhauer's abhorrence; and he was wont to maintain, strangely enough, that one result of the honour and respect paid to ladies of the higher ranks in Europe is that the women of the lower classes there are more unhappy than those in the East. No arguments, however, have been adduced by him in support of this extraordinary statement.[1]

It must not, however, be supposed that all the writers of the Pessimist school endorse these extravagancies of their master. The asceticism recommended by Schopenhauer has not met with the approval of von Hartmann. Low as is his estimate of female virtue and intellect, the latter philosopher strongly maintains that proper female society is more beneficial to young men than intercourse with persons of their own sex, and that such society is of essential importance for men inclined to philosophical studies. The loss of male society can, in his opinion, be compensated for by the study of books, that of women never. The philosopher who dispenses with female society is like a man who seeks to obtain an acquaintance with real life only by reading books.[2] The ideas of von Hartmann on this point are in accordance with the Sanskrit proverb which says, "women are instructed by Nature, the learning of men is taught by books," or again, "Nature is woman's teacher, and she learns more sense than man, the pedant, gleans from books."[3] Venetianer justly

---

[1] Schopenhauer, *Parerga und Paralipomena*, Band 2, cap. xxiv. "Ueber die Weiber." Sämmtliche Werke, 6ter Band, p. 649 ff.

[2] E. von Hartmann, *Die Philosophie des Unbewussten*, 3te Aufl. Berlin: 1871, p. 370.

[3] *Eastern Proverbs and Emblems illustrating Old Truths*, by Rev. J. Long, Member of the Bengal Asiatic Society, F.R.G.S. London: Trübner & Co. 1881.

considers Schopenhauer's hatred of women philosophically absurd, inasmuch as at least one-half of the human race consists of women. He asks, "Is the love of a mother, the devotion of a sister, the fidelity of a wife, worthy of being despised as only common selfishness, and gratitude towards him who feeds them? Schopenhauer has not indeed omitted to instance the fact, that a mother's love may go so far as to sacrifice her own life, as a proof of the strength of the animal instinct in humanity!"[1]

Such is the manner in which the new Atheistic philosophy seeks to lower the estimation of the female sex. Such lucubrations might be despised, if they had not an important practical bearing. But, in matters of morality, "facilis descensus Averno."

We have already noticed the fact (p. 170) that Schopenhauer and von Hartmann maintain that the natural instinct of men is in favour of polygamy, while the feeling of women is in favour of monogamy. Both writers bear testimony to the present degraded state of men in general, notwithstanding the ameliorating influences of modern civilization. They assert as an undeniable fact that by far the larger majority of men in the present day are, at least for a season, virtual polygamists. Bad as unregenerate human nature is, even in professedly Christian lands, we cannot but hope that such a statement is to a large extent an exaggeration. But, if the principles of Pessimism, and of Atheism in general, should continue to spread (and such principles are spreading in an alarming degree), a largely increased crop of immorality must be the result. Schopenhauer, with that boldness and freedom of speech on all subjects which is so remarkably characteristic of his writings, is not ashamed to praise the Mormons,

---

[1] Venetianer, *Schopenhauer als Scholastiker*, p. 272. Venetianer remarks that Schopenhauer's chapter upon women might usefully be read aloud for pastime and amusement on the occasion of a feast, or on the evening of Purim.

because they have made converts by throwing off what he terms the unnatural bondage of monogamy. He maintains that the practice of polygamy, though opposed to the *esprit de corps* of women in civilized lands and against the interests of individual women, is on the whole a benefit to the female sex. It must not be forgotten that his writings, as well as those of von Hartmann, are shortly to appear in an English translation.

It need not create any surprise that, boldly avowing such detestable sentiments, Schopenhauer should maintain that women ought to possess no real property, that at most they should, when unmarried, be permitted to enjoy an income for life, that they should be always placed under guardians, and in no case be permitted to act as sole guardians of their own children. He quotes the opinion of Aristotle (*Politic.*, ii. 9), who maintained that the liberty granted to women in Sparta, and the large dowries and inheritances of which they came into possession, were among the causes which led to the downfall of that state. Schopenhauer himself maintains, and history on this point supports his opinion, that the French Revolution was brought about by the corruption engendered by female influence. Woman, concludes Schopenhauer, is by nature intended to obey, and she is wont to place herself under some master by whom she permits herself to be ruled and directed; "if she is young, it is a lover; if she is old, a confessor."

It is important, though melancholy, to note the degradation of male and female which, sooner or later, is ever the outcome of atheism. St. Paul has vividly described the state of the heathen world who "knowing God, glorified Him not as God" (Romans i. 21 ff.), and his description may be regarded (*exceptis excipiendis*) almost as a prophecy of the results that always follow in the wake of atheism and false philosophy.

"Amongst the heathen," writes the great German reformer, "there was a saying—*tria mala, mala pessima, ignis, aqua, femina*—that is, there can be nothing worse than what these three can do, to wit, fire, water, and woman. But these and many like sayings against the female sex have been vomited forth by the devil out of pure hatred and venom towards God and His work, meaning in this way to disgust every man with the married state and with God's word." But, as Samson is said to have obtained honey in the carcase of the lion, we may deduce from this saying of the ancients something higher and nobler. How could the world, ruined as it is by sin, exist at all without fire to warm us, water to refresh us, and woman to comfort us. A French writer, Jouy, quoted by Schopenhauer, well says: "Without women the beginning of our life would be deprived of its succour, the middle of our life of pleasure, and its end of consolation." The student of the Holy Scriptures need not be reminded of the numerous examples of noble women mentioned in Old Testament Writ, or of the devoted heroines of New Testament days. Their names stand forth conspicuously, side by side with those of men, in the muster-roll of the "noble army of martyrs," concerning which our Christian poet has sung:—

"A noble army, men and boys,
  The matron and the maid,
Around the Saviour's throne rejoice,
  In robes of light arrayed;
They climbed the steep ascent of heaven,
  Through peril, toil, and pain;
O God! to us may grace be given,
  To follow in their train!"

CHAPTER VIII.

*THE CLOSING SECTION OF THE BOOK OF KOHELETH.
—THE DAYS OF LIFE AND THE DAYS OF DEATH.*

CHAPTER VIII.

The closing section of Koheleth, 217—Its poetic character, 217—Koheleth on the duty of submission to kings, 218—Woe to the land whose king is a child, 219—The importance of noble birth in a ruler, 220—The ruin often caused by the revelry of king and nobles, 221—Koheleth's book no encouragement to rebellion, 222—"Curse not the king," 222—Words uttered in secret, 223—Casting bread on the waters, 223—Hitzig's explanation untenable, 224—Koheleth supposed to recommend merchants to engage in foreign enterprises, 224—Objection to this interpretation, 226—The passage in Koh xi. 1, 2 an exhortation to beneficence, 226—Anecdote from the Kabus, 227—Thin cakes of bread, 227—Beneficence should be generous and not stinted, 228—Advantages of beneficence from a worldly point of view, 228—The uniformity of the laws of nature, 229—False interpretation of Koh. xi. 3 by Bridges, 229—Opportunities not to be neglected, 230—The way of the wind and the secrets of embryology, 231—Constant occupation a blessing, 231—The sweetness of life, 232—The darkness of the grave, 233—Cheerfulness commended in youth, 234—The advice not ironical, 234—The direction of the Law and the advice of Koheleth, 234—The judgment of the future, 235—The condemnation of anger and peevishness, 237—The evil of the flesh, 238—Cheerfulness of mind and early piety, 238—The importance of piety, 238—The days of evil, or man's passage to the tomb, 239—Death like a winged Pegasus, 240—Koheleth's description of "the evil days," 240—The absence of pleasure, 240—The Hebrew mode of speaking of the seasons, 242—The allegorical explanation of the light of the sun, etc., 242—The watchers of the house, 243—The house the body of man, 244—The grinding maids ceasing from work, 244—The organs of sight, 244—The doors shut to the street, 245—The sound of the mill ceasing, 246—The rising up at the voice of a bird, 247—The weak voice of old age, 248—The storm theory of the passage, 249—The daughters of song, 250—The fears on the way, 251—Hahn's exposition of the passage, 252—The night of death and the terrors of the grave, 253—The prophetical exposition of the passage given in the Midrash, 255—The almond-tree in blossom, 257—Plumptre on "the tree of wakefulness," 259—The various explanations of the locust, 260—Objections adduced, 261—Plumptre's strange exposition, 261—The anecdote of the Talmud, 262—The song of the grasshopper, 262—The reference to the caperberry, 263—Its use, 263—The objectionable views of Hitzig, 263—The mourners going about, 265—The silver cord, 266—The golden bowl, 266—The shivering of the pitcher, 268—The end of man and the beast, 268—The new interpretation, 269—The evil days of man, 269—The Palestinian winter, 270—"The days of the old woman," 271—The legends on which the phrase is based, 271—The division into seven stanzas, 272—The days of advance to the grave, 272—The slave and the master, 272—The maid and her mistress, 272—The advent of spring, 273—The two pictures, death and life, 273—Free translation of the whole passage, 274.

CHAPTER VIII.

THE CLOSING SECTION OF THE BOOK OF KOHELETH.—THE DAYS OF LIFE AND THE DAYS OF DEATH.

THE various sections of the Book of Koheleth are not always distinctly marked off from one another, and it is a matter of considerable uncertainty at what precise point the last section of the book really commences. Chapter xii. cannot be regarded as forming in itself a complete section, for it is clearly connected with the two concluding verses of chap. xi. And even these verses are in their turn connected, though not so intimately, with those preceding them. Delitzsch considers the final section to begin at chap. x. 16. As the question is not of any great importance, we may assume the latter opinion to be correct, and regard that as the commencement of the closing portion of the book.

No survey of the Book of Koheleth in relation to modern criticism would have any claim to be regarded as complete even as an introduction to the study of the work itself, if it passed over in silence the conflicting interpretations given of the 12th chapter. We may indeed fairly refer the student who wishes to learn our opinion on other passages to the commentary appended to this work, but it is necessary here to attempt to give a general outline of the contents of the closing chapter. This chapter is so intimately connected with the passage that precedes it, as to render it hopeless for a critic to maintain with any plausibility that it is the work of another writer. And yet it exhibits powers of poetical expression so remarkable, when compared with the heavy diction of the other parts of the book, as ought to make critics cautious in asserting (as is often done too rashly) the incapacity of a writer, whose general style on some subjects may be dull and prosaic, to rise at other times to the level of poetry.

If, as has been maintained in the preceding chapters, the Book of Koheleth is to be regarded as a production of the later portion of the Persian era, it is worthy of special notice that, just as the Apostle Paul in the days of Nero exhorted Christians to exhibit a ready obedience to the temporal rulers of the Roman Empire (Rom. xiii. 1–7), so Koheleth, at the very time when the Persian rule must have been felt most galling, advised his readers to submit to that authority under which Providence had placed them.

The views of Koheleth as to the wisdom and duty of submission to the king are so decided, that Hitzig, believing that such opinions cannot be reconciled with the severe remarks on unworthy princes and nobles contained in chap. x. 16, 17, ventures to assert that these strictures ought to be regarded as part of the speech of the fool spoken of in the preceding verse.

But Hitzig's judgment is here seriously at fault. Koheleth may well maintain on the one hand that kings and those in authority ought to be respected and obeyed, and yet condemn in scathing terms the effeminacy and immorality often exhibited by princes, and the drunkenness and debauchery too generally practised by the nobles at the Persian courts, and well known to all the subjects of the empire. The prophets of the Old Testament, though ever ready to uphold the lawful authority of princes, were, as Delitzsch observes, no less ready to rebuke with bold frankness the impiety and oppression often shown by those in high places. Thus, Elijah boldly rebuked Ahab; Isaiah was not behindhand in reproving Ahaz; and the solemn denunciations of

Jeremiah against the unrighteous acts of Jehoiakim, Jehoiachin, and Zedekiah are sufficient of themselves to prove, that respect for the office and person of a monarch is not inconsistent with a manly condemnation of the sins of men placed in the loftiest earthly position.

The expression of Koheleth, "Woe to thee, O land, whose king is a child" (chap. x. 16), is partly an echo of the saying of Isaiah (iii. 12), "as for my people their ruler (נגשׂיו) is a wilful child, and women rule over him (*i.e.* the child)." In place, however, of referring, as Isaiah does, to the misery of a land whose prince is under the government of women, Koheleth directs attention to the misfortune of a country whose ruler spends his time in the society of revellers. "Woe to thee, O land, whose king is a child, and whose princes eat in the morning," that is, who "rise early in the morning that they may follow strong drink, and continue till night, till wine inflame them " (Isaiah v. 11).

It is no wonder that so striking an aphorism as that of Koheleth has often been referred to at various epochs of history. Delitzsch notes that Salomon, Bishop of Constance, alluded to it as fulfilled in the time of Louis III., surnamed the Child, the last of the Carlovingian emperors of Germany. Catharine de Medici made frequent mention of it when she spoke of the state of France in the early portion of the reign of Charles IX.[1] There is a Rabbinical proverb formed by the combination of the thought in the aphorism of Koheleth with the saying of Isaiah before quoted, "Woe to (or, unhappy is) the generation, whose leader (דַבְּרִיתָא) is a woman;" and its spirit is breathed in another Jewish proverb, "Woe to the generation which has lost its leader (מנהיגו), woe to the ship which has lost her steersman." [2]

---

[1] See Henry White's *Massacre of St. Bartholomew*. London: John Murray, p. 151.

[2] See Dukes' *Rabbinische Blumenlese*, pp. 120, 89.

The truth of the aphorism was strikingly exemplified in the early part of the reign of Rehoboam the son of Solomon. But this fact is not, as some have imagined, an argument in favour of the Solomonic authorship of the book, but rather the reverse. The writer was, as has been already noticed, well acquainted with all the incidents of the reign of Solomon and of his successor.

The proverb which immediately follows, "Happy art thou, O land, whose king is a son of nobles" (chap. x. 17), is strongly suggestive of the later period of Jewish history. Koheleth, in another place (chap. x. 7), expresses his disgust at beholding slaves unduly exalted, while nobles were forced to occupy humble positions. He pronounces that land fortunate, whose ruler is born and trained up in the higher ranks of society, and is not a mere upstart slave or low-born eunuch, elevated like Bagoas by atrocious crimes to lofty estate.[1] That slaves should occupy the place of nobles, and nobles should be degraded from the position due to their rank, was in his eyes a reversal of the proper order of things. Men born to the purple have not, indeed, always acquitted themselves with honour; but, as a general rule, men are best fitted to be rulers of men who by early education and training have been prepared for such office and authority. The phrase made use of by Koheleth might, indeed, be interpreted metaphorically to indicate men of noble character. But the literal sense is well suited to the passage. For though nobility of blood has in no age been any certain guarantee of nobleness of action, or of the possession of the wisdom desirable for one invested with royal authority, the history

---

[1] Bagoas was raised for his valuable services to the most eminent position in the state by Artaxerxes Ochus. He afterwards murdered that monarch (B.C. 338) and all his sons save Arses, whom he placed on the throne of Persia, but murdered also shortly after. He was put to death himself by Darius Codomannus—whom he had placed upon the throne in room of Arses—shortly after the accession of that monarch.

of the Persian empire abounds with illustrations of the truth that persons raised from a state of slavery to the place of authority have generally proved the most terrible oppressors of their fellow-men. It need not cause any surprise that, as is usual in such aphoristic maxims (see p. 205), the writer should have spoken in general terms of the advantage to a country of its ruler being of noble blood, and should have passed over without notice the numerous exceptions presented in history.

Koheleth also does not forget to remark on the evil consequences which are the result of a monarch and his nobles abandoning themselves to sensuality and revelry. Men ought to eat and drink in order to refresh themselves for the higher work they may have to perform. When the king and nobles, through indolence or debauchery, neglect their proper duties, the whole fabric of the empire soon falls into a ruinous condition ; just as the timberwork of a house, the repairs of which have been neglected, rapidly decays, and its roof becomes leaky and useless (ch. x. 18).

Under such pictures the writer portrays the danger which arises from those apparently harmless feasts, spread for purposes of pleasure, which frequently prove nets to catch and destroy the simple. In the round of such festivities rulers and men of high position have often drowned themselves and their country in destruction and perdition. The winebowl gladdens for a season the life of such gay revellers, and they yield themselves to all the blinding joys of sensuality (ch. x. 19). Men who are rich are able for a season to make provision for the flesh to fulfil the lusts thereof (Rom. xiii. 14), by the means of money which renders it possible for them to obtain that which they lust after ; for little is denied to those wealthy transgressors who can pay handsomely the slaves of their passions.

In days when a state is plainly falling to pieces by

reason of the dissolute conduct of its prince, the thought must needs arise in many a heart whether it be not advisable to seek to hurl the unworthy monarch from his throne. But Koheleth did not intend his work to be an encouragement to rebellion. While, therefore, he censures the wretched king and nobles, and drops a lament over the land cursed with such a plague, he calls to mind the truth alluded to in several parts of his book, namely, that God has a proper time and season at which He will punish men for their transgression (ch. iii. 17). The individual sufferer must wait for that season, and make the best use he can of the trial which the "King of nations"[1] (Rev. xv. 3,) hath given to men to exercise them therewith. Like St. Paul in a later day—whose teaching seems founded on Koh. viii. 2, though the Apostle nowhere quotes the book—Koheleth, at a much earlier period, urged as a matter of conscience the duty of submission to lawfully constituted authority. It would have been simple madness had Jewish believers, through indignation at the sensuality or immorality of any of the Persian monarchs, burst out into rebellion against their rule. The weapons with which they were armed were far nobler than merely carnal ones; the latter would have been unsheathed in vain; their success by means of the former would ultimately have been certain.[2]

Hence it was that Koheleth, under the guidance of a higher than human inspiration, warned his readers not even in their inner consciousness to curse the king, or in their bed-chambers to execrate the rich man, however unworthily either might act. The dictum "vengeance belongeth unto

---

[1] The reading, "king of saints," followed by our A.V., is unsupported by Greek MSS., and was smuggled into the Greek text of the New Test. from the Vulgate by Erasmus. See Delitzsch's *Handschriftliche Funde*, 1stes Heft, p. 40. Delitzsch has consequently, in his Hebrew New Test., adopted the reading מֶלֶךְ הַגּוֹיִם. The Revised English Version of the N. T. follows in its text the reading ὁ βασιλεὺς τῶν αἰώνων, *king of ages*, which is that adopted by Westcott and Hort in their edition of the Greek Testament (Cambridge, 1881).

[2] See remarks in my *Bampton Lectures on Zechariah*, pp. 240, 247, 252.

Danger of words uttered in secret.

me : I will recompense, saith the Lord," which is so strikingly commented on by St. Paul (Rom xii. 19 ff.), is one of the great sayings of the Law, and necessary to be obeyed for the sake of conscience towards God, and also for the sake of one's own personal safety in dangerous days. Men sometimes fancy they are alone when they are not. Words uttered in secret are often proclaimed on the housetops. The curse denounced against the monarch may be carried by the fowls of heaven screaming in the open air, and the winged creatures may publish the secret to the outer world.[1] "There are ears on the road and ears in the wall" open to listen to imprudent expressions ; and, though the wise man should not take heed to every bitter word that may be spoken against himself in secret (if he accidentally overhears such language), but should act as if he heard it not (Koh. vii. 21, 22), he need not expect an immoral tyrant to exhibit such magnanimity.

There is considerable difference of opinion as to the sense of the opening verses of the eleventh chapter. There is no allusion there, as was long supposed by popular commentators, such as Bridges and others, to the sowing of seed upon the waters which takes place in Egypt during the inundation of the Nile. This interpretation, however, is as old as Jerome, and probably older. It is scarcely possible to explain the phrase "over the face of the waters" as equivalent to "beside all waters" (Isa. xxxii. 20), though the word translated *bread* is sometimes used in the sense of *seedcorn* (Isa. xxviii. 28, xxx. 22, and Ps. civ. 14). But the verb

---

[1] Compare the story told of Ibycus, who having been set upon by robbers near Corinth called upon a flock of cranes which were flying over head to avenge his death. Soon afterwards, when the people of Corinth were assembled in the theatre, a number of cranes appeared hovering over the heads of the spectators, and one of the murderers exclaimed : "Behold the avengers of Ibycus!" This exclamation led to the discovery of the crime. The expression "the cranes of Ibycus" afterwards passed into a proverb. See for authorities, *Smith's Dict. of Greek and Roman Biography and Mythology*.

which occurs in the passage does not mean to *cast* or *scatter abroad* seed, but to *send*, or send *forth*. It is used of the sending forth of plagues, wild beasts, or famine upon a land, and of the sending forth of a king by God in judgment as a scourge against a country. It is technically used in a few passages of the sending forth of arrows from the bow (1 Sam. xx. 20), or of the sending or casting forth of the fire of judgment into a city (Amos i. 4 ff.) in order to consume it; but this latter usage does not afford any help in the explanation of the passage of Koheleth.

The verb also occurs in the sense of *casting away*, and Hitzig considers it has that signification in the passage before us. But the direction "cast away thy bread upon the face of the waters" is scarcely defensible on exegetical grounds. For the passage cannot be interpreted with Hitzig as a recommendation to those who desire to see their hopes fulfilled to cherish no expectation of success, and to have no faith in their best exertions. Hitzig imagines that Koheleth is urging on his readers the wisdom of being prepared for adversity, and he quotes as a parallel the words of Æneas, " una salus victis nullam sperare salutem (Virg. Æn. ii. 354). But the language of the passage is not certainly that of desperation.

Hitzig's interpretation has not found much favour among expositors. But there are two other explanations of the passage for which much can be said. The view which Delitzsch has taken is a modification of that formerly held by Martin Geier, J. D. Michaelis and others—namely, that Koheleth recommends the practice of the prudent merchant, who sends forth his merchandise in ships, which go over the face of the waters to distant lands, with the expectation that on their return he will receive his own with an increase. He regards the word *bread*, which is expressed in the first clause of the verse, and is represented by the pronoun in the second, to signify in the former the means of making gain, and in the latter "the bread of acquisition," or that gained by trading. The word *bread* cannot, indeed, be translated *wealth* or *property*, as was maintained by some of the earlier expositors who took this view of the passage. It might be urged that *bread* is scarcely a suitable expression for the gains of the merchant who naturally seeks to obtain a large return from his enterprises. But Proverbs xxxi. 14 may be cited in defence of the aphorism being so understood. For the wise woman is there said to be "like the ships of the merchant, she bringeth her food (לַחְמָהּ, *her bread*) from far." Delitzsch compares Psalm cvii. 23, where mention is made of those who go down to the sea in ships, and do business in the great waters. The picture, according to him, is taken from the corn-trade of a maritime city. Mendelssohn maintains that Solomon is here urging on the Israelitish merchants of his day the advantage to be obtained from foreign commerce, with an under reference to the practice which he first introduced into Israel, of sending ships to Ophir and Tarshish in search of the products of distant lands.

If the first verse be so interpreted, the second must bear a similar sense. It has, therefore, been explained by Mendelssohn, Preston, Delitzsch, etc., as a continuation of the advice to those inclined to engage in foreign ventures. Koheleth recommends a person to "divide the portion into seven, yea eight portions, for thou knowest not what evil will occur upon the earth." The precept, according to Delitzsch, enjoins a speculative prudence similar to that displayed by Jacob on a critical occasion (Gen. xxxii. 9), and its sense is: do not commit all your goods to one ship. The proverb thus understood is equivalent to our maxim, "Do not put all your eggs into one basket."

The critical arguments by which Delitzsch defends this interpretation will be seen in our commentary. The great objection to it is, that the phrase *to give a portion* or *a part to a person* (נָתַן חֵלֶק לְ, Josh. xiv. 4; xv. 13) is used elsewhere in a different signification, namely, as synonymous with *to give gifts to* (נָתַן מָנָה לְ, 1 Sam. i. 4, 5; 2 Chron. xxxi. 19; Esther ii. 9). Moreover, it may be fairly questioned whether, if the writer had intended to refer to disaster by sea, he would have used the phrase in the second clause, "thou knowest not what evil shall happen on the earth." It is rather far-fetched to suppose that in the latter he had in his mind the possibility of the disasters which might happen to a caravan on land.

Hence we are disposed rather to agree with those who explain both verses 1 and 2 as exhortations to beneficence. The earliest comment on the passage is that of Ben Sira, who, in a maxim of his, extant only in Chaldee, observes "strew (זְרֹק) thy bread upon the surface of the water and on the dry land, and thou shalt find it in the end of days."[1] It will be observed in this earliest comment upon the verse that the difficulty of considering the verb to refer to sowing of seed was felt even at that time, and an attempt made to obviate it by translating the word in a sense in which it certainly occurs. Bishop Lowth in his work on *Hebrew Poetry* has explained the phrase as equivalent to the Greek expression *to sow the sea*. But the aphorism of Koheleth was not meant as an exhortation to engage in labour though apparently fruitless. Its signification is better conveyed in the Arabic proverb quoted from Diez by several commentators, "Do good, cast thy bread into the water, at some time a recompence will be made thee." Delitzsch observes that the same proverb has been naturalised in Turkish, "Do good, throw it into the water, if the fish does not know it, God does." A very suitable parallel is quoted by Herzfeld from Goethe's *Westöstlich. Divan*,

---

[1] Dukes' *Rabbinische Blumenlese*, p. 73. See on this proverb of Ben Sira our remarks on p. 46.

> "Was willst du untersuchen,
> Wohin die Milde fliesst!
> Ins Wasser wirf deine Kuchen:
> Wer weiss, wer sie geniesst!"

A similar interpretation is found in Voltaire.[1] Dukes gives in his note the following story, quoted from the Kabus by Diez (*Denkwürdigkeiten von Asien*, 1 Th. p. 106 ff.), which, whether it be a fact or a fiction, well illustrates the meaning of the Arabic proverb.

The caliph Mutewekkil in Bagdad had an adopted son Fettich of whom he was very fond. As the latter was bathing one day, he sank under the water and disappeared. The caliph offered a large reward to any one who should recover the boy's body. A bather was fortunate enough after seven days to discover the boy alive in a cavern in a precipitous mountain by which the river flowed. On investigation, the caliph ascertained that the boy was kept from starving by cakes of bread borne to him over the surface of the water, on which cakes was stamped the name of Mohammed ben Hassan. The caliph, having summoned Mohammed ben Hassan into his presence, asked him what induced him to throw the bread into the water. Mohammed ben Hassan replied, that he had done so every day for an whole year in order to test the truth of the Arabic proverb already cited. The caliph, according to the story, was so pleased with his conduct, that he made over to him on the spot five villages in the neighbourhood of Bagdad.

It must be borne in mind that bread in the East is generally made in the form of thin cakes, which, if cast into the water, would remain for a considerable time on

---

[1] In his *Précis de l'Ecclésiaste en vers*, Voltaire paraphrases:
> Repandez vos bienfaits avec magnificence,
> Même aux moins vertueux ne les refusez pas.
> Ne vous informez pas de leur reconnoissance ;
> Il est grand, il est beau de faire des ingrats.

the surface and be easily carried along by the current of the stream.

The second verse is best explained in the same way as an exhortation to the practice of a benevolence towards others that does not stop at any precise limits, but is willing to exceed "the seven times" which might satisfy the mere legalist (Matt. xviii. 21). Nothing is more opposed to the spirit of the passage than the objection made by Preston, who considers such an exhortation inconsistent with the large-hearted liberality recommended in the previous verse. On seven and eight as indicative of a large but indefinite number see Micah v. 4. Compare the expression in Job v. 19: "He shall deliver thee from six troubles, yea, in seven there shall no evil touch thee."

The advantage of beneficence, even considered purely from an utilitarian point of view, is glanced at in the close of the verse. In times of evil and calamity the kind and the good often escape when others find no place of refuge. "Peradventure for the good man some one would even dare to die" (Rom. v. 7). Many misfortunes occur which fall upon the most deserving as well as upon the most worthless of mankind. Man knows not when he may need the help of his fellow; and it is well to act kindly and liberally in the day of prosperity.[1] True philanthropy is not, indeed, based on a calculation of chances. But, though there are higher motives to impel men to do good unto others, the lower motives cannot be altogether left out of consideration. "St.

---

[1] Compare our Lord's direction to the rich tax-gatherers or publicans who, touched by His acts of grace and words of kindness, avowed themselves His disciples, "make to yourselves friends by means of the mammon of unrighteousness (*i.e.* money often gained by and spent in unrighteousness); that, when it shall fail, they may receive you into the eternal tabernacles" (Luke xvi. 9), that is, spend your riches in doing good in this world, seek to make friends of the poor and the maimed, the lame and the blind, by doing acts of kindness, and distributing to their necessities (Luke xiv. 12–14), that they may welcome you when you shall enter the mansions of the blessed.

Paul," writes Cox, "urges us to help a brother who has fallen before temptation (Gal. vi. 1) on the express ground that we ourselves may need similar help some day: and *he* was not in the habit of appealing to mean and base motives." Self-love is implanted in man's nature, and men who affect to despise such a motive are often themselves, with all their professed loftiness of aim, actuated by no higher objects than those of pleasure, fame, or advancement. When a country is visited by some great calamity, the rich and the great are often the first to suffer. It is wise, therefore, for those in prosperity to remember that they may themsevles taste the bitterness of adversity.

If this be the meaning of verses 1 and 2, it will be seen that there is a close connexion between these thoughts and that brought under notice in verse 3, where Koheleth reminds his readers of the uniformity of the laws of nature. The good and bad alike are exposed to the action of these laws. If the clouds are full of heavy showers, these showers must discharge themselves in due course upon the earth; and if a tree falls in the north or the south, in the place where the tree falls there it will lie.

The last remark proves that the uniformity of natural law was the thought uppermost in the writer's mind. The future depends on laws beyond the control of man, and a prudent individual ought to be prepared for all contingencies. Knobel imagines that the first clause refers to the refreshing showers which come from the clouds when they are full of rain, and considers that the writer exhorts those who are rich in this world's good to be equally ready to communicate out of their abundance to those who are in need. But the second clause shows that this is not here the meaning of the writer; for it will scarcely bear the interpretation put upon it by Knobel, that no generous action is performed without some benefit resulting to the doer, since the tree is always found in the place where it falls, and can be utilised for the good of the owner. Bridges explains the passage as teaching that "there is good security for the return of well-principled benevolence." But he suggests at the close of his note that "the accommodation of Solomon's figure" in this passage brings vividly the truth before one's eyes that death may soon strike and then "our state is unchangeably fixed for eternity; where the tree falleth there shall it be. Death changes, purifies nothing." This is a glaring example of a meaning assigned to a text which the commentator did not feel himself at liberty to reject, but well knew it never was intended to bear. Bullock is perfectly correct when he says that "there is nothing in the text to indicate that the common application of the image of the fallen tree to the state of departed souls (see St. Bernard, *Sermones de Diversis*, lxxxv.) was in the mind of the inspired writer." In the interests of evangelical truth one must protest strongly against all such popular misinterpretations of Scripture.

The wise man, while he must not be unmindful of dangers ahead, but prudently seek to provide against them, ought not be too anxious about the future. There is, as Lord Bacon observes, no greater impediment to action than an overcautious observance of times and seasons. Such calculations often defeat their own purpose. The man who puts off the sowing of his fields from day to day, through fear of the wind or the rain, will at last lose his harvest. There is no absolute certainty in human affairs.[1] Opportunities, as Bacon notes, are as often made as found. A man "must have faith and courage to run some risk; the conditions of success cannot be reckoned on beforehand; the future belongs to God, the all-conditioning" (*Delitzsch*).

The latter is the idea presented in the next verse (verse 5).

---

[1] "Probability," as Bishop Butler has well remarked in his work on *The Analogy of Religion*, "is the very guide of life."

"As man knows not what is the way of the wind," the ways and working of which are concealed from mortal knowledge, as is also the way in which "the bones come into being in the womb of her who is with child, even so man cannot understand the work of God who maketh all." The context shows that it is not the "*spirit*" which Koheleth here speaks of, as our Auth. Version, following the Targum, has translated the word. The wind is mentioned in the preceding verse, and the writer speaks of it in chap. i. 6, and in viii. 8. Man knows not the way of the wind (John iii. 8), because he has not the control over it, and man only knows that which he governs (*Delitzsch*). The secrets of the wind are as profound as are those of embryology, the latter being always regarded as some of the deep things of nature which cannot be searched out to perfection. If such secrets exist in the works of nature, the acts of the God of nature must necessarily be inscrutable. He overrules the future as well as the past. "The growth of the child in the workshop of the mother's womb is compared to the growth of the future in the bosom of the present, out of which it will be born (Prov. xxvii. 1, comp. Zeph. ii. 2)"—*Delitzsch*.

Since, therefore, the future rests in the power of One who arranges all things, but who does not act arbitrarily, and since a finite being cannot unravel the secrets of the Infinite, man should act faithfully, and perform energetically his appointed task. "Whatsoever thy hand findeth to do, do it with all thy might" (chap. ix. 10). This is the thought which reappears here. Man should sow his seed in the morning, and continue his work till evening (Ps. civ. 23). Agriculture is used as a synonyme for work of every kind. Man's work is often spoken of as a sowing of seed; for, whether he will or nill, he is working for the future, sowing seed of one kind or another (Gal. vi. 7, 8). It was the curse pronounced upon him after his fall that in the sweat of his face he should eat bread (Gen. iii. 19). But the curse can be transformed into a blessing. Constant occupation, without too much anxiety for the future, is a blessing here on earth. Man knows not, indeed, whether his individual work shall prosper; but he knows that, as in the natural world "seedtime and harvest" do not cease (Gen. viii. 22), so men, as a general rule, do not labour in vain. The harvest they reap is usually proportionate to their exertions.

So far as we have gone in our explanation of the chapter, an intimate connexion exists between each of the verses. This is true also with respect to the verses on the exposition of which we have now to enter (chap. xi. 7 ff.).

Koheleth proceeds further to speak of the pleasures of life which lie within the grasp of men, and which they ought thankfully to enjoy, inasmuch as they come from the hand of God. The honest and earnest worker has a full right to enjoy such harmless pleasures as life affords him. "This joy of life, based upon fidelity to one's vocation, and sanctified by the fear of God, is the truest and highest enjoyment here below" (*Delitzsch*). The previous admonitions to be diligent in earthly business are closely connected with the exhortation to enjoy life. Though St. Paul may not have had man's ordinary labour in view in his remarks in Rom. xii. 11, 12, the sequence of his thoughts in that passage is very similar to that of Koheleth.

The spirit which actuated the writer was the very opposite to that of the modern Pessimist. This is shown by the remark of Koheleth : "And sweet is the light, and good it is for the eyes to behold the sun, for, though a man live many years, let him rejoice in them all, and let him remember the days of darkness, for they shall be many. All that cometh is vanity."

The light here commended as sweet is the light of the upper world, the light of life (comp. Ps. lvi. 14, A. V. verse

13; Job. xxxiii. 30), the glorious light of the sun. The enjoyment of life is confined to no special season of human existence, though it may be less at one season than at another. As long as the eyes can drink in the light of day, it is good for them to behold the glory of the sun. Days of evil may come; clouds may, during long hours of sorrow, obscure the glory of the sun; but even if a man live many days he should endeavour to rejoice in them all; and all the more so, if a long night of darkness awaits him ultimately at the close of his earthly career. By the days of darkness, which Koheleth in chap. xi. 8 says "shall be many," he does not mean the days of sorrow in this life, or even the days of old age. To explain the passage in such a way would be to make it self-contradictory, for Koheleth asserts that a man ought to rejoice all the days of his life. Nor would he be justified in asserting that the days of darkness in every man's case are "many," if days on this side of the grave are signified. He evidently refers to the state after death; "all that cometh," that is, whatever comes in the future after the life on earth is over, is but vanity. A long, shadowy, unsubstantial existence was all that, with his limited knowledge, Koheleth saw before man. The darkness which shrouded the future state had not then been illumined by the light which now shines brightly from the sepulchre of the Redeemer, from whose door the stone was rolled away by a mighty angel (Matt. xxviii. 2). Job similarly describes the land beyond the grave as it appeared in his eyes, as "a land of darkness and of the shadow of death, a land of darkness, as darkness itself, and of the shadow of death, without any order, and where the light is as darkness" (Job x. 21, 22).[1]

Inasmuch as a long dark night, a life which seemed to be only a shadow of life, appeared to Koheleth to be the future which awaits all men, he urges on young men the wisdom of

[1] See our remarks in chap. vii. p. 197 ff.

taking all the legitimate enjoyment possible in early years, and of plucking those flowers of pleasure which grow alongside the path of life. Hence the section begins with the words :

> Rejoice, young man, in thy youth,
> And let thy heart cheer thee in the days of thy youth,
> And walk in the ways of thy heart,
> And according to (lit. *in*) the sight of thine eyes,
> But know, that for all these God shall bring thee into the judgment.

A merry heart maketh a cheerful countenance (Prov. xv. 13); and the heart of the young man should be full of joy in the days of youth. If he cannot enjoy himself in early days of health and vigour, it is unlikely, should his time be prolonged upon the earth, that he will be able to rejoice in all the days of his mortal life, which Koheleth, in the verse immediately preceding, affirms to be a bounden duty of man. The life which begins in a self-created gloom will probably be dark and gloomy up to its close. If a man does not seek to cultivate a cheerful spirit while young, he will be still more morose and discontented in advancing years.

The language of Koheleth in this passage has been often explained as ironical. But this idea does not suit the context. His advice is meant seriously. Koheleth was far from recommending the young man, either in jest or in earnest, to make provision for the flesh to fulfil the lusts thereof (Rom. xiii. 14). Men were forbidden in the Law of Moses to follow after the inclination of their heart and their eyes (Num. xv. 39). The opposition between the recommendation of Koheleth and the direction of the Lawgiver is, indeed, more apparent than real. What is signified by the ways of the heart in the two passages is by no means identical. Koheleth was not an ascetic, and disapproved of all attempts to drive men into courses contrary to nature. But he was very far from being a sensualist. While the young are bidden to enjoy the morning of life, they are at the same time admonished in all things to have the fear of God before their eyes.

It is interesting to note that the LXX. (if, as is probable, the original text of that version be faithfully represented by the Vatican Codex) have ventured to amend the recommendation of Koheleth into: "and walk blameless in the ways of thy heart and not after the sight of thine eyes." The Arabic version has followed the Vatican text. But the negative μή is wanting in the Cod. Alex. and other MSS.[1] The Targum exhibits the same disposition to explain away the meaning of the writer, paraphrasing the text: "walk humbly (lit. in humility) with the ways of thy heart, and be cautious (prudent) in the seeing of thine eyes, and look not on evil."[2]

All such emendations are, however, unnecessary. For Koheleth adds: "and know thou that for all these things God will bring thee into the judgment." Hitzig imagines the writer to refer to the fact that the sins of youth are often punished by Providence by sickness and premature old age. And Winzer and Knobel cite in defence of the idea that the writer refers to a judgment in this present life, such passages as chap. iii. 17: "I said in my heart, God shall judge the righteous and the ungodly, for there is a time there for every purpose and for every work." Compare also chaps. ii. 26; vii. 17, 18, 26.[3] But something further seems to be intended.

---

[1] Cod. B (the Vatican) omits after ἐν ὁδοῖς the words καρδίας σου. A (the Alex. MS.), C (the Codex Ephraemi Rescriptus), and S² (the secondhand of the Cod. Sinaiticus), along with the Complutensian, omit μή. See Nestle, *Veteris Test. Græci Codices Vat. et Sin. cum Textu Recepto Coll.* (Lipsiæ: F. A. Brockhaus, 1880).

[2] The LXX. read καὶ περιπάτει ἐν ὁδοῖς καρδίας σου ἄμωμος, καὶ μὴ ἐν ὁράσει ὀφθαλμῶν σου. The Targum is וַאֲזֵל בְּעִנְוְתָנוּתָא עִם אוֹרְחֵי לִבָּךְ וּתְהִי זְהִיר בְּחֵזְיוֹנֵי עֵינָךְ וְלָא תִסְתַּכַּל בְּבִישׁ. The Vulg., Jerome and the Syr. follow the reading of the Hebrew.

[3] Reference may also be made to chap. viii. 5, 6, although that text is not a distinct parallel. The same truth is taught in many other places of the Old Testament, as Ps. vii. 7-9; ix. 5, 20; Isa. lxvi. 16; Ezek. xxi. 30.

We do not lay stress upon the use of the article, "the judgment," because it occurs in cases where no reference is intended to the judgment in another world (as in Job ix. 32; xxii. 4). But Koheleth notices on several occasions the fact that sin is not always punished in this world (chap. viii. 14), while he affirms at the same time that God has His own time and season for everything, and will ultimately execute vengeance on transgressors. This consideration is especially urged on the attention in chap. iii. 16, 17. The thought of a judgment to come reappears, too, in the epilogue (chap. xii. 14), where at first sight the expression seems to be more general than that in the passage before us (chap. xi. 9). But, if in the latter the noun is rendered definite by the article, it is no less clearly defined in the former by the words with which it is connected. Had the writer, argues Winzer, intended to refer to a judgment after death, he would not have spoken so briefly on such a topic. But brevity is one of the peculiar characteristics of the writer, and it is noteworthy that the epilogue (whether its writer be identical or not with the author of the work) contains an equally brief though most distinct allusion to the final judgment. Although therefore it cannot be denied that the same phraseology is used in other books of the Old Testament in a general signification,[1] we are fully justified in maintaining that Koheleth refers in this passage to a final judgment after death. This is the view of the passage taken by J. D. Michaelis, Rosenmüller, and Delitzsch. Of the time and nature of this final world-judgment Koheleth, indeed, had no clear perception. His faith in God led him to affirm its truth as a moral necessity,

---

[1] Thus for instance the Psalmist prays that God would not enter into judgment with him וְאַל־תָּבוֹא בְמִשְׁפָּט אֶת־עַבְדֶּךָ (Ps. cxliii. 2). And Job complains (chap. xiv. 3) that "Thou bringest me into judgment with Thee" וְאֹתִי תָבִיא בְמִשְׁפָּט עִמָּךְ. So in Job. ix. 32. נָבוֹא יַחְדָּו בַּמִּשְׁפָּט, "let us enter together into the judgment," and in chap. xxii. 4. יָבוֹא עִמְּךָ בַּמִּשְׁפָּט, "will He enter with thee into the judgment?"

though he did not possess the clearer light of Messianic days.

Koheleth's advice to the young is based upon the fact that both "youth and manhood are vanity." The opportunities for enjoying life presented in youth are fleeting, and will soon be past. Hence the joys peculiar to that season must be embraced then or never. Koheleth's advice is summed up under three heads—"banish moroseness from thy heart," "remove evil from thy flesh," and "remember thy Creator in the days of thy youth."

The first recommendation is rendered by the ancient versions, and in the margin of the A.V., by "put away anger from thy heart."[1] The translation in the text of the Authorised Version is much to be preferred: "put away sorrow from thy heart." But the word is even better rendered in this place by *moroseness* or *peevishness*, which is often the outcome of a mind discontented, and therefore angry, on account of the conditions of life in which its lot has been fixed by an overruling Providence. For the opposite to cheerfulness and joyousness is that which is meant by the writer. The bane of youth is a certain peevishness which, when no real sorrows or troubles are present, often embitters the heart and oppresses the individual by evils of its own creating. The state of the heart has much to do with the health of the body. For, where peevishness and moroseness of disposition obtain the mastery, the individual becomes often careless as to his bodily health. Life becomes to a great degree irksome, and

---

[1] This "anger" has been explained by some to refer to the wrath of God, by others to that excited in the breast of youth when called away from pleasure and reminded of the fear of God. Bishop Wordsworth has ventured to translate the word (בַּעַס) by *provocation*, which sense, that of *incitement to anger*, it bears in some passages (1 Kings xv. 30; xxi. 22; 2 Kings xxiii. 26, etc.) He explains the passage to mean: "take heed lest thou provoke God by the thoughts of thy heart." But the Bishop is unmindful of the fact that when the word is used in such a signification its meaning is defined by the words with which it is united, and that the word has not that meaning when used absolutely, as in this passage.

the youth speaks and acts as if it were a matter of indifference when his earthly existence may terminate.

The second admonition " remove evil from thy flesh " refers rather to physical than to moral evil. The days of evil (in chap. xii. 1) are days of sorrow and calamity, which our Lord speaks of as an evil (ἡ κακία), " sufficient unto the day is the evil thereof " (Matt. vi. 34). The ancient versions (such as the LXX., Vulg. and Jerome, Targ. and Syr.) agree in explaining the evil alluded to in the passage to be "*wickedness.*" But this does not harmonise with the expression "the evil days," which immediately follows (chap. xii. 1). But, if it be borne in mind that Koheleth often speaks of sorrow and trouble as directly caused by sin, it is highly probable that he includes under the expression those sins common to youth which the Apostle characterises as "sins against the body " (1 Cor. vi. 8).

If Koheleth in his advice to young men urges the importance of cheerfulness of mind, and of the proper care of the body, he is still more emphatic in pressing upon them the importance of piety as a guide in the days of youth and a solace in "evil days."[1] For he adds : "and remember thy Creator in the days of thy youth." The plural in the original Hebrew is the plural of excellence.[2] The older Christian interpreters sought to explain all such expressions as having reference to the plurality of persons in the Godhead, and Bishop Wordsworth has recently adopted that view. It cannot, however, be sustained by a critic. Some of the older critics ventured to delete the plural י, and on the authority

---

[1] So Job xxxv. 10, אַיֵּה אֱלוֹהַּ עֹשָׂי, "*where is God my maker,*" and in Isaiah liv. 5 כִּי בֹעֲלַיִךְ עֹשַׂיִךְ יְהוָה צְבָאוֹת שְׁמוֹ, "*for thy husband is thy maker, Jahaveh (the God) of hosts is His name ;*" also Ps. cxlix. 2. Comp. Josh. xxiv. 19.

[2] It might be somewhat fanciful to trace in this threefold admonition, in which directions are given with respect to the mental, bodily, and spiritual requirements of youth, any distinct intention to set forth the doctrine of the tripartite nature of man.

of a few MSS. to read the word in the singular. But the reading of the Masoretic text is unquestionably correct.[1]

The Midrash Koheleth states on the authority of R. Joshua ben Levi that the following saying in the Treatise Aboth (iii. 1) was founded on this text: "Consider three things and thou wilt not come into the hands of transgression, know from whence thou comest; and whither thou art going; and before whom thou art to give account and reckoning." "Remember בְּאֵרְךָ, *thy source*, בּוֹרְךָ, *thy grave*, בֹּרַאֲךָ, *thy Creator*." This Talmudic exposition was, as Dr. C. Taylor has well noted, only designed as a mnemonic.[2] But the hint given has been eagerly caught at by Graetz, who arbitrarily asserts that the form of the word in the accepted Hebrew text is "abstruse," and maintains that the wife of youth is metaphorically referred to under the term בּוֹר or בְּאֵר.[3]

"The days of evil" described by Koheleth in these and the following verses are the days of old age. He refers to the bodily decrepitude which usually marks the closing scenes of a long life. There is, however, much difference of opinion as to whether the writer relates literal facts, or whether the verses are an allegorical representation of the decay in old age of the various parts of the human frame. We do not consider the anatomical interpretation satisfactory. But there are also difficulties in the way of regarding this last strain of Koheleth—a strain which exhibits many of the characteristics of real poetry—as a formal "dirge of death."

---

[1] It is incorrect to refer to the ancient versions in a case like this as affording evidence in favour of the singular reading. For they could not do otherwise than render the word in the singular, whatever reading they might have had before them. The suggestion of Schmidt and Nachtigal that בוראים might be taken as an abstract noun in the sense of *existence*, as if the writer bid the young man rejoice in his existence, is untenable; as is also the alternative suggestion of the former critic that the word is to be connected with the cognate root in Arabic, and explained to signify the years of health and vigour.

[2] See C. Taylor, *Sayings of the Jewish Fathers*, p. 57. The saying is also cited in the Jerus. Talmud, Sotah ii. 2, and elsewhere.

[3] So also A. Geiger, *Urschrift u. Uebersetzungen der Bibel*, p. 405.

It seems to us to speak of man's progress to the tomb, through days of gloom and trial, through days of darkness and bitterness, at a season even when all nature around is blithe and gay. Death itself, though present throughout to the mind of the writer, and contemplated by him as the last and greatest "evil," is not distinctly mentioned until near the close of his verses. In every day of earthly trial man's thoughts naturally turn towards his grave. Death, like a "winged Pegasus," as a quaint writer expresses it, "posts and speeds after men, easily gives them law, fetches them up again, gallops and swallows the ground he goes (over), sets out after every man as soon as he comes into the world, and plays with him, as the cat with the mouse, as the greyhound with the badger; sometimes he follows fair and afar off, lingers aloof, and out of sight; anon he spurs after, and by and by is at the heels in some sickness, and then, it may be, gives us some breath again, but in the end overtakes us, and is upon us with a jerk, as the snare over the fish or the fowl."[1]

In discussing the sense of the closing passage of this remarkable book, it is necessary to review briefly, in detail, the various conflicting interpretations, proposed by eminent scholars for each verse, ere we present a connected picture of our own views.

Koheleth thus commences his description of "the evil days" and of the years in which all joy is gone and man is forced to exclaim: "I have no pleasure." He bids the young to remember their Creator—

> Ere the sun is darkened, and the light; and the moon and the stars,
> And the clouds return after the heavy shower (הַגֶּשֶׁם);
> In the day that the keepers of the house tremble,
> And the men of power bend themselves,
> And the grinding women cease because they are few,
> And the women that look-out through the lattices are darkened.

---

[1] Samuel Ward's *Life of Faith in Death*, in Ward's Sermons and Treatises at the end of the 3rd vol. of *Thomas Adam's Works* (J. Nichol, 1862).

The oldest interpreters consider this and the following verses to be an allegorical description of old age. But, while they thus agree in the general outline of their exposition, they manifest in the details the utmost difference of opinion.[1]

Modern commentators have generally, though not always, avoided the extravagancies of the earlier Jewish interpreters. Knobel draws attention to the fact that the darkening of the sun and the moon is descriptive of a change of days of joy into days of mourning. He quotes such passages as Job xxx. 26: "For I looked for good, and there came evil, and I waited for light and there came darkness." Compare also Job xxix. 2, 3; and the language of Isaiah (xiii. 10, 11) in speaking of the downfall of Babylon; "For the stars of heaven and the constellations thereof shall not give their light. The sun shall be darkened in his going forth, and the moon shall not cause her light to shine." Similar is the language of the prophet Ezekiel when predicting the overthrow of Egypt: "And when I put thee out, I will cover the heaven and make the stars thereof dark, I will cover the sun with a cloud and the moon shall not give her light. All the bright lights of heaven will I make dark over thee, and set darkness upon thy land, saith the Lord Jahaveh" (Ezek. xxxii. 7, 8). And Joel, in writing of the coming of the terrible locusts, describes the day as "a day of darkness and of gloominess, a day of clouds and of thick darkness, as the

---

[1] Thus the Talmud (*Shabb.* 151 *b* and 152 *a*) interprets the sun and light to signify the forehead and the nose, the moon to be the soul, and the stars to be the cheeks;—while the Midrash on Koheleth explains the sun and light to be the countenance and the nose, the moon to be the forehead (these latter are transposed in the Midrash Vayikra), while the stars are explained to be the corners of the cheeks which fall in in old age. According to the Targum the sun and light are the brightness of the countenance and the light of the eyes, the moon and stars are the comeliness of the cheeks and the apples of the eyes. The Talmud and Midrash agree in explaining the last clause with the Targum—" thy eyelids drop down tears like clouds after rain." Other interpretations, like those of Wedel (in Schleuchzer, *Physica Sacra*, tom. iv.) and Witsius, etc., which explain the clouds to mean severe attacks of catarrh, need only be alluded to here.

The seasons according to the Hebrews.

morning spread upon the mountains . . . Before their face the people shall be much pained; all faces shall gather blackness. The earth shall quake before them; the heavens shall tremble: the sun and the moon shall be dark, and the stars shall withdraw their shining." [1]

Vaihinger draws attention to the fact, that, while in the West four seasons of the year are generally spoken of, the Hebrews usually spoke only of two, summer and winter. They were also wont to talk of youth and age as contrasted, understanding under the designation of "youths" persons below forty years of age, and under the designation of "old men" persons sometimes not much over fifty. According to this expositor, the writer is contrasting the winter of man's existence with the morning of life referred to in chap. xi. 10. His similes are drawn from the gloomy winter of Palestine, when heavy storms of rain succeed one another in rapid succession, and darken the whole face of nature. Under such imagery Koheleth portrays the time when the heavy sorrows and storms of life set in, and the joy of existence is obscured by its gloomy earnestness.

Hitzig, Ewald and Zöckler take substantially the same view. Delitzsch considers the passage as allegorical throughout. He explains the sun to mean the *spirit* of man (רוּחַ or נְשָׁמָה), and calls attention to the fact that רוּחַ, *the spirit*, like שֶׁמֶשׁ, *the sun*, is both masculine and feminine. The spirit of man, according to the Book of Proverbs (Prov. xx. 27), is the candle of Jahaveh, which with its light of self-examination and self-knowledge pierces through the innermost parts of our nature. He compares our Lord's description of the spirit,—" the light that is in thee" (τὸ φῶς τὸ ἐν σοί, Matt. vi. 23). The "light" is accordingly explained to be the activity of the spirit in its unweakened intensity, sharp com-

---

[1] Compare also Amos viii. 9, 10, and by way of contrast, Job xi. 17; Isaiah xxx. 26, and lx. 10.

Allegorical exposition of the lights of heaven. 243

prehension, clear thinking, true and serviceable memory. The moon on the other hand represents the *soul*. For the moon (whether termed יָרֵחַ or לְבָנָה) when contrasted with the sun is a feminine symbol.¹ The animal soul by means of which the spirit becomes the principle of the bodily life (Gen. ii. 7) when viewed in relation to the spirit is, according to Delitzsch, "the weaker vessel." Hence the spirit cheers the soul with the words, "why art thou cast down, O my soul (נַפְשִׁי)? (Ps. xlii. 6). As Koheleth was acquainted with the seven planetary gods of the Babylonian-Assyrian astrological system, namely, the sun, moon, and the five planets, Delitzsch thinks it probable that the writer considered the five stars to be allegorical of the five senses by which the soul has cognizance of the outer world. The clouds which return after the rain are explained by Delitzsch to be those attacks of sickness and bodily weakness which in old age confuse thought, obscure self-consciousness, and which, when they have once seized hold of the frame, though they may for a time cease, return again, and hinder the aged one from enjoying perfect health.

The third verse admits of easy explanation on the lines of the allegorical interpretation. The watchers of the house are, according to this view, the ribs and the loins, or the knees; "the men of power" the bones, and those that look out at the windows, the eyes. The Midrash explains the watchers to be the ribs, "the men of power" the arms, and the grinding women the organs of digestion,² while the teeth are regarded as the subject of the verb "are few." The Targum

---

¹ Compare Gen. xxxvii. 9, ff, where the sun in the dream of Joseph symbolizes the patriarch Jacob, and the moon Leah.

² The Midrash Koheleth has הממס, which, though the word possibly may have a Semitic origin (vid. Levy's *Neuheb. W. B.*), is probably derived from the Latin *omasum*, the *gut*, or *intestines*, which in Midrash Lev. rab. sec. 4, is said to serve to grind up the food. The Midrash divides the two clauses of the last sentence of verse 3, "the grinding maids cease because they are few," into "the grinding maids stand still, that is the digestive organs, and are few, that is, the teeth."

more naturally considers the watchers to be the aged knees which tremble, the men of power the arms, the grinders the teeth. Both agree in explaining the lookers out at the windows to be the eyes.

Knobel, Ewald and Delitzsch consider the body of man to be here pourtrayed as a building threatened from within with impending ruin. (Compare Job iv. 19, and the Apostle's language in 2 Cor. v. 1, etc.) They explain the keepers or watchers of the house to be the hands and arms; and the verb "tremble" might very suitably be used in reference to the limbs of the old and palsied man. They further interpret "the men of power" to be the feet and legs, in accordance with the language of the Psalmist (Ps. cxlvii. 10, compare Cant. x. 15); and the expression "bend themselves" harmonizes well with this explanation.

Nor can it be denied that the expression "the grinding maids cease," might naturally mean that the teeth can no longer perform their ordinary work.[1] Female slaves in the East generally perform the duty of grinding the corn for the daily consumption of the family.

The clause may be rendered "the grinding women cease because they are few," which is the translation of all the ancient versions (except the Targum), and thus the statement might refer to the loss of teeth in old age. The verb has also been rendered transitively, as Dr. C. Taylor translates it: "the grinding maids cease when they have wrought a little," that is, according to his idea, they have little to do because, at the approach of death, entertainments are no longer given.[2]

---

[1] The molar teeth are termed in Arabic and Syriac, as by us, *the grinders*, and the word for teeth, though masculine in the ancient Hebrew is, as Delitzsch observes, feminine in the later or Mishnaic. He notes that the Greeks also used the expression μύλαι or μύλοι for the teeth, and compares the translation of the LXX. of Psalm lvii. 7, τὰς μύλας τῶν λεόντων.

[2] The Targum renders loosely: "and the teeth of thy mouth are destroyed until they cannot chew food." The piel מעטו may be intransitive, according to

The lookers-out at the windows.

"Those that look out at the windows" might without violence be interpreted of the organs of sight, whose windows are the eyelids with their accompanying eye-lashes, behind which the eyes are partly concealed. In any description of old age some reference would certainly be expected to be made to the common infirmity of loss of sight.

But serious difficulties beset the allegorical interpretation in the explanation of the fourth and following verses. We may here render the fourth verse:—

> And doors are shut in the street
> When the sound of the mill is low (*or* ceases);
> And one rises at the voice of the bird,
> And all the daughters of song are humbled.

The Targum explains the first line of the old man being no longer able to go out into the street.[1] Some, as Knobel, have explained it of the old man's silence. Delitzsch lays stress on the fact that the word for *doors* is dual, and, there-

---

the analogy of קָהָה, *to become blunt*, in chap. x. 10. Taylor, however, in his critical notes on Aboth iv. (*Sayings of the Jewish Fathers*, p. 16), maintains that the constant usage of the Mishna is in favour of the transitive sense of the verb in question. In Aboth iv. 14, it is contrasted with בטל : "Rabbi Meir used to say, have little business (וֶהֱוֵי מְמַעֵט בְּעֵסֶק), and be busy in the Thorah (in reading and studying it) . . . and if thou ceasest from (studying) the Thorah (וְאִם בָּטַלְתָּ מִן הַתּוֹרָה), thou wilt have idlers many against thee," or, perhaps, as Levy, *Neuheb. W. B.*, translates the clause, "many disturbing things will set themselves against thee." But the verb can scarcely be regarded as a transitive in the passage in question; for the כִּי, which is "*for*," "*because*," not "*where*," and the perfect tense seem to require the intransitive sense. In Strack's edition of the *Sprüche der Väter*, the passage is Aboth iv. 10. Strack has retained the numeration found in the editions of the Mishna. A different numeration of the sections is to be found in the editions of the Jewish Prayer Book (סִדּוּר). Dr. C. Taylor follows in his arrangement the Cambridge Manuscript.

[1] The ancient Jewish interpreters in the Talmud and Midrash explain the doors to be the openings in the human body for the purposes of excretion, which are closed in old age when the teeth can no longer masticate, or the stomach digest, the food. In the morning prayer of the Jews there is a thanksgiving as follows: "Blessed be thou, Lord our God, King of the world, who hast wisely formed man and created in him many openings and orifices (וּבָרָא בוֹ נְקָבִים נְקָבִים חֲלוּלִים חֲלוּלִים)." But a poet would scarcely introduce such representations into his verses.

fore, points to a pair of similarly fashioned and related members of the body. He also insists on the point that the expression "in the street," or "towards the street," indicates that the members referred to are such as are generally exposed to view, and not those which decency requires to be screened from ordinary gaze. Hence he follows here in the main Jerome's interpretation. The jaws of the leviathan are termed "the doors of his face" (Job xli. 6, A.V. xli. 14), and the Psalmist prays that God will " keep the door " of his lips (Ps. cxli. 3). A similar phrase, but not identical, is used by Micah (chap. vii. 5). Hence Herzfeld and Delitzsch consider the lips or jaws to be compared to a double-leaved door, and the passage to refer to the lips closing together in old age in consequence of the loss of the teeth, which while they remain keep the jaws and lips apart. Zöckler takes the same view; but his American editor Tayler Lewis remarks that the dual is just as applicable to the eyes and the ears as to the lips. The latter considers the interpretation of Hengstenberg more in accordance with the context. Hengstenberg explains it of the ear, which in old age is closed to external sounds, and Tayler Lewis of all the various senses being closed to ordinary impressions, the senses being the avenues to the outer world.

Delitzsch translates "the doors are shut towards the street" or "on the street side," referring the clause, as already noted, to the closing together of the jaws from loss of teeth. Ewald and Vaihinger also refer it to the closing of the mouth; but the former considers the allusion to be to the shutting of the mouth against food, while the latter thinks that the reference is to the silence of the aged man.

Ewald, Delitzsch and others interpret the sound of the mill becoming low as signifying that, when the old man masticates his food, the jaws of the toothless mouth being closed, the dull sound of munching is all that can be heard. Hitzig's objection to this interpretation seems valid, namely, that no great noise is usually made in chewing, and such a trifle is unworthy of notice by a poet. Hitzig himself explains the passage of the weakness of the voice in age. But, if the teeth are interpreted to be the grinding maids, the mouth must (to be consistent) represent the mill; and, if it be unpoetical to regard the clause as referring to the dull munching noise made by the old man in masticating his food, this fact discredits the allegorical interpretation.[1]

According to our view, the clause "when the sound of the mill is low" is best regarded as a note of time.[2] The words that follow, translated in our Authorised Version, "and he shall rise up at the voice of the bird," have been variously rendered and expounded. The true reading of the Hebrew text is the imperfect jussive, and not the imperfect indicative, as printed in the ordinary Hebrew Bibles.[3] The importance of this fact will be noticed presently.

The Talmud, Midrash and Targum render the clause, as our A.V., "and he shall rise up at the voice of the bird," or, as St. Jerome explains it, at cock-crowing.[4] The objection urged by Ginsburg against this interpretation is not for-

[1] It is curious to notice that Prof. Tayler Lewis asserts that the grinding maids undoubtedly represent the teeth, and yet maintains that the grinding itself, or "the mill is not so much metaphorical as illustrative," and is to be taken in its primary sense as showing the old man's dulness of hearing, by whom "the most familiar and household sounds, such as that of the grinding mill, are faintly distinguished."

[2] The word שְׁפַל in this sentence has been regarded by all the ancient versions (except that of Symmachus) as a noun. It is, however, manifestly the infinitive construct. The form in a is rare, though it occurs in a few verbs which have a in the imperfect, or whose second radical is a guttural. See Gesenius-Kautzsch, § 45, 1 a; Böttcher, Lehrb. § 987, 5; König, Lehrg. § 21, 4; Stade, § 619 a. The LXX. have erroneously regarded הטחנה as a participle.

[3] That is, וְיָקוּם, and not וְיָקוּם, vid. crit. comm. See Ges.-Kautzsch § 72, rem. 4; König, Lehrgeb., p. 442. The Masora magna notes that the word occurs twice, once with cholem (milel), and once with a short vowel, kametz-chatuph (milra). See Ochla-ve-Ochla, no. 5; Levita's Massoreth ha-Massoreth, p. 208 ed. Ginsburg.

[4] The rendering of the Targum is: "and thou shalt awake from thy sleep at the sound of a bird, as at thieves that go about during the night." The last clause is significant as showing an attempt to combine two opposing interpreta-

midable, namely, "that, though aged people may easily be awakened by a slight noise, yet they do not rise up at the sound of a bird." For the phrase may simply mean that the old man's sleep is broken by the first chirping of the birds in the early morning.

If, however, the clause that follows be supposed to refer to deafness as a characteristic of old age, which prevents the aged man from taking pleasure any longer in female singers, there is an apparent incongruity. For the old man would be represented in one clause as having his slumbers broken by the chirping of the birds, and in the next as too deaf to hear the songs of women. There is no difficulty in explaining the first clause of the singing of birds in the early morning as a note of time, the idea of the passage being that one wakes early in the morning when the birds begin to sing.

Hitzig, Ewald and Zöckler consider the allusion in the passage to be to the weak voice of the aged man. The verb is regarded by them as impersonal, inasmuch as no previous mention is made of the voice. They accordingly translate: "and it seems (lit. riseth) like the voice of a sparrow," or, as Kleinert, "and when it raises itself it is as the chirping of a bird,"[1] understanding the allusion to be to the piping, whispering voice of old age, "his big manly voice, Turning again towards childish treble."[2] Ewald refers in illustration of the idea to Isaiah xxix. 4, where Cheyne translates: "thy speech shall be subdued (coming) from the dust, and thy voice shall be as that of a ghost from the ground, and from the dust thy speech shall come chirpingly."[3] In support of the

tions. Jerome's words are: "porro consurgere cum ad vocem volucris ostendit, quod frigescente jam sanguine et humore siccato, quibus materiis sopor alitur, ad levem sonitum evigilet, noctisque medio, quum gallus cecinerit, festinus exsurgat."

[1] Ginsburg's statement that the rendering of Ewald, Hitzig, and others, "the noise of the mill rises to the voice of a sparrow" is at least open to misconception.

[2] Shakespeare, *As you like it*, Act ii. 7.

[3] On the supposed chirping and muttering of ghosts, see Cheyne' on Isaiah viii. 19.

rendering of the phrase used in the original as signifying *to pass from one state to another*, Hitzig refers to Zeph. iii. 8; I Sam. xxii. 13; Micah ii. 8. But these references are unsatisfactory.[1] Delitzsch observes that, whenever the words "at the voice" or "at the cry" (לְקוֹל) are connected with a verb denoting motion, whether bodily or mental, the exciting cause of the movement is referred to. Thus the Israelites are represented as fleeing at the cry (לְקֹלָם) of those who were swallowed up in the earthquake (Num. xvi. 34). The coasts, suburbs, or fleets belonging to Tyre (whatever be the meaning of מִגְרָשׁוֹת), are represented by Ezekiel (chap. xxvii. 28) as trembling at the sound of the cry (לְקוֹל זַעֲקַת) of the Tyrian pilots; while Job speaks of the children who rejoice at the sound (לְקוֹל) of the pipe (Job xxi. 12). See also Habb. iii. 16.

According to Umbreit, Koheleth depicts in these verses the advance of death under the imagery of an approaching storm, which darkens the heavens, startles even men of power, and puts a stop to all work. He translates the clause in question, "and the bird raises its voice to a shriek." Ginsburg adopts this view, and, regarding the swallow as the bird referred to, renders "and the swallow shall rise to shriek," in allusion to the cries of that bird before a storm. But this is opposed to the Hebrew accentuation.[2] The use of the jussive is also against this rendering. For that form indicates that the clause is to be viewed as conditional, and connected either with the "in the day when" of verse 3, or the "before that," or "ere," which is twice repeated in the previous verses.

---

[1] For in the latter two passages the ordinary signification of *rising up* is the true one; as also in Zeph. iii. 8, where it is necessary, in order to extract the sense given to the passage by Hitzig (namely, "unto the day, when I come forward as witness"), to abandon the traditional vocalization of the Hebrew text, and on the authority of the LXX. and Syr. to read לְעֵד instead of לָעַד. Similarly the LXX., Targ. and Syr., read in Isaiah xxx. 8 לְעֵד in place of לָעַד.

[2] According to which קוֹל is the construct governing הַצִּפּוֹר in the genitive.

250   *The expositions of "the daughters of song."*

The phrase does, indeed, sometimes mean to rise up for the purpose of performing an action.[1] But, had the writer intended to say "the swallow shall rise to shriek" (*Ginsburg*), or "the bird of evil omen (the owl or raven) raises his dirge," (*Taylor*), he would have used a different construction.[2]

The Talmud explains the last clause in the verse, "and all the daughters of song shall be brought low," to mean that music and songs appear to the old man like ordinary chattering, while the Targum considers the clause to refer to the man himself, "thy lips will lower themselves (וְיִתְרַפְסוּן) from singing a song." Several modern scholars have followed the rendering of the Targum, though without referring the words to the lips. Thus Hitzig understands "the daughters of song" to mean the simple songs which the old man tries to sing, but for which he finds that his voice is no longer equal; and Ewald translates the phrase "daughters of song" by "singing birds," but considers the voice to mean allegorically the old man's song, and his words[3] to be the singing birds, once loud and distinct, now feeble like the chirping of a small bird. Singing, however, is not such a common ac-

---

[1] Ginsburg refers in proof of this to Psalm lxxvi. 10, where the phrase קוּם לַמִּשְׁפָּט occurs in the sense of *to rise to judgment*, i.e. to rise in order to execute judgment. So also קוּם לַמִּלְחָמָה, *to rise up for war*, Jer. xlix. 14. But the third passage he refers to, Ps. cxxxii. 8, קוּמָה יְהוָה לִמְנוּחָתֶךָ is somewhat doubtful. The Arabic construction قَامَتْ تَنُوحُ, *she began to lament*, cited by Taylor is not *ad rem*. See W. Wright's *Arab. Gram.*, ii. § 42 rem. g. (p. 118, 2nd ed.). Taylor, however, observes justly that the idea of rising for *the purpose of speaking* is a very ordinary one, but the verb would be then used without לְקוֹל or any such equivalent. It is moreover open to serious doubt whether that noun would thus, without any qualification in the context, be used in the sense of a *shriek* or a *screech*.

[2] He would have written, as Delitzsch has observed יָקוּם הַצִּפּוֹר לָתֵת קוֹלוֹ, or at least יָקוּם הַצִּפּוֹר לָקוֹל.

[3] Ewald considers the מִלִּים, *words*, which is feminine, to be pointed to by the בְּנוֹת.

That expression must refer to singing women. 251

complishment as to justify a poet speaking of the loss of voice as one of the striking features of old age.

Ginsburg, who adopts the view of Umbreit as to the general meaning of the passage, explains with Ewald the "daughters of song" to be "singing birds," although he takes the phrase literally. But, as Taylor observes, "the word שִׁיר is only used of articulate song." It can be applied to a "song" such as those of David, but not to the song of a bird. The daughters of song are evidently "singing women," like those of whom Barzillai spoke when he said that he was unable by reason of his advanced age any longer to hear "the voice of singing men and singing women" (2 Sam. xix. 36).[1]

If the fourth verse has been variously interpreted, much more the fifth, which we may here render,—

> Even they are afraid of that which is high,
> And all-kinds-of-fears are in the way;
> Then the almond-tree is in bloom,
> And the locust drags-itself along,
> But unavailing is the caperberry;
> For the man is going to his eternal house,
> And the mourners go about in the street.

Delitzsch regards the explanation of the first clause given by the Talmud and Midrash as correct in the main. These Jewish authorities refer it to the dread which aged persons have of hills on the road, which are magnified by their fears

---

[1] The verb used in the passage for "are humbled," or "brought low" is יִשַּׁחוּ, from the stem שָׁחַח. This form, however, has been explained as an imperfect kal formed after the Aramaic fashion by the doubling of the first radical. So *Olshausen*, § 243 *d.*, *Ges.-Kautzsch*, § 67, rem. 3, *Stade*, § 490 *a*. But, inasmuch as an imperfect kal in *o* of the same verb, יָשֹׁח, is in use, and has a transitive force, it is better with Rödiger, Böttcher, König and others, to regard יִשַּׁח as a regular imperfect niphal. The niphal may be viewed as the regular passive of kal, the latter being used in the sense of being *bowed down with sorrow*; or it may be explained after the analogy of Isaiah xxix. 4, where the subdued sound of the voice is signified. The majority of the ancient versions understand it in the sense of "being humbled." So the LXX., Syr. and Aquila; but the Vulg. and Jerome interpret it in the sense of being *hushed* into silence (*obsurdescent, obmutescent*). Umbreit and Elster explain it as referring to the birds who lower themselves in the air, fly low, and flutter about uneasily in dread of the coming storm.

into veritable mountains, so that every journey appears formidable. The Midrash observes that, if an old man is asked to a feast, the first question he asks is, how many steps will he have to mount to get to the banqueting room? Such an explanation scarcely suits the dignity of the poem. Delitzsch understands the passage to mean that the old man is afraid of any hill, for his breath fails him and his legs are unequal to the strain.

A similar view is taken by the ancient versions, and by Ewald in his later editions.[1] Umbreit, Elster, and Ginsburg explain the clause as depicting the storm gathering overhead. The rendering of the Targum seems like an attempt to combine in one idea two different interpretations. It is "thou shalt even be afraid to call to mind the actions (done) before this (time), and a small ascent shall be in thy estimation like a great mountain when thou art walking on the road." Plumptre observes: "to be afraid of a hill expresses not merely, or chiefly, the failure of strength of limb to climb mountains, but the temper that, as we say, makes mountains out of molehills; that, like the slothful man of Proverbs xxii. 13, sees a lion in the path." But the view of the passage propounded by Taylor seems to us preferable, namely, that the expression "from on high" in the former part of the sentence is contrasted with "in the way" in the second. The thought would then be similar to that in the Book of Job (chap. xviii. 11), "the terror not only lowers upon them from above, but lurks also beneath their feet."[2]

It may be worth while here to notice the peculiar interpretation which Hahn has given of the whole passage. He

---

[1] See note on p. 254.

[2] Taylor aptly compares the passage in the Koran (Sura vi. 65). "Say, He it is that hath power to send upon you punishment from above you and from beneath your feet." He refers also to Isaiah viii. 21, 22, where a similar contrast is found: "they shall fret themselves, and curse their king and God, and look upward. And they shall look unto the earth; and behold trouble and darkness."

rightly rejects the idea of Hengstenberg, adopted by some later expositors of less note, that Koheleth had in view the old age of the ungodly; or, as others have suggested, that the last days of a worn-out sensualist are here depicted. Had the writer had either the one or the other idea in view, he would not have expressed himself in such general terms. Moreover, as Hahn notes, the old age of the wicked is not always miserable. Job speaks of it as the very reverse (xxi. 7 ff.). Hahn maintains that "the night of death" is here described. Man, according to him, emerged at his birth from darkness to the light of day, and Koheleth refers to this fact when he speaks of the clouds of darkness returning after the destructive storm (Ezek. xiii. 11; comp. Isa. xxv. 4) which destroys the building.

In common with the other allegorists, Hahn maintains that the house is the body of man in which his spirit resides. But he interprets the watchers and strong men to be the powers of life which have their root in the spirit and pervade the whole body,—which, instead of resting by night, as do the legs and arms, continue always to discharge their appointed tasks. It is when these become powerless that death forces its way into the building.

Hahn explains the grinding women to be the vital powers pervading the frame, which provide for its wants and assimilate the food necessary for its support. The street, according to him, is the outer world; the doors thereto are the senses. So far the interpretation seems to run smoothly enough; but, when the sound of the mill becoming low is explained as a reference to the heart and its pulsations, one sees how much better it would have been had the sound of the mill been viewed as merely part of the drapery of the allegory; for the more noiselessly the heart performs its functions, and the less it forces itself into notice, the more healthy and vigorous is the life of the individual.

But far more objectionable is his explanation of the next clause, where he supposes the soul to be compared to a bird in a cage, and renders, " and the bird rises (from its earthly prison) at the voice," *i.e.* of God, which calls it to return (comp. Ps. xc. 3). There is no article in the original (לְקוֹל), and it is almost impossible that the soul, which, according to this interpretation, has been all along spoken of as the master directing the watchers and men of power, and ruling over the grinding maids, etc., should, without warning, be suddenly compared to a bird in a cage. Nor is there anything to justify the explanation of " the daughters of song " as meaning " songs, which are his daughters."

Hahn's translation of verse 5 is unique, and unlikely to find favour with Biblical interpreters : " Also they are afraid before the High One (God),[1] as well as of the terrors on the way " ; namely, the terrors of death, which intervene between that which is on this side and the other side of the grave ; for Hahn considers the way spoken of to be that which leads from earth to the High and Lofty One who is throned in heaven. In order to extract this sense from the passage he is forced to reject the translation " almond tree " or " almond fruit," which is the uniform sense of the Hebrew noun in verse 5, and to take it in the signification of " the watchful one "[2] as an appellation of the soul of man " whose

---

[1] To bring out this meaning Hahn arbitrarily supplies מִן before הַתְּחִתִּים out of the preceding מִגָּבֹהַּ. Hahn says that Ewald takes the same view of מִגָּבֹהַּ, referring it to God, and appeals to Koh. v. 7. The absence of the article in itself makes this translation improbable. Whatever Ewald's earlier opinions may have been, in his *Dichter des Alten Bundes* he rejects this view, as he explains his translation "vor dem Hohen" to mean "was schwer zu ersteigen ist." In his *Ausf. Lehrb.* (8te Ausg. 1870) § 179 *a*, note, he says, " Erschrecken ist am Wege d. i. man erschrickt vor dem Wege (aus Altersschwäche) ist der sicherste Sinn der Worte Qoh. xii. 5, ähnlich wie das vorige Glied sich auf die Furcht vor dem Emporsteigen bezieht." It may be noted that Ibn Ezra also gives this turn to the passage, as he says that the fear alluded to is that the old man's thoughts tell him that his spirit must soon quit his body and go to the high heaven.

[2] Note Plumptre's rendering of this word, which is commented on at p. 259.

The prophetical exposition of R. Levi.

being is watchfulness, self-consciousness and freedom." The verb in the clause he translates "*to get feathers.*"[1] Thus the sense is explained to be, "the watchful one obtains pinions, and the locust disburdens itself," this expression being regarded as synonymous with "the butterfly emerges from its chrysalis," "and the poor (one)[2] breaks forth"; *i.e.* the spirit breaks its earthly shell, "the body of our humiliation" (Phil. iii. 21), "for man goeth to his eternal house," the kingdom of glory, which would be almost equivalent to that which the Apostle speaks of in 2 Cor. v. 1, 2.

This attempt to ingraft New Testament ideas upon the book of the Old Testament philosopher cannot be regarded as successful. However ingeniously worked out in its details, it cannot stand the test of any critical examination; and, independently of this fact, it is in itself too fanciful. Its very originality is its most decisive condemnation.

A remarkable prophetical exposition of the chapter is given by R. Joshua of Sikhnin, in the name of R. Levi, in the Introduction to the Midrash on the Book of Lamentations (sect. 23). It explains "the days of youth" in verse 1 of the period of Israel's prosperity, "the days of evil" of the time of the exile. The darkening of the "sun" describes the obscuration of the glory of the Davidic house (comp. Ps.

---

[1] יָנֵאץ is explained as equivalent to יָנֵץ from הֵנֵץ, which Hahn regards a denominative from נוֹצָה, *a pinion* (Job xxxix. 13). See on this verb, note on p. 258.

[2] Hahn takes אֲבִיּוֹנָה to be the feminine of the adjective אֶבְיוֹן. The daghesh forte in the י is no decided objection to this view. For the word might be regarded as a strengthened form of אֶבְיוֹנָה. Compare, on this use of the daghesh, Böttcher, *Lehrb.* § 295, 2. But the peculiarity of punctuation was more probably adopted by the punctuators to preserve the true traditional view of the passage, according to which the word was regarded not as the feminine of אֶבְיוֹן, but as a noun denoting the *caperberry*, although the Rabbinical word used for the latter in the Talmud is pronounced exactly in the same way as the feminine adjective referred to. See p. 263. Compare the difference between עֵדֶן and עֶדֶן, which, though slight in itself, is highly significant. See Friedrich Delitzsch, *Wo lag das Paradies?* p. 3 ff.

lxxxix. 37); "the light" is the Law (Prov. vi. 23); "the moon," the Sanhedrin; "the stars," the Rabbis (Dan. xii. 3); "the clouds returning after the rain," the troubles predicted by Jeremiah. "The watchers of the house" are the watches of the Priests and Levites (Num. viii. 21); "the sound of the mills," the great Mishnaioth, "few" of which are contained in the Talmud; or, according to others, the Israelites themselves, busied day and night about the Law (Josh. i. 8); "the lookers out of the windows" who are "darkened," the Jewish exiles scattered among the nations. "The voice of the bird" is explained to be that of the cruel Nebuchadnezzar, whose actions caused the songs of "the daughters of song" to cease throughout the land (Isa. xxiv. 9); "the fears in the way" are interpreted of the difficulties which Nebuchadnezzar dreaded when seeking to discharge that work of judgment which he was commissioned by the Most High to perform. (Comp. Ezek. xxi. 26 ff., A.V. xxi. 21 ff.). The blossoming of "the almond" tree is explained, after the analogy of Jer. i. 11, of the hastening of the day of wrath; the "locust" being "burdensome" of the golden image of Nebuchadnezzar (Dan. iii. 1); the powerlessness of "the caperberry" of the merit of the fathers as of no avail to stay the destruction. The clause "for man goeth to his house of the world" (for so the phrase in verse 5 is evidently understood), is explained of Babylon itself; while the mourners are interpreted of the weepers for Jeconiah or Jehoiachin.[1] The "silver cord" is explained of "the chain of genealogies" (שלשלת יוחסין); "the golden bowl" of the words of the Law (Ps. xix. 11); the "pitcher at the fountain" either of the pitcher of Baruch at the fountain of Jeremiah, or of the pitcher of Jeremiah at the fountain of Baruch (Jer. xxxvi. 18). The "wheel broken at the cistern" is also interpreted

כי הולך האדם אל בית עולמו מבבל היו ושם חזרו . וסבבו בשוק הסופדים .
זה גלות יכניה.

of the destruction at Babylon (comp. Jer. li. 49). The dust returning to the earth as it was is explained of the return to Babylon. "They were from Babylon and they returned there."[1] "'And the spirit returns to God,' etc., that is, the Holy Spirit. When the Holy Spirit was taken away from them, they went into captivity, and, when they went into captivity, Jeremiah's lamentation arose over them, 'how doth the city sit solitary' (Lam. i. 1)."

Kaiser, in his curious book on Koheleth,[2] in which he endeavours to make out that the work describes under various forms the history of Israel from the time of Solomon to the exile, naturally explains the 12th chapter in reference to the downfall of the Jewish State. His interpretation, though not by any means identical with that given in the Introduction to the Midrash nor borrowed therefrom, is in some respects similar. Such prophetical interpretations, though strained in a few particulars, require scarcely more violence to be done to the original than is done in the endeavour to interpret the whole chapter as an allegorical picture of old age.

But to return. A review of all the various expositions suggested for the clause in the 5th verse rendered by us, "and the almond-tree flourishes," or "is in bloom," would here be impossible. The explanations of the Talmud, Midrash, and Targum are too far-fetched to require special notice. The noun in the sentence is used to denote both the almond-tree and the nuts which grow thereon. This in itself opens the door to a variety of interpretations. The verb is rendered by Gesenius "*shall be despised*," and that scholar considers the writer to refer to the almonds which the old man can no longer eat, his teeth being gone. The fact, however, that the correct reading of the passage has the

---

[1] מבבל היו וישם חזרו.
[2] *Koheleth, das Collectivum der Davidischen Könige in Jerusalem, ein historisches Lehrgedicht über den Umsturz des jüdischen Staates* (Erlangen, 1823).

verb in the jussive is a serious difficulty in the way of this and many other interpretations.[1] The best translation of this verb is unquestionably that given by the majority of the ancient versions, inclusive of the LXX., Vulg. and partly of the Syr., and adopted by our A.V., namely, *is in blossom ;* and the peculiar form which appears in the Hebrew text is to be regarded either as caused by an early blunder of some scribe, or as having arisen from an old marginal reading.

Ewald, Delitzsch, and many modern as well as ancient commentators, regard the clause as picturing the snowy hair

---

[1]. Gesenius in his *Thesaurus* regards יָנֵאץ as the hiphil of נָאַץ, for יַנְאִיץ. Similar instances can be cited in which an א gives its vowel to a vowelless consonant preceding. There is, however, a second irregularity in the word, namely, the ֵ in place of the ִ־. The verb is regarded by other scholars as the impf. hiphil of נָצַץ, *to shine, to bloom ;* the perfect hiphil of this verb occurs, though with a peculiarity of punctuation, in Cant. vi. 11. But the form in Koheleth is altogether irregular, as the א cannot be satisfactorily accounted for. The vowels appended to the word show that the punctuators connected it with נָצַץ. The instances, however, adduced by Ewald and Delitzsch, in order to prove that the form in the Hebrew text is simply an incorrect mode of יָנֵץ are not satisfactory. Kimchi's derivation of the verb from נָאַץ, an unused stem, as if it were a denominative from נִצָּה, *a blossom,* affords no assistance. The form is, perhaps, best viewed as a simple blunder, if the vowels of the text be not regarded as belonging to an unnoticed k'ri, as Böttcher has suggested in several cases, and which König (*Hist.-krit. Lehrgeb. der heb. Spr.,* pp. 313, 314) considers probable here. It has been thought that the punctuation was the result of an early attempt to amend the text. For Böttcher and König maintain that שָׁקֵד, *the almond,* is a euphemism for the *phallus,* and that it was considered desirable to give a better turn to the passage. The authority of the ancient versions is against this notion, which, besides having no evidence on which it can be based, is in itself repulsive in the extreme.

If the vowels attached to the word be regarded as belonging to an unnoticed k'ri, the word in the text must, as in all such cases, be treated as unpointed. The word then must be connected with נָאַץ, but can be read in several ways. (1) As יִנְאַץ imperf. kal used impersonally, "*one despises the almond.*" Hitzig renders the clause thus pointed, "and the almond-tree," an allegorical name for the youthful maiden, "refuses," *i.e.* to give its fruit to the aged man. This explanation, like many of Hitzig's, is remarkable for its perverse ingenuity. (2) The word may be regarded as the imperf. hiphil יַנְאִץ, scriptio defectiva, or יַנְאֵץ, or (3), which would be the easiest mode of pointing, as יִנָּאֵץ, the impf. niphal, *will be despised,* a view taken by several critics.

on the head of the aged man. The blossoming almond-tree would thus indicate what is expressed by the Latin poet:

"Temporibus geminis canebat sparsa senectus."—*Virgil, Æn.* v. 416.

The objection urged against this interpretation by Knobel, and repeated by Plumptre, namely, that the colour of the blossoms of the almond-tree is pink and not white, has long ago been answered by Ch. F. Bauer (1732). The latter has noted that the almond blossoms turn to a snowy white ere they fall from the tree. The American missionary Thomson, who was well acquainted with this appearance of the almond-tree in Palestine speaks of it (in his *Land and the Book*) as often completely covered with white blossoms.[1] Plumptre, who "records but only to reject" the opinion that the almond blossoms represent the white hairs of old age, falls back, with Symmachus and the Syr., upon the original meaning of the stem שָׁקֵד, *to watch, to be watchful*, and maintains that "the true meaning is to be found in the significance of the Hebrew name for almond-tree (Shaked = the early waking tree), comp. Jer. i. 11." His idea is that "the enigmatic phrase describes the *insomnia* which often attends old age. The tree that flourishes then is the tree of *Vigilantia* or Wakefulness." But, as the noun in question is never used in any other sense than that of the almond-tree, or the almond-nut, all interpretations which seek to assign another signification to it may be worthy of record, as proof of ingenuity, but must be rejected.

The noun used in the next clause (חָגָב) certainly means *the locust*, and it is so rendered by the LXX., Syr., Arab. and Vulg. It is found in four other passages (Lev. xi. 22; Num. xiii. 33; Isa. xl. 22; 1 Chron. vii. 17). It occurs

---

[1] Ewald in his footnote cites a passage from Bodenstedt (1001 *Tage im Oriente*, ii. p. 237), where that traveller incidentally speaks of the white blossoms falling off the almond-trees like flakes of snow.

in the list of animals, which, according to the Mosaic Law (Lev. xi. 22), might be used for food. Jewish interpreters have, however, explained it to signify the bone at the extremity of the spine, or even the *joints*,[1] while Jerome imagined that the swollen legs of the old man were meant. Hitzig, Böttcher, and Graetz, with a critical nose degenerating (to use Delitzsch's strong expression) into a hog's snout, have sought to interpret it of the *phallus*.[2] Delitzsch translates the sentence, "the locust crawls along," or is "with difficulty dragged along," the hithpael, יִסְתַּבֵּל, being regarded here almost as equivalent to a passive. Comp. chap. viii. 10. The allusion is supposed to be to the loss of elasticity in the hips, and their inability to bear any weight. In this interpretation Delitzsch substantially adopts the view of the Talmud, regarding the locust as being the *coxa*, the *hips*, or the back part of the pelvis, in which the muscles used in rising and walking are concentrated. Delitzsch thinks that this part of the body is so termed because its mechanism is somewhat similar to that in the locust. But this interpretation appears to us too artificial. We can scarcely conceive that a poet would choose under such an image to depict the stiffness felt by old men in the morning, which they attempt to remedy when getting out of bed, or when rising from a seat, by putting their hands behind their backs, and thus pushing themselves forward.

The verb used in this sentence can only mean to *drag oneself* along, or to *crawl along*, or to *load oneself* with something. It is doubtful whether it can convey the sense of

---

[1] The Talmud however explains the *locust* to mean עֲנָבוֹת, *nates;* the cognate word to this in Arabic signifies the *os coccygis*, or the bone at the extremity of the spine; while the Midrash explains it by "*these are his joints*" (אֵלּוּ קַרְסוּלָיו), Targ. אִסְתַּוְרֵי רַגְלָךְ, *the ankles of thy feet*. The Targum makes use of the word קַרְסֻלִּין in Lev. xi. 21 to denote the joints above the feet of the locusts, used by them in springing from the ground.

[2] See note on p. 263.

Strange interpretation of Dean Plumptre.

"being a burden to another," or of *becoming troublesome*, or dull. The ancient translators have indeed taken the word in the sense of being *burdensome*, not to others, but *to oneself*. Under the influence of the allegorical exposition (which was adopted in very early times) the LXX., Vulg. and Syr. deduced from this signification the meaning of *becoming fat*. Tyler seems to coincide with this view. It was only going a step further to explain the locust itself, rapacious as is its appetite, to signify the *stomach*.

Some commentators have maintained that the locust is referred to as a favourite kind of food. They consider the sense of the passage to be that all such luxuries are no longer attractive, either by reason of the terror inspired by the gathering storm (*Ginsburg*), or by the failure of appetite in old age. But the locust, though occasionally eaten in Palestine, is not regarded there (as in Arabia) as an agreeable kind of food.[1] Zöckler considers that the locust is mentioned simply on account of its littleness (comp. Isa. xl. 22; Num. xiii. 33), and that the aphorism is equivalent to "the gnat becomes a burden, or the fly," or, as the Germans say, "a fly on the wall annoys him." Professor Tayler Lewis has defended the popular exposition of the phrase found in our English version, "the grasshopper shall be a burden," as if it meant to describe the old man as so feeble that he cannot bear the smallest weight. So Wardlaw. One would have thought such an interpretation unlikely to find favour with critics; but it has actually been adopted by Dean Plumptre, who observes, "that which is least weighty is a burden to the timidity of age. Assuming the writer to have come in contact with the forms of Greek life, the words

---

[1] An interesting story told by Palgrave of the relish which the Arabs exhibit for this food is given by Prof. E. Percival Wright, M.D., in his popular work on *Animal Life, being a series of descriptions of the various sub-kingdoms of the Animal Kingdom*, p. 493.

may receive an illustration from its being the common practice of the Athenians to wear a golden grasshopper in their heads as the symbol of their being autochthones, 'sprung from the soil.' Such an ornament is to the old man more than he cares to carry, and becomes another symbol of his incapacity to support the least physical or mental burden." We may safely predict that such an explanation will in time find its proper place in a museum of curiosities of Biblical exposition.

We must here pass over Ewald's interpretation of the clause. But the following anecdote, cited in the Talmud (*Shabbath* 151ᵇ, 152ᵇ) in connexion with its interpretation, presents the allegorical exposition in the most favourable aspect, and hence deserves quotation. An anecdote somewhat similar is given in the Midrash. "The Emperor asked Rabbi Joshua ben Ḥananyah, How is it that you do not go to the house of Abidan (בי אבידן)?" a place where learned discussions and disputations on religious questions were wont to be held. "He said to him (in reply), The mountain is snow (my head is white); the hoar frosts surround me (my whiskers and beard are also hoary); its dogs do not bark (I have lost my wonted power of voice); its millers do not grind (I have no teeth); the scholars ask me, whether I am looking for something which I have not lost?" referring, probably, to the old man feeling here and there, on account of his shortness of sight, as if looking for something.[1]

We are not unmindful of the fact that this clause has been ingeniously explained by Taylor to refer to the chirping of the grasshopper, or the song of the τέττιξ, which was much admired by the ancients. The passage alludes, indeed, to the time of spring when the τέττιξ gives forth its notes. But,

[1] א״ל קיסר לרבי יהושע בן חנניא מ״ט לא אתית לבי אבידן א״ל טור
תלג סחרוני גלידין בלבוהי לא נבחין טחנוהי לא טוחניי בי רב אמרי אדלא
אבידנא בחייטנא.

The use of the caperberry.

as no mention is made in Biblical literature of the chirping of the locust, or the grasshopper, as a sound admired by the Hebrews; and moreover, as the conjugation of the verb presents a difficulty in the way of this interpretation, we regard it as more than doubtful.

The allegory passes on, according to Delitzsch, in the next clause to describe the dying out of the sensitive desires and the decay of the organs which minister to these wants. Koheleth speaks of the caperberry as no longer able to excite the sluggish appetite. It is certain from the renderings of the LXX., the Syr., and the Vulg., that אֲבִיּוֹנָה is *the caperberry*, whose flower-buds and berries were used as a relish in ancient as well as in modern times. The caperberry was also used as an aphrodisiac in the middle ages, but no conclusive evidence has been adduced that the ancients employed it for that purpose.[1] אֲבִיּוֹנָה in the Talmud denotes

[1] Pliny, though he says much about the capparis (Nat. Hist. xiii. 44, and xx. 55) and describes its medical properties, does not mention this use of it. Gesenius and Hitzig refer to Plutarch (*Symp.* vi.; *Quæst.* 2), but, though it is there spoken of as a provocative to appetite, the other use is not mentioned. His words are πολλοὶ τῶν ἀποσίτων ἐλαίαν ἁλμάδα λαμβάνοντες, ἢ κάππαριν γευσάμενοι ταχέως ἀνέλαβον, καὶ παρεστήσαντο τὴν ὄρεξιν. The Talmud renders the word here by חמדה, *desire*, the Midrash by another synonyme (see n. 3, p. 264). The Targum, both according to Walton's text and that of Lagarde, has כַּשְׁבְּנָא, which Ginsburg renders by *rest*, Winzer better by *tabernaculum*. The word does not occur in the former signification, and in the latter is not suitable here. Delitzsch quotes the Targum according to the reading of the Antwerp Polyglott, משבבא. Böttcher (*Aehrenl.* pp. 98, 99) regards all three words (*almond, locust*, and *caperberry*) as having concealed references to the sexual organs. This is the view of several old Jewish commentators, and of Graetz, who refers to the use of the word for *caper* in Arabic. But the Arabic كَبَر, *the caper*, is used of several aromatic plants (see Lane's *Arab. Lex.*), and there is not the slightest necessity for supposing such allusions. Koheleth was, as Delitzsch well observes, no Martial or Juvenal to delight in such references. On the rapidity of growth of the caper, see the anecdote from the Talmud given on p. 23. The word used for the plant in that passage is צָלָף. There does not appear to be any authority for the statement made by Buxtorf that אביונה occurs in the meaning of *olive-berries*, although that translation is adopted by Taylor. The latter scholar explains, however, that he has used the word *olive* in his translation merely because it is "a more familiar poetical symbol."

caperberries. The translation, "desire shall fail," given in our A.V., on the authority of the Jewish lexicographers, and defended by Knobel and others among the moderns, is condemned by Delitzsch as "impossible," on the ground that the form of the word would be "unexampled and incomprehensible."[1]

The verb which occurs in this sentence[2] is used elsewhere in the sense of *breaking, bursting,* and also with reference to the *making* a covenant *invalid,* and the declaring of a vow null and void. Koheleth employs it here in the sense of *becoming void,* becoming fruitless, or ineffective. This is in accordance with the usage whereby that which is viewed by the Shemitic people as an *act,* is regarded by Europeans as a *state.* If the context admitted of the meaning, the clause might be translated, "and the caperberry bursts," in allusion to the bursting of the ripe caperberries, from which that plant receives, according to Wetzstein, its Syro-Arabic proper name, i.e. שְׁפָלָח, *the burster,* a term which for a similar reason is also applied to over-ripe dates.[3] Ewald translates the clause literally, "and the caper bursts." He explains it however, allegorically. According to his view, the soul, which in the former clause is compared to a locust beginning

---

[1] That is, the feminine form cannot denote *desire* in the abstract, but must refer to something which has, or arouses, desire.

[2] תָּפֵר, the imperfect hiphil from פרר, *to break.* The hiphil is also used in the same sense. Gesenius in his *Thes.* describes the hiphil as here intransitive. But see König's *Lehrgeb.,* § 27, and compare W. Wright's *Arab. Gramm.,* vol. i. § 45, rem. c. Some have proposed to read here וְתֻפַּר, the hophal.

[3] Hence the translation of the LXX. καὶ διασκεδασθῇ ἡ κάππαρις. The Syriac gives a double rendering ܟܒܪܐ ܘܬܬܒܛܠ . ܩܦܪ ܘܬܬܒܪ "and the caperberry shall burst, and want shall cease." The translation of Symmachus, καὶ διαλυθῇ ἡ ἐπίπονος, has much exercised the ingenuity of scholars. Dr. Abr. Geiger, in his able article on *Symmachus der Uebersetzer der Bibel,* in his *Jüdische Zeitschrift,* vol. i. (1862) p. 57, prefers the reading ἡ ἐπιγονή, which he explains as identical with the exposition of the Midrash, זו התאוה המטלת שלום בין איש לאשתו, but Field, in his edition of *Origen's Hexapla,* has clearly shown that

to fly, is here likened to the caperberry which has burst its capsule.

But it is far more probable that Koheleth speaks here of the caperberry as powerless any longer to excite the appetite of the dying man. The idea of Hitzig, that the poet refers to the uselessness of the caperberry as an aphrodisiac in extreme old age, must be unhesitatingly rejected. For, even if the Jews were acquainted with that use of the plant, the writer would not naturally have referred to it, unless he were giving a picture of the last days of a miserable sensualist. This is certainly not the theme of Koheleth's verse, or some reference would have been made in the poem to the sensualist's former habits of life. But, as Renan truly observes, the Book of Ecclesiastes is never immoral or obscene, its author was "not a professor of libertinism." [1]

We have already spoken of the name here (verse 5) given to the grave, namely man's "eternal house" (see p. 201). The mourners have been explained often as the relations of the deceased man, but the verb in the passage (סָבְבוּ) is more suitably applied to the going up and down, or the going in procession, of the hired mourners who were wont to accompany the rich to their graves, often moving onward with funereal music, singing dirges for the dead. Classical scholars will naturally think of those "*qui conducti plorant in funere*" (*Horat. Ars Poet.*, 431). The Targum regards the

---

this is impossible. Symmachus has probably taken the Hebrew word in the sense of "miserable," and the word ζωή may be understood after ἡ ἐπίπονος, or the reference may be, as Delitzsch thinks, to the spirit of man. The word, as Field observes, is found nowhere else in the Greek versions except in a fragment of Symmachus on Isaiah liii. 3, where he renders "a man of sorrows and acquainted with grief," by ἀνὴρ ἐπίπονος καὶ γνωστὸς νόσῳ. On the caperberry see u. on p. 263.

[1] "C'est un livre de scepticisme élégant ; on peut le trouver hardi, libre même ; jamais il n'est immoral ni obscène. L'auteur est un galant homme, non un professeur de libertinage, et c'est ce qu'il serait vraiment si la fin du livre renfermait les étranges sous-entendus admis par M. Graetz."—Renan, *Étude sur l'Ecclésiaste*, p. 72.

סוֹפְדִים, *the mourners*, as the persons who go about here and there to gather information concerning the life of the deceased man, to be worked up for the funereal dirge, and thinks at the same time, that, while those on earth are busied about such matters, the angels are also going about to investigate on their part the deeds done in life by the departed.

The sixth verse presents some difficulties which, however, do not affect much the interpretation.[1] Almost all commentators agree in assigning to the verb, however it may be read, the signification of breaking. The allegorists have explained the silver cord variously as the spine, the spinal cord, the nerves, or the vital powers in general. Delitzsch interprets it to mean the soul, which like a cord holds up the body (the lamp); the spirit, according to his notion, being the oil contained therein.

It is impossible to discuss here with any fulness these or other interpretations. Our view is that Koheleth, who (as we shall shortly point out) in the first five verses portrays death as slowly but surely advancing in old age, in the sixth

---

[1] The text must be read either kal, יֵרָחֵק, or niphal, יֵרָחֵק. As there is a k'ri, the vowels attached to the consonants of the word in the text belong to that in the margin. רחק signifies *to go away from*, or *to be far off from*, so the clause with the imperfect kal may be rendered, as Zöckler, "before that the silver cord gives way." The Græcus Venetus translates the verb as a niphal, μακρυνθῇ, probably thinking of the cord being stretched out until it finally snaps asunder. Winzer renders the niphal "before that the silver cord be removed," while Knobel regards the niphal as used in the same sense as Zöckler has rendered the kal. Delitzsch prefers the reading of the margin, which is יֵרָתֵק, though he confesses it is not without its difficulties. That verb in kal signifies *to bind together*, *to chain*, and is used of the binding of prisoners (Nah. iii. 10). The Targum explains the clause to refer to the tongue, and paraphrases "ere thy tongue is lamed so that it cannot speak." Rashi and Ibn Ezra consider the idea to be rather that of *contracting*. The notion of Kimchi and others that the niphal ought to be regarded as a negative of kal, and that the verb signifies in kal *to bind*, and in niphal *to loose*, is in violation of the laws of the language. The ancient translators have all, more or less explicitly, given the verb the sense of *breaking*. There is no necessity whatever to alter the text, and to read יִנָּתֵק with Pfannkuche, Gesenius, and Ewald, or, by transposing the consonants, to read with Hitzig, יֵחָרֵק.

and the breaking of the golden lamp. 267

verse speaks of it as coming suddenly, with little or no warning. The idea of the golden bowl (גֻּלָּה) or reservoir for oil seems to be borrowed from the fifth of Zechariah's visions. In that vision Zechariah beheld a candlestick of gold, similar in most respects to that of the Mosaic tabernacle, with, however, some remarkable differences. No ministering priests were there to supply its lamps with oil, but its oil flowed directly from two olive-trees which stood on either side of the candlestick and discharged their oil through two golden channels into a common reservoir, or bowl (a גֻּלָּה), from which by means of pipes it was conveyed to each of the seven lamps.[1] The oil that fed the lamps of Zechariah's candlestick was in Koheleth's mind a fit emblem of the spirit, which, as Delitzsch rightly notes, is termed (in Prov. xx. 27) a lamp of God. The lamp in Koheleth's picture is, however, supposed to hang from the top of a tent, or from the ceiling of a house, suspended by a silver cord. The oil (not mentioned by Koheleth, but the pouring out of which is necessarily implied in the picture) is thought of as contained in the golden bowl. But suddenly the silver cord snaps asunder, the golden lamp falls, the precious oil is poured out like water, and the light which once shone in the dwelling is extinguished.[2]

The fact that a vessel of gold cannot be shivered in pieces need create no difficulty, for the writer may have thought of some merely gilded lamp. Moreover the verb is also used of things which may be "crushed in," and not actually broken in pieces. Comp. קָנֶה רָצוּץ, *a bruised reed*, in Isaiah xlii. 3.

The next picture under which the sudden death of man

[1] See my *Bampton Lectures on Zechariah and his Prophecies*, p. 81 ff.
[2] The conjecture of Taylor that גֻּלָּה is nearly synonymous with גָּלִיל is surely unnecessary. He argues that גָּלִיל in some passages might mean *roller* and then גֻּלָּה might mean *a reel;* and hence he translates the two clauses, "Ere the silver thread escape, and the golden reel hasten," *i.e.* spin round rapidly when the wheel is released from the strain put upon it. But conjectures of this kind are to be avoided except in cases where the passage will otherwise afford no good sense.

is pourtrayed is that of a pitcher shivered at the fountain,[1] so that in the breaking thereof there is not found "a sherd to take fire from the hearth or to take water withal out of the pit." (Isa. xxx. 14). The noun (כַּד) is used both of a pitcher and a bucket, but it is evident that the first is its real meaning here.

The third image presented by Koheleth is that of a wheel suspended over a well for the purpose of lightening the operation of drawing up water from the depths below. An ancient expositor cited in the Midrash makes mention of the wheel whereby the water was drawn up from the deep well at Sepporis. The well of Sychar will at once suggest itself to one's mind. The word in the original (גַּלְגַּל) is to be taken in its ordinary meaning of a wheel. There is no necessity whatever for seeking to assign to it the signification of *bucket*. The last word in the verse may be explained to be either a well artificially constructed, or a cistern. Death is thus likened by Koheleth to the sudden breaking down of the wheel during the process of drawing water, whereby bucket, rope, wheel and all, are precipitated into the well.

The end of man, however, is not like that of the beast. If the dust returns to its kindred dust, the spirit of the dying man goes not downwards (chap. iii. 21) but upwards. This reference back to the passage in the former part of the work proves that the writer does not teach the absolute cessation of man's existence. In that case there would be no difference between man and the beast; the comparison of the two passages shows that the writer believed in the existence of a real difference. The paraphrase of the Targum is, as Delitzsch notes, in full accordance with the teaching of the book, "thy

---

[1] The word (מַבּוּעַ) is used in the signification of *fountain* or *spring* in the two other passages where it occurs (Isaiah xlix. 10; xxxv. 7). Taylor thinks there is some propriety in the use of עַל *over* the מבוע. Our A.V. renders simply "at," "*at the fountain.*"

Concluding sketch of the passage.

spirit will return to stand in judgment before God who gave it to thee." And, as that expositor says, in this connexion of thought Koheleth expresses more than Lucretius (ii. 998 ff.)

> "Cedit item retro, de terra quod fuit ante,
> In terras, et quod missum est ex ætheris oris
> Id rursum cœli rellatum templa receptant."

A comforting thought lies, as Delitzsch goes on to observe, in the words "who gave it." What God gives He repents not of having given (Rom. xi. 29). If He takes back any gift, He takes it back in order to restore it again more glorious than before.

It now remains for us to give a brief sketch of what we think to be the true interpretation of the entire passage.

In the verses with which he concludes his remarkable book, Koheleth depicts man's days of sorrow in contrast with the joyous days of boyhood and early manhood. Such days form part of that sore trial which God hath given to man to be exercised therewith. In contrast with the days of youth, our poet describes first the gradual waning away of life in old age; and then, in a few rapid touches, that sudden death which carries off many ere they have arrived at the utmost span allotted to mortals here below.

The first seven verses of chap. xii. may be regarded as a description of the evil days of man. Considered as a whole they naturally fall into seven short sections or stanzas of unequal length, not however exactly corresponding with the seven verses of the Masoretic text. Three of the sections begin with the phrase "*ere*" (עַד אֲשֶׁר לֹא), and one is distinguished by commencing with "*in the day when*" (בַּיּוֹם שֶׁ). Two others are sufficiently marked out by וְ (*and*, or *then*, etc.), followed by the imperfect jussive, which form proves that the clauses with which it commences are conditional, and that we must supply either the "*ere*" which occurs in the first verse, and whose force is felt from the beginning to the end, or the alternative expression "in the day when," made use of in verse 3. In the fifth and remaining section, which, as we maintain, consists of verse 5 (with the omission of the opening clause) the imperfect indicative is found; but it is plain from the context that this also is to be regarded as forming in itself a complete stanza.

The imagery employed in the first five verses is drawn from the closing days of the Palestinian winter. The seven last days of that season (though viewed as the heralds of the approaching spring), are peculiarly dreaded in Palestine as fraught with death to persons advanced in years. The following facts noticed by Consul Dr. J. G. Wetzstein [1] as to certain striking peculiarities of that season cast considerable light upon the poetry of Koheleth.

In Europe the autumnal season is the period of the year which is most dangerous for the old. But it is very different in Palestine. The months of October, November, and part of December are mild and pleasant, and the rain which occasionally falls imparts new life to the vegetation scorched by the summer sun. In the end of December the weather begins to be unpleasant, and the Palestinian winter with its piercing cold, accompanied by frequent storms of rain and snow sets in in January, and continues until late in February. There are, however, in February occasional intervals of more genial weather. But in the latter days of that month an after winter occurs with undeviating regularity. It lasts generally for seven days, during which the cold is bitterly felt, especially as it always comes after warm weather. These seven days are noted as dangerous to the aged, and are styled in the native almanacks the أمّ العجوز, *the days of the old woman.*

---

[1] See the valuable *Excurse* which are to be found in the German edition of Delitzsch's *Commentar über das Hoheslied u. Koheleth*, but not in the English translation. I deeply regret that this valuable work is so marred and misrepresented in the English version. See note on p. 119.

The seven "days of death." 271

The legends connected with this name are given by Wetzstein and Lane.[1] The appellation is a very ancient one, and (as founded upon popular experience) may have been well-known in the days of Koheleth. But, whether the special appellation be as old as his time or not, Koheleth, as a native of Palestine, must have been well acquainted with these seven "days of death."

In his description of the evil days of man, Koheleth derives much of the imagery he employs from the features which characterise this deadly week. With that partiality for the number seven, which the sacred writers often exhibit,

---

[1] Wetzstein notes that these days are noted in the native almanacks, "*the scale of the times*" (Deregat el-aukât). He observes that the locusts crawl out in Syria in the early days of spring, and that the native almanacks mention this fact. On the signification of the term applied to these days, he quotes a native Arabic rhyme, in which February is represented as speaking to March, " O March, dear cousin, the old women are mocking at me. Three [days] of thine and four of mine, And we will bring the old people to singing [another tune.] " The old women mock at February on account of its mild weather, for so many fine days occur in that month that old women, who are susceptible of the least cold, are represented as treating the month as devoid of danger. Hence February asks the loan of a few days from March, in order to put an end to the merriment of the old. With respect to the one month borrowing days from another, it may be worth noting that the idea is found even in sayings current in the north of Ireland, where it is said that March having undertaken with its cold winds to "skin a cow," was compelled to borrow three days from April in order to accomplish the task completely; and hence the first three days of April are called in many parts by the name of "the borrowing days." The legend given by Beidâwî, and quoted by Lane in his *Arabic English Lexicon*, book i. p. 1961, is that during the seven days before alluded to the people of the tribe of 'Ād in Arabia perished, according to the tradition of the Koran (Sur. lxix. 7), by a scorching wind which prevailed seven days and eight nights, and the days are so called as being in the latter part (عَجُز) of winter; or from an old woman (عَجُوز) of 'Ād who concealed herself in a subterranean excavation, from which the wind dragged her forth on the eighth day and destroyed her. Another legend given by Wetzstein, from Thaʻâlibî (A.H. 400), is that the old woman who gave the name to these days wished to marry again, and to prove that she was strong enough, determined at the advice of her seven sons to sleep out seven bad nights in the open air, on the seventh of which she died. The days in question are called also the أَيَّامُ الْعَسُومِ, the *days of the cutting off*, *the unlucky days*, or the *deadly days* of the old. See Wetzstein, and Lane, p. 569.

Koheleth (probably in allusion to the seven days of death of the Palestinian after-winter), divides his verses into seven stanzas, all of which more or less distinctly savour of decay and death.

The first stanza alludes briefly to those days of evil wherein man exclaims, "I have no pleasure;" a marked characteristic of the season referred to. The second stanza depicts the darkening of the atmosphere, the pouring rain, and the return of storm and rain after the clouds seemed to have passed away. The gloom of life increases, and man feels he is wending his way towards the place whence he will not return (Job xvi. 22). In the third stanza the picture drawn is still more vivid. It describes the effects of the bitter weather upon all. The men-servants tremble; the men of power, their masters, also bow themselves together. For death is beginning to cast its dark shadow over the high and the low alike, and the limbs both of the noble and peasant tremble when they feel the touch of that "king of terrors."

But these "days of evil" affect also "the weaker sex." The grinding maids cease for a time from their task of grinding corn, either "because," their fellow-companions being prostrated with sickness, "they are but few"; or "when they have worked but little," for the sickness common to the season has weakened their bodily frames. The ladies, too, who were wont to gaze out at the lattices are darkened. Like the Nazarites, or princes, described in the Book of Lamentations, once brighter than snow and whiter in appearance than milk, but whose countenances by reason of terrible sorrow had become darker than blackness itself—so the faces of these gazers at the lattice-windows are now darkened, as they too have to look into the face of death. Hence the doors are shut towards the street, and the sound of the mill ceases. The voice of mirth is gone, and the voice of gladness, the sound of the millstones, and the light of the lamp (Jer. xxv. 10). The ordinary occupations of man and woman are at an end. Every house is shut up, all joy is gone, "as with the slave, so with his master, as with the maid, so with her mistress " (Isa. xxiv. 2, 10).

The fourth stanza begins in the middle of verse 4, where the jussive form shows that the phrase "in the day when" is to be supplied. In it Koheleth describes the passing away of the severe season and the advent of spring. The after-winter has done its work, and the old men and women are now dying. Nature has its spring, but there is no spring for the aged. There is hope for the tree, as Job says, but man dieth and wasteth away, he lieth down and riseth not (Job xiv. 7, 10, 12). At the approach of spring, when those yet in the vigour of manhood rise early at the glorious concert of birds, with whose melody the humbled daughters of song cannot compete, the aged sick in their chambers are beset with all sorts of fears from above and below. Tennyson almost expounds the words of Koheleth when he says:

> "Ah sad and strange, as in dark summer dawns
> The earliest pipe of half-awakened birds
> To dying ears, when unto dying eyes
> The casement slowly grows a glimmering square;
> So sad, so strange the days that are no more."—
> *The Princess.*

The writer presents two pictures, the one death in life, the other nature re-awakening from its temporary grave. The almond-tree is in blossom, and the locusts are crawling out, as they are wont to do at this season, coming forth from the holes in which they were hatched, and just beginning to prepare for their destructive flights. But in yon chamber the old man is lying, and even the caperberry cannot arouse his failing appetite. The food lies untouched, for the man is going to his eternal home; and lo! the mourners, ready to be hired to escort him to his last earthly resting-place, are going to and fro in the street not far off from the house of death.

But remember thy Creator, young man, cries Koheleth, in the days of thy youth, for death may advance upon thee unawares. The silver cord that suspends from the ceiling that shining lamp with its golden bowl may suddenly snap; the pitcher often borne before to the spring for water may fall and be shivered into pieces in the very place from whence the refreshing draught was so often procured; the wheel set up with care to draw up from the depths of earth the cool waters may suddenly give way and fall itself into the well. Therefore remember thy God, and prepare while here to meet Him, "before that the dust shall return upon the earth, dust as it was; for the spirit shall then return to the God who gave it.

We close with a translation of the whole passage.

Rejoice, young man, in thy youth,
And let thy heart cheer thee in the days of thy youth,
And walk in the ways of thy heart
And according to the sight of thine eyes !
But know—that for all these God shall bring thee into the judgment.

Therefore banish moroseness from thy heart,
And put away evil from thy flesh,
    For boyhood and manhood are vanity—
And remember thy Creator in the days of thy youth,

(1)

Ere there come the days of evil, and years approach
In which thou shalt say, I have no pleasure !

(2)

Ere the sun is darkened, and the light, and the moon, and the stars,
And the clouds return after the pouring rain.

(3)

In the day when the keepers of the house tremble,
And the men of strength bow-themselves-together—

And the grinding-maids cease because they are few,
And the ladies that look out at the lattices are darkened !
And doors are shut towards the street,
When the sound of the grinding-mill ceases.

(4)

When one rises at the voice of the bird
And all the daughters of song are humbled !
    Even they fear from on high, and all-sorts-of-terrors are in the path.

(5)

Then there blossoms the almond,
And crawls out the locust ;
    But unavailing is the caperberry—
For the man is going to his eternal house,
And there go the mourners about in the street !

(6)

Ere the silver cord be snapped asunder,
And the golden bowl break—
And the pitcher be shivered upon the spring,
And the wheel be broken (and fall) into the well ;

(7)

And *ere* the dust return upon the earth as it was ;
For the spirit shall return to the God who gave it.

THE BOOK OF KOHELETH.

*A NEW TRANSLATION, ARRANGED IN SECTIONS,
WITH A CRITICAL AND GRAMMATICAL
COMMENTARY.*

PRELIMINARY NOTE ON THE TITLE KOHELETH.

It is unnecessary to give any extended notice of the various interpretations proposed for the name Koheleth, as such will be found in the commentaries of Knobel and Ginsburg. See, however, our remarks on pp. 84 ff. The word is the active participle fem. which has two forms קוֹטְלָה (in pause קוֹטֵלָה) and קֹטֶלֶת, often found together in the same verb, as יוֹשְׁבָה and יֹשֶׁבֶת. Chap. vii. 27 is often referred to in proof of the name having been given to Solomon as the personification of wisdom, since the noun is there construed with a feminine verb. But the ordinary reading of that passage is considered by Olshausen, Böttcher and Delitzsch to be a blunder. Had the author desired to pourtray Solomon in such a character, he would hardly (as Delitzsch rightly argues) have made him speak as in chap. i. 16–18, and vii. 23 ff. Moreover, the language of chap. vii. 27 is not that of wisdom personified. One would have expected in that passage some stress to have been laid upon the masculine gender of the speaker. Several explanations of the noun, such as "the penitent one" (*Cocceius*), "the congregation, academy" (*Bauer, Döderlein, Nachtigal, etc.*), "old man" (*Simonis, Moldenhauer*), have been long since abandoned.

The word is of the same formation as the following proper names of men, viz. סֹפֶרֶת *Sophereth*, "*scribe*," Neh. vii. 57, and פֹּכֶרֶת *Pokereth*, in the compound name פֹּכֶרֶת הַצְּבָיִם "*the hunter of gazelles*," Ezra ii. 57, where our A. V. has incorrectly "Pochereth of Zebaim." Böttcher considers such fem. participal forms to be feminine abstract nouns used as titles of honour, like the titles *Majesty, Excellency, Highness, Grace*, which in German and other kindred languages are feminines (Majestät, Excellenz, Hoheit, etc., *Lehrb.*, § 645). But the feminine appears to be used in such cases, as in Arabic, to intensify the meaning (see W. Wright's *Arab. Gramm.*, 2nd edit. vol. i. p. 157, and p. 203. Comp. Ges.-Kautzsch, § 107, 3 *c*). The feminine is often found in Hebrew in a neuter signification. Nouns of the form of the fem. part. active were originally regarded as neuters, and then applied to persons as possessors in a high degree of the particular quality specified by the verb. Hence such names occur with the article. So הַסֹּפֶרֶת in Ezra ii. 55; the article is not expressed in our A. V. The article too before the second word in the compound name פכרת הצבים renders the first definite according to the well-known Hebrew idiom. The use, however, of proper nouns of this form to denote men is rare, and seems to belong to a late stage of the language, for such forms do not occur in early Hebrew. As an example of the same form as a fem. proper name we may cite מֹלֶכֶת used with the article, 1 Chron. vii. 18, and צֹבֵבָה, used similarly with the article, 1 Chron. iv. 8. But the limited extent of the induction does not permit such a statement to be made with any degree of certainty. The observations of Rev. D. Johnston in his *Treatise on the Authorship of Ecclesiastes* are beside the question, and exhibit a strange misunderstanding of the point of Delitzsch's remarks, which he attempts to controvert. To the names *Sophereth* and *Pochereth* mentioned by Delitzsch, Johnston adds "and Mispereth in Neh. vii. 7," a name not quoted by that scholar, and not of the same grammatical form as the others. Feminine nouns of other forms are, indeed, made use of in early Hebrew as proper names (Olshausen, *Lehrb.*, p. 224), but the use of the fem. of the part. active as such constitutes the special peculiarity in the name Koheleth. Delitzsch observes that the language of the Mishna not only uses the feminine of participles active as proper names of men, but even makes use of the fem. of the part. pass. in an active signification in place of the proper active part., and moreover employs plurals of the form of the fem. part. pass. (קְטוּלָה) in a masc. signification. He cites as instances הַדְּרוּכוֹת "*those who tread the wine-press,*" Terumoth iii. 4, הַפְּשׂוּהוֹת, "*the reapers,*" Erub. iv. 11. These subjects are construed with masculine predicates. See, for similar instances, Geiger, *Lehrb. zur Sprache der Mischnah*, § 16, 6, p. 44.

Hebrew feminine forms, like סֹפֶרֶת, פֹּכֶרֶת and קֹהֶלֶת, applied to men, correspond exactly both in grammatical form and signification with the Arabic nouns رَاوِيَة *a hander-down of traditions, a traditionary*; دَاعِيَة, *an emissary*, or *missionary*; بَاقِعَة *a deep investigator*. See

W. Wright's *Arab. Gram.*, vol. i. § 233, rem. *c.*, p. 157. Delitzsch considers Koheleth to be an official title of a *preacher*. So the Assyr. has the fem. plural form *ḥazanâti* in place of the Hebrew חַזָּנִים. In Ethiopic, masculine nouns which signify an office, business, or profession, take in the plural a feminine termination. See Dillman, *Gramm. der Æthiop. Spr.*, § 133. The verb קהל is only used in the sense of *collecting together* persons, and not in reference to things, and the nouns, like קָהָל, derived from that stem, are used in a similar signification, the noun קֹהֶלֶת is not therefore to be taken in the sense of a *collector of proverbs*, or one who gathers wisdom, or of one who seeks to combine various opinions. The LXX. render it by ἐκκλησιαστής, Aquila κωλέθ, not συναθροιστής (as Knobel has erroneously stated) as Rödiger (in Gesenius' *Thes.*), and Field (in *Origen. Hex.*) have pointed out. Symmachus is said to have rendered the word by παροιμιαστής in chap. xii. 10, but the reading given there as that of Symmachus was probably taken from Aquila's version of the preceding verse. See Field *in loco*. The Gr. Ven. has rendered it by ἡ ἐκκλησιάστρια in chap. i. 1, 2; vii. 27, and in chap. xii. 8; but by ἡ ἐκκλησιάζουσα in both chap. xii. 9 and 10. Vulg. *ecclesiastes*. Jerome notes: "ἐκκλησιαστής græco sermone appellatur qui cœtum *i.e.* ecclesiam congregat: quem nos nuncupare possumus concionatorem, eo quod loquatur ad populum et ejus sermo non specialiter ad unum, sed ad universos generaliter dirigatur." Kleinert regards the word as a denominative from קָהָל *an assembly, congregation*, like בֹּקֵר *a shepherd* from בָּקָר, *cattle*, and considers it to signify δημαγωγός, *one who speaks to the people, a preacher*, in contrast to the כֹּהֵן who represents the congregation before God. The feminine ending *he* explains not as denoting an *office*, but as indicating the wisdom personified in the sayings of Solomon (*Ewald, Hitzig, Hengstenberg*). He refers in proof to chap. vii. 27, and to the predicates used in chap. xii. 8 ff. Similarly Hoelemann, save that he regards the fem. as indicating the personified voice of the preacher (referring to John i. 23). We prefer, however, Delitzsch's explanation.

In an article on Renan's work on Ecclesiastes, Dr. Paulus Cassel, in the No. of *Sunem* for May 19th, 1882, referring to Renan's remarks on the letters of Koheleth (see p. 127), draws attention to the fact that the numerical value of the letters in קהלת is 535, while the value of שלמה בן דוד המלך is 536. He thinks that the comparison is interesting. It would be so if the numbers corresponded exactly, but in this case one might use the English proverb, "a miss is as good as a mile."

THE JEWISH DIVISION OF THE BOOK.

The Masora divides the Book of Koheléth into four sections, or סדרים, containing in all 222 verses. The mnemonic word which contains this number is כְּבָר (כ, 20 + בּ, 2 + ר, 200 = 222) in the phrase מַה־שֶּׁהָיָה כְּבָר נִקְרָא שְׁמוֹ, chap. vi. 10, which is the middle of the book. The first two sections are of equal length, each containing 57 verses, the first embracing chap. i. 1—chap. iii. 13, the second chap. iii. 14 to chap. vi. 12. The conclusion of chap. vi. is the logical end of a section, but so much cannot be said in reference to the artificial break at chap. iii. 13. The third section, which contains 52 verses, ends at chap. ix. 6; and the fourth, containing 56 verses, runs on to the end of the book. These divisions have been made without respect to the logical connexion of thought presented in the work, and afford little or no help in any attempt to arrange the book into its component parts.

THE BOOK OF KOHELETH.

A NEW TRANSLATION.

§ 1. *The absolute vanity of everything earthly. Earthly phenomena like a circle with no real progress.*

I. 1 The words of Koheleth, son of David, king in Jerusalem.
2 Vanity of vanities, saith Koheleth, the whole is vanity.
3 What profit is there to man in all his toil (in) which
4 he toileth under the sun? A generation is going, and a generation coming, and the earth is abiding for ever [*i.e.*
5 continually]. And the sun rises, and the sun sets, and even (when going) to its place, longing it is to arise there!
6 Going towards the south, and circling towards the north, the wind is going, circling, circling; and the wind is (ever) returning to its circlings.
7 All the streams are going to the sea, and the sea— it is not full; to the place whither the streams are going, there they are again going.
8 All things have become weary, no man can express it; the eye will not be satisfied with seeing, and the ear will not be filled with hearing.
9 That which hath been is that which shall be; and that which hath been done is that which shall be done; and
10 there is nothing new under the sun. Is there a thing of

which one says, "See this is new!" it was already for
11 ages which were before us. There is no remembrance
of those (persons who lived) in former times, and even of
those in after times who shall come into being, there will
be no remembrance of them with those who shall be in
the after time.

§ 2. *Koheleth's first discovery.—The vanity of wisdom.*

12 I Koheleth have been king over Israel in Jerusalem.
13 And I gave my heart to search into and to seek out
by wisdom with regard to all that is done under the sun;
it is a woful exercise which God has given to the sons of
14 men wherewith to exercise themselves. I have seen all
the works which are done under the sun, and behold!
the whole is vanity and a striving after wind.
15 "The crooked cannot be straightened,
And a deficit cannot be counted in" [*i.e.* counted as a
part of the whole].
16 I spake [communed] with my heart, saying, Behold I
have become great, and have gathered wisdom, above all
(the rulers) who were before me over Jerusalem, and my
(own) heart has seen abundantly wisdom and knowledge.
17 And therefore I have given my heart to know wisdom,
and to know madness and folly. I perceived that even
18 this was a striving after wind. For in much wisdom
is much sorrow, and he who increases knowledge increases pain.

§ 3. *Koheleth's second discovery.—The vanity of pleasure and
riches.*

II. 1 I said in my heart, Come now, I will test thee by joy,
therefore enjoy [lit. *see*] good! And behold! even this
2 was vanity. To Laughter I said, It is mad; and to Joy,

3 What doeth it? I searched out [lit. spied out] in my heart (how) to attract my flesh with wine, while my heart was acting [guiding] with wisdom, and to take hold of folly, until that I should see what might be good for the sons of men, which they should do under the sun during the number of
4 the days of their life. I undertook great works; I built
5 for myself houses, I planted for myself vineyards. I made for myself gardens and parks; and I planted in them trees
6 of all sorts of fruit. I made for myself pools [tanks] of water; in order to water by them a wood sprouting out
7 (with) trees. I procured servants and maidens, and I had also "sons of the house" [slaves born in my house]; also herds, oxen and sheep in abundance belonged to me:
8 above all those who were before me in Jerusalem. I gathered for myself even silver and gold, and the peculiar treasure of kings, and of the countries; I got for myself singing-men and singing-women, and the delights of the
9 sons of men, a wife and wives. And I became great, and I increased above all who were before me in Jerusalem:
10 moreover my wisdom remained with me. And all that which my eyes asked, I did not keep back from them; I did not deny my heart any joy, for my heart had joy from all my toil, and this was my portion from all my toil.
11 And I turned towards [*i.e.* turned to contemplate] all my works which my hands had made, and towards my toil with which I toiled to make them; and behold! all was vanity and striving after wind, and there was no advantage under the sun.

§ 4. *Koheleth's third discovery.—(a) The vanity of wisdom, since the end of the wise man and the fool is alike.*

12 And I turned to behold wisdom, and madness, and folly, for what is the man, who shall come after the king,

13 him whom they made (king) long ago! And I saw that there is an advantage to wisdom over folly, like the
14 advantage of the light over the darkness. As regards the wise man, his eyes are in his head; and (as for) the fool, he walks in darkness.

And I perceived, even I, that one chance happens to
15 them all. And I said in my heart, As the chance of the fool, even to me will it happen; and for what (end) have I then been exceedingly wise? So I spake in my heart, that this also is vanity.
16 For there is no remembrance of the wise man more than of the fool for ever. In the days which are coming [it will be said by and by], "The whole (of them) are long ago forgotten!" and how dieth the wise man like the fool!
17 Therefore I hated life, for evil to me [*i.e.* in my eyes], was the work which was done under the sun, for the whole is vanity and striving after wind.

(*b*) *Riches though obtained by much toil are vanity.*

18 And I hated all my toil with which I was toiling under the sun, because that I shall leave it, (even) to the man
19 who shall be after me. And who knows whether he shall be a wise man or a fool? And he shall rule over all my toil for which I have toiled, and in which I have
20 wisely acted, under the sun. Even this is vanity. And I turned round to give my heart up to despair, concerning
21 all the toil with which I had toiled under the sun. For there is a man whose work is (performed) with wisdom, and with knowledge, and with success; and to a man who has not toiled therein must he give it as his portion.
22 Even this is vanity and a great evil. For what is to be the result to the man in all his toil, and in the striving of

23 his heart, wherewith he is toiling under the sun. For all his days are pains, and trouble is his occupation, even by night his heart does not rest. Even this is vanity itself.

(c) The conditions necessary for cheerful enjoyment.

24 There is nothing better among men than that one should eat and drink and that his soul should see good in his toil. Even this have I seen, that it is from the
25 hand of God. For who can eat and who can enjoy
26 himself without Him? For to a man who is good in His sight He has given wisdom and knowledge and joy; but to the sinner the exercise to gather, and to collect together, in order to give it to one who is good before God. Even this is vanity and a striving after wind.

§ 5. *The shortsightedness and powerlessness of men before God, the Disposer and Arranger of all things.*

III. 1 To everything there is a season, and a time for every purpose under the heavens.
2   A time to have children [or, to be born], and a time to die.
    A time to plant, and a time to root up what is planted.
3   A time to kill, and a time to heal,
    A time to break down, and a time to build up.
4   A time to weep, and a time to laugh,
    A time to mourn, and a time to dance.
5   A time to throw stones (over the fields), and a time to gather up the stones,
    A time to embrace, and a time to draw off from embracing.
6   A time to seek, and a time to lose,
    A time to guard, and a time to throw away.

7   A time to rend, and a time to sew,
    A time to be silent, and a time to speak.
8   A time to love, and a time to hate.
    A time of war, and a time of peace.
9   What profit has he who is acting in that with which
10 he is toiling. I have seen the exercise which God has
    given to the sons of man in order that they may exercise
11 themselves with it. The whole of this [or, Everything]
    He hath made beautiful in its season, even Eternity hath
    He put into their heart, so that man cannot find out
    from the beginning to the end the work which God hath
    made.
12 I perceived that there is nothing good among them
    [men], except to be glad, and to do good in one's [lit. his]
13 life. But also that every man should eat and drink, and
14 see good in all his toil, it is a gift of God. I perceived
    that everything which God doeth, it shall be for ever, to
    it it is not (possible) to add, and from it it is not (possible) to take away ; and God has made it so that they
15 may fear before Him. That which has been, long ago
    it is (in existence), and that which is to be, long ago it
    has been, and God seeks after that which has been driven
    away [*i.e.* the past].

§ 6. *The unrighteous actions of men when left to themselves.
Men compared to the beasts that perish.*

16 And again I saw under the sun the place of judgment,
    (that) iniquity was there ; and the place of righteous-
17 ness, (that) iniquity was there. I said in my heart: the
    righteous and the wicked shall God judge ; for there is a
18. time for every purpose, and for every work THERE. I said
    in my heart, it happens according to the manner of the
    sons of men, in order that God may test them, and in

order that they may see that they are beasts, they with
19 respect to themselves. For a chance are the children of men, and a chance is the beast, and the same [lit. one] chance happeneth to them: like the death of the one, so is the death of the other; and one breath is to all; and a superiority of the man over the beast there is not; for all
20 is vanity. All are going to one place, all were from the
21 dust, and all are returning to the dust. Who knoweth with regard to the spirit of the sons of men whether it ascendeth upwards, and with regard to the spirit of the beast whether it descendeth downwards to the earth?
22 So I saw that there was nothing better than that man should rejoice in his works, for that is his portion. For who can bring him to see that which shall be after him.

§ 7. *The misery common to man*—(a) *The oppression of man by his fellow.*

IV. 1 And again I saw all the oppressions which were done under the sun, and behold! the tear of the oppressed, and they had no comforter; and from the hand of those who are oppressing them (proceedeth) violence, and they
2 have no comforter! And I praised the dead which were dead long ago, more than the living who are living
3 still. And better than both of them is he who does not yet exist, who has not seen the evil work which is done under the sun.

(b) *The rivalry and useless toil of man.*

4 And I saw all the toil, and all the superiority of work, that it is the rivalry of man over his fellow—even this
5 is vanity, and a striving after wind. The fool foldeth
6 his hands together, and eateth his own flesh. Better is

the full of a hand with rest, than the full of two (closed) hands with toil and striving after wind.

§ 8. *The disadvantages of a man being alone by himself, and the benefit of companionship.*

7, 8 And I saw again vanity under the sun. There is one without a second, even son and brother he has not, and there is no end to all his toil, even his eyes are not satisfied with riches ;—And for whom am I toiling and depriving my soul of good? Even this is vanity 9 and a woful exercise it is. The two are better than the one, because they have a good reward in their toil. 10 For, if they fall, the one will lift up his companion ; and woe to the one who falls, and there is not a second 11 to lift him up. Moreover, if two lie together, then they 12 are warm; but how can one be warm (alone)? And if any make an attack on the one, the two will stand up against him ; and the threefold cord will not quickly be broken.

§ 9. *The vanity of popular enthusiasm for a new monarch.*

13 Better is a youth poor and wise than a king old and foolish, who does not any longer understand how to be 14 warned. For out of the house of the prisoners goeth he [the youth] forth to reign ; though even in his [the old 15 monarch's] kingdom he was born poor. I have seen all the living who walk under the sun on the side of the youth, the second [person just mentioned], who stands up 16 in his [the old monarch's] room. There is no end to all the people, to all those at whose head he is. (But) truly those who come after [the people of a younger generation] shall not delight in him. For even this is vanity and a striving after wind.

§ 10. *Vanity in Religion—Divine worship, and vows.*

17 Keep thy foot when thou goest to the house of God, for to draw near to hear is (better) than the fools offering sacrifices; for they are ignorant [lit. do not know], so
v. 1 that they do evil. Be not hasty with thy mouth, and let not thy heart hasten to utter a word before God; for God is in the heavens, and thou upon the earth,
2 therefore let thy words be few. For the dream cometh by reason of much occupation; and the voice of a fool in consequence of many words.
3 When thou vowest a vow to God, defer not to fulfil it, for there is no delight in fools—that which thou
4 vowest fulfil. Better is it that thou dost not vow, than
5 that thou shouldest vow and not fulfil. Suffer not thy mouth to cause thy flesh [thyself] to sin, and say not before the angel [the priest] that it was an error; wherefore should God be angry on account of thy voice, and
6 destroy the work of thy hands? For in the multitude of dreams are also vanities, and (in) many words (as well); but fear God.

§ 11. *The vanity of riches (a) in a state under despotic rule; (b) riches are little advantage in themselves, and (c) are gathered for others.*

7 If thou seest oppression of the poor and robbery of judgment and righteousness in the province, be not surprised at the matter; for there is a high one over a
8 high one watching, and higher persons over them. And an advantage of a land in all respects it is (to have) a king devoted to the field [*i.e.* agriculture].
9 He who loveth silver shall not be satisfied with silver, and he who loveth riches has no fruit (of them). Even
10 this is vanity. When the property increaseth, those that

consume it increase also; and what advantage pertains to
11 its possessor except the seeing of his eyes? Sweet is the
sleep of the husbandman, whether he eats little or much;
but the abundance of the rich, it does not allow him
to sleep.
12   There is a sore evil I have seen under the sun, riches
13 preserved by the owner thereof to his misfortune. And
these riches perish through bad circumstances; and he has
14 begotten a son, and there is nothing in his hand. As he
came out of his mother's womb, naked shall he return
again, just as he came; and nothing shall he take by his
15 toil that he can bring with him in his hand. And even this
is a sore evil, that in all respects as he came, so he must
go; and what profit has he that he toils for the wind?
16 Even all his days he eateth in darkness, and has vexed
17 himself much, and (oh!) his sickness and anger! Behold
what I have seen good, which is beautiful, (namely,) to
eat and to drink, and to see good in all his toil with
which he toils under the sun, during the number of the
days of his life which God has given him; for this is
18 his portion. Also for every man to whom God hath
given riches and treasures, and hath given him rule over
it in order to eat of it, and to take his portion, and to
19 rejoice in his toil; this (indeed) is a gift of God. For he
does not think much about the days of his life, for God
answers in [*i.e.* corresponds with] the joy of his heart.

§ 12. *The ultimatum—the vanity of possessing riches without
enjoying them.*

VI. 1 There is an evil which I have seen under the sun, and
2 it is great upon man: A man to whom God gives riches,
wealth, and honour, and he denies himself nothing of all
that he desires; but God does not give him the power to

eat thereof,—for a man, a stranger, eateth thereof.—This
3 is vanity and an evil disease. If a man begets a hundred (children), and live many years; yea, however numerous may be the days of his years, if his soul be not satisfied with that which is good, and he has also no burial—I say,
4 better than he is the untimely birth. For it came into nothingness, and it goes into the darkness, and with the
5 darkness shall its name be covered. Even the sun it saw not, and knew not—the rest (that falleth) to the one is
6 more than (that which falleth to) the other. And [the same thing is true even] if he lived a thousand years twice (told), and did not see good. (For) are not all going to one place?

§ 13. *The insatiability of desire.*

7 All the toil of man is for his mouth, and even the soul
8 is not filled. For what advantage hath the wise man above the fool? What (has even) the poor man who
9 knoweth how to walk before the living? Better is the sight of [*i.e.* that which is seen by] the eyes, than the wandering to and fro of a soul. Even this is vanity and striving after wind.

§ 14. *Human powerlessness and shortsightedness with respect to destiny.*

10 That which has been, long ago has its name been pronounced, and known is that which a man shall become; and he cannot contend with Him who is stronger than
11 he. For there are many words which increase vanity;
12 what profit (are they) to man? For who knoweth what is good for man in life, during the number of the days of the life of his vanity, for he spends them as the shadow? For who can point out to man what shall be after him under the sun?

§ 15. *Proverbs concerning things to be preferred by man.*

VII. 1 Better is a name than good [*i.e.* perfumed] oil, and the
2 day of death than the day of one's birth. Better is it
to go to a house of mourning than to go to a house of
feasting; because that is the end of every man, and the
3 living will lay it to his heart. Better is sorrow than
laughter, for through the sadness of the face the heart
4 is made better. The heart of wise men is in a house
of mourning, and the heart of fools in a house of mirth.
5 Better is it to hear a reproof of a wise man, than that
6 a man should be hearing a song of fools. For, like the
noise of the nettles under the kettle, so is the laughter of
the fool. Even this is vanity.

§ 16. *Patience and wisdom the best preservatives in the time of oppression and adversity.*

7 Because oppression maddeneth a wise man, and a gift
8 [a bribe] destroyeth [breaketh] (his) heart, better is the end
of a matter than its beginning; better he who is patient
9 in spirit than he who is haughty in spirit. Be not hasty
in thy spirit to be angry, for anger rests in the bosom of
10 fools. Say not, How is it that the former days were
better than these? for not with wisdom dost thou ask
11 after this. Wisdom is good along with an inheritance,
12 and an advantage to those who behold the sun. For in
a shade [shelter] is wisdom, in a shade [shelter] is money,
yet an advantage of knowledge is that wisdom gives life
13 to those who possess her. Consider the work of God;
for who can make that straight which He hath made
14 crooked? In a day of prosperity be in good spirits;
and in a day of adversity consider that even God hath
made this [the evil day] as well as that [the day of prosperity], in order that man may find out nothing of that
(which shall come) after him.

§ 17. *The importance of keeping "the middle mean," and the practical advantages of wisdom.*

15 All (sorts of things) have I seen in the days of my vanity. There is a righteous man perishing in (spite of) his righteousness, and there is a wicked man prolonging
16 (his life) in (spite of) his evil-doing. Be not righteous to excess, and do not show thyself too wise; why wilt thou
17 ruin thyself? Be not wicked to excess, and be not a
18 fool; why wilt thou die before thy time? Good (is it) that thou shouldest lay hold on this [proverb]; and also from that withdraw not thy hand; for he who feareth God fulfilleth [or, shall come out of] them all.
19 Wisdom proves stronger to the wise man than ten
20 rulers which are in the city. For a man there is not (so)
21 righteous on earth who doeth good and sinneth not. Also give not thy heart [thy attention] to all the words which they say, that thou hear not (about) thy servant cursing
22 thee. For many times even, thy heart knoweth, even thou hast cursed others.
23 All this have I proved by wisdom; I said: Wise will
24 I become, but it was far from me. Far [from man's comprehension] is that which is, and deep, deep, who can discover it.

§ 18. *The snare by which men are generally caught. The wicked woman.*

25 I turned myself (to another matter); and my heart was to know and to spy out, and to seek wisdom and (knowledge based on) reckoning; and to know wickedness (to
26 be) folly, and foolishness (to be) madness. And I find more bitter than death the woman who is snares, and a net [lit. nets] is her heart, fetters are her hands—he who is good before God shall be saved from her; but a sinner
27 shall be caught by her. See, this have I found, saith the

Koheleth, adding one to one to find out the reckoning, 28 what still my soul hath sought, and I have not found, one man out of a thousand I have found, but a woman 29 among all those I have not found. Only, this see! I have found: that God made man upright, but they have sought out many devices [lit. reckonings].

§ 19. *The benefit of wisdom in days of oppression.—The wise man will be obedient and patient, knowing that there is a God who judgeth the earth.*

VIII. 1 Who is as the wise man? and who understands the explanation of a thing? The wisdom of a man causes his face to shine, and the coarseness of his face is changed. 2 I (say), observe the command of a king, even on account 3 of the oath of God. Hasten not to go away from him, stand not in an evil affair; for all that he desires he will 4 do. For a word of a king is powerful, and who can say to him, What doest thou (there)? 5 He who observeth (his) commandment shall experience no evil thing; and time and judgment knoweth the heart 6 of a wise man. For to every purpose there is a time and judgment; for the wickedness of man is heavy upon him; for there is no one who knoweth that which shall be; for, 7 how it shall be, who can tell to him? There is no man who has power over the wind so as to restrain the wind; 8 and there is no ruler in the day of death; and there is no discharge in the war; and wickedness does not deliver its masters. 9 All this have I seen, even by applying my heart to all the work that is done under the sun, at a time when 10 man ruleth over man to his hurt [*i.e.* of the latter]. And thus [under such circumstances] have I seen wicked men buried; and they came (into being); and from the place of the holy they went (to their graves); and they are forgotten in the very city where they acted thus (wickedly). Even this is vanity.

11 Because sentence against the work of wickedness is not executed speedily, therefore the heart of the sons of men
12 within them is full [has full courage] to do evil: because a sinner commits evil a hundred times, and prolongeth (his days) for it; although indeed I know that it shall be well
13 for those that fear God, who fear before him: and well it shall not be for the wicked, and he shall not prolong his days, (he shall be) like the shadow, because he feareth not before God.
14 There is a vanity which is done upon the earth, (namely) that there are righteous men to whom it happeneth according to the work of the wicked; and there are wicked men to whom it happeneth according to the work of the righteous. I said, that this indeed is vanity.
15 And I commended joy [cheerfulness], because there is nothing better for man under the sun than to eat, and to drink, and to enjoy himself; and that this should accompany him in his work during the days of his life, which God hath given to him under the sun.

§ 20. *Man knows not the work of God, but is in all things conditioned by a higher power than his own, which permits the same things to happen to all men alike.*

16 As I gave my heart to know wisdom, and to see into the business which is done upon the earth, for even by day or by night, there is no seeing sleep in his
17 [man's] eyes,—then have I seen all the work of God, that man is not able to find out the work which is done under the sun; because that man labours to seek it, and does not find it; and even if the wise man says that he knows it, it is not to be found out.

IX. 1 For all this I have laid to my heart, and I strove [lit. I have been about] to test [prove] all this: that the righteous and the wise and their actions are in the hand of God; even love or hatred man knoweth not, all lies 2 before them. All (is) like that which (is) to all, one fate [chance] happens to the righteous and to the wicked, to the good, and to the clean and to the unclean, both to the man who sacrificeth and to him who sacrificeth not; as is the good (man) so is the sinner, the man who sweareth is as he who fears an oath.

§ 21. *The fate that awaits all, the state of the dead. Men ought therefore to enjoy life, while working for their daily bread. The uncertainties of life, and the certainty of death in an unexpected time.*

3 This is an evil in all that is done under the sun; that one fate [chance] happens to all, and also that the heart of the sons of men is full of evil, and madness is in their hearts during their lives, and after it [*i.e.* their life]—to the dead!
4 For he who is joined to all the living [*i.e.* to all living beings] has hope, for even a living dog is better than the 5 lion which is dead. For the living know that they shall die; but as for the dead, they know nothing, and they have no more a reward, for their memory is forgotten.
6 Even their love, yea their hatred, and their rivalry, long ago has perished; and they have no portion more for ever in all that which is done under the sun.
7 Go, eat with gladness thy bread, and drink with good heart thy wine; for, long ago, God hath approved of thy 8 doings [in this matter]. At every time let thy garments be white, and let oil upon thy head not be wanting.
9 Enjoy life with a wife whom thou lovest all the days of the life of thy vanity, which God hath given to thee under

the sun; all the days of thy vanity, for this is thy portion in life, and in thy toil, wherein thou toilest under the sun.
10 All that thy hand may find to do with thy strength, do; for there is no work, nor reckoning, nor knowledge, nor wisdom in Sheol, whither thou art going!
11 I came back even to see under the sun that the race belongs not to the swift, nor the battle to the heroes, nor even bread to the wise, nor even riches to the prudent, nor even favour to the knowing; for time and chance
12 befall all of them. For indeed man knoweth not his time; like the fishes which are caught in an evil net, and like the birds which are caught in the trap;—like these are the sons of men ensnared in a time of evil, like that which [or, when it] falls upon them suddenly.

§ 22. *The poor wise man, and the benefits of wisdom.*

13 Even this have I seen as wisdom under the sun, and it
14 was great in my estimation; a little city, and men in it but few, and there came to it a great king, and encom-
15 passed it, and built against it great intrenchments; and found in it a poor wise man, and he [the latter] delivered the city through his wisdom, and not a man remembered that same poor man.
16 Then said I, Better is wisdom than strength; but the wisdom of the poor is despised, and his words are not heard.
17 Words of wise men (uttered) in quiet are heard, better
18 than the shout of a ruler among fools. Better is wisdom than weapons of war; and one sinner destroyeth much good.

§ 23 *The usefulness of wisdom and the danger of folly, shown by various proverbs.*

x. 1 Poisonous flies make the oil of the perfumer to stink

and ferment; heavier than wisdom, than honour, is a
2 little folly. The heart of a wise man (inclines) towards
3 his right, and the heart of a fool towards his left; and
even on the road, as [or, when] the fool is going along,
his heart [understanding] fails him, and he says to all that
he is a fool.
4   If the spirit of the ruler rise against thee, leave not
thy post; for patience puts an end to great transgressions.
5   There is an evil which I have seen under the sun, like
6 an oversight which proceedeth from the ruler. Folly is
placed on great heights, and rich men sit in lowliness.
7 I have seen slaves upon horses, and princes walking like
slaves upon the earth.
8   He who digs a pit may fall into it, and he who breaks
down a wall a serpent may bite him. He who heweth
9 out stones may be hurt by them; he who cutteth down
trees may be endangered by them.
10   If the iron has become blunt, and he has not whetted
the face (of it), then must he put forth strength; a
superiority in setting right (has) wisdom.
11   If the serpent bites before enchantment, then there is
no use for the master of the tongue [*i.e.* the snake-charmer].

§ 24. *The fool noted for his useless talk and aimless toil.*

12   The words of a wise man's mouth are grace, but the
13 lips of a fool swallow up himself. The beginning of the
words of his mouth is folly, and the end of his mouth
14 wicked madness. And the fool multiplieth words,
(although) man knows not that which shall be, and that
15 which shall be after him [*i.e.* after his death], who can
narrate to him? Fools-work [*i.e.* foolish philosophizing]
wearies him who does not know (even) how to go to the
city.

§ 25. *The misery of a land cursed with a foolish king, and the necessity of prudence in the subjects of such a monarch.*

x. 16 Woe to thee, O Land, whose king is a child, and whose
17 princes eat in the morning! O thy happiness, O Land! whose king is a son of nobles; and thy princes eat at the (right) time in strength, and not in drunkenness.
18 Through great indolence the beam-work sinks, and by
19 laziness of hands the house leaks. For merriment they make feasts [lit. bread], and wine gladdens life, and money grants all (they desire).
20 Even in thy consciousness, curse not a king, nor in thy bed-chambers curse a rich man; for the fowl of the heaven shall carry the voice, and the possessor [lit. master] of wings [the winged birds] shall tell the word [or, expression].

§ 26. *The wisdom of beneficence. The future belongs to God, but man ought to labour and enjoy life while he can.*

XI. 1 Cast thy bread upon the surface of the waters, for in
2 the (course of) many days thou shalt find it. Give a portion to seven, yea even to eight, for thou knowest not
3 what evil shall be upon the earth. If the clouds are full of heavy showers, they will empty themselves upon the earth; and if a tree falleth in the north or in the south, in the place where the tree falleth, there it will
4 be [or, let it be]. He who observeth the wind shall not sow, and he who looketh at the clouds shall not reap.
5 As thou knowest not which is the way of the wind, like the bones in the womb of her who is with child, even so
6 knowest thou not the work of God who maketh all. In the morning sow thy seed, and until evening slack not thou thy hand, for thou knowest not whether this shall

prosper, either this or that, or if both together shall be good.

7 And sweet is the light, and good for the eyes it is to
8 see the sun. For, if the man lives many years, let him rejoice in them all, and let him remember the days of darkness, for they shall be many. All that which is coming is vanity.

§ 27. *The Song of Koheleth. The Days of Life, and the Days of Death.*

9 Rejoice, young man, in thy youth,
And let thy heart cheer thee in the days of thy youth,
And walk in the ways of thy heart,
And according to the sight of thine eyes!
But know—that for all these God shall bring thee into the judgment.
10 Therefore banish moroseness from thy heart,
And put away evil from thy flesh,
For boyhood and manhood are vanity;

XII. 1 And remember thy Creator in the days of thy youth:

ERE there come the days of evil, and years approach,
Of which thou shalt say, "I have no pleasure in them!"

2 ERE the sun is darkened, and the light, and the moon, and the stars,
And the clouds return after the pouring rain.

3 IN THE DAY WHEN the keepers of the house tremble,
And the men of strength bow-themselves-together,
And the grinding-maids cease because they are few,
And the (ladies) that look out at the lattices are darkened!
4 And doors are shut towards the street,
When the sound of the grinding-mill ceases.

WHEN one rises at the voice of the bird,
And all the daughters of song are humbled,
5 Even they fear from on high, and all-sorts-of-terrors are in the path.

Then there blossoms the almond tree,
And crawls forth the locust ;
But unavailing is the caperberry—
For the man is going to his eternal house ;
And there go the mourners about in the street !

6 ERE the silver cord be snapped asunder,
And the golden bowl break—
And the pitcher be shivered upon the spring,
And the wheel be broken (and fall) into the well ;

7 And ERE the dust return upon the earth as it was ;
For the spirit shall return to the God who gave it.

§ 28. *The Epilogue.*

8 Vanity of vanities, saith the Koheleth [Solomon], the whole is vanity.
9 And, moreover (note), that Koheleth [the writer] was a wise man ; further, he taught the people knowledge, and pondered-over [lit. weighed], and investigated, [yea] ar-
10 ranged many proverbs. Koheleth sought to discover words of pleasantness, and what was written in uprightness, words of truth.
11 Words of wise men are like the goads ; and like nails firmly-driven-in are the masters of [*i.e.* persons well versed in] " collections " (of such sayings). They [the "collections"] are given from One Shepherd.
12 And, moreover (note) more than that : my son, be

warned, of making many books there is no end, and much study is a weariness of flesh.

13 The end of the matter when all is heard is, Fear God and keep His commandments, for this ought every man to
14 do. For God shall bring every work into a judgment, (which shall pass) upon all that is concealed, whether good or whether evil.

CRITICAL AND GRAMMATICAL COMMENTARY.

CHAPTER I.

1. "The words of Koheleth, son of David, king in Jerusalem." The greater distinctive zakeph is placed in the Hebrew over *David*, to point out that the words following are in apposition to *Koheleth*, and not to David. The smaller distinctive (pashta) over דברי is necessary, for zakeph-katon, as a general rule, requires to be accompanied by its minor. מלך is rendered definite by the following בירושלם. The expression is peculiar. On the name Koheleth, see prelim. note on p. 287 ff. One would have expected, "king of Israel in Jerusalem," or, as in the 12th verse, "king over Israel in Jerusalem." Comp. 2 Kings xiv. 23. See remarks on p. 88 ff.

2. הֲבֵל הֲבָלִים. The full phrase occurs three times, twice in this verse and once in chap. xii. 8. The concluding words הכל הבל are, however, to be found also in verse 14, in chap. iii. 19, and in xi. 8, in a modified form, בל שבא הבל. The expression is used in a superlative sense. Compare the phrases "heaven of heavens," 1 Kings viii. 27; "servant of servants," Gen. ix. 25; "ornament of ornaments," Ezek. xvi. 7; "song of songs," Cant. i. 1. Compare מִפְּנֵי רְעַת רֲעַתְכֶם, Hos. x. 15. It is to be regarded as an accusative of exclamation; not as a nominative, as if a kind of predicate, LXX., Vulg., etc., and by Rosenmüller among the moderns, "vanissima inquit Concionator, vanissima sunt omnia." The form of the construct הֲבֵל is peculiar. It is best explained with Delitzsch after Ewald, § 32 *b*, as an Aramaising form like, עֲבֵד, צְלֵם, ܓܠܵܐ. Zöckler compares אֲבֵל in Ps. xxxv. 14, but that word is not a segholate, nor

are the instances cited by Olshausen, § 154 *a*, in which the original vowel reappears between the second and third stem letters. See Kalisch, § xxvii. 2 *b*. Jerome seems to have read הֲבַל from his remarks "in Hebræo pro vanitate vanitatum ABAL ABALIM scriptum est." There is some uncertainty as to the translation of the other Greek translators, for Jerome quotes their rendering as ἀτμὸς ἀτμίδων sive ἀτμῶν, while others give it as ἀτμὶς ἀτμίδων or ἀτμὸς ἀτμῶν. See Field. In Heb. and Chald. הבל is used in the sense of *breath* or *vapour*, or a slight breeze (Isa. lvii. 13), such as that which comes from the mouth, and it is frequently used in a figurative sense for *vanity*. The signification of *mist* assigned to it in some passages of Koheleth (chap. vi. 4; viii. 14; xi. 8) is more than doubtful.

אמר may be taken either as a past or a present, but the latter signification is more suitable here.

הכל ה׳. *All is vanity.* Some writers have considered the reference here to be the *universe*, but Koheleth speaks only of the things done under the sun, or of those matters which affect the earth and man.

As to the subject matter of the verse, suitable parallels are found in Ps. xxxix. 5–7; xc. 3–10; cii. 25–28. Comp. also Gen. xlvii. 9.

3. מה יתרון. The word יִתְרוֹן occurs nine times in this book, and in this only; viz. chap. i. 3; ii. 11, 13 (bis); iii. 9; v. 8, 15; vii. 12; x. 10. But the shortened form יֶתֶר (comp. Olshausen, § 215 *g*) occurs as a proper name (*Jethro*) in Exod. iii. 1; xviii. 1, 5, 6, 9, 12, called also once יֶתֶר, Exod. iv. 18. יִתְרוֹ might, however, be explained otherwise as an apocopated form of יִתְרוֹן, like שִׁילֹה from שִׁילוֹן. Hence it cannot be fairly asserted that the word is later Hebrew. The Chald. and post-Biblical word for יִתְרוֹן is יוּתְרָן, Syr. ࠌࠓࠕࠊ. It signifies *that which remains over and above, gain, profit, advantage*, and, when construed with מִן, as in chap. ii. 13, *pre-eminence*. In chap. iii. 19 the noun מוֹתָר, derived from the same stem, occurs as a synonyme. LXX. literally, τίς περισσεία τῷ ἀνθρώπῳ. The LXX. always so translate the word. Aq. and Symm. here τί πλέον τῷ ἀνθρώπῳ. Symm., in chap. v. 15, translates it by περισσόν, and in chap. x. 10 by προέχει. A primary form יָתְרוֹן (comp. כָּרוֹן, const. כְּרוֹן, בְּלָיוֹן, const. בִּלְיוֹן, vid. Böttcher, *Lehrb.*, § 751 *f*) is unknown, vid. note on verse 11. Delitzsch observes that Simson the punctuator (Cod. 102 *a*, of Leipzig Univ. Lib.) blames those that use וְיִתְרוֹן in a liturgical prayer for the Day of Atonement.

Ch. i. 3, 4] *Critical and Grammatical Comm.* 307

Kleinert translates מה יתרון לא, *man has nothing abiding*, a translation *quoad sensum*. Its peculiarity lies in the rendering of מָה by *not*, a force which it seems to have in some few instances, as Job xxxi. 1; Cant. viii. 4; 1 Kings xii. 16, when compared with 2 Sam. xx. 1. See Ewald, § 325 *b*. Ewald, however, does not assign that meaning to מה in this passage. Compare the negative ل in Arabic. The negative meaning has arisen out of its interrogative sense. See Ewald, *Gram. Crit. Arab. Ling.*, § 698. Comp. Böttcher, *Lehrb.*, § 532.

In all his work. Hahn translates "*notwithstanding*," or "in spite of all his work," appealing to Isa. v. 25, where בכל זאת is rendered "*for all this.*" But this is unnecessary.

שיעמל. ש does not here denote the accusative of the manner, but of the object (*Delitzsch*). The same expression recurs in chap. v. 17, and a cognate expression עָמָל עָמֵל, chap. ii. 19, 20.

Under the sun. See p. 142. This formula is frequently found in Koheleth, and is peculiar to it, See verse 9, 14; chap. ii. 11, 17, 18, 19, 20, 22; iii. 16; iv. 1, 7; v. 13, 18; vi. 1, 12; viii. 9, 15; ix. 6, 9, 11, 13; x. 5. Compare the phrases "*under heaven*" and "*upon the earth.*" The former occurs in verse 13; ii. 3; iii. 1, and is an expression often found elsewhere, as in Exod. xvii. 14; Deut. vii. 23; ix. 14; xxv. 19; xxix. 20; 2 Kings xiv. 27, as well as in the Chaldee verse in Jer. x. 11, and in Lam. iii. 66. The phrase occurs also in Greek in Baruch ii. 2; Luke xvii. 24; Acts ii. 5; iv. 12; Col. i. 22. The cognate expression "under the whole heaven" is used in Deut. ii. 25; iv. 19, and several times in the Book of Job (xxviii. 24; xxxvii. 3; xli. 11). The phrase "*upon the earth*" על־הארץ is found in chap. viii. 14, 16; xi. 2, and often elsewhere, as in Gen. viii. 17. Compare the kindred expression על האדמה in Exod. x. 6. See Deut. iv. 4 and 36.

4. הלך to *go*, to *depart*, hence to *die*, chap. v. 15; Job x. 21; Ps. xxxix. 14. On the subject matter of this verse comp. Sir. xiv. 19.

עמדת, *is abiding.* Comp. Ps. xix. 10. The copula in this sentence may intimate "*whilst.*" The earth "remains standing as it is, with its entire order and arrangement. He does not deny that there is movement within, but it is movement in a circle which leads to nothing" (*Hitzig*). Delitzsch considers that this is not the meaning of the verse, which is rather that the earth fulfils its destiny by remaining immovable. It is the only thing that remains unmoved while generations go and come. The thought, dwelt on by the Psalmist, of the contrast between the unchangeableness of God and the changeableness of all things earthly, is foreign to the object which Koheleth had in view. Jerome thus comments on the passage: "quid hac vanius vanitate quam terram manere, quæ hominum causa facta est, et ipsum hominem, terræ dominum, tam repente in pulverem dissolvi." It is unnecessary, with Zöckler, to suppose that the writer is thinking of the earth as founded upon pillars, Ps. xxiv. 2; civ. 5; Job xxxviii. 6. Graetz maintains that the earth here signifies the inhabitants thereof, which still continue to exist, though one generation succeeds another.

5. The LXX., Vulg., Targ., Luther, Herzfeld, Hitzig, Hahn, connect ואל מקומו שואף with the preceding, translating the clause substantially as: "*and hastens to its place where it also arises.*" In this case the relation אשׁר is considered to be understood before שָׁם, אֲשֶׁר שָׁם, signifying *where*. The LXX. translate שואף by ἕλκει, Vulg. *revertitur*. Jerome remarks: "pro eo autem, quod Vulgatam ed. sequentes posuimus, *ad locum suum ducit*, in Hebræo habet *soeph*, quod Aq. interpretabatur εἰσπνεῖ, id est *aspirat*; Symm. vero et Theod. *recurrit*." The transl. of Symm. and Theod. is generally given as ἐπαναστρέφει, but Field (*Orig. Hex.* in loco) points out that Symm.'s rendering here, and even that of Aquila, is somewhat doubtful. But the accentuation distinctly connects שואף with the second part of the sentence, as if "*and the sun rises, and the sun sets: and* (going) *to its place* [namely, the place of its rising]; *panting, rises* (the Heb. has also here the participle) *he there.*" Ewald renders "and the sun arises, the sun goes down, and thither back again where it arises panting." But, as Delitzsch observes, the verb שאף does not signify *panting* from fatigue so much as *panting* after something. This is the meaning in which the word occurs in Isaiah xlii. 14; Job vii. 2, and Ps. cxix. 131. The picture drawn by Koheleth is not the same as that in Psalm xix. 6, where the sun is represented as rising, rejoicing as a hero to run his race. Delitzsch translates, "and the sun goes down, and to its place it goes panting back in order to arise there." The place where the sun goes is most naturally conceived as the place of its setting. Delitzsch considers the idea of the passage to be, that the sun hurries back to the place where it is again to arise, and must continue both day and

night on its constant course, however wearied it may be. Kleinert regards the two participles as expressing together one idea. So in the rendering given above, "and (the sun goes) even to its place, longing it is to arise there." Somewhat similar is the rendering of Ginsburg, "and though it pantingly goeth to its place, it riseth there." Similarly Herzfeld, who notes that the Syr. likewise renders: ܘܐܦ ܐܙܠ ܠܐܬܪܗ ܢܣܒ. The objection to this is that the שָׁם would naturally be regarded as connected with the preceding suffix (מְקוֹמוֹ). A similar construction with two participles occurs in 1 Sam. xvi. 16, יֹדֵעַ מְנַגֵּן, *one who understands playing*. See Ges.-Kautzsch, § 142, 4, Kalisch, § c. 2. On the meaning of שֹׁאֵף compare Habb. ii. 3, where it is said of a vision וְיָפֵחַ לַקֵּץ "*and it pants for the end.*"

Graetz, regarding all attempts to extract a satisfactory meaning out of שֹׁאֵף as vain, proposes to read שָׁב אַף. The meaning of the clause would then be, "and to its place it returns, rising there again." There is, however, no necessity for this alteration. Clericus unsuitably compares the *panting horses of the sun*, spoken of by Ovid (*Metam.* xxi, 418) and Virgil (*Georg.* i. 250), but such an idea is totally foreign to the Hebrew conception. Rosenmüller more suitably adduces Catulli Carm. v. 4 ff:—

"Soles occidere et redire possunt;
Nobis, cum semel occidit brevis lux,
Nox est perpetua una dormienda."

Jerome observes: "Sol iste, qui in lucem mortalibus datus est, interitum mundi ortu suo quotidie indicat et occasu. Qui postquam ardentem rotam Oceano junxerit, incognitas nobis vias ad locum, unde exierat, regreditur, expletoque noctu circulo rursum de thalamo festinus erumpit."

זוֹרֵחַ הוּא On the pronoun see Ewald, § 311 *a.* (1). The Book of Koheleth is remarkable for the partiality which the writer exhibits for the participle. See chap. i. 4, 6, 7; ii. 14, 19, 21; iii. 20; iv. 5; v. 7, 9; vi. 12; viii. 12, 14, 16; ix. 5, 10, 16, 17, etc. The personal pronoun is also frequently used with such participles, even when there is no emphasis whatever to account for its use, as well as with finite verbs. This use of the personal pronoun, and the fact that it is placed after the word and participle, is indicative of a late stage of the language. וּמוֹצֶא אֲנִי, *and I find*, chap. vii. 26, so here, זוֹרֵחַ הוּא,

he rises. Verbal adjectives are also used by Koheleth with the personal pronouns to express the present tense, as אֲנִי עָמֵל *I weary myself,* chap. ii. 18; iv. 8; אַתָּה עָמֵל, chap. ix. 9; הוּא עָמֵל, chap. ii. 22; iii. 9. In all these cases the pronoun is preceded by the relative. When a negative is required, the writer expresses such by אִין, to which the personal pronoun is appended as a suffix, as אֵינֶנּוּ יֹדֵעַ, *he knows not,* viii. 7 (so also with verbal adj., chap. vi. 2; viii. 13); אֵינָם יוֹדְעִים, *they know not,* chap. iv. 17.

6. The first part of this verse is referred to the sun by the LXX., Targ., Syr., Vulg., and, among the moderns, by Gejer and Graetz. But the verse division of the Hebrew is evidently correct. The writer adduces the wind as a fresh example of motion which continually repeats itself. The use of the participles adds life indeed to the picture, but it gives at the same time the impression of weariness. Wolfg. Menzel (in his *Naturkunde in christ. Geiste aufgefasst*, i. 270) considers that Dove's law of the circuits of the winds is here alluded to. We agree with Zöckler in thinking otherwise, though not with the reason he gives, namely, that the author in verse 4 depicts the earth as standing unmoved. Hahn considers that the author refers to the constant change between hot and cold winds, the cold wind blowing from the north and going toward the south (comp. Job xxxvii. 9; Sir. xliii. 20), and the warm wind coming up from the south (Job xxxvii. 17; Luke xii. 55). He supposes these winds to symbolise respectively prosperity and adversity in the life of man; but the verse, however, does not suggest any such symbolism.

In the fourth verse all the predicates are participles. In the first part of the fifth verse two perfects occur, followed in the second clause by two participles. In the fourth verse, יָשׁוּב in the last clause is most probably the participle. So the Syriac regards it. In such verbs ע״ו, the participle active is identical in form with the perfect. The participle expresses habit and continuance more distinctly than the perfect. It will be noted that the subjects in ver. 4 precede the predicates in all three cases. In ver. 4 they follow, and similarly in ver. 6.

The wind, according to Hitzig, is described as blowing from north to south, the sun being spoken of in connexion with the two other quarters of the heavens, namely the east and west. But the clause that follows "circling, circling goes the wind," proves that the

Ch. i. 6, 7.] *Critical and Grammatical Comm.* 311

winds were not conceived by the writer as blowing only from north and south, but as blowing from all quarters of the heaven. The repetition of the participle סובב סובב denotes the repetition of the phenomena. See Ewald, § 313 *a*. Comp. Ges.-Kautzsch, § 108, 4. The sense is merely the same as that of סָבִיב סָבִיב, *round and round*, Ezek. xxxvii. 2. The comparison of the two passages led Jerome to translate *gyrans gyrando vadit spiritus*.

ועל ס' שב הר'. Knobel and Ewald translate, "returns upon its circles," *i.e.* returns by the same paths again. But it is better to construe על with the verb, after Delitzsch and Zöckler, as in Prov. xxvi. 11 (comp. Mal. iii. 24; Ps. xix. 7). So Hitzig "the wind returns to its circlings," *i.e.* begins the same course over again, its movements constantly repeating themselves anew.

7. נחלים is a general term which includes all streams. The statement that all the streams flow into the sea is a general one. It does not involve the error which the Targum has fallen into that the ocean surrounds the earth like a ring, or that the rivers regain their sources by subterranean channels (*Ginsburg*, after the Targ.), or that the sea replenishes the fountains from which they flow (*Hitzig*). Nor is there necessarily any allusion to the fact, probably well-known even in that day, that the water rises from the sea in vapours, and is collected in rain-clouds (Job xxxvi. 27, 28) and thus replenishes the streams and causes the rivers to flow on continously (*Delitzsch*). This view is, however, preferable to the others. Koheleth's instances are selected from common experience, and would have lost much of their force if any facts not generally known had been alluded to. The phenomenon referred to is the same as that noted by Aristophanes, Nubes, 1291 ff.

Strepsiades: καλῶς λέγεις.
τί δῆτα; τὴν θάλατταν ἔσθ' ὅτι πλείονα
νυνὶ νομίζεις ἢ πρὸ τοῦ;
Amynias: Μὰ Δί', ἀλλ' ἴσην,
οὐ γὰρ δίκαιον πλεῖον' εἶναι.
Streps.: κᾆτα πῶς
αὕτη μὲν, ὦ κακόδαιμον, οὐδὲν γίγνεται,
ἐπιρεόντων τῶν ποταμῶν, πλείων; κ.τ.λ.

אֵינֶנּוּ מָלֵא. On construction vid. n. on p. 5. Delitzsch observes that איננו, Mishnaic אינו, has the reflexive pronoun, as in Exod. iii. 2; Lev. xiii. 34, and elsewhere.

אֶל־מָקוֹם שֶׁהַנְּ׳. On the construct state before the relative compare chap. xi. 3, and see Ges.-Kautzsch, § 116, 2; Gesenius, *Lehrg.*, p. 679; Ewald, § 332 *c*; Kalisch, § 87 *f.*

The שָׁם in the second part of the verse is not to be combined with the preceding relative and translated *whence* or *from whence* (as Symm. ἀφ' οὗ, Vulg. *unde*, Grotius, Umbreit, etc.), which would require מִשָּׁם. The relative in descriptions of places often means by itself *in which*, i.e. *where*, Gen. xxxix. 20, or *to which*, i.e. *whither*, Num. xiii. 27; 2 Kings xii. 2 (where our A.V. has incorrectly "*for*"), but never *from which*, or *whence*. But, as Delitzsch observes, שָׁם after verbs of motion (*e.g.* after שׁוּב in Jer. xxii. 27, and after הלך in 1 Sam. ix. 6) has frequently the signification of שָׁמָּה. Hence the passage is "*to the place whither* (שֶׁ׳ in שֶׁהֵם) *the rivers are going, thither* (שָׁם) *they go again*," that is, they flow on ever again and again into the all-devouring sea. In combination with another verb, שׁוּב is often best rendered by the adverb "*again.*" The verb qualified is placed either in the same tense, and (1) connected with ו, as in 2 Kings i. 13; or (2) without ו, as Gen. xxx. 31. Or, (3) as here, followed by ל with the inf., Hosea xi. 9; Job vii. 7, etc. The use of the participle is intentional, as continuity is intended to be expressed. See n. on verse 6. Compare Lucretius vi. 631–638:—

> "Postremo quoniam raro cum corpore tellus
> Est, et conjuncta est, aras maris undique cingens,
> Debet, ut in mare de terris venit humor aquai,
> In terras itidem manare ex aequore salso;
> Percolatur enim virus, retroque remanat
> Materies humoris, et ad caput amnibus omnis
> Confluit; unde super terras redit agmine dulci
> Qua via secta semel liquido pede detulit undas."

8. כָּל־הַדְּבָרִים יְגֵעִים. The word דָּבָר, the plural of which is found here, may either mean *word* or *thing*. In the latter sense it is found in the next verse, as also in chap. vi. 12; vii. 8; Josh. v. 4, etc. The LXX., Syr., Targ., with many modern commentators, translate it here by "*words.*" But the expression would be strange, if the meaning sought to be conveyed is that given by Gesenius (in the

Thes.) "*all words are wearied*," that is, the man would be wearied who should endeavour to declare all these things in words. Equally strange is it if the translations of Winer, Knobel, etc., be adopted, "*all words weary*," *i.e.* render the ears of those weary who hear them; the adjective being regarded as active. Knobel, after Rosenmüller, urges in defence of this rendering that words of a similar form are often active in signification, as עָמֵל, *a workman*, Judges v. 26; עָרֵב, Ps. xlix. 6; שֹׁהֵד Job xvi. 19; אָשֵׁם, Ezra x. 19. This explanation is, apart from other considerations, scarcely consistent with the close of the verse where the writer speaks of the ear, not as wearied, but as never satisfied with hearing. Graetz renders "all things weary themselves," *i.e.* in the same way as related, by ceaselessly going the same rounds. Not dissimilarly Delitzsch, "all things weary themselves," *i.e.* working with all their might and main, or, in other words, "all things are in activity." He compares the signification of the noun יְגִיעַ, *work, labour*, used specially of hard toil (comp. the verb in piel, chap. x. 15). The fem. noun יְגִיעָה occurs in same sense in chap. xii. 12. This is better than Rosenmüller's "*omnes res fatigantur h.e. in perpetua versantur vicissitudine qua fatigantur quasi.*" יָגֵעַ signifies not *causing weariness*, but *suffering from weariness*. So in Deut. xxv. 18; 2 Sam. xvii. 2, which are the only other passages where the adjective occurs. Closely related however is the adjective יָגִיעַ, which occurs once in plural, Job. iii. 17, also in an intransitive sense; unless indeed יָגֵעַ and יָגִיעַ be regarded as identical, vid. Böttcher, *Lehrb.*, § 751 *a*, § 994, 8. Perowne, in the *Expositor*, translates "all things are weary," and observes: "this is the poetry of the heart. The weary spirit sees its own weariness reflected on all sides. Man interprets nature,—reads into it his own unrest and dissatisfaction, and weary, profitless, laborious monotony." But the explanation of Delitzsch seems more in accordance with the context.

The object to be supplied after לְדַבֵּר is כֹּל. The restless activity exhibited by the things of nature communicates itself also to man, and makes him restless; his eye is not satisfied with what it sees, nor his ear content with what it hears. The expression about the eye is not used in the same sense as in Prov. xxvii. 20. Hitzig and Zöckler render מִשְּׁמֹעַ, "so that it will no longer hear," lit. "away from hearing." But this is unnecessary. שָׂבַע is construed with מִן of the thing with which one is satiated or satisfied. (See chap. vi. 3; Job xix. 22; Ps. civ. 13.) Similarly נִמְלָא is construed with מִן preceding the object of which anything is full. See Ezek. xxxii. 6, and comp. the verb in kal in Isaiah ii. 6; in piel, Jer. li. 34; Ps. cxxvii. 5.

9. מַה שֶׁהָיָה. The LXX. render מַה־שׁ interrogatively in both parts of the verse, τί τὸ γεγονός; αὐτὸ τὸ γενησόμενον· καὶ τί τὸ πεποιημένον; αὐτὸ τὸ ποιηθησόμενον; and similarly Vulg. So the Arab., Grotius, Bauer and others. So מַה־שֶּׁ is a phrase indicative of a late period of the language. It means *that which*, identical with Aram., ܡܢ, מָה דִּי, מָה דְ, Dan. ii. 28, 29, 45; Ezra vii. 18. Comp. Koh. iii. 15; x. 14. The older language uses in this sense the simple relative אֲשֶׁר, and כֹּל אֲשֶׁר in that of *whatever* (chap. vi. 10; vii. 24). מה though properly interrogative, was in certain cases used to denote *whatever* (quodcunque), Job xiii. 13 (in which sense the more definite דְּבַר־מַה, Num. xxiii. 3, is also employed), also to denote *something, anything* (aliquid, quidquam), Gen. xxxix. 8; Prov. ix. 13, and מִי or מִי אֲשֶׁר is used in the sense of *quisquis, whoever*, Exod. xxiv. 14; xxxii. 33. These references are those of Delitzsch. See also Ewald, § 331, 3; Ges.-Kautzsch, § 124, 2; Kalisch, § 80, 11. In הוּא שֶׁ, (compare הוּא אֲשֶׁר, Gen. xlii. 14), Delitzsch notes the meanings *id (est) quod* and *idem (est) quod* are combined. הוּא is sometimes used to denote that two things are placed on the same footing, as Job iii. 19, or are the same, Ps. cii. 28. הָיָה is used throughout the book specially with reference to events or circumstances in nature which occur of themselves, or independently of the will of man (chap. iii. 15, 22; vi. 10, 12; viii. 7; x. 14; xi. 2); עָשָׂה of events which are the results of human action (i. 13, 14; ii. 17; iv. 3, 8; ix. 3, 6). Koheleth by no means, however, affirms here the Stoic doctrine of a recurring cycle of human history as set forth in Virgil, Ecl. iv.

אֵין כָּל חָדָשׁ. *There is nothing new.* Comp. Dan i. 4; Num. xi. 6; Deut. viii. 9; and in N.T. οὐ πᾶς, Matt. xxiv. 22; Luke i. 37; Apoc. xxi. 27. See Ges.-Kautzsch, § 152, 1; Ewald, §323 *b*; Kalisch, § 106 *f.*

The same thought appears in the Roman and Greek authors. Thus Seneca, Epist. xxiv.: "Nullius rei finis est, sed in orbem nexa sunt omnia; fugiunt ac sequuntur. Diem nox premit, dies noctem; æstas in autumnum desinit, autumno hiems instat, quæ vere compescitur. Omnia transeunt ut revertantur, nihil novi video, nihil novi facio. Fit aliquando et hujus rei nausea. Multi sunt qui non acerbum judicent vivere, sed superfluum." So Marcus Aurelius: Lib. vi. 37, ὁ τὰ νῦν ἰδὼν πάντα ἑώρακεν, ὅσα τε ἐξ ἀϊδίου ἐγένετο, καὶ ὅσα εἰς τὸ ἄπειρον ἔσται· πάντα γε ὁμογενῆ καὶ ὁμοειδῆ; vii. 1, οὐδὲν καινόν, πάντα καὶ συνήθη καὶ ὀλιγοχρόνια; xii. 26, πᾶν τὸ γινόμενον οὕτως ἀεὶ ἐγίνετο καὶ γενήσεται καὶ νῦν πανταχοῦ γίνεται. The same thought occurs in Justin Martyr, Apol. i. 57, though his words are too general to be regarded as a distinct reference to this text: οὐ γὰρ δεδοίκαμεν θάνατον· τοῦ πάντως ἀποθανεῖν ὁμολογουμένου, καὶ μηδενὸς ἄλλου καινοῦ ἀλλ' ἢ τῶν αὐτῶν ἐν τῇδε τῇ διοικήσει ὄντων. See a remarkable parallel also in Manilius, *Astronomica*, i. 522 ff.

10. יֵשׁ דָּבָר "*Is there anything. etc.*" יֵשׁ = Assyr. *isu*, has here the force of a hypothetical antecedent, granted that there is a thing of which one might say—*Delitzsch*. On דָּבָר see n. on verse 8. LXX. have ὃς λαλήσει καὶ ἐρεῖ, and similarly Syr. ܟܕ ܢܬܒܠ ܟܠܕ; Knobel considers they read שֶׁיְדַבֵּר וְיֹאמַר. The Vulg. paraphrases the verse "nihil sub sole novum, nec valet quisquam dicere."

יֵשׁ is used after רָאָה as its object in chap. vii. 27, 29, in the second of which cases it is preceded as here by makkeph, but in both cases connected with the following word by a conjunctive. Here, though substantially the subject referring to that which follows it is marked with a distinctive (tippecha), as if "*see this, new it is.*" דָּבָר See our glossary. לְ לָעֹלָמִים expresses the rule or measure with which the comparison is made. אֲשֶׁר הָיָה מִלְּפָנֵנוּ. The irregularity here of the singular verb instead of the plural, עֹלָמִים being the antecedent, is best explained by regarding the verb as neuter. So chap. ii. 7, בְּנֵי בַיִת הָיָה לִי, and vid. Ges.-Kautzsch, § 147, rem. 2. Ewald and others suppose the relative to be understood, "that which has occurred before our eyes was already long ago." See also Ewald, § 294 *b* 2, and § 295 *d*. Comp. Gen. xxxv. 26; xlvi. 22; 1 Chron. ii. 9; iii. 1. Several MSS. have corrected the irregularity, and Renan would read also the plural here and in verse 16. On מִלְּפָנֵינוּ compare מִלְּפָנִים, Isa. xli. 26; לְפָנִים, Deut. ii. 10, 12, etc.; מִפָּנִים, 2 Sam. x. 9. That which is considered new in one generation sometimes turns out to have been known in another, and afterwards to have fallen into oblivion, so that the old, when it re-appears, seems to be new.

11. אֵין זִ לָרִאשֹׁנִים. זִכְרוֹן is generally regarded as placed in the construct before לְ owing to the intimate connexion. So Gesenius, Elster, Knobel. See Ges.-Kautzsch, § 116, 1; Philippi, *Stat. Const.*, p. 59. זִכְרוֹן may be viewed with Delitzsch as in the absolute state, being then regarded as another form of זִכָּרוֹן, and one more common in later Hebrew. Comp. יִתְרוֹן, verse 3, פִּשְׁרוֹן, chap. ii. 21; iv. 4.

ראשנים and אחרנים are often regarded, especially by the older comm. as neuters, and so Graetz among the modern. In such cases the fem. would be expected, as in Isaiah xlii. 9; xliii. 9, 18; xlvi. 9. Elster and Herzfeld think both men and things are referred to. Knobel, Delitzsch, etc., consider the reference to be to persons. ראשנים is used for *those of former time* (Deut. xix. 14) and אחרנים for *those of later generations* (chap. iv. 16; Job xviii. 20.) Comp. also Gen. xxxiii. 2. The article is used with both words, hence the kametz under the לְ. Compare קַדְמֹנִים used of persons, 1 Sam. xxiv. 14, and קַדְמֹנִיּוֹת used adverbially, Isa. xlviii. 18; and even in this very verse the masc. לֹ and לֹא in the first part are contrasted with לָאַחֲרֹנָה in the close.

Marcus Aurelius (Lib. iv. 34) speaking of the names of great men as mere words which need interpretation, says ἐξίτηλα γὰρ πάντα καὶ μυθώδη ταχὺ γίνεται· ταχὺ δὲ καὶ παντελὴς λήθη κατέχωσεν. Of the ordinary class of men he notes, οἱ γὰρ λοιποὶ ἅμα τῷ ἐκπνεῦσαι, ἄϊστοι, ἄπυστοι, and in cap. 35 he observes, πᾶν ἐφήμερον, καὶ τὸ μνημονεῦον καὶ τὸ μνημονευόμενον. So in Lib. ii. 17 he remarks, ἡ ὑστεροφημία δὲ λήθη.

12. See our remarks on this verse p. 88 ff. and specially note on p. 93. Graetz translates "I Koheleth am king," and calls attention to the fact that היה often means to *become* as well as *to be*. He regards the word as signifying that the person represented here as the speaker is described as a parvenu king. "I have become king." But, even if Graetz's theory were true that Herod the Great was depicted under the person of Koheleth, this explanation would not suit the passage, for the speaker is relating actions performed in the past, and is not speaking of his condition at the moment of writing. The expression "king over (עַל) Israel" is occasionally found in the earlier books, 1 Sam. xv. 26; 2 Sam. xix. 23; 1 Kings xi. 37. The more usual expression is "king of Israel."

13. נָתַן לֵב לְ is to *give one's heart* or *mind to* a matter. The phrase

occurs in chap. i. 13, 17; vii. 21; viii. 9. 16, also in Dan. x. 12; 1 Chron. xxii. 19. Similar phrases are שִׁית לֵב לְ, Ps. xlviii. 14; הָכִין לֵב לְ 2 Chron. xii. 14. Compare נָתַן אֶל־לִבּוֹ, ἐν φρεσὶ θεῖναι, Koh. vii. 2; ix. 1. The synonyms דָּרַשׁ and תּוּר do not refer to a lower or higher degree of investigation (*Zöckler*), but to two different methods; דרש signifies to search into the root of matters (the word implying *rubbing, testing*), תּוּר rather to investigate on all sides. So Delitzsch. Hence the latter word is suitably used of the spies searching the land of Canaan (Numb. xiii. 1, 16, 17), and in this passage figuratively of intellectual research. The Midrash Shir-ha-Shirim, chap. i. 1, considers the word תּוּר to be used by Koheleth in reference to the work done by the spies spoken of in Numbers, to which he figuratively compares his work. One would have expected the author to have used in this place and in verse 16 (also in chap. ii. 5, 9, 12, 13, etc.; iii. 22; iv. 1, 7; viii. 17; ix. 15, etc.), the imperf. with vav conversive, instead of which he has made use of the perfect with simple vav. See Ewald, § 343 *c.*, Driver, *Heb. Tenses*, § 133. See especially the note of the latter in his 2nd edit. p. 191.

הוּא עִנְיַן רָע. *This is an evil business*, or *exercise*, *i.e.* the investigation and search after those things which are done under the sun. הוּא is subject as chap. ii. 1. It is generally used in this book as a predicate. The ordinary reading is עִנְיַן רָע in which case ע is the construct, and רע either the adj. or the noun (see Ewald, § 287 *a*, 1). But the better MSS. and the older editions, as Delitzsch mentions in his *Anhänge*, have עִנְיָן with kametz, and so also in chap. v. 13.

עִנְיָן, *trouble, business, occupation*, in Biblical literature occurs only in Koheleth, where it is found eight times, chap. i. 13; ii. 23, 26; iii. 10; iv. 8; v. 2, 13; viii. 16. It is very common in Rabb. Hebrew, where it is used in the sense of business in the largest sense of the word, for instance in that of the subject-matter of a discussion. See examples cited by Delitzsch and Graetz. In Chaldee it is used (as sometimes in the Targ. of the Psalms) in the signification of *circumstances, thing, kind, affair*. It is found in the Targg. in Ps. xix. 5; xli. 2; Cant. i. 11. Jerome observes "verbum ANIAN Aquila, LXX., et Theod., περισπασμὸν similiter transtulerunt, quod in *distentionem* Latinus interpres expressit, eo quod in varias sollicitudines mens hominis distenta lanietur. Symm. vero ἀσχολίαν, id est, *occupationem*, transtulit." אשר נתן אלהים וגו' for נתן אלהים׃אלהים.

14. רְעוּת רוּחַ. The word רְעוּת occurs seven times in this book, chap. i. 14; ii. 11, 17, 26; iv. 4, 6; vi. 9, in all these cases followed by רוּחַ. The word occurs elsewhere only in the Chaldee parts of Ezra (v. 17; vii. 18). It has been erroneously derived from רָעַע or רוּעַ, to *make a noise*, to *break*, and hence rendered by *perturbation of mind*, or *afflictio spiritus* (Vulg.), or by kindred phrases in the Syr. and Targ.; Symm. in vi. 9, κάκωσις πνεύματος. But רְעוּת as well as רַעְיוֹן, chap. ii. 22 (used also in a parallel formula, רַעְיוֹן רוּחַ verse 17; chap. iv. 16) are both derived from רָעָה. Renan would in all these cases read רְעוּת. But the two distinct words are in existence, and רַעְיוֹן occurs frequently in the Chaldee of Daniel (ii. 29, 30; iv. 16, etc.). רְעוּת is the fem. of רֵעַ or רְעִי (in רְעוּאֵל) like מְתוּ (in מְתוּשֶׁלַח) = מְת or מַת (Böttcher, *Lehrb*. § 704). The *ûth* is the abstract feminine ending like מַלְכוּת, which in Aramaic was apocopated into מַלְכוּ. רָעָה means both to *feed* and to *delight in*. Hence some have rendered the phrase here a *"feeding on wind."* So Aq. and Theod., νομὴ ἀνέμου, Symm. (chap. i. 14), βόσκησις ἀνέμου, which rendering he gives for ר' רעיון in chap. iv. 16. The LXX. render both phrases alike by προαίρεσις πνεύματος. Compare on the sense, Hosea xii. 2, אֶפְרַיִם רֹעֶה רוּחַ, which is explained by the parallel וְרֹדֵף קָדִים, and Jer. xliv. 20. רֹעֶה אֵפֶר, *he strives after ashes*.

15. מְעֻוָּת לֹא יוּכַל לִתְקֹן. *The crooked cannot be straightened*. Knobel adduces the proverb from Suidas ξύλον ἀγκύλον οὐδέποτ' ὀρθόν. תָּקַן occurs in two other passages of this book, viz. chap. vii. 13, and xii. 9, both piel. The word is not found elsewhere in Bibl. Heb. It occurs in the Chald. of Dan. iv 33, in hophal, and is of frequent occurrence in both Chald. and Syr. in the sense of to *arrange*, to *set in order*. Delitzsch notes that it is common in the Mishna. A derivative תִּקּוּן in later Hebrew is the technical term for *arrangement, order*, תִּקּוּן סוֹפְרִים, *the arrangement of the scribes*, תִּקּוּן הָעוֹלָם, *the order of the world*. Note the intransitive inf. in *o*, תְּקֹן instead of תְּקַן. Delitzsch compares נְפֹל, יְקֹד, יָבֹשׁ; compare יָשֹׁן, in chap. v. 11. The sentiment of this passage recurs again at chap. vii. 13. The LXX. διεστραμμένον οὐ δυνήσεται ἐπικοσμηθῆναι. The Targ., Vulg., Syr. and some later commentators have misunderstood the passage to refer to the sins or immoralities of man.

Ch. i. 15, 16.] *Critical and Grammatical Comm.* 319

15. חֶסְרוֹן. An ἅπαξ λεγ. in the Biblical writings. The idea is expressed in the other books by מַחְסוֹר, a derivative from the same root. 'ח itself occurs frequently in Rabb. Hebrew to signify *a loss, a deficit*, the phrase חֶסְרוֹן כִּים being commonly used for a *deficit in the purse*, or *loss of money*. See Levy, *Neuheb. W. B.*, s. v. Delitzsch in his glossary quotes the words of the high priest in the prayer on the Day of Atonement: "Should loss (חסרון) befall us on this day or this year, may our loss be one caused by good works (יהא חסרוננו בחסרון של מצוות)."

The meaning of the niphal הִמָּנוֹת must here be *to be brought to the full number*. The phrase means "a deficit cannot be counted," *i.e.* as a whole, and is similar to the proverb, "where there is nothing, there is nothing to count." So Delitzsch, similarly Kleinert, and, among the ancient interpreters, Theod. καὶ τὰ ὑστεροῦντα οὐ δύνανται, *numerari calculo.* Syr. Hex. ܠܡܛܠܐ ܣܡܟܐ ܠܐ ܡܨܝܢ. See Field's *Hexapla*. Knobel takes מָנָה in the signif. of the Chald. מְנִי *to set up*, and explains the sense to be: the wants in life are innumerable, and what is once wanting in circumstances of life for a full enjoyment thereof cannot be made up by human efforts. Symm. renders (καὶ) ὑστέρημα μὴ δυνάμενον ἀναπληρῶσαι ἀριθμόν. LXX. καὶ ὑστέρημα οὐ δυνήσεται ἀριθμηθῆναι. Bridges supposes the passage to refer to man as being "a creature of so many wants." The latter idea is, however, quite foreign to the text. Renan and Plumptre are probably correct in regarding this verse as a quotation of an aphorism either common in the writer's day or borrowed from an earlier writer.

16. דברתי אני. The אני is pleonastic, see Ges.-Kautzsch, § 137, 3, rem. 2, and Excurs. 4. דבר עם ל, means most probably, as the לאמר following shows, to *speak to the heart*, but the phrase might be used in the sense of *to speak in the heart*, as Deut. viii. 5; comp. דבר על ל, 1 Sam. i. 13. See Delitzsch's *Bibl. Psych.*, p. 134 (Engl. ed. p. 293).

הגדלתיוהוספתי. The second verb might be regarded as the complement of the first, the phrase implying "I became very great in wisdom. See Ges.-Kautzsch, § 142, 3 *a*, Ewald, § 285 *a*, Kalisch, § 103, 2. Kleinert renders the perfects here, after הִנֵּה, as futures, "I will become great, etc.," and refers to 1 Kings iii. 12, the phraseology of which is imitated here. See Ewald, § 135 *c*. The employment, however, of the perfect in the next clause is some objection to this. על כל־א' היה. On the sing. היה vid note on verse 10.

אֲשֶׁר לֹא־הָיָה עַל־כָּל־מֶלֶךְ. Compare 1 Chron. xxix. 25, אשר ה' לפני על ירו'
לְפָנָיו עַל־יִשְׂרָאֵל. The phrase in Koheleth if strictly construed would imply that there were more kings than one before Solomon who reigned over Jerusalem, and is therefore to be regarded as a slight anachronism. But the phrase in Chronicles construed strictly could be justified by fact, inasmuch as Saul as well as David ruled over Israel, though not over Jerusalem. See on the whole passage our remarks in pp. 88–95.

ולבי ראה וגו'. *To see wisdom, etc.*, to have knowledge and apprehension of it. Compare the cognate phrase ידע חכמה, chap. viii. 16, and John ii. 21, οἴδατε ἀλήθειαν. See on the expression, Delitzsch's *Bibl. Pyschology*, p. 254 (Engl. ed. p. 276).

הַרְבֵּה prop. inf. hiph., used also as an adverb, Ges. *Lehrg.* p. 627, Ges.-Kautzsch, § 100, 2 *d*, Ewald, § 240 *c*, § 280 *a*. König, *Lehrg.*, p. 536. It qualifies both verbs and nouns, but is placed after and not before the word qualified. It is here used as an adverb qualifying the ראה which precedes, and not the חכמה which follows it. See 2 Kings x. 18; 2 Sam. viii. 8; 1 Kings v. 9. In Koheleth it is used as an adjective with nouns, chap. ii. 7; v. 6, 16; vi. 11; ix. 18; xi. 8; xii. 9, 12; as an adverb, chap. v. 19; vii. 16, 17. Hence the transl. "My heart saw much wisdom and knowledge" (*Ewald, Ginsburg, Plumptre*) is incorrect. The Gr. Ven. in translating ἡ καρδία μου τεθέαται καταπολὺ σοφίαν καὶ γνῶσιν has shown a nice perception of Hebrew Grammar. See Delitzsch's Pref. to Gebhardt's edition of the Græcus Venetus, p. viii. חכמה and דַעַת differ as σοφία and γνῶσις, sapientia and intelligentia; the former indicates practical wisdom, the latter theoretical insight (*Knobel*).

17. וָאֶתְּנָה. The cohortative ending gives here an intensive meaning to the imperfect. The cohortative הָ‍ is really the remains in Hebrew of the energetic form of the imperfect in Arabic. See W. Wright's *Arab. Gram.*, § 97, rem. *c*. On the form in Hebrew see Ewald, § 232 *g*, and better Stade, *Lehrb.*, § 480, especially rem. 2. The form is often used after the strong vav or vav conversive. The imperfect with vav conversive occurs only three times in this book, viz. chap. i. 17; iv. 1, 7, whereas the perfect with simple vav occurs repeatedly. Comp. remarks on chap. ii. 5. Driver remarks that "this circumstance, estimated in the light of what is *uniformly* observable in other parts of the Old Testament, is of itself,

Ch. i. 17.]   *Critical and Grammatical Comm.*   321

though naturally it does not stand alone, a strong indication of the date at which that book [Koheleth] must have been composed." *Hebrew Tenses*, § 133. See his note in the second enlarged edition in reply to the arguments adduced by Johnston in his *Treatise on the Authorship of Ecclesiastes*. The vav conversive denotes in this case the chronological sequence of the statement in the verse in its relation to that in the preceding verse. See Driver, § 74 a.

וְדַעַת הֹלֵלוֹת וְשִׂ׳. In consequence of לָדַעַת having been used in the previous sentence, דַּעַת is used as an infinitive without the repetition of the לְ. There is no occasion to strike out the words which follow (הללות ושכל), as Ginsburg does in his translation. He considers that they "crept into the text through the carelessness of a transcriber," and with the LXX. he views דעת as a noun connected with the preceding חכמה. It is certain, however, from the ancient versions that the words so rejected were in the text. The LXX. render them παραβολὰς καὶ ἐπιστήμην, not unnaturally regarding שִׂכְלוּת to be the same as שֵׂכֶל *understanding;* the Gr. Ven. has similarly rendered it by νόησις. Hence Graetz would read מְשָׁלוֹת וְשִׂכְלוּת. But שִׂכְלוּת is, according to the Masora, the same as סִכְלוּת; which latter form occurs frequently in this book. See Delitzsch on this passage, and Ewald, § 50 a. Many MSS. have סִכְלוּת contrary to the Masora. We find הוֹלֵלוֹת, independently of this passage, coupled with 'ס in chap. ii. 12. It follows והסכלות in chap. vii. 25. It occurs without 'ס in chap. ix. 3, while in chap. x. 13 the form הוֹלֵלוּת occurs. These are the only cases in which the word appears; it is found only in this book. הוֹלֵלָה in the same signification occurs once at least in the Midrash Koheleth. The form in וּת is that of the abstract sing.; the form in וֹת is, as Delitzsch has pointed out, that of an intensive fem. plur. as בִּנוֹת Zeph. iii. 4, בִּינוֹת, חָכְמוֹת, vid. Böttcher, § 700 c. The LXX. render it here by παραβολαί, which rendering is followed by the Syr., but in chap. ii. 12, and vii. 25 by παραφορά. Aquila, πλάναι.

זֶה הוּא רֵע. Compare 1 Chron. xxii. 1, זֶה הוּא בֵית יְיָ. The personal pronoun is generally regarded in such cases as equivalent to the substantive verb; the הוּא is placed as copula between the subject and the noun which is used as predicate, as Gen. ii. 14; ix. 18 and here, and sometimes after both, as chap. ii. 23; Gen. xxxiv. 21.

Y

Vid. Ges.-Kautzsch, § 121, 2, but see Driver's *Hebrew Tenses*, second edit. § 201, 3.

רעיון. See note on verse 14.

18. יוֹסִיף is more easily explained as a participle kal for יוֹסֵף, than as a participle hiphil for the regular מוֹסִיף which is found Neh. xiii. 8. Böttcher has maintained the latter view, *Lehrb.*, § 994, 3. But see Ewald, § 169 *a*, Stade, § 214 *b*, and § 100, and specially König, § 36, 1 (p. 404). For similar forms, reference is made to Isa. xxix. 14; xxxviii. 5; Ps. xvi. 5. But Delitzsch, in his comm., points out that in all these passages the verb can be explained as the imperfect, and so Ges.-Kautzsch, § 50, rem. 1. In reply to Böttcher's assertion that there is no other example where two imperfects taken impersonally follow one another, Delitzsch adduces Prov. xii. 17, יָפִיחַ אֱמוּנָה יַגִּיד צֶדֶק. Hoelemann notes that this verse is a striking contrast to "sapere aude" and the panacea of the present day.

Renan regards this verse as an aphoristic quotation from some older source, but this is improbable. Delitzsch notes that the proverb "much learning causes headache" may be suitably compared with chap. xii. 12, but not here where mental grief and pain is that implied by both the nouns which are made use of.

CHAPTER II.

1. אמר א בלבי. Vid. note on chap. i. 16.

אֲנַסְּכָה imperf. piel of נסה. The Vulg. renders *et affluam deliciis*, connecting it in some way (like Ibn Ezra) with נסך, *to pour out* (as if אֶסְּכָה niphal, see Delitzsch on Ps. ii. 6). The signification of the latter verb, however, will not admit of this. נסה is construed with בְּ of the means, or instrument, by which the trial is made, chap. vii. 23; 1 Kings. x. 1. Hengstenberg thinks that the germ of the parable of our Lord in Luke xii. 16–21 is contained in the first two verses of this chapter. The כָה, the fuller form of the suffix ךְ, is used, (1) to make the suffix more distinct in words which end in caph, *e.g.* אֶרְכָּה, 1 Sam. ii. 22, (2) to lengthen in writing shorter words, as בָּאְכָה, Gen. x. 19, (3) less frequently, as in this passage, in longer words, which last usage may be a mark of later date. See Böttcher, § 871. וּרְאֵה בְטוֹב. Words which refer primarily to the senses are often used in a figurative sense of any experience however derived. Hence *to see* is often used in the signification of *to experience* and *to enjoy*. Comp. in N.T. Luke ii. 26 ; John iii. 36 ; viii. 51. Knobel notes that the idea of enjoyment which is sometimes supposed to lie in ראה when construed with בְּ does not necessarily belong to that phrase, as it is also employed with respect to experiences by no means pleasurable (Gen. xxi. 16 ; xliv. 34). וּרְאֵה is the imp. and forms part of the address to the heart. It cannot be the infinitive, as Graetz regards it.

2. Joy and laughter are personified ; the words spoken to them are put in the *oratio obliqua*. Knobel understands the passage differently, and translates לְ by *in reference to*, appealing to Ps. iii. 3 ; xxii. 31; Isa. v. 1, etc. Pleasure in general is signified by "joy," and unrestrained merriment by "laughter"; which latter often appears to be folly, if not worse, to an unconcerned looker-on. Compare Seneca, Epist. 23, "Animus debet esse alacer et fidens, et super omnia erectus. Res severa est verum gaudium. Ceteræ hilaritates non implent pectus, sed frontem remittunt ; leves sunt, nisi forte tu illum judices gaudere, qui ridet."

מְהוֹלָל part. poal *mad*, comp. Ps. cii. 9. It is masculine and not neuter, hence Hitzig's rendering "dummes Zeug," a *foolish thing*, is incorrect. The hithpoal is used in the sense of *to be mad* in 1 Sam. xxi. 14; Jer. xxv. 16 ; li. 7. The Greek translators have all understood the word in the sense of *error*, and so Vulg., but the old Latin better, *amentia*.

מַה־זֹּה עֹשָׂה. On זֹה see Ges.-Kautzsch, § 34. זֹה is a shortened and later form of זֹאת. It occurs in 2 Kings vi. 19 ; Ezek. xl. 45, and in several places in this book. It must not be confounded with זוּ another form of זִי, which is of the common gender. Nor is it identical with the זֹה found in the phrase כָּזֹה וְכָזֶה, *thus and thus*, Jud. xviii. 4. See Böttcher, *Lehrb.*, § 897 *a*. Delitzsch observes that the use of זֶה in Koheleth is similar to that in the Mishna. For Koheleth uses it regularly without the article in cases similar to those in the Mishna, זֶה דִינָר, *this dinár*, זֶה מִדְרָשׁ, *this interpretation*. In cases where the writer does not use the masculine זֶה in a neuter sense (such as chap. vii. 10, 18, 29 ; viii. 9 ; ix. 1 ; xi. 6), he employs in this signification no other feminine form than זֹה, Mishnaic זוֹ, as in chap. ii. 2 ; v. 15–18 ; vii. 23 ; ix. 13. The use of the pronouns is also, as Delitzsch notes, in other points akin to that of the Mishna. So in chap. i. 10, זֶה הוּא is like the Mishn. וְהִי, *this is.*

עָשָׂה is the feminine of עָשׂ agreeing with שִׂמְחָה. The Syriac renders freely, ܥܒܕܐ ܗܢܐ *to what use?* But there is no reason to suppose it had a different rendering. עָשָׂה is used in the sense *to get, to obtain*, Ezek. xxviii. 4; Judg. xiii. 15. Hitzig regards the meaning as equivalent to עָשָׂה פְּרִי. Delitzsch compares the use of the noun מַעֲשֶׂה to signify the result or effect of work in Isaiah xxxii. 17.

Renan views this verse also as a quotation, but it is scarcely probable.

3. See p. 145. תַּרְתִּי. The verb תּוּר does not mean to *prove* (as Hengstenberg), but to *spy out*, to *explore*, to *look round about*, etc. See Num. x. 33, and many other passages. The word occurs three times in Koheleth (chap. i. 13; ii. 3; vii. 25), in the sense of *seek out* and *discover* by mental effort. It means scarcely *to purpose* or *to resolve*. The verb מָשַׁךְ, with which it is connected, literally means *to draw*, and has been variously explained as signifying *to strengthen* the body in the sense of Horace's *se benignius tractare* (so *Gesenius* in *Thes.*), or *to hold fast* the sensual desires by wine, *i.e.* to give free indulgence to them (*Knobel*). But these and other meanings assigned to the word rest on no sufficient basis. The passage is loosely paraphrased in our A.V. "I sought in mine heart to give myself unto wine." Hitzig considers that the writer in this verse compares his body in the first clause to a carriage, wine, as the motive power, being thought of as the horse; while in the second clause he compares wisdom to a coachman placed on the box, in order to prevent the steed from throwing the carriage into a pit or morass. Later writers, as Tayler Lewis, in the English edition of Zöckler, and Perowne, in the *Expositor*, have improved on this by comparing the supposed picture drawn by Koheleth to the beautiful parable of Plato (*Phædrus*, 54 *f*) of the νοῦς or Reason as a charioteer driving his two horses, the fierce steed being the flesh with its lusts, and the gentle one Platonic love. But the resemblance is purely fanciful. For, as Delitzsch has pointed out, מָשַׁךְ does not mean to *draw* in this sense, but to *draw towards oneself*, to *attract* by sensual delights. Similarly Syriac ܠܡܒܣܡܘ ܒܚܡܪܐ ܒܣܪܝ, *to delight my flesh with wine.* This seems to be the sense put upon the passage by the Targ. "*to draw out* (לְנַגְדָּא) *my flesh in the house of the banquet of wine,*" and of the more literal rendering of the Græc. Ven., ὡς ἕλκοιμι ἐν οἴνῳ τὴν σάρκα μου.

Ch. ii. 3.]   *Critical and Grammatical Comm.*   325

מָשַׁךְ is often employed in this signification in Rabb. Heb. Buxtorf quotes the phrase מֶשֶׁךְ אַחַר תַעֲנוּגִים as equivalent *to indulge in pleasures.* Comp. also Chagiga 14 *a*. אֵלּוּ בַעֲלֵי אַגָּדָא שֶׁמּוֹשְׁכִין לִבּוֹ שֶׁל אָדָם בְּמַיִם "*these are the masters of the Aggada who draw* (*entice, refresh*) *the heart of man as water does.*" Tayler Lewis' explanation, "I sought diligently when my flesh was furiously driving on *in wine*, or pleasure [בַּיַּיִן being supposed to signify the state or condition] to draw it, to restrain it, to bridle it, to keep it, in the path of temperance" is, for many reasons, perfectly impossible. מָשַׁךְ is nowhere used in such a signification. Graetz alters the text, rendering לִמְשׁוֹחַ. He notes, indeed, that that verb is used chiefly of *anointing* with oil; but, inasmuch as it occurs also in the sense of *painting* with vermilion (Jer. xxii. 14), he translates the text so amended by "*to embrocate my body with wine,*" and observes that herein lies a raffinement that, while others were satisfied to anoint themselves with oil, Koheleth wished to do so with wine. Delitzsch remarks on this that Koheleth might with more propriety have spoken of bathing himself in wine, and, if such a conjecture were admissible, the text might even further be improved by reading בְּיוֹנִי in place of בַּיַּיִן, *i.e.* in *Grecian* (wine), *e.g.* Chian, Falernian, Champagne!! The idea of the Breslau professor is about as good as that of a well-known temperance advocate who, unable to answer the argument of those who were defending the moderate use of strong drink, drawn from St. Paul's advice to Timothy to "use a little wine for his stomach's sake" (1 Tim. v. 23), had the hardihood to affirm that the Apostle intended the wine to be used as an embrocation!! The LXX. translation is unsuitable, καὶ κατεσκεψάμην εἰ ἡ καρδία μου ἑλκύσει ὡς οἶνον τὴν σάρκα μου, but it is evidence in support of the present reading. Aquila and Theod. also translate לִמְ' by ἑλκῦσαι. The Vulg. expresses the very opposite of the sense of the passage "cogitavi in corde meo abstrahere a vino carnem meam."

The clause "my heart acting with wisdom" is to be regarded as a kind of parenthesis, as is evident from the use of the participle נֹהֵג and from the וְלֶאֱחֹז, which is connected with לִמְשׁוֹךְ, and, like it, under the government of תַּרְתִּי. The sense of the passage has been given on p. 145. A variety of translations have been assigned to נָהַג, but it is pretty evident that it is used in the sense of *to act, to conduct oneself*, a meaning common in the language of the Mishna. See

Glossary. LXX. καὶ καρδία μου ὡδήγησεν ἐν σοφίᾳ. Incorrectly Symm. ἵνα τὴν καρδίαν μου μεταγάγω εἰς σοφίαν.

By *folly* in this verse the sensual pleasures are evidently intended which are afterwards mentioned in detail. Nachtigal, and after him Kaiser, maintained that idolatry was here meant by folly. But of this there is no proof whatever.

עד איזה אראה. The expression is old Hebrew—*Delitzsch.* אי־זה טוב *What might be good.* אי־זה is the interrogative *which? what?* used both in direct questions as 1 Kings xiii. 12, or in indirect, as here and in chap. xi. 6. See Ewald, § 326 *a*. אשר יעשו means either *that which they do,* or, *that which they should do.* Perhaps the latter rendering ought, with Delitzsch, to be preferred on account of the parallel passages in chap. ii. 24; iii. 22; v. 4, 5, 18. מספר ימי ח׳. "*During the number of the days of their life.*" מִסְפַּר is in the accusative, Ges.-Kautzsch, § 118, 2, Kalisch, § 86 *f.* So chap. v. 17; vi. 12; Job xv. 20. Knobel translates, "*during the few days of their life,*" as מ׳ is used for "*few*," "*some*" (Num. ix. 20; Job xvi. 23; Isa. x. 19. But this idea is hardly suitable to the passage; and moreover מִסְפָּר when so employed does not precede the noun in the construct state as here, but either follows it in the genitive, or is used as a predicate.

4. הגדלתי מ׳. See note on chap. i. 16. On the buildings of Solomon see 1 Kings vii.; ix. 15-22; 2 Chron. viii. 3-6. It is not surprising that the writer, in making reference to the buildings of Solomon erected to gratify his sensual tastes, should abstain from all mention of the building of the temple. But, had the book been an autobiography, some allusion would necessarily have been made to that great fact in Solomon's history. The Targum introduces a reference to it in its rendering of this passage.

בָּתִּים is to be read not *bottim* but *battim.* It is often pointed בָּתִּים, the daghesh after heavy metheg serving to distinguish the word from בָּתִים part. of בּוּת. See Ges.-Kautzsch, § 16, 2 *b*, and the other authorities quoted in my critical note in *Zechariah and his Prophecies,* p. 594.

Mention is made of David's vineyards in 1 Chron. xxvii. 27. A vineyard belonging to Solomon is referred to in the Song of Songs chap. viii. 11, and in such a manner as to suggest the idea that the vineyard had been given up or sold. Whether this be a correct interpretation of that passage or not, there is no ground, with Knobel, to accuse the writer as guilty here of exaggeration. David's vineyards passed into the possession of Solomon, and there is little doubt that Solomon added to their number. He was peculiarly fond of gardens, as the references to them in the Song of Songs, chap. vi. 2, and also in 1 Kings iv. 33, abundantly prove.

5. גנות ופ׳. See previous note. Gardens of herbs are spoken of in Deut. xi. 10; 1 Kings xxi. 2; and the king's garden, which was undoubtedly a resort of pleasure, is frequently referred to in the historical books (*e.g.* 2 Kings xxi. 18; xxv. 4; Neh. iii. 15; Jer. xxxix. 4).

פַּרְדֵּס, which occurs only here and in Cant. iv. 13; Neh. ii. 8, was introduced from the Persian into Greek by Xenophon in the form παράδεισος. The Greek word is used several times by the LXX. as the translation of גן (Gen. ii. 8 ff; xiii. 10; Num. xxiv. 6, and of גַּנָּה, Jer. i. 30). The word is borrowed also not only by the Aram. but by Arabic and Armenian. Whether it be derived from the Zend *pairidaêza* or from the Sanskrit *paradêça* is yet a matter of dispute. See Friedr. Delitzsch, *Wo lag das Paradies?* pp. 95 ff. The plural in the Mishna language is פַּרְדֵּסוֹת. It is certain that it means a park planted with trees. Observe here the simple perfect with ו, where one would have expected the imperf. with vav conversive. Ewald, § 343 *c*. See note on chap. i. 17. עֵץ כָּל פְּרִי. *Trees of all sorts of fruit.* Comp. Ges.-Kautzsch, § 111, 1, rem.

6. בְּרֵכָה, a *pool, tank*, or *pond*, artificially constructed. Arab. بِرْكَة, plural, בְּרֵכוֹת (בִּרְכוֹת is the plural const. of בְּרֵכָה, abs. בְּרֵכוֹת) possibly from the stem בָּרַךְ, *to kneel*, as if a place where the camels kneel down to drink water; or from that stem in the sense of *to continue*, because of the continuance of the water therein (see Lane's *Arab. Lex.*); or better as meaning *to spread out*, in the sense of an extended surface of water, as Delitzsch explains the Arabic lexicographers (see his *Comm. über d. Genesis*, 4te Ausg. p. 98). "The king's pool" is mentioned in Neh. ii. 14; and the בְּרֵכַת הַשֶּׁלַח (identified by the Vulg. and by the A.V. with the pool of Siloam, but probably not identical with it), is spoken of in Neh. iii. 15 as belonging to the king's garden (לְגַן הַמֶּלֶךְ). Solomon's pool is spoken of by Josephus (*Bell. Jud.*, lib. v. 4, § 2). There are three pools of Solomon still in existence, near the ancient Etam. Comp. Joseph. *Antiq.*, viii. 7, 3. The pools mentioned here were constructed "in

order to water from them a forest of trees." מֵהֶם instead of מֵהֶן (the word for *pool* is feminine), which latter in its turn, as Delitzsch observes, is employed in the Mishna in place of מֵהֶם. See Geiger, *Lehrb. d. Mischn.*, § 13. Knobel, however, considers the pronoun to refer to מים.

יַעַר צומח ע׳, *a wood sprouting out trees*, in place of *sprouting out with trees*. Verbs which signify growth, flowing, swimming, etc., instead of using prepositions, take after them nouns in the accusative specifying the completion of the idea conveyed by the verb. See Ewald, § 281 *b*, Ges. *Lehrg.*, p. 809, Ges.-Kautzsch, § 138, 1, rem. 2, Kalisch, § 102, 7. So Isa. v. ; 6 xxxiv. 13 ; Prov. xxiv. 31.

7. קניתי ע׳, refers here evidently to procuring by purchase (comp. Gen. xvii. 12), although Knobel conceives the idea to be more general, and to include the home-born slaves. These are, however, mentioned in the second clause. A distinction was generally made between the slaves born in the house and those procured in any other way. Home-born slaves are termed here, and in Gen. xv. 3, בְּנֵי־בַיִת, more usually יְלִידֵי בַיִת (Gen. xiv. 14 ; xvii. 23, 27). The LXX. render both phrases οἰκογενεῖς. The servants and attendants of Solomon are specially noted in 1 Kings iv. 27, 28, and in 1 Kings x. 5, as having excited the astonishment of the Queen of Sheba. Many who performed such service were Canaanites reduced to slavery (1 Kings ix. 20, 21), so that there is no occasion to treat the statement here, with Knobel, as "free fiction."

היה לי for היו לי. See note on chap. i. 10.

מִקְנֶה. The construct מִקְנֵה בקר וצאן would have been naturally expected here (comp. Gen. xxvi. 14 ; xlvii. 17, 18 ; 2 Chron. xxxii. 29), and such is the reading of several MSS. and editions. The correct Masoretic text has, however, the absolute, as Delitzsch has pointed out. He observes that מ׳ must be regarded as in apposition, like זבחים שלמים, Exod. xxiv. 5; הבקר הנחשת, 2 Kings xvi. 17, though the nouns that follow here might be regarded as accusatives of closer definition (Ewald, § 281*c*, Ges.-Kautzsch, § 139, 2, rem., Kalisch, § 86 *d*), herds consisting of oxen and sheep. Delitzsch regards such a construction as too artificial for a book of so late a date. Solomon seems to have been in possession of enormous flocks and herds, as is proved by the sacrifices performed on the occasion of the consecration of the temple (1 Kings viii. 63), and from the account given of the daily provision for his table (1 Kings iv. 22 ff). The Israelitish kings were also often possessors of extensive flocks (1 Chron. xxvii. 29-31).

The mention made in this verse of "all that were before me in Jerusalem," as also the same phrase in ver. 9, would naturally be explained as referring to previous kings, if chap. i. 16 (or 1 Kings iii. 13; x. 23) be kept in view. But the phrase here may be understood more generally.

8. כנסתי. This verb is common to all the Shemitic languages, inclusive of Assyrian, and, though specially used in the later Hebrew, cannot be regarded as one peculiar to the later language.

וסגלת מ' והמדינות. Herzfeld seeks to explain the absence of the article with מלכים and its presence with המדינות as owing to the fact that, although kings changed, the districts of the empire or country remained the same. Graetz arbitarily maintains that some word like משמני (Dan. xi. 24) must have fallen out before המדינות. The use or disuse of the article may here have no special significance, though it is possible that in the phrase "of kings and of the countries," the former is used in a more partial, the second in a more general sense. Hitzig and Zöckler consider that its use with המר' has special reference to the twelve districts into which Solomon divided the land of Israel for the purpose of taxation (1 Kings iv. 7 ff). But the "districts" referred to were evidently not exclusively those of the land of Israel, nor is the word מ' used in 1 Kings iv., where these divisions are spoken of. The Persian empire is stated in Esth. i. 1 to have been divided into 127 such "districts" (מדינות). Owing to the large extent of these districts the word appears to be employed in the more general signification of "*lands*," "*countries*." מרינה does not occur in any book of a date earlier than the exile. It is very frequently used in the Book of Esther, but occurs in Koheleth only in one other place, chap. v. 7.

Johnston calls attention to the fact that the only other place where סגלה occurs, in the sense of material wealth or treasure, is in 1 Chron. xxix. 3; where David speaks of the treasure of gold and silver available for the building of the temple. He considers this fact "deeply significant" and as "one of the delicate and conclusive evidences of the fact that the author of Ecclesiastes can have been none other" than Solomon! See our remarks on p. 115.

שׁדה ושׁדות. The expression only occurs here, and has given rise to a large number of conjectures. It is, however, tolerably clear that women of various sorts are signified, who are referred to in the preceding expression "the delights (תַּעֲנוּג, plur., תַּעֲנוּגִים, only here תַּעֲנֻגוֹת) of the sons of men." A verb *shadâdu* has been found in Assyrian, and perhaps this explains the phrase, which probably means "*a love and loves*" (see Friedr. Delitzsch, *Paradies*, p. 145). The word may be explained, with Mühlau and Volck, from שׁדד, *to be strong*, or from שׁי=שׁיד (Olshausen, *Lehrb.* § 83. *e*.) שָׁדָה being, i.q. שִׁידָה, comp. Arab. مَسِيدَة, *mistress, domina*, the addition of the word in the plural in one passage denoting abundance of such "delights," like the Arab. expression مال وأموال, *abundance of riches*. The reference to Isa. iii. 3, and to Ewald, § 172 *b*, does not bear upon our passage, as there is no difference of gender here between the words. Knobel considers *women* spoken of, but connects the word less suitably with an Arab. root to *shut up*, as a designation of the wives of an eastern monarch. Rosenmüller connects it with שַׁד, *the breast*, comparing the expression, רַחַם רַחֲמָתָיִם, Judges v. 30. The word was a puzzle to the ancient translators. Aquila rendering κυλίκιον καὶ κυλίκια; and so Vulg. "scyphos et urceos." Symm. (known here only by Jerome's transl.) "*mensurarum species et appositiones*," possibly connecting it with the Chald. שְׁרִי or שְׁרָא, *to pour out*. The Targ. probably connected it with the same stem, explaining it as "baths and bath-houses (having) channels which poured forth (וְשָׁדְיָן) lukewarm water, and channels which poured forth warm water." The LXX. seem to have connected the word with the same root, though they render differently οἰνοχόον καὶ οἰνοχόας, *male and female cup-bearers*, reading, perhaps, the words as participles שָׁדֶה וְשֹׁדוֹת (comp. 1 Kings x. 5 ; 2 Chron. ix. 4). So Syr. ܡܫܩܝܐ ܘܡܫܩܝܬܐ. Others have assigned the word the meaning of *music* (after the Arab. شدا, *to sing*). So Græc. Ven. σύστημα καὶ συστήματα, *harmony and harmonies*. So Kimchi, Luther, Nachtigal. Rashi explains the phrase as *beautiful carriages, litters*, connecting it with the Talmudic שִׁדָּה, *an ark*, or *chest*; and Böttcher, in his *Exeg.-krit. Aehrenlese* for 1849, connects it with the same, regarding שׁדה ושׁדות to be *chest and chests* used in the sense of *abundance of anything*. See above. In his *Neue Aehrenlese*, he connects it with the same word, but considers that the phrase means "*palanquin and palanquins.*" Graetz takes nearly the same view, and refers to the Talmud Babli, *Gittin*, 78 *a*, where it is said that the word was understood in Palestine to mean *chests*, or *sedan-chairs*, but in Babylon was considered to signify שִׁדָּה וְשִׁדּתִין, *demons both male and female;* the regular fem. plural is שֵׁדָה. See also the Midrash Shir-ha-Shirim on chap. iii. 8. Delitzsch observes that this Hagadic interpretation is at least on the right track, שֵׁד, *a demon*, being connected with the root שׁוד in the sense of *to be strong*.

Ewald suggests that שִׁדָּה is probably equivalent to Arab. شِدَّة, *power, strength*, in the sense of a strong or high degree of any quality, in which sense the Arabic-word also occurs (see Lane's *Arab. Lex.*). So Hahn. The sentence would then mean: "*and the delights of the sons of men in great abundance.*" In support of this idea, Ewald observes that at the end of a long enumeration some such phrase would be natural. We adhere, however, to the opinion first mentioned.

9. וגדלתי והום׳. vid. n. on chap. i. 16. היה for היו, vid. n. on chap. i. 16. עמדה לי, *remained with me, i.e.* in spite of all my folly. The verb occurs in this sense construed with בְּ in Isaiah xlvii. 12, also Jer. xlviii. 11. So Knobel, Delitzsch and others. Vulg. *perseveravit mecum*. But Kaiser, Heinem., Herzfeld, Ewald, Graetz, prefer to render "*assisted me.*" Herzfeld compares the Chanuka-prayer, עָמַדְתָּ לָהֶם בְּעֵת צָרָתָם; and Graetz adds that in the Agada for the Passover evening the expression occurs וְהִיא שֶׁעָמְדָה לַאֲבוֹתֵינוּ וְלָנוּ. Comp. Dan. xii. 1, where the verb is construed with עַל. Herzfeld argues that Solomon's wisdom was superfluous while he directed his efforts toward what was sensual, but not, however, his ability, which assisted him in carrying out his plans. But the verse evidently recites the carrying out of the design spoken of in verse 3, and hence the former rendering is to be preferred.

10. מהם in place of מהן. Gesenius (*Lehrgeb.*, p. 731) ascribes this to an incorrectness of speech common in ordinary language, in which masculine pronominal suffixes were not uncommonly used with reference to feminines. So Gen. xxvi. 15; xxxi. 9; xxxii. 16; Job i. 14; Prov. vi. 21. Herzfeld observes that the masc. was often used where the distinction between the genders was not necessary for the sense. Comp. chap. x. 9; xi. 8; xii. 1. See Kalisch, § 77, 21.

ראיתי—מכל וגו׳. *I kept back my heart from no joy.* Comp. Num. xiv. 11. Graetz would here alter the text and read, כי לבי שמח in place of כי לבי שמח. But the change is unnecessary, and is supported by no authority save the Professor's "must." Hahn and others translate "*after all my labour.*" But מן expresses here rather the origin and cause of joy.

11. שעמלתי לעשות. Vid. Ges.-Kautzsch, § 45, 2, § 142, 2, Kalisch § 98, 5, comp. Gen. ii. 3.

ופניתי א׳ בכל. The more usual construction is פָּנָה אֶל־ *to turn to*, *i.e.* in the direction of any person or thing. פנה בְּ here, as in Job vi. 28, is a kind of *constructio prægnans*, to turn towards in order to fix the attention upon something as an object of contemplation.

12. Mendelssohn's translation is impossible, "I turned myself from the contemplation of philosophy (wisdom) in unison with madness and folly," so Preston's translation; or, as Delitzsch translates Mendelssohn's Hebrew, "I therefore gave up my attempt to desire to combine wisdom with folly and madness." Such a translation would require פניתי מלראות. Moreover, the ellipsis of כן cannot be defended. Mendelssohn maintains a similar ellipsis at chap. vii. 29, which is also impossible. Hitzig translates, "I turned myself to behold wisdom, and lo! it was madness and folly." This would require the insertion of *and lo!* (והנה) in Hebrew as well as in English. The passages he appeals to do not justify the translation. The two vavs are, as Delitzsch says, conjunctive and not correlative.

The second clause of the verse is best explained as we have done, after Delitzsch, on p. 147: "For what is the man that is to come after the king whom they made long ago?" Who can have greater knowledge than Solomon, made king long ago amid the acclamations of the people? The words are most suitably put into the mouth of Solomon, who is represented as speaking of his wisdom as exceeding that of all before him (chap. i. 16), and who had been promised wisdom above all those who should come after him (1 Kings iii. 12). The verse might well be cited as one of those which are inconsistent with the traditional idea of the Solomonic authorship of the book. On את אשר, see Köhler on Zech. xii. 10, and the critical note in my *Bampton Lectures on Zechariah*, p. 588. See also Ewald, § 332 *a*. Koheleth, in verse 19, speaks of himself as not knowing whether his successor would be a wise man or a fool; and hence it would have been inconsistent for him to have referred to his successor as a man certain to follow a course of folly; or, as some commentators explain the text, as a man inheriting the throne but not the wisdom of his sire. Ewald, Heiligstedt, and Elster regard the את here as the preposition, and translate, "*And I turned myself round to see wisdom and folly and madness, namely, what the man would be* [*i.e.* what kind of a fool he would be] *who should come after the king, compared with him* (Solomon) *whom they have already made*" king, *i.e.* compared with his predecessor. But, as Delitzsch notes, there is no proof of את in this pregnant sense, at least in the Book of Koheleth, which does not employ את as a preposition. There is perhaps less objection to the transl. given by our A. V., Rosenmüller, Knobel, Hengstenberg, and Zöckler, "*for what can the man do that cometh after the king? even that which hath already been done.*" But any reference to a successor to Solomon is foreign to the context of the passage. According to that idea, there would be little or no connexion between the two clauses of the verse. Hitzig would alter the vocalization, reading עָשׂוּהוּ (after Exod. xviii. 18) instead of עָשׂוּהוּ. On this alteration Delitzsch remarks, "that a writer of the age of Koheleth would, instead of such an anomalous form, have used the regular עָשׂוּתוֹ. Moreover, אֵת אֲשֶׁר־כְּבָר עָשׂוּהוּ *he will do*, or *act that which long ago was his doing* (mode of action), is not Hebrew; it must at least be בַּעֲשׂוֹתוֹ כְּבָר בֶּן יַעֲשֶׂה, or at least עָשָׂהוּ." The meaning of the clause, according to Hitzig, would be, he shall act like a fool, as he has been long doing. The verse, however, states simply that Solomon gave himself up to contemplate the relative value of wisdom on the one hand, and of madness and folly on the other, knowing that he was qualified for this task by reason of that wisdom with which he had been endowed far above his fellows. The expression עָשׂוּהוּ presents no difficulty, for the writer of 1 Chron. (chap. xxix. 22) had no hesitation in speaking of Solomon as made king by the people. The ancient versions seem quite at sea as to the meaning of the passage. The LXX translate ὅτι τίς ἄνθρωπος ὃς ἐπελεύσεται ὀπίσω τῆς βουλῆς, τὰ ὅσα ἐποίησεν αὐτήν; and Symm. τί δὲ ὁ ἄνθρωπος, ἵνα παρακολουθήσῃ βουλῇ, both connecting המלך with the Chald. and late Hebrew מְלַךְ (מְלָךְ), *council*. Aquila, correctly, ὃς εἰσελεύσεται ὀπίσω τοῦ βασιλέως; the Vulg. thinks of God as the Creator, "quid est, inquam, homo, ut sequi possit regem Factorem suum?" Similarly

Jerome, and also Syr. ܡܳܢܰܐ ܂ܓܶܝܪ ܒܰܪܢܳܫܳܐ ܂ܕܢܺܐܙܰܠ ܒܳܬܰܪ ܡܰܠܟܳܐ ܂ܒܕܺܝܢܳܐ ܂ܟܰܕ ܥܰܠ ܥܳܒܽܘܕܶܗ *for what is man that he should go after the king in judgment, and then* (afterwards) *with his Maker?* Strangely the Targ. "For what use it is for a man to pray after the decree of the king and after punishment? behold, it is already decided with respect to him, and it has been done to him."

מֶה. See on this form König, *Lehrgeb.*, § 19, 2 *b*, Stade, *Lehrb.*, § 173 *c*, Ewald § 182 *b*. According to the Masora מֶה occurs twenty-four times, generally before ה and ע. In eight instances, as Delitzsch observes, this form occurs before other letters; three of these are found in Koheleth, in all of which מֶה precedes the letter ה, namely, chap. ii. 12, 22, and chap. vii. 10.

13. בִּיתְרוֹן for כְּיִתְרוֹן which is the reading of some MSS. Good MSS. read also כְּיֳתָרוֹן (see Delitzsch, *textkrit. Bemerk.*). On יתרון see Glossary and note on chap. i. 3.

14. See remarks on p. 148. Note the use of the participles as denoting that which is habitual. On מקרה, see Glossary. On the thought in the verse comp., John xi. 10, and Cicero, *de Nat. Deorum*, ii. 64, "totam licet animis tamquam oculis lustrare terram." Zöckler takes the גם in this verse (גם אני) as adversative, "*yet I perceived.*" But, as Delitzsch notes, גם in this sense should stand at the commencement of the sentence. See Ewald, § 354 *a*. The גם אני is here emphatic.

15. See note on chap. i. 16. גם אני is the accusative, in apposition to the suffix in יִקְרֵנִי. Vid. Ges.-Kautzsch, § 121, 3. It precedes here for emphasis, comp. Gen. xxiv. 27; Ezek. xxxiii. 17. ולמה ל asks after the object or design, מדוע after the reasons for that object. —*Delitzsch.* יֹתֵר See Glossary. שגם־זה ה. *That this also is vanity,* namely, that there is no distinction often between the lot of the wise man and the fool. The LXX. have attempted to give a different turn to the latter clause of this verse. They connect אז יתר with the words following, and render περισσὸν ἐλάλησα ἐν καρδίᾳ μου ὅτι καί γε τοῦτο ματαιότης, διότι ὁ ἄφρων ἐκ περισσεύματος λαλεῖ, making the verse that follows to be the expression of the fool's thoughts. The words διότι ὁ ἄφρων κ.τ.λ. are an exegetical gloss not in the Hebrew, devised apparently to get over the difficulty of the passage. The Syr. similarly adds at the beginning of v. 16, ܡܳܢܳܐ ܂ܕܝܰܬܺܝܪ ܥܰܠ ܥܰܒܕܳܐ ܂ܡܶܢ ܚܰܟܺܝܡܳܐ. The same turn is given to the passage in the Vulg.

(and in the comment. of Jerome), "locutusque cum mente mea animadverti quod hoc quoque esset vanitas."

16. See p. 148. זכרון. See n. on ch. i. 11. Koheleth is speaking here of wise men in general, not of the few examples of persons whose names have been immortalised in history. שכבר. *Long ago*. See Gloss. under כבר. The writer transports himself in thought into the distant future. Comp. Aesch. *Agam.*, 579. הימים הב׳ acc. of time. הכל, *all, the whole of them*, used of persons, as Ps. xiv. 3, or כֻּלָּם in verse 14. It might, possibly, refer to all of the events in the history of the persons referred to. איך וגו׳, "*how dieth the wise man as the fool!*" איך used sarcastically, as Isa. xiv. 4; Ezek. xxvi. 17. See p. 148. עם is in both cases used as a particle of comparison, as in chap. vii. 11; Job ix. 26; xxxvii. 18. Delitzsch compares יַחַד, Ps. xlix. 11. But it might mean in the second clause, "*how dieth the wise man along with* (in company with) *the fool?*" Less suitable is the rendering, "*How dieth the wise man? As the fool!*" given in the English translation of Zöckler, but not in the German original. נִשְׁכָּח might, as far as form goes, be explained as the perfect. But it is better to regard it as the participle which is used to express that which ordinarily happens in human experience.

17. רע עלי "*evil to me*," *i.q.* רַע בְּעֵינַי, similar to טוב על in Esth. iii. 9. This construction belongs to a late stage of the language. Comp. חָבִיב עָלֶיךָ, *dear to thee*, Aboth 2, 10 (2, 14 in Taylor's ed.). See Ewald, § 217 *i*, p. 566. Hitzig explains the expression as, *it was evil upon me*, *i.e.* like a heavy weight resting on me. So LXX. πονηρὸν ἐπ' ἐμέ.

18. The author expresses himself in this verse in a manner inconsistent with the theory of the Solomonic authorship. Solomon, as Delitzsch has well observed, would not have spoken of his successor in such an undefined and unsympathetic manner.

שאניחנו לאדם וגו׳. "*Because I will leave it to the man who shall be after me.*" The suffix נּוּ‎ refers to the עָמָל of the previous sentence. On the two forms of the hiphil of נוח, and their various meanings, see the Lexicon, and Ewald, § 114 *c*.

19. שלט׳ vid. Glossary.
On the double interrogative vid. Ges.-Kautzsch, § 153, 2, rem.

20. וסבותי וגו׳. Compare in verse 12 וּפָנִיתִי ל׳. The difference between the two verbs, according to Delitzsch, is that פָּנָה simply

means to *turn oneself round;* and סָבַב, when used in that sense, means to *turn oneself round from* one thing to another which might present something new, worthy of special attention. On יאש see Glossary.

21. שֶׁעֲמָלוֹ בְּחָכְמָה וגו׳. Ewald translates "*whose toil is about wisdom and knowledge,* etc." But the writer is speaking about a work the result of which could be handed down to another to inherit. Hence this translation is unsuitable. On construction, see Ewald § 309 *b*. On כשרון see Glossary.

22. כִּי מֶה־הֹוֶה ל׳. "*For what is to be the result to the man, etc.?*" Lit. "*what is becoming,*" *about to happen to?* The participle of הוה for היה only occurs elsewhere in Neh. vi. 6, the participle of היה only once, Exod. ix. 3. On the pointing מֶה vid. Ges.-Kautzsch, § 37.

שֶׁהוּא. The reading of the better MSS. is שֶׁהוּא, like שְׁהֶם chap. iii. 18. See Delitzsch (*textkrit. Bemerk.*). In the latter case this pointing occurs before makkeph, scarcely however, as Böttcher supposes, from a desire to avoid the cacophony of ־ֲ־ (*Lehrb.*, § 263); but more probably as Ewald thinks (§ 181 *b*) because the שׁ is regarded as a separate word, and when used as the relative is pronounced as short as possible. See also Kalisch, § xx. 2.

23. Abstract substantives are often similarly used as predicates. Comp. chap. x. 12; Ps. v. 10; Isa. v. 12. The parallelism proves that וָכַעַס is the predicate. The ו in וכעס has kametz, because, according to Delitzsch, a monosyllabic word, or a word which has the tone on the penult (such as a segholate noun), when it immediately precedes a word with athnach, takes kametz in the syllable before the tone. See Lev. xviii. 5; Prov. xxv. 3; Isa. lxv. 17.

24. אֵין טוֹב וגו׳. אֵין טוֹב must not be taken interrogatively, inasmuch as it implies a direct affirmation in the negative. The interrogative would require הֲלֹא טוֹב. Hence the Vulg. "*nonne melius est comedere et bibere,* etc.," is incorrect. The translation of our A. V. is with slight modifications that approved of by most scholars. But it requires a slight alteration to be made in the received Hebrew text. In place of אין ט׳ באדם שֶׁיֹּאכֵל we must read אין ט׳ באדם מִשֶּׁיֹּאכֵל. As the text stands, it must be rendered, "*it is not good among men that one should eat and drink and that his soul should see good,* etc.," which would be directly contrary to chap. iii. 12, 13; viii. 15. Some have proposed with the Targ. and Syr. to insert כי אם before the verb, after the analogy of the latter passage. But כי אם ש׳ is scarcely

Hebrew. It is better with Ewald, Hitzig and Delitzsch to insert the simple מִן after the analogy of chap. iii. 22. בָּאָדָם is not, however, to be regarded with Hitzig (and our A.V. "*for a man*") as indicating the object or purpose, but more simply, with Delitzsch (after the analogy of אֵין טוֹב בָּם, chap. iii. 12, and that of מוֹשֵׁל בָּאָדָם, 2 Sam. xxxiii. 3), as signifying "*among men.*" It is interesting, observes the latter scholar, to see how the usages of the older and the later language appear here side by side, without the former passing altogether over into the latter. Thus, after מִשֶּׁיֹּאכַל, *quam ut edat*, normal perfects follow, according to that peculiarity of the old syntax which Ewald once very suitably termed the fading off of the coloured into grey.

הראה את נ׳ טוב is the same as הֵיטִיב לוֹ, Ps. xlix. 19, and is the causative of the phrase found in chap. iii. 13, or of that found in chap. v. 17; vi. 6.—*Delitzsch.* Koheleth commends in this verse as best for man, not a lazy life of pleasure (note especially the significant addition בַּעֲמָלוֹ) but a life which duly combines work and pleasure, a life in which a man eats and drinks and enjoys whatever work it may be his lot to perform. This power, however, to enjoy the ordinary pleasures of life, which are common to man, and to find pleasure in his daily task is, the writer notes, a gift from the hand of God.

25. ומי יחוש חוץ ממנו. The traditional text has here מִמֶּנִּי. But Ewald and Delitzsch are certainly right in reading, with the Syr. and many MSS., מִמֶּנּוּ. The sentence, "*Who can eat and can enjoy himself better than I?*" would be a most lame conclusion here, and it is highly questionable whether that meaning could be extracted from the Hebrew phrase חוּץ מִן, which means properly *outside of, apart from, except, without,* equivalent to the Chald. בַּר מִן. On the other hand the thought, "*who can eat and who can enjoy himself without Him?*" *i.e.* God, is one which would naturally follow that of the preceding verse. Man even in the commonest matters is absolutely dependent on the will of a higher power. Hoelemann has lately sought to interpret the passage as a penitential confession on the part of Solomon. We cannot coincide with his interpretation, and if true it would not tell much in favour of the traditional theory as to the authorship of the work.

The verb יָחוּשׁ is translated by the LXX. and Syr. by *drink*. But the rendering cannot be justified. Ewald is inconsistent with himself. In his translation he gives "*enjoy*" (geniessen) as the interpretation of the word, but in his notes he approves of the rendering of the LXX. and Syr., connecting the Hebrew with the Arab. حسا = حسا, to *sip*, or *sup*. But the verb in question does not appear in Hebrew. חוּשׁ, in the sense of *hasten*, is tolerably frequent, and Dale would translate here after the A.V. "*who can hasten* (thereunto)." But what is more to the point is that the verb חוּשׁ (and חָישׁ) occurs in Chald. and in Talmudic, in the sense of to *think over*, to *reflect on*, to *suffer* (prop. to *experience*). See Levy's *Neuheb. W.B.* The Rabb. חוּשׁ is also used for *sense*, as חוּשׁ הטעם, *the sense of taste*, pl. חוּשִׁים *the* (*five*) *senses*. So Arab. حاسّة, pl. حَوَامس. Aquila and Symm. (according to Field) translate φείσεται, which reading has crept into MSS. of the LXX.

26. גם זה הבל. The reference in "*this also is vanity*" seems to be to the collecting and heaping together of riches by the sinner just mentioned. The author returns to the point touched on before. The "this" can scarcely refer to the striving after enjoyment in, and through means of, work (*Delitzsch*); because that striving, though spoken of in verse 24, is too remote. The writer does not (as Knobel thinks) refer to the arbitrary distribution of good from the hand of God, for such cannot be described as "*a striving after wind*"; nor (as Bullock) to the gifts of God to the righteous, as well as to "the travail of the sinner"; for the gifts of God, though they may in some respects come under the description of "vanity," cannot be spoken of as "a striving after wind."

CHAPTER III.

1. Time and season (וְעֵת זְמָן) are here contrasted. The former designates rather the point of beginning, the latter the period embraced by the event or matter spoken of. The former is the more general appellation for time, the latter points out rather a special season or portion of time. The LXX. expresses the first by χρόνος, the second very suitably by καιρός. Καιροὶ καὶ χρόνοι is the rendering of the LXX. and Theod. in Dan. ii. 21, עִדָּנַיָּא וְזִמְנַיָּא. The words occur in the reverse order in Acts i. 7; 1 Thess. v. 1. Comp. the use of the sing. in the LXX. transl. of Dan. vii. 12 (עִדָּן וּזְמָן). The Targ. uses in the present passage זִמְנָא וְעִדָּנָא. There may pos-

Ch. iii. 1, 2.] *Critical and Grammatical Comm.* 339

sibly be a reference to this verse in Wisdom viii. 8, where the writer says of wisdom that she foreseeth ἐκβάσεις καιρῶν καὶ χρόνων "*the events of seasons and times.*" The derivation of עֵת is a matter of uncertainty, as it may be regarded either as a contraction of עֶרֶת from the stem יָעַד = וְיָעַד, or of עֵנָת, Ezra iv. 10, from a stem עָנָה, Talm. עִנְתָּא.

Koheleth seems to return in this chapter to the thought expressed in chap. i., and points out that there are laws made by a higher power than that of man which regulate human actions; which actions, though in many cases the result of free agency, are, considered as a whole, under the control and guidance of that God who is over all and conditions all things.

On חֵפֶץ see Glossary.

2. עֵת לָלֶדֶת would naturally signify *a time to bear*, and, since the verb is used not only of *bearing* or *bringing forth*, but also of *begetting* (Gen. iv. 18 and Ps. ii. 7), it might be translated generally "a time to have children." If this be so, the writer begins his catalogue of the times and seasons of man with the season of full maturity, with which he contrasts the season of death. Those, who at one time give life to others, at another have themselves to yield to the law of death. So LXX. καιρὸς τοῦ τεκεῖν. Syr., obscurely, ܘܙܒܢ ܠܡܛܒܚ though most probably referring only to the mother. The Targ. also takes the word in the active sense, but translates it, contrary to the usage of the language, by לָמוּת, *to kill*. "There is a time to beget sons and daughters, and a time to kill disobedient and blasphemous children." The active meaning of the verb is upheld by Knobel, Hitzig, and others. Hitzig and Zöckler argue in support of this opinion that חֵפֶץ denotes a conscious or intentional purpose; but, as Delitzsch justly remarks the לַכֹּל "*for everything,*" which stands at the beginning of the verse, comprehends both doing and suffering, and death itself (apart from suicide, which is certainly not referred to) is not an intentional act, but an event very frequently encountered in a state of unconsciousness. The infinitive active is sometimes, though rarely, used in a passive signification. So לִטְבֹחַ, Jer. xxv. 34. See Ewald, § 304 c. Delitzsch observes that לֵדָה, which is properly an infinitive active, is used in Hosea ix. 11, in the sense of *birth*, and that in Assyrian *li-id-tu, li-i-tu, li-da-a-tu* means "*offspring.*" Hence

it is quite possible to render the clause with Ewald, Ginsburg, Delitzsch, etc., "*a time to be born*," and the contrast contained in the other clause, "and a time to die," is possibly more in favour of this rendering, although no instance can be cited in which the inf. active of this particular verb is used in a passive sense.

By *the time to plant* (עֵת לָטַעַת) the season of planting or sowing is indicated, and the time of the harvest is not obscurely pointed out under the expression, "a time to pull up that which is planted." The form טַעַת only occurs here; the form נְטַע, or נְטוֹעַ, occurs four times, Isa. li. 16; Jer. i. 10; xviii. 9; xxxi. 28.

3. "A time to kill" probably refers to the execution of individual offenders and not to slaying in war, for the time of war is mentioned afterwards in verse 8. Hahn has endeavoured to explain these "times and seasons" spiritually. חפץ in verse 1 is rendered by him *desire*, and applied to the efforts of those who seek after righteousness. Hence birth is interpreted of moral regeneration, and *death* of the death of "the old man"; the planting of the previous verse is understood spiritually in reference to the heart, and the uprooting to signify the destruction of the plants of evil; the killing similarly is explained of the mortification of sin (Rom. vii. 4); the healing is supposed to mean recovery from the sickness of sin, etc. This exposition, however, does violence to the obvious sense of the passage. Its complete novelty is a proof of its want of any solid foundation on which to rest. No other interpreters before Hahn have sought thus to explain the passage, nor has he had (as far as we know) any followers in this peculiar line of exposition.

The "times and the seasons" spoken of are those appointed for human actions and human purposes; such times are all arranged by, and under the control of, God who is above. The Ruler of men, the Most High has appointed death as the punishment for certain offences. He has also imparted to man a knowledge of the art of healing as well as of husbandry and agriculture. Compare on the former, Exod. xvi. 26; Deut. xxxii. 39; Hosea vi. 1; Isa. xxxviii. 21; and on the latter, Isa. xxviii. 23-29. For similar expressions used metaphorically, see Ps. xliv. 3; lxxx. 3, 4, 13, 14; Jer. xxiv. 6. See our remarks on pp. 187 ff.

4. Compare on this verse, Luke vi. 21; John xvi. 20.

On mourning as appointed by God, see Zech. xii. 10, and Matt. ix. 14, 15. Dancing was made use of on occasions of festivities, and occasionally in religious festivals. On the manner and times of dancing, see the Biblical Dictionaries.

5. *To throw away stones* (הִשְׁלִיךְ אֲבָנִים) has probably reference to the marring of fields and rendering of them unfit for agicultural purposes by casting stones on them. The Israelites acted thus in the land of Moab (2 Kings iii. 25), "and upon every good portion they cast every one his stone" (וַיַּשְׁלִיכוּ אִישׁ אַבְנוֹ). By the gathering together of stones the author probably refers to their being collected together with the intention of removing them from the fields. Compare Isa. v. 2. Some have supposed that our Lord alludes to this passage in Mark xiii. 2, but it is scarcely probable. Zöckler maintains that "*to throw away* stones" in this passage is equivalent to קִפֵּל in Isa. v. 2; lxii. 10, and has reference to the throwing of them away from the fields. He has forgotten, however, that the exact phrase occurs in the opposite meaning in 2 Kings. The expression "*to collect stones*" might refer to the purposes of building; but the connexion in which the expression here occurs is in favour of the general interpretation.

חבק seems to be used here, as in Prov. v. 20, without any special reference to women, but to mean any affectionate embraces of men by men. Compare its use in Gen. xxix. 13; xlviii. 10. The thought of the writer is that there is a time for the manifestation of friendship and a time to refrain from all such manifestations. Compare the arrangement made by Jonathan with David (1 Sam. xx. 19-22), which, however, accidental circumstances permitted afterwards to be modified (verses 37-41).

6. The seeking in this passage has reference to the search after riches and honour, or after such things as are commonly sought by men. That which is sought carefully is often lost again. אִבַּד piel is used generally in the sense *of destroy*, and so even in chap. vii. 7. This is its older signification. In the signification of *to lose* it is found only in this passage. Its use, however, in the latter signification is very common in later Hebrew. See Levy, *Neuheb. W.B.*, s.v.

7. "*A time to rend and a time to sew.*" In the former the reference is to the rending of garments in token of sorrow (Gen. xxxvii. 29; 2 Sam. xiii. 31). Knobel thinks there is an allusion in the passage to the Jewish practice of sewing up the rent made in token of sor-

row, at the conclusion of the days of mourning. Herzfeld, however, doubts whether the latter custom (not that of the *rending of garments*, as Ginsburg supposes him to refer to) can be traced as far back as the days of Koheleth.

With respect to the time for silence here spoken of, note the silence of the Psalmist under deep sorrow (Ps. xxxix. 2, 9), the long-protracted silence of Job and his friends (Job ii. 13), and that of the servants of Hezekiah in 2 Kings xviii. 36. On times for boldly speaking out, compare Isa. lviii. 1; Acts xviii. 9. Compare too Prov. xxvi. 4, 5.

8. The time to hate and the time to love probably correspond with the times of war and peace in the next clause. In time of war, whatever secret love one may have towards the enemies with whom he may contend in battle, must practically be laid aside. Is it impossible that this verse formed the basis of the saying of "the men of old" referred to by our Lord in Matt. v. 43? Compare also Luke xiv. 26.

Renan has printed this catalogue of " times and seasons " (verses 2-8) as if it were a quotation made by the writer from some earlier source. But there appears little in favour of that view.

Comp. Marc. Aurelius, xii. 23, τὸν δὲ καιρὸν καὶ τὸν ὅρον δίδωσιν ἡ φύσις.

10. The עִנְיָן, or *troublesome business*, which God has given to man is, that he must work under the conditions prescribed for him by these "seasons and times," which like other " times and seasons " referred to by our Lord (Acts i. 7), are appointed by Divine authority and power. Man is conditioned by this constant change of times and circumstances which he cannot alter. The acts of man, like those of nature, must be again and again repeated. As in nature (chap. i.) so in human affairs, all things seem to move in a circle. From a higher standpoint there may be progress and a steady advance towards some end which finite understanding cannot grasp, though it is ever striving to do so. From the lower plain on which the ordinary observer has to stand (however great minds may, by the erection of some mighty pyramid of science, elevate themselves a little), there often seems to be little or no progress, and sometimes even progress in the wrong direction.

11. See remarks in chap. vii., pp. 188 and 194 ff. Hoelemann considers the author to refer to the Divine statement in reference

to the creation recorded in Gen. i. 31. He thinks that the writer suggests the idea that the work of creation is still going forward, and that ultimately (בְעִתּוֹ) even the sorrows of humanity will be found among the things which are truly beautiful. As a suitable parallel to the thought of Koheleth here, compare Milton's Paradise Lost, Book ii. 146-8:—

"Sad cure! for who would lose
Though full of pain, this intellectual being,
These thoughts that wander through eternity."

The noun עולם is rendered by the ancient translators (LXX. αἰών, Syr. ܥܳܠܡܳܐ, Vulg., *mundus*) by *the world*, and so our A.V. The word has this meaning in later Hebrew, but it is nowhere found in such a signification in the Biblical language. See note 1, p. 196, and our comm. on chap. ix. 6. עולם occurs in five other passages in Koheleth (לְעוֹלָם, chap. i. 4; ii. 16; iii. 14; ix. 6; עֹלָמוֹ chap. xii. 5). Gaab and Spohn take עֹלָם in the sense of *understanding*, and so Hitzig reading עֵלֶם, Arab. عِلْم. No such word, however, exists in either Bibl. Heb., nor have examples of it been found in Chald., Syr., or Rabb. Heb. Graetz translates the word by *ignorance* (the stem עלם signifying to *conceal*). But neither is the word found elsewhere in that sense. It is true that R. Achva bar Zira, as noted in the Midrash Koheleth, referring to Exod. iii. 15 and to the meaning of the stem, explains this passage of the *concealment* from men of the true pronunciation of the שם המפורש, or the Sacred Name יהוה. The Targ., with a similar reference to the meaning of the stem, paraphrases the passage, "and even the day of death He (God) concealed from them in order that that which shall happen in the end might not be known to man from the beginning." But even this rendering proves the Targumist to have taken the word in its ordinary signification. Rab is said (*Berach.*, 43 *b*) to have explained the passage to mean that God permits every man to be pleased with his own special work; *e.g.* the tanner with tanning.

מִבְּלִי, מבלי אשר לא. is used as a conjunction in interrogative sentences with הֲ prefixed, and followed by אֵין, in Exod. xiv. 11; 2 Kings i. 3, 6, 16, "*is it because that there is* (or *that there was*) *not?*" In this verse it is used as a preposition governing אֲשֶׁר, in the sense of "*without that not*" (Gr. Ven. ἄνευ τοῦ ὅτι). סוֹף is a word of later

Hebrew, for which קֵץ and תַּכְלִית are used in the earlier language. See Glossary.

12. אֵין טוֹב בָּם corresponds with אֵין־טוֹב בָּאָדָם, chap. ii. 24. The suffix might, however, also refer to the things enumerated before by the writer. Hoelemann regards the joy spoken of by the writer as identical with that alluded to by the Apostle in Phil. iv. 4. Man ought to "rejoice evermore," in all states, in joy and sorrow, "to lie passive in God's hand," and to submit to His will. But such an idea is not in accordance with the sentiments elsewhere expressed by the writer, and forms rather part of that grace brought unto man by the revelation of Jesus Christ.

עָשָׂה טּוֹב in this verse has been regarded as equivalent to רָאָה טוֹב in the first clause of the next verse, meaning *to enjoy good*. So Luther, Knobel, Hitzig, Ginsburg, Delitzsch, and others. But the ancient versions (the LXX., Syr., Targ., and Vulg.) have understood it of *moral good*, and this is the uniform meaning of the expression. The analogy, therefore, of chap. ii. 24; iii. 22; v. 17; viii. 15 and ix. 7 (in every one of which passages other expressions are made use of), cannot blind us to the fact that here, where we would least have expected it, though not as fully as might be desired, Koheleth speaks of the necessity of morality as forming an essential part of man's happiness. The statement is a preparation for the conclusion arrived at in the epilogue of the work (chap. xii. 13, 14). This is the view of the expression taken by Rosenmüller, Elster, Vaihinger, Hengstenberg, and Zöckler. Comp. Ps. xxxiv. 14; xxxvii. 3, 27, etc.

13. וְגַם. *But also*, adversative. Comp. chap. vi. 7; Neh. v. 8. The construction of the passage is similar to that in chap. v. 18.

כל האדם, properly, *the whole of mankind*. The expression used here and in chap. v. 18; xii. 13, signifies "*every man*"; the article in this case qualifying the genitive, and not, as is more usual, the governing word. Comp. חֶלְקַת הַשָּׂדֶה, *a portion of the field*, or in the example cited by Delitzsch, בְּתוּלַת יִשְׂרָאֵל, where the first word is undetermined, while the second is definite of itself.

כל האדם is here almost like a *casus pendens*, separated as it is from its predicate by the שֶׁ which precedes it (שֶׁיֹּאכַל).

14. "Everything which God does (or "will do," not, as Ginsburg, "hath made"), it shall be for ever." Koheleth refers not to the work of creation, but to the arrangements of Divine Providence with reference to human actions mentioned in the previous

part of the chapter. These exist for ever (לעולם), *i.e.* man cannot alter them. Compare on the thought of the passage chap. i. 4; Isa. xlvi. 10; Ps. xxxiii. 11. Ben Sira gives a good comment on the passage when he says (Sir. xviii. 6), "It is not possible to take from (οὐκ ἔστιν ἐλαττῶσαι οὐδὲ προσθεῖναι), nor to add to, and it is not possible to track out the wondrous works of the Lord."

עָשָׂה שֶׁ, *fecit ut*, as Ezek. xxxvi. 27; ποιεῖν ἵνα, Apoc. xiii. 15; שייראו מלפני. So also chap. viii. 12, ff. Compare 1 Chron. xvi. 30 with Ps. xc. 9.—*Delitzsch.* By fear *reverence* is here signified.

15. אשר להיות. *That which is to be*, in the future, τὸ μέλλον. See Ges.-Kautzsch, § 132, 3, rem. 1.

אֶת־נִרְדָּף The article would have been expected here after את. But compare אֶת־לֵב, chap. vii. 7; Ewald, § 277 *d.* נ means literally that which has been *driven away, the departed, the past;* Vulg. "*Deus instaurat quod abiit.*" God seeks the past, and brings it again into being. He alone can bring that back which was once past and gone. This explanation coincides with the previous part of the verse. The expression, however, only occurs in this passage, and has been variously explained. Hengstenberg, after the LXX. (ὁ Θεὸς ζητήσει τὸν διωκόμενον), Aquila, Symm. (with slight variations), Syr. and Targ., render " *God seeks the persecuted.*" This idea does not fall in with the context. The Gr. Ven. renders literally, ὁ Θεὸς ζητήσει τὸ ἀπεληλαμένον. So most modern scholars. In Arabic a *synonyme* of a word is technically called its مُرَادِف, and the expression for *synonymous words* is أَلْفَاظٌ مُتَرَادِفَةٌ. In post-biblical Hebrew נִרְדָּפִים signifies *synonymes.*

16. מקום המש, the *place of judgment, i.e.* in the place where judgment ought to be administered. It is, perhaps, best to regard מקום as the object after ראיתי. The accentuation is not against this view, as may be seen from a reference to the accentuation in Gen. i. 1. Hitzig, Ginsburg, and others regard מ as an adverbial accusative of place, equivalent to בִּמְקוֹם (Ges.-Kautzsch, § 118, 1; Ewald, § 204 *a*), "*I saw under the sun, in the place of righteousness, etc.*" It is difficult to harmonise the statements of this verse with the traditional view of the authorship of the book by Solomon.

17. The שָׁם at the close of the verse is best referred to God, who is spoken of in the preceding clause. Comp. Gen. xlix. 24. It

cannot well be regarded as an adverb of time, *then*, *i.e.* in the day of judgment (as Vulg. and Targ.). The general sense of the passage is in either case the same, for in both cases the writer is supposed to refer to the future judgment. Ewald refers the adverb to past time, "there is a time for everything, and (=and indeed) a judgment for every work (done) there" in time past. Houbigant, Hitzig, and others, propose to read שָׂם perf. of שׂוּם; the passage then signifying, "*a time for every purpose and for every work hath He* (God) *appointed.*" But neither the MSS. nor the ancient Versions give any countenance to this conjecture, all of them being in favour of the traditional reading. Herzfeld, followed by Fürst and Vaihinger, leaving the text as it is, has sought to explain שָׁם as perfect of שׂוּם, in the Talmudic sense of *estimating, judging*. But, as Delitzsch observes, the verb in question is construed with the accusative, and not (as in this passage) with לְ and עַל; and, according to this idea, the thought of Koheleth must be conceived as here broken in upon, although he proceeds in the next verse further to develop and expand it. In later Hebrew the construction with עַל is used indifferently alongside of אֶל and לְ. See Ewald, § 217 *i*.

18. עַל דברת וגו׳. "*According to the manner of the sons of men.*" Compare Ps. cx. 4; LXX., badly, περὶ λαλιᾶς υἱῶν τοῦ ἀνθρώπου, and so the Syriac. Johnston considers (*Treatise*, p. 128) that the fact that the expression עַל דברת only occurs in Ps. cx., outside the Book of Ecclesiastes, "deserves notice in connexion with the question of authorship."

לְבָרָם. *In order to try them.* בַּר is the infinitive construct in *a*, from the stem ברר. Similar examples are רָד, Isa. xlv. 1, and שַׁר, Jer. v. 26. An infinitive from בוּר is found in chap. ix. 1. This is the only instance in which an infinitive const. of this form is found with suffixes. See Böttcher, *Lehrb.*, § 987, 5 γ; König, *Lehrgb.*, § 34, 2 and 6, pp. 339, 358; Ewald, § 255 *d.*, § 238 *b*; Ges.-Kautzsch, § 67, rem. 3. The meaning *prove*, or *try*, given to ברר by the Vulg., Targ., Gesenius (in *Thes.*) *explorare*, is preferable to the translation of the word by Rosenmüller and Knobel as *declarare*, or that assigned by Ginsburg, namely, *to choose*. Not much differently the LXX. ὅτι διακρινεῖ αὐτοὺς ὁ Θεός. האלהים is to be regarded as the subject after the infinitive according to Ges.-Kautzsch, § 133,

2, 3, and rem. at the end. See also Ewald, § 309 a. Compare לְהָאִיר עֵינֵינוּ אֱלֹהֵינוּ (Ezr. ix. 8).

וְלִרְאוֹת. *And in order that they may see.* The LXX., Syr. and Vulg. translate this as hiphil (וּלְהַרְאוֹת = וְלַרְאוֹת), which reading is approved by Ginsburg; the Masoretic reading is rightly preferred by Delitzsch.

שָׁהֶם־. Delitzsch notes that the Frankfort cod. reads שְׁהֵם, as mentioned in Michlol, 216 a. הֵמָּה may be regarded as the copula, Ges.-Kautzsch, §121, 2. Ewald regards the accumulation of pronouns in this passage as a sort of ironical gradation, like Lat. *ipsissimi*, § 315 a. הֵמָּה seems purposely introduced because of its alliteration with בְּהֵמָה. This play upon words, remarks Delitzsch, musically accompanying the thought, remains, even if המה be connected with the להם immediately following, as in the Frankfort MS., which exhibits the accentuation שְׁהֶם בְּהֵמָה הֵמָּה לָהֶם. The להם is rightly explained by him to be the dative of relation, as in Gen. xvii. 20 (וּלְיִשְׁמָעֵאל), Ps. iii. 3, etc.

19. מִקְרֶה occurs three times in this verse. In the first two cases the LXX. have regarded it as the construct (מִקְרֵה) governing the word following the genitive. It is better, however, with the Masorites, the Targ., etc., to regard the word as the predicate in all three cases. On the thought of the verse compare Ps. xlix. 13, 21, and the words of Solon to Crœsus, πᾶν ἐστι ἄνθρωπος συμφορή (Herod. i. 32). See our remarks on the allusion to this passage in the Book of Wisdom, on p. 68 ff. Böttcher, *De Inferis*, p. 246, regards the expression as adverbial, in which case the similarity between this passage and Wisdom ii. 2 is more close. But we prefer to render it uniformly as the predicate.

The writer does not affirm, as Hitzig imagines, that men and beasts are the results of mere "blind chance," nor does he mean simply to affirm that both are subjected to the same law of transitoriness (Elster, Zöckler), but rather that mankind, being conditioned by circumstances over which there can be no control, are subject in respect to their whole being, actions and sufferings, as far as mere human observation can extend, to the law of chance, and are alike destined to undergo the same fate, *i.e.* death.

20. See our remarks on p. 44, and on pp. 191 ff.

הַכֹּל שָׁב. שָׁב is the participle active, corresponding to הוֹלֵךְ in the first clause of the verse.

21. See our remarks on p. 190 ff. The ה in הָעֹלָה and in הַיֹּרֶדֶת was not designed by the Masorites to represent the interrogative,— the הַ in the first word being lengthened into הָ before the ע, as it is lengthened in three cases before א, Judges xii. 5; vi. 31; Num. xvi. 22. See Ges.-Kautzsch, § 100, 4, rem., and especially Stade, *Lehrb.*, § 175 *a*. Kalisch, however, cites this passage as an instance of the interrogative, § xx. 4 *a*. Geiger (*Urschrift*, pp. 175, 176), instances the pointing of this text, and that of Ps. xlix. 12, as intentional alterations of the text for dogmatic purposes. In the latter passage the LXX., Targ. and Syr. read קִבְרָם, "*their grave is their house for ever*," in place of the Hebrew pointed text, "their inward thought (קִרְבָּם) is that their houses shall be for ever." But see Delitzsch's Comm. on the Psalms on the latter passage.

22. לִרְאוֹת בְּ. See note on ch. ii. 1, and on מָה, Ges.-Kautzsch, § 37.

CHAPTER IV.

1. וְשַׁבְתִּי אֲנִי וָאֶרְאֶה. This is the second instance of the vav consec. found in the book. Lit. *I returned and saw*, i.e., I saw again. The same phrase occurs in verse 7. See on construction, Ges.-Kautzsch, § 142, 3 *a*, rem.; Ewald, § 285 *a*; Kalisch, § 103, 2. Comp. also ch. ix. 11. שַׁבְתִּי וְרָאֹה.

הָעֲשׁוּקִים. In the first instance in which this word occurs in this verse it signifies *oppressions*, and it is used in this sense in Job xxxv. 9 and Amos iii. 9. It is properly the participle passive used abstractively, the plural number denoting the many individual cases which are combined in the one idea. See Böttcher, *Lehrb.*, § 698. It is construed here with the plural אֲשֶׁר נַעֲשִׂים, but this need not be regarded as strange, seeing, as Delitzsch notes, that even חַיִּים is construed (as in Ps. xxxi. 11; lxxxviii. 4), with a plural predicate. The LXX. and Syr. have in their translations noted correctly the difference in meaning of the word in the two clauses of the verse. But Ginsburg, after Symmachus (who translates in both places הע by τοὺς συκοφαντουμένους), with Herzfeld and others, renders the word in both clauses alike by "*the oppressed*." Hence he is driven to translate אשר נעשים by those "*who are suffering*" (literally, "*who were made so*"); but this latter rendering cannot be regarded as correct.

דִּמְעַת. Used collectively. Rosenmüller quotes Cicero, *De Partit.*, vii. 17, "cito arescit lacryma præsertim in malis alienis." A more suitable comparison is Isaiah xxv. 8, דִּמְעָה מֵעַל כָּל־פָּנִים, imitated in Rev. xxi. 4.

The expression וּמִיַּד עֹשְׁקֵיהֶם כֹּחַ is somewhat peculiar. It is to be connected with the preceding הִנֵּה. The Vulgate, viewing the clause as affected by the אֵין in the preceding sentence, has rendered, "*nec posse resistere eorum violentiæ.*" But the repetition here of the thought previously expressed is more in accordance with the usage of the writer. Comp. ch. i. 6; ii. 10; iii. 16. כֹּחַ is always used in the signification of *power* and not in that of *violence*.

2. וְשַׁבֵּחַ. Knobel and others explain this form as the participle piel shortened from מְשַׁבֵּחַ, after the analogy of the participle pual, in which the מ of the participle is sometimes dropped. See Ges.-Kautzsch, § 52, rem. 6; Kalisch, § xliv. 1, 7. But Delitzsch maintains that the מ of the participle piel is not dropped; the only example being מַהֵר, Zeph. i. 14; but in that passage *et festinanter valde* is the same as *et festinanter valde veniens*, the adverb being virtually an adjective. Herzfeld considers the form a verbal adj. like קָם. This seems to be the view of Kimchi, who says (*Michlol*, 58 *b*), "it is an adjective instead of a participle." The question is treated most fully by König, *Lehrgeb.*, § 32, 5, p. 292. It is only the rareness of the construction which has made scholars consider the form which occurs here as the participle. But the form is unquestionably that of the inf. absolute, which is used in continuing a narrative, the pronoun being here added as the subject of the verb. Ewald (§ 351 *c*) quotes an exact parallel, וְנַהֲפוֹךְ הוּא, Esth. ix. 1. Compare also Prov. xvii. 12. See Ges.-Kautzsch, § 131, 4, rem. 1; Olshausen (§ 249 *a*) would correct the text to מְשַׁבֵּחַ. ערנה, vid. glossary, s. עֶרֶן.

On the subject of the verse, comp. ch. vii. 1; Job iii. 13 ff. See our remarks on p. 150. Knobel cites as parallels, Herod. i. 31. διέδειξέ τε . . . ὁ Θεὸς, ὡς ἄμεινον εἴη ἀνθρώπῳ τεθνάναι μᾶλλον ἢ ζώειν, and Menander, ζωῆς πονηρᾶς θάνατος αἱρετώτερος.

3. את אשר־ע וגו'. The accusative here is governed by וְשַׁבֵּחַ in the preceding verse. The LXX. (ὅστις οὔπω ἐγένετο), Syr., Gr. Ven. regard it as the subject, את being sometimes, though rarely, used to give prominence to the subject of the sentence (see Böttcher, *Lehrb.*, § 516). But the former is the simpler explanation.

הָרָע has always the double kametz, except in Ps. liv. 7 ; Mic. vii. 3. *Delitzsch*.

Many classical parallels to the idea expressed in this verse could be quoted. Thus Theognis, 425-428.

> πάντων μὲν μὴ φῦναι ἐπιχθονίοισιν ἄριστον
> μηδ' ἐσιδεῖν αὐγὰς ὀξέος ἠελίου·
> φύντα δ', ὅπως ὤκιστα πύλας Ἀΐδαο περῆσαι·
> καὶ κεῖσθαι πολλὴν γῆν ἐπαμησάμενον.

Or Sophocles, *Œd. Col.* 1225-1228.

> μὴ φῦναι τὸν ἅπαντα νικᾷ λόγον· τὸ δ', ἐπεὶ φανῇ
> βῆναι κεῖθεν ὅθεν περ ἥκει,
> πολὺ δεύτερον, ὡς τάχιστα.

So also Cicero, *Tusc.*, i. 48, where the sentiment is ascribed to Silenus, "Non nasci homini longe optimum esse; proximum autem quam primum mori."

4. כשרון. Vid. Glossary.

Koheleth does not deny that labour and toil effect something for man, but he observes that the superior excellence of the work performed arises in most cases from the envious desire on the part of a man to surpass his fellows. Consequently he asserts that there is in general no lasting good attained by the individual worker. Man, however, is compelled to labour; for, although toil produces little result, idleness proves the ruin of an individual. קִנְאָה is active in meaning, and signifies *envy, jealousy*. Our A.V. departs, in its translation, widely from the sense of the original, "I considered all travail, and every right work, that for this a man is envied of his neighbour." The ambiguity of the expression "right work" has led to the passage being expounded by Bridges, Young, Bp. Wordsworth, and others, to mean that "for *doing right* multitudes have been envied and persecuted." But Koheleth does not refer in the passage to moral rectitude, but to superiority in work or workmanship. Gesenius, in *Thes.*, regards קנאה to mean an *object of envy*, and so Vaihinger. The latter renders מֵרֵעֵהוּ, *before his fellow*, but "the מִן is evidently comparative, like אָמֵן מִן, Ps. xviii. 18, etc., *æmulatio qua unus præ altero eminere studet.*"—*Delitzsch*.

5. "The fool foldeth his hands together," in slothfulness and

sleep" (Prov. vi. 10; xxiv. 33), instead of working as he ought. He destroys himself by his own laziness, "eats his own flesh." Ginsburg has strangely interpreted the aphorism, "The sluggard foldeth his hands and yet eateth his meat," as if he considered Koheleth to contrast the enjoyment of the easy sluggard with the toilsome labour of the envious. Ginsburg maintains that "אָכַל בָּשָׂר, *to eat meat*, is frequently used in Scripture as indicative of an ample and delicate repast." In proof of this he refers to Exod. xvi. 8; xxi. 28; Isa. xxii. 13; Ezek. xxxix. 17. In all of these passages, however, the eating of flesh is contrasted with the use of other food, and in none of the examples cited is the phrase equivalent to "*eating his meat*" (or, "*his food*"), in the English sense of that expression. Ginsburg has been incautiously followed by Plumptre. It is true that the Hebrew phrase is not used in the sense condemned by Plumptre, that is, of "pining away under the corroding canker of envy and discontent," as Gesenius suggested in *Thes.* (s.v. אכל), comparing Il. vi. 202, ὃν θυμὸν κατέδων, Plaut., *Trucul.*, 2, 7, 36, "quisnam illic homo est, qui ipsius se comest, tristis oculis malis." Gesenius says that such a person is called in Arab. آكَلَ نَفْسَهُ, but he has quoted no examples of this usage. Plumptre is justified in saying that we have no authority for this in the language of the Old Test. But Gesenius stands almost alone in such an interpretation. The other interpreters regard the phrase as equivalent to "*destroys himself.*" Instances of similar Arab. phrases in the latter sense may be seen in Lane, *Arab. Lex.* The phrase "*to eat men,*" and "*to eat the flesh of men,*" is found in Arabic in the sense of defamation of character. The meaning of the expression in Koheleth is sufficiently explained by the Psalmist when he speaks of his enemies as coming upon him "to eat up his flesh" (Ps. xxvii. 2), or by Micah who speaks of those who "eat the flesh of my people" (Micah iii. 3). Zechariah speaks of the evil, or worthless shepherd (not "idol shepherd," see my *Bampton Lectures*, p. 346 ff), who devoured the flesh of the Jewish flock (Zech. xi. 16), in contrast with the true Shepherd. This usage is in direct accordance with the denunciation (Isaiah xlix. 26), "I will feed them that oppress thee with their own flesh." The simple meaning of Koheleth is that the indolent by their indolence feed upon their own flesh and destroy themselves.

6. There is no difficulty as to the translation of this passage. Its meaning has, however, been strangely misconceived by some expositors. Plumptre describes it as expressing the thought which might be conceived "as rising in the mind of an ambitious statesman or artist striving after fame, as he looks on the *dolce far niente* of a *lazzarone* at Naples, half-naked, basking in the sun, and revelling in the enjoyment of his water-melon. The one would at such a time almost change place with the other, but that something after all forbids." Mendelssohn and others consider the passage to contain a dialogue between the industrious man and the sluggard, the fifth verse being the statement of the industrious, and the present verse the reply of the lazy. Similarly Hitzig explains verse 5 as containing an objection, to which verse 6 supplies the answer. Zöckler coincides in the main with Hitzig. The latter critic considers that the writer is probably citing a proverb in verse, while Renan looks upon verse 5 altogether as a quotation. Delitzsch calls attention to the fact that נַחַת does not mean the rest of laziness, but rest in contrast with that excessive occupation in business, that hunting after gain and honour, which can never be satisfied, and which impels a man unceasingly to strain every effort in order to overtop and outrival his fellows. The rest which Koheleth commends is a quiet stillness (chap. ix. 11), and a cessation from the toil which man imposes upon himself, and which ultimately proves his destruction (Isa. xxx. 15). Thus the two verses are not opposed to one another. In the former, the author notes how the fool consumes by idleness his own vital powers; while in the latter he observes that a little real rest is better than all the results achieved by that striving occasioned merely by the spirit of rivalry and jealousy which permits a man to take no rest, and yet ends in nothing. "*Better is the full of a hand*" (כַּף, the flat open hand), *with rest, than the full of two* (bent) *hands with toil and striving after wind.*" חָפְנַיִם occurs in Biblical Heb. only in the dual; the singular חֹפֶן is not found in Hebrew, but occurs in Chaldee, חָפְנָא, Syr. ܚܘܦܢܐ, Arab. حَفْنَة, Assyr. *huppunnu, the fist, the closed-up hand.* נַחַת, עָמָל, and רְעוּת רוּחַ, are all accusatives of respect. See Ges.-Kautzsch, § 118, 3; Kalisch, § 86, 4 *b*; מְלֹא is a noun followed in each of the two clauses by a genitive.

Knobel suitably compares the saying of Publius Syrus, "quam felix vita, quæ sine negotiis transigit!"

8. וְאֵין שֵׁנִי. וְאֵין here has almost the meaning of *without*. Delitzsch compares וְאֵין מִסְפָּר, Ps. civ. 25; cv. 34.

On וְאֵין, for which, with the conjunctive accent, we would have expected וְאֵין (as in Prov. xvii. 17 with merca), compare וְאָט with kadma as contrasted with וְאָט Hosea xi. 4. Delitzsch also compares וְצָאן, chap. ii. 7, with mahpach, and on the contrary, chap. ii. 23, וָכַעַס with pashta.

The correction in the K'ri of עֵינָיו into עֵינוֹ is occasioned by the following verb (לֹא־תִשְׂבַּע) being singular. When the reference is made to things, not persons (the *pluralis inhumanus*), the verb is frequently used in the singular. Vid. Ges.-Kautzsch, § 146, 3; Kalisch, § 77, 9.

ומחסר את־נ׳ מ׳. On the const. compare Ps. viii. 6. Renan supposes that the author refers here to his own personal circumstances, but no solid reason can be assigned for this opinion.

For classical parallels, comp. Juvenal, *Sat.*, xiv. 139; Horat., *Od.*, ii. 13, 14. See our remarks on the passage at p. 206.

9. The article in השנים refers to two persons such as are alluded to in the previous verse, and the article in האחד is used to denote one individual like the person who is there more fully described.

10. אם־יפלו, taken partitively, *when one or the other*. Knobel compares the formula, וַיֹּאמְרוּ אִישׁ אֶל־רֵעֵהוּ (Gen. xi. 3; Judg. vi. 29, etc.).

וְאִילוֹ, for וְאִי לוֹ, *and woe to him!* אִי־לָךְ, *woe to thee!* chap. x. 16. The Masora magna notes that there are five cases in which munach and rebhia occur together on one word, namely, Gen. xlv. 5; Exod. xxxii. 31; Zech. vii. 14; Eccl. iv. 40; Dan. i. 7. Graetz, after the Targ., would explain אִילוֹ as the later Hebrew אִלּוּ. The latter occurs in this book in chap. vi. 6. The meaning would then be "*and when.*" But the LXX., Syr., Vulg. are in favour of the traditional punctuation. הָאֶחָד in the clause ואילו האחד, is in apposition to the suffix preceding, as in Ps. lxxxvi. 2 in a less appropriate manner. It is not necessary to repeat the preposition in apposition. See Gen. ii. 19; ix. 4. Exceptions sometimes occur, such as Ps. xviii. 51; lxxiv. 14.—*Delitzsch.*

11. The passage evidently refers to the sleeping together of two friends for mutual warmth and comfort in the winter season.

Delitzsch notes that (in the Aboth of R. Nathan, chap. viii.) sleeping with a person is regarded as a sign of friendship. וחם להם used impersonally, "*it is warm to them*," i.e. "*they are warm.*" Comp. Job iii. 13; Isaiah xlix. 20.

12. יִתְקְפוֹ for יִתְקְפֵהוּ, Job xv. 25. Compare, יְרִדְפוֹ Hosea viii. 3. See Ges.-Kautzsch, § 60, rem. 2. König, *Lehrgeb.*, § 29, 2, p. 224. Ewald, § 249 *b*. The verb תקף is probably used here in the sense of *to make an attack on*. Others take it in sense of *prevail against*, in the A.V., *si quispiam prævaluerit contra unum*, regarding the suffix as pleonastic, and הָאֶחָד as the accusative. Graetz and many expositors, after the Syr. and Targ., take הָאֶחָד as the subject (Graetz reads, יתקפם); but it is better, with Knobel and Delitzsch, to regard it as the object, as a permutative referring to the previous suffix, as Exod. ii. 3, וַתֵּרְאֵהוּ אֶת־הַיֶּלֶד.

13. There is no necessity to suppose that Koheleth had in view any particular historical incident, such as that of Joseph in Egypt, Saul and David, Jeroboam and Rehoboam. These and many other parallels have been adduced by various commentators, but none of them are quite satisfactory. Graetz refers the incident in this and following verses to Herod and his son Alexander, whom the Jews wished to have as king. But it is more probable, inasmuch as similar instances are so common in history, that Koheleth speaks here in general terms.

14. מִבֵּית הָסוּרִים is no doubt for מִבֵּית הָאֲסוּרִים, which reading is found in some MSS. of Kennicott. Compare הָרַבִּים, 2 Chron. xxii. 5, in place of הָאֲרַמִּים, found 2 Kings viii. 28. See Gesenius, *Lehrg.*, p. 377; Ewald, § 73 *c*. Stade (*Lehrb.*, § 112 *a*) regards this mode of writing as phonetic for הָאֲסוּרִים. Delitzsch notes that the later Hebrew is fond of the elision of א, as אֶפְּלוּ = אִם אֵלּוּ, אַף אֵלּוּ = אֶלְתָּר = אַל־אַחֵר. In his *Dichter des alt. Bundes*, Ewald translates, aus dem Hause der Niederen, "*out of the house of the lower* (classes)," explaining הַסּוּרִים as "*the cast-off,*" after Isa. xlix. 21 (גֹּלָה וְסוּרָה). Hitzig takes the word in the sense of *fugitives*, referring to Judg. iv. 18, regarding "the house of fugitives" as a description of Egypt when Jeroboam fled from the vengeance of Solomon. Both explanations are highly artificial and improbable. Equally strained is Hitzig's later exposition in the 14th vol. of Hilgenfeld's *Zeitschrift für wissenschaftl. Theologie*, where the youth is interpreted of David and the old and

foolish king of Saul. Hitzig there explains בית הסורים as "*the house of the escaped*," or estranged, as in Jer. ii. 21; xvii. 13. Hahn has made a very ingenious but unsuccessful attempt to explain the whole passage of Messiah's lowly birth and universal sway. It would be certainly strange that in a Messianic passage, after mention having been made of His people as innumerable, there should follow a statement such as "those that come after will not delight in him," and still stranger that the usual refrain, "for even this is vanity, etc.," should also follow such a prediction.

יָצָא is to be regarded as a perfect, "*he goes forth*," otherwise the comparison would be lame. Graetz, however, takes it as *future*, "*he will go forth to reign*," referring to the hopes the author had, according to Graetz's theory, of Alexander's succession to the throne of Herod.

כי גם וגו'. "*When even in his kingdom he was born poor*," i.e. although he was originally born as a poor individual in the kingdom of the old and foolish king, over which he now goes forth to rule as king. It is highly probable that the suffix in בְּמַלְכוּתוֹ refers to the old king, inasmuch as the suffix in תַּחְתָּיו (verse 15) must refer to him.

The translation given by Ginsburg, "for a prisoner may go from prison to a throne, whilst a king may become a beggar in his own kingdom," must be rejected, because to express such an idea the imperfect would have been employed. It is very questionable whether נוֹלַד can be taken with Herzfeld in the sense of the Greek γίγνομαι, *to become*. No instances can be adduced in which it is used in this signification.

Renan regards this verse as a quotation, but this is unlikely, from the close connexion in which it stands with the preceding verse.

15. The author describes that which usually takes place on such occasions just as if he had actually beheld it himself. The language employed is such as could only have been used by a person living under one of the great world-monarchies. Hence the subjects of the empire are spoken of as "all the living who walk under the sun." The intensive form הַמְהַלְּכִים (part. piel) is employed instead of the participle kal, which latter is more usual. Compare הֹלְכִים, Is. xlii. 5. Ewald considers that the expression הַשֵּׁנִי (*the second*) refers to the title הַמִּשְׁנֶה (*the second*), met with in Gen. xli. 43. But in that case the instance adduced by the author would have to be regarded

as distinct from that brought forward in verses 13, 14. The use of the word יֶלֶד shows, however, that the same person is referred to in both places. The youth described as coming out of prison to reign could not be described as "the second" person in the kingdom; not at least in the sense in which that expression is used in the Book of Genesis. Hitzig and Delitzsch are, therefore, correct in regarding the "young man" (יֶלֶד) as termed הַשֵּׁנִי (*the second*), the king himself being regarded as the *first*. It is true, as Delitzsch writes, that there is some incorrectness in the expression which has at least the appearance of referring to two persons, each entitled to the appellation of "youth." This inaccuracy in diction, he notes, is similar to that found in Matt. viii. 21, when by ἕτερος τῶν μαθητῶν is meant "another person, and that one also one of His disciples," or that in Luke xxiii. 32, ἤγοντο δὲ καὶ ἕτεροι δύο κακοῦργοι σὺν αὐτῷ ἀναιρεθῆναι. The translation of Ginsburg "the sociable youth" cannot be justified, and moreover partakes somewhat of the ludicrous. The preposition עִם denotes "*by the side of.*" Koheleth represents the people as ranging themselves on the side of the youth who has been raised from low estate to royal dignity. Ewald regards the עִם as a kind of comparative, appealing to the use of עִם in chap. ii. 16 ; vii. 11. On the impf. here in the sense of *successurus erat*, see Ewald, § 136 *d*.

16. See remarks on p. 86. לְכֹל אֲשֶׁר־הָיָה לִפְנֵיהֶם. Ewald maintains that the reference of the writer is to "*all those who preceded them*," *i.e.* the two kings just mentioned. Others, as Gesenius, Rosenmüller, and Ginsburg, consider the young king to be the subject of the verb (היה), and regard היה לפני to convey the sense of *to be over*. They translate the clause "*there is no end to all* (the people) *over whom he ruled.*" Similarly Delitzsch renders the last words, "*at whose head he was*," comparing the phrase כִּי הוּא יוֹצֵא וּבָא לִפְנֵיהֶם, 1 Sam. xviii. 16 ; so also 2 Chron. i. 10 ; Ps. lxviii. 8, etc.

גַּם הֵא. *Also, i.e.* notwithstanding all the court paid to him by the men of his day and generation—*those who come after, i.e.* the men of a later generation *shall not rejoice in him*, for his memory shall also perish. On וְגַם compare chap. vi. 7, and see Ewald, § 354 *a* ; Ges.-Kautzsch, § 155, 2 *a*. הָאַחֲרוֹנִים. Comp. chap. i. 11 ; Isa. xli. 4. The events here related do not coincide exactly with any known incidents of history. The attempts made to explain the passage

Ch. iv. 16, 17.] *Critical and Grammatical Comm.* 357

as referring to Saul and David, or to Solomon and Jeroboam, or to Seleucus and Antiochus the Great, all break down when subjected to close examination. Worst of all, perhaps, is the attempt of Graetz to trace a reference to the history of the Herodean family. Hahn considers the passage to be a prophecy of the Messiah, who was born poor, and came forth from the prison to reign. He consequently maintains that the expression in verse 15 refers literally to all those who dwell on the earth. He regards the first king mentioned in the passage as meant collectively of all the kings of Israel, from David onwards, compared with whom Messiah is "the second," inasmuch as he founds a second and an everlasting kingdom. The 16th verse is then regarded as a description of the hatred exhibited by the ungodly against the Messianic rule. But the exposition is so manifestly forced, and so opposed to the whole character of the work, that it is unnecessary to enter upon its formal refutation.

17. It is almost a matter of indifference whether we follow the reading of the written text רגליך (*thy feet*, plural) or that of the K'ri רגלך (*thy foot*, sing.). Both are admissible, compare Ps. cxix. 59 and 105, the singular being more common.

By בית האלהים the temple may possibly be meant (see note 2, p. 115), though it is not unlikely the reference is here to the synagogue, inasmuch as the writer speaks of *listening* to preaching, which was no part of the temple cultus. The priests gave instruction to the people on matters of religion (Lev. x. 11; Deut. xxxiii. 10; Mal. ii. 7), but they did not preach or teach at the public temple services. The cantillation of the Psalms, and the reading of lessons from the Law and probably also from the Prophets, no doubt formed a portion of the temple service in the days of Koheleth. But the passage seems to refer to the ordinary synagogue services held everywhere throughout the land. The writer affirms that a diligent listening to the teaching imparted in the synagogue is of more real value than the "sacrifices" offered up in the temple by "fools."

וקרוב לשמע. 'ק is inf. abs. kal, not piel, as Olshausen, § 249 *c*, and Ewald, § 240 *b*, maintain. See König, *Lehrgeb.*, p. 175. The infinitive absolute may be used either as an object or subject. See Ewald, § 240 *a*. Böttcher (*Neue Aehrenlese*, No. 1649) disputes the latter statement. He renders the clause, "*take heed to thy foot whenever thou goest into God's house, and of drawing near to hear more than etc.*" Delitzsch notes that in that case the words following should rather have been מִתֵּתְךָ כַּכְּסִילִים זָבַח. He regards the inf. absol. as the subject of the sentence, "*and to draw near to hear is* (*better*) *than that the fools should give sacrifice.*" The inf. abs. is used in a wide manner in Koheleth. Comp. chap. iv. 2. Owing to the הכסילים following, קָרוֹב is not to be translated as an imperative. In the latter case it would be necessary to insert טוֹב before מִתֵּת, as is done by the Syr. and Vulg. The latter combines two translations, "et appropinqua ut audias. Multo enim melior est obedientia quam stultorum victimæ." מתת הכסילים is rendered by the LXX., ὑπὲρ δόμα τῶν ἀφρόνων θυσία σου, and so, substantially, Aquila, Theod., and Jerome, "donum enim insipientium sacrificium," reading מַתַּת *a gift* instead of מִתֵּת. שמע must not be translated "*obey,*" as Ginsburg and Zöckler, and the Vulg. in its second rendering. When the verb has that signification, words are added to show the sense in which it is used, or such words can easily be supplied from the context, as in 1 Sam. xv. 22.

In the last clause of the verse כִּי־אֵינָם יוֹדְעִים לַעֲשׂוֹת רָע we may read, after the analogy of chap. iii. 12, viii. 15, כי־אינם יודעים [כי אם] לע׳ ר׳. So Renan, who considers the omission of the words in brackets was caused by similarity of the ending of the יודעים immediately preceding, in which case the meaning is "*for they do not know except to do evil.*" The text as it stands is to be explained with Delitzsch, "*they* (the fools) *do not know* (*i.e.* they are ignorant, comp. Ps. lxxxii. 5; Isa. lvi. 10), *in order to do evil*" = "*so that they do evil.*" That is, their ignorance leads them to do evil. This is preferred by Plumptre. The translation in our A.V., "*they consider not that they do evil,*" is substantially that of Elster, Dale, Zöckler, Bullock. But, as Delitzsch notes, this would require עֲשׂוֹתָם רָע (comp. Jer. xv. 15). The only case he remarks which has been adduced to defend the explanation of לעשׂות רע as an accusative with inf., as if *se facere malum*, is וַיִּשְׁאַל אֶת־נַפְשׁוֹ לָמוּת (1 Kings xix. 4) which is not a parallel, for לָמוּת does not there signify *se mori* but *ut moreretur*. The translation of the Vulg. "*qui nesciunt quid faciant mali*" is still worse. Herzfeld renders, "*for they understand not to do evil,*" which would be the most natural translation of the words if they stood alone.

But his explanation cannot be justified. For he explains "they" to refer to the subject supposed to be implied in לִשְׁמֹעַ, which he renders *to obey*. Hence he assigns the meaning to the passage, "*those who obey commit no sin*," which has been adopted by Ginsburg.

The expression used here, "*to give a sacrifice*," is peculiar, and may possibly have some reference, as Delitzsch has suggested, to the feasting connected with the offering up of sacrifices. Comp. Prov. i. 14. נָתַן is used in connection with *sacrifice* in Psalm li. 18.

CHAPTER V.

1. The construction of בָּהֵל with עַל may suitably be compared (with Delitzsch) to the German and English construction to *fly upon wings*, or to the phrase found in Ps. xv. 3. רָגַל עַל לְשֹׁנוֹ, "*to slander with* (lit. *upon*) *his tongue*. Delitzsch also compares the post-Biblical term הַתּוֹרָה שֶׁבְּעַל פֶּה, the *oral law*. The writer warns against rash and hasty vows, or professions made carelessly in prayer. The piel בָּהֵל here is intensive, not causative; as Rosenmüller and Ginsburg regard it, rendering "*do not hasten on thy mouth.*" בָּהֵל is used with a reflexive accus. in 2 Chron. xxxv. 21. Compare with this verse Matt. vi. 7-9.

On Ben Sira's imitation of the saying, see on p. 43. In Berachoth, 68 *a*, it is stated that Rab Huna said in the name of Rab, "Let the words of a man be always few (מוּעָטִין) before the Holy One, blessed be He! according as it is written," and then follow the words of Koheleth in this passage. מְעַטִּים. See Glossary, s.v.

2. "*A dream comes* (בָּא is probably the participle indicating the result of frequent experience) *in* (as the consequence of) *much occupation* (*i.e.* bustling about many things), *and the voice of a fool in consequence of many words.*" It is difficult in English to render בְּרֹב alike in both sentences. A man who is very far from being a fool, may through much speaking make himself appear for the time being to be one. Comp. chap. x. 14. Symmachus renders ברב עניו by διὰ πλῆθος ἀνομίας, reading עָוֹן. Hitzig and Ginsburg take קוֹל כְּסִיל as equivalent to "*foolish talk*," but כסיל (as Delitzsch observes) is always used of living *persons*, never in reference to *things*.

3. The language of this and the next two verses is closely akin to that in Deut. xxiii. 22–24. On Ben Sira's imitation of it, see p. 43.

אין חפץ בכ׳. "*There is no pleasure* (or delight) *in fools*," namely, on the part of God. Compare כִּי־חָפֵץ יְהוָה בָּךְ in Isaiah lxii. 4. The idea is far from being "trivial," or from being a "tame anticipation" of the declaration in verse 5. The Lord first ceases to delight in a man, and then after long forbearance, gives him over to destruction. Compare, too, Psalm cxlvii. 10, 11. The translation of Herzfeld, "keine Bereitwilligkeit ist in den Thoren," and that of Ginsburg, approved of by Plumptre, "fools have no fixed will," are both opposed to the usage of חֵפֶץ.

4. טוב אשר. On the use of אשר for כי see Ewald, § 336 *a*. Knobel refers to the prohibitions of the Talmud (in Tract. *Nedarim*) against frequent vows, as sometimes leading men to commit perjury.

5. See p. 18. Delitzsch correctly explains this verse in accordance with the passage in Deut. xxiii. 22, 23 (A. V. 21, 22), upon which it is manifestly based. The passage in Deut. contains a warning against rash vows as likely to lead to serious transgression (וְהָיָה בְךָ חֵטְא). But the remark there follows: "if thou shalt forbear to vow, it shall be no sin in thee," לֹא־יִהְיֶה בְךָ חֵטְא. Similarly in this passage in Koheleth the meaning is, "*let not thy mouth cause thee* (lit. *thy flesh* בְּשָׂרְךָ, used for the whole personality) *to sin*," *i.e.* bring thee into sin, and consequently into punishment. The passage in Job xxxi. 30, is an exact parallel. The phrase נתן ל with the inf. is there used in the sense of *to suffer, to permit*, as in this passage and in Judges i. 34, וְלֹא־נָתַתִּי לַחֲטֹא חִכִּי לִשְׁאֹל בְּאָלָה נַפְשׁוֹ, "*and I did not suffer my mouth* (lit. *my gums*) *to sin by cursing his life*," and thus seeking his death. On the syncopated hiphil infinitive, vid. Ges-Kautzsch, § 53, rem. 7; Kalisch, § xlv. 2 *d*. The idea is not that "the sensuality of man is simply excited by the sins of the tongue or the mouth" (*Zöckler*); for, independently of the fact urged by Delitzsch that the formula "*the flesh sins*" is not in accordance with Old Test. ideas, a reference here to such sins as Zöckler alludes to is quite out of place in this connexion. The sin of one member of the body can bring ruin upon the whole (comp. Matt. v. 24). The use of בָּשָׂר is akin to that in chap. ii. 3; xi. 10; Prov. xiv. 30. Gesenius, in *Thes.*, rightly refers to Deut. xxiv. 4; Isa. xxix. 21, and to the present passage, as instances

in which הֶחֱטִיא is used in the sense of to *make one guilty*. Cheyne, however, disputes the correctness of that rendering in Isaiah xxix.

There is little doubt that the priest is meant by the הַמַּלְאָךְ (rendered in our A.V. "*the angel*") in the second clause, and that לִפְנֵי הֹמ׳ is equivalent to לִפְנֵי הַכֹּהֵן, Lev. xxvii. 8, 11, although Mal. ii. 7 is the only other case in which the priest is so termed in the Old Test. המלאך in the passage might also signify the ruler or Chief Rabbi of the synagogue. Zöckler is right in maintaining that ἄγγελος is used in Rev. i. 20; ii. 1 ff. in "essentially the same signification." Tayler Lewis, indeed, maintains that the word is to be taken in its usual meaning "as an angel of God, visible or invisible, supposed sometimes to appear in terror, the avenging angel, as 2 Sam. xxiv. 16, who came to punish Israel and their king for his rash words. There may be an express reference here by Solomon to his father's fatal error; and the words וְאַל תֹּאמַר may be rendered very easily as a caution, *that thou mayest not have to confess thine error* as David did (2 Sam. xxiv. 17). It must have made a deep impression on the young mind of the Prince." It is scarcely necessary to point out that the writer of Koheleth cannot possibly refer to any such supernatural appearances; nor is the idea of the Targumist possible, that the angel meant is "the avenging angel" in the great day of judgment. Tayler Lewis further suggests as possible that "the angel" might be "Gad, the *messenger* sent to David." Equally erroneous is the view of Ginsburg that it is "the angel presiding over the altar." The angel in the text must necessarily mean some one connected with the temple or synagogue, to whom application might be made for a release from the vow rashly made, on the ground that it was a שְׁגָגָה, a sin of weakness. The only difficulty lies in the fact that though, according to the Mosaic law, a husband could in certain cases of his own authority dissolve the vow of his wife, or a father that of his daughter (Num. xxx.), no mention is made of a *priest* having any special power in such matters. They had, however, a kind of oversight with regard to vows. See Lev. xxvi. 8, 12, 14, 18, 23. According to a passage in the Talmud, quoted by Delitzsch (*Bekhoroth*, 36 *b*), a learned man (חָכָם), or even three laymen, could release from a vow. Hence we are disposed to regard the word as meaning not only a priest, but any authorised teacher of religion. Whether the author had in his mind the case of one who desired to be freed entirely from his rash vow, or of one willing to offer up some lesser sacrifice in lieu of a larger, promised in a moment of rashness, cannot be determined with any certainty. But the excuse offered is certainly one contemplated by the author as made at some public religious service to some person officially accredited by the Church, and looked upon as God's representative, and hence termed המ׳ "*the messenger*," or "*angel.*" The writer cannot refer to some invisible angel supposed to be present in the temple. The LXX. explain the phrase as meaning "*in the presence of God,*" and so the Syr. and Arab., which coincides with our explanation. Vulg., literally *coram angelo*, and Jerome *in conspectu angeli*. Prophets were often called by the term מלאך, as Isa. xliv. 26; Hag. i. 13; Mal. iii. 1.

By "thy voice," in the close of the verse, is probably meant not " thy idle talk " (Ginsburg), but "the voice of thy supplication," or prayer.

Graetz maintains that there is a reference in these verses to the common superstition, that in case of evil dreams it was necessary to offer up a sacrifice of some sort in order to avert the evil consequences threatened. The custom referred to was prevalent among the Greeks, but unknown, as Graetz admits, to the Jews in pre-exilian times. The saying of Rab, which Graetz quotes from the Talmud (*Shabbath*, 11 *a*; *Taanith*, 12 *b*), that "fasting is serviceable to make evil dreams innocuous," is also insufficient to prove that the Greek custom of ἀποτροπιασμός was common among the Jews of later days, and it is fanciful to suppose that Koheleth in this passage ridicules such folly. Graetz renders חַבֵּל by "*estimate,*" in allusion to the law of Lev. xxvii., where, however, a different word is made use of. But the verb in question is evidently used in this passage in the far stronger sense of *destroying*, as in Isa. xiii. 5; liv. 16, etc. Compare מַלְאֲכֵי חַבָּלָה, *angels of destruction*, a common name used in the Talmud and Midrash for the organs of Divine justice.

Renan asserts, that when vows were solemnly made in the temple, and any delay occurred as to their performance, the priests were wont to send agents to claim the money due. He considers that the verse refers to this practice. But he has given no authority for such a statement.

6. The verse as it stands is somewhat obscure and rugged in its

construction. It cannot well mean, as Symmachus, Vulg., Luther, Ewald, "*for in the multitude of dreams there are also vanities and many words.*" For the verse professes to assign a reason against rash speaking and especially against rash vows, which so translated it would not give. And why should the writer affirm that in dreams there are "many words?" According to the Hebrew accentuation, the word הבלים seems to be a genitive dependent on בְּרֹב. So the Græc. Ven., ἐν γὰρ πλήθει ὀνείρων καὶ ματαιοτήτων καὶ λόγοι πολλοί. Hence ודברים הרבה is to be regarded as the predicate. The same objections, however, lie against this translation. Hitzig and Knobel supply בְּ from the first clause before דברים in the second, thus rendering "*for in the multitude of dreams are also vanities, and in many words also.*" Knobel compares Exod. xvi. 6; Prov. xxiv. 27; Job xxxvi. 26. Not very dissimilarly Rosenmüller. As the text stands, this seems the best rendering, although the supply of the בְּ is somewhat harsh, and the clause is uneven. Tayler Lewis renders, "*though* (כִּי, *notwithstanding*) *in multitude of dreams*," or "*though dreams abound, and vanities and words innumerable, yet* (כִּי) *fear thou God.*" Such a rendering is impossible. According to it there would be no verb at all in the passage. For Tayler Lewis does not intend the clause to be understood as if it was literally, "there are also vanities and words," etc. (which would be also questionable), but he distinctly denies that the copulative ו has here "an assertive force." The LXX. render literally ὅτι ἐν πλήθει ἐνυπνίων καὶ ματαιοτήτων καὶ λόγων πολλῶν, ὅτι σὺ τὸν θεὸν φοβοῦ, leaving it to be inferred that some such word or expression as *which are deceptive*, or *vain*, is to be mentally supplied. So the Syr. inserts after ורב׳ הרבה the word ܘܣ̈ܓܝ. Herzfeld, after the Arab. version, followed by Ginsburg and Bullock, would supply after the opening כִּי the pronoun היא, used for the substantive verb. They render the clause as if it were כִּי הִיא בְרֹב וגו, "for *it is* (or, it happens) *through the multitude of idle thoughts, and vanities, and much talking.*" Herzfeld considers the reference to be to the foolish speaking noticed in verse 2. Ginsburg seems to include also "the wrath of God and the punishment consequent thereon," spoken of in the preceding verse. But this is harsh and unsuitable. Graetz regards the text as corrupt, and would delete the first כִּי, thus making the verse one with the preceding. Delitzsch considers that it is probable that the text is dislocated, although the ancient versions seem to have had the existing text before them. He would arrange the text as follows : כי ברב חלמות ודברים הרבה והבלים, *i.e. "for in the multitude of dreams and many words there are also divers vanities."* This last is the rendering found in our Auth. Version.

7. See on p. 150. Graetz maintains that this verse is out of its place, and belongs to another group than that in which it stands. Like Hitzig, considering that the second clause refers to the authorities of the land or empire, he regards that clause as ironical. He further considers it impossible to view גֵּזֶל as the construct governing משפט וצדק as genitives expressing the object (signifying, *robbery of judgment and righteousness*), though he does not state the ground of his objection. If, as is probable, he objects on the ground that such an expression is not found elsewhere, such an objection is not decisive, since גֵּזֶל (const. גֵּזֶל, here and in Ezek. xviii. 18) only occurs six times in the O.T., and גְּזֵלָה only the same number. The ancient versions have found no difficulty in the word, and it is quite arbitrary to insert מקום as an accusative of place, "*in the place of*," before the two united genitives, as Graetz has proposed, and as is approved of by Renan.

On חפץ and מדינה, see Glossary. Rosenmüller, Knobel, Ewald, Elster, Zöckler, etc., translate גבהים עליהם, "*there is the High One above them*," regarding 'ג as the plural of majesty, after the analogy of chap. xii. 1, or according to similar analogies in Prov. ix. 10 ; xxx. 3; Dan. vii. 18, 22. The Targ. refers the first גָּבֹהַּ to *God*, and some English commentators have explained the text according to this view. But Delitzsch correctly regards the second clause of the verse as conclusive against this opinion, for אל־תתמה is simply "*be not surprised thereat*" (LXX. μὴ θαυμάσῃς), and the verse evidently means, as explained at p. 150 : Do not be surprised at the corruption and baseness of the lower officials, inasmuch as the same corruption prevails among those in far higher positions. Koheleth is not here seeking to cheer up the sufferer by bidding him look higher ; he is describing the evil state of affairs everywhere existing in the empire in his own day. Hahn fancifully explains הַמְּדִינָה in this verse to mean the kingdom of God; but Renan is not far wrong when he observes that the feudal system in force at the time appeared to Koheleth to be the principal cause of the wretched administration of affairs glanced at in this verse.

[Ch. v. 8, 9.] *Critical and Grammatical Comm.*

8. Graetz would insert before this verse the passage in chap. vii. 11, 12. But it is improbable that any such dislocation could have ever taken place. The rendering of our A.V., "*the profit of the earth is for all; the king himself is served by the field,*" has this in its favour, that it coincides with the Hebrew accentuation. It is substantially the same as that given by R. Samuel ben Meir (Rashbam). Its difficulty lies in the rendering of בַּכֹּל, *for all*, as if it were לַכֹּל. בַּכֹּל is best explained as meaning "*in everything,*" in all respects, i.q., *always*. Comp. Gen. xxiv. 1; Ezra x. 17, which latter is incorrectly explained in the A.V. The difference in this verse between the K'thibh and K'ri is merely that the written text is הִיא, and the K'ri reads הוּא in order to agree with יִתְרוֹן, which is masculine. The K'ri note does not extend at all to בכל, as the remarks of Hitzig and Zöckler would lead the reader to conceive. The first clause is best rendered, "*and an advantage of a land in all respects it is (to have) a king devoted to the field,*" or to agriculture. See Rosenmüller, Dathe, Delitzsch. Other translations of the latter clause are: (1) *a king honoured by the land, i.e.* by his subjects. See Gesenius, De Wette, Knobel, etc. But no instance can be adduced of שָׂדֶה being so employed. Knobel compares Ps. lxxviii. 12 where שָׂדֶה stands in parallelism to אֶרֶץ. (2) Hahn, explaining this verse of the future heavenly king of Israel, renders "*a king will be honoured as wide as the field,*" *i.e.* over the whole land. This translation is excessively forced, and in every respect faulty. (3) Ewald, Heiligstedt, Elster, Zöckler, translate "*a king made by the field,*" "*rex agro factus, terræ præfectus, i.e.* in omnibus injuriis, quibus terra premitur hoc ei est utilitati, quod rex ei præest, qui illas injurias comprimere et punire potest."—*Heiligstedt*. But, as Hitzig urges, neither the expression עָשָׂה מֶלֶךְ nor עָבַד מֶלֶךְ is used for *to make a king*. (4) Hitzig regards נֶעֱבָד as qualifying שָׂדֶה, and renders accordingly, "*a king to the tilled field*. See LXX. βασιλεὺς τοῦ ἀγροῦ εἰργασμένου. It is a point in favour of this that the niphal of עָבַד in the other three places in which it occurs (Ezek. xxxvi. 9, 34; Deut. xxi. 4) is used in the sense of "*tilled*."

9. Though the aphorism in this verse does not appear at first sight naturally to follow the subject mentioned in the preceding verses, a little closer examination shows that it is intimately connected with it. The oppressions noticed in ver. 7 are such as were occasioned by "the love of money." But a king fond of agricultural pursuits would

be unlikely to be a man inordinately fond of gain. And the love of riches, continues Koheleth, brings no satisfaction to the man who abandons himself to the pursuit of them, he obtains no real תְּבוּאָה, or return for his exertions, to be compared with the *produce* or *fruit* afforded by the land (Josh. v. 12), or with that of the threshing floor (Num. xviii. 30), which are enjoyed by the tiller of the soil. Koheleth speaks of *silver* not of *gold*, because כֶּסֶף *silver*, is, as Delitzsch observes, the specific word for coin. The construction אָהַב בְּ in the second clause is worthy of note, as it is only found in this passage. The בְּ strengthens the idea, and is in accordance with the analogy of רָצָה בְּ, חָפֵץ בְּ, etc. Compare רָאָה בְּ, *to look upon* with pleasure. הָמוֹן is used for a *multitude* of persons, and also, as here, for *abundance* of wealth. So in Ps. xxxvii. 16; 1 Chron. xxix. 16. Hitzig, after the LXX., with Spohn and others, translates this last clause interrogatively "*And who hath joy (or delight) in (that) abundance which produces nothing?*" But it is better with the Vulg. (*qui amat divitias fructum non capiat ex iis*), Syr., Targ., and most commentators to regard לא תבואה as the simple predicate of the sentence viewed as a statement of fact, "*and he who loves wealth has no fruit,*" or advantage from it. On the use of אֹהֵב in the first clause along with מִי אֹהֵב in the second, see Ewald, § 331 *b*. Compare Horat., *Epist.*, i. 2, 56, "Semper avarus eget,".Ovid, *Fasti*, i. 211, 212.

"Creverunt et opes et opum furiosa cupido
Et, cum possideant plurima, plura petunt."

10. ברבות הטובה, *when prosperity increases*. רבות inf. const. of רָבָה to *be many, to increase*. Comp. Prov. xxix. 2, 16. רַבּוּ 'א *those that consume it increase also*, *i.e.* become many, or are many; probably a reference, as Zöckler supposes, to the numerous servants of a rich household. Comp. Job i. 3; 1 Kings v. 2, ff. Ginsburg suitably compares the anecdote narrated in Xenophon, *Cyrop.*, viii. 3, 35-44. There is no substantial difference between the reading of the K'thibh (רְאִית) and that of the K'ri (רְאוּת).. Both nouns occur and stand related to one another as שְׁבוּת, K'thibh, Ps. cxxv. 4, and שְׁבִית, which is found there in the K'ri. בְעָלִים is used here in a singular signification, as in verse 12; chap. vii. 11; viii. 8; Exod. xxi. 29 : Isaiah i. 3, etc. Similar is the use of אֲדֹנִים in the plural as a singular.

11. The advantage of agricultural pursuits is here again touched on. הָעֹבֵד is the *husbandman.,* Comp. Gen. iv. 2; Prov. xii. 11. When work in general is referred to, עָמָל is the verb used. The LXX. (not the Syr.), followed by the Arab., translate *slave* (עֶבֶד), a reading which has been adopted by a few critics. The more general word, however, suits the passage better, the free labourer as well as the slave enjoys sleep as the result of toil. In the expression והשבע ל׳ in the next clause no reference is made to the overloaded stomachs of the rich, as Jerome, Rosenmüller, Hitzig and others have supposed, led astray by the allusion to eating in the first clause. For the overloading of the stomach would produce the same effect in the case of the poor as in that of the rich. "*The abundance of the rich*" (comp. שָׂבָע in Prov. iii. 10; Gen. xli. 29), is rather the abundance of their riches, which bring with them cares and anxieties which prevent slumber. הַשָּׂבָע לֶעָשִׁיר is a circumlocution for the genitive. See Ges.-Kautzsch, § 115, 2; Kalisch, § 87, 14 *a*. Delitzsch notes that the nouns צָמָא, רָעָב and שָׂבָע have no construc' state, and hence the necessity for this construction. שְׂבַע is the const. of שָׂבָע. But it may be noted that רְעָבָם (Neh. ix. 15) shows that it is quite possible to say for example רְעַב הָאֶבְיוֹן; compare also צְמָאִי, Ps. lxix. 22; צְמָאָם, Ps. civ. 11. Ginsburg is mistaken in regarding לֶעָשִׁיר as a dative. Classical parallels for the thought in the second clause may be found in Horat., *Sat.,* i. 1, 70–79, Juvenal, *Sat.,* x. 12, 13, or xiv. 304, "misera est magni custodia census," and the maxim of Publius Syrus, "avarum irritat, non satiat pecunia." On the former clause we may compare Hor., *Od.,* iii. 20–24, Virg., *Georg.,* ii. 467–474, or, with Plumptre, Shakespeare, *Henry VI.,* act ii. scene 5.

13. רָעָה חוֹלָה, *a sore evil,* חוֹלָה is the feminine participle of חלה, *to be sick.* Compare חֳלִי רָע, chap. vi. 2; מַכָּה נַחְלָה, Jer. xiv. 17; Neh. iii. 19. שמור לב׳, *preserved by the owner.* See Ewald, § 295 *c*. Ginsburg's rendering "*hoarded up by the rich for the owner*" is possible, in accordance with the analogy of 1 Sam. x. 24, the only other passage where the construction שָׁמוּר לְ occurs. But the idea thus introduced into the text is not natural, and, as similar constructions occur, as has been pointed out by Ewald, it is rash with Ginsburg to condemn on the authority of a single passage, as "ungrammatical," a

construction so obviously intended here, and one which has the support of the ablest critics, such as Knobel, Ewald, Hitzig, Heiligstedt, and Delitzsch. On בעלים used in a singular signification, see note on ver. 10. See our remarks on this passage on p. 149.

וְהוֹלִיד. The perfect is used in order to bring into prominence a further aggravation of the hypothetical instance adduced by the writer, "*and should he have begotten a son, then* (ן) *there is nothing in his hand*," *i.e.* wherewith to support the child. Others suppose that the suffix *his* refers to the son, but this is not so good. On the use of the perfect, Delitzsch compares the clause in Gen. xxxiii. 13, וּמֵתוּ כָּל־הַצֹּאן. See also Driver, *Heb. Tenses*, § 149.

14. This verse is closely connected with the preceding, and does not introduce a new subject, as Rosenmüller supposes; the author evidently refers to Job i. 21. Comp. Sirach xl. 1, in which a reference is made to this passage. כְּשֶׁבָּא for כַּאֲשֶׁר בָּא. וּמְאוּמָה לֹא־יִ בעֲ. מְאוּמָה precedes the לֹא for emphasis in the sense of "anything," *quidquam*. Compare the clause at the end of the preceding verse with the phrase וּמְאוּמָה אֵין בְּיָדוֹ in Judges xiv. 6. Some expositors regard the בּ in בַּעֲמָלוֹ as partitive, "*taking nothing from his work.*" So Vulg., Ibn Ezra, Luther, our A.V., Ginsburg, etc. But it is better with the Targ., Knobel, Ewald, and Delitzsch, to regard it as the בּ *pretii*, "*taking nothing by his work.*"

שֶׁיֵּלֵךְ. One of the few instances of the jussive (see Excursus, No. 4) which occur in this book. Other instances occur in ch. x. 10 (וַיָּגֵד), and ch. xii. 4 (וְיָקוּם), see note 3 on p. 247. Hitzig would read שֶׁיֵּלֶךְ, kal instead of hiphil, on the authority of the LXX. ἵνα πορευθῇ, Symm. ὃ συναπελεύσεται. But this reading would scarcely signify (as Hitzig explains it) *which would go with him*, as a reward for his trouble. A fitting parallel to the thought of the passage is found in 1 Tim. vi. 7, compare also Propertius, iii. 35, 36,—

"Haud ullas portabis opes Acherontis ad undas;
Nudus ab inferna, stulte, vehere rate."

15. זֶה. Vid. n. on ch. ii. 2. כָּל־עֻמַּת שֶׁ. Vid. glossary under שֶׁ. Delitzsch notes that the Cod. Heidenheim writes כְּעֻמַּת שֶׁ as one word, probably under the mistaken presupposition alluded to by Kimchi, that it is a composite word compounded of the כְּ of comparison and

לְעָמַת (which frequently occurs in Hebrew), and therefore ought to be pointed בְּלְעָמַת. On עָמָּה see Gesenius' Lexicon.

16. Instead of "*eats in darkness*," בַּחֹשֶׁךְ יֹאכֵל, the LXX. and Vulg. read בַּח' וְאָבֵל (καὶ ἐν πένθει, *atque tristitia*). This reading is approved by Spohn, Heiligstedt, and Ewald. Böttcher proposes to read וְאָכֹל. Hitzig regards כָּל־יָמָיו as the accusative of the object, *i.e.* "*he eats* (consumes) *all his days in darkness*." The passages, Job xxi. 13, יְבַלּוּ יְמֵיהֶם בַּטּוֹב, or יְבַלּוּ בַטּוֹב יְמֵיהֶם, Job xxxvi. 11, do not justify this explanation. The expressions *to sit in darkness* (Micah vii. 8), and *to walk in darkness* (Isaiah ix. 2; l. 10), coupled with such phrases as "*the bread of affliction and the water of affliction* (1 Kings xxii. 27), justify the retention of the reading of the text, which corresponds with the thought in Virg., *Aen.*, ii. 92, "afflictus vitam in tenebris luctuque trahebam." Ginsburg gives some curiosities of interpretation in his note on the passage.

וְכָעַס in the Masoretic text is the verb. It cannot be taken (as Tayler Lewis has done) as a noun with the pathach lengthened into kametz. The tone being milra forbids this. The noun as a segholate must be milel. Delitzsch observes that in the Cod. Heidenheim the note is added to the word מלרע 'ב, *i.e.* "*twice milra*," the verb occurring in the perfect here and in Ps. cxii. 10. The perfect, according to Hebrew syntax, suitably follows the imperfect in the previous clause. But the conclusion of the sentence is thus somewhat abrupt. The LXX. render the clause, καὶ θυμῷ πολλῷ καὶ ἀρρωστίᾳ καὶ χόλῳ. Hence Hitzig would read : וְכָעַס הַרְבֵּה בְּחָלְיוֹ וְקִצְּף. In this case the copula would be regarded as uniting "all his days" in the former sentence with (כעס) "vexation" here. But this would be a strange combination of ideas. Ewald, Burger, and Böttcher would also point כַּעַס as the noun, and read in the latter part simply וְחֳלִי. Delitzsch, however, well remarks that in this case the reading וְחֳלִי לוֹ would be necssary. Zöckler (who is here misinterpreted by his English translator), Delitzsch, and others preferably regard וְחָלְיוֹ וְקִצְּף as an exclamation, "*and oh !* (thereto must be added) *his sickness and anger!*" Delitzsch compares similar exclamations in Isa. xxix. 16; Jer. xlix. 16. See Ewald, § 328 *a*. See before, p. 149.

17. The text as accentuated in the Hebrew presents a difficulty. The word "good" would naturally be construed with the verb "saw,"

"*Behold that which I saw to be good.*" But the accent closes the first sentence with rebhia. Hence אֲנִי in pause is there אָֽנִי. The טוֹב must then be connected with what follows. But טוֹב אֲשֶׁר־יָפֶה cannot be translated with the Targ., Syr., and the A.V., "*it is good and comely, etc.*" Hence the assertion of Graetz that we have here the Greek καλὸν κἀγαθόν is unproved. Better, as in the marg. of the A.V. after the LXX., ἰδοὺ εἶδον ἐγὼ ἀγαθὸν ὅ ἐστι καλὸν κ.τ.λ., "*there is a good which is comely,*" or "*beautiful.*" Even in the latter case we would have expected a distinctive accent at יָפֶה, in place of munach. Rosenmüller follows the LXX. (so also Tayler Lewis) and appeals with Kimchi to Hosea xii. 9, as a parallel, עָוֹן אֲשֶׁר חֵטְא, "*a transgression which is sin.*" The parallel is, however, unsatisfactory, inasmuch as that passage probably means "iniquity which deserves punishment." Hence it is safer, with Delitzsch and most modern critics, to disregard here the accentuation, and regarding the second אשר as referring back to the first, to translate "*Behold what I have seen good, which is beautiful (namely), etc.* This passage is one of those relatively long verses in which no athnach is found. The accentuation is somewhat peculiar. The suffix in עֲמָלוֹ refers to the subject of the preceding infinitives. See Ewald, § 294 *b*, 2. מספר וגו׳, acc. of time, comp. chap. ii. 3. Knobel compares with this verse Marc. Aurel. ii. 1, where that emperor says of himself τεθεωρηκὼς τὴν φύσιν τοῦ ἀγαθοῦ ὅτι καλὸν κ.τ.λ.

18. The גַּם with which the verse commences is to be regarded as referring to each clause of the same. נְכָסִים. This word occurs in Josh. xxii. 8, and, therefore, although generally used by later writers, is not to be cited as one of the proofs of the composition of Koheleth in post-Solomonic times.

19. It is unnecessary, with Herzfeld whom Ginsburg has followed, to suppose that the הַרְבֵּה really belongs to את־ימי ח, and not to יִזְכֹּר· For similar instances of attraction Ginsburg refers to chap. ii. 24; iii. 21. The text, however, requires no transposition. Koheleth simply affirms that the man, who enjoys the blessings spoken of in the former verse as proceeding from the hand of God, does not, as a fact of ordinary experience, "*much remember,*" or *think of*, "*the days of his life;*" although he knows full well (as stated in ver. 17) that they are but few in number. The blessings which God bestows upon man so occupy his attention that he does not often trouble himself with the thought that all such enjoyments are fleeting. The second

clause of the verse presents some difficulties, though the general drift of the passage is tolerably clear. Ewald considers that the hiphil is here used in the sense of the kal, and, appealing to Ps. lxv. 6, for the construction of עֲנֵה בְ, translates, "*God grants to him the joy of his heart*," *i.e.* the joy of heart which man possesses is God's gift. Similarly Heiligstedt. The passage in Ps. lxv. 6 cannot be regarded as a proof of this, for ענה is construed there with a double accusative, and the בְּצָרְקָ which follows in that passage is best explained as an adverbial designation of the mode and manner. LXX. ὅτι ὁ θεὸς περισπᾷ αὐτὸν ἐν εὐφροσύνῃ καρδίας αὐτοῦ, "*God occupies him in the joy of his heart.*" So Vulg., "eo quod Deus occupat deliciis, etc." Similarly Vaihinger and Knobel. Others, as Köster, "*God makes him sing in the joy of his heart.*" But if it had been the author's intention to express this idea he would certainly have made use of a less ambiguous verb. For ענה unites the significations of being *bowed down*, and of *replying* and of *singing*. In the last signification it is identical with the Arab. غنى. "*God makes him sing*" would have been expressed by מַעֲנֵהוּ. Fürst translates "*God witnesses to the joy of his heart*," but what is the meaning of that? Ginsburg, desiring to uphold the causative sense of the hiphil, renders, "*God causeth (him) to work for the enjoyment of his heart.*" But, as Delitzsch remarks, עֲנָה בְ in Koheleth does not mean simply, *to busy oneself with a matter*, but *to weary oneself* with it, so that the hiphil does not express the desired meaning. It is on the whole better to explain the phrase with Delitzsch, "*God answers (corresponds with) the joy of his heart,*" *i.e.*, as interpreted by Plumptre, "is felt to approve it as harmonizing, in its calm evenness, with His own blessedness."

CHAPTER VI.

1. Koheleth often introduces new experiences with יֵשׁ; either followed by אֲשֶׁר, as here and at chap. viii. 14, or without אֲשֶׁר, as in chap. iv. 8; v. 12; x. 5.

ורבה היא על ה׳. The use of this phrase in chap. viii. 6 seems decisive in favour of the translation, "*it is great upon man*," that is, lies heavy upon him. Compare chap. ii. 21. The phrase has also been interpreted to mean, *it is common among men*. So the Vulg. *frequens apud homines*, our A.V., and many commentators.

2. The phrase "riches and wealth and honour" is evidently borrowed from the narrative concerning Solomon in 2 Chron. i. 11, where the three words are found similarly united. This fact is conclusive against the translation of כָּבוֹד by *abundance*, given by Herzfeld, Ginsburg, and others. Ginsburg asserts that the translation *honour* "is incompatible with the verb לֶאֱכֹל, inasmuch as it would be preposterous to say, *he cannot eat his honour*:" but the same remark would be applicable to the other nouns *riches* and *wealth*. To *eat* is used metaphorically in the sense of *to enjoy*.

The Vulg., Targ., etc. render אֵינֶנּוּ חָסֵר, *there is nothing wanting*, the suffix being treated as pleonastic (Gen. xxx. 33; xxxix. 9, are quoted as instances of this usage, but incorrectly). The LXX. render καὶ οὐκ ἔστιν ὑστερῶν τῇ ψυχῇ αὐτοῦ. The literal translation is "*and he lets not his soul want of all, etc.*" חָסֵר is a verbal adjective. לְנַפְשׁוֹ is the dat. commodi, *for himself*, a sense which נֶפֶשׁ with suffixes frequently has: נַפְשִׁי, *myself*, נַפְשְׁךָ, *thyself*. The מִן is best regarded as partitive, as in Gen. vi. 2. אִישׁ נָכְרִי, *a stranger, one of another family*, and not the legal heir. There is no occasion to take the word with Heiligstedt in the sense of *a foreigner*. חלי רע, compare רָעָה חוֹלָה, chap. v. 12.

3. אִישׁ, *a man*, used indefinitely for *one, any one*, Ges.-Kautzsch, § 124, 2, rem. 2; Kalisch, § 82, 4. יוֹלִיד מֵאָה. The word בנים is evidently understood. Comp. 1 Sam. ii. 5; Gen. v. 3. Knobel, however, thinks that the numeral is to be taken adverbially, appealing to Gesenius, *Lehrgeb.*, p. 703, but this would rather be expressed by מֵאַת. Comp. chap. viii. 12. The expression *a hundred* is to be regarded as a round number (Gen xxvi. 12; 2 Sam. xxiv. 3; Prov. xvii. 10). Several of the kings of Israel and Judah had a large number of children. The number of Solomon's sons is not given, but Rehoboam had eighty-eight children (2 Chron. xi. 21) and Ahab had at least seventy sons (2 Kings x. 1). Bernstein, Delitzsch and Plumptre trace in the passage an allusion to Artaxerxes Mnemon (B.C. 405–362) who had, according to Justin (x. 1), 115 sons by various concubines besides the three begotten in lawful marriage. His son and successor Artaxerxes Ochus, who reigned from B.C. 362 to 339, was murdered by Bagoas and had no funeral, his body being thrown to the cats.

In the phrase וְרַב שֶׁיִּהְיוּ יְמֵי־שָׁנָיו the שֶׁ is redundant, it is really connected with the preceding אִם; רַב can scarcely to be regarded with Hitzig as the verb, but is the adjective taken adverbially. So Heiligstedt, "*et si multum est, quod fuerint,* i.e. et si multi fuerint dies annorum ejus." The phraseology seems to be a reminiscence of the וַיִּהְיוּ יְמֵי which recurs so often in Genesis v. Knobel and Vaihinger take רַב in the sense of *powerful, mighty,* understanding the phrase to be, "*and great as he may be while his years last.*" Similarly the Targum. Ginsburg, however, renders correctly, "yea, numerous as may be the days of his years."

The clause, "and also he has no grave," or burial, has occasioned difficulty to some commentators. Hitzig considers that it gives the impression as if the writer asserted that if the rich miser received a decent burial, his lot would be better than an untimely birth, a statement opposed to the whole tenor of the context and of verse 6. Hence he would strike out the clause. Others have sought to interpret it metaphorically, or to explain the loss of the grave as caused by the ultimate poverty which overtakes the rich man, or on account of the meanness of his relatives or heirs, or their hatred of him. Ginsburg has interpreted the passage, "even if the grave did not wait for him," that is, even supposing he had a very long life. But the passage in Job xvii. 1 does not prove that the clause is equivalent to *shall not see death* (Ps. lxxxix. 49), or *shall not see the grave* (Ps. xvi. 10; xlix. 10), the latter phrase being very different from that in our passage. קְבוּרָה means *the grave* or *burial,* קְבוּרַת חֲמוֹר, *the burial of an ass,* is spoken of as the most dishonourable, in Jer. xxii. 19. Hengstenberg is scarcely correct in maintaining that the grave of an ass is the flaying ground, and that allusion is here made to such a catastrophe as is spoken of in Ps. lxxix. 3 or Jer. viii. 2; ix. 21, etc. It is possible that there may be a historical allusion in the passage to the fate of Ochus already noticed, but, whether this be or be not the case, it is certain that the want of burial in the grave of one's ancestors was looked upon as a loss. Comp. 1 Kings xiii. 22; Isaiah xiv. 18–20. Kleinert gives a very different sense to the passage, maintaining that Koheleth returns here to the thought expressed in the first clause, and that the words "and that he hath no burial" form the climax, thus meaning that even if such a man were to require no grave, or in other words, were immortal, his lot is not to be envied.

אָמַרְתִּי. *I say.* Ges.-Kautzsch, § 126, 3; Ewald, § 135 *b*; Kalisch, § 93, 3.

4. The contrast here between the perfect and imperfect tenses ought to be preserved in translation. Compare the reference here to the untimely birth, with that in Job iii. 16; Ps. lviii. 8. There is no necessity to interpret "*name*" here of *memory*. The lifeless fœtus receives no name, but always, as Delitzsch observes, remains a nameless thing, and is forgotten as if it had never been. The translation *a mist, an exhalation*, given by Gesenius and others here for הֶבֶל, and assigned also as the rendering of that word in chap. viii. 14; xi. 8, cannot be justified. הַהֶבֶל seems here to be used of human existence which the writer repeatedly declares is in itself, "vanity," "nothingness."

5. נחת לזה מזה. Lit. *the rest that is* (belongs) *to this* (one) (the untimely abortion) *is more than this* other, *i.e.* the rich man. Compare on זֶה — זֶה chap. iii. 19. נַחַת is a segholate noun from the stem נוּחַ. The LXX. has striven to preserve the construction of the Heb., καὶ οὐκ ἔγνω ἀναπαύσεις τούτῳ ὑπὲρ τοῦτον. But Symmachus has translated the clause, καὶ οὐκ ἐπειράθη διαφορᾶς ἑτέρου πράγματος πρὸς ἕτερον, Vulg. *neque cognovit distantiam boni et mali*. Delitzsch has explained the rendering of Symmachus as arising from the common Talmudic construction of נוֹחַ, *quiet, mild* (an adjective from the same stem), with לְ in the sense of "*better than*." The first example of this cited in Levy's *Neuheb. und Chald. W.B.*, from *Erub.* 13 *b*, has a direct bearing on the passage before us. For two years and a half there was a controversy between the school of Shammai and that of Hillel: "the one (party) said (נוח לו לאדם) it was better for man that he had not been created than (in the condition) that he was created; and the other said, it was better for man (נוח לו לאדם) that he was created rather than not to have been created. Their votes were counted, and they decided (נמנו ונמרו), that it was better for man (נוח לו לאדם) if he had not been created, rather than to have been created; but, inasmuch as he had been created, he ought to lead a blameless life." The reader will observe how much further the Jewish theologians were disposed to go in this point than even Koheleth with all his pessimism. The expression of the writer, remarks Delitzsch, cannot stand the test of exact thought. Koheleth is not, however, to be looked upon

in the light of a calm logical debater, and he nowhere lays claim to being such. But reflections such are here indulged in are common to man, however defective they may appear when weighed in the balances of pure reason.

6. וְאִלוּ, vid. Glossary. פעמים, vid. Ges.-Kautzsch, § 120, 5. Ka-lisch, § 91, 7. Ibn Ezra regards אלף שנים פעמים to mean a thousand years multiplied by a thousand, *i.e.* a million. Delitzsch notes that the Targ. explains שִׁבְעָתַיִם, in Isa. xxx. 26, as signifying 343 = 7 × 7 × 7, "the light of the sun shall in future shine three hundred and forty-three times more brightly." He remarks that Ibn Ezra is possibly right, for why should the author not have written אֲלָפַיִם שָׁנָה? There is no other instance in Biblical Hebrew of פְּעָמִים used after a numeral, so that the requisite data are wanting to enable one to arrive at any definite conclusion on the matter.

וטובה לא ר׳. The reference of the writer is not to moral or spiritual good, but to the enjoyment of life referred to in verse 3. The Targum, however, refers the passage to higher things, rendering "and if the days of the life of the man were two thousand years, and he did not study the Law, and did not perform judgment and righteousness by means of the oath of the Word of the Lord, in the day of his death his soul will descend to Gehenna, to the place where all sinners are going."

Compare on the last clause of the verse the Horatian expression, "omnes eodem cogimur" (*Carm.*, ii. 3, 25), and Ovid, *Metam.*, x. 33,

"Tendimus huc omnes, sedem properamus ad unam."

7. לפיהו is rendered by some "*in proportion to him*," "*according to his measure*." Comp. לְפִי in Exod. xii. 4; Gen. xlvii. 12. But this rendering does not suit the context. "*For his mouth*" is equivalent to for his enjoyment. Zöckler maintains that mouth and soul are here contrasted as representatives—the former of the purely sensual enjoyments, the latter of deeper, spiritual joys. But, as Delitzsch notes, נֶפֶשׁ (*soul*) and פֶּה (*mouth*) are so little thought of as contrasted with one another that in Prov. xvi. 26 the phrase "*his mouth*" in one sentence corresponds to "*his soul*" (A.V. *himself*) in the other. So also Isaiah v. 14; xxix. 8. Delitzsch observes also that the expression נפש היפה, "*the excellent soul*" is used (in *Chullin*, iv. 7) of a good appetite, *i.e.* an appetite which is not fastidious.

The expression לא תמלא is used here figuratively of the soul just as it is in chap. i. 8 used of the ear.

8. H. G. Bernstein (*Quæst.*, p. 21) and Ginsburg consider that the מִן in the first clause is to be supplied before יוֹדֵעַ, in which case the second clause would mean "*what advantage has the poor man over him who knoweth to walk before the living?*" Bernstein, in support of this construction, refers to Zech. xiv. 10; 2 Chron. xv. 9; Hab. ii. 8, 17; Ps. xvii. 9, etc., but the passages appealed to are not strictly parallel. Ginsburg explains the clause "him who knoweth to walk before the living," as meaning one who leads a public life, a chief, a magnate, but such an expression is unparalleled elsewhere. We have no authority from the usage of the book to explain, with the Targum, "the living" to mean "the righteous in paradise." Nor can we adopt such forced explanations as that of Graetz who makes עָנִי the *poor man* to be an ascetic, one who afflicts his soul (עִנָּה נֶפֶשׁ, Isa. lviii. 3), and regards נֶגֶד as used in an adversative sense, rendering the latter clause "to walk against life," or to act differently from the ordinary course of life. הַחַיִּים must, as elsewhere in this book, be rendered *the living*, and the sentence יוֹדֵעַ לַהֲלֹךְ נֶגֶד הַחַיִּים must be construed together, notwithstanding the zakeph katon on the first and the tiphcha on the second word. Delitzsch cites Gen. vii. 4 as an instance in which the same consecution of accents does not interfere with their close grammatical connexion. The form הֲלֹךְ for the inf. const., which occurs here and in the next verse in place of the more common לֶכֶת, is found in five other passages, Num. xxii. 13, 14, 16; Exod. iii. 19, and Job xxxiv. 23. The LXX., Vulg. and Syr. all regard חיים as used in the sense of *life*, and seem, as Ginsburg has noted, to have been influenced by the mystical explanation of the passage to the life beyond the grave. But their rendering in detail is not easy of interpretation. The LXX. render, ὅτι περισσεία τῷ σοφῷ ὑπὲρ τὸν ἄφρονα, διότι ὁ πένης οἶδε πορευθῆναι κατέναντι τῆς ζωῆς. Vulg. "quid habet amplius sapiens a stulto? et quid pauper, nisi ut pergat illuc, ubi est vita?" Ewald translates, "*what advantage hath the wise man over the fool, the intelligent sufferer that he walks before the living?*" This translation would be scarcely intelligible without the interpretation of its author, who paraphrases it as follows: the wise understanding sufferer, or pious man, has in this an advantage which makes life

("walking before the living") endurable to him, that he does not permit strong desire so destructive (to peace) to rule over him, but is contented to enjoy life in quiet contemplation. But the idea of the passage seems to be, the desire of man is insatiable, he is never really satisfied; the wise man, however, seeks to keep his desires within bounds, and to keep them to himself, but the fool utters all his mind (Prov. xxix. 11). Even the poor man who knows how to conduct himself in life, and understands the right art of living, though he keeps his secret to himself, feels within himself the stirrings of that longing, which is destined never to be satisfied on earth below.

9. By מראה ע, *the sight of the eyes*, may be understood the things which are seen by the eyes, the enjoyment of what we can see with the eyes, the good and the beautiful. Or the sight of the eyes may be explained of that which is present as contrasted with that which is often desired after. So Elster, Zöckler. The wandering to and fro of the soul may even be explained (with Zöckler) as the seeking after high things (Luke xii. 29; Rom. xii. 16) which is characteristic of the man discontented with his present lot. Luther has not unsuitably rendered the idea as equivalent to, "*it is better to enjoy the good that is present, than speculate about some other,*" like the dog in the fable who snapped at the reflection of the meat in the water, and lost the piece he had in his mouth. Delitzsch objects to the explanation of הלך־נפש, as an equivalent to the rioting of desire, *grassatio, i.e. impetus animæ appetentis*, the ὁρμὴ τῆς ψυχῆς (of Marc. Aurelius, iii. 16), as it explained by Knobel, Heiligstedt, and Ginsburg. For he observes that הלך means *grassari* only with certain subjects, such as fire, pestilence, etc., and in certain forms, as יְהַלֵּךְ for יֵלֵךְ, to which הָלַךְ = לֶכֶת does not belong; but it means rather *erratio*, the going out abroad, roving in the distance (comp. הֹלֵךְ, *a traveller*) the ῥεμβασμὸς ἐπιθυμίας of Wisdom iv. 12. The attempt, however, to draw a distinction in meaning between the various forms in use of the verb הָלַךְ is somewhat too subtle. Graetz strangely renders "*better the feeding of the eyes* (present enjoyment) *than consumption of the body*" by ascetic practices. But this is certainly not the sense of the writer. Renan, however, follows Graetz, rendering "mieux vaut vivre à sa guise que de s'exténuer," and proceeds to explain the גם־זה (*even this*) which follows by rendering, "*too much virtue is also a vanity.*" But the

section is descriptive rather of the insatiableness of desire than "the vanity of virtuous efforts." Moreover Koheleth nowhere regards asceticism as a virtue. Knobel compares Marc. Aur., iv. 26, τὸ δ' ὅλον, βραχὺς ὁ βίος· κερδαντέον τὸ παρὸν σὺν εὐλογιστίᾳ καὶ δικῇ· νῆφε ἀνειμένος, also Horat., *Epist.*, i. 18, 96–99.

10. According to Hahn and others, Koheleth here returns partially to the thought expressed in chap. i. that there is nothing really new under the sun. Hahn, comparing Gen. viii. 21, considers the author to refer to the evil which has taken place since the fall of man. A reference, however, to the fall of man would be here strangely out of place. Tayler Lewis imagines an allusion to be made to the name of Adam as derived from the earth, אדמה (Gen. ii. 7), names having been given of old to things to denote their real nature. Koheleth seems rather to point to the fact that man cannot alter the conditions under which he is placed by the predetermination of God, and to urge that he would act wisely in submitting himself to the will of his Maker. It is not so much the weakness or mortality of man which is referred to, as that man is a being placed under conditions both as to time and place (comp. Acts xvii. 26). The phrase קרא שם may have a reference to Gen. ii. 19. As to the niphal participle נודע, Bullock has well compared the expression in Acts xv. 18, γνωστὰ ἀπ' αἰῶνός ἐστι τῷ Θεῷ πάντα τὰ ἔργα αὐτοῦ.[1] "As מה after ידע denotes *quid*, so אשר after ידע may mean *quod* = that which (comp. Dan. viii. 19, although there is no need of a proof), and *id quod homo est* will express that which a man is—it is impossible to translate the הוא without expressing a definite idea of time—namely that the whole existence of a man, whether of this or that person, at all times and on all sides, is previously known."—*Delitzsch*. The thought of Koheleth is very similar to that in Isaiah xlv. 9 ; Rom. ix. 20 ff. Indeed the Apostle seems almost as much to refer to this passage in Koheleth as to that in Isaiah. The Midrash Shemoth § xl. considers the calling of Bezaleel to make the tabernacle and its furniture (Exod. xxxi. 1, 2) an illustration of this saying of Koheleth.

The K'ri has שֶׁתַּקִּיף, omitting the article, which occurs in the

---

[1] That reading of the passage in Acts, however, is not considered the most correct one. Westcott and Hort, with Alford and others before them, read λέγει Κύριος ταῦτα ποιῶν γνωστὰ ἀπ' αἰῶνος, and this is the reading which has been adopted in the new Revised Version, "saith the Lord, who maketh these things known from the beginning of the world."

Ch. vi. 10, 11.] *Critical and Grammatical Comm.* 379

K'thibh, שֶׁהַתְקִיף. That the reading of the latter ought to be thus pointed, and not with Herzfeld, שֶׁהִתְקִיף, the hiphil of תָּקַף viewed as a denominative verb from תֹּקֶף (vid. Ges.-Kautzsch, § 53, 2), is plain from the passages in chap. x. 3, 20, as also Lam. v. 18, where similar marginal corrections occur in which the article is omitted. Had we not the analogy of these passages to guide us as to the sense in which the written text was understood, the opinion of Herzfeld would be defensible. For, though the hiphil of תקף does not occur in Bibl. Hebrew, it is found, as Delitzsch notices, in the Talmud, and the aphel is in use in the Targum.

11. The contention alluded to in the former verse is here further explained as one carried on by *words;* for we must not, as many commentators have done, render דברים in this passage by *things*, thereby obscuring the whole significance of the verse. The ancient versions (LXX., Vulg., Syr.) have rightly seen this. The Targum alone interprets the noun to mean *things*. Elster and Delitzsch with great probability consider that the reference of the author is to the school-learning of the Jews which was then coming into notice. According to Josephus the problem of man's freedom and the decrees of God formed a subject of dispute between the Pharisees on the one hand and the Sadducees on the other, the former maintaining an intimate connexion between the Divine decrees (*fate*, or εἱμαρμένη), and the acts of man; the Sadducees denying that there was any such thing as fate at all (Σαδδουκαῖοι δὲ τὴν μὲν εἱμαρμένην ἀναιροῦσιν). The Pharisees, however, did not maintain that all human actions were the subject of the Divine decrees (οἱ μὲν οὖν Φαρισαῖοί τινα καὶ οὐ πάντα τῆς εἱμαρμένης εἶναι λέγουσιν ἔργον, τινὰ δ' ἐφ' ἑαυτοῖς ὑπάρχειν, συμβαίνειν τε καὶ οὐ γίνεσθαι), but in contradistinction to the Essenes (who believed that all things were predestined) they seemed to have maintained that in matters of morality men were free. See Joseph., *Antiq.*, xiii. 5, 9; xviii. 1, 3, 4; *Bell. Jud.*, ii. 8, 14. According to Delitzsch, the Talmud gives us no insight into this controversy among the Jewish theologians, save that in *Berachoth*, 33 *b*, the remarkable saying of Rabbi Chanina is preserved, הכל בידי שמים חוץ מיראת שמים, "All is through the hand of Heaven except the fear of Heaven," *i.e.* absolute freedom has been given to man to choose his own course with respect to matters of religion and morality. See also *Aboth*, iii. 24 (iii. 15). On these latter points man is fettered by no Divine decrees impelling him to any special course of action.

St. Paul, as Delitzsch notes, has taken his stand on the same side (Rom. ix.), and the author of the Book of Koheleth could have countersigned the statements of the Apostle as his own, inasmuch as the exhortation to "fear God" (chap. xii. 13) is "the stone and star" (Kern und Stern), the pith and marrow, of his pessimistic book.

12. Man knows not what is good for him in this life. What he does in the present will bear fruit after he has passed away; and yet who can point out with certainty to an individual the line of action he should adopt in all cases, seeing that man does not know the secrets of the future? מִי יוֹדֵעַ, *who knows?* is a strong negative. Comp. chap. iii. 21. מִסְפַּר יְמֵי ח. Acc. of time, vid. chap ii. 3. הַבְלוֹ. Comp. chap. vii. 15; ix. 9. וְיַעֲשֵׂם. The phrase עָשָׂה יָמִים means to *spend time*, like ποιεῖν χρόνον, Acts xv. 33. Comp. James iv. 13, and Prov. xiii. 33 (LXX.). The clause here is to be considered as relative. כַּצֵּל means *as the shadow* passes, so chap. viii. 13; Job xiv. 2, not, as Delitzsch remarks, *like to a shadow* (although the days of a man's life are elsewhere likened to a shadow, as in Ps. cxliv. 4, etc.), for the latter construction does not suit the verb (עָשָׂה) here employed. The Hebrew phrase, though corresponding with the Greek, and with the Latin *facere dies* (Cicero, Seneca, etc.), must not be regarded, with Zirkel and Graetz, as a Græcism (*Delitzsch*).

CHAPTER VII.

1. The writer, having virtually asserted in the last verse of the previous section that it is impossible to tell what is "good" (טוֹב) in life (a truth which, in the sense in which the assertion is made, cannot seriously be called in question), now proceeds to point out that, however impossible it may be to know with certainty the best course for an individual to pursue, there are certain things connected with human affairs which may safely be pronounced "good," and even "better than" other things.

The first clause of verse 1 is not to be rendered with the Midrash, A.V. and Luther, "*a good name is better than precious* (lit. good) *ointment.*" For the order of the words and the analogy of the proverbs which follow (verses 2, 3, 5, 8) show that the first טוֹב (*good*) is the predicate. So Vulg. "melius est nomen quam unguentum bonum," and the Targum. שֵׁם is occasionally used without a qualify-

Ch. vii. 1–3.] *Critical and Grammatical Comm.* 381

ing adjective in the sense of *a good name, renown*. So Prov. xxii. 1; Gen. vi. 4; comp. with the latter Job. xxx. 8. See remarks on p. 151. The paronomasia between שֵׁם and שֶׁמֶן is intentional; so also in Cant. i. 3. יוֹם הִוָּלְדוֹ, "*the day of his*" i.e. one's "*birth*." Compare on the suffix chap. viii. 16. See remarks on the verse on p. 151 and p. 158.

2. וְהַחַי. The ה of the article is correctly pointed with pathach before ח. The Masora magna notes three exceptions, Gen. vi. 19; Isaiah iii. 22; xvii. 8. See Baer and Delitzsch, crit. ed. of the Heb. text of Isaiah (Lepizig, 1872), on chap. iii. 22. נתן אל לבו, *to lay it to his heart*, corresponds to שִׂים אֶל־לֵב, 2 Sam. xiii. 33; שִׂים עַל־לֵב, Isa. xlii. 25; שִׂים בְּלֵב, 2 Sam. xxi. 13. The Vulg. paraphrases the clause "*et vivens cogitat quid futurum sit;*" LXX., literally but strongly, ὁ ζῶν δώσει ἀγαθὸν εἰς καρδίαν αὐτοῦ. The Talmud (*Berachoth*, 6 *b*) quotes a saying of Rab Papa, "*the advantage of (i.e. which accrues from a visit to) the house of mourning is silence,*" namely, a solemn stillness, which Dukes (*Rabb. Blumenlese*, p. 87) considers to be a comment on this verse.

Delitzsch remarks on this passage that the Talmudists have split their heads in the endeavour to harmonise this saying with the ultimatum of Koheleth (chap. ii. 24), "there is nothing better than to eat and to drink." But the solution is easy. Koheleth's ultimatum does not speak unconditionally of the enjoyment of life, but of the enjoyment of life coupled with the fear of God. See remarks on p. 232. When man contemplates the fact of death, two things present themselves to him; (1) that he should make use of his brief life, and (2) that he should use it in contemplation of his end, and, therefore, like one who has to give account of himself to God. Comp. Ps. xc. 12.

3. כַּעַס in contrast to שְׂחוֹק evidently means *sorrow*, which produces the outward impression of *melancholy*. On the expression רֹעַ פָּנִים compare פָּנִים רָעִים in Gen. xl. 7; see also Neh. ii. 2. The Vulg. takes כַּעַס in the sense of *anger*, and translates, "melior est ira risu, quia per tristitiam vultus corrigitur animus delinquentis," "*anger is better than laughter; because by the sadness of the countenance the mind of the offender is corrected*" (*Douay Version*). But this is certainly not the sense of the passage, though, possibly, derived from the Targum, which explains the *anger* and *laughter* here

of God; God's anger against the righteous resulting in their purification, and His laughter at the wicked being a token of impending ruin (Ps. xxxvii. 13). The purifying and sanctifying power of grief, especially in contemplation of the grave, seems, however, to be the real point which the writer has here in view.

4. Delitzsch observes that the reason why zakeph katon is used to divide this verse in place of athnach is that none of the words which follow אֵבֶל are trisyllabic. Compare on the contrary, verse 7.

5. The reproof of a wise man naturally refers to such warnings as are naturally uttered in the house of mourning concerning the duties of the living. For the song of fools with which it is here contrasted is not to be understood with the Vulg. to signify the flattery of fools (*stultorum adulatio*), but the boisterous song of the reveller in "the house of mirth" spoken of in the previous verse. In place of מִשְׁמֹעַ, which would have been naturally expected in the second part of the verse, the phrase מֵאִישׁ שֹׁמֵעַ is employed, because the "hearing" in the two cases is thought of as connected with two different individuals.—*Delitzsch*. The expression, *the hearing of rebuke*, like many other similar phrases, is borrowed from the Book of Proverbs (Prov. xiii. 1, 8), but Johnston has erred widely in regarding such borrowed expressions as evidences of unity of authorship.

6. We have endeavoured in our translation to preserve the play of words which occurs in the first clause in the Hebrew, כְּקוֹל הַסִּירִים תַּחַת הַסִּיר. It has also been preserved in the German rendering of Vaihinger, Knobel, Delitzsch by rendering *Nesseln, Kessel*; Ewald has *knistern, kichern*. It must be borne in mind, however, that סִירִים properly means *thorns;* it is used in the sense of a *thorn-hedge* in Hosea ii. 8, A.V. ii. 6. The stalks of dry thorns, or even nettles, make a crackling noise and produce a bright flame. Symmachus strangely renders, διὰ γὰρ φωνῶν ἀπαιδεύτων ἐν δεσμωτηρίῳ γίνεταί τις. Knobel considers that he probably read הַכְּסִילִים instead of הַסִּירִים. On this rendering, Field, in his edit. of *Orig. Hex.*, writes: "Nobil. affert: Schol. διὰ γὰρ φωνῶν ἀπ. (non τῶν ἀπ. ut Montef. post Drusium edidit) κ. τ. ἑ. Contenderimus scholium esse hujus aut præcedentis versus, nisi diserte affirmarit Hieron.: 'Symmachus pro eo quod nos posuimus, *Quia sicut vox spinarum sub olla, sic risus stulti,* . . . ait: *Per vocem enim imperitorum vinculis quispiam colligatur.*' Etiam sic vix credibile est, Symmachum Hebræa tam

Ch. vii. 6, 7.] *Critical and Grammatical Comm.* 383

clara adeo perverse interpretatum esse, præsertim cum juxta Syrum nostrum idem interpres posteriorem clausulam sic verterit: οὕτως καὶ γέλως τῶν ἀπαιδεύτων. In contrariam partem Schleusnerus monet, vocem קִיר in lingua Chald. et Syr. de *vinculis* et *carcere* adhiberi." See Buxtorf, *Lex. Chald et Talm.*, s. v. קִירָא.

7. The כִּי at the commencement of the verse would be most naturally explained as introducing a reason for the aphorism immediately preceding. But the verses have no real connexion with one another. Ginsburg would connect the "for" with the first clause of verse 5, but this seems to be strained. The same view, however, has been taken by Tayler Lewis, who considers עֹשֶׁק to mean *annoyance* or *perverseness*, appealing to Ps. lxxiii. 8, and to Isaiah lix. 13, but these proofs cannot be viewed as satisfactory. Ewald proposed formerly to read עֹשֶׁר *riches* in place of עֹשֶׁק *oppression*. But this he maintains in his last edition to be unnecessary, for a *gift* or a *bribe* would be given to the wise in order to induce him to participate in unlawful oppression. Ewald there renders עשׁק by *injustice.* The idea, which Zöckler here introduces, of the wise man being drawn from the path of probity in consequence of the evil examples of the ungodly (introduced in order to connect the verse with the preceding), does not explain the passage. There is no connexion between the boisterous song of the foolish reveller, and the subject of this aphorism. Plumptre thinks the "latent connexion" is that "the 'song' and 'laughter' of fools, *i.e.* evil-doers, like those of Prov. i. 10–18, and Wisd. ii. 1–20, leads to selfish luxury, and therefore to all forms of unjust gain. The mirth of fools, *i.e.* of the godless, is vanity, *for* it issues in oppression and bribery." This explanation does not satisfy us. Renan quietly omits the "*for*" in his translation. With the exception of the words "this also is vanity" in verse 6, he regards the first eight verses of this chapter to be proverbs quoted by Koheleth from various sources, each more or less distinct from one another, but all tending to show "the vanity of the philosophy which proclaims that all is vanity." There is much to be said in favour of Delitzsch's idea that there is a gap in the text between verses 6 and 7, and that verse 7 forms the second half of a tetrastich, the former half of which has been lost, but which probably began with טוב, like the verses preceding. The missing words he considers probably conveyed some such thought as that in Prov. xvi. 8, "*Better is a little with righteousness than much produce without right; for oppression maketh the wise man*

mad, and a gift (bribe) *destroys the heart."* Inasmuch, however, as no trace of such a hiatus is found in the ancient versions (albeit that fact is by no means decisive in such a question), we incline with the older expositors to connect the verse with what follows instead of with that which precedes. The translation of ' by "surely," given in our A.V., cannot be sustained, for כִּי in that sense must be connected with a preceding clause. It may, however, be rendered "because," inasmuch as a sentence which expresses the cause is sometimes placed first, as in Gen. iii. 14, 17. The sense of the passage would then be : "oppression maketh (even) the wise man mad, drives him to do foolish acts through indignation against the oppressor (compare the use of the part. poal in Ps. cii. 9), and a gift (a bribe given to pervert judgment) ruins the heart" *i.e.* of the wise, *i.e.* utterly breaks down his spirit under the sense of injustice. Comp. יֹאבַד לֵב הַמֶּלֶךְ, Jer. iv. 9. The Psalmist speaks of a *smitten* and a *wounded* heart (Ps. cii. 4, cix. 22), and Nabal's heart "died" within him (1 Sam. xxv. 37), when he heard the news which Abigail communicated. So the spirit is said, in Prov. xv. 13, to be broken by reason of sorrow of heart ; and in numerous passages the heart is spoken of as melted by reason of grief or terror.

Modern critics have generally supposed the verse to speak of the wise man becoming perverted by stooping to oppression for the sake of gain, and thus ultimately becoming a fool by yielding to his passions. The text is regarded as an echo of Exod. xxiii. 8 ; Deut. xvi. 19. In order to illustrate the expression of *destroying* the heart, Delitzsch refers to Hosea iv. 11, where it is said that "whoredom and wine and new wine take away the heart," or, even more appropriately, to the expression used in *Bereshith Rabba*, § 56, סבא סבא אובדת ליבך. "*Age! age! thou hast destroyed thy heart*," *i.e.* lost thy understanding. The LXX., Vulg. and Targ. all understand the writer to speak, not of a change in the wise man's character, but of some attack made upon the wise man himself. The LXX. and Vulg. render עֹשֶׁק by συκοφαντία, *calumnia ;* compare their rendering of chap. iv. 1. The Targ. explains the passage of an attack made by robbers. The Syr., however, supports the opinion of the later critics, ܡܛܠ ܕܚܣܡܐ ܡܛܥܐ ܠܚܟܝܡܐ ܡܣܚܦ ܠܗ ܠܠܒܗ. On the want of agreement in gender between יְאַבֵּד and מַתָּנָה see Ges.-Kautzsch, § 147 *a* ; Ewald, § 316 *a* ; Kalisch, § 77, 15.

Ch. vii. 8-11.] *Critical and Grammatical Comm.* 385

8. This proverb seems to stand in close connexion with the preceding. The end of a matter is often better than its beginning, and even out of evil good sometimes arises. For Koheleth adds, *better is he who is forbearing in spirit* (comp. אֶרֶךְ אַפַּיִם, Exod. xxxiv. 6) *than he who who is haughty of spirit.* Both אֶרֶךְ and גְּבַהּ are adjectives in the construct state. On the form גְּבַהּ, on account of the guttural, vid. Ewald, § 213 *d*; Kalisch, § xxvii. 1, *c*. Böttcher thinks that it comes from a form גָּבֵהּ, *Lehrb.*, § 378, 4. The English translation of Delitzsch here utterly misrepresents that scholar's opinion. Hitzig regards אֶרֶךְ as a noun and גְּבַהּ as the inf. const. This is possible, but unnecessary. The man who can quietly endure oppression is sure to come off best in the end (comp. Matt. v. 38-41). At the same time the proverb can be taken also in the general sense assigned to it in p. 151, though the former appears to us to be its primary sense in the connexion in which the aphorism here occurs. If it be thus expounded, it stands in intimate connexion with the aphorism which immediately follows. Ginsburg renders דבר by *reproof*, translating "the end of a reproof is better than its beginning." But the examples he cites for that meaning (Prov. iv. 4, 20; 2 Sam. xvii. 6; 1 Kings i. 7) are certainly no proofs of such a signification.

9. In times of oppression a wise man ought to learn to keep down his anger; and much more should he thus act in times when he is assailed by lesser provocations. On חֵיק comp. Job xix. 27. לִבְעוֹס infinitive, compare לִישׁוֹן chap. v. 11.

10. Every age has its peculiar difficulties, and a man inclined to take a dark view of things will always be able to compare unfavourably the present with the past. But a readiness to make comparisons of that kind is no sign of the possession of real wisdom. There is light as well as darkness to be seen in every age. The young men that shouted for joy at the rebuilding of the temple acted more wisely than the old men who wept with a loud voice (Ezra iii. 12, 13). Compare on the thought, Horat., *De Arte Poet.*, 173, 174:

> "Difficilis, querulus, laudator temporis acti
> Se puero, censor castigatorque minorum."

11. This aphorism has been differently understood by expositors. It is generally translated "*wisdom is as good as an inheritance.*" So Knobel, Ginsburg, Tyler, Zöckler, etc. But in that case one would

have expected the writer to have expressed himself rather in the terms of Prov. viii. 11. The real sense of the passage is the most natural one, and that which is assigned to it by the LXX., Vulg., Targ., etc., "*wisdom is good along with an inheritance.*" The saying corresponds with that of Menander, μακάριος ὅστις οὐσίαν καὶ νοῦν ἔχει· χρῆται γὰρ οὗτος εἰς ἃ δεῖ ταύτῃ καλῶς. It is no objection to this view that Koheleth in other passages declares all to be vanity. He speaks here of that which is useful while men are alive and behold the light of the sun. The proverb, as Delitzsch observes, is formed exactly on the lines of that in Aboth, ii. 2, יָפֶה תַלְמוּד תּוֹרָה עִם דֶּרֶךְ אֶרֶץ, *beautiful is the study of the Law combined with worldly occupation.* In the second clause of the verse, יֹתֵר is to be rendered as a noun signifying *advantage.* See Glossary, s. v. Herzfeld, Hitzig and Hengstenberg, however, translate that clause "*and even better*" is the possession of wisdom "*for those who behold the sun.*" The former exposition best harmonizes with the verse which follows.

12. Some commentators regard the particle in בְּצֵל as the בְּ *essentiæ*; but Delitzsch preferably considers בְּצֵל like בְּצֵל of Jonah iv. 5, and translates, *in the shadow is wisdom, in the shadow is money.*" That is, he who possesses wisdom finds himself in a shadow, shielded from many dangers, and similarly the man who has possession of money. Compare Ps. xci. 1; cxxi. 4; Isa. xxx. 2, 3; xxxii. 2; xxxiv. 15, etc.

13. See remarks on p. 145. Comp. chap. i. 15. רָאָה, *see,* is here used almost in the signification of *consider.* Hitzig takes כִּי in the sense of *that,* and so extracts the sense "that no one can straighten," etc. So also Ginsburg. But this can scarcely be the meaning of כִּי מִי, which is simply "for who can," etc. The idea of the verse is, submit yourself to the arrangements of Divine providence, for it is impossible for you to alter them. The LXX. and Vulg. gave a false turn to the passage, under the impression, which is shared by the Targ., that Koheleth is speaking of physical defects of the body, but the passage has a far deeper significance. LXX. has ὅτι τίς δυνήσεται κοσμῆσαι ὃν ἂν ὁ Θεὸς διαστρέψῃ αὐτόν; Vulg. "*quod nemo possit corrigere quem ille despexerit.*"

14. Compare on this verse Sirach. xiv. 14. הֱיֵה בְטוֹב, *be in good spirits* (comp. Ps. xxv. 13), *i.q.* chap. ix. 7, בְּלֶב־טוֹב, 1 Kings viii. 66. ראה גם וג׳. This second clause is best understood with Ginsburg, Zöckler and Delitzsch, "*consider that even God hath made this*

(*i.e.* the day of evil) *as well as that*," the day of good. So Job ii. 10, "What, shall we receive good at the hands of God, and shall we not receive evil?"

The final clause, "*that man may find nothing after him*," is easy to translate, but not so easy to explain. Zöckler, with others, considers the meaning to be that man does not know that which lies before him. But אַחֲרָיו is used always with reference to that which happens after this present life (chap. iii. 22; vi. 22; Job xxi. 21). Hitzig explains the text to mean that God designs man after his death to be done with all things, hence He puts upon him evil in the period of his life, and permits it to alternate with good, instead of punishing him after death. This idea is opposed, however, to the teaching of Koheleth respecting a future judgment. Delitzsch explains the verse to mean that God causes man to have experience of both good and evil here in order that he may pass through the whole school of life; and that when he departs therefrom, there may be no experience outstanding which he has not encountered. The writer seems to us even to go further, and to assert that God has so mixed up this present life with good and evil that man cannot find out by his own powers, or by all his meditations on the present state, what the lot of mankind will be in a future state of existence. The secrets of the state after death lie utterly beyond the ken of mortal man. The contemplation of the present life with its mixture of good and evil affords no clue whatever to the future.

15. אֶת־הַכֹּל. Zöckler explains this as "*everything possible*," everything that can come under consideration. Luther, Vaihinger, etc., better "*all sorts of things*." The "all" is no doubt afterwards spoken of as falling under two heads; but this fact does justify the translation "both," given by Preston and Ginsburg. "*The days of my vanity*." Compare chap. vi. 12. Some have interpreted this as a penitential expression on the part of Solomon. But it is unnecessary to comment on such an interpretation. The בְּ in בְּצִדְקוֹ and בְּרִשְׁעָתוֹ is to be translated with Herzfeld, Delitzsch, etc., as equivalent to *in*, i.e. *in spite of*. Delitzsch pertinently adduces בַּדָּבָר הַזֶּה, Deut. i. 32. The translation "*through*," "*by means of*," defended by Hitzig, does not harmonize with what follows. כַּאֲרִיךְ is used both with and without the following יָמִים. So chap. viii. 12, with verse 13.

16. By צַדִּיק הַרְבֵּה, *too just*, according to Heiligstedt, is meant too sharp and bitter in passing judgment on others. Koheleth, how-

ever, probably had in view the tendency to asceticism prevalent in his day, which drove men to deny themselves all pleasures through fear of sin. There is always danger of exaggeration in matters of religion. וְאַל־תִּתְחַכַּם. On the form of imperf. hithp. vid. Ges.-Kautzsch, § 54, rem. 1. *Do not show thyself too wise.* Compare Exod. i. 10. On this signification of the hithpael, compare הִתְחַזַּק *to show oneself strong*, 2 Sam. x. 12; הִתְאַנַּף, *to show oneself angry*, Deut. i. 37; הִתְנַכֵּל, *to act subtilly*, Ps. cv. 25. Some would render "*affect not to be wise*," but this translation is not in accordance with the general usage of the hithpael (although the conjugation has that signification in Prov. xiii. 7), and does not suit here. The translation *clement, merciful,* assigned here to צדיק by the Targ., the Midrash Koheleth, and other Jewish authorities, is unwarranted. Even in Dan. iv. 24 צִדְקָה is not ἐλεημοσύνη. תִּשּׁוֹמֵם. The form has two anomalies, (1) the assimilation of the final ת in the תִּת of the hithpoel (Ges.-Kautzsch, § 54, 2; Kalisch, § xlvi. 8 *b*), and (2) the hithpoel is the only reflexive form of the finite verb which preserves the tzere in pause. Comp. Ges.-Kautzsch, § 54, rem. 1. The infinitive hithpael has tzere in pause, as 2 Chron. xx. 6; Isa. xxviii. 20; lx. 21; lxi. 3; so also the participle, Isa. xxx. 23; Job xv. 20. See König, *Lehrg.*, p. 350; Stade, *Lehrb.*, § 129 *d*; Böttcher, *Lehrb.*, § 1030. Hitzig, followed by Ginsburg, renders, "*thou wilt only make thyself to be forsaken.*" But this is scarcely the meaning. Nor is the LXX. rendering, μήποτε ἐκπλαγῇς, or that of the Vulg. *ne obstupescas*, at all suitable.

There is no necessity to regard this with Plumptre, as "a distinct reproduction of one of the current maxims of Greek thought, μηδὲν ἄγαν (*ne quid nimis*, "*nothing in excess*"), of Theognis, 402, and of Chilon (*Diog. Laert.*, I. i. § 41). The thought is similar, but far from being identical. Nor is there a reference, as Zöckler imagines, to the differences between the Pharisees and Sadducees, already, perhaps, beginning to develope themselves. The contrast in this and the next verse between צדקה and רשעה was not, as Delitzsch points out, one of the differences between those parties; the overstraining of the Pharisees referred to the ceremonial and not to the moral law. One may compare the well-known aphorism, *summum jus summa injuria;* or the Aristotelian doctrine, that virtue lies in the middle mean, μεσότης δὲ δύο κακιῶν, τῆς μὲν καθ' ὑπερβολήν, τῆς δὲ κατ' ἔλλειψιν (*Ethic. Nicom.*, ii. 6), which is repeated by Ovid, *Metam.*, ii. 137, "medium tenuere beati, medio tutissimus ibis"; and by Horace, "virtus est medium vitiorum utrinque reductum" (*Epist.*, i. 18, 9).

17. According to Zöckler, Koheleth does not here commend a certain moderation in wickedness as allowable, but, recognising the fact that all men are more or less sinful by nature (verses 20-22), he warns his readers against malicious wickedness. Delitzsch, in allusion to the original meaning of the verb, regards the aphorism to mean, while avoiding a narrow rigorism do not be too lax. This is, indeed, the sense of the passage; but the difficulty of thus translating the passage lies in the fact that there is no instance in which the verb is used in such a signification. Plumptre imagines that "the difficulty vanishes, if we will but admit that the writer might have learnt the art of a playful irony from his Greek teachers." It was not, however, necessary to have recourse to Greek teachers to learn irony. Herzfeld translates, "*be not too unrighteous*," and explains it as a caution not to lose oneself too much in worldly affairs. Herzfeld does not, however, go the length of Ibn Ezra, who affirms "that *wicked* here means to be engaged in worldly matters." See Ginsburg. While it is clear from other passages that Koheleth does not wink at any indulgence in "little sins," as they are termed, it can scarcely be questioned that he is in the text before us warning men against excess in wickedness, and that he was led into this mode of expression by the aphoristic form in which the former verse was cast. One might be tempted to compare the warning of St. James, to "put off all filthiness and περισσείαν κακίας" (chap. i. 21), which certainly was never meant to convey the idea that κακία in any sense or shape was to be willingly retained. Proverbial expressions are not to be measured too exactly. Compare the remarks on p. 205. The man is a "fool" who permits himself by ungodly excesses to be swallowed up in the waves of sensuality, which drown many before their time. If it be borne in mind that Koheleth speaks in this verse from the practical standpoint of a "man of the world," in the good sense of that term, there is no need to be astonished at his warning, or to be offended at the terms in which it is set forth.

18. "It is good that thou shouldest lay hold on this" course, namely the plan of pursuing with moderation the paths of righteousness and wisdom, "and also that thou shouldest not withdraw from

the other" course, namely, that of avoiding all those excesses which prove ruinous to many. Compare 1 Pet. iv. 4. Very differently Kleinert, who refers the זה and זה to what follows, the first "this" referring to "he that fears God escapes all;" the second to the clause, "wisdom gives more strength to a wise man," etc. But such long and involved sentences are not characteristic of our writer. The last clause of the verse has been explained, "*he that fears God shall come out of them all*," that is, will escape "all the perplexities of this life" (*Tyler, Bullock*) caused by over-rigorism on the one hand and over-laxity on the other. Zöckler similarly supposes the writer to allude to the evil consequences of a hypocritical righteousness, and of a defiant immorality. The construction of יצא here with the accusative has been often compared to that in Gen. xliv. 4; Exod. ix. 29, 32, etc. But the comparison, as Ginsburg has noted, is "inapposite," for the sense of the phrase is not identical. The translation of Hitzig, though adopted by Ginsburg ("*will make his way with both*"), introduces an expression unexampled in Biblical literature. Delitzsch explains the verb in the final clause after the usage of the Mishna, in which יצא often occurs in the meaning of *fulfilling* one's duty. *E.g.* יצא ידי חובתו, *he fulfilled his duty*, lit. *went out of* (escaped) *the hands of his duty*, by a performance thereof; or also elliptically יוצא בה, *he fulfils thereby his duty*, אינו יוצא בה, *he does not thereby fulfil his duty*. See Levy, *Neuheb. und Chald. Wörterbuch*, s.v. יצא. Hence the passage means, "*he that fears God fulfils them all*," i.e. the duties previously mentioned, and avoids the extremes on both sides. Compare our Lord's remarks in Matt. xxiii. 23. The truly pious man keeps "the golden mean."

The LXX. translate somewhat freely, but there is no reason to suppose that they had a different reading. The Vulg. erroneously supposes the writer to speak of the duty of supporting the upright man and not deserting him, "bonum est te sustentare justum, sed et ab illo ne subtrahas manum tuam."

19. עזז is either transitive, as Ps. lxviii. 29, *to strengthen*, or here followed by ל, better rendered intransitively, *proves itself strong.* שליט is akin to the Assyrian śa-laṭ, which is used both in the sense of a *stadtholder* and a *commander*. See Schrader, *Keilinschriften und das A. T.*, 1st edit., p. 370. [The 2nd edition of this important

Ch. vii. 19-22.] *Critical and Grammatical Comm.* 391

work is now announced as ready.] There is probably an allusion here to some political or other arrangements of the time with which we are imperfectly acquainted. Tyler remarks that ten means a full number, "comp. Gen. xxxi. 7; Job xix. 3. In the Mishna (*Megillah*, i. 3) a great city is defined as one in which there are ten men of leisure. Ten men were required for the formation of a synagogue."

20. There is a reference here to the words used in the prayer of Solomon, 1 Kings viii. 46. כי אדם אין וגו' is for כי אין אדם, for the sake of emphasis. The connexion between this verse and its context has given rise to much difference of opinion. See remarks on p. 147. It is unnatural to consider that the writer speaks of wisdom as protecting against the justice of God by teaching man his sinfulness even in his best estate. Hitzig and Delitzsch seem to have caught the true sense of the passage in supposing the thought of the writer to be, that man is fallible, and the wisest at times commit mistakes, but their wisdom enables them to get the better of their mistakes and protects them against the evil consequences which happen in such cases to the unwise. This exposition not only connects the passage with what precedes, but also with that which follows. For the wise man who is conscious of having made mistakes himself, and of having been guilty of transgression, will act kindly and leniently to his fellows, and not make them offenders for a word. Comp. Isa. xxix. 21. See Delitzsch on the latter passage, which Cheyne would, however, expound differently.

21. Do not pay attention (lit. *give not thy heart;* see note on chap. i. 13) to evil reports about other persons, which people in general (not only the *ungodly*, which nominative the LXX., Targ., Syr., here supply before the indeterminate verb יְדַבְּרוּ, vid. Ges.-Kautzsch, § 137, 3) rashly circulate without examining at all into their truth or falsehood. There is no necessity with some commentators to restrict the application of the passage by mentally supplying "about thyself." Compare on this passage, *Marc. Aurel.*, Lib. vi. 20. מְקַלֶּלְךָ. This is no Græcism, vid. Ewald, § 284 *b*.

22. כי גם. The גם is to be connected with לְבָּךְ. Delitzsch compares on its position here, Hosea vi. 11; Zech ix. 11 (see crit. comm. at end of my *Bampton Lectures*, p. 571), and even Job ii. 10. פְּעָמִים רַבּוֹת. Accusative of time, not the accusative of the object.

On the inversion of the clause for emphasis, see Ewald, § 336 b. Compare ver. 20; chap. iii. 13; v. 18. ידע לבך. Compare 1 Kings ii. 44. Johnston (*Treatise*, p. 109) considers the fact that this phrase is only found in that passage and in Prov. xiv. 10 (and in Koh. viii. 5) to be an argument in favour of the Solomonic authorship, but see p. 87.

נם־אתּ. Delitzsch observes in his critical notes on the text that the אתּ should, according to the Masora, on account of the half pause, have the accent on the penult, and not on the last syllable, אתּ, as in the ordinary text. The K'ri gives the full form, אתּה.

The LXX. has here ὅτι πλειστάκις πονηρεύσεταί σε (Knobel conjectures that they read יָרַע instead of יָדַע, or the imperf. of רוֹעַ), καὶ καθόδους πολλὰς κακώσει καρδίαν σου. Montfaucon observes (see Field's *Hexapla*) that in this passage two versions are combined, the first being that of the LXX., the latter that of Aquila, who constantly renders פעם by κάθοδος. He observes that many of Aquila's renderings have been foisted into the text of the LXX. See our remarks on pp. 51, 52.

23. אָמַרְתִּי אֶחְכָּמָה. This is the only instance in the book where the cohortative occurs. It expresses here strong resolve, "*I said, wise will I become.*" It must not be rendered "*I have become wise,*" or, what is equivalent, by *sapio*, as Rosenmüller, who explains it, "jam mihi persuadebam me ad fastigium sapientiæ adscendisse." Symm. well renders: ὑπέλαβον σοφὸς γενέσθαι. Koheleth determined to increase his natural wisdom, and to unravel the perplexities of this life, but he found the attempt vain. Ginsburg considers the two verbs are subordinated in accordance with the principle explained in Ges.-Kautzsch, § 142, 3 c. But this can scarcely be regarded as an instance of that construction. Ginsburg's rendering, "*I wished to be wiser,*" is weak.

24. See our remarks on p. 202. Delitzsch rightly regards מַה־שֶּׁהָיָה as expressing an idea in itself, "*that which was,*" or "*that which exists,*" chap. i. 9; iii. 15; vi. 10; in the former signification forming a contrast to מַה־שֶּׁיִּהְיֶה, "*that which will be,*" chap. viii. 7; x. 14 (comp. iii. 22); in the latter, the opposite to that which does not exist, because it has yet to come into being. So Hengstenberg explains it "that which has being," wisdom being τῶν ὄντων γνῶσις ἀψευδής, Wisd. vii. 17. The ancient versions have misunderstood the author's meaning. The translation of Rosenmüller, de Wette, Knobel, and others, "*what is far and deep*" does not so suit or

harmonise with the order of the Hebrew. Nor does the view of Zöckler commend itself to our judgment, namely, that the author here refers to wisdom, " far is it what she is," *i.e.* the real innermost essence of wisdom is far from human comprehension. Comp. Job xxviii. 12 ff.; Sirach xxiv. 38, 39; Baruch iii. 15 ff. On the repetition of the adjective to express the superlative degree, see Kalisch, § 75, 8; Ges.-Kautzsch, § 119, 2, rem.

25. סבותי. See chap. ii. 20. ולבי is not to be connected with the preceding אני, as the majority of interpreters have done. The word caused difficulty to the ancient interpreters. Hence arose the reading found in many MSS., בְּלִבִּי, which seems to have been that of the Targ., Symm., as quoted by Jerome (*sensu meo*), and Vulg. *animo meo*. The A.V. and Luther have freely rendered, "*and I applied my heart*," as if there was no copula before the לבי. The Heb. accentuation also connects אני with לבי, and disconnects the latter from לדעת. But such an expression is without a parallel. Ibn Ezra, Herzfeld, Moses Stuart and Delitzsch connect the ולבי with the following word, "*and my heart* (my longing) *was to know*." ולתור. See n. on chap. i. 13. חשבון. See Glossary. In the phrase וְלָדַעַת רֶשַׁע כֶּסֶל, the first accusative is that of the object, and the second is the predicate, "*to know wickedness to be folly*." See Ewald, § 284 *b*. Ginsburg incorrectly regards הסכלות הוללות to mean, *that folly which is madness*.

26. ומוצא אני. See n. on chap. i. 5, p. 309. On the form, see Ges.-Kautzsch, § 75, 21 *a*; König, p. 611; Kalisch, § lxvi. 21. Comp. chap. viii. 12. The *finding* of a wife is spoken of as a treasure in Prov. xviii. 22. Hence, as Delitzsch mentions in his *Comm. on Proverbs*, it was a custom in Palestine to ask concerning the bridegroom, מצא או מוצא, *i.e.* has he found (מצא) a treasure, as in Prov. xviii. 22, or has he found a snare (מוצא), as in Koh. viii. 26? See Talmud Babli, *Jebamoth*, 63 *b*; *Berachoth*, 8 *a*. מר ממות. The adjective referring to " the woman " afterwards spoken of is masculine, because it precedes, vid. Ges.-Kautzsch, § 147 *b*. On the phrase אשר היא מצודים, Hitzig observes that היא is the copula between the subj. and pred., which for the sake of contrast precedes the predicate and gives emphasis to it. It must not be regarded with Ginsburg as a nominative, nor is אשר to be viewed as a conjunction. אֲשֶׁר הוּא,

or אֲשֶׁר הִיא, as Delitzsch observes, is never used as the representative of the subject previously named and taken up again by a suffix pronoun referring back thereto. אסורים, *fetters, chains,* so in Judg. xv. 14. The singular אָסוּר occurs in Jer. xxxvii. 15. See remarks on this passage on p. 202. Comp. Ben Sira, Heb. fragm. 4 in Delitzsch's *Gesch. d. jüd. Poesie,* p. 204, כֵּן תִּלָּכֵד בִּמְצוּדָתָהּ.

27. ראה זה. Comp. verses 14, 29. אָמַר הַקֹּהֶלֶת. So the text ought to be read with the LXX. and Syr., instead of אָמְרָה קֹהֶלֶת. The Targ. supports the ordinary reading. The Vulg. *dixit Ecclesiastes* cannot be cited for either. See on the name Koheleth, the prelim. note, pp. 279 ff. Delitzsch well observes that Ginsburg vainly contends in favour of the Masoretic text, that personified wisdom might be as well represented as a feminine as masculine; but especially here, where the female sex is spoken of in disparaging terms, the designation of wisdom as feminine would be peculiarly unsuitable. Delitzsch also notes that similar errors of transcription are found 2 Sam. v. 2; Job xxxviii. 12. In the two latter cases the error is corrected in the K'ri, and acknowledged by the punctuators.

28. See remarks on p. 203. "*What my soul hath sought,*" not *is seeking,* which would require the participle. Delitzsch, in his textual remarks, observes on בִּקְשָׁה, that all the piel forms of בקש ought Masoretically to have the ק marked with raphe, with the exception of the imperative בַּקְּשִׁי. Comp. Luzzatto, *Gramm.,* § 417; König, *Lehrg.,* p. 188. The consecution of the accents in the clause, אדם א' מאלף מצאתי is the same as in Gen. i. 9, except that gereshayim is used instead of geresh on אדם. For the reason of the latter see Davidson's *Heb. Acc.,* § 12, 3, and § 11, 2.

29. לבד ראה זה מ'. The order of the words is here inverted. זה is the accus. governed by מ' and לבד (see Glossary) qualifies it.

CHAPTER VIII.

1. מי כהחכם. *Who is as the wise man?* Not identical with the expression מִי חָכָם *who is wise,* Hosea xiv. 10; Ps. cvii. 45, but "*who is like the wise man?*" Comp. Exod. xv. 11, מִי כָמוֹכָה *who is like thee?* On the absence of the usual syncope of the article after כְּ, see Ges.-Kautzsch, § 35, rem. 2; Kalisch, § xxi. 5; Ewald, § 244 *a*. This omission of the syncope occurs chiefly in the later

Ch. viii. 1.] *Critical and Grammatical Comm.* 395

books. The accent under 'מִ in the beginning of the verse is yethibh, prepositive and disjunctive, hence the daghesh in 'פה. וּמִי יוֹדֵעַ. Knobel and others consider the בְּ is here understood, but this is unnecessary. פֵשֶׁר דָּבָר. On פ see Glossary. This is translated by Hitzig and many others, "*the interpretation of the proverb*," namely, of that which follows. The absence of the article is, however, a decided objection to this. דָּבָר ought to be rendered indefinitely, and is better understood in the sense of *thing*, as in chap. i. 8; vii. 8. The ancient versions render it here *word*, but inasmuch "as the explanation, or interpretation פֵּשֶׁר = تفسير), refers to the actual substance of that which is spoken, *word* and *thing* in this case coincide" (*Delitzsch*).

Wisdom enlightens the face, because the light that is within makes itself partially visible without (comp. Ps. xix. 9; cxix. 130). עֹז פָּנִים, from the comparison of the similar phrases in Deut. xxviii. 50; Dan. viii. 23; Prov. vii. 13, seems to signify *fierceness, impudence, coarseness of countenance*, or, *of the expression of face*. Delitzsch refers in illustration of the idea to the Talmud, *Shabbath*, 30 *b*, and *Taanith*, 7 *b*. In the latter it is said אמר רבה בר רב הונא כל אדם שי"ש לו עזות פנים מותר לקרותו רשע שנאמר העז איש רשע בפניו רב נחמן בר יצחק אמר מותר לשנאותו שנאמר ועז פניו ישונא (יְשֻׁנֶּא) אל תקרי ישונא אלא ישנא (יִשָּׂנֵא). That is, "Rabbah bar Rab Huna says, with respect to every man who has עַזּוּת פָּנִים (*impudence of expression*) it is lawful to call him *wicked*, for it is written (Prov. xxi. 29) '*a wicked man hardens* [makes impudent] *his face.*' Rab Naḥman bar Isaac says, it is lawful *to hate him*, for it is written '*and the coarseness* [impudence] *of his face is changed.*' Read not [in his case] ישונא (*changed*), but ישנא (*hated*)." This passage of the Talmud proves that the present reading of our text is the original. The gloss, however, of Rab Naḥman explains the rendering of the LXX., καὶ ἀναιδής (reading עַז instead of עֹז) προσώπῳ αὐτοῦ μισηθήσεται, which is followed by the Syriac. Dale explains the Heb. verb after the LXX. But the Masoretic note is correct, א' במקום ה', "א *is in place of* ה." Similar cases occur in ל"ה verbs. See Ges.-Kautzsch, § 75, rem. 22; Kalisch, § lxvii. 20; Ewald, § 142 *c.*; König, p. 532. It is unnecessary to read the piel, with Zirkel and Hitzig. The proverb of Ben Sira, based on this saying of Koheleth and alluded to p. 41, has the piel in the original Hebrew, which has been in this case preserved, לֵב אָדָם

יְשַׁנֶּה פָּנָיו בֵּין לְטוֹב בֵּין לְרָע, "*the heart of man changes his countenance as well to good as to evil.*" See Delitzsch, *Gesch. der jüd. Poesie*, p. 205; Dukes, *Rabb. Blumenlese*, p. 78. Ewald's translation of this passage in Koheleth, namely, "the brightness of his countenance is doubled," must, independently of other considerations, be rejected, on account of the passages cited which show the real meaning of עֹז פָּנָיו.

2. The אֲנִי standing alone at the commencement of the verse is peculiarly strange. The simplest method of explaining it is to suppose that אָמַרְתִּי is omitted. If the omission be not regarded as an ancient blunder of some copyist, the ellipsis is without a parallel elsewhere. The omission of נִגְלָה in Isa. v. 9 (compare chap. xxii. 14), or of לֵאמֹר in Jer. xx. 10, are not really similar. Kleinert notes that Ewald compares 1 Chron. xxviii. 2, which is scarcely parallel. In his *Dichter d. alt. Bundes*, 2te Ausg., Ewald renders, "*Ich:* den Mund des Königs beachte." Kleinert himself renders the אֲנִי, *my judgment is*"; Dale gives, "*As for me, a royal word observe.*" Neither translation is defensible. The LXX., Syr. and Targ. solve the difficulty by simply omitting the אֲנִי; the LXX. and Syr. preserving the order of the Heb. words, στόμα βασιλέως φύλαξον; but in such a command the verb would have been placed first. Fidelity even towards heathen monarchs was commanded by the prophets of Israel, 2 Chron. xxxvi. 13; Ezek. xvii. 15. See our remarks on p. 222. The mention made by Josephus (*Antiq.*, xii. 1) of the fact that Ptolemy Lagus required the Jews in Egypt to take an oath of allegiance to him does not imply that such an oath had not previously been exacted by other kings. R. Levi, in the Midrash Koheleth, refers the passage to God (followed in this particular by Hengstenberg and others), and explains it as אֲנִי אֶשְׁמֹר. Similarly Luther, though rightly considering an earthly sovereign to be spoken of (Ich halte das Wort des Königs), after the Vulg., *ego os regis observo*. The Vulg. may have read the word as the participle (שֹׁמֵר), which Hitzig views as the correct reading. But the traditional reading of the word as the imperative is to be preferred, because Koheleth nowhere adduces his own conduct as an example for others to follow.

3. On the construction אַל תִּבָּהֵל מִ׳ תֵּלֵךְ, see Ges.-Kautzsch, § 142, 3 *b*; Kalisch, § 103, 2; Ewald, § 285 *b*. Koheleth seeks in this place

to dissuade his readers from casting off their allegiance to the king, or taking part with the enemies of the monarch under any hasty impulse whatever. So Rosenmüller, Knobel and Delitzsch explain the passage. On this sense of הלך מפני, compare Gen. xxxvi. 6, or Hosea xi. 2, "*they* [the prophets] *called them, but they* [the people] *went away from them* (הָלְכוּ מִפְּנֵיהֶם), *they sacrificed to Baalim, and burned incense to graven images.*" Heiligstedt is not justified (on the slender induction of particulars which is possible in this case) in maintaining that the niphal of בהל cannot be used in the same sense as the piel. The explanation given by Zöckler and others, namely, that the clause warns against a timid withdrawal from the royal presence when the king is unfavourably disposed, does not, in our opinion, suit the passage. The advice of Koheleth is similar to that in chap. x. 4. דְּבַר רָע is best explained like verse 5, as "*an evil thing,*" not, as several expositors have maintained, "*an evil word.*" עָמַד בְּ, as is proved by comparison of the phrases in Ps. i. 1; 2 Kings xxiii. 3; Ps. cvi. 23, and Jer. xxiii. 18, might well be used of entering into a wicked conspiracy against the monarch. The Targum on this verse supposes that the king referred to is God above, and so Hengstenberg, Hahn, Dale. But this is opposed to the context, as is also the idea that Koheleth refers here to cases like that of Cain, who fled from the presence of the Lord (Gen. iv. 16), or Jonah (i. 3, etc.). Hitzig's translation "*do not hesitate at a bad command* (to obey the king)," is contrary to the use of the phrase. He maintains that the writer intentionally adopts a "servility" of tone when speaking of the king, and refers to him in language used by other writers in reference to God (see n. on next verse). But the "servility" of tone exists only in the imagination of the critic.

4. The author is speaking of a monarch who possesses absolute power. It is no real argument against this view of the text that the same phrase which occurs in the second clause of the verse is applied to God in Job ix. 12; Isa. xlv. 9. Comp. Dan. iv. 32; Wisd. xii. 12. בַּאֲשֶׁר, as Delitzsch observes, is used here in the beginning of the verse to introduce a *reason* for the remark made at the close of the preceding; like בְּשֶׁ, chap. ii. 16, compare Gen. xxxix. 9, 23; Greek, ἐν ᾧ and ἐφ' ᾧ. שִׁלְטוֹן, see Glossary. The use of this word as an adjective is very peculiar.

5. The commandment alluded to is that of the king mentioned in

verse 2, not the Law of God, which some commentators wrongly consider to be referred to. When Koheleth says that the man who obeys the king's command "will experience no evil thing," or that no harm will come to him, he is, of course, speaking generally (like St. Paul in Rom. xiii. 1-5), and not contemplating the case of kings requiring obedience to decrees contrary to the Divine laws, such as those of Nebuchadnezzar (Dan. iii.) or Darius (Dan. vi.). The יֵדַע in both clauses of the verse ought to be translated uniformly, not as a future in one clause, and a present in the other, or *vice versâ*. לב חכם might be either *a wise heart*, or the *heart of a wise man*. The connexion of this verse with verse 1 is in favour of the latter rendering. The writer in the last clause does not assert that the wise man will wait patiently for a change in the royal dynasty (he might, in many cases, have to wait long enough!), but that such a person will wait patiently (Lam. iii. 26) for the time and the season (chap. iii. 1, 11, 17) of judgment, which God hath put in His own power. עֵת וּמִשְׁפָּט is regarded by the LXX. as an hendiadys, καιρὸν κρίσεως, *time of judgment*.

6. Four of the sentences in verses 6 and 7 begin with כִּי. This opens the door for a variety of interpretations; because כִּי is susceptible of different renderings. It is perhaps better, with Delitzsch, to regard the four כִּיs alike as members of a single chain of proofs. The sense of this and the following verse is: The heart of the wise will know the time and judgment and will keep quiet, for (1) there is a time and a judgment appointed by God in which the wicked ruler will be duly punished. Comp. chap. iii. 17; (2) the wickedness of man is heavy upon him (man), and will entail its own punishment; (3) No man knows the future, or that which will take place, and, therefore, no despot is able absolutely to guard himself against the stroke of vengeance; for (4) who can tell him how the vengeance will be brought about; he may look in this direction and in that for the longed-for information, but in vain (comp. Isaiah xlvii. 13 ff.); one thing, however, is certain, that whilst the wicked "are drowned in their carousing they shall be consumed like stubble fully dry" (Nahum i. 10).

The LXX. and Theod. have ὅτι γνῶσις τοῦ ἀνθρώπου πολλὴ ἐπ' αὐτόν, reading דַּעַת instead of רָעַת, which, however, affords no sense.

7. The paraphrase of the Vulg., though not verbally correct,

expresses the sense of the passage, "*quia ignorat præterita, et futura nullo scire potest nuntio.*" See note on the previous verse.

8. Koheleth has in the previous verses given four distinct proofs that the heart of a wise man knoweth time and judgment. He now proceeds to point out that there are four things known to be impossibilities which conduct to the same conclusion. (1) There is no man who has power over the wind to check it in its course or to restrain its violence. Judgments are often likened to the wind (Isa. xli. 16; lvii. 12; Jer. iv. 11–13; xxii. 22), and the Divine judgments can be as little kept back (לכלוא) as the mighty wind be prevented from bursting forth. (2) There is no one who has power over the day of death, or is able to avert the arrival of that "king of terrors" (Job xviii. 14); the pestilence walketh forth in darkness, and the sickness wasteth at noon-day (Ps. xci. 6). (3) There was no discharge granted from the ranks in time of war under the rigorous law of Persia, and the Divine law of requital cuts off with equal certainty all hope of escape from the guilty transgressor; and lastly, (4) wickedness will not deliver its master. When the hour of Divine vengeance strikes, the sinner shall receive the meet reward of his actions. "The wages of sin is death" (Rom. vi. 23).

The word רוּחַ in the first clause has generally been explained by the commentators, with the Targ. and Vulg., to mean the *spirit* of man. Delitzsch's argument against this interpretation is not satisfactory, namely, that man has the power to put an end to his own life at any time by suicide. For the passage, as generally explained, only asserts the inability of man to deliver himself from death. He may shorten but he cannot protract his days. But, on the other hand, Mendelssohn appears to be right in considering that Koheleth has in view something similar to the three causes of death referred to by David in 1 Sam. xxvi. 10; death by the wind, or storm, which brings with it the plague (הֱיֵה נֶגֶף, compare נֶגֶף, the *pestilence*), or death in the ordinary course of nature, and death in battle. The three clauses of Koheleth are not properly speaking parallel (hence Ginsburg's objection on this score is invalid). The fourth clause may be regarded as a general statement including the others. The wind is not only one of God's grandest creations (Amos iv. 13), but one of his special instruments of power (Nahum i. 3); and power over the wind is one of the things kept in God's hand and not conceded to man (Prov. xxx. 4).

The LXX., Vulg., and Syr. take שִׁלְטוֹן as an abstract noun for *power*. So Ginsburg and others; but, as Delitzsch notes, שַׁלִּיטוֹ is rather to be regarded here as the concrete *"ruler"* (as in Dan. iii. 2 ff. and above in verse 4, and everywhere in the Talmud and Midrash) in contrast with the abstract שִׁלְטָן, which is formed after the analogy of אָבְדָן, דִּרְבָן, פִּלְחָן, פִּרְקָן, קְרָבָן. On מִשְׁלַחַת vid. Glossary. Graetz would read עֹשֶׁר *riches*, instead of רֶשַׁע, *wickedness*. The proposed alteration does not suit the passage so well as the received text, to which the ancient versions bear witness. Renan adopts Graetz's conjecture in his translation, though he does not specially notice the alteration of the text in his Appendix. בעליו is plural, but might refer to the despotic king. Compare chap. v. 10, 12; vii. 12; Prov. iii. 27.

9. This verse does not, as Renan imagines, begin a new section. Koheleth refers by את־בל־זה to that which was mentioned before. נָתוֹן is the inf. abs. which is used either adverbially, Ges.-Kautzsch, § 131, 2; Kalisch, § 97, 5, or for the same tense of the finite verb which precedes (*i.e.* here the perfect), Kalisch, § 97, 3; Ges.-Kautzsch, § 131, 4; Ewald, § 351 *c*. On the special phrase see note on chap. i. 13. עֵת, Accusative of time, as Jer. li. 33. So Ewald, Graetz, Delitzsch, Renan, etc. Delitzsch compares Ps. iv. 8, and notes that the relative of עֵת אֲשֶׁר is like מָקוֹם אֲשֶׁר, chap. i. 7; xi. 3. Many commentators (with the A.V.) erroneously regard עֵת as commencing a new sentence, "there is a time, etc." לְרַע לוֹ. The suffix is referred by Symm. (εἰς κακὸν αὐτοῦ), the Vulg., the A. V., Grotius, Herzfeld, etc., to the ruler spoken of before, but the LXX., Theod. (τοῦ κακῶσαι αὐτόν), Syr., Targ., and most modern commentators refer it correctly to the second noun. See our translation.

10. This verse is beset with difficulties, and a full survey of the various opinions of scholars in ancient and modern times would occupy more space than is here available. The phrase אֲשֶׁר כֵּן־עָשׂוּ is rendered by most modern critics "*those who acted right*," *i.e.* the righteous, who are supposed to be contrasted with the ungodly mentioned in the opening of the verse. This translation can be justified by an appeal to 2 Kings vii. 9, where the phrase occurs, לֹא־כֵן אֲנַחְנוּ עֹשִׂים, "*we are not acting rightly*." Comp. Gen. xlii. 11. But most of the ancient versions regard כֵּן in the second part of the verse as identical with כֵּן in the beginning, in the phrase בְּכֵן (Symm.

indeed, renders, ὡς δίκαια πράξαντες). In that case the אֲשֶׁר כֵּן עָשׂוּ must be rendered, "*who did* (or, *acted*) *thus.*" The accentuation of the verse seems to show that the punctuators took the same view. The main difficulty in the way of regarding the writer as contrasting the fate of the wicked with that of the godly is, that we must in that case explain the וּבָאוּ "*and they went in,*" or "*entered*" (with Hitzig, Ewald, and Delitzsch, etc.), as an elliptical expression for "*they entered into rest,*" in reference to Isaiah lvii. 2. But the ellipsis is harsh. To explain further, with Ewald and Heiligstedt, the verb following, יְהַלֵּכוּ (as piel used for the hiphil), as an impersonal 3rd person, "*they cast them* (the righteous) *away,*" is doing violence to the passage. Ewald explains "the holy place" as "the holy burying-place;" but, as Delitzsch observes, no such name for a cemetery can be discovered amongst the numerous designations in use among the Jews. See Hamburger, *Real-Encycl. für Bibel und Talmud*, Abtheil. I., s. v. *Grab*. Delitzsch explains that phrase of the going forth of the righteous, probably to a foreign country (compare Amos vii. 17). He rightly explains the מְקוֹם קָדוֹשׁ, *holy place*, either as meaning Jerusalem, termed in the second part of Isaiah, Nehemiah, Daniel, and St. Matthew (xxvii. 53), *the holy city* (עִיר הַקֹּדֶשׁ), or the holy ground of the temple of God, the τόπος ἅγιος (Matt. xxiv. 15), as Aquila and Symm. translate the phrase. We explain with Knobel the coming (בָּאוּ) and going (יְהַלֵּכוּ) after the analogy of chap. i. 4, though we do not agree in other points with his exposition. We cannot coincide with Ginsburg in explaining the בָאוּ as referring to the coming back of the wicked in the persons of their children; "these wicked ones are perpetuated by their children when they die." Our explanation of the verse is, "*And in such a way* (בְכֵן, *under such circumstances*) *have I seen wicked men buried* [possibly with the accompaniments of pomp and show; comp. chap. vi. 3], *and they came* (into being), *and from the place of the holy* (from Jerusalem) *they went away* [one generation coming, and another going, in constant succession], *and they are forgotten* [with the greater part of their oppressive actions] *in the very city where they so acted; even this is vanity,*" namely, that despite of all their wickedness, there is no difference often made between the dealings of Providence with such tyrants and his dealings with other men. (See Job xxi.; Ps. lxxiii.) "The wise man," however, knows that "God shall judge the righteous and the wicked, for there is a time THERE (with the Most High) for every purpose and every work " (chap. iii. 17). In spite of all appearances to the contrary, "there is a time and a judgment." The LXX., Aq., Symm., Theod., and Vulg. read וַיִּשְׁתַּבְּחוּ, from שָׁבַח, "*and they were praised*," which is the reading of several Heb. MSS. collated by Kennicott and De Rossi. The reading harmonises well with our reference of the entire verse to the ungodly oppressors. On the change of construction in the beginning of the verse from the participle to the perfect see Ges.-Kautzsch, § 134, 2, rem. 2; Ewald, § 350 b. Delitzsch notices that the punctuation וּבָאוּ instead of וּבָאוּ is used because the distinctive rebhia takes the fuller form. Comp. Isaiah xlv. 20 with Job xvii. 10.

11. אֲשֶׁר. *Because*, as in chap. iv. 3; vi. 12. פִּתְגָם. So pointed, according to Delitzsch, in good MSS. and in the older editions, as also in Esth. i. 20; Dan. iii. 16. The פ has no daghesh, because of the נַעֲשָׂה preceding. See on פתגם in Glossary. Delitzsch notes that the long *a* of פִּתְגָם, as Esth. i. 20 shows, is unchangeable. The word is here in the construct. The zakeph is no objection to this, for the accents are often used only for the purpose of cantillation, and in Esth. i. 4 a similar instance occurs of a zakeph between a construct state and the governed genitive. The governing word indeed has rightly a distinctive accent when the genitive governed which is connected with it consists of several members. Under such circumstances pashta occurs in Isa. x. 12. See for instructive examples Isa. xxviii. 1–4. But מעשה הרעה might be regarded as an accusative of respect. The נַעֲשָׂה which precedes פתגם is the fem. of the participle niphal, and not the 3rd pers. sing. perf., which could not be construed with אֵין. פתגם, which is masc. in the only other place in which it occurs in Hebrew (namely, in Esth. i. 20, as also in Chald.) is here to be regarded as feminine. Hitzig would read the masc. participle נַעֲשֶׂה. But, as Delitzsch observes, the foreign word פתגם, like the Arab. فِرْدَوْس *paradise*, is of both genders (see Ewald, § 174 g). LXX. ἀπὸ τῶν ποιούντων τὸ πονηρόν, Vulg. *contra malos*, reading מֵעֹשֵׂי הר׳. מְהֵרָה, properly a noun signifying *haste*, is here taken as an adverb, as Num. xvii. 11; Judg. ix. 54.

12. The אֲשֶׁר with which the verse commences is to be rendered, with Hitzig and Delitzsch, *because*. The LXX. badly ὃς ἥμαρτεν. Ewald, followed by Heiligstedt, Zöckler, and others, adopts the view

Ch. viii. 12-14.] *Critical and Grammatical Comm.* 403

of the Vulg., which has *attamen*, "*although*," and so our A. V. See Ewald, § 362 *b*. Though אֲשֶׁר could thus be rendered in an antecedent sentence (Lev. iv. 22 ; Deut. xviii. 22), the imperfect ought to follow, and not the participle as here. חֹטֶא. On form see chap. vii. 26 and the references there. Hitzig suggests that the punctuation with seghol is on account of the following guttural. The רַע following עֹשֶׂה ought to have kametz according to the Masora. מְאַת, *a hundred times*, פְּעָמִים being understood. Compare אַחַת, Job xl. 5. It is not, as Delitzsch notes, to be translated with Hengstenberg, an *hundredfold*, which would require מֵאתַיִם; or, as Ginsburg, after the Targ., *a hundred years*, which would be rather מֵאָה, *scil.* שָׁנָה. But see Ges.-Kautzsch, § 120, 1 rem. ; Kalisch, § 90, 6. The LXX. (ἀπὸ τότε), instead of מאת seem to have read מאז. Aquila, Symm., and Theod. seem to have read it מֵת, as they render it by ἀπέθανεν. מַאֲרִיךְ. supply יָמִים. See n. on chap. vii. 15. Mendelssohn would supply אַף, and refer the clause to God. So Vulg. *et per patientiam* (scil. *Dei*) *sustentatur*. This is also the sense of the transl. of Symm. and Theod., μακροθυμίας γενομένης αὐτῷ. But this is wrong, as appears by the verse following, and by chap. vii. 15. לוֹ *for it*, or *for himself*, the dat. ethicus. Our view of the whole verse coincides in the main with that of Delitzsch, and will be seen from our translation. Appearances, Koheleth saw clearly enough, were against him, yet his faith was strong even under all such difficulties, and through it he was victorious. Comp. 1 John v. 4 ; and, on the last clause of the verse, see Jer. v. 22.

13. The A. V. follows correctly the division of the verse given by the accentuators. So Ewald, Delitzsch, etc. The Vulg. renders the clause, "*sed quasi umbra transeant qui non timent faciem Domini.*" This precative rendering is incorrect. But the division of the verse, by putting the stop in the middle at יָמִים, given by the Vulg., has been followed by Hitzig, Zöckler, and others. Hitzig asks, Is then the shadow therefore קְצַר־יָמִים, because it does not יַאֲרִיךְ יָמִים? They render the second clause less suitably, "He is as a shadow who feareth not before God." Man is often compared to the shadow that fleeth away, which is the idea of this passage. Comp. chap. vi. 12 ; Ps. cxliv. 4 ; Wisd. ii. 5. The LXX., led astray perhaps by the use of צֵל in chap. vii. 12, render οὐ μακρυνεῖ ἡμέρας ἐν σκιᾷ.

14. On מַגִּיעַ אֶל see Glossary, s.v. נָגַע.

15. Compare chap. ii. 24; iii. 12, 22; v. 17. On לְוָה vid. Glossary. Delitzsch observes either וְהוּא יְלֻוֶּנּוּ begins a new sentence, and the imperfect is then to be rendered imperatively, "*let this accompany him*"; or it is to be connected with the previous infinitives, and the imperfect is to be translated as a subjunctive, as in our rendering. The Greek versions regard it as an indicative, and so many modern critics, as Ewald, Ginsburg, Zöckler, "*and this will cling to him*," etc., or "*this will follow him*."

16. On נתן לב ל and on עִנְיָן see n. on chap. i. 13. This verse with that which follows forms one long period, which the Masorites have rightly divided. שֵׁנָה is governed by the act. part. רֹאֶה at the close of the verse. On the expression to *see sleep*, compare, with Rosenmüller, Terent., *Heautont.*, Act. iii. Sc. i. 82 "somnum hercle ego hac nocte oculis non vidi meis." Rosenmüller also refers to the expression of Cicero (*Epist. ad divers.*, vii. 30), "fuit mirifica vigilantia, qui toto suo consulatu somnum non vidit," but it must be noted that Cicero there uses the language of fact not of metaphor. C. Caninius Rebilus was made consul for only a portion of a day by Julius Cæsar (B.C. 45); Cæsar himself and Antonius entered into office the very next day. Compare, also, on the expression in Koheleth, Ps. cxxxii. 4; Prov. vi. 4; Gen. xxxi. 40.

17. בְּשֶׁל אֲשֶׁר. Ewald proposes here to read בְּכֹל אֲשֶׁר, "*for all that*," maintaining that the present reading of the text is meaningless. See his *Lehrb.*, § 362 c. Ewald is partly supported by the rendering of the LXX. ὅσα ἄν, Vulg. *et quanto plus*. Similarly Syr. But, as Hitzig and Delitzsch remark, the alteration is unnecessary. The latter observes that בְּשֶׁל אֲשֶׁר is Hebrew exactly equivalent to the Aram. בְּדִיל דְּ, as in Onk., Gen. vi. 3, בְּדִיל דְּאִנּוּן בִּשְׂרָא, *because that they are flesh*; and further that Rashi and Kimchi (*Michlol*, 47 b) have rightly explained it by בִּשְׁבִיל שֶׁ and בַּעֲבוּר שֶׁ. Compare with the contents of these verses the exclamation of the Apostle, Rom. xi. 33.

CHAPTER IX.

1. נתתי אל לבי. See n. on chap. i. 13. וְלָבוּר inf. const. of ברר after the analogy of verbs ע"י. vid. Ges.-Kautzsch, § 67, rem. 3, Kalisch, § lxii. 12. Knobel and others take the inf. with ל as used here, like the inf. absol. for the finite verb. But see Ges.-Kautzsch,

Ch. ix. 1.] Critical and Grammatical Comm. 405

§ 132, 3, rem. 1; Ewald, § 237 c. הָיִיתִי must be understood before לָבוּר, as in chap. iii. 15, הָיָה before לִהְיוֹת. It is a mistake to suppose that the inf. const. with ל is used in place of the finite verb. Delitzsch, in his comm. on Habakkuk, i. 17, observes that the inf. with ל is used in three significations: הָיָה לַעֲשׂוֹת may mean (1) *est facturus*, "he is about to do," (2) *est faciendum*, "it is to be done," and (3) *est faciendo*, "he is in the position of doing." See this construction well explained in Driver's *Hebrew Tenses*, 2nd edit., Append. v. pp. 300, 301. ברר has the meaning of sifting, testing, thoroughly examining into, not that of *digging through* (which Plumptre assigns to it), but of *separating* and *dividing* one thing from another, and thus thoroughly understanding each. See Mühlau and Volck's *Ges. Lex.* The LXX. have translated the phrase as if they had read ולבי ראה, καὶ καρδία μου σύμπαν εἶδε τοῦτο (on the σύμπαν see note on p. 51). So Syr. ܘܟܠܗ. On עבדיהם vid. Glossary, s.v. עָבַד. See remarks on p. 189, where we have explained the passage as meaning that no man knows what will be the objects of his love or hatred in life. Man fixes his love or hatred on persons or things, not according to his own self-determination, but according to the circumstances under which he comes into relation with them, which, rightly or wrongly, draw forth his love or hatred. Man is no automaton, but a being tested by circumstances, which cause him either to manifest his character to others, or reveal himself to himself. In the expression "*all lies before them*" the emphasis is to be put on the word "*all.*" The meaning is not that men are deprived of all freedom whatever, but that events of all kinds lie before them, and God arranges that which shall happen to them. But the moral and religious condition of man is not thought of here by the writer. See our note on chap. vi. 11. Others have explained the text to mean that men do not know whether they will be the objects of the Divine love or hatred. But, as Delitzsch notes, the expressions "love" and "hatred" are too general for this. Moreover the translation does not suit the general drift of the passage. This, however, substantially is the sense given by the Vulg. "et tamen nescit homo utrum amore an odio dignus sit."

Knobel compares Marc. Aurelius, xii. 11. ἡλίκην ἐξουσίαν ἔχει ἄνθρωπος μὴ ποιεῖν ἄλλο, ἢ ὅπερ μέλλει ὁ θεὸς ἐπαινεῖν καὶ δέχεσθαι πᾶν, ὃ ἂν νέμῃ αὐτῷ ὁ θεός.

2. The first clause of this verse in the LXX., and the first word in Syr., Aq., Symm. is connected with the preceding. The Syr., Aq., Symm. in place of הכל have read here הבל (Syr. ﻫܒܠ, Aq. ματαιότης, Symm. ἄδηλα). The reading of the present text of the LXX., ματαιότης ἐν τοῖς πᾶσι, seems to be compounded of Aquila and the original LXX. (compare note on chap. ii. 25 ; vii. 22). The Vulg. rendering has similarly incorporated the ἄδηλα of Symm. at the end of the clause : "*sed omnia in futurum servantur incerta.*" The הַכֹּל at the commencement of the verse is to be regarded as neuter, *the whole, everything* which happens, referring to the הבל in the previous verse ; the כל in לַכֹּל on the other hand refers to persons, as in chap. x. 3, "*all (is) like that which (is,* or *happens) to all.*" There is no difference, speaking generally, in the circumstances in which men are placed; all are on the whole treated alike. Men are here classified into five pairs of different individuals, each contrasted with the other (comp. Isaiah xxiv. 2), the righteous and the wicked, the clean and the unclean (both ceremonially and morally, comp. Hos. v. 3 ; Ezek. xxxvi. 25), the man who brings sacrifices and he who does not, the good man and the sinner, the profane swearer (see Exod. xx. 7 ; Matt. v. 34 ff) and he who keeps aloof from such profanity, reverencing the solemn oath (Isa. lxv. 16). The construction is, however, varied in each of the last two couplets. The participle (יָרֵא) follows here the accusative which it governs, as in Isa. xxii. 2 ; Nah. iii. 1. Delitzsch compares with שְׁבוּעָה יָרֵא the expression of the Mishna יָרֵא חֵטְא.

3. זֶה רַע בְּכֹל. Knobel, Ginsburg and others, after the Vulg. *hoc est pessimum inter alia*, regard this as a kind of superlative. See Ewald, § 313 *c*; Kalisch § 89, 6, 7. But the article would in such a case naturally have been used, as in Cant. i. 8; Josh. xiv. 15 ; Judg. vi. 15 ; although perhaps not absolutely necessary, Obad. 2 ; Lam. i. 1 ; though it may be questioned whether in the latter passages the superlative sense is intended. In our passage the superlative meaning is unnecessary, and, indeed one might almost say, opposed to chap. viii. 11. The word מָלֵא, as Delitzsch observes, might be an adj., for this adjective is often construed with an accusative, Deut. vi. 11 ; xxxiii. 23 ; xxxiv. 9 ; and is only once (Jer. vi. 11) construed with a genitive. [The English translation of Delitzsch's Comm. on Eccl. here, as in several other places, expresses a sense exactly opposed to the meaning of the German original.]

But, as Delitzsch remarks, inasmuch as it is not a *state* but an *act* which is here spoken of, it is better to regard מָלֵא as a verb, as in chap. viii. 11. והוללות. On this noun see n. chap. i. 17. According to the Heb. accentuation found in five MSS. collated by Michaelis, and in two of the best MSS. noticed by Delitzsch (which have רֹע with kadma instead of רֹע with geresh), the ה would be regarded as a genitive combined with the previous word. So Vulg. and Symm. as quoted by Jerome. But the LXX., Syr., Aq. and Targ. are correct in viewing it as commencing a new sentence. אַחֲרָיו may be explained with Hitzig, Ewald, etc., after Jer. li. 46, *afterwards* (Vulg. *post hæc*), the suffix being taken in a neuter sense; but, inasmuch as the expression is used in chap. iii. 22; vi. 12; vii. 14, to refer to man, it is perhaps better to take it also here, with Delitzsch, in the same sense, "*after him*," *i.e.* after man's life is ended. The plural suffix in בְּחַיֵּיהֶם is no objection to this, as there is the same mixture of singular and plural in verse 1, in chap. iii. 12, etc. The long-suffering of God with sinners leads them too often to indulge in sin almost without restraint during their lives, and then they go away to the dead. (See p. 189.) Renan maintains that such passages as this prove the writer to have had no faith whatever in a state of existence after death. According to his idea, Koheleth conceived the Divine Being as so great as not to be troubled, unless in case of gross wickedness, with man's actions. The notion of man's immortality was in his view one of the greatest follies, and, so far from being a pious dogma, was an offence against God and common sense. The common people believed in *refaim*, ghosts, and apparitions, who could sometimes be evoked by sorcery, but Koheleth here laughs at all such folly. Renan regards chap. xii. 7 as teaching only the separation of soul and body, not the continued existence of the former. He has seen clearly enough that the denial of a future state is almost equivalent to a denial of the justice of God, for the righteous are not always rewarded or the wicked punished in this world. But Koheleth, according to him, stopped short of drawing any such conclusions. As a practical man, his "religion," such as it was, did not lead him to seek a solution of such difficulties. Renan's conception of Koheleth's opinions we hold to be distinctly opposed by that writer's statements in chap. iii. and in chap. viii. 11 ff., as well as in other places. See our remarks on pp. 192-195 and on pp. 197-200.

4. The attempts to extract a suitable meaning from the reading of the K'thib יבחר are utterly vain. Rosenmüller and others render "*nam quis* (est) *qui eligatur,* ut scilicet non ad mortuos abeat, *i.e.* nemo excipitur.*"* And so Ginsburg, "*for who is excepted?*" attaching the words to the end of the preceding verse. It is true that if the word be read יְבָחֵר (or יָבְחַר as Hengstenberg), it will mean, "*who is chosen out,*" but the idea of being excepted by no means naturally follows from this. Scarcely better is the rendering of Elster (reading יִבְחַר), "*for who is he that can choose, i.e.* to whom does the choice stand open?" The K'ri reading has יְחֻבַּר, by transposition of the two middle letters of the word, and this is upheld by the LXX. τίς ὃς κοινωνεῖ πρὸς πάντας τοὺς ζῶντας; and the Syr. More freely Symm. τίς γὰρ εἰς ἀεὶ διατελέσει ζῶν, rendered by Jerome, *quis enim potest in sempiternum perseverare vivens?* Still further from the original words, though evidently still based on the reading of the K'ri, is the rendering of the Vulg. *nemo est qui semper vivat.* The K'ri is mentioned and explained in the Jer. Talmud (*Berachoth,* 13 *a,* col. 2): "Rabbi Johanan said, For why is it that יחובר (יְחֻבַּר) is read instead of יבחר, except that all the living have hope (בטחון), for a man has expectation (תקוה) as long as he is alive, but when he is dead his expectation perishes. For what foundation is there in the death of a wicked man, for his expectation perishes." See Strack, *Proleg. Crit. in V. T. Heb.*, p. 82. The accentuation of the verse, which cuts off יחבר from what follows by the great distinctive accent zakeph katon, has been regarded by Rosenmüller as in favour of the reading of the K'thibh. But Delitzsch points out that the accentuation does not really refer to the textual reading, but proceeds from some such explanation (however contrary it may be to the context) as the following: he who will be received into communion with God has to hope for the full life on the other side of the grave. So the Targ. "*for who is the man who associates* (דִי אתחבר) *himself with all the words of the Law, and has hope to obtain the life of the world to come?*" The interrogative מִי אֲשֶׁר, *quis est qui,* acquires from that signification the force of a relative *quisquis* (quicunque), and may be taken in the same way as here (compare the single מִי chap. v. 9), in both senses in Exod. xxxii. 33; 2 Sam. xx. 11; the latter of these two passages is in the form of its apodosis similar to that before us. The sense of the passage seems to be, *he who is joined to all the living, i.e.* to all living beings of whatever kind they may be, by

Ch. ix. 4-7.] *Critical and Grammatical Comm.* 409

being himself a partaker of the grace of life, *has hope, for a living dog is better than a dead lion.* The ל is used before כלב for the sake of emphasis. See Ewald, § 310 *b*; 1 Chron. iii. 2; vii. 1; 2 Chron. vii. 21; Isa. xxxii. 1. Rosenmüller, Herzfeld, and Graetz prefer to regard ל as used in its usual signification, like Symm. κυνὶ ζῶντι βέλτιόν ἐστιν ἢ λέοντι τεθνηκότι. But in that case, as Delitzsch observes, the Hebrew should have been כלב חי טוב לו מן האריה המת. The dog was made use of by the Hebrews as an emblem of reproach (1 Sam. xvii. 43; 2 Sam. iii. 8; ix. 8; xvi. 9), while the lion was regarded as an emblem of greatness and power (Isa. xxxi. 4), as being the hero among beasts (Prov. xxx. 30). Koheleth in other places speaks of death as preferable to life (chap. iv. 2, 3; vii. 1), when taking a view of the sorrows which so often fall to the lot of humanity; here from another standpoint he regards life as preferable to death, because it affords opportunities of enjoyment.

5. See remarks on pp. 197 ff. אינם—מאומה. comp. chap. v. 13. Knobel calls attention to the paronomasia between שָׂכָר and זִכְרָם. As to the difficulty which has often been raised as to such expressions being used by a writer who had any belief in a future state, see pp. 199 ff.

6. The expressions, אַהֲבָתָם, *their love*, etc., need not, with Knobel and Ginsburg, be explained of the affections themselves which men have while they live; nor with Luther as if Koheleth affirmed that one does not love or hate or envy the dead any more; nor simply that they have no more objects to love or to hate, for such sentiments have ceased for them, because as רפאים they are destitute of all affections and interests. So Rosenmüller, Zöckler, Delitzsch, comp. Isa. xxxviii. 18. See the paraphrase of this passage given in our remarks on pp. 197 ff.

The rendering of the Vulg. in the second clause, *nec habent partem in hoc sæculo*, is erroneous. It is, however, followed by Luther, who translates עוֹלָם here by *world*, and is also found in the Targ. Independently of other considerations (see note on chap. iii. 11) the Hebrew would require to be בָּעוֹלָם הַזֶּה.

7. It is vain to try to evade the real meaning of the passage by explaining it with Hengstenberg, as containing the voice of the spirit in opposition to the voice of the flesh. But at the same time Koheleth does not here set forth the doctrines of Epicurus, as many

commentators affirm. Inasmuch as he had no bright hopes to communicate with respect to the future state, Koheleth simply urges upon his readers the practical wisdom of seeking to enjoy cheerfully the present (see remarks on p. 201), and to have no scruples whatever in so doing, provided they remembered in all things to "fear God and keep His commandments," for God has long ago permitted such enjoyments, and designed in His good Providence such pleasures for man on earth as the rightful use of food and wine. So rightly Ibn Ezra, Hitzig, Delitzsch, etc. מעשיך may be taken with Hitzig as a singular (comp. 1 Sam. xix. 4), but it may equally well be translated as plural. The works referred to are the eating and drinking just mentioned. No reference whatever is here made to moral conduct, as some commentators suppose. The writer is addressing men as men. God has graciously given man certain capacities of enjoyment of which he may lawfully make use, without torturing himself with self-imposed scruples. כְּבָר *already, long ago*, is emphasized by being accentuated with the zakeph katon. Compare on the thought, chap. ii. 24; iii. 12, 13, 22; v. 17 (A. V. v. 18); viii. 15.

8. White garments used to be worn in times of joy, after days of sorrow were over (2 Sam. xii. 20; xix. 24; comp. Rev. iii. 4, 5; vii. 9). Fragrant oil was also used on such occasions (Ps. xxiii. 5; xlv. 8; Prov. xxvii. 9; Isa. lxi. 3). Knobel and Ginsburg give many references to Greek and Roman writers. The Talmud and Midrash explain the directions here to refer to a pure and holy life. In *Shabb.*, 114 *a*, in the course of explanations about the things belonging to baths, the anecdote is narrated that R. Jannai said to his sons, "bury me not in white robes, nor yet in black robes; not in white robes, because I may not be of the righteous, and (then) I shall be as a bridegroom among the mourners, nor in black, because I may be of the righteous, and I shall be as a mourner among the bridegrooms; but (bury me) in robes scented with fine oil (בכלים אוֹלְיָירִין, *in vestibus oleariis*), which come from the district of the sea," *i.e.* from lands beyond the sea.

9. See p. 206. On ראה חיים see n. on chap. ii. 1. The article is intentionally omitted both before חיים and אשה (comp. Ps. xxxiv. 13), for the writer is speaking generally. He recognises, however, the fact distinctly, that in ordinary cases for man's happiness a "helpmeet" is needed. The advice of Koheleth is similar to, and based

on, that in Prov. v. 18, 19; xviii. 22. His condemnation of women in chap. vii. 23, is in like manner founded on Prov. ii. 18. See remarks on p. 202. Ginsburg is certainly wrong in maintaining that not a *wife*, but "a *favourite* woman" is here recommended, and consequently that the writer does not refer at all to the married state. The majority of critics, including all the best, differ from him on this point. Plumptre observes that "we should say naturally, 'live with a wife whom you love.'" The latter scholar must be regarded as mistaken in the view, propounded in his Introduction, p. 73, that the sayings of the writer of the Book of Wisdom (chap. iii. 14; iv. 1) were levelled against the possible misunderstanding of this passage of Koheleth. The relative in the clause שאר נתן־לך may either refer to the *wife* mentioned in the previous sentence (as Michaelis, Rosenmüller, Heinem. and others explain it), in which case Gen. ii. 22 was probably in the author's mind; or to *the days of thy life*, as the LXX., Vulg., Knobel, etc., which is more in accordance with chap. v. 17. The LXX., Syr., Targ., omit the second כל ימי הבלך, which, however, are expressed by the Vulg. and the Arab. The reading of the text is most probably correct, though the repetition of the phrase is regarded by some critics as heavy, but by others as being emphatic, and by Tayler Lewis as "a most exquisite pathos in view of the transitoriness and poverty of life!" The Oriental MSS. read, in the end of the verse, כִּי הִיא חֶלְקֵךְ, a like difference as Delitzsch notes in his *Textkrit. Bemerk.* as in Nah. ii. 12. It would be quite possible here to interpret that reading as referring to the wife previously spoken of. The analogy of chap. iii. 22; v. 17 (A.V. v. 12), and even chap. vii. 2, however, is decisive against that interpretation. Geiger (*Urschrift*, pp. 236 ff) considers this variety of reading in passages not belonging to the Pentateuch as a proof that the form הוא was formerly used for the feminine in other books as well as the Pentateuch, in which books less care was taken to preserve the original forms. He calls attention to the fact that the Babylonian and Oriental MSS. have in many places הוא where the Western MSS. read היא.

10. See remarks on p. 231. תמצא ידך. Comp. Lev. xii. 8; Judg. ix. 33; 1 Sam. x. 7; xxv. 8. According to the accentuation, the בְּכֹחֲךָ belongs to that which precedes. It is not exactly בְּכָל־כֹּחֲךָ, as in Gen. xxxi. 6, though it is not essentially different. The "all"

has accidentally crept into our quotation of the passage on p. 231. בְּכֹחֲךָ is scarcely to be rendered with Ginsburg after Rashi, "*whilst thou art able.*" Koheleth, so far from recommending an easy indifference, prescribes for man honest, earnest labour in his calling, combined with such enjoyments as God's providence spreads before him. The punctuation וְיָדַעְתָּ, instead of וְדַעַת, is, as Delitzsch has noted, because of the conjunctive accent. The rule may thus be stated: In the case of two words connected together by the copula, if the second word be accented on the penult, and is marked with a disjunctive, וְ is pointed וָ. So in chap. i. 16; Isa. xxxiii. 6; Prov. xxii. 20. The two apparent exceptions referred to by Delitzsch are Ps. lxv. 9 and Koh. ii. 26. In the former, וְעֶרֶב with a conjunctive is for וְעֹרֶב (rebhia mugrash), comp. Baer, *Accentuations-system*, cap. xviii. 1 (in Delitzsch's *Comm. über die Psalmen*, vol. ii. p. 503, Leipzig, 1860). Therefore the וְ is correct. In the latter (Koh. ii. 26) וְדַעַת has indeed a disjunctive (tiphcha), but a third word is connected with the two preceding. Hence that, too, is no exception. See also note on chap. ii. 23.

11. The expression שַׂכְתִּי וְרָאֹה corresponds to the simple שַׂבְתִּי וָאֶרְאֶה, which occurs in chap. iv. 1. Comp. Ges.-Kautzsch, § 142, 3, with § 131, 4. Perhaps there is a slight difference between the two constructions, the second expressing more definitely the notion of two distinct actions. Compare the same construction in chap. viii. 9. The construction in chap. ix. 1 is scarcely *ad rem*. By the use of this phrase the writer connects the observations that follow with his own personal experiences previously commented on. The last occurrence of רָאִיתִי, which precedes that in the text, is in chap. viii. 17. The use of מֵרוֹץ, the abstract masc. found here only, instead of מְרוּצָה, the fem. noun used in older Hebrew, may be an indication of a late date, vid. Böttcher, *Lehrb.*, § 628, 3 *c*. Neither word necessarily means "*a race*," i.e. a formal game of that kind. The latter is used in the more general signification even in post-Biblical Hebrew. Hence Plumptre's notion, that the author might be referring to the Greek games introduced into Palestine in the Grecian period, is quite out of place. A far better parallel is found in the race between Ahimaaz and Cushi, narrated in 2 Sam. xviii. 27. The phrase at the end of the verse, עֵת וָפֶגַע וגו׳, is rendered in the A.V., "*time and chance happeneth to them all.*" But the עֵת refers back to the "times and seasons" appointed by God (chap.

iii.) for every human purpose, in consequence of which the swift do not always out-run the slow, nor heroes always win the battle, nor human wisdom and knowledge always prove successful. פֶּגַע only occurs twice in Scripture, in this place and in 1 Kings v. 18 (A.V. v. 4), and does not convey the same idea as the English word *chance*, but may be used of *a stroke* (פָּגַע, to *strike*), *accident*, or *incident*, caused by a higher power. Both Ps. iii. and xci. are termed in *Shebuoth*, 15 *b*, שיר של פגעים, *a song against accidents*, or against the attacks of evil spirits. Koheleth does not here mention God, because he makes use of the language of an ordinary observer, and not distinctly that of a man of faith. The sentiments of a man of the latter stamp are found in 1 Sam. xvii. 47; Ps. xx. 8 [A.V. ver. 7]; xxxiii. 16. The pathach under לַחֲכָמִים must here be regarded as that of the article, as is proved by the fact that all the other nouns with which the word is connected in the verse have the article. Compare also chap. ix. 1; Exod. xxxvi. 4; Esther i. 13. Delitzsch observes that, as the idea of mental superiority is here expressed by three distinct terms, so in Isa. xi. 2, among the gifts of the spirit חכמה, בינה and דעת follow one another. The imperf. יִקְרֶה is masc. agreeing with פֶּגַע; עֵת is occasionally masculine, as Cant. ii. 12; Ezek. xxx. 3. See Böttcher, *Lehrb.*, § 648.

12. The particle כִּי is marked with a distinctive accent to note that it is not to be connected with the following גַּם; comp. chap. viii. 12. The כִּי governs the whole sentence, while the גַּם, as Delitzsch notes, is to be referred to the אֶת־עִתּוֹ. The latter expression has been explained by Knobel, etc., as the *proper time* for working, by Ginsburg as the *time of misfortune*; but the context shows that the rendering of Jerome, *nescit homo finem suum*, approved by most critics, is correct, and that the writer refers to the day of death. Death comes generally in an unexpected moment. Men look for it as little as the fishes when they are caught in the net, or the birds when taken in the trap. The sudden and unexpected approach of death is elsewhere depicted by the writer under other figures, see p. 274. In one of Rabbi Akiba's remarkable sayings, preserved in *Aboth*, iii. 25 (Taylor's edit., or *Aboth*, iii. 16, in that of Strack, see note on p. 245), reference is made to this passage as follows: "Everything is given on pledge, and a net (וּמְצוּדָה) is spread over all living" (comp. Isa. xxv. 7); *i.e.* man has no permanent posses-

sion on earth, he is already enclosed in a net, and must give account for the debts which he owes to heaven. Instead of the reading האחוות with ו dageshed, the word ought, with the best MSS. and older editions, to be marked with raphe. יוּקָשִׁים is for מְיֻקָּשִׁים, the participial מ being rejected, and the vowel of the first radical prolonged to compensate for the omission of daghesh, Böttcher, § 296 β; 924, 10, 997, 2 e; Ewald, § 169 d; König, p. 408; Kalisch, § xliv. 1, 5; Ges.-Kautzsch, § 52, rem. 6; Stade, § 220. Stade suggests that it is possible in this case that the כ of the preceding כָּהֵם may have been intended to do duty also for the מ of the participle following. See his *Lehrb.*, § 23 b, rem.

13. The example cited by Koheleth in this and the following verses is given to show that however beneficial wisdom may be, it does not in all cases secure advantages for its possessor. On זו see note on chap. ii. 2. Hitzig would read זֶה, and place a great distinctive there, "*also this have I seen: wisdom, etc.*" So the Gr. Ven. But there is no necessity to depart from the Hebrew accentuation. The passage, indeed, ought not to be rendered with Ginsburg and others, "*even this wisdom have I seen*," for the order of the words points to something different from the usual concord of the demonstrative and substantive. Jerome has observed the peculiarity of the order of the words in his rendering, *hanc quoque sub sole vidi sapientiam*; but, as Delitzsch remarks, the phrase here is equivalent to, "*also in this have I seen wisdom*," the demonstrative pronoun (גַּם־זֹה) being, as in chap. v. 15 (comp. also chap. v. 18), put in the same gender as the חכמה, inasmuch as it is related to it as its predicate. So the LXX. καί γε τοῦτο εἶδον σοφίαν ὑπὸ τὸν ἥλιον. On the construction גְּדוֹלָה אֵלָי compare Esth. x. 3, where Mordecai is called גָּדוֹל לַיְּהוּדִים corresponding to גָּדוֹל בְּעֵינֵי פ׳ Exod. xi. 3, or גָּדוֹל לִפְנֵי פ׳ 2 Kings v. 1. LXX. καὶ μεγάλη ἐστὶ πρὸς μέ, Symm. better καὶ μεγάλη δοκεῖ μοι.

14. See p. 148. The historical fact present to the mind of Koheleth, which formed the basis of the incident here adduced, was the deliverance of Abel-Beth-Maacha through the wisdom of "a wise woman" (2 Sam. xx. 15–22). Compare the historical allusions made to events fresh in the memory of the Jewish people in our Lord's parable of the pounds, as recorded in Luke xix. 12 ff. (note especially verses 14 and 27), which, slightly transformed, form part of the

parable itself. The name of the "wise woman" who delivered the city Abel from the horrors of war had been forgotten when the 2nd Book of Samuel was written. This instance of popular ingratitude to a benefactress seems to have formed the real basis of Koheleth's parable. He has substituted "a poor man" in place of "a wise woman," because the anecdote corresponds better thus with the sentiment of verse 11, which it was intended to illustrate. By the use of the expression, מֶלֶךְ גָּדוֹל, "*great king*," the writer depicts the incident as having occurred in his own days. All attempts have utterly failed to make out that the writer is literally narrating some historical fact, which perhaps occurred at the siege of Dora by Antiochus the Great, as Hitzig asserts without any evidence; or to Themistocles' treatment by the Athenians, as Ewald more hesitatingly puts forward. It may, of course, possibly refer to some event which is not recorded in history, but well known to the public for whom Koheleth primarily wrote (*Graetz*). It is certainly wrong to treat it as an allegory, with the Midrash, and after its example many Christian interpreters, as Hengstenberg. There is not the slightest difficulty in regarding it as a parable founded on fact, but modified by the writer in order that the story might suit better the special object which he had in view. See remarks on verse 18.

On the structure of the sentence, Delitzsch aptly compares Ps. civ. 25. He adduces the literal translation of the Vulg. *civitas parva et pauci in ea viri, venit contra eam rex magnus*, observing that the former (*civitas parva*) is the subject and the latter (*pauci in ea viri*) the predicate, the object (the city) stands out rigid as a statue, and then follows the recital of that which happened to it. On the meaning of בּוֹא אֶל, comp. Gen. xxxii. 9. In place of מְצוֹדִים, two MSS. of De Rossi read מְצוּרִים *walls, fortifications*, which Döderlein and some other critics prefer. But that reading is, as Delitzsch notes, a mere error of transcription. For the plural of מָצוֹר is מְצָרוֹת, feminine, not masculine as here. The LXX. render here χάρακας, *palisades*, Symm. ἀποτείχισμα, Vulg. *munitiones per gyrum*. מְצוֹדִים, more often used in the sense of *nets*, as in chap. vii. 26, means here *intrenchments*, so called from being the places in which the army of the besiegers lie in wait to seize (צוּד) the besieged as their prey. מְצוֹדָה is used in the sense of *stronghold* in Isaiah xxix. 7. See also Ezek. xix. 9.

15. וּמָצָא. The verb here is regarded by many expositors as impersonal, "*and one found,*" i.q. "*and there was found.*" But this is unnecessary. The natural subject of the verb is the "great king" spoken of in the verse before. מָצָא is used not of the king having discovered the poor wise man after searching for him, but in the sense of having *come across* him contrary to all expectation. Comp. the use of the same verb in Deut. xxiv. 1; Ps. cxvi. 3. חָכָם is used as an adjective qualifying the person spoken of before, אִישׁ מִסְכֵּן. Hence the pashta on the word preceding. Delitzsch compares 2 Chron. ii. 13. We might express the force of the disjunctive by rendering, "*a poor man, (but) wise.*" In place of וּמִלַּט־הוּא, the perfect with simple vav, the older language would have written וַיְמַלֵּט, the impf. with vav conv. See n. on chap. i. 13. On the form מִלַּט with pathach, vid. Ges.-Kautzsch, § 52, rem. 1; Kalisch, § xliv. 1; König, § 23, 2, p. 187. Delitzsch observes that instead of אָדָם לֹא the older language would have preferred אִישׁ לֹא, but perhaps the writer wished here to avoid the repetition of the אִישׁ; although he uses also אָדָם אַיִן instead of אִישׁ אַיִן, chap. vii. 20, where no such reason can be assigned.

16. The participles are made use of in this verse to express a fact commonly true in human experience. Plumptre suitably compares Juvenal, *Sat.*, i. 74, "*probitas laudatur et alget.*" The Vulgate introduces at the beginning of Wisdom vi. 1 a heading, which has crept there into the text, partly borrowed from this passage and partly from Prov. xvi. 32, "*melior est sapientia quam vires, et vir prudens quam fortis.*" See Grimm and Deane's notes.

17. There is no discrepancy whatever between this verse and the preceding. If the multitude will not listen to the voice of the wise, there will always be found some persons among them who will listen and learn wisdom. The comparative is expressed in this verse, as in chap. iv. 17, by the simple מִן. Some explain the clause to mean, "*words of the wise heard in quiet.*" So Vulg. *verba sapientium audiuntur in silentio.* Others preferably explain the clause to mean, "*words of the wise, (uttered) in quiet, are heard.*" The latter corresponds more strictly to the contrasted clause, "*the shout of a ruler among the fools,*" as also to the Hebrew accentuation, which places a disjunctive (tiphcha) on בְּנָחַת. By the latter clause is clearly meant (as the parallel cases מוֹשֵׁל בָּאָדָם 2 Sam. xxiii. 3, and גִּבּוֹר בַּבְּהֵמָה,

Prov. xxx. 30, abundantly prove), that the ruler spoken of is himself a fool of the first class. Compare in illustration of the verse, the contrast presented in Isa. xlii. 2 ; Matt. xii. 19, and on the *quiet* of our text, Isa. xxx. 15.

18. The moral drawn in this verse is evidently the conclusion which Koheleth desired his parable to impress upon the mind of his hearers. Hence it is evident that "the poor wise man" was not supposed to have displayed his wisdom by inventing weapons of war, like Archimedes. The weapons of war were all on the other side, and they were turned back by the wise man's wisdom. There was "one sinner" who sought to destroy "much good," and who exercised a powerful influence for evil, which was only overcome by the wisdom of his antagonist. All these incidents are strikingly illustrated in the story of Abel-Beth-Maacha, on the occasion of the wicked and causeless rebellion of Sheba the son of Bichri (2 Sam. xx.), who sought to break up again the union re-established between the tribes, which had been severed by the rebellion of Absalom. Hence we adhere to the view already stated, that Koheleth's illustration is a parable founded on that fact. חוֹטָא is here pointed after the analogy of ל״ה verbs, and this form is, according to the Masora, the correct form throughout this book (with the exception of chap. vii. 26); even in chap. ii. 26, where the ordinary text has וְלַחוֹטָא with zere. See Excursus No. 4, § 1.

CHAPTER X.

1. The aphorism with which this chapter commences has reference to that with which the last closes. Just as "one sinner destroys much good," a little folly may utterly mar the influence of a wise man. זְבוּבֵי מָוֶת may mean either *dead flies* or *poisonous flies*. The former is the rendering of the Vulg., Syr., Arab., Symm., Rosenmüller, Ginsburg, and others, and has been adopted by our A.V. The latter rendering is that of the LXX., the Targ., Gesenius, Knobel, Delitzsch, etc. The latter is to be preferred, being more in accordance with the other compound expressions into which מָוֶת enters, as כְּלֵי מָוֶת, *deadly weapons*, Ps. vii. 14 ; חֶבְלֵי מָוֶת, *the snares of death*, Ps. xviii. 5. In favour of the former it has been maintained that dead flies, whether poisonous or not, would have an equally delete-

rious effect upon a pot of ointment. In the East, flies of all sorts corrupt and destroy the ointment or food they settle on, even if they do not themselves become entangled therein, and perish. The writer might, therefore, term such in disgust "*poisonous flies*," whether they were of a really poisonous character or not. Had he, however, meant merely *dead flies*, he would have chosen the more simple expression זְבוּבִים מֵתִים. As to the singular verb יַבְאִישׁ, Delitzsch observes that in cases in which the idea of the plurality of the individuals is subordinate to that of unity of kind the singular is often made use of; as in Gen. xlix. 22; Joel i. 20; Isa. lix. 12. See Ges.-Kautzsch, § 146, 4; Ewald, § 319 a. There is, therefore, no occasion to read with Hitzig זְבוּבֵי, the singular with the archaic termination ־י, which does not harmonise with the time in which the writer lived, or even, with Luzzatto whom Graetz follows, זְבוּב יָמוּת. Ewald, however, considers the singular reading more correct, and expresses it in his translation, as does Renan. The translation given by Ginsburg of יַבְאִישׁ יַבִּיעַ וגו׳, "*maketh sweet ointment stinkingly to ferment*" is strange English; although it is quite true that the first verb may be regarded as used adverbially to qualify the second. Vid. Ges.-Kautzsch, § 142, 3 b; Kalisch, § 103, 1, 2. The LXX., Targ., Symm., Syr. and Vulg. do not express the יַבִּיעַ, but the omission is caused simply by the difficulty of translating such an expression. Ginsburg's "sweet ointment" is similarly a free rendering of the "oil of the perfumer." רָקַח properly means, *to pound*, *to crush*, specially spices; hence רֹקֵחַ is a preparer of sweet smelling oil, as is evident from the context here and in Exod. xx. 33. We have rendered it by *perfumer*. The verbal asyndeton יבאי״שׁ יביע in the first clause corresponds with the nominal asyndeton מחכמה מכבוד in the second. Some MSS. and editions insert in the second clause the copula between the nouns; but the true Masoretic reading omits it, as Delitzsch points out in his *Textkritik. Bemerk.* The Vulg., Syr., and Targ. express the *and*, but, after the liberties of translation taken by them in the former clause, they cannot be safely adduced as evidence in this case of such a reading. The adjective יָקָר is taken in its original meaning of *heavy*, *weighty*, and, inasmuch as it precedes the subject, is in the masculine, instead of agreeing in gender with its subject סכלות at the end of the sentence. The thought of the passage is akin to that in 1 Cor. v. 6, with this exception, that while Koheleth speaks of an individual, the Apostle speaks of a community of persons. The idea is that a little folly cast into the scale on the other side overweighs a great deal of wisdom. The ancient translators curiously misunderstood the clause as stating that in some way or other folly was better than wisdom.

2. This verse does not mean, as often expounded, that the heart of the wise is in its right place, while that of the fool is in the wrong side ; nor is it to be explained with Rosenmüller, Ginsburg, Bullock, etc., as meaning that the mind of the wise man is at his right hand, ready to help and protect him, while that of the fool is out of its proper place. Nor can we discover in this passage, as Plumptre imagines, "another trace of the Greek influence which pervades the book," as if the writer referred to right and left respectively as the lucky or unlucky quarter. The preposition made use of (לְ) indicates direction, and the meaning of the saying is, as Knobel, Delitzsch, and others explain it, the heart of the wise leads him always to the right or the proper side, while the heart of the fool leads him to the left, *i.e.* in the wrong direction. Delitzsch mentions in a note that the verse is jocosely applied among the Jews to the study of a book (of course written in the Hebrew language, and consequently read from right to left, and not from left to right) : " *The heart of the wise man is towards the right*" of the book, that is, he turns the leaves over backwards, and reads over again what he has already read ; " *the heart of the fool is towards the left,*" or the end of the book. The fool turns the leaves forwards, endeavouring superficially to anticipate that which he has not read, having scarcely patience to wait for the end of the work.

3. The K'ri considers the occurrence of the ה of the article after שֶׁ to be incorrect, and directs it to be omitted as redundant. It is not, however, clear but that the ה was purposely inserted by the writer to avoid the cacophony of the two sibilants coming together. But see on chap. vi. 10. The writer in this verse speaks more fully of the progress of the fool in the wrong direction whither his foolish heart inclines him to go. In order to emphasise the path of error, the clause is inverted, and בַּדֶּרֶךְ is placed before כְּשֶׁסָּכָל. The writer, as Hitzig justly remarks, does not describe the fool on a journey, but the fool in the common path of life. If he were only to keep at home, his folly would remain undetected, but he must needs go out of doors, and then he is sure in some way or other to proclaim himself a fool. Comp. Prov. xvii. 28. חֲסַר־לֵב *deficient in heart*, or *understanding*, is

a phrase which occurs eleven times, and always in the Book of Proverbs, where it is applied to a fool, as Prov. vi. 32; vii. 7, etc.; and so Herzfeld and Ginsburg explain this passage in Koheleth. But the order of the words and the suffix is, according to Delitzsch, against this view, and hence we must render, not "*he lacks his heart,*" but "*his heart* (his understanding) *fails him.*" On the various significations in which the word heart (לֵב) occurs in Scripture, see Delitzsch's *Biblical Psychology*, chap. iv. § 12, on the "heart and head." The clause וְאָמַר לַכֹּל סָכָל הוּא signifies "*and he says to every one that he himself is a fool*" (*se esse stultum*). The expression is, as Delitzsch notes, similar to that in Ps. ix. 21, "*that the heathen may know,* אֱנוֹשׁ הֵמָּה. *that they are* (mere) *men.*" But the Vulg. renders *omnes stultos æstimat*, and Symm., as known here from Jerome's transl., *suspicatur de omnibus quia stulti sunt*. Köster, Knobel and Ewald render סָכָל הוּא by "*it is foolish,*" to which Hitzig rightly objects that כֹּל is not used of actions or things.

4. This verse commences a new section. רוּחַ is used here in the sense of *anger*, as in Judg. viii. 8; Isa. xxv. 4; Prov. xxix. 11; Zech. vi. 8. See my *Bampton Lectures on Zechariah*, p. 139. מְקוֹמְךָ, *thy place, post*, or *position*. The use of מָקוֹם in this signification is peculiar, but the translation is justified by the analogy of מַצָּב and מַעֲמָד, both used in a similar sense in Isa. xxii. 19. Compare the use of מָקוֹם in the closely related passage in verse 23 of that chapter. So Herzfeld, Delitzsch, etc. But Knobel, Hitzig and others render, "*do not lose thy self-possession;*" there are, however, no analogies to justify that translation. Others suppose the author refers to actual locality. Comp. 1 Sam. xix. 10; xx. 25, 27. מַרְפֵּא, which appears also in the form מַרְפֶּה, Jer. viii. 15, is generally used in the sense of *healing*, and this is the sense in which the word is taken by the LXX., Vulg., Syr. and Targ. Such a meaning, although defended by Dale, is not suitable here. Symmachus renders here ὅτι σωφροσύνη παύσει ἁμαρτήματα πολλά. The word is used in Prov. xiv. 30; xv. 4, in the sense of *mildness, calmness*. So Herzfeld, Zöckler, Delitzsch. Zöckler is unintentionally misrepresented in the English edition of his comm. as if he gave the rendering *yielding*, which is in the A.V. Graetz, connecting מרפא with רִפְיוֹן, renders it by *laziness*, making the passage to mean that the indolence which abandons a post too readily gives rise to suspicion on the part of the king

that great offences have been really committed by the individual who acts in such a manner. Renan seems also to adopt this view. Herzfeld is correct in considering that the "great sins" or "offences" spoken of in the passage are not those of the monarch, for an Oriental would not thus express himself, but rather the "sins" or "blunders" of the subject who has fallen, justly or unjustly, under royal displeasure. In some aspects the advice is similar to that in Prov. xv. 1. Comp. the language of James v. 20.

5. After being led to allude to the mistakes which draw forth anger on the part of the ruler, and can often be pacified by calmness on the side of the subject—for the proper demeanour of a subject frequently leads a monarch to pass over even serious offences—Koheleth now proceeds to notice blunders on the other side. He approaches this subject with evident caution. The simplest rendering of the passage before us appears the best, "*there is an evil that I have seen under the sun, like an oversight which proceeds from the ruler.*" This verse of Koheleth is referred to in *Kethuboth*, 23 *a*, on which passage compare the very important remarks of Biesenthal on quotations from the Scriptures in the Talmud, in his *Trostschreiben des Apostels Paulus an die Hebräer*, p. 57. The prep. in כִּשְׁגָגָה is not to be rendered with Knobel, and others, "*in consequence of.*" The writer only touches lightly on the point. He does not affirm in the previous verse that the anger of a king is always to be justified, though he drops a suggestion as to how the royal anger may be pacified, even in cases where the subject is to be blamed. So here he does not assert that the mistakes noticed are really due to the monarch, but merely says that there are cases in which they appear to come from that quarter. Ginsburg's rendering of שגגה by *outrage* is far too strong. יֹצָא for יֹצְאָה, part. fem. of יצא after the analogy of verbs ל״ה, vid. Ges., *Lehrgeb.*, p. 418; Ges.-Kautzsch, § 75, rem. 21 *c*; Ewald, § 189 *f*; Kalisch, § lxvi. 1 *b*. הישליט. See Glossary. This does not refer to God, as several Jewish commentators and Hengstenberg suppose, but to an earthly monarch.

6. הַסֶּכֶל is here abstract from concrete, personified and impersonated folly. The LXX., Aq., Symm., Syr., Vulg., Targ. either read הַסָּכָל, *the fool*, or have given that translation as expressing the real sense of the passage. Graetz maintains that there is no contrast between the סכל and עשירים, and, therefore, proposes to amend the text by

rendering הישפל, *the man of low degree*, which arbitrary alteration has been endorsed by Renan. במרומים רבים. Not "*in many heights*," but "*in great heights*," the רבים stands as it were in a sort of apposition, and hence has not the article, vid. Kalisch, § lxxxiii. 15 *c*; Ges.-Kautzsch, § 111, 2 *b*. עֲשִׁירִים, *rich*, is used in the sense of *nobles*. Comp. the similar use of שׁוֹעַ in Isa. xxxii. 5.

7. Riding on horses was a mark of the nobility, Jer. xvii. 25; 2 Chron. xxv. 28; Esth. vi. 8, 9. Compare on the thought here, Prov. xix. 10. Justin says of the Parthians, "equis omni tempore vectantur. . . . Hoc denique discrimen inter servos liberosque est, quod servi pedibus, liberi non nisi equis incedunt" (Lib. xli. 3). Graetz sees in this verse a vivid picture of the days of Herod the Great.

8. It is impossible within our limits to attempt to give a sketch of the opinions of scholars of various times on the connexion between these verses and the foregoing. The verses, on the consideration of which we are now entering, seem specially to recommend prudence by pointing out the dangers which beset even the most necessary actions. On גוּמָּץ, which only occurs here, see Glossary. יפול might here indicate the future, and express a necessary consequence, as in Prov. xxvi. 27, in which case the first clause of the aphorism would be identical in sense with the maxim there set forth; but it may also be taken, with Delitzsch, as intimating a result that is merely possible, which is more in accordance with the aphorisms to be found in the immediate context. The second clause tends to show that Koheleth does not refer to the case of one who plots the ruin of another but falls himself into the pit he has made. For the wall mentioned in the second clause is not a neighbour's landmark, or a fence through which one breaks to steal his neighbour's fruit, but some old wall or fence which requires for some cause to be renewed, in the crannies and nooks of which, however, serpents have been wont to make their nests, so that the man who breaks it down incurs the danger of being bitten, and ought, therefore, to go cautiously about the work. It is quite beyond the object of the writer to allude under these similitudes to the dangers encountered in all attempts to subvert the structure of a despotic government, which Ginsburg considers to be the drift of the passage. The moral intended to be enforced is rather, be cautious and circumspect, and make due provision in

all cases in order to guard against dangers which may naturally be anticipated.

9. These aphorisms are to the same effect. מַסִּיעַ אֲבָנִים is *one who removes stones*, after the analogy of 2 Kings iv. 4; or *one who breaks or cuts stones*, after that of 1 Kings v. 31. The latter is most likely the real meaning. יֵעָצֵב בָּהֶם, *may be hurt by them*, alludes probably to the accidents which happen to stonecutters. Hence we are inclined to regard בּוֹקֵעַ עֵצִים as signifying the *woodman* or *forester*, *he who splits or cuts down trees*. עֵצִים might mean pieces of wood used for firewood, Lev. i. 7; iv. 12, but it can also mean *trees*, as in chap. ii. 6. It seems more probable that the writer has in view the dangers of accidents happening to the woodcutter such as mentioned in Deut. xix. 5, rather than the lesser dangers experienced in chopping firewood. יִסָּכֶן, *shall be endangered*. See Glossary. The LXX. rightly, κινδυνεύσει ἐν αὐτοῖς. Less correctly the Vulg. *vulnerabitur*.

10. This, linguistically speaking, is confessedly the most difficult passage in the Book of Koheleth. קֵהָה is an intransitive piel, and means *to be blunt*, as is evident from the use of the cognate verbs in Chald. and Syr. It occurs in kal in reference to the teeth, in Jer. xxxi. 29, 30; Ezek. xviii. 2, in the three places in the same form, and is rendered by our A.V. by "*set on an edge*." The former transl. is, however, more correct, though, according to our manner of speaking, less appropriate. פָּנִים, which properly means the *face, countenance*, has been explained as evidently used here in the signification of *edge*. This idea is elsewhere expressed by פֶּה, *the mouth*, then *edge*, in the oft-used expression, פֶּה " *the mouth* (or *edge*) *of the sword*." The plural פִּים is likewise used in the sense of *edge*, 1 Sam. xiii. 21, as is also a second plural form, פֵּיוֹת, Prov. v. 4. Compare פִּיפִיּוֹת, Isa. xli. 15. In spite of Graetz's objection, לֹא פָנִים, *without an edge*, would be a phrase, as Hitzig observes, formed exactly on the model of לֹא בָנִים, *without children*, 1 Chron. ii. 30, 32; Ewald, § 286 g. Ewald, in the latest edition of his *Dichter d. alt. B.*, has adopted the translation "*without a point*," in place of his former idea, followed by Ginsburg and others, that פָּנִים is for לְפָנִים, and means *beforehand*. The latter translation is from the Vulg. *et retusum fuerit ferrum, et hoc non ut prius;* but, as Delitzsch maintains, such a rendering is impossible and leads to nothing, inasmuch as לפנים means *formerly*, but not *before that*, like וְלִפְנֵי מִזֶּה, Neh. xiii. 4. See

Ewald, § 220 a. Delitzsch considers that פָּנִים is used in a wider signification than merely the *edge*, and that it is rather employed here in the sense of the *face* of the iron. Viewing קֵהָה as a piel in an inchoative sense (see Ewald, § 120 d), and the הוּא as referring to the labourer rather than to the iron, he connects the לֹא with קִלְקַל (which is fully justified by 2 Sam. iii. 34; Num. xvi. 29), and brings out the meaning of the first clause, "*if the iron has become blunt, and he has not whetted the face thereof, etc.*" קִלְקַל, which also occurs in Ezek. xxi. 26, is the pilpel of קלל, with pattach instead of tzere on account of the ק, vid. Böttcher, *Lehrb.*, § 1021 β. The kal means *to be light*, the pilpel *to sharpen*, moving lightly and swiftly up and down (vid. Mühlau and Volck's edit. of *Ges. Lex.*), hence the LXX. ἐτάραξε, and Syr. ܫܚܠ, which renderings, however, afford no sense, though they are evidence in favour of the correctness of the Masoretic text. Graetz tries conjecturally to amend the text in the first clause, and brings out, "*when he has made the iron blunt, then he pitches it into the face, and increases wounds,*" while he abandons the second clause as hopeless. We must not render וַחֲיָלִים יְגַבֵּר with Ginsburg by "*he shall only increase the army*," following the LXX. καὶ δυνάμεις δυναμώσει, if that obscure rendering does not look quite another way. Such a translation requires the interpolation of a considerable exposition in order to render it intelligible. Delitzsch, after Abulwalid and Kimchi, preferably interprets the phrase of the putting to of more strength, the increasing of effort. גִּבֵּר means *to strengthen*, Zech. x. 6, 12, and the rendering of חֲיָלִים, plural of חַיִל, *by strength*, is supported by גִּבּוֹרֵי חֲיָלִים, *mighty heroes*, 1 Chron. vii. 5, 7, 11, 40. Hence this second clause may well mean "*then* (וְ) *he must put forth efforts of strength.*"

The word הַכְשִׁיר in the concluding sentence of the verse is the infinitive absolute hiphil of כשר. It stands here in the genitive governed by יִתְרוֹן, with which it is connected by the accentuation, and is treated as a hiphil noun. The absolute is used instead of the construct; for in the latter case חכמה would be governed by it as an object, whereas it is the predicate of the sentence. Hence the disjunctive accent upon הכשיר. Hitzig would alter the punctuation and read הַכְשִׁיר, the inf. const. governing חכמה in the accusative. He regards the predicate of the sentence to be הַכְשִׁיר הַכְמָה. So also Elster and Zöckler. The clause would then be rendered, "*it is a profit wisely to handle wisdom.*" Delitzsch considers such a combination as absolutely impossible. הַכְשִׁיר, see Glossary, s.v., means "to set in the right position," "to pre-arrange;" and the sentence, according to Delitzsch, means, *the advantage of pre-arranging rightly*, or *of putting to rights, is wisdom*, that is, wisdom brings with it this advantage, that it teaches a man to arrange everything rightly beforehand, and a wise man acts accordingly in this way. It would be possible to explain הִכְשִׁיר (like the hiphil הצליח and הִשְׂכִּיל) causatively, *makes to succeed*. So Knobel, *the advantage of success* (or *of obtaining prosperity*) *is wisdom, i.e.* wisdom is that which secures this gain. But, as Delitzsch argues, the meaning of *making fit* or *equipping*, which is common in post-Biblical Hebrew, is more suitable to the example from which the writer deduces this corollary.

11. The translation of our A.V., "*surely the serpent will bite without enchantment, and a babbler is no better,*" incorrectly renders the אִם. That particle is conditional, "*if the serpent will bite without enchantment.*" בעל הלשון in itself might well be a designation of a *babbler*, as Munster and others of the older expositors explained it. But this does not harmonise with the former clause, nor with the context in which the aphorism occurs. The interpretation of the LXX. and the Syr. is, therefore, to be preferred, who regard the *snake-charmer* as here termed the *lord of the tongue* (LXX., ἐπᾴδων, Syr. ܠܥܣܠ). This designation of the snake-charmer, which is only one of many, is not given, as Delitzsch observes, without a reason, for the tongue is an instrument, like the iron of ver. 10. There is no occasion whatever to suppose that the LXX. and Syr. read בַּעַל לָחַשׁ; they simply interpreted the Hebrew expression. The phrase in our text has been interpreted by the Vulg. of the secret calumniator or slanderer, "*si mordeat serpens in silentio, nihil eo minus habet qui occulte detrahit.* The Targ. renders similarly *a slanderer* (גְּבַר אָכֵל קוּרְצִין). Delitzsch refers in illustration of this rendering to the fable in *Taanith*, 8 *a*, "In the future all the animals will gather together, and go to the serpent and say, 'The lion treads down (his prey) on the ground and devours it, the wolf tears it and devours it, but what advantage hast thou for thy poison?' And the serpent shall say to them, [quoting the words of this text] 'the slanderer also has no profit.'" The fable is given at fuller length from the *Tanchuma* in Dukes' *Rabbin. Blumenlese*, p. 201. By the serpent biting בְּלוֹא לָחַשׁ,

is meant its biting before the charmer has time to make use of his skill in charming (compare בְּלֹא יוֹמוֹ, Job. xv. 32, *before his time has come*). For there are serpents which will not hearken to the voice or tongue of the charmer (Ps. lviii. 5.). Hence, when the passage is examined more closely, one sees that the passage in Sirach (xii. 10) alluded to on p. 41, though at first it appears to have no connexion with this passage in Koheleth, is really based on it, namely, τίς ἐλεήσει ἐπαοιδὸν ὀφιόδηκτον καὶ πάντας τοὺς προσάγοντας θηρίοις; the point of the aphorism of Koheleth is, no skill or wisdom is of any avail if made use of too late. "It is too late to lock the stable-door when the steed is stolen."

12. The lips of a wise man bring favour to him, as well as preserve him (Prov. xiv. 3), but the lips of a fool swallow him up, *i.e.* lead to his ruin. הֵן, abstract used for emphasis, comp. chap. ii. 23. שִׂפְתוֹת. This plural construct form (the absol. שְׂפָתוֹת does not occur) is considered by Knobel and Böttcher (*Lehrb.*, § 684, 8) to be later Hebrew in place of the older dual construct שִׂפְתֵי, but the statement is based on arbitrary assumption. On שִׂפְתוֹת from שָׂפָה, compare קְשָׁתוֹת רִישָׁתוֹת, and אוֹת, אֲתוֹת, in which words also the plural וֹת is attached to the fem. ending. On the sing. verb. תְּבַלְּעֶנּוּ, comp. chap. iv. 18. The suffix. refers to the fool, and not to הֵן; as Schmidt and Umbreit explain it.

13. The fool begins with talking folly, and ends with mischievous madness. His words injure himself and others. Compare Prov. xv. 2; x. 8, 21; xviii. 7. The expression used in the next verse suggests the idea that the writer may be referring to that vain discussion about matters too high for man's understanding which was a striking characteristic of his day. See p. 189, and n. on chap. vi. 11, p. 379.

14. The *and* at the beginning of the verse has almost the force of *moreover*. The word used for the fool (הַסָּכָל) has reference to his *confusion* of thought. He is termed before הַכְּסִיל in reference to his *stupidity* and dulness of comprehension. His words were declared in the previous verse to have their beginning in סִכְלוּת, hence he is himself characterised as a סָכָל. Tayler Lewis, after Rashi, considers the "words" of which the fool is full, to refer to those boasting assertions with regard to the future which are condemned by St. James in ch. iv. 23, and to which our Lord alludes in Luke xii. 20.

These are certainly comprised under the general expression, which includes far more than merely "endless loquacity." The language used by St. James is probably founded on the expression in the verse following. One would have expected גַּם before the לֹא־יֵדַע, but the clause, as Delitzsch notices, signifies here the state or condition, and is directly subordinated to the principal clause after the analogy of Ps. v. 10. In the expressions that follow, מה־שיהיה ואשר יהיה מאחריו, there is a kind of tautology, which is best explained, after Delitzsch, by considering the מה־שיהיה to be more distinctly defined by the words following. That clause proves that the writer is referring to what may occur after the individual's death. Comp. chap. vi. 12·; vii. 14. Hitzig explains the word as meaning, "*man does not know what will happen,*" what consequences his words may have in the immediate future, "*and what may happen after that,*" *i.e.* the more remote consequences, that is, he knows not whether his expressions may damage him now or hereafter. But the sense in which the writer elsewhere employs אחריו is against this view. Ginsburg explains מה־שיהיה to refer to the future in this life, and the second clause to the future after death. In this point he is supported by the Targ. and Ibn Ezra. The ancient versions either have sought to paraphrase the passage loosely, and thus remove the tautology; or have read the perfect (שֶׁהָיָה) instead of the imperfect of the Masoretic text (שיהיה); the LXX. translating τί τὸ γενόμενον καὶ τί τὸ ἐσόμενον, Vulg., *quid ante se fuerit, et quid post se futurum sit.* Similarly the Syr., Symm. and Arab. The Targ. alone keeps to the Heb. text, although it is unlikely that the other translators had any other reading actually before them.

15. עֲמַל הַכְּסִילִים תְּיַגְּעֶנּוּ. Though עמל is masculine, it is here construed with a feminine verb. The idea of Kimchi, that ע is thought of in the sense of יְגִיעַת עָמָל, is rightly viewed by Delitzsch to be impossible. Böttcher considers that עמל is regarded (*Lehrb.*, § 657, 4), as a noun of unity, which is scarcely possible here; or (*Neue Aehrenlese,* No. 1659), that it expresses the collective sense, "*all kinds of toil,* even the slightest." Hitzig maintains that the writer treated the word as fem. to avoid the cacophony of the double yod, which, in other cases when vav conversive precedes, is often avoided by dropping one of the yods. Comp. Neh. i. 4; Lam. iii. 33, and the K'ri in 2 Chron. xxxii. 30. But forms with double yod,

as Delitzsch remarks, are used elsewhere without hesitation, as יָחֵל (Mic. v. 6), יְסָדְנָּה (Josh. vi. 26). A similar instance, perhaps, is מוּסָר which is treated as a fem. in Prov. iv. 13; possibly, according to Böttcher, because the writer there thoroughly identified the מוּסָר, or *instruction* treated of, with *wisdom* or חָכְמָה. (*Neue Aehrenlese*, No. 1279). Delitzsch refers to the fact that the similarly formed noun צָבָא is also of two genders. If עמל הכסילים be understood to mean "*the toil of the fools*," the singular suffix after תִיגְעֶנּוּ must be regarded as a case in which the plural passes over into the distributive or individualising singular. Delitzsch compares Isa. ii. 8; Hos. iv. 8. On the other hand, the clause may be explained, with Herzfeld and others, as "*fools'-work*," or toil such as fools have, and the singular noun may be used in reference to the fool (הַסָּכָל) mentioned in verse 14. Or, it may be explained "fools'-work (vain philosophizing, see n. on verses 13, 14) wearies the man who does not know how to find the way to the city." For עמל הכסילים would then express a single idea, and therefore be feminine, and there would be no synallage of number.

Many interpretations have been proposed for the last clause. It is unnecessary to do more than to allude to the attempts to explain the word עִיר from the Arabic, as signifying *a crowd* or a *caravan*. עִיר is *the city*, and not to know the way to the city is not to know the very simplest matter. The fool is smitten with a judicial blindness, like that poured on the Syrians at Dothan, 2 Kings vi. 18-20. Many perplex themselves with difficult matters, who have no comprehension of even the simplest things. "Isaiah's description of the road to the restored Jerusalem as being such that 'wayfaring men, though fools, shall not err therein' (Isaiah xxxv. 8) supplies," writes Plumptre, "an interesting parallel." Ewald thinks that the writer is complaining of bad government, "a government in which the toil of fools, *i.e.* the wretched heathen ruler, wearies the poor countryman who does not know how to go to the city." He regards the saying as a proverbial expression, signifying that the peasant does not understand how to bribe the great lords in the city (chap. vii. 19), where men rule who are unworthy, riotous, indolent, and sell everything for gold. This is, however, certainly not the meaning of the writer; nor is it necessary to interpret the passage with Hitzig, Elster and Zöckler, of going to the city as the seat of the rulers and officers from whence oppression indeed proceeds, but where redress also may be obtained. Graetz's idea that the writer refers to the peculiarities of the Essenes, who were wont to avoid cities, "living by themselves" (Joseph., *Antiq.*, xviii. 1, 5), is not too farfetched to prevent its being endorsed by Renan. אֶל־עִיר is for אֶל־הָעִיר, and sounds, as Delitzsch remarks, vulgar; πόλις is used in Greek as definite in itself and Athens is generally termed ἄστυ without the article. The very name of Stambūl (Constantinople), however, adds that scholar, signifying as it does εἰς τὴν πόλιν, may serve as an illustration of the proverbial saying, "*not to know how to go* אל־עיר."

16. See remarks on pp. 218, 219. On אִי, see Glossary. "Instead of שֶׁמַּלְכֵּךְ נַעַר the older language would have rather said אֲשֶׁר נַעַר מַלְכָּהּ" (*Delitzsch*). Note the relative used in the genitive in reference to the second person both here and in the following verse. See Ges., *Lehrg.*, p. 745. Ges.-Kautzsch, § 123, 1, rem. 1; Kalisch, § 80, 1; König, p. 136. The analogy of Prov. xxx. 22, would have permitted the use of עֶבֶד here in place of נַעַר; but, as Delitzsch notes, not by any means in the sense in which Graetz expounds it, namely, as a reference to Herod as "the slave of the house of the Hasmonæans." For, though Ziba who was a servant was also called נַעַר (2 Sam. xix. 18, A. V. 17), the noun נַעַר does not mean *a slave* as such, but is identical with the מְעוֹלֵל of Isaiah iii. 12. Renan has in his translation here also followed Graetz. By the *eating* (אכל *i.q.* אכל לחם, Ps. xiv. 4) is evidently meant banqueting such as is alluded to by Isaiah (chap. v. 14).

17. See remarks on p. 220. אֶשֶׁר is only found in the construct plural; the plural being used contrary to general rule not only before the heavy but also before the light suffixes. Thus we find alike אַשְׁרֶיךָ and אַשְׁרֵיכֶם. The form אַשְׁרֶיךָ which here occurs might possibly be regarded as an incorrect mode of writing אַשְׁרֶךָ, in which case it might be viewed as an example of the occurrence of the singular. If viewed as plural it must stand for אַשְׁרָיִךְ. One instance of the singular may be אַשְׁרֵהוּ, Prov. xix. 18, unless that be regarded as defective for אַשְׁרֵיהוּ. The form אַשְׁרֵי occurs in Prov. xiv. 21; xvi. 20. Böttcher (*Lehrb.*, § 699), regards it as a plural of extension (in thought); Delitzsch explains the employment of the plural as having arisen from the use of the word as a kind of exclamation. It properly means *fulness of happiness;* when used as an exclamation it signifies, *O his happiness!* like Aram. טוּבִי, טוּבוֹהִי, טוּבוֹי בן־חורים

might be used metaphorically, see *Ges. Lex.*, s. v. בן. We prefer to take it literally. בעת, *at the right time*, elsewhere expressed by בְּעִתּוֹ (chap. iii. 11), here equivalent to the Gr. ἐν καιρῷ, lit. *in tempore*, perhaps caused by the contrast with בַּבֹּקֶר.—*Delitzsch.* בגבורה ולא ב׳ש׳ is not to be rendered *"for strength and not for feasting"*—as ב does not denote the object (see note on chap. ii. 24)—but rather with Delitzsch, *in manly strength*, i.e. as the strength of a man requires (comp. the plural בִּגְבוּרוֹת, Ps. lxxi. 16, to indicate fulness of strength, or fulness of measure, as in Ps. xc. 10), and not only בַּשְׁתִי, in such a manner that the feast has drinking for its main object. So Kleinert, *"as men and not as drunkards."* בַּשְׁתָה. From שָׁתָה, which is akin to שִׁית, *to set, to place*, comes שְׁתִי, *the warp*, used frequently in Lev. xiii.; from שָׁתָה *to drink*, comes שְׁתִי, *drinking, carouse*, only found in this place, though the fem. שְׁתִיָּה occurs in Esth. i. 8. The LXX. have here καὶ οὐκ αἰσχυνθήσονται, the translators either confounding בשתי with בֹּשֶׁת, or having in mind the known consequences of drunkenness. The Targ. renders בְּחַלָּשׁוּת, *in weakness, neglect*, and similarly the Midrash בְּתָשִׁישׁוּ.

18. Note remarks on p. 221. עצלתים. The dual is most probably *intensive*, so that the word means *great indolence*, and does not refer (as Ewald and others explain it) to the *two idle hands*. See Böttcher, *Lehrb.*, § 687, and specially his *Neue Aehrenlese*, No. 1660, in which he criticises the view advocated by Ewald and Hitzig. See also Kalisch, § 85, 4. יִמַּךְ. On the difference between מבך and מוך, the former being used in a literal signification, the latter in a metaphorical, see Böttcher, § 1147. הַמְּקָרֶה, with the daghesh in the מ, is the noun, *the beam-work*. Hence the remark of the Masora here לית דניש; on the contrary הַמְקָרֶה in Ps. civ. 3 (Masora, לית רפה) is the participle. See Delitzsch, *Textkrit. Bemerk.*

19. See p. 221. עֹשִׂים, indet. third pers. pl. like אֹמְרִים Exod. v. 16, referring, no doubt indirectly (not directly) to the persons spoken of in the preceding verses. לִשְׂחוֹק. The ל denotes the object, *for laughter, for the purpose of merriment*. It can scarcely be regarded as an adverbial clause, as Hitzig views it, after Lam. iv. 5; nor is the clause to be rendered, with Ginsburg, *"they turn bread and wine, which cheereth life, into revelry."* עשה לחם is *to make a feast*, or *prepare a meal*, as Ezek. iv. 15 and in Chald. עֲבַד לְחֶם רַב, Dan. v. 1. Comp. אכל לחם, Gen. xxxi. 54; Exod. xviii. 12, and ἐσθίειν ἄρτον, Matt.

xv. 2, also עָשָׂה מִשְׁתֶּה, Gen. xxi. 8. The clause ויין יש׳ ח׳ is not to be regarded as a relative, but as a co-ordinate clause. So rightly the Hebrew accentuation. יַעֲנֶה might be regarded either as the imperf. kal, or as the imperf. hiphil. Hitzig prefers the latter, explaining it, money "*makes all hear*" him that hath it, *i.e.* "*provides everything*" for him. It is, however, better to take it with Delitzsch as the kal, and את־הכל as the accus. of that sought for, "*money grants all*," answers every wish. Vulg. *pecuniæ obediunt omnia.* Symm. ἀργύριον δὲ εὐχρηστήσει εἰς ἅπαντα. The LXX. give a wide paraphrase of the verse, εἰς γέλωτα ποιοῦσιν ἄρτον, καὶ οἶνον καὶ ἔλαιον τοῦ εὐφρανθῆναι ζῶντας, καὶ τοῦ ἀργυρίου ταπεινώσει ἐπακούσεται τὰ πάντα. The Syr. has also, "*bread and wine and oil are made for gladness, that they may gladden the living.*" Both versions express "oil" which is not in the Heb., and take חיים as an adjective. But the Syr., as Janichs notes, read the passive part. while the LXX. read עֹשִׂים with the Heb. Classical parallels abound, such as Horat., *Epist.*, i. 6, 36, 37, or the passage from Menander, quoted by Clericus, "*but I supposed that the gods which were useful to us were silver and gold only ; for having once established them in the house* (εὖξαι τι βούλει, πάντα σοι γενήσεται), *pray for what you wish, all will be thine.*"

20. See remarks on pp. 222, 223, and the story of Ben Buta given on p. 20. On מַדָּע, see Glossary. On גם comp. Deut. xxiii. 3. בעל הכנפים. The K'ri erases the article as unnecessary. So in verse 3, chap. vi. 10, and in 1 Sam. xxvi. 22. This expression for a *bird* is found also in Prov. i. 17. יַגֵּיד. So according to the Masora ; it belongs to the few jussive forms to be found in the book. In his note on p. 432 in connexion with the critical remarks on the text, Delitzsch asks why did the punctuators, notwithstanding the presence of the י, point the יגיד as jussive (subjunctive)? He remarks, when we consider more closely such questions, the punctuation appears one of the greatest problems of literary history. The jussive may here give a sort of climax to the passage. May not the reading יַגִּיד be regarded as K'thibh, and the punctuation יַגֵּד be considered as a case of an unnoticed K'ri? Comp. שְׁנַיִם שְׁתַּיִם for שְׁתֵּי, שְׁנֵי. See Ges.-Kautzsch, § 97, 2, and note 1 on p. 258.

Parallels cited by Knobel and others are Juvenal, *Sat.*, ix. 102 ff.; Publius Syrus : Nullum locum sine teste esse putaveris. Plumptre compares on the reference to the birds, Aristophanes, *Aves*, 50, 575 ; as also Anacreon's ode to a pigeon.

CHAPTER XI.

1. This passage has been sufficiently treated in pp. 223-227. It is not necessary with our interpretation to explain שַׁלַּח in the sense of *cast away*, it can equally well be taken in the sense of *send*, or *send forth*. The word cannot mean to *scatter* seed. Hitzig, who disputes the correctness of referring the passage to beneficence, urges against the latter view the fact that מצא does not mean *to find again*; but, as Kleinert observes, when one finds that which one has cast away, the idea of *finding again* lies in the very circumstance itself. Hence the signification of the verb is no conclusive argument against the ordinary interpretation.

2. See remarks on pp. 225-228. Delitzsch would explain the phrase נָתַן חֵלֶק לְשִׁבְעָה *divide the portion into seven*, etc. after the analogy of Gen. xvii. 20, וּנְתַתִּיו לְגוֹי גָּדוֹל. He considers the חלק to be the portion which the person addressed has in his possession.

3. See on pp. 190, 229, 230. In *Abodah Zarah*, 31 *a*, this verse is explained by R. Johanan to mean where there is a distinguished teacher one always find traces of his teaching. See also the German transl. of that treatise by Dr. F. C. Ewald, p. 222. הֶעָבִים ought, as Delitzsch notes, to have the accent merca which occurs in the best MSS., and not mahpach, as in the ordinary editions of the Hebrew Bible. Michaelis reads merca, though the majority of his MSS. have the other accentuation. The accentuators rightly connect גשם with the conditional clause. The older language would, according to Delitzsch, in this case have preferred the use of the perfect in both clauses (Ewald, § 355 *b*) to indicate that, as often as the one fact occurs, the other invariably follows. See Driver's *Heb. Tenses*, § 12.

In the second clause the protasis as it lies before us consists in itself of two related parts (compare the two וְאִם, Amos ix. 3), "*and if a tree falls on the south side, and (or) if it fall on the north side,*" i.e. whether it falls on the one side or the other. The athnach, which would have more correctly been placed at יריקו, marks off in a more emphatic manner the protasis from the apodosis; ואם יפול unquestionably begins a new sentence, but there was a necessity for a distinctive of high power to be placed upon the בצפון.—*Delitzsch*.

מָקוֹם acc. of place, followed by שׁ, as in chap. i. 7; compare Esth. iv. 3; viii. 17, where אשר follows. The שָׁם is not here to be con-

Ch. xi. 3-5.] *Critical and Grammatical Comm.* 433

nected with the relative שׁ which precedes, but, as the accents indicate, with the יְהוּא following. So also in chap. i. 7. יְהוּא is the jussive from הָוָה, imperf. יְהָוֶה (though this form actually does not occur), jussive יְהוּ, the vav receiving its kindred vowel, even as yod under the same circumstances is pointed with chirik (יְהִי). The א at the end is only an orthographic addition, found in Arabic in certain cases (Wright's *Arab. Gramm.*, vol. i. § 7, rem. *a*). See on this usage in Hebrew, Ges.-Kautzsch, § 23, 3, rem. 3, and § 32, rem. 6. The form in this particular case, which is variously explained by grammarians, is most satisfactorily treated by König, *Lehrg.*, p. 597. The participle of the verb הוה occurs in chap. ii. 22, see note there. Delitzsch does not regard יְהוּא in this place as jussive, but notes that יְהוּא thus written approaches near to the Mishnaic inflexion of the imperf. of הוה, whose singular is יְהֵא, and plural יְהוּ. Hence certain Jewish expositors regard the form here as plural. The context, however, requires the singular. Ewald (§ 192 *b*) regards the form as Aramaic, הֲוָה always being there used for היה, and the ה passing over into א (§ 142 *c*), the formation being after the analogy of a ו״ע verb, like בּוֹא.

4. See p. 230.
5. See remarks on p. 231. מְלֵאָה see Glossary. In his *Textkritisch. Bemerk.* Delitzsch calls attention to the following facts, viz.: that הַמְּלֵאָה has the daghesh in the מ, while on the contrary in Deut. xxii. 9 and Amos ii. 13, the הַמְלֵאָה has the מ with raphe. Dunash, in his work *Sefer Teshuboth*, written against Saadia (edited by Schröder, 1866), p. 35, maintains that the cause of the daghesh lies in the pausal accent. Delitzsch suggests that the probable cause is the same as noted in chap. x. 18 on הַמְּקָרֶה. With daghesh the word is the substantive, not the participle. Observe the nice distinction between the use of the participial אֵינְךָ יוֹדֵעַ in the protasis, and the use of the imperfect לֹא תֵרַע in the apodosis, as when we say, if thou dost not know that, consequently thou wilt also not know this.— *Delitzsch.* Comp. Ps. cxxxix. 15. See on this subject the remarks in Wisdom vii. 1 ff., and the observations of Marcus Aurelius, x. 26. ταῦτα οὖν τὰ ἐν τοιαύτῃ ἐγκαλύψει γενόμενα. A remarkable parallel to this passage occurs in the New Test. in John iii., where in verses 3 and 6 the necessity of a new birth is insisted on, and in verse 8 the expression is made use of, "the wind bloweth where it

listeth, and thou hearest the sound thereof, but canst not tell whence it cometh or whither it goeth; so is every one that is born of the Spirit."

6. See remarks on p. 231. On אי זה יכשר וגו, see Ewald, § 361. On כשר see Glossary; and on באחד, see also the Glossary under that heading. שניהם refers to the זה and זֶה immediately preceding, which are regarded as neuters. Comp. chap. vii. 18; on the other hand זֶה and זֶה are treated as masculine in chap. vi. 5.

7. See p. 232. There are many parallels to be found in the classic writers. Thus Theognis, 569, λείψω δ' ἐρατὸν φάος ἠελίοιο. Euripides, *Iphig. in Aulid.*, 1218, 1220, ἡδὺ γὰρ τὸ φῶς λεύσσειν. The Masora in 1 Sam. xvi. 7 and here, according to Delitzsch, has לְעֵינַיִם, while in Gen. iii. 6 and Prov. x. 26 it reads לְעֵינָיִם. Comp. Kimchi's *Michlol*, 53ᵇ.

8. See remarks on p. 233. כי אם־שׁ. Knobel and others translate כִי here by *yea*, appealing to Hosea x. 5; Job vi. 21, etc. Heiligstedt renders *immo*. But the ordinary meaning of *quia*, "*for*," assigned by Rosenmüller and Delitzsch, is more suitable. The כִי and אִם are to be taken apart "*for, if,*" as in Exod. viii. 17. The כִי in the second part of the verse is, as Delitzsch notes, the explicative *quod;* comp. chap. ii. 24; iv. 4, 8, 17, etc. Compare Horat., *Carm.*, Lib. I. iv. 16, 17; xi. 7, 8. כָּל־שֶׁבָּא, *all that which is coming, i.e.* in the future. Delitzsch compares *Sanhedrin*, 27 a, מכאן ולהבא *from the present and to the future*, for which the expression לעתיד לבא occurs elsewhere.

9. See remarks on pp. 234 ff. בְּחוּרוֹת only occurs here and in chap. xii. 1. It is a later form of the earlier בְּחוּרִים found in Num. xi. 28. So נְעוּרוֹת, Jer. xxxii. 30 instead of the common נְעוּרִים.

והלך וגו׳. See notes on p. 235. וּבְמַרְאֵי. So the Kethibh has the word in the plural, which is found in Cant. ii. 14. Gesenius regards such plurals as poetic, *Lehrgeb.*, p. 665. The K'ri prefers the singular. The former refers rather to the multiplicity of objects seen, the latter comprehends all in a single point of view. Many MSS. have the K'ri reading. The ancient versions ought not to be adduced as evidence in favour of that reading. במשפט. See remarks on p. 235, and footnote 3, and on p. 236. Hoelemann observes that this verse is the original of one of the most popular of the student songs of Germany, the "Gaudeamus igitur," the early form of which was that of a penitential song of two stanzas. See Du Meril, *Poësies latines du moyen âge* (1847); Schwetschke, *Zur Geschichte des Gaudeamus igitur* (Halle, 1877). The first and third stanzas are :—

"Gaudeamus igitur, juvenes dum sumus;
Post exactam juventutem, post molestam senectutem,
Nos habebit humus."

"Vita nostra brevis est, brevi finietur,
Venit mors velociter, rapit nos atrociter,
Nemini parcetur."

10. והסר כעס. See remarks on p. 237 and footnote. והעבר וגו׳, see p. 238. The sentence of Publius Syrus, quoted by Knobel, is a suitable parallel to the sentiment in the first part of this verse, namely, "tristitiam, si potes, cave ne admiseris." הַשַּׁחֲרוּת. This word only occurs here. It is, as Delitzsch observes, not to be connected with שַׁחַר, *the dawn*, with most expositors, comparing מִשְׁחָר Ps. cx. 3, as in that case it would be identical with the preceding יַלְדוּת, and be tautological, but with the adj. שָׁחוֹר *black*, denoting the time of black hair (Targ. rightly, יוֹמֵי אוּכְמוּת שְׂעַר, *the days of black hair*), in contrast with the days when the hair is grey or white. Hence we render "*manhood*." See Glossary. The LXX. render ὅτι ἡ νεότης καὶ ἡ ἄνοια ματαιότης, thus translating הש׳ by ἡ ἄνοια, which is followed by the Syriac. Janichs considers that the LXX. so translated the word because they derived it from the root שָׁחַר, *to be black*, understanding it metaphorically to refer to the mind of youth as enwrapped in darkness. Johnston seeks (*Treatise*, p. 128) to draw an inference in favour of the Solomonic authorship from the occurrence of יַלְדוּת and מִשְׁחָר in Ps. cx., and that of יַלְדוּת and שַׁחֲרוּת in this passage. But this is verily a grasping at straws.

CHAPTER XII.

1. בוראיך. On the plural and its significance see pp. 238 and 239, and footnotes on both pages. A critic has privately suggested to me that the clause might be rendered "*remember those shaping thee*," and thus be synonymous with "*thy parents.*" But such an interpretation is simply impossible. ברא is never used of *parents*, but is always used

of a *Divine* creation. The singular בֹּרְאֶךָ "*thy Creator*," occurs with reference to God in Isaiah xliii. 1, and בֹּרֵא in the usual participial sense elsewhere in Amos iv. 13, and twice in Isaiah xlv. 7, always in reference to God. The use of the plural here causes no difficulty whatever, see footnote on p. 238.

2. See remarks on pp. 239-245, and footnotes, also pp. 249, 253, 255-272.

3. See remarks on pp. 243 ff. and footnotes, also pp. 253, 256, 262, 272.

4. See remarks on pp. 245-251 and footnotes, pp. 254, 256, 262, 273. The expression on בישפל קול הט' is there sufficiently explained. See on יִשַּׁפֵּל the note on p. 247. Some interpreters have ventured to assign to the verb the signification of "*standing*," in the sense of *ceasing;* appealing to the use of the expression, כְּמוֹ עֵינַיִם, used of *blindness*. But the cases are not parallel. Hence Schmidt and Schelling's translation, "*the sound of the mill stands* (ceases) *at the voice of the cock*," or at cockcrowing, and, what is still worse (inasmuch as the verb is masculine and the noun for *mill* is feminine), the translation, "*the mill itself ceases*," are to be rejected. וְיָקוּם. Delitzsch notes (in his *Textkritisch. Bemerk.*) that this reading, which is the reading which accords with the directions of the Masora, is found in the Frankf. Cod. and the Cod. Heidenheim. The MSS. in general have וְיָקוֹם, contrary to the Masora. See n. 3 on p. 247. It might be possible to regard וְיָקוֹם as an imp. indicative in *o* (vid Ges.-Kautzsch, § 72, rem. 2), but the existence of an impf. in *o*, alongside of an imperf. in *u*, in the same verb would be anomalous.

5. See remarks on pp. 251 ff., 254-5, 256, 257-266, 273-4, and footnotes. The noun חֲתַחְתִּים is explained as a plural of intensity by Böttcher, § 762. The plural signification of such words is not, however, lost sight of. Thus עַפְעַפַּיִם, *the eyelids*, retains its dual force, while the kindred nouns סַלְסִלּוֹת, *all kinds of baskets*, תַּלְתַּלִּים, *palm-branches*, קַשְׂקַשִּׂים, *scales*, etc., all preserve the plural sense.

אל־בית עלמו. See remarks on p. 201. Delitzsch notes that the grave, according to Diodorus Siculus (i. 51), was also called by the Egyptians "an eternal house": τοὺς δὲ τῶν τετελευτηκότων τάφους ἀϊδίους οἴκους προσαγορεύουσιν. Knobel observes that "*domus æterna*" is found in Latin inscriptions (*Inscript. ap. Gruter*, pp. 790, 5; 903, 6; 913. The Targ. Jonathan (on Isaiah xlii. 11) terms the tombs of the dead, בָּתֵּי עָלְמֵיהוֹן, "*their eternal houses.* So Tobit (iii. 6) styles the grave τὸν αἰώνιον τόπον. Delitzsch cites the expressions, *Sanhedrin*, 19 *a*, בית עלמין דהוצל *the cemetery* (*eternal house*) *of Husal*; בחד בית עולם, *in one eternal house*, or *cemetery;* בנו בית עולם, *within the cemetery*; בתרע בית עולם, "*at the door of the cemetery*," *Vayyikra rabb.*, c. xii. See other cases in Glossary under בֵּית עֹלָם. These facts prove the truth of the statement on p. 201. The Syriac translator did not, however, like the expression, and accordingly substituted for it ܒܝܬ ܥܡܠܗ, "*the house of his toil*," comp. Job iii. 17. There is no reason to suppose that the translator had a different reading before him, but it is worth noticing that a critic of authority has suggested to us that the true reading of chap. iii. 11, may have been את־העמל instead of את־העלם. The suggestion does not, however, commend itself to our judgment.

6. See remarks on pp. 266-8, especially the footnotes there, and on p. 274. There is no difficulty whatever in the derivation of the verbal forms תָּרָץ in the second clause, and נָרֹץ in the fourth clause from רצץ, although they are forms properly belonging to a verb ע"י. For it is a well-known fact that verbs ע"ע and ע"י frequently borrow forms from one another.

7. See remarks on pp. 192, 268, 269. וְיָשֹׁב. Jussive, connected with the עַד אֲשֶׁר לֹא of the preceding verse. The contrast in meaning between the jussive, which is used in a subjunctive signification, and the imperf. indicative in the second clause, which speaks the language of fact, has been preserved in our translation. In the *Missing Fragment of the Latin Transl. of the Fourth Book of Ezra*, edited by R. L. Bensly (Cambridge, 1875), there is a remarkable reference to this passage in verse 78 : "nam de morte sermo est : quando profectus fuerit terminus sententiæ ab Altissimo ut homo moriatur, recedente inspiratione de corpore ut dimittatur iterum ad eum qui dedit adorare gloriam Altissimi primum." Justin Martyr seems to refer to this passage of Koheleth in his *Dial. cum Tryph.*, cap. vi., where he says, ἀπέστη ἀπ' αὐτῆς τὸ ζωτικὸν πνεῦμα καὶ οὐκ ἔστιν ἡ ψυχὴ ἔτι, ἀλλὰ καὶ αὐτὴ ὅθεν ἐλήφθη ἐκεῖσε χωρεῖ πάλιν.

8. It is a matter of considerable doubt whether this verse ought to be regarded as the conclusion of the book itself, or as the beginning of the epilogue. There is much to be urged in favour of the former view. We, however, incline to the latter; inasmuch as the

repetition here of the words with which the book opens appears to be a reflection naturally suggested by the stanza with which the previous section closes, rather than designed to be the close of that section itself. The "*and*," with which verse 9 opens, is thus more naturally explained. Delitzsch, however, maintains the opposite view, and his opinion is probably that of the majority of expositors.

The abruptness with which the epilogue is introduced, and its didactic character, have led many critics to maintain that it is an addition by a later hand than that of the author of the book. So Döderlein, Schmidt, Bertholdt, Umbreit and Knobel, as well as Krochmal, Fürst, Graetz, and Renan, who belong to a different category. Knobel assigns the following arguments in defence of this opinion: (1) The entire addition is superfluous, and, in the case of a book like Koheleth, absolutely objectless. (2) Koheleth speaks of himself in this appendix in the third person, while in the book he always speaks of himself in the first person. But note chap. i. 1, 2. This is the more peculiar, since the author, in the epilogue (verse 12), assumes the character of a teacher addressing his hearer as "*my son*." (3) The writer of the epilogue regards piety and the fear of God as the great objects of the teaching of the wise. For, although Knobel admits that the fear of God is recommended in the former part of the book, he maintains that such is not the main object for which the work was written. We need not discuss this subject here, as it has been treated sufficiently in the earlier part of our work. (4) Knobel maintains that the teaching of the epilogue on the question of a future judgment does not accord with the doctrine of the book. But see our remarks on pp. 235, 236. (5) He argues further that the complaint "*of making many books there is no end*" scarcely comes with propriety from a writer who probably lived in the Persian era. Hence the epilogue, according to Knobel, is to be viewed as the work of a later hand.

In favour of the epilogue having been composed by the author of the work, Delitzsch justly urges the fact that the Hebrew in which it is written is indeed akin to the language of the Mishna, but decidedly of an earlier type. The phrases used in it are commented on, sentence by sentence, in the Talmud, as points in the explanation of which there was considerable uncertainty. Delitzsch moreover adduces the following expressions which occur in the epilogue and in the book itself. In verse 13 the words יְרָא אֶת־הָאֱלֹהִים

are repeated from chap. v. 6; while the phrase זֶה כָּל־הָאָדָם is formed on the same model as וְנוֹדָע אֲשֶׁר הוּא אָדָם in chap. vi. 10. יֹתֵר, which is found twice in the epilogue (in verses 9 and 12), occurs no less than five times in other parts of the book (chap. ii. 15; vi. 8, 11; vii. 11, 16), and only twice in any other part of Scripture (1 Sam. xv. 15; Esth. vi. 6). The phrase בעלי אספות in verse 11 is akin to the phrases בעל הלשון in chap. x. 11, and בעל כנפים, chap. x. 20. In verses 9, 10, 11, after two ideas connected together with the copula, a third idea follows, attached ἀσυνδέτως; and the same peculiarity of construction is found in chap. i. 7; vi. 5. The unconnected beginning בהיש קהלת (verse 10), is also like דברתי אני, chap. i. 16, etc.

Other peculiarities might be adduced (and the force of what has been already mentioned will be understood more fully when the passage is examined clause by clause), but these are strong arguments in favour of the unity of authorship of the book and the epilogue, which has never been called in question until comparatively modern times. Such peculiarities could scarcely be invented.

9. וְיֹתֵר. Hitzig observes that this phrase is identical with that in verse 12, save that here it is followed by the indirect narrative, and in verse 12 by the direct. See Glossary. יֹתֵר is properly a participle. Ewald and Hitzig render it as an adjective (übrig ist), "*and over and above (this)* there is to say," etc. Gesenius, Knobel, Delitzsch, and others regard it with equal propriety as taken adverbially in combination with the שׁ which follows. The punctuators have put a great distinctive, zakeph gadhol, on the word in order to sever the connection with the שׁ. Hence we have in our translation rendered "*and moreover (note), that,*" etc. LXX. καὶ περισσὸν ὅτι. Symm., (καὶ) ὑπερβάλλον.

The question arising out of this verse is, who is Koheleth? According to our view, "Koheleth," used here without the article, is contrasted with "the Koheleth" of the preceding verse, which has the article (see pp. 100 ff.). Comp. ch. vii. 27. There would be nothing new in a writer of a later date informing his readers that Koheleth was a wise man, if Solomon were the person referred to, and no fresh information is imparted by the remark that Solomon taught the people knowledge. Both statements would be evident truisms, conveying no additional facts of any kind to the reader. The statements of the verse, too, are peculiarly unsuitable, if supposed to come from the pen of Solomon himself. Nor do they impart much information if supposed to intimate that "the Koheleth," who is represented in the book before us as "a wise man," is the same person who composed the comprehensive people's book, the Proverbs. The expressions appear to us too indefinite to be regarded as a reference to that book. Moreover, every reader of the Book of Koheleth, in which Solomon is unquestionably adduced throughout as the speaker, would certainly be acquainted with the fact that the authorship of the Book of Proverbs was also ascribed to that king. If this be all which the words convey, they may indeed be characterised, with Knobel, as "superfluous" and "objectless." Explained, however, in the sense assigned to them on p. 101, the words are neither "superfluous" nor "objectless." If the author of the book took any share himself in the final redaction of the Book of Proverbs by "the men of Hezekiah" (see pp. 4, 5), and was led, as a result of such work, to apply himself to make a further collection of "wise sayings," the words in question would have far more significance than is ordinarily assigned to them. We cannot, however, go so far as to assert anything as a fact for which no evidence can be adduced. All traces of the author's activity outside the limits of the book before us have unfortunately been obliterated by the hand of time, but we nevertheless abide by the interpretation of the verse presented on p. 101. Johnston, in his *Treatise*, calls attention to the fact that חקר occurs in Prov. xxv. 2, among the first of the proverbs copied out by "the men of Hezekiah," and to the coincidence that in Prov. xxii. 20, 21 כתבתי occurs, corresponding with כתוב in Koheleth, and אמרי אמת corresponding also with דברי אמת.

עוד למד־ד׳ את־העם. On לִמַּד for קִמַּד, see Ges.-Kautzsch, § 52, 2, rem. 1. Kalisch, § xliv. 1; Böttcher, *Lehrb.*, § 1021 γ; comp. מִלֵּט, chap. ix. 15. LXX. ὅτι ἐδίδαξε γνῶσιν σὺν τὸν ἄνθρωπον, which reading האדם for העם Graetz prefers. Aquila and Symm. have λαόν. Field notices that two MSS. (Codd. 23, 253) have in the text καὶ ἐδίδασκε γνῶσιν σὺν τὸν λαόν, which shows the manner in which Aquila's readings crept into the LXX. It was, as is known, the habit of Aquila to translate את when used as a mark of the accusative by σύν with an accusative following, according to a hermeneutic rule of the Talmud. Comp. Derenbourg, *Essai sur l'Hist. et la Geog. de la Palestine d'après les Talmudes et les autres sources Rabbiniques* (Paris, 1867), p. 397. Graetz, *Gesch.*, iv. p. 437. See n. on ch. ix. 2.

Ch. xii. 9-11.] *Critical and Grammatical Comm.* 441

ואזן והקר ת׳. LXX. καὶ οὖς ἐξιχνιάσεται κόσμιον παραβολῶν, which gives little sense, but probably ought to be read, as Prof. Delitzsch has suggested to me, κόσμον παραβολῶν = תִּקֵּן מְשָׁלִים. They must also have read אָזֵן. The Syr. translates אזן by ܐ̇ܙܢ, *he heard*. Aquila, καὶ ἠνωτίσατο, καὶ ἠρεύνησε, καὶ κατασκεύασε παροιμίας. See the Glossary on אזן. On the construction, וחקר תקן מ׳, see above. On תקן, see the Glossary, and on משלים הרבה, the note on chap. i. 16, p. 320.

10. See remarks on p. 101. בקש ק׳. Comp. דברתי אני, chap. i. 16. דברי־חפץ, *pleasant words*, scarcely "*words of comfort*," (*Ginsburg*), comp. אַבְנֵי־חֵפֶץ, Isaiah liv. 12. LXX. λόγους θελήματος, Aq. λόγους χρείας, in the sense of *useful words*. וְכָתוּב יֹשֶׁר. Hitzig would prefer to read וְכָתוֹב, inf. absol., which would be quite possible, but unnecessary. LXX. καὶ γεγραμμένον εὐθύτητος, reading וּכְתוּב. כָּתוּב can scarcely with Ginsburg be translated by the finite verb, "*wrote down*," for being the passive participle it cannot be made to govern דברי אמת as its object. Aquila, the Vulg. and the Syriac, which thus translate, probably read וּכְתוֹב, if not וְכָתַב. כָּתוּב is the participle taken in the neuter sense, *that which was written*, יֹשֶׁר being the accusative of manner. Ges.-Kautzsch, § 118, 3; Kalisch, § 86, 4 c. On the asyndeton in this verse see note on v. 8, p. 439.

11. See remarks on pp. 102 ff. כַּדָּרְבֹנוֹת. The LXX., Aq., Theod., translate ὡς τὰ βούκεντρα, Gr. Ven., ὥσπερ βουπλῆγες. The word, notes Delitzsch, is one of the three names for goads mentioned in the Jerusalem Gemara (*Sanhedrin*, x. 1), דרבן from דרב, ذرب, *to sharpen, to point;* מַלְמָד, from למד, *to teach, to exercise in;* and מַרְדֵּעַ, from רדע, ردع, *to hold back, repellere.* He calls attention to the fact that the ָ is *ā*, or more precisely the full vowel, like Swedish å; not ŏ, as Gesenius, Ewald and Hitzig have erroneously regarded it, for the so-called light metheg, which under certain circumstances can be changed into an accent (munach, merca, etc.), and kametz-chatuph mutually exclude one another. See Baer's *Metheg-Setzung*, § 18 and § 27 end, in Merx's *Archiv.* See also Ges.-Kautzsch, § 9, rem. 2. Kautzsch observes that this fact is confirmed by the Babylonian punctuation, as well as by the original Jewish grammarians, though not on rational grounds. See Kimchi's *Michlol*, ed. Fürth, 153 *b* and 182 *b*. In his *Textkritik. Bem.*, Delitzsch notes that the kametz is great kametz (קמץ גדול opposed to קמץ חטוף), and can,

therefore, have the accent munach in place of metheg. Gesenius (in *Thes.*), Hitzig, Heiligstedt and others explain the word as meaning *pricks*, the words of the wise being so termed because they penetrate deep into the memory and hearts of men. But, as Delitzsch observes, for *pricks*, *aculei*, the Hebrews used קוֹצִים, while the דרבנות were goads used for driving onwards, therefore *stimuli*, as the Vulg. renders. He calls attention to the paronomasia between דברי and דרבנות. On משמרות and נטועים see Glossary. On the בעלי אספות, see remarks on pp. 102 ff. and notes. Heiligstedt explains the term as "*lords of collections*," i.e. sayings which are collected, or *collected sentences*. Kimchi, Grotius, Michaelis, Schmidt, and others interpret the phrase as *collectors of sentences*. Not very dissimilarly Tyler, "*editors of collections*," learned men who collect together proverbs as ears of corn, gathering up the sayings of the sages before them. Graetz (see p. 98) proposes to read בעלי אספות נתנום, explaining it, the members of the Sanhedrin have handed them down from one Shepherd. In the former clause he would also read תקועים in place of נטועים.

Kleinert renders the passage, "words of the wise are as spikes (Spiesse) and as nails driven in as protectors of the treasure-chambers, placed by one Shepherd." He explains the אספות to be equivalent to the אספים of 1 Chron. xxvi. 15, 17; Neh. xii. 25, meaning *storehouses*, and the בעלי אספות to be *the keepers*, or *protectors of those treasure chambers* of the temple. He calls attention to the fact that the doors of the temple were provided with מִסְמְרִים (מַסְמְרוֹת, 2 Chron. iii. 9; i.q. כַּמַּשְׂמְרוֹת in this passage), *nails*. He considers Koheleth to compare his proverbs to such nails as guarding the sacred storehouses; the meaning being that no person without a commission from heaven should touch or add to the sacred collection of proverbs. The writer, according to him, closes his book with a warning like that in Rev. xxii. 18, 19. Kleinert thinks that the incorrect explanation of this verse gave rise to the tradition regarding "*the fence*," or סְיָג which the Jews of later time strove to erect round the Law (see p. 10 and p. 464). The translation and explanation are ingenious, but withal too recondite. As to the "assemblies" which other learned men have dreamed of here, we read nowhere else about them; and the word אספות, as the cognate אספים (1 Chron. xxvi. 15, 17; Neh. xii. 25) shows, is used of *collec-*

tions of things, not of *persons*. See Böttcher, *Lehrb.*, § 719, 8, vol. i. p. 518.

The Syriac rendering, ܥܳܬܒܳܐ ܕܥܰܠ is explained by Dean R. Payne Smith in his *Thes. Syr.*, as "*qui ad limina sedent*, sc. in consessu sapientum." The Greek translators have all incorrectly regarded בעלי as a preposition (and so throughout this book, comp. the LXX. rendering of chap. v. 12; vii. 12; viii. 8), παρὰ τῶν συνθεμάτων; Aq., παρὰ τῶν συνταγμάτων; Symm., παρὰ τῶν συναχθέντων. The Gr. Ven. better, δεσπόται ξυναγμάτων.

נתנו מרעה אחד. Hitzig reads נִתְּנוּ מִרְעֶה, comparing for the construction Isaiah li. 12. He understands the whole clause to be, "*and like driven-in nails the collected (proverbs), which are presented united as a pasture,*" a very extraordinary statement, signifying that the united proverbs afford a pasture in which one may feed. But the traditional punctuation, מֵרֹעֶה אֶחָד, is supported by the LXX., ἐδόθησαν ἐκ ποιμένος ἑνός, the Vulg. and Syr.; and, moreover, Hitzig's conjecture destroys the very point of the passage, which is to show that the collection of proverbs by Koheleth, as well as the earlier collection by Solomon, is to be traced up to the same Divine origin. See p. 104.

12. See remarks on p. 105. On ויתר see note on verse 8. Hitzig translates the clause, "and for the rest, by these, my son, be instructed," *i.e.* by these sayings of Koheleth (verse 10), not by the sayings of the wise spoken of in verse 11, hence הֵמָּה, not אֵלֶּה. But, as Delitzsch notes, נִזְהַר does not mean *to be instructed*, but is used in the sense of *to be admonished, to be warned*, and מִן, though it might be connected with a niphal, as in Gen. ix. 11; Isa. xxviii. 7, yet after יתר is naturally to be connected with it, and with the verb following (comp. Esth. vi. 6, *Sota* vii. 7, comp. Ps. xix. 12). The מהמה is probably *what is more than these* things, which have already been mentioned. See note on p. 105 and p. 469. Buxtorf, in his work, *De Abbreviaturis Hebraicis*, p. 226, notes that the saying common among the Rabbins, בני הזהר בדברי סופרים יותר מדברי תורה, "*my son, attend to the words of the scribes more than to the words of the Law,*" is founded upon this text.

The second part of the verse is rightly subdivided by the Hebrew accentuation into two clauses, "*of making many books there is no end, and much study is a weariness of flesh.*" The statements are commented on at p. 105. They are well summed up in the words of C. A. Bode (1777), quoted by Delitzsch, *polygraphiœ nullus est finis, et polymathia corpus delassat*, and are well rendered by the LXX., Aquila, and Symm., τοῦ ποιῆσαι βιβλία πολλὰ οὐκ ἔστι περασμός, καὶ μελέτη πολλὴ κόπωσις σαρκός. It is highly probable that in an age of mental unrest like that in which Koheleth lived there were writers who ventured to handle the problems touched on in his work in a different spirit from his own, and that the writer may have here had such in view. It is unlikely that there is any reference whatever, as Zirkel supposes, to the philosophical works of the heathen. It is quite possible that the writer may have had in his mind the numerous works of Solomon alluded to in 1 Kings v. 12, 13. Tayler Lewis's idea, defended at length in his Appendix to Zöckler's Introd. pp. 31 ff., that ספרים is here used in the sense of *chapters* or *sections* of the preceding books, and that the clause means "*of making many chapters, sections, cantos, or books, there is no end,*" is utterly unsupported by the usage of the word, and was plainly invented to answer Zöckler's argument in favour of the late date of the book drawn from this allusion to a numerous literature; an argument however, to which only a very subordinate weight is to be allowed on account of the very scanty information we possess on the subject. Hitzig would render the sentence, "*of making books without end is a weariness of the flesh.*" But Delitzsch remarks that "the *nomen actionis* [inf. const.] עֲשׂוֹת with its object is the subject of the sentence, of which it is said, אֵין קֵץ, *it is without end;* the assertion of Hitzig that it (in this case) should be אֵין לָהּ קֵץ is not justified, because אֵין קֵץ is a virtual adjective, *endless*, as אֵין עָוֶל, Deut. xxxii. 4, etc., and as such is the predicate of the substantival sentence." On להג, which is not to be rendered, with Luther and Herzfeld, by *preaching*, see Glossary.

13. The initial letter in this verse is printed in the Hebrew text large, סוֹף, probably in order to draw attention to the importance of the passage. סוֹף is used here in the sense of the *final word*, the *sum* of the words of Koheleth; LXX., τὸ τέλος λόγου, τὸ πᾶν ἄκουε; Vulg., *finem loquendi pariter omnes audiamus*, and so the Gr. Ven. But הַכֹּל for כֻּלָּנוּ, as Delitzsch observes, is contrary to the Hebrew style, and moreover in the whole book הכל is used generally of things, not of persons. Hitzig renders: "*let us hear the end of the*

whole book," which is possible, but would probably have been otherwise expressed; Ewald translates (*Lehrb.*, § 291 *a*), "*the last word of all*" is. וְנִשְׁמָע is regarded by Ewald, § 168 *b*, as a participle in the sense of *audiendum*; but נשמע as participle is only *auditum, that which is*, or *has been heard*, and can have the sense of *audiendum* only when that sense suits the context in which it occurs; that is, in cases where the participle can be rendered as well *auditum* as *audiendum*, which is not the case in this passage. Comp. Lat. invictus = *invincible*. נִשְׁמָע may be here regarded as the pausal form of the perfect, in which case the literal rendering would be "*the end of the matter, all is heard,*" or, as Hoelemann, "enough, all is heard, since, etc.," for what is contained in the book is the essence of all knowledge, and is summed up in the two following doctrines. It is, however, better to take the word, with Delitzsch, as the participle, and render it as on p. 105. The Syr. translate after the LXX. the נשמע by the imperative rendering, "*the sum of the matter in its end is, Hear everything!*" After "fear God and keep His commandments," the Syr. adds at the end of the verse, "for this [namely, 'keep His commandments'] is that which is given by the one Artificer [*i.e.* Maker] to every man," ܣܟܠܐ ܘܗܘ ܝܗܒ ܡܢ ܐܠܗܐ ܠܟܠܢܫ. Ginsburg notes that the הכל נשמע corresponds exactly with הכל נשכח, chap. ii. 16. On the circumstantial clause here comp. chap. x. 11; Deut. xxi. 1; see Ewald, § 341 *b*. "After סוף דבר הכל נשמע, the athnach stands where we would put a colon; the mediating *hocce est* is omitted, as in chap. vii. 12."—*Delitzsch.*

כי זה כל האדם. Hitzig explains this sentence as if a negative clause were omitted, "*and not them only, but this ought every man to do.*" It scarcely means, as Ewald, Herzfeld, after the Vulg. *hoc est enim omnis homo*, for "*this is the whole man,*" that is, the end of man's earthly existence. Similarly LXX., ὅτι τοῦτο πᾶς ὁ ἄνθρωπος; and Symm., πᾶς ὁ ἄνθρωπος; and the anonymous transl. mentioned in Field's *Hexapla*, τοῦτο γὰρ ὅλος ὁ ἄνθρωπος. So Dale and Bullock, after our A. V., "*this is the whole duty of man.*" Tyler explains the clause after the formula of the Mishna זה הכלל, "*this is the general rule,*" or "*this is the universal law.*" These and other interpretations are all open to the objection urged by Delitzsch, "that כל האדם never signifies the whole man or the whole (all) of man.

It means either *all men* (πάντες οἱ ἄνθρωποι, οἱ πάντες ἄνθρωποι, οἱ ἄνθρωποι πάντες), as chap. vii. 2, הוּא סוֹף כָּל־הָאָדָם; or it is equivalent to כָּל־אָדָם, *every man* (πᾶς ἄνθρωπος), as chap. iii. 13; v. 18 (LXX. etc., chap. vii. 2, τοῦτο τέλος παντὸς ἀνθρώπου), and it is more than improbable that the more common expression should have been used here in a meaning unexampled elsewhere." The clause means literally "*this is every man,*" and has been explained "*this is of every man,*" *i.e.* the duty of every man. Zirkel (p. 50) explains it as a Græcism like τοῦτο παντός ἀνθρώπου (ἐστί χρῆμα). Others supply a verb from the preceding clause. Hitzig supplies יִשְׁמְרוּ after the analogy of Deut. xx. 19; and Ginsburg יִשְׁמֹר. Similarly Böttcher (*Coll. Heb.*, p. 176), who regards the predicate omitted here as perfectly intelligible from the connexion of the words. Delitzsch considers the construction as most easily explained from the habit in the Shemitic languages of subject and predicate being often simply united together without any connecting link, it being left to the hearer or reader himself to supply the relation between the two. Thus, Ps. cx. 3, עַמְּךָ נְדָבֹת, "*Thy people (are) freewill offerings,*" *i.e.* offer themselves willingly; Ps. cix. 4, וַאֲנִי תְפִלָּה, "*and I (am) prayer,*" *i.e.* give myself entirely to prayer. So Koh. iii. 19, "*the children of men are a chance.*" So here, "*this is every man,*" i.e. *this is every man's duty.* In *Berachoth*, 6 *b*, the question is asked, "what is the meaning of זה כל האדם? R. Eleazar said, 'the Holy One said, blessed be He! the whole world would not have been created except on account of this (אלא בשביל זה).' R. Abba bar Kahana said, that 'this word is of equal importance as the whole world.' R. Shimeon bar Azzai said (some say, R. Shimeon ben Zoma), 'the whole world would not have been created, save for this command to be given.'"

14. See pp. 105, 106, also p. 236. The article is omitted here with בְּמִשְׁפָּט, while it is expressed in chap. xi. 9, but the "judgment" referred to is determined by the description which is annexed, and, therefore, does not require the article.

על כל־נעלם Comp. κρίνει ὁ Θεὸς τὰ κρυπτὰ κ.τ.λ. Rom. ii. 16, καὶ φωτίσει τὰ κρυπτὰ κ.τ.λ. 1 Cor. iv. 5. The Syriac adds after נעלם the gloss ܘܢܓܠܐ, *i.e.* "*and manifest,*" וְנִגְלָה. The על should not be ignored in translation. It has a special significance here. The athnach, as Delitzsch observes, stands correctly on נעלם, as that word is not closely connected with what follows; the אם־טוב ואם רע belongs to the כל־מעשה which precedes, which is accentuated with zakeph katon to emphasize its importance.

The Book of Koheleth is one of the books referred to in the Masoretic mnemonic יתקק. The books so noted are Isaiah, indicated by the י, the Minor Prophets by the ת (תריסר, *the Twelve*), the double ק denoting severally Koheleth and Lamentations (קינות). In reading these books in the synagogue, in order to avoid the harsh expressions with which they close, the verse preceding the last is required to be repeated by the reader at the end.

APPENDIX.

EXCURSUS I.—The Talmud and the Old Testament Canon, with special reference to the Hagiographa.

EXCURSUS II.—On the Talmudic statement that "the Holy Scriptures defile the hands."

EXCURSUS III.—"The Men of the Great Synagogue."

EXCURSUS IV.—Grammatical peculiarities of the Book of Koheleth, and Glossary.

EXCURSUS I.

THE TALMUD AND THE OLD TESTAMENT CANON.

THE principal passage of the Talmud which speaks of the Canon is as follows. The difficulties experienced with respect to the Book of Ecclesiastes will be found noticed in § 3.

§ 1. THE TRADITION AS TO THE CANON :—

The great passage generally appealed to as giving the opinion of the Synagogue with respect to the Canon occurs in *Baba Bathra*, 14 *b* and 15 *a*. In order that it may be better understood we have thrown it into paragraphs with explanatory remarks, noting, after the example of Strack,[1] the questions and objections it contains.

"*Our Rabbis have handed down* (ת"ר i.e. תנו רבנן) *that the order of the Prophets* (סדרן של נביאים) *is Joshua, and Judges, Samuel and Kings, Jeremiah and Ezekiel,*[2] *Isaiah and the Twelve* [Minor Prophets].

"[*Question.*] Hosea is the first [of the Minor Prophets], because it is written, *The beginning of the word of the Lord to Hosea* [Hosea ii. 1]. And how [did he speak first] to Hosea? Rabbi Johanan[3] says that he was the first of four prophets who prophesied at the same time, and these were, Hosea, Isaiah, Amos, and Micah. Should then Hosea stand first [*i.e.* before Jeremiah, or

---

[1] See his article on the *Kanon des Alten Testaments*, in Herzog-Plitt, *Real-Encyklopädie f. protest. Theologie und Kirche*. 2te Aufl. Band vii. (1880).

[2] Jeremiah occupies this place because his work contains many chapters which are a continuation of the history contained in the Second Book of the Kings. Considerable variation prevails as to the order in which the books of the greater prophets follow one another in Hebrew MSS. See Strack, pp. 433, 441. It may be well here to note that the Baraitha itself (ת"ר), i.e. the text of the old tradition, is given above in italics in order to distinguish it from the observations made thereon by the later Talmudists.

[3] That is R. Johanan ben Nappacha. Strack notes that he was brother-in-law of the Resh Lakish.

before Isaiah as the first of the four contemporaneous prophets] at the commencement (ואיקדמיה להושע ברייתא) ? [*Reply.*] Forasmuch as his prophecy was written (כיון דכתיב נבואתיה גבי חגי וגו׳) along with Haggai, Zechariah and Malachi, and that Haggai, Zechariah and Malachi are the end of the prophets, it was reckoned along with them (חשיב ליה בהדייהו). [*Objection.*] But it might have been written by itself (וליכתביה לחודיה), and (have been placed) at the beginning [*i.e.* before Jeremiah]? [*Reply.*] Because it is so small it might be lost (איידי דזוטר מירכס). [*Question.*] Then Isaiah (lived) before Jeremiah and Ezekiel, (therefore) Isaiah stands first at the beginning (before both)? [*Reply.*] Forasmuch as (the Book of) Kings ends with destruction, and all Jeremiah is about destruction, and the beginning of Ezekiel is about destruction, and its close about consolation, and all Isaiah is about consolation, we join destruction to destruction, and consolation to consolation [*i.e.* the Book of Isaiah is for this reason placed according to the Jewish order immediately after the Books of the Kings].

"*The order of the Kethubim* [the Hagiographa] *is: Ruth*[1] *and the Book of the Psalms, and Job, and Proverbs, Koheleth, the Song of Songs, and Lamentations, Daniel, and the Roll of Esther, Ezra, and the Chronicles.*

"[*Question.*] And if any one says Job was in the days of Moses, therefore Job should be first at the commencement (of the Hagiographa)? [*Reply.*] It [the book of Job] begins with misfortune, we do not (thus) begin [a division of the Scriptures]. [*Objection.*] Ruth even (tells of) misfortune [to wit, famine and exile, the death of Elimelech and his sons]. [*Reply.*] It is misfortune which has a happy end (היא פורענות דאית ליה אחרית). For Rabbi Johanan says, Wherefore was her name called Ruth? Because David descended from her who refreshed [שֶׁרִוָּהוּ, lit. *caused him to drink*] the Holy One, blessed be He! with songs and praises.[2]

"[*Question.*] And who wrote them [*i.e.* the various books of Holy Scripture]? [*Reply.*] Moses wrote his book and the section concerning Balaam [containing, as Rashi notes, "his prophecy and his parables,

---

[1] It is placed thus at the beginning because it closes with the genealogy of David, the author of the majority of the Psalms.

[2] This derivation of רוּת from Heb. רָוָה, Chald. and Syriac רְוִי, is ingenious, but, of course, not the real etymology of the word.

§ 1. *The Talmud and the Old Testament Canon.* 453

although they are not necessary parts of Moses and his Law, and the series of his doings "]. Joshua wrote his book and the eight verses of the Law [Deut. xxxiv. 5–12]. Samuel wrote his book, and Judges, and Ruth. David wrote the Book of Psalms with the assistance of [or, in the place of, י״ע, *i.e.* על ידי [1]] ten elders, with the help of Adam the first [part of Ps. cxxxix. is ascribed to him, especially vv. 15, 16, 17], with the help of Melchizedek [Ps. cx.], and with the help of Abraham [2] [Ps. lxxxix.], Moses [Ps. xc.], Heman [Ps. lxxxviii.], Jeduthun [Pss. xxxix., lxii., lxxvii.], Asaph [Pss. l., lxxiii.–lxxxiii.], and the three sons of Korah [Pss. xlii.–xlix., lxxxiv., lxxxv., lxxxvii., lxxxviii.]. Jeremiah wrote his book, and the Books of Kings and Lamentations. Hezekiah and his college wrote ([3] חזקיה וסיעתו כתבו ימש״ק סימן) Isaiah, Proverbs, the Song of Songs and Koheleth. The Men of the Great Synagogue wrote ([4] אנשי כנסת הגדולה כתבו קנד״ג סימן) Ezekiel and the Twelve (Minor Prophets), Daniel, and the Roll of Esther. Ezra

---

[1] Ethan the Ezrahite (הָאֶזְרָחִי), the author of Ps. lxxxix., is identified (*Baba Bathra*, 15 *a*) with Abraham, on the supposition that Abraham is referred to in Isaiah xli. 2, "who hath raised up the righteous man from the east (מִמִּזְרָח)."

[2] Strack and other scholars render על ידי "*with the help of*," and the phrase is often used in that signification. But it is also used in the sense of "*in the room of,*" and so Bloch explains the phrase in this place in his *Studien zur Gesch. der Sammlung der altheb. Lit.*, pp. 126 ff. He quotes *Shekalim*, i. 6, 7, השוקל על יד אשה על עני על יד, עבד על יד קטן פטור מקולבן. "he who pays the temple-shekel on behalf of a woman, for a poor person, for a servant, for one under age, is free from the exchange" charged on such occasions. So in *Megilla*, 24 *a*, ואם היה קטן אביו או רבו עובדין על ידו, *and if he is young, his father or his teacher shall do it in his stead.*" Hence Bloch explains the passage above to mean that David wrote the Psalms in question for the ten elders whose names are found mentioned in their titles, *i.e.* he put these Psalms in their mouths, and wrote, as it were, from the several standpoints which those older patriarchs might have been supposed to have severally occupied. If this be the meaning of the passage, it shows that the Talmud recognised such literary devices as perfectly lawful and in no way inconsistent with Divine inspiration.

[3] ימש״ק is the mnemonic word (סימן) for the books whose names follow : י for *Isaiah*, מ for משלי *Proverbs*, ש for שיר השירים *the Song of Songs*, and ק for *Koheleth.*

[4] The mnemonic קנד״ג or קנד״ג is very peculiar, as the letters of which it is composed are not the initials as in the former case, but are in most cases medials. Strack and others explain it thus, ק for יחזקאל, *Ezekiel*, נ for שנים עשר, *the Twelve* (Minor Prophets), ד for *Daniel* (the only *initial* letter used in the mnemonic) and ג for מגלת אסתר, the Roll of Esther.

wrote his book and the Genealogies (וַיַחְסֵם) of the Book of Chronicles down to himself.[1] This is a proof in favour of Rab; for Rab Jehudah said on the authority of Rab, that Ezra did not go up from Babylon until he had written out his genealogy, and then he went up. And who completed it [the Book of Ezra]? Nehemiah ben Hachaliah. Mar [supposed by some to have been the author of this Baraitha, or supplementary addition to the Mishna] says, Joshua wrote his book, and eight verses of the Law. The tradition is, as one might say, that Joshua wrote the eight verses of the Law from, *and Moses the servant of the Lord died there* [Deut. xxxiv. 5]. . . . And Joshua wrote his book; and the writing, *and Joshua the son of Nun the servant of the Lord died* [Joshua xxiv. 29 ff.], Eleazar finished it. And the writing, *and Eleazar the son of Aaron died* [Jos. xxiv. 33], Phinehas finished. Samuel wrote his book. And the writing *and Samuel died* [1 Sam. xxv. 1 ff], Gad the seer finished and Nathan the prophet.

This passage in the Talmud (as may be seen from its perusal *in extenso*) does not profess to impart information respecting the manner in which the Old Testament canon was formed. It does, however, contain a list of all the books regarded as canonical, and proposes to give information as to the mode in which they assumed their present shape and appearance. But it is taken for granted that throughout the books referred to are books *sui generis*, books of authority, whether handed down originally in writing, or committed to the memory of faithful disciples, and thus transmitted to posterity long prior to the time when the prophecies alluded to were written in a book and arranged in the order in which they now appear in the Jewish Scriptures.

It is clear, as Strack observes, that the sense of the passage above entirely depends upon the signification assigned to the word כָּתַב, *to write*, which in one form or other occurs so frequently within its compass.[2] Herzfeld has strangely endeavoured to show that it is used here in five distinct significations, but his views on this point have rightly been rejected by scholars. It is also putting violence on the word to regard it, without some qualifying statement in the

---

[1] עד לו. Rashi explains the clause to mean "as far as his (Ezra's) own genealogy. But R. Chananel says that לו here stands for ולו, the first word of 2 Chron. xxi. 2, which verse Ezra had prefixed to his own genealogy. See Levy, *Neuheb. u. Chald. W.B.*, s. v. כתב.

[2] See his article on the Canon, p. 418.

§ 1. *The Talmud and the Old Testament Canon.*

context, as signifying to *write in*, or *to introduce* into the canon.[1] Strack rightly maintains that Rashi in his Comm. on the passage in *Baba Bathra*, has given the correct interpretation of the word. A summary of Rashi's comments as given in Buxtorf's *Tiberias*, p. 91, will be found in pp. 5, 6. But it may be well to give here a full translation of his remarks. They are also cited in Strack's article.

"The college of Hezekiah wrote the Book of Isaiah, for Isaiah was put to death by Manasseh, but the prophets wrote their books first before [*i.e.* not until immediately before] their death (שלא היו הנביאים כותבים ספריהן אלא לפני מותן) . . The Men of the Great Synagogue, Haggai, Zechariah, Malachi, Zerubbabel, Mordecai, and their comrades, wrote the Book of Ezekiel. I know not any other reason why Ezekiel himself did not write it [his book], except that his prophecy was not designed to be written outside (of Palestine). They wrote therefore his prophecies after they went to the [Holy] Land. And so with the Book of Daniel who lived in exile, and with the Roll of Esther. The Twelve Prophets, because their prophecies were short, did not write them, (that is) each prophet (did not write) his own book. When Haggai, Zechariah, and Malachi went up (from Babylon), and saw (וראו שרוח הקדש מסתלקת) that

---

[1] The word seems, however, to be used in that signification in *Megill.* 7 *a*, where we read: שלחה להם אסתר לחכמים בתבוני לדורות [in place of לד׳, Levy, *Neuheb. W.B.*, s. v. gives from a MS. the reading בספר] כתבתי לך הלא לה שלחו [Levy reads לה, omitting מקרא] מקרא לו שמצאו עד רבעים ולא שלישים שלישים כתוב בתורה כתב זאת זכרון בספר כתב זאת מה שכתוב כאן ובמשנה תורה זכרון מה שכתוב בנביאים בספר מה שבחוב במגלה, "Esther sent to them, to the learned men [the Scribes], write [copy] me for the generations (to come)," or, according to Levy's reading, "write me in the book," *i.e.* receive me (my book) into the Canon. "They sent to her, Have I not written for thee three [שלישים— pointed as שָׁלִישִׁים, Prov. xxii. 20—is here interpreted שְׁלִישִׁים, *threefold*] but not four [which Levy explains in reference to the three divisions of the Canon, viz. Pentateuch, Prophets, and Hagiographa, to which no fourth part could be added]; until that they discovered [as authority] for it [or, *for her*, according to Levy's reading] a passage written in the Law, '*write this as a remembrance in the book* [Exod. xvii. 17],' '*write this*' (זאת) that which is written here and in the Second Law [Deut. xxv. 19]; '*as a remembrance*' (זכרון), that which is written in the Prophets [1 Sam. xv. 2 ff.]; '*in a book*' (בספר), that which is written in the Roll [Levy reads במגלת אסתר, *in the Roll of Esther*];" the latter referring to the fact that the destruction of Haman the Agagite, *i.e.* an Amalekite, is recorded in the Book of Esther. But even in this passage it is the context alone which gives the peculiar significance to the verb "*to write.*"

the Holy Spirit was departed [from Israel], and that they were the last prophets, then they rose up and wrote their prophecies [i.e. those of the Minor Prophets], and they united together the short prophecies, and they made a large book (כתבו נבאותיהם וצירפו נבואות קטנות עמם ועשאום ספר גדול), that they [the books of the lesser prophets] might not perish because of their small size."

The sense of the passage in the Talmud evidently is, that the college of Hezekiah first wrote out and edited for popular use, copies of the Books of Isaiah, the Proverbs, the Song of Songs and Koheleth. In the case of the Book of Proverbs, there was added in the edition thus issued, a number of additional aphorisms, which either had not been written down previously, though preserved by having been committed to memory, or actually found by these early editors existing in separate manuscripts. These proverbs were added to the original book drawn up by Solomon (Prov. xxv. 1). A similar work was performed at a later period by the Men of the Great Synagogue for the prophecies of Ezekiel and Daniel, and of the Minor Prophets, as well as for the Book of Esther ; the contents of these several books having been in former times, committed to memory by disciples interested in the preservation of these sacred relics of antiquity. The preservation in this manner of important works need occasion no surprise, since we know that the body of tradition, comprehended under the name of the Mishna ("*the Second Teaching*") was actually in existence, and taught orally to Jewish scholars, long prior to the time when it was committed to writing by R. Jehudah the Holy ; and moreover that the Mishna itself only comprehended the heads of the various subjects treated of more fully in the Gemara (or, "*Perfection*"), which, though committed to writing several centuries later than the earlier portion of the Talmud, yet contains within its compass material which dates as far back (if not further) as many ordinances found in the earlier collection. Neither the Mishna nor Gemara would have been committed to manuscript, had not the circumstances of the era imperatively demanded the adoption of such a course, which had been long opposed by the Jewish scholars (see p. 482).

Bloch calls attention to the fact that the Baraitha already quoted from *Baba Bathra* was not observed by the strictest Talmudists. The order of the Scriptures followed in most Hebrew MSS. is not that laid down in this part of the Talmud, though it is found in a few

§ 1. *The Talmud and the Old Testament Canon.*

MSS. See Strack, p. 441. For this and other reasons, Bloch maintains in his *Studien* (pp. 19 ff.), that this Baraitha was only the private opinion of some individual teacher, the directions in which, not being backed up by sufficient authority, were not regarded as binding.

The Tosafoth (a commentary on the Talmud) on *Baba Bathra*, 15 *a*, says: "Hezekiah and his college wrote Isaiah: because Hezekiah caused them to busy themselves with the Law, the matter was called after his name. But he [Hezekiah] did not write it (the Book of Isaiah) himself, because he died before Isaiah, since Manasseh, his successor, killed Isaiah." The words are: חזקיה וסיעתו כתבו ישעיה לפי שחזקיה גרם להם לעסוק בתורה נקרא הדבר על שמו אבל הוא לא כתבו שהרי מת קודם לישעיה דמנשה בן ביתו הרג לישעיה:

Fürst, in his work (*Der Kanon des alt. Test. nach den Ueberlieferungen in Talmud und Midrasch*), maintains that the Hezekiah mentioned in *Baba Bathra* as having written or edited the Books of Isaiah, Proverbs, the Song of Songs and Koheleth, was Ḥananyā ben-Ḥiskiyā ben-Garon, or (if the name be transcribed after the fashion of the English Bible), Hananiah the son of Hezekiah the son of Garon, who lived in the time of Hillel and Shammai, in the century before Christ. The Talmud (*Shabb.* 13 *b*), says that "Ḥananyā ben Ḥiskiya ben Garon and his college" (חנניה בן חזקיה וסיעתו) wrote the Megillath Taanith, or the Chronicles of the Fasts, in which the later festivals are pointed out on which fasting was forbidden. The authority of Ḥananya on questions connected with the interpretation of scripture was held in high repute.[1] He is said to have been visited in his old age by Hillel and Shammai and their disciples in the upper chamber of his house, where with his assistance eighteen enactments forbidding all intercourse with the Gentiles were drawn up. This story contains an anachronism (see p. 457). But as Ḥananya is said to have, after much study, harmonised the contradictions supposed to exist between the Book of Ezekiel and the Pentateuch,[2] and mention is made of his "College," Fürst maintains that that body is to be identified with "Hezekiah and his college." Fürst's ideas on this

---

[1] On Ḥananya ben Ḥiskiya, see Bacher's interesting articles on *Die Aggada der Tannaiten*, in Graetz's *Monatsschrift für Gesch. u. Wissenschaft des Judenthums*, for March, 1882, p. 118.

[2] The asserted contradictions are enumerated in *Menachoth*, 45*a*, where the remark is made that Elijah will explain them when he comes. They consist chiefly in differences between the various measures mentioned in connexion with the offerings spoken of in Ezekiel xlvi., and those commanded in the Law of Moses.

point have been generally rejected by scholars. The use of the phrase וסיעתו, and of the name "Hezekiah" in both cases, is a slender foundation on which to erect such a superstructure. The word סיעא denotes *a society* of any kind, whether it be a body of learned men, or of youths under instruction, or even of soldiers. The proper names moreover are far from identical. According to the ordinary reading of the Talmud (*Shabb.* 13 *b*), the teacher referred to was Hananya, whose father's name was Hezekiah. But, according to Graetz (*Gesch. der Juden*, vol. iii. pp. 494–502), his proper name was Eleazar, his father's name being Hananya and his grandfather's Hezekiah.

The Jewish synod, in which the eighteen enactments were passed forbidding all intercourse with the Gentiles, was an assembly in which the doctors of the law belonging to the school of Shammai were more numerous than those belonging to that of Hillel, and in which the decision of the majority was finally accepted at the point of the sword.[1] The Synod met in the stormy days which preceded the final rebellion of the Jews against the Roman power in the days of Trajan. The Megillath Taanith, of which Hananya ben Hiskiya ben Garon was the author, was, according to Graetz, directly connected with that insurrection. An attempt was made about the same time to strike out of the Canon certain books which seemed to contradict passages in the Law of Moses, and the Book of Ezekiel was retained in the Canon mainly through the strenuous exertions of Hananya, Shammaite though he was. In consequence, however, of the efforts of the national party, a ban was placed, probably not for the first time, upon the study of apocryphal writings and of Greek learning in general, which had up to that time been cultivated by many Jews.[2]

§ 2. THE THREEFOLD DIVISION OF THE JEWISH SCRIPTURES.—The triple division of the Jewish Scriptures is mentioned by Josephus in his work *Against Apion* (Lib. i. § 8.), written about A.D. 100.

---

[1] See Jerusalem Talmud, *Shabbath*, i. 6; also Talmud Babli, *Shabbath*, 13 *b*.

[2] Dr. M. Joël, in his *Blicke in die Religionsgeschichte zu Anfang des zweiten christl. Jahrhunderts* (I. Der Talmud und die griechische Sprache), maintains that the opposition to Greek learning and to the Greek translation of the Scriptures, dates really from the time of the great rebellion against Trajan. It is highly probable that the hatred against the Greek language existed at a much earlier period, but that it was revived in the era referred to, when the Romans stepped into the position of the Greeks as oppressors of the Jewish nation. See n. on p. 38.

§ 2. *The Threefold Division of the Scriptures.* 459

He speaks there of the Jewish canon, not as a canon recently agreed upon, but one recognised as authoritative for centuries. "For we have not myriads of books, differing with and opposing one another, but twenty-two books only, containing the history of all past time, which are justly believed to be divine (τὰ δικαίως θεῖα πεπιστευμένα), and of these five are those of Moses, which contain the laws and the tradition concerning the generation of men (καὶ τὴν τῆς ἀνθρωπογονίας παράδοσιν) down to his own death. This period of time embraces nearly three thousand years. But, from the death of Moses to the reign of Artaxerxes, the king of the Persians after Xerxes, the prophets who came after Moses wrote the events which occurred in their time in thirteen books; but the four remaining books contain hymns to God (ὕμνους εἰς τὸν Θεόν), and precepts of life for men (καὶ τοῖς ἀνθρώποις ὑποθήκας τοῦ βίου). But, from the time of Artaxerxes down to our own time, all events have indeed been written; but they (the books) are not deemed worthy of the same credit as those before them, because there was not the exact succession of the prophets (τὴν τῶν προφητῶν ἀκριβῆ διαδοχήν)."

The number 22, here assigned to the Sacred Books, is generally supposed to have been chosen by Josephus as being that of the letters of the Hebrew alphabet (as suggested by Jerome in his *Prolog. galeatus*). Strack, however, considers Josephus simply to have followed in this particular the Alexandrian manner of reckoning. The thirteen books are counted up in the following way—(1) Joshua, (2) Judges and Ruth, (3) 1 and 2 Samuel, (4) 1 and 2 Kings, (5) Job, (6) Isaiah, (7) Jeremiah, and the Lamentations, (8) Ezekiel, (9) The Twelve Minor Prophets, (10) Daniel, (11) Ezra and Nehemiah, (12) 1 and 2 Chronicles, (13) Esther. The four books of hymns and ethics are the Psalms, Proverbs, Ecclesiastes, and Canticles.[1]

[1] The ordinary arrangement of the books in the Hebrew canon is in three great divisions; I. "The Law," called also, "the five-fifths of the Law," namely, Genesis, Exodus, Leviticus, Numbers, Deuteronomy. II. The Prophets—(*a*) the earlier Prophets: Joshua, Judges, 1 and 2 Samuel, 1 and 2 Kings (reckoned altogether as forming four books), (*b*) the later Prophets: Isaiah, Jeremiah, Ezekiel, the Twelve, *i.e.* the Twelve Minor Prophets (all the later Prophets being thus regarded as comprising four books). III. The Hagiographa (or Holy Writings), or Kethûbîm (the Writings), consisting of (*a*) the Poetical Books: Psalms, Proverbs and Job, (*b*) the five Megilloth or "Rolls," to wit, Song of Songs, Ruth, Lamentations, Koheleth, Esther, and (*c*) the three books which have no common name, Daniel, Ezra and Nehemiah (the two latter being counted as one), and 1 and 2 Chronicles, reckoned also as one book, thus making in all twenty-four books.

The statement of Josephus agrees substantially with what Jerome says in his preface to the Book of Kings, which preface is commonly known as the *Prologus galeatus.* Jerome sought to discover a reference to the twenty-two Hebrew letters in the twenty-two books of the Old Testament, and saw also a connexion between the fact that in the Hebrew Alphabet five letters have a double form, the second exclusively employed at the end of a word (ך, ם, ן, ף, ץ,) and the fact that in the Old Testament there are five books which are double, namely, 1 and 2 Samuel, 1 and 2 Kings, 1 and 2 Chron., 1 and 2 Ezra (Ezra and Nehemiah), and lastly, Jeremiah with his Lamentations. The order of the several books mentioned here by Jerome as that adopted by the Jews of his time, is somewhat peculiar. First, the "Thorath" or the five Books of Moses. Next the Prophets, comprehending Joshua, Judges and Ruth (as one Book), 1 and 2 Samuel, 1 and 2 Kings, Isaiah, Jeremiah, Ezekiel, the Twelve Prophets. Thirdly, the Hagiographa, namely, Job, Psalms, the three books ascribed to Solomon, viz. Proverbs, Ecclesiastes (Accoeleth), and the Song of Songs, Daniel, 1 and 2 Chronicles, Ezra (Ezra and Nehemiah), Esther, which is the last in his arrangement, thus making in all 22. He notes, however, that some reckon Ruth and the Lamentations among the Hagiographa, and thus make 24 books, corresponding to the four and twenty elders of the Book of the Revelation. Jerome further observes that the double books were often (*a plerisque*) counted separately,[1] thus making the number of books, 27, as is now generally done. In his Preface to the Book of Daniel he seems to prefer reckoning the books as 24 ; namely, 5 in the Law, 8 in the Prophets, and 11 in the Hagiographa.

Inasmuch as Graetz maintains that the Canon of the Old Testament was not finally settled until the Synod of Jamnia (A.D. 90), he is forced to question the conclusions usually drawn from the statements of Josephus. According to Graetz's contention, the Book of Job could not have formed one of the historical books referred to by Josephus. He denies that Ruth and Lamentations were reckoned parts of Judges and Jeremiah. He would regard Ruth as one of the historical books alluded to by Josephus, and transfer Job to the third division, as one of the books which contained " hymns to God

---

[1] But in this latter point Jerome is incorrect. See Strack, pp. 437-8.

§ 2. *The Threefold Division of the Scriptures.* 461

and precepts of life." Inasmuch as Graetz maintains that the Canticles cannot be included under such a description, he regards that book to have been excluded from the canon of Josephus. He has his doubts whether Koheleth was included therein or not, inasmuch as the four books described by Josephus might be Job, Psalms, Proverbs, and Lamentations, or Job, Psalms, Proverbs, and Ecclesiastes.

Graetz's opinions on this point have not met with the approval of the critics. The testimony of Jerome shows that in his day the Books of Ruth and Lamentations were regarded by some as forming part respectively of the Books of Judges and Jeremiah. It must be borne in mind that, in counting the books as 22, Jerome followed the authority of the LXX. There is nothing strange in the idea that Josephus should have regarded the Book of Job as historical, though, as he nowhere directly refers to that book, we cannot be certain as to his ideas regarding it. The Book of Job is cited by Philo as one of the sacred books. The main object which Josephus had in view in his work *Against Apion*, was to point out the historical faithfulness of the Jewish records, and this naturally led him to speak of the historical and prophetical books as one class. They are alluded to, moreover, only in general terms in one simple sentence, "the prophets after Moses wrote down what was done in their day, in thirteen books;" and the critic who ventures to deny that such a description does not suit the Book of Job as well as the volume of the Twelve Minor Prophets is not deficient in hardiness.

The evidence of Josephus is decisive in favour of the view that the canon of the Old Testament had been closed long previous to his time. For, in the clauses which immediately follow the passage already quoted, Josephus remarks: "but it is evident, indeed, how we believe in our own Scriptures. For, although so long a period has already elapsed, no one has dared to add or to take away anything from them, or to change them. But it is implanted in all Jews directly from their very birth to esteem these books as oracles of God (Θεοῦ δόγματα), and to abide by them, and if necessary, even to die for them." And Josephus contrasts the manner in which the Greeks regarded their literature with the reverence exhibited by the Jews towards the Sacred Writings.

Although modern criticism has made it impossible to endorse in all their details the statements of Josephus on this subject, yet it may safely be maintained that he would not have ventured to use such language had the Canon of the Old Testament been only finally settled at the Synod of Jamnia (A.D. 90).

The only real argument which Graetz adduces in support of his view is that the Palestinian canon of the Prophets consisted only of eight books. In defence of this assertion he adduces the statement in *Baba Bathra*, 13 *b*, that " Boethos ben Zonin had the eight Prophets in one volume."[1] These eight prophets Graetz recounts as Joshua, Judges, Samuel, Kings, Isaiah, Jeremiah, Ezekiel, and the Twelve Minor Prophets. The argument seems to be a *petitio principii*, for it is impossible to prove that both Ruth and Lamentations were not included in the volume as part and parcel of Judges and Jeremiah, which the statements of Josephus, Melito, Origen and Jerome seem to show was an ordinary custom. The number *eight*, on which Graetz lays such great weight proves nothing, as the same enumeration of "eight books of the Prophets," is found in Origen and Jerome.

Following up the hint thrown out by de Wette, that in the expression contained in Dan. ix. 2, "I understood by the books" (בִּינֹתִי בַּסְּפָרִים), reference is made to a collection of the prophetic writings in one volume, Graetz draws an important argument in favour of his peculiar views from the fact that in the old Talmudic writings the prophetic books, as distinguished from the Law, were called ספרים (*The Writings*), which name was only used to denote the books used publicly as lessons in the synagogue, and therefore excluded the Hagiographa, which, with the exception of the Book of Esther, were not thus used.

But Delitzsch has well pointed out that in *Baba Bathra*, i. 6, all the canonical books, without exception, are designated by the appellation כתבי הקדש, " *Holy Scriptures*," and also that in *Megilla*, i. 8; iii. 1, and *Shabbath*, 115 *b*, all the sacred books, with the exception of the Thorah, are spoken of under the term ספרים, "*the books.*" In *Shabbath* 115 *a*, a distinction is made between the Holy Scriptures (כתבי הקדש) in which they read and those in which they do not read (בין שקורין בהן ובין שאין קורין בהן), that is, as Rashi expounds the clause,

---

[1] מעשה בביתוס בן זונין שהיו לו שמונה נביאים מדובקין בא' על פי ראב״ע that is, באחד על פי ר' אלעזר בן עזריה. The Boethus (בְּיתוֹם, Βοηθός) mentioned here was, according to Müller (*Soferim*, p. 44), not the founder of one of the sects of the Sadducees (see p. 131), spoken of in the *Aboth R. Nathan*, chap. v., but a well-known teacher of the Law, who lived in the time of R. Jehudah the First.

§ 2. *The Threefold Division of the Scriptures.*

between the books out of which the haphtaroth, or lessons for public service, are read, and the books from which no haphtarah, or lesson, is selected.[1]

The triple division of the Jewish Scriptures was distinctly referred to by our Lord under the name of "the Law of Moses, and the Prophets, and the Psalms" (Luke xxiv. 44). But it must be noted that it is by no means certain that all the books of the third division in general are included under the heading "Psalms." It is quite possible that our Lord referred only to the Book of the Psalms as being the most important book of that division, and the one in which the most numerous Messianic prophecies are found. See the important observations of Strack on the New Testament evidence in favour of the Canon, on p. 427 of his article. In the New Testament the Jewish Scriptures as a whole are usually spoken of as "the Law and the Prophets," or as "Moses and the Prophets," even in cases in which quotations are made from the Book of the Psalms, which was included in the third division or Hagiographa (Matt. v. 17; vii. 12; xi. 13; xxii. 40; Luke xvi. 16, 29, 31; John i. 45; Acts xiii. 15, 39, 40; xxiv. 14; xxviii. 23; Rom. iii. 21). All the books of the Old Testament are also sometimes spoken of under the title of "the Law" (John x. 34; xii. 34; xv. 25; 1 Cor. xiv. 21), although the Mosaic writings are in general specially referred to under that name.

A like usage may be observed in the Talmud. Though the Pentateuch is specially designated as the Thorah, or "Law," the Holy Scriptures in general are sometimes alluded to under that appellation. Thus, in *Jebamoth*, 7 *b*; *Pesachim*, 92 *a*, the Books of Chronicles are spoken of as Thorah, and so with regard to the Book of Proverbs in *Aboda Zarah*, 58 *b*, while the expression תורה שבכתב, the *Written Law*, is commonly used of all the Old Test. writings. Bloch has (*Studien*, p. 7) also given further instances.

The writers of the Old Test. Scriptures are generally designated in the New Test. as "prophets" (Luke xxiv. 25; Acts xiii. 27;

---

[1] Dr. Joel Müller in his *Masechet Soferim, der Talmudische Tractat der Schreiber* (Leipzig, 1878), pp. 41 ff., has pointed out that the Mishna often designates the Nebiim [the Prophets] and the Kethubim [the third division or Hagiographa] by the one and the same expression, and observes that, while the old Tanaites according to the Mishna (*Yadaim*, iii. 5), designate all the Scriptures by the expressions כתבי קדש, *Holy Scriptures*, and also כתובים, the Baraitha and Tosefta (*R. Hashana*, ii.) speak of the collection of the Prophets and Hagiographa as strictly separated from one another.

Rom. i. 2; xvi. 26; Heb. i. 1), and in the Old Testament, Ezra (chap. ix. 10 ff.), quotes the directions of the Pentateuch as the commands of "the prophets." One may compare with this usage the passages cited by Bloch from the Targums and Midrashim (*Studien*, p. 12) in which the writers of the Hagiographa are similarly designated, and their sayings ascribed to Divine inspiration.

The testimony of Ben Sira to the Jewish canon has been already discussed briefly on pp. 40 ff.[1] For a satisfactory discussion of the various modes of enumeration of the books of the Old Testament as forming 22, 24, and 27 books, we must refer to Strack's able article on the Canon, in which the statements of the Talmud, as well as the testimonies of Philo, Melito, and Origen (which must here be passed over) will be found duly discussed. The student will find these also noticed in Bleek's *Einleitung*, as well in the second and third editions edited by Kamphausen, as in the fourth by Wellhausen. We can here only briefly refer to the evidence of the 2nd Book of Maccabees (chap. ii. 2, 3, 13, 14), which, though regarded by Geiger and Graetz as worthless, is, in spite of the legendary matter with which it is connected, of great importance on account of the testimony borne to the Jewish canon, and the mention there made of the collecting together of the Sacred Writings in the days of Nehemiah, and in the early days of the Maccabees. The writer mentions the Law or Pentateuch in verses 2 and 3, and the other two divisions of the Old Testament Scriptures in verses 13 and 14. The latter are spoken of as "the (writings concerning) the kings and prophets (τὰ περὶ τῶν βασιλέων καὶ προφητῶν)," the former probably denoting the books of the writers styled by the Jews "the former prophets," and the latter the books of "the later prophets," the two ordinary sub-divisions of the writings known as "the prophets." The third division of the Jewish Scriptures is alluded to by the writer of 2nd Macc. as "the (writings) of David (καὶ τὰ τοῦ Δαυίδ)," so called (as, perhaps, in Luke xxiv. 44) from the first book in that division. The epistles of the kings concerning the holy gifts (καὶ ἐπιστολὰς βασιλέων περὶ ἀναθεμάτων) which were deposited in the library of Nehemiah, were probably the decrees of the Persian monarchs having reference to the restitution of the Temple service in Jerusalem.[2]

[1] See on the points connected with the Talmud and Ben Sira, p. 467.
[2] See the observations of Pusey on this head, in his *Daniel the Prophet*, pp. 305, ff.

§ 3. *The Aboth of R. Nathan.*

Nor is the testimony of the Fourth Book of Ezra (Second Esdras) without its value, as that book was probably composed by a Hellenistic Jew of Palestine at the close of the first century after Christ. It bears witness in favour of the 24 books of the Jewish canon in the curious passage in chap. xiv. 44-48. The correct reading in verse 44 is "nonaginta quatuor," *ninety-four* in place of the common reading "ducenti quatuor," *two hundred and four*, found in the A.V. translation. The "seventy" writings which were to be preserved and delivered only to the wise men of the Jewish people, added to the twenty-four canonical books which were to be published, in order that all, worthy or unworthy, might read them, make up together the "ninety-four" books spoken of in the vision.[1]

§ 3. THE ABOTH OF R. NATHAN.—We must here quote the passage from the Aboth of R. Nathan alluded to on p. 11. This tract in the Talmud follows the Treatise Aboth, and is a kind of commentary on it, interspersed with numerous legends and interesting anecdotes. In its exposition of the second saying of the Men of the Great Synagogue (see p. 10), "be deliberate in judgment," it says: "In what way is a man taught that he should be deliberate in judgment? That every one who is deliberate in judgment is quiet in judgment (שכל הממתין בדין מיושב בדין), as it is written, '*even these are proverbs of Solomon which the men of Hezekiah king of Judah copied out*' [Prov. xxv. 1], and not only because they copied them out (שהעתיקו), but because they were deliberate (אלא שהמתינו) in doing so. Abba Shaul says, not because they were deliberate, but because they interpreted them (שפירשו).[2] At first there were persons who said that the Proverbs and the Song of Songs and Koheleth were apocryphal (גנוזים היו), because they [the books] spake parables [homely proverbs], and were not of the Kethubim [the Hagiographa]; and some stood up and declared them apocryphal (ועמדו וגנזו אותם), until the Men of the Great Synagogue came and interpreted them; as it is written,

---

[1] See Fritzsche, *Libri Apocryphi Veteris Testamenti Græce* (Leipzig, 1871), and Strack's article on the Canon, pp. 414 ff. On a reference made in the missing fragment of the 4th Book of Esdras, discovered by R. L. Bensly of Cambridge, see our crit. comm. on chap. xii. 7.

[2] In interpreting העתיקו to mean "*they were deliberate*," the verb is regarded as the causative of עתק *to be old*. The men of Hezekiah are regarded as having acted according to the Horatian precept, "nonumque prematur in annum" (*Ars Poet.*, 388). Abba Shaul takes the verb in its more usual meaning of *to copy out*, or *to translate* and *explain*.

'*and I beheld among the simple ones, etc.*' [here follows Proverbs vii. 7–20, with the omission of verse 8, the homely plain-spoken language of which gave offence, see p. 11]; and it is written in the Song of Songs, '*Come, my beloved, let us go forth into the field, etc.*' [here follows Cant. vii. 11–13, which passage also gave offence, and then immediately after]; and it is written in Koheleth, '*Rejoice, young man in thy youth, etc.*' [Koh. xi. 9, see remark on p. 12, and then follows]; and it is written in the Song of Songs, '*I am my beloved's, and his desire is toward me*' [Cant. vii. 10]. All which is a proof [הוי] that it was not that they [the Men of the Great Synagogue] were deliberate only, but that they interpreted."

This passage is very different as it appears in the edition of the Aboth of R. Nathan, edited by Salomon Taussig.[1] It there runs as follows: "They said three things, be deliberate in judgment, that they should persevere and produce when suitable (לייישבו ולהוציאו על אופניו), and thus they found with the men of Hezekiah as it was written, '*even these are the proverbs of Solomon*' [Prov. xxv. 1]. What is the doctrine taught in '*even these?*' Is it not that they were deliberate in judgment? '*Which the men of Hezekiah king of Judah copied out.*' But why is it so said? Because, I say, the Proverbs, and the Song of Songs, and Koheleth were apocryphal (גנוזים היו) until that they were among the Kethubim (עד שהן בכתובים). In the Proverbs why does he say, '*she is loud and stubborn*' [Prov. vii. 11]? In the Song of Songs, [why] '*a bundle of myrrh is my well-beloved unto me*' [Cant. i. 13]? In Koheleth, [why] '*Rejoice young man in thy youth*'? Another explanation of '*which they copied out,*' is not that they copied out, but that they *interpreted* or *expounded.*"

It is worthy of note here that Bloch (*Studien*, pp. 130 ff.) explains the "three things," or "three words," ascribed to the Men of the Great Synagogue, differently than generally interpreted. According to him the first saying, "*be deliberate in judgment,*" refers to the establishment of tribunals for the promotion of justice and righteousness; the second, "*raise up many disciples,*" to the setting up of schools of sacred learning; while the third, "*make a fence to the Thorah,*" or

---

[1] נוה שלום. *I. Theil, enthaltend Aboth di Nathan in einer von der gedruckten abweichenden Recension, Seder Tannaim w'Ammoraim und Varianten zu Pirke Aboth.* Aus Handschriften der Königl. Hof- und Staatsbibliothek zu München herausgegeben und erläutert von Salomon Taussig aus München (München, 1872, K. Hofbuchdruckerei, E. Huber).

§ 4. *The Talmud and the Book of Ben Sira.* 467

Law, he regards as a direction to take care above all things to secure the correctness of the sacred text in general. He maintains that the expression, "Law," is used in this passage not of the Pentateuch as distinct from the other portions of the Sacred Writings, but of all the Holy Writings (see p. 463). In this particular, Bloch has adopted the view of Krochmal and Hartmann.[1] That תורה can be taken in the sense of מצוה, and that reference is made to such ordinances as those of the late Rabbins, may be questionable, especially if we regard the "three words" as actually those of the Men of the Great Synagogue. According to Bloch's explanation the sentences are full of deep significance. The latter clause need not be interpreted with Krochmal as referring to the settlement of the Masoretic text, but may refer to the sending forth of correct copies of the Sacred Writings, and even to the establishment of a fixed canon of Holy Scripture.

§ 4. THE BOOK OF BEN SIRA.—The passages on which Graetz and others have maintained that the Book of Ben Sira formed at one time a portion of the canon have been given in note 2, on p. 48. But it is necessary here to observe that there were two distinct classes of "extraneous books," or of books outside the canon, which were severally regarded with very different feelings.

The most important passage which speaks of these books is that in the Jerusalem Talmud, *Sanhedrin*, x., alluded to on p. 47. The Mishna of that chapter says (27 *a*), "All Israel has a portion in the world to come. But these persons have no portion in the world to come, namely, he who says there is no resurrection of the dead in the Thorah, or that the Thorah is not from heaven, or (he who is) an Epicurean. Rabbi Akiba says, he also who reads in the extraneous books, and he who mutters over a wound, and says [as a charm], '*I will put none of these diseases upon thee which I have brought upon the Egyptians, for I am the Lord that healeth thee*' [Exod. xv. 26].[2] Abba Shaul says, and he who pronounces the Name [יהוה] according

---

[1] A. Th. Hartmann, *Die enge Verbindung des Alten Testament mit dem Neuen.* Hamburg, 1831, pp. 130 ff.

[2] It is interesting to note that this passage alludes to the cures performed by early Christians. St. James once desired to cure a sick Jew, but was not permitted to do so. See Jer. Talmud, *Abodah Zarah*, ii. fol. 40 *b*. See the translation of the passage in F. C. Ewald's *Abodah Sarah* (Nürnberg, 1868), p. 198, and Smith's *Dict. of Bible*, under article "*James.*" On R. Akiba's position, see Graetz, *Gesch. der Jud.*, iv. p. 108.

to its letters." In the explanation of part of this given in chap. x.
28 a, " Rabbi Akiba says, even he who reads in the extraneous
books,¹ as for instance the books of Ben Sira (כנון ספרי בן סירא), and
the books of Ben Laanah (וספרי בן לענה), but the books of Hamēram
(אבל סיפרי המירם), and all the books which were written from that
time and onwards, we may read in them as one reads in a letter."

Inasmuch as there was only one book of Ben Sira, Graetz, Joel,
and other Jewish scholars would read here and in the Talmud Babli,
Tosephta Yadaim, cap. ii. (ed. Zuckermandel, p. 683), the singular
ספר in place of the plural ספרי.² Graetz proposes considerable
transpositions in this passage, reading ספרי המינים, "*the books of the
heretics*," in place of "*the books of Ben Sira*" in the first clause; and
then inserting the clause אבל ספר בן סירא, "*but the book of Ben Sira*,"
before "*the books of Ben Laanah;*" and for "*the books of Hamēram*"
(see p. 470) reading ספרי המירם, and translating "*the day-books.*"
But Dr. M. Joel maintains that the correct reading in place of "*the
books of Ben Sira*," which may have been introduced from *Yadaim*
ii., is "*the books of Ben Satda*" (ספרי בן סטרא), i.e. *the Christian
books*.³

According to the *Tosephta Yadaim*, the Book of Ben Sira, though
held in high favour, stood on the border line which separated the
canonical from the non-canonical, or extraneous books.⁴ The Jews
were permitted to read it and other non-inspired books cursorily,
just as one might read an ordinary letter from a friend. But such
books were not to be studied too much. The command of the Law
was that the Divine Word was to be the constant subject of study
(Deut. vi. 6 ff.); David meditated therein day and night (Ps. i. 2;
comp. Jer. xxxiii. 25). There was, therefore, no time to waste in
the minute examination of other writings. Heretical books were to

---

¹ Joel observes (*Blicke in die Religionsgeschichte, Der Talmud und die griechische
Sprache*. p. 70, note) that the Gemara instead of the *extraneous books*, has here
כפרי הצדוקים, "*the books of the Sadducees*," but the correct reading is certainly
ספרי המינים, "*the books of the heretics.*"

² See note 1 on p. 49.

³ Satda, or Sateda, Soteda, סוֹטְדָא, כטדא, is the name given in the Talmud
to the Virgin Mary, and contains a reflection on the Virgin as an apostate or a
woman unfaithful to her husband. The passages in which the Blessed Virgin is
thus spoken of, and the Lord Jesus is called *Son of Soteda*, or worse, *Son of Pandera*,
his supposed father, are among the saddest found in the Talmuds.

⁴ See note on p. 48, and also Strack's article on the canon, pp. 430, 431.

§ 5. *The Talmud and the Book of Koheleth.*

be altogether avoided; other extraneous writings, even when unobjectionable, or of value, were to be but lightly regarded in comparison with the Holy Scriptures. In the passage immediately following that cited from the Jerusalem Talmud, reference is made to Koh. xii. 12, in order to prove that such books might be used indeed for study but not for the weariness of the flesh. The Midrash Koheleth, possibly reflecting the greater strictness of a later age, says, "Every one who brings into the middle of his house more than the 24 books [of the Canon] brings confusion (מהמה in Koh. xii. 12 is here interpreted מְהוּמָה) into his house, as for example the Book of Ben Sira and the Book of Ben Tiglah, for much study (לַהַג הַרְבֵּה) is a weariness of the flesh, and those books are intended for meditation (להגות נתנו) but not for weariness of the flesh," or intense study. It is not necessary to do more than call attention to the paronomasia in these passages both in Talmud and Midrash.

5. THE BOOK OF KOHELETH.—The length to which our Excursus has extended forbids us here to quote the passages in full which bear on the Book of Koheleth, some of which have been alluded to in our work. But we must here add from Bloch's interesting treatise on the *Ursprung und Entstehungszeit des Buches Kohelet*, p. 144, a list of the following passages of the Talmud in which sayings of Koheleth are quoted as authoritative Scripture by ancient teachers of the Law,—*Berach.* 16 *b*, *Shabb.* 30 *b*, 151 *b*, *Pesach.* 53 *b*, *Chagg.* 15 *a*, *Jebamoth* 21 *a*, *Kethub.* 72 *b*, *Kid.* 30 *a*, 33 *b*, 40 *a*, *Nedarim* 15 *a*, *Menach.* 110 *a*, *Sebach.* 115 *b*, *Sanhed.* 101 *a*, *Baba Bathra* 14 *a*, *Sheb.* 39 *b*, *Abodah Zarah* 27 *b*, *Jerus. Berach* vii. 2 ff., *Tosefta Berach* cap. 2. Bloch calls attention to the fact that the book was cited by Hillel and Simeon ben Shatach, which is a conclusive proof that the hypothesis of Graetz as to its origin in Herodean days is purely imaginary.

EXCURSUS II.

ON THE HOLY SCRIPTURES DEFILING THE HANDS.

THE question is asked in *Shabbath* 14 *a*, why the Holy Scriptures are included among those things to which uncleanness is imputed according to the Rabbinical regulations (גזרות)? The answer given there is, in order to prevent the Holy Scriptures being kept along with the heave-offerings, a practice which had arisen from the notion that all holy things ought to be kept in the same place, and which had led to injury being done to the Scriptures. The uncleanness referred to is that of the second degree, that is, the Holy Scriptures are not supposed to render anything unclean for ordinary use, but to render it unfit to be given as an offering to the priests.

This regulation was made while the temple was still standing, as is evident from the reference made to the Terumah or the heave-offering. It was one of the regulations of the School of Shammai, and was universally acknowledged by the Pharisees. The Sadducees, however, seem to have turned it into ridicule.

Thus in *Yadaim* iv. 6 we read: "The Sadducees say, 'we object against you, Pharisees, that you say the Holy Scriptures make the hands unclean, but the books of Hamēram [heretical writings] do not make the hands unclean.' Rabbi Jochanan ben Zaccai said, 'and have we nothing else against the Pharisees but this alone, for behold they say the bones of an ass are clean, but the bones of Jochanan the high priest are unclean?' They [the Sadducees] said to him, 'According to their estimation (*i.e.* value, worth) so is their uncleanness, in order that a man may not make the bones of his father and mother into spoons. He said to them, even so the Holy Scriptures, according to their estimation [*i.e.* the value in which they are held] is their uncleanness; the writings of Hamēram which are not esteemed, they do not make the hands unclean."

The phrase translated here "the writings of Hamēram" is usually read in the Talmud ספרי המירם. But the reading is doubtful; another reading is with an ס, "the books of Hamēras," which latter has sometimes been incorrectly emended into הַמִירוֹם, Gr. "Ομηρος or *Homer*. Graetz, in his Koheleth, defends the second reading, which he explains as being the Gr. ἡμερήσια βιβλία, *day-books*. Dr. J. Levy, in his *Neuheb. und Chald. W.B.* (under articles המירם, and מרום), maintains that the correct reading is ספרי מירם, and that Merom (מֵרוֹם or מִירָם) was the name of a heretical writer whose writings are not now extant, but who composed works similar to those of Ben La'anah (בן לענה [1]) and Ben Sira. If, however, the reading ספרי המירם be correct, the ה cannot be regarded as the article, but must be viewed as an integral part of the proper name.

Delitzsch calls attention to the fact that the same maxim is spoken of in Nidda 55 *a*, where it is made the subject of the following jest: "The skin of an ass is clean, but the skin of a man has been declared by the wise as unclean, in order that no one may use the skin of his father or mother for the saddle of an ass."

The controversy in the Jewish schools concerned three books of Scripture, namely, the Song of Songs, Koheleth, and in some aspects the Book of Esther. The question in dispute was, not whether these books should be received for the first time into the Canon of Scripture, but whether, having been admitted into the Canon at a earlier date, they had been properly so admitted, and whether there was not sufficient proof from internal evidence to justify their exclusion from that Canon.

Delitzsch observes that the principal places of the Talmud which speak of this controversy are as follows: *Yadaim* iii. 5,—" All Holy Scriptures (כל כתבי הקדוש), or, according to the preferable reading כל כתבי קדש) defile the hands [or render them unclean]. The Song of Songs, and Koheleth defile the hands. Rabbi Jehudah says the Song of Songs defiles the hands, but as to Koheleth there is a dispute (וקהלת מַחֲלוֹקֶת). Rabbi Jose says, Koheleth does not defile the hands, and as to the Song of Songs there is a dispute. Rabbi Simeon says Koheleth is one of the lax points of the school of Shammai (*i.e.* one of the points on which that School is more lax than that of Hillel) and of the rigid points of the School of Hillel. Rabbi

---

[1] לענה, means *wormwood*, but who Ben La'anah was, or what was the nature of the work, termed elsewhere the Book of Ben Tiglah (ספר בן תגלה) is unknown. Some suppose them to have been works of an apocalyptic character.

Simeon ben 'Azzai says, I received by tradition from the mouth of the seventy-two elders in the day when they inducted Rabbi Eliezer ben 'Azariah into the seat of patriarch, that the Song of Songs and Koheleth defile the hands. Rabbi 'Akiba said, Mercy and peace (חס וישלום)! no man of Israel disputed concerning the Song of Songs that it did not defile the hands, for the whole world is not equal to the day on which the Song of Songs was given to Israel, for all of the Kethubim (שכל הכתובים, the Hagiographa) are holy, but the Song of Songs is holy of holies;[1] and if they have disputed, they have not disputed except with regard to Koheleth. Rabbi Jochanan the son of Joshua, the son of the father-in-law of Rabbi 'Akiba, said, According to the words of Ben 'Azzai thus they disputed, and thus they decided," *i.e.* they disputed with regard to the two books, the Song of Songs and Koheleth, and ultimately decided that both the books defiled the hands, or in other words were worthy to be retained in the sacred Canon.

The same controversy is alluded to in *Ediyoth*, v. 3 (9 a), in the following terms, which throw some light upon the previous quotations: "Rabbi Ishmael said three opinions were of the lax points of the school of Shammai, and of the rigid points of the school of Hillel; (*viz.*) Koheleth does not defile the hands according to the opinions of the school of Shammai, while those of the school of Hillel say it defiles the hands. What then was the sin which their commandments made? The school of Shammai pronounced (them) clean and the school of Hillel pronounced them defiled. Coriander seed the school of Shammai pronounced clean and the school of Hillel pronounced unclean, and so with respect to tithes."

The final decision arrived at on this special controversy between the two schools as regards the Books of Koheleth and the Song of Songs, was, therefore, according to the account of Ben 'Azzai, that the validity of the rule כל כתבי הקדש מטמאין את הידים was acknowledged to include these books as well as the other books of the Hagiographa.

Another important passage in the Talmud referring to this controversy is that in *Megilla*, 7 a.

[1] See A. Geiger, *Urschrift und Uebersetzungen der Bibel*, p. 398. R. Akiba also says (in *Tosephta Sanhed.* c. 12), "he who sings the Song of Songs at a drinking festival, and so makes it an ordinary song, has no part in the world to come."

"Rabbi Jehudah [the editor of the Mishna] said, says Samuel [ben Manasseh, his contemporary] that Esther does not defile the hands.[1] Did Samuel intend to say that Esther was not spoken in the Holy Ghost (ברוח הקודש נאמרה)? But Samuel says, yes, Esther was spoken in the Holy Ghost. It was spoken [thus] to be read [in the public services on the feast of Purim], and it was not spoken that it should be written down (ולא נאמרה לִיכָּתֵב). Rabbi Me'ir says that Koheleth does not defile the hands, and that the dispute is about Koheleth. Rabbi Simeon says that Koheleth is one of the lax points of the school of Shammai, and one of the rigid points of the school of Hillel, but that Ruth, and the Song of Songs, and Esther defile the hands. But he [Samuel] says (the same) as Rabbi Joshua has taught [namely, with regard to the public reading of Esther]. R. Simeon ben Manasseh says: Koheleth does not defile the hands, because its wisdom is that of Solomon [*i.e.* it was only such wisdom as belonged to Solomon as a man, not as an inspired writer]. They said to him [*i.e.* to R. Simeon, in answer to this objection], Is this (Koheleth) the only book which he (Solomon) spoke? And is it not already said [1 Kings iv. 12] 'and he spoke 3,000 proverbs,' and he [Solomon] says 'add not to his [God's] words' [Prov. xxx. 6]. Wherein lies then the proof? for if you would say right, he spoke much; had he wished it would have been written down, even much; had he wished it would not have been written down [hence it is argued it is incorrect to regard Koheleth as merely an accidentally written monument of Solomon's human wisdom, for that idea is refuted by the verse quoted], come, hear! 'add not to his words' [by which saying Solomon was considered to have explained his own proverbs as Divine words written by inspiration of the Holy Ghost]. Rabbi Eliezer taught, saying, Esther was spoken in the Holy Ghost, because it is said, 'and the matter was made known to Mordecai [Esther ii. 22] etc.'"

In what follows an attempt is made to prove that Esther must have been written under Divine inspiration, on the ground that that work not only relates known events, but also secret matters, which could not have been known except by means of a knowledge higher than human. Delitzsch observes that the nature of the controversy respecting the Book of Esther was wholly different from that with

---

[1] On this expression see Levy, *Neuheb. W.B.*, s. v. טמא.

respect to the Song of Songs and Koheleth. With regard to the Book of Esther, no doubt was entertained as to its inspiration, though Rabbi Samuel maintained that the Book of Esther did not defile the hands, on the supposition that that work was intended not to be read in private, but to be listened to when recited in the public services on the feast of Purim.

The foregoing is in great part the working up of an article by Prof. Franz Delitzsch on the subject, entitled "Talmudische Studien," published in the *Zeitschrift für lutherische Theol. u. Kirche, herausgeg. von Dr. A. G. Rudelbach u. Dr. H. E. F. Guericke*, 15ter Jahrgang, 1854. Leipzig: Dörffling u. Franke. The extracts from the Talmud, are, however, given above at somewhat greater length, together with a few additional observations.

EXCURSUS III.

THE MEN OF THE GREAT SYNAGOGUE.

"THE Men of the Great Synagogue" form an important link in the history of the Canon of the Old Testament. They are, as we have seen (pp. 453 ff.), mentioned in the tradition of the Talmud which treats of the order and arrangement of the Sacred Books,—and also as (p. 465) having taken an important part in removing the difficulties connected with the Books of the Proverbs, Canticles, and Koheleth.

The principal works on the question of the Men of the Great Synagogue, in addition to those specially referred to in this Excursus, are as follows: Joh. Eberh. Rau, *Diatribe de Synagoga Magna*, Utrecht, 1727; C. Aurivillius, *Dissertationes* (ed. by J. D. Michaelis), Götting. und Leipzig, 1790, pp. 139–160; Ant. Theod. Hartmann, *Die Verbindung des Alten Test. mit dem Neuen*, Hamburg, 1831, pp 120-166; C. Taylor, *Sayings of the Jewish Fathers*, Excurs. II.

According to tradition, the "great Synagogue," or "Council," was convened by Ezra, after the return from Babylon, for the purpose of arranging the affairs connected with the Jewish Church and people. Among the first members were Ezra and Zerubbabel, Joshua the High Priest, Nehemiah, Mordecai (Ezra ii. 2; Neh. vii. 7), with the prophets Haggai, Zechariah, and Malachi. Elias Levita[1] maintained that the period during which "the Men of the Great Synagogue" presided over the Jewish Church and the nation, did not last more than forty years. This statement of Levita seems to have been based on the opinion held by many of the Jews, that Simon the Just, mentioned in the Treatise Aboth as among the last of "the Men of the Great Synagogue" (pp. 9 ff.), was high priest in the days of Alexander the Great. Hence, ignorant of the long period which intervened between the time of Ezra and Alexander, they imagined that the visit of the latter monarch to Jerusalem took

---

[1] See his *Massoreth ha-Massoreth, edited by Ginsburg*, pp. 108 ff. (London: Longmans, 1867).

place forty years after the erection of the Second Temple (see Buxtorf's *Tiberias*, p. 92). Later scholars have, however, pointed out that the Great Synagogue, if its existence be regarded as an historical fact, must have lasted at least two hundred years.

"The Men of the Great Synagogue," according to the Jewish tradition, performed many important services for the Jewish Church and nation. To them is ascribed the closing of the Old Testament canon and the settlement of the text handed down to us by the Jewish Church. The statements of Elias Levita on these points were, for a long time, accepted by scholars of all shades of opinion, Jewish, Roman Catholic, and Protestant, as indisputable facts of history. But the rise of the critical school has subjected all such statements to a rigid examination, and the whole story of "the Men of the Great Synagogue," and their work, was declared fabulous by some scholars in the last century, such as Franz Buddæus and J. D. Michaelis, as well as by later critics, such as de Wette and Bleek. Budde of Halle attached peculiar importance to the fact that no mention of such a body is made in the apocryphal Books of Ezra, or in the works of Josephus. But little weight is to be assigned to the silence of Josephus, as such a point scarcely comes within the scope of his history. Prof. Kuenen, of Leyden, notes that "the Great Synagogue" is not alluded to in 1 Macc., though the writer speaks of a great assembly (συναγωγὴ μεγάλη) of the priests and people and rulers of the nation and the elders of the land (1 Macc. xiv. 28)—which, however, was a very different assembly from that spoken of in the Talmud. Nor do any other books of the Old Test. Apocrypha refer to the Great Synagogue of which the Talmud speaks. It may be well to observe that the Hebrew expression rendered in 1 Macc. by the Greek συναγωγή would be, as Kuenen observes, עֵדָה, or קָהָל, and not כְּנֶסֶת, which latter is the term used in the expression, "the Great Synagogue." The word συναγωγή, which occurs frequently in the LXX. in the meaning of a *collection* or *gathering* of any kind, does not occur there in the sense it afterwards assumes in the New Test. It is used in the signification of "congregation" in Sirach i. 30; iv. 7.

Kuenen's views have been endorsed by Prof. W. Robertson Smith,[1] who maintains that "the whole idea that there ever was a body called the Great Synagogue holding rule in the Jewish nation is

---

[1] See the notes on p. 6.

The Men of the Great Synagogue.

pure fiction," and that the legend can be traced back to the account in the Book of Nehemiah of the great assembly there recorded as being been convened in Jerusalem. Kuenen's theory is based to a considerable extent on the articles of Nachman Krochmal, in the Hebrew journal, *Kerem Chemed* (see note 2 on p. 82). The Great Synagogue (כנסת הגדולה) according to Kuenen is to be identified with the great assembly (קְהִלָּה גְדוֹלָה) convoked by Nehemiah with the object of suppressing the usury under which the poorer Jews groaned (Neh. v. 7), or with the greater convocation convened by Ezra in order to induce the Jews to put away the strange wives (Ezra x. 7 ff.), or with that general assembly of the returned exiles of Israel mentioned in Neh. ix. and x., at which a solemn covenant was signed. In both the latter cases, however, no expression similar to "the great synagogue" occurs in the narratives of Ezra and Nehemiah. The solemn supplication and covenant recorded in Neh. ix. 5-38 are indeed frequently referred to as having been drawn up by "the Men of the Great Synagogue." Kuenen cites a passage from the Midrash Tanchuma [fol. 19 a, on Exod. i. 1, p. 162 of the Stettin ed.] where it is said that "the Men of the Great Synagogue came and said let them praise [comp. Neh. xi. 17] the name of Thy glory which is exalted above all blessing and praise." In this quotation the reference to Neh. ix. 5 is unmistakably clear. The words of Neh. ix. 6 are ascribed in the Midrash Bereshith to "the Men of the Great Synagogue," and treated as an explanation of Gen. i. 17. "The Men of the Great Synagogue" are similarly said (*Bereshith Rabba*, § lxxxviii. on chap. xxxii. 27, 28) to have called the patriarch by the name of Abram instead of Abraham, where reference is made to Neh. ix. 7. The expression used in the prayer in Neh. ix. 18, "they wrought great provocations," is said to have been an interpretation of Exod. xxxii. 8 by " the Men of the Great Synagogue " (*Shemoth Rabba*, § xli. on Exod. xxxi. 18). Similarly the words made use of in Deut. x. 17, "the great God, mighty and terrible," which recur again only in Neh. ix. 32, are said three times in the Babylonian Talmud, and twice in the Jerusalem Talmud, to have been formulas of prayer adopted by "the Men of the Great Synagogue."[1] So also in the Midrash Shemoth, § li. (on Exod.

---

[1] Talm. Babli, *Berach.* 33 b, *Megilla* 25 a, *Joma* 69 b, and in the Jerus. Talm. *Berach.* vii. 4, *Megilla* i. 5.

xxxviii. 21), the confession of Nehemiah (chap. i. 7) is quoted as that of "the Men of the Great Synagogue."

All that is clearly proved by these quotations is that Ezra, Nehemiah, and their colleagues, were reckoned among the number of those belonging to the body thus designated. This, however, is part and parcel of the tradition itself. But the passages do not prove more than this, which is admitted on all sides.

The Great Synagogue is sometimes said to have consisted of 120 members, at other times of 85 only. In *Megilla*, 17 b, and the Jerusalem *Berachoth*, ii. 4, the former number is mentioned; while the latter number is that given in the Jerus. *Megilla*, i. 5, and in the Midrash on Ruth (§ 3, on chap. ii. 4; the number 84 occurs in the Warsaw edit.). Kuenen points out that these numbers also have been derived from the records preserved in Neh. viii.–x. Eighty-four names of persons are mentioned in Neh. x. 2–28, as having sealed or subscribed their names to the solemn covenant there spoken of. The number 120 is made up by adding together the 102 heads of the houses of the fathers, Ezra ii. 2–59, with the 15 *additional* names mentioned in Ezra viii. 1–14, plus Haggai, Zechariah, and Ezra, the latter being identified with Malachi by many of the Jews. Or to the number 84 in Neh. x. 2–28, add the 33 names of the companions of Ezra and the Levites given in Neh. viii. 4, 7, and ix. 4, 5, who with the three prophets, Haggai, Zechariah, and Malachi, mentioned in Ezra v. 1, make up 120.[1]

Dr. M. Heidenheim has treated this matter very fully in his article on the *Origin of the Seventy Elders*.[2] We need not here discuss the mode in which Heidenheim explains the repetition of certain names in the lists given in the Book of Ezra, inasmuch as our object here is merely to point out the source from whence the Talmudists derived the special numbers, and not the historical correctness of that tradition. The numbers mentioned in connexion with "the Men of the

---

[1] These numbers vary slightly. Instead of 84 as in the Hebrew in Neh. x., 83 names occur in the LXX. The number of the names in Neh. viii. and ix. is sometimes reckoned at 35, and at other times at 34. In Neh. x. 10 it has been supposed that the repetition of the copula (וישוע) renders it probable that a name has there fallen out, or by others that the name of Ezra is to be added. See also Herzfeld, *Gesch. d. Volkes Israel*, vol. ii. p. 381.

[2] See his essay, "Ueber die Entstehung der 70 Aeltesten und Rechtfertigung meiner Ansicht über die Synagoga Magna," in his *Deutsche Vierteljahrsschrift*, Band ii. Gotha, 1875.

The Men of the Great Synagogue.

Great Synagogue" may be admitted to be fictitious without the whole story of the existence of the body, which included all the leading teachers of the Law from Ezra to Simon the Just, being relegated to the realms of fable. The assembly spoken of in the Books of Ezra and Nehemiah was convened not for the purpose of making new laws, but simply to revive the practice of the ancient laws of Moses. "The Men of the Great Synagogue" are, on the other hand, said in the Talmud to have enacted laws relative to matters both of religious worship and of ordinary life (*Sanhedrin*, fol. 104 *b*). Kuenen, of course, would maintain that the latter statement is but a legendary amplification of the former history.

In maintaining the Great Synagogue and the Great Convocation to be identical, and in arguing that the statements of the Talmud and Midrash as to the former are simply legendary accretions to the latter story, Kuenen and Robertson Smith attach considerable importance to a passage in the Midrash on Ruth, which contains an exposition of the clause, "and behold Boaz came from Bethlehem" (Ruth ii. 4). The Midrash says: "Three things they decided in the lower court of judgment, and they agreed with them in the upper court of judgment; and these were: 1. to salute in the Name (of the LORD); 2. (to receive) the Megillath (or the Book of) Esther; and 3. (to reinstitute) tithes." The authority on which these decisions were arrived at is then set forth. It is only necessary here to notice the third. "Tithes. On what authority? Rabbi Berachiah in the name of R. Krizpa (says): they made known the sin (in the matter) of heave-offerings and tithes. Shimon bar-Abba in the name of R. Jochanan says: when they [Ezra and his colleagues] made it known they [the people] were dismissed [Neh. viii. 8–13], and they declared themselves guilty by their lamentations [Neh. ix. 1, 2]. What did the Men of the Great Synagogue do? They wrote a book [containing the solemn covenant with God], and they spread it out in the court (of the temple), and in the morning they stood up, and found it sealed. This is that which is written, '*and for all this we make a sure covenant, and write it, and upon the sealed document*' [ועל החתום, in the sing. Neh. x. 1, A.V. ix. 38]. One verse says, '*and upon the sealed document*' [sing. Neh. x. 1], and another verse is '*and upon the sealed documents*' [plural, ועל החתומים, verse 2]. Why is it only ועל החתום [in the first passage]? This is the upper house of judgment [which agreed to the covenant]. And why וְעַל הַחֲתוּמִים [plural in the second]? This is the lower house of judgment?"

We have quoted this passage at greater length than given in the essay of Kuenen or in the work of Robertson Smith,[1] and have inserted a few explanatory remarks, in order that its import may be the better understood. But all that can be proved thereby is that Ezra and his colleagues, being according to the tradition the first members of the Great Synagogue, are referred to under the designation of "the Men of the Great Synagogue." There is nothing whatever unnatural in this fact, which, as already noticed, has never been called in question. But, though the acts of Ezra, Nehemiah, and their co-workers in the restoration of the Jewish Church and polity are often cited as acts of "the Men of the Great Synagogue," many other works are referred to as those of the Men of the Great Synagogue which must have been executed in the period previous to the Grecian conquest, and could not have been performed by Ezra and his colleagues.

It has always been regarded as a fact that the formation of the body known in later times by the name of "the Men of the Great Synagogue" is recorded in Ezra x. 16. "The chief," or "heads of the fathers," in that passage and in Neh. xii. 22, are identical with the "rulers" or "princes of the people," spoken of in Neh. xi. 1. The prophets Haggai, Zechariah, and Malachi are sometimes classed among "the Men of the Great Synagogue," and other "prophets" are said to have belonged to that body; whereas at other times (as in *Aboth*, i. 1) "the Men of the Great Synagogue" are spoken of as having received the Scriptures from the prophets, in which latter case, of course, the later members of the body, such as Simon the Just, are referred to (see p. 486).

The commission granted by Artaxerxes empowered Ezra to appoint magistrates and judges to judge in the districts of Judæa (Ezra vii. 25). According to Talmud Babli (*Sanhedrin*, 104 *b*), the Men of the Great Synagogue appointed both instructors of the young and judges of the people. The statement corresponds well with Bloch's interpretation of *Aboth* i. 1 (see p. 466). The judges of that day had not merely to administer the law, but, under the circumstances of the times, in many cases virtually to enact the law. Hence it was a correct instinct on the part of the early Jewish teachers to ascribe

---

[1] See notes on p. 6.

The Men of the Great Synagogue.

the latter work not merely to Ezra and the men of his day, but to "the Men of the Great Synagogue," including under that term not only the contemporaries of Ezra, but those also who succeeded them in office and authority,

The Jews of that period were not left without regular government; and the "heads of the people," or "the Men of the Great Synagogue," in that and the succeeding ages must have exercised a mixed civil and ecclesiastical authority. It is highly probable, as Bloch argues, that they definitely appointed the three daily services or times of prayer, in accordance with the pious habits of the Psalmist (Ps. lv. 18) and the practice of Daniel (Dan. vi. 17),—a practice no doubt derived from earlier antiquity. The tradition that traces back to the same period the settlement or re-institution of set forms of prayer, is not to be regarded as unhistorical, although it is impossible exactly to point out the liturgy of that day. The form of prayer, however, comprehended in all probability the " Hear, O Israel" (שמע יש׳ וגו׳ Deut. vi. 4-9) and the Decalogue (*Berachoth*, 12 a). The opening of the first treatise of the Talmud, namely, *Berachoth*, treats of the time when the former prayer ought to be used. Bloch (*Studien*, p. 114) notices that the "eulogies" which precede and follow the reading of this prayer, and which comprehend some of "the finest pearls of the Jewish liturgy," as well as those used at the opening and close of the services of the Sabbath and holy days, are distinctly ascribed to "the Men of the Great Synagogue" (*Berachoth*, 33 a; *Pesach.*, 117 a; *Megilla*, 17 b). Those, he remarks, who doubt this fact can never have read the prayers in question. "Not only their brevity, and purity of language, but even their contents, and many of their peculiar expressions, if one only has the ancient readings before him, point back to the Persian period."

To adduce the proofs cited in support of this statement would require a more lengthened discussion than we can here afford. The blessing used by the priests when they changed the watches in the Temple, namely, " He whose Name dwells in this house cause love and brotherhood and peace and friendship to abide between you," must have been composed at a time long prior to the destruction of the Temple. The magnificent eulogy of Simon the high priest, the last of "the Men of the Great Synagogue" (see p. 36), in Sirach l., makes use of expressions which prove that the liturgical service of the Jewish Church was at that early period fully established in all its grandeur and beauty. This corresponds with the statements made in the Talmud, with respect to at least a portion of the work performed by "the Men of the Great Synagogue." To them also is ascribed in the Talmud (*Megill.*, 17 *b*), the composition of the eighteen benedictions still in use in the ordinary Morning Prayer of the Jews. It is highly probable, as Krochmal, Bloch and others think, that the selection of the Psalms for liturgical purposes belongs to the same period.[1] Bloch calls attention to the fact that Graetz interprets the warning of Ben Sira (Sirach vii. 14) as directed against an attempt made in his day to alter the ancient forms of prayer, which were distinguished not only for their purity of diction, but also for their brevity.

The Men of the Great Synagogue, according to *Berach.*, 33 *a*, ordained for Israel forms of blessing and prayer, of consecration and of benediction at the conclusion of the Sabbath and holy days (ברכות ותפלות קדושות והבדלות). They are likewise said to have prohibited the unnecessary heaping up of epithets in addressing the Almighty in prayer (*Berach.*, 33 *b*; comp. *Pesachim*, 117 *a*). In the latter place reference is made to the special epithets employed in Neh. ix. 32. It is quite in accordance with Jewish usage that advantage should be taken of such an opportunity to cite in support of this prohibition an incident recorded in the Sacred Writings, and it is hypercriticism to regard the reference there made as another proof of the identity of the Great Synagogue with the Great Assembly mentioned in the Book of Nehemiah.

Many things undoubtedly are ascribed to Ezra and "the Men of the Great Synagogue," which were the work of scholars of a far later era. Such are, for instance, the marginal readings (the K'ri) ascribed to that early period even by Elias Levita; also "the corrections of the scribes" (the תקון סופרים) attributed to the Great Synagogue by the Midrash Tanchuma (fol. 26 *a*).[2] The vocalization and accentuation of the Hebrew Scriptures Elias Levita saw clearly enough was the work of scholars in the early centuries of the Christian era. But the adoption of the square Aramaic alphabet in place of the ancient alphabet, which was akin to the Phœnician and which in a more

---

[1] J. S. Bloch (*Studien*, p. 115) refers also to *Pesachim*, 111 *a*, 136 *a*; *Berach.*, 33 *a*; *Succa*, 38 *b*; and *Sota*, 30 *b*.

[2] See on the latter, Strack's *Proleg. Crit. in Vet. Test. Heb.*, p. 87; Geiger *Urschrift*, pp. 309 ff.; and my *Bampton Lectures on Zechariah*, p. 541.

embellished shape is preserved in the Samaritan, must have been the work of scholars several centuries before the Christian era. The ancient character still kept its place on the coins of the Maccabean period, and may have been employed in ordinary writing, but the use of the new alphabet in the copies of the Sacred Scriptures was probably much earlier. Such changes are not introduced all at once, and meet generally with considerable opposition. Bloch has called attention to the fact that in later days the square alphabet was regarded as the more ancient, and that the assertion was made that the really older alphabet with its unsightly forms was a Divine punishment from which Israel was delivered in the days of Ezra. The directions that the Law should be written in the Assyrian character (*Zebachim*, 62 *a*), and the prohibition to use for that purpose the older alphabet, called contemptuously the רע״י, must have been promulgated in a very early era. The most honourable title given to Ezra in his book, besides that of "priest," was that he was "a ready scribe in the Law of Moses" (Ezra vii. 6), or, as he was styled by Artaxerxes, "a scribe of the Law of the God of heaven" (ch. vii. 21), and one of the most important works of the members of the Great Synagogue must (even if no tradition could be adduced on the point) have been the copying out of the Sacred Writings from the few copies in the hands of the people, and multiplying the same throughout the land. The scribes would naturally begin with the books of the Law itself, and afterwards issue the other sacred writings. According to *Baba Bathra*, 14 (see p. 453), they "wrote Ezekiel, the Twelve Prophets, Daniel, and Esther," which may mean either that they committed these books for the first time to writing, or that they first copied them out for general circulation. A considerable number, if not all in later times, of the members of the Great Synagogue must have been "scribes." We are not inclined to agree with Bloch's idea that they concerned themselves with compiling the prayers and inscriptions intended for the door-posts and for phylacteries. Yet there may be some historical basis for the curious statement in *Pesach.*, 50 *b* (although it savours indeed of the legendary), given on the authority of R. Joshua ben Levi, that the Men of the Great Synagogue ordained twenty-four fasts, על כותבי ספרים תפילין ומזוזות שלא יתעשרו שאילמלי מתעשרין אין כותבין, "on account of those who wrote books, prayers and Mezuzoth (inscriptions for the door-posts) in order that they might not grow

rich, for if they were to grow rich they would not have written."
The first beginnings at least of a Jewish Lectionary were settled in
their day (*Megilla*, 31 *b*; Jer. *Megilla*, i. 1), and they certainly instituted the Feast of Purim, and arranged the Book of Psalms as the
Hymn-Book of the Jewish Church. The beginning of a system of
schools for the young is naturally ascribed to them (*Sanhedrin*,
104 *b*). It is an interesting fact, whether historically correct or
not, that *Baba Bathra*, 21 *b*, 22 *a*, ascribes to Ezra a peculiar direction, that no one should attempt to prevent a teacher of children
from opening a school in any district on the plea that other schools
were in existence, inasmuch as קנאת סופרים תרבה חכמה, "*the emulation of scribes increases wisdom.*"

If it be enquired why did not the Great Synagogue, if its members
were so active and their work so important, leave behind them some
distinct record of their actions? the answer is easy. The fact is,
as Bloch has pointed out (*Studien*, p. 120) that it was strictly forbidden to commit to writing religious laws and ordinances not
contained in the Scriptures. All such laws and ordinances were
taught by word of mouth. We have before referred to the fact (see
p. 456) that even in later days it was long before such a scruple was
overcome. The Talmud itself, with its voluminous directions and
interpretations, was only by degrees committed to writing. How
keenly the teachers of an earlier period felt on this question appears
from the saying, כותב הילכות כשורף תורה, "*he who writes down the
ordinances is like one who burns the Law.*" The result of all this is
patent. Not one of the great Rabbis, from the days of Simon the
Just till long after the period of Hillel and Shammai, left behind
him any written memorials of his learning. Their teaching was oral,
and their decisions on the most difficult matters were intrusted only
to the memory of faithful disciples. Very many of their precious
sayings, which passed for ages from mouth to mouth, are treasured
up in the treatises of the Talmud. But though they did not actually write books, and though some of the traditions concerning them
may be legendary, no one has yet been found hardy enough to maintain that the account of their words and actions contained in the
Talmuds and Midrashim is in the main to be regarded as fabulous.
We consider it almost equally rash and uncritical to question the
existence and authority exercised by "the Men of the Great Synagogue."

Closely connected with this question is that concerning the institution of the Sanhedrin, discussed also by Kuenen in an earlier article.[1] Dr. David Hoffmann, Docent in the Rabbinical Seminary in Berlin, has in a recent essay, in which he reviews the theory put forward by the Dutch Professor,[2] ably pointed out that the existence of a supreme court of justice in Israel prior to the Babylonish captivity is placed beyond doubt by the statements of Deut. xvii. 8 ff. and 2 Chron. xix., and moreover, that, according to the Jewish tradition (noticed in Josephus and the Talmud), a body exercising similar authority was in active existence from the time of Moses down to the final overthrow of the Jewish polity by the Romans, and even long after that event.

According to Kuenen, the Jewish Council known commonly under the Hebraized name of the Sanhedrin (συνέδριον) did not exist prior to the Greek period (B.C. 330), and was first known by the name of the Gerusia (γερουσία) or Senate. His arguments appear to be mainly drawn from the supposed silence of Ezra and Nehemiah on the point, and from the fact that Josephus does not mention such a body when describing the reception of Alexander the Great (*Antiq.*, xi. 8, 5), while he makes mention of "Senate" when narrating the reception of Antiochus III., which occurred about a century afterwards (*Antiq.*, xii. 3, 3). It must not be forgotten, however, that Josephus speaks of the high priest as having been accompanied on the former occasion by the priests and the multitude of the citizens (μετὰ τῶν ἱερέων καὶ τοῦ πολιτικοῦ πλήθους). In opposition to the idea expressed by Jost, Graetz and others, Kuenen maintains that the statements of the New Test. and Josephus, which speak of the Sanhedrin as an aristocratic body, do not harmonize with those of the Talmud, according to which the Sanhedrin was composed mainly of Doctors of the Law, admitted to that body solely on account of their learning, and presided over by two distinguished Doctors of the Law, the President of the body being styled Nasi, or "*Prince*," and the Vice-President, Ab-Beth-Din, "*Father of the House of Judgment.*"

Hoffmann maintains that there is no real contradiction between

---

[1] *Over de Samenstelling van het Sanhedrin* in the *Verslagen en Mededeelingen der Koninklijke Akademie van Wetenschappen.* Afdeeling Letterkunde x.. Amsterdam: 1866.

[2] *Der oberste Gerichtshof in der Stadt des Heiligthums* in the *Jahres-Bericht des Rabbiner-Seminars für das orthodoxe Judenthum* pro 5638 (1877-1878). Berlin.

the statements of the Greek and the Talmudic authorities referred to. The fact of noble birth had, indeed, considerable influence in procuring admission to the Sanhedrin, and this point is not gainsaid in the Talmud. But an acquaintance with the laws and ordinances such as was required by the terms of Ezra's commission (Ezra vii. 25, 26), and is alluded to in the Book of Sirach (chap. xliv. 4 ff., xxxviii. 24 to xxxix. 11), was primarily required. Hoffmann points out at considerable length that the historical character of the Talmudic accounts respecting the Nasi and the Ab-Beth-Din ought not reasonably to be doubted. These officials of the body are often referred to as "the pairs" (הזוגות). They seem indeed to have been first appointed about B.C. 170, for the chiefs of the Sanhedrin, from Jose ben Jo'ezer and Jose ben Jochanan to Hillel and Shammai (B.C. 170-30) are known by that appellation. These "Pairs" are said in *Peah*, ii. 6, to have been the link immediately following "the prophets" in the chain of tradition, which statement Kuenen adduces in order to strengthen his argument as to the legendary character of "the Men of the Great Synagogue." But, under the designation "prophets," in *Peah*, ii. 6, "the Men of the Great Synagogue" (mentioned in *Aboth*, i. 1 as the link which followed "the prophets") seem to have been included.[1] For the succession of "the prophets" had not ceased when "the Great Synagogue" was organized; but, on the contrary, prophets were among the most conspicuous members of that body in the earlier period of its existence. The decisions of the Sanhedrin during the time of "the pairs" are, according to Hoffmann, referred to as ordinances made by "the pairs" themselves.

Hoffmann further argues that even in the Books of Ezra and Nehemiah mention is made of a senate at Jerusalem under various names (Ezra x. 8; vi. 7, 14; Neh. x. 1; xi. 1, etc.). The governing body was then composed of priests and Levites under the headship of the High Priest, and of Israelitish laymen under the headship of the Prince of the House of Judah. "The elders of the House of Israel" were all probably "scribes" skilled in the Law like Ezra himself (Ezra vii. 25). Such a body would naturally be renewed from time to time, and the name of "the Great Synagogue" was

---

[1] The *Aboth* of R. Nathan, 69 a, speaks of the Men of the Great Synagogue as having derived the tradition from Haggai, Zechariah, and Malachi.

The Men of the Great Synagogue.

given to it in later days, not only on account of the important work it performed in the re-constitution and preservation of the Jewish Church and State in troublous times, but also because its members were originally more numerous than those of the Sanhedrin of a later period, or even of the council of elders which occupied its place in earlier and happier days.[1] Though we cannot narrate the history of the disruption of the Great Synagogue, it is highly probable that after the death of Simon the Just it was shattered by internal dissensions, caused by the disposition of many men of position at that time to yield to heathen customs which were then widely introduced into Jewish national life owing to the intercourse with the Greeks. If the eighteen Greek Psalms known as the Psalter of Solomon, the original language of which was in all probability Hebrew, could be satisfactorily shown to belong to the Maccabean period, or to have been composed shortly after that date, the fourth Psalm of that remarkable collection, which speaks of the unholy and impure sinner ἐν συνεδρίῳ (בית דין, or דין הגדול), would well describe the character of the men whose conduct broke up the early council, or of those who, notwithstanding their ungodliness and sensuality, were during the troubles of that day able to obtain seats in the later body. "The Great Synagogue" was broken up some years previous to the heroic struggles of the Maccabees; and after that era the governing body of the Jewish Church was reorganised by Hyrkanus and termed the Sanhedrin.

[1] Dr. M. Heidenheim, in his interesting article before alluded to, has pointed out that the reason why this council originally consisted of seventy elders was, that the families and the "captains" or "princes" of the tribes given in Num. i. 5 ff., and in Num. xxvi. 7 ff., were exactly seventy. For Reuben 5, for Simeon 7, for Gad 8, for Judah 6, for Issachar 5, for Zebulon 4, for Manasseh 9, for Ephraim 5, for Benjamin 8, for Dan 2, for Asher 6, for Naphtali 5. Total 70. The reasons why the numbers allotted to the several tribes varied so curiously can only be a matter of pure conjecture.

EXCURSUS IV.

GLOSSARY OF WORDS AND FORMS PECULIAR TO THE BOOK OF KOHELETH.

§ 1. GRAMMATICAL PECULIARITIES OF THE BOOK.

THE following grammatical peculiarities in the Book of Koheleth are specially worthy of notice as belonging mainly to the modern period of the Hebrew language.

Verbs ל״א, which occasionally in all periods of the language interchange forms with verbs ל״ה (see Ges.-Kautzsch, § 75, rem. 20–22), are in the Mishna regularly inflected as verbs ל״ה. See Geiger, *Lehrb. zur Sprache der Mishna*, p. 46. Compare in Koheleth יֹצֵא fem. part. for יֹצְאָה, or יֹצֵאת, chap. x. 5; מוֹצָא for מוֹצֵא, chap. vii. 26; חֹטֵא and חוֹטֵא, chap. viii. 12; ix. 18, and also according to the Masora in chap. ix. 2; ii. 26, though in these two latter passages the regular form חוֹטֶה occurs in the common text, which according to the Masora ought only to appear in chap. vii. 26. The form יִשְׁנֶא for יִשְׁנֶה occurs in chap. viii. 1.

Attention has also been called by Delitzsch and others to the fact that the use of the moods in Koheleth is more restricted. The cohortative only occurs once, in chap. vii. 23; the jussive, which is used in prohibitive clauses, such as chap. vii. 16, 17, 18; x. 4, occurs elsewhere only in chap. v. 14; x. 20, and xii. 7. Other cases have been cited by some scholars, namely יְהוּא chap. xi. 3, and יָגֵן chap. xii. 5, but see our crit. comm. on these passages. The disuse of the imperfect with vav conversive is still more significant, see notes on chap. i. 13, p. 317, chap. i. 17, p. 320. That construction occurs only in three cases, chap. i. 17; iv. 1, 7, notwithstanding the frequent use of the perfect with simple vav. Note also the way in which the inf. absolute is employed in chap. iv. 2, 17. See pp. 349, 358.

The personal pronouns are used after the verb where no contrast or emphasis can have been designed, thus, אֲנִי follows the verb in the first person in chap. i. 16; ii. 1, 11, 12, 13, 15, 18, 20; iii. 17,

18; iv. 1, 4, 7; v. 17; vii. 25; viii. 15; and הוא in chap. ix. 15. Delitzsch notices that the same peculiarity occurs in Hosea, but in that case the personal pronoun precedes the verb, as for example, Hosea viii. 13; xii. 11. So also in Ps. xxxix. 11; lxxxii. 6, etc. In one case אני in the nominative is preceded by גם for emphasis, see note on chap. ii. 14. In chap. ii. 15 גם אני is the accusative, see our note.

The frequent use of the participle in the book, and the employment of the personal pronouns after the participle to indicate the subject, is a noteworthy characteristic of the book. So also is the use of verbal adjectives with the pronouns. See note on chap. i. 5.

So likewise the mode in which the demonstrative זֶה is employed is similar to the Mishna, and the fact that the feminine used in the book is זֹה, Mishnaic זוֹ. See note on chap. ii. 2. The employment of מַה־שֶּׁ in chap i. 9 is a sign of a late period; and the use of מָה is peculiar. See note on chap. ii. 12.

As marks of peculiarity of style the frequent employment of יֵשׁ may be noted (chap. i. 10; ii. 13, 21; iv. 8; v. 12; vi. 1, 11, etc.); the common use of the personal pronouns in place of the substantive verb, as in chap. i. 5, 7, 10; iii. 18; v. 18, etc., and the more constant use of particles such as גַּם, פִּי, כְּ, אֲשֶׁר, בַּאֲשֶׁר, etc. The frequency with which these occur is significant of the late period of the writer, though they are by no means exclusively found in the later Hebrew. We do not adduce here the expressions necessitated by the subject matter of the book itself, as to do so would be a *petitio principii*.

Other instances will be found given in the commentary, all pointing towards the conclusion arrived at by the critical school, namely, that the work was composed at a period far later than that of Solomon.

The Glossary which follows is, with the exception of the words and clauses within brackets and the references to our commentary, a translation of Delitzsch's " List of Hapaxlegomena and of words and forms in the Book of Koheleth indicative of a later period of the language." I had originally intended to give a glossary only based on that of Delitzsch, but on consideration I have considered it better simply to translate Delitzsch's list, which is only partially and very imperfectly given in the English translation of his work (see n. 2 on p. 119). But I have included in it many remarks which in the original German are not to be found in the Glossary but in the work itself.

§ 2. Glossary of Words and Forms.

[אָבַד. See note on chap. iii. 6.]

אֲבִיּוֹנָה, *caper*, or *caperberry*, the flower-buds of the caper plant, only chap. xii. 5. See notes pp. 263, 264. Compare *Ma'seroth*, iv. 6; *Berachoth*, 36 *a*, where a distinction is made between אביונות, *the caperberries*, and קפריסין the husks of the fruit of the caper. [Note the allusion to the caper (עלף) on p. 23.]

אדם, *man*, opposed to אִשָּׁה, only chap. vii. 28.

אָזַן. *To weigh*, only in chap. xii. 9. Not used in this sense in Talmudic [Buxtorf notes that the pual אֻזַּן is used in the sense of *trutinari, probari* apud arithmeticos: יְאוּזַּן זה המין, *probabitur hæc species*. The writers alluded to by Buxtorf are those of the middle ages, but their usage is unimportant in considering the significance of the term in earlier Rabbinic].

אִי, *Wo!* chap. v. 16. אִילוֹ, *woe to him!* chap. iv. 10, see crit. comm. instead of the older אוֹי. Comp. הִי Ezek. ii. 10, as אי להם, *Shemoth Rabba*, § 46. אי מה ביישין, *Ah, how evil!* Targ. Jer. on Lev. xxvi. 29. אי שמים, *Ah, heaven!* *Rosh ha-shana*, 19 *a*. אי עניו, *Alas! the meek one!* *Berachoth*, 6 *b*, or compare הי עניו, *Sanhedrin*, 11 *a*.

אִלּוּ, *if*, chap. vi. 6, Esth. vii. 4; compounded of אם (אִין) and לוּ לֹא (read לֹא Ezek. iii. 6), Targ. Deut. xxxii. 29 = Heb. לוּ, common in the Mishna, *e.g.*, *Maccoth*, i. 10, אילו היינו בסנהדרין, *if we had been in the Sanhedrin*.

אֲסוּרִים, see note on chap. vii. 26.

אֲסֻפּוֹת, in the phrase בַּעֲלֵי אֲסֻפּוֹת [see p. 98 note, p. 99, pp. 102, 103] only in chap. xii. 11, as in *Sanhedrin*, 12 *a*, of those assembled together to arrange the calendar. See Jer. *Sanhedrin*, x. 28 *a*, [quoted in note 1, p. 103]. In his crit. remarks on the text Delitzsch notes as follows: אֲסֻפּוֹת has daghesh in the פ like הָאֲסֻפִּים, 2 Chron. xxxvi. 15; בְּאַסֻפֵּי, Neh. xii. 15. Menahem ben-Saruk in his Lexicon, under אסף, states this distinctly; the Masora, on the contrary, affixes the note לית [*i.e. not elsewhere*], to all the three forms. The sing. is אֲסֻפָּה, like אֲגֻדּוֹת, from אֲגֻדָּה.

Glossary of Words and Forms. 491

בְּהֵל, *to hasten*, in this sense found only in chap. v. 1; vii. 9, so hiphil Esther vi. 14; compare the transitive use of the piel, Esth. ii. 9, like Targ. בַּהֵל (= אִתְבְּהֵל) and בְּהִילוּ, *haste*.

בּוּר, *to search out*, only chap. ix. 1; compare the Talmudic עַל בּוּרְיוֹ, *pure, thoroughly free from faults and failures*.

בְּחוּרוֹת, *the period of youth*, only chap. xi. 9; xii. 1; comp. מִבְּחֻרָיו, Num. xi. 28.

בְּטֵל, *to cease, to be inactive*, chap. xii. 3, elsewhere only in the Chaldee of the Book of Ezra, common in the Mishna, *e.g. Aboth*, i. 5, בוטל מדברי תורה, *ceasing from the study of the Law* [see note, p. 245]. LXX. chap. xii. 3, ἤργησαν = ἀεργοὶ ἐγενήθησαν.

בֵּית עוֹלָם, *the eternal house* (comp. Ezek. xxvi. 20), *i.e. the grave*, chap. xii. 5 [see p. 201] as *Tosefta Berachoth*, iii. המפטיר בבית עולמים אינו חותם ברוך, *he who delivers the farewell address at a cemetery does not close with the blessing*. [Compare the phrase נאספה לבית עולמה האשה in the first line of the Aden inscription (A.D. 718) in Plate xxix. of *The Oriental Series of Facsimiles of Ancient MSS.*, edited for the Palæographical Society by Prof. Wm. Wright, noticed also by M. A. Levy, *Zeitschrift der D. M. G.* xxi. pp. 156–160.] Comp. בֵּית עָלַם, Targ. Isaiah xiv. 18; xlii. 11 [see crit. comm. on chap xii. 5, pp. 436, 437].

בְּכֵן, *then, thus*, chap. viii. 10; Esth. iv. 16, elsewhere only in the Targum, as Isaiah xvi. 5, בְּכֵן מְשִׁיחָא דְיִשְׂרָאֵל יְתַקֵּן בְּטוּב כּוּרְסוֹהִי, *then will the Messiah of Israel erect his throne in goodness*.

בַּעַל הַלָּשׁוֹ, *one who has a peculiar tongue* by which he can charm serpents, chap. x. 11, comp. בעל בשר, *a corpulent person*, Berachoth, 13 b; בעל גבר, *one who is manly*, Bechoroth, vii. 5; בעל החוטם, *a man with a fine nose*, i.e. holding his head (nose) high, Taanith, 19 a.

גַּבֵּר, *to strain, to apply one's strength to a thing*, only in chap. x. 10; in other passages it means *to make strong*.

גּוּמָץ, *pit*, only in chap. x. 8 [In use both in Chald., Syr. and Arab. غَمْص].

דִּבְרַת, see under שׁ.

הֹוֶה, *what will be, i.e.* what is the result, chap. ii. 22, as in the Mishna, *e.g. Shabbath*, vi. 6; *Erubin*, i. 10; *Jebamoth*, xv. 2, of that which actually occurs, what happens according to one's experience, what usually happens.

הוֹלֵלוֹת and הוֹלֵלוּת, *folly*, only found in Koheleth, see note on chap. i. 17.

זִכָּרוֹן, see note on chap. i. 11.

עֵת, *time*, chap. iii. 1 ; Neh. ii. 6 ; Esth. ix. 27, 31, elsewhere only in Biblical Chaldee; along with שָׁעָה, ὥρα, the usual word in the Mishna for καιρός and χρόνος. See note on chap. iii. 1.

חוֹלָה, fem. part. kal of חלה, chap. v. 12, 15, the niphal participle is used in Isa. xvii. 11 ; Jer. x. 19 ; Nah. iii. 19 ; xiv. 17.

בֶּן־חוֹרִים [*a son of nobles*, chap. x. 17, see p. 220], *one free born* (*liber*, opposed to עֶבֶד, *a slave*), the usual word in the Talmud [בני חורין, *free persons*, Baba kam., 14 *b*], used of the owners of possessions, like *prædium liberum*, *ædes liberæ* in Roman law [נכסים בני חורין, *farms free of mortgages*, Baba kam., 14 *b*]. Compare חרות, *freedom*, upon the coins struck during the revolt against the Romans.

חוּץ מִן, *outside of, except*, only in chap. ii. 25 (Chald. בַּר מִן, Syr. ܠܒܪ ܡܢ), common in the Mishna, *e.g. Middoth*, ii. 3, חוץ משל אולם, *outside* (the steps of) *the porch*, חוץ משער ניקנור, *except the gate of Nikanor*.

חוּשׁ, *to enjoy*, chap. ii. 25. See note there. Generally used in Talm. and Syr. of painful *experiences*, comp. Job xx. 2.

חֲיָלִים, *strength*, chap. x. 10 [see note there]. It means everywhere else, also in Aram. (חֵילְתָא, חֵילַיָּא), *armies*, except in Isaiah xxx. 3, where it signifies *opes*, *riches*.

חֶסְרוֹן, *a loss, deficit*, see note on chap. i. 15, p. 319.

חֵפֶץ, *desire, matter, business, thing*, chap. iii. 1, 17 ; v. 7 ; viii. 6. Comp. Isa. lviii. 3, 13. The original unweakened signification is to be found in chap. v. 3 ; xii. 1, 10. The weakening of the original meaning, *delight, pleasure*, may have already begun early. In the Book of Koheleth it has already proceeded as far as in the language of the Mishna, *e.g. Mezi'a*, iv. 6, בכמה חפץ זה, *how much does this cost?* or *Berachoth*, 5 *a*, אדם מוכר חפץ לחברו, *a man sells a thing to his fellow*.

חֶשְׁבּוֹן, *reckoning, account*, sing. chap. vii. 25, 27 ; ix. 10, a well-grounded *knowledge* based upon careful reckoning up of matters ; נתן חשבין is the Mishnaic for the N. T., λόγον ἀποδιδόναι. Plural חִשְׁבֹּנוֹת, *machinations*, "*devices*," chap. vii. 29, used also

Glossary of Words and Forms. 493

in 2 Chron. xxvi. 15, but in the sense of *machinæ bellicæ* [Gesenius compares the later Latin *ingenia*, "engines," from which ingénieur, "engineer"]; but in *Shabbath*, 150 a, however, there occurs the expression similar to that in the Book of Koheleth, namely, חשבונות של מצוה מותר לחשבן בשבת, *one may make on the Sabbath calculations about a good work*. דין וחשבון is the general Mishnaic expression for *calculation, reckoning*. [The word is not to be explained with Grotius in chap. vii. 29, as meaning "*rationes* ac *causas* multas cur a primæva ista simplicitate deflecterent."]

חַתְחַתִּים, *terrors*, only chap. xii. 5. See note there.

מַחֲנָה, *mill*, chap. xii. 4, comp. טְחוֹן, Lam. v. 13, a word foreign to the language of the Mishna, but corresponding even with the old רֵחַיִם, as the vulgar Arabic مَطْحَنَة and طَاحُون used in place the older رحا [See Eli Smith in Delitzsch's *Jüdisch-arabische Poesien aus vormuhammedanischer Zeit* (1874), p. 40].

יֵאֵשׁ Piel, *to give up* (one's heart) *to despair*, only chap. ii. 20 [The niphal occurs in several other passages]. The older language uses the niphal in the sense of *to give up hope;* the Talmudic uses the niphal and also a hithpael נִתְיָאֵשׁ (*Kelim*, xxvi. 8), and also the piel יִאֵשׁ, *Mezî'a*, 21 b, from which it is apparent that יֵאֵשׁ (chap. ii. 20) is not to be regarded as a causative (like the Arabic), but as a simple transitive after which לִבּוֹ is to be supplied. In place of לְיָאֵשׁ, Delitzsch observes that לְיָאֵשׁ with pathach should be read as in the Biblia Rabb., the Mas. parva according to MS., and in the St. Petersburg MS. [So also several of the MSS. collated by Michaelis.]

יְגִעָה, *weariness*, only chap. xii. 12.

יוֹתֵר, as participial adjective, *what remains, the rest* (comp. 1 Sam. xv. 15) = *advantage, profit*, chap. vi. 11; vii. 11, or *preference, pre-eminence*, chap. vi. 8. As an adverb, *more* (comp. Esth. vi. 6), *exceedingly, too*, chap. ii. 15; vii. 16: וְיֹתֵר שֶׁ־, *and moreover that*, chap. xii. 9; וְיֹתֵר מֵהֵמָּה, *and moreover more than that*, chap. xii. 12. In Talmudic Hebrew יותר [in fem. יוֹתֶרֶת] is used in the signification of *superfluous* (*Kiddushin*, 24 b), and is common [followed by מִן] as an adverb in the signification of *more* or *more than*, e.g. *Chullin*, 57 b.

יָפֶה, *beautiful*, of that which is good and right, chap. iii. 11; v. 17, as in Jerus. *Pesachim*, ix. 1 (Babl. *Pesachim*, 99 *a*): "beautiful," or " becoming (יפה) is silence to the wise, how much more to the fools!"

[יצא. See note on chap. vii. 18.]

יִתְרוֹן, *preference, advantage*, chap. ii. 13 (twice); vii. 12 (synon. מוֹתָר, chap. iii. 19), more often, of real *profit*, chap. i. 3; ii. 11; iii. 9; v. 15; x. 10, *pre-eminence and advantage*, chap. v. 8; peculiar to the Book of Koheleth, and borrowed in Rabbinic from it. [See note on chap. i. 3.]

כְּאֶחָד, *together, alike*, chap. xi. 6; Isa. lxv. 25; Chron., Ezra, Neh. Chald. כַּחֲדָא, Syr. ܐܟܚܕܐ, frequent in the language of the Mishna, as רואה את החדר ואת העליה כאחד, *he who sees the room below and the garret together*, i.e. squints with one eye, *Bekhoroth*, vii. 4. Similarly כאחת, *e.g. Kilayim*, i. 9. It is also common in the later language. So, in the last of "the eighteen benedictions," ברכנו אבינו כולנו כאחד, *bless us, our Father, all of us together!*

כְּבָר, *size, length*, as adverb, *long ago*, chap. i. 10; ii. 12, 16; iii. 15; iv. 2; vi. 10; ix, 6, 7; so generally in the Mishna, as שכבר הייתי מסתכל, *I have long ago perceived*, *Erubin*, iv. 2. In Aram. more frequent in the meaning of *perhaps* than in that of *formerly*.

כָּשֵׁר, *to be good, prosperous*, chap. xi. 6; Esth. viii. 5; in the language of the Mishna the common word for that which is ritually suitable, or legally admissible. The hiphil verbal noun הַכְשִׁיר, *setting-right*, occurs only in chap. x. 10. In the Mishna it is the usual word for the *arrangement* according to the written directions, *e.g.* of the firstfruits, of the tabernacle, of the festal nosegay, in the heading of the Treatise מכשירין of *the making liable* to uncleanness. Compare *Menachoth* 48 *b*, אין דנין דבר שלא בהכשירו מדבר שבהכשירו, *i.e.*, one draws no conclusion with regard to a thing which is not set right according to the rule from a thing which is set right according to the rule. הכשיר is generally pronounced הֶכְשֵׁר, but הִכְשִׁיר is more correct.

כִּשְׁרוֹן, *success, superiority*, chap. ii. 21; iv. 4; *advantage*, chap. v. 10. Only found in Koheleth.

לְבַד [common in other books of Scripture, either with suffixes, or when used with reference to a preceding noun, as Exod. xxvi. 9], used

Glossary of Words and Forms. 495

absolutely in the sense of *only* in chap. vii. 29. Similarly, but not exactly alike is Isa. xxvi. 13.

לַהַג, *study* [not *preaching* as Luther and Herzfeld], only found chap. xii. 12, not Talmudic, from לָהַג, Arab. لَهَجَ *to gape, to long for*, Syr. ܠܗܓܐ, *vapor*, from breathing out, *exhalare*. Connected in meaning הֶגֶה) הִגָּיוֹן) [See note on chap. xii. 12].

לָוָה, *to accompany* (elsewhere in kal in sense of *to lend* or *borrow*), chap. viii. 15. The verb is used similarly in the Mishna, in piel or hiphil, *e.g. to accompany a guest, to accompany a traveller*, to accompany a corpse to the tomb, whence the saying, לווי ילונניה, "he who accompanies a dead body, to him will one also give the same honour," *Kethuboth*, 72 *a*. So the noun לְוָיָה, *company*, לְוָיַת הַמֵּתִים, *the conducting of the dead* to the tomb.

מְדִינָה, see note on chap. ii. 8.

מַדָּע, *knowledge, consciousness,* συνείδησις, chap. x. 20, and elsewhere, only in the Chronicles and in the Book of Daniel; Targum מַנְדַּע. See note on chap. x. 20.

מְלֵאָה, *pregnant*, chap. xi. 5 only, as in the Mishna, *e.g. Jebamoth*, xvi. 1, יצתה מלאה, "she was already pregnant on her departure." [So in Lat. plena, "plena patris thalamis excedit," Ovid, *Metam.*, x. 469. So in Greek, πληροῦν γυναῖκα.]

מַלְאָךְ, *messenger* (angel) of priests, chap. v. 5 [see note there], comp. Mal. ii. 7, in the sense of the later שְׁלוּחַ שָׁמַיִם (שליח דרחמנא, *Kiddush*, 23 *b*), delegate of God. Plural everywhere שְׁלוּחִים (not שְׁלִיחִים). See Delitzsch, *Die Discussion der Amtsfrage in Mischna und Gemara* in the *Lutherische Zeitschrift*, 1854, pp. 446–9.

מִסְכֵּן, *poor, brought down*, only chap. iv. 13; ix. 15, 16, compare, however, מִסְכֵּנוּת, *poverty*, Deut. viii. 9, and מִסְכָּן, *impoverished*, Isa. xl. 20.

מַשְׂמְרוֹת, *nails*, chap. xii. 11 [see note], *i.e.*, מַסְמְרוֹת, Jer. x. 4, comp. Isa. xli. 7; 1 Chron. xxii. 3; 2 Chron. iii. 9. The word is written with שׂ in Koheleth, from which the Talmud takes occasion to interpret משׂמרות, *nails*, in Jer. *Sanhedrin*, x. 1, as משׁמרות, *ordinances*.

מְעַטִּים, *few*, chap. v. 1, a plural which occurs elsewhere only in Ps. cix. 8.

מִקְרֶה, *hap, accident* (from קרה, *to meet, happen*), is *quidquid alicui accidit* (in the later philosophical terminology the *accidens;* Gr. Ven. συμβεβηκός), in Koheleth, as the context shows, that which finally puts an end to life, the final event of death. More frequently used in Koheleth than in any other book. See especially chap. iii. 19, and note there.

מרוֹץ, *race*, only in chap. ix. 11. See note there.

מָשַׁךְ, *to draw, to attract*, chap. ii. 3 [see note there]. Compare the expression מישך את־הלב, *to entice the heart*, *Chagiga*, 14 *a*, *Sifri*, 135 *b*, ed. *Friedmann*.

מִשְׁלַחַת, *discharge*, chap. viii. 8, different from Ps. lxxviii. 49.

נָגַע. Hiphil construed with אֶל, *to strike against* any one, *to happen*, chap. viii. 14, like Esth. ix. 26. Aram. מְטָא לְ, *e.g.* Targ. Jerus. Exod. xxxiii. 13.

נָהַג, *to conduct oneself, to act*, as in the language of the Mishna, *e.g. Aboda zara*, iii. 4, את שנוהג בו משום אלוה, *one against whom one behaves as against a God*, also 54 *b*, עולם כמנהגו נוהג והולך, *the world acts and proceeds according to its usual course*. Comp. Targ. Koh. x. 4, דִּי הֲוֵיתָ נָהֵג לְמְקָם בֵּיהּ, *leave not thy good post where thou wert accustomed to stand*.

נַחַת, *rest*, chap. vi. 5, rare [see note], as in the usual נחת רוח, Assyr. *nuḥ libbi*. Sometimes a synonyme of טוב, as נוח לו שלא נברא, *it were better for him not to be born*, Jer. *Berachoth*, i. 2. This נוח לו is common in place of Koheleth's נחת לו.

נָטַע, *to fix, to drive into*, chap. xii. 11 (for which Isa. xxii. 23 has תָּקַע, Mishnaic קבע, Jer. *Sanhedrin*, x. 1), as Dan. xi. 45.

סבל, Hithpael, *to drag oneself*, only chap. xii. 5 [see p. 260].

סוֹף, *end*, chap. iii. 11; vii. 2; xii. 13; Joel ii. 20; 2 Chron. xx. 16, the later word which afterwards drove out of use the older אַחֲרִית, which also occurs in Koheleth chap. vii. 8; x. 13. So in the first Mishna, *Berachoth*, i. 1, עד סוף האשמרת הראישונה, *unto the end of the first night watch*. It does not always correspond with אחרית, for אחרית דבר could not be used for סוף דבר, chap. xii. 13 (compare the expression common in the Palestinian Talmud, לֹא סוף דברי . . . אלא אפילו, *that is not all . . . but also*"), which has the sense of *summa summarum* (Mishnaic synon. כְּלָלוֹ שֶׁל דבר).

Glossary of Words and Forms. 497

סָכָל, *fool*, chap. ii. 19; vii. 17; x. 3 (bis), 14; Jer. iv. 22; v. 21; in the Book of Koheleth it is a synonym of the more frequently used כְּסִיל, for which it is the word in the Targums.

סֶכֶל, *folly*, only found chap. x. 6.

סִכְלוּת, *folly*, chap. i. 17, with שׂ [see note there], ii. 3, 12, 13; vii. 25; x. 1, 13 (synon. כְּסִילוּת, Prov. ix. 13).

סכן, Niphal, *to be endangered*, chap. x. 9. [The verb has this meaning only here, in Chald. it is frequent in Pael, Aphel, and Ithpa.] Compare *Berachoth*, i. 3, סיכנתי בעצמי, *I brought myself into danger*, whence מְסֻכָּן, *in danger, dangerously ill*, סַכּוּן and סַכָּנָה, *danger*. The Ithpael, אִסְתַּכַּן, found in the Targ. and Talmud, corresponds to the Niphal.

עֲבָד, *deed, work*, only in chap. ix. 1, like the Syr. ܥܒ݂ܳܕ݂, Jewish Aram. (עוּבָּד) עוֹבָד.

עֲדֶן (contracted from עַד־הֵן), *yet*, with לֹא, *not yet*, chap. iv. 3.

עֲדֶנָה, or according to another reading עַדֶנָּה (from עַד־הֵנָּה), *yet*, chap. iv. 2. Mishnaic עֲדַיִן, *e.g. Nedarim*, xi. 10, עדיין היא נערה, *she is yet a girl*, similar to, and of the same meaning as, the Syr. ܥܕ݂ܰܟܺܝܠ, which also means with the negative *nondum*, like the Mishnaic עֲדַיִן לֹא.

עָוַת, Hithpael, *to bow oneself*, only chap. xii. 3.

עָמַד, *to stand still, to remain*, chap. ii. 9; viii. 3, as Jer. xlviii. 11; Ps. cii. 27.

עָמַת, see under שׁ.

עָנָה, see crit. comm. on chap. v. 19; x. 19.

עִנְיָן, *toil, business*, only in the Book of Koheleth. See note on chap. i. 13, p. 317. This is one of the most common words of the post-biblical Hebrew, primarily used of the subject of business, as עסוקין באותו ענין, *employed with this matter, Kiddushin*, 6 a, also Aram. they came to speak, מעניינא לעניינא, *from one matter to another, Baba Bathra*, 114 b.

עַצַלְתַּיִם, only chap. x. 18. See note there.

עָשָׂה with לֶחֶם, *to give a feast*, chap. x. 19, as Dan. v. 1, עֲבַד לְחֶם, N.T. ποιεῖν δεῖπνον, Mark vi. 21. In Ezek. iv. 15, עָשָׂה לֶחֶם is used of the preparing of food. In chap. vi. 12 the verb is used like ποιεῖν (= διάγειν) χρόνον, Acts xv. 33. Followed by טוֹב it

K K

means not only *to do good*, chap. vii. 20, but also *to enjoy good, to pass an agreeable life*, chap. iii. 12 [but see our note on that passage].

[פַּ֫גַע, see note on chap. ix. 11.]

פַּרְדֵּס (Cant. iv. 13; Neh. ii. 8), plural, chap. ii. 5, פַּרְדֵּסִים, *parks, gardens of trees*, as *Mezi'a*, 103 *a*, פרדיסי [see note on chap. ii. 5].

פֵּ֫שֶׁר, *interpretation, explicatio*, chap. viii. 1, elsewhere only in the Chaldee portions of the Book of Daniel, an Aramaism for the older פִּתְרוֹן and יֵ֫בֶר, for which the Targum has פִּ֫שַׁר and פּוּשָׁרָן, Talmud. פְּשָׁרָה, *the disentanglement* or *making up of a matter of strife*.

פִּתְגָּם (פִּתְגָם), a Hebraized Persian word occurring in the Books of Ezra and Daniel, but elsewhere only in Koh. viii. 11 [see note there] and in Esth. i. 20, *message, saying, decision*; used in the Targums, in which the Decalogue is called עֲשָׂרָה פִתְגָּמִין, and in Syriac, but not naturalised in Talmudic.

קִלְקַל, Pilpel, derived from the adjective קָלָל (*smooth, shining*, of brass), which occurs in Ezek. i. 7; Dan. x. 6, *to sharpen*; only found in this sense in chap. x. 10; used in Ezek. xxi. 26 in the sense of *to shake* [see note on chap. x. 10].

רָאוּת, *seeing*, only chap. v. 10, *K'ri* for which the text has ראית [see note there], which may be read רָאֲיַת, רָאִית (comp. Ezek. xxviii. 17) or also רְאִיַּת; the last two forms are naturalized in the language of the Mishna, and have there peculiar meanings arising out of the idea of *seeing*, *e.g.* God in His sanctuary, or *seeing* with one's own eyes, which is the meaning of the root.

רדף, Niphal participle נִרְדָּף, only in chap. iii. 15 [see note].

רָעוּת. See note on chap. i. 14.

רַעְיוֹן, used in the Chaldee parts of Daniel and in the Targum, רִעְיוֹן and רַעְיָן. See note on chap. i. 14.

שֶׁ. This form of the relative is by no means a later form, as is shown by the Babyl.-Assyrian *sa*, the Phœnician אש [which is not to be regarded as a shortened form of אֲשֶׁר, see Schröder, *Phönizische Sprache*, § 65], but a relative (originally a demonstrative) belonging to the oldest period of the language, which in the Mishna has entirely supplanted the אֲשֶׁר of the older written Hebrew language. It is already used in the Book of Koheleth in the

Glossary of Words and Forms. 499

same way as in the Mishna, but in such a way that it stands in the same line as אֲשֶׁר, and disputes its supremacy. שׁ according to Herzfeld occurs 68 times; אֲשֶׁר, 89 times; comp. for example chap. i. 13 ff.; viii. 14; x. 14, where both are used promiscuously. The use of אֲשֶׁר as a relative pronoun and a relative conjunction in Koheleth is not different from the manner in which it is used in the older literature: עַד אֲשֶׁר לֹא in the sense of *before that*, chap. xii. 1, 2, 6, Mishnaic עַד שֶׁלֹּא, is only a natural application of the root-meaning, *until that not* (2 Sam. xvii. 13; 1 Kings xvii. 17); so that it is only a matter of accident that further proofs cannot be cited for מִבְּלִי אֲשֶׁר לֹא, *without that not (nisi quod non) = so indeed that not*, chap. iii. 11 (comp. בִּלְתִּי, *without that = so indeed that*, Dan. xi. 18), for which וּבִלְבַד שֶׁלֹּא is used in the Mishna, *e.g. Erubin*, i. 10. How far, however, the use of שׁ has extended itself the following list will show, from which all cases of שׁ standing alone as a relative, or as a relative conjunction, have been excluded.

בְּשֶׁכְּבָר, *long ago*, chap. ii. 16.

בְּשֶׁל אֲשֶׁר, *because that, eo quod*, chap. viii. 17 (comp. Jon. i. 7, 8, 12), corresponding to the Talmudic בְּדִיל דְּ.

כֹּל שׁ, *all which*, chap. ii. 7, 9; *all what*, chap. xi. 8 (כָּל־שֶׁבָּא, *everything future*).

בְּל־עֻמַּת שׁ, *in all respects as*, chap. v. 15, corresponding to the Chaldee כָּל־קֳבֵל דְּ, Dan. ii. 40, etc.

כְּשׁ, *as*, chap. v. 14 (כְּשֶׁבָּא, *as he came*), chap. xii. 7 (כְּשֶׁהָיָה, *as he has been*), and *when, quum*, chap. ix. 12; x. 3.

מַה־שׁ, *that which*, chap. i. 9 [see note there]; iii. 15; vi. 10; vii. 24; viii. 7; x. 14. מָה שׁ, chap. iii. 22.

מִשׁ, *than that*, chap. v. 4 (מִשֶּׁתִּדּוֹר, *than that thou shouldest vow*).

עַל דִּבְרַת שֶׁלֹּא, *in order that not*, chap. vii. 14 (comp. chap. iii. 18; viii. 2).

שֶׁגַּם, *that also*, chap. ii. 15; viii. 14.

שִׂדָּה and שִׂדּוֹת, only chap. ii. 8 [see note].

שַׁחֲרוּת, *youth*, only in chap. xi. 10 [see note].

שָׁכַח, Hithpael, *to be forgotten*, only chap. viii. 10, the common word in Talmudic, *e.g. Sanhedrin*, 13 *b*.

סִכְלוּת‎, see שִׂכְלוּת‎.

שָׁלַט‎, *to have power, to rule,* chap. ii. 19; viii. 9; elsewhere only in the books of Nehemiah and Esther (comp. *Bechoroth,* vii. 6, etc.); Hiphil, *to give power,* chap. v. 18; vi. 2; elsewhere only Ps. cxix. 133.

שִׁלְטוֹן‎, *powerful, a ruler* [Assyr. *siltannu,* "a ruler;" Arab. سلطان‎] chap. viii. 4, 8 [see notes there], nowhere else in Old Test. Hebrew, but in the Mishna, *e.g. Kiddushin,* iii. 6. אדבר עליך‎, לישלטון‎, *I will speak for thee to the prætor.*

שַׁלִּיט‎, followed by בְּ‎, *having power over,* only in chap. viii. 8 (comp. Ezek. xvi. 30), on the contrary in chap. vii. 19; x. 5, as in Gen. xlii. 6, in the political sense, *a ruler* [see n. on chap. vii. 19].

שׁמם‎, Hithpoel in a peculiar sense, see note on chap. vii. 16.

שִׁפְלוּת‎, *sinking-down,* chap. x. 18, elsewhere only in Targ. Jer. xlix. 24.

שְׁתִי‎, *drinking,* only chap. x. 17 [see note].

תַּחַת הַשֶּׁמֶשׁ‎, chap. i. 3 [see note there, p. 307] corresponding with the Greek ὑφ᾽ ἡλίῳ or ὑπὸ τὸν ἥλιον.

תָּקִיף‎, only in chap. vi. 10, not found elsewhere in Biblical Hebrew, but it occurs in Chaldee, in the Targums and Talmud.

תָּקַן‎, *to be straight, to straighten,* chap. i. 15 [see note there, p. 318]. Piel, *to make straight, to arrange,* chap vii. 13; xii. 9, a word common in the Mishna, both in Piel and Hiphil, *to arrange* (*e.g. Gittin,* iv. 2), as well as its derivatives תִּקּוּן‎ and תַּקָּנָה‎; the latter noun is used also in sense of *welfare* (*Gittin,* iv. 6), *ordinances* (*Shabbath,* 30 *a*). For the former compare the phrase תקון סופרים‎, *the ordinance of the scribes,* see p. 48.

INDEX OF TEXTS.

ILLUSTRATED AND NOT MERELY REFERRED TO

OLD TESTAMENT.

GENESIS.	PAGE
i. 31	343
iii. 14, 17	384
,, 16	25
,, 19	25, 44, 232
v.	373
xxix. 9	47
xxxii. 9	225
xli. 43	355
xlix. 24	345

EXODUS.	
ii. 22	93
xv. 26	4
xxiii. 8	384
xxxi. 1, 2	378

LEVITICUS.	
xxvi. 8, 12, ff.	361

NUMBERS.	
i. 5, ff.	487
xi. 16	98, 103
xv. 39	234
xxx.	361
xxxii. 10	199

DEUTERONOMY.	
xvi. 19	384
xix. 5	423
xxiii. 22–24	360

JUDGES.	PAGE
xi. 3	47

1 SAMUEL.	
xvii. 47	113
xx. 19–22	341
xxvi. 10	396

2 SAMUEL.	
xviii. 27	412
xix. 36	251
xx. 15–22	414

1 KINGS.	
iii. 7, 8	86
,, 12	332
iv. 7, ff.	329
,, 27, 28	328
,, 33	327
v. 12, 13	444
viii. 1	85
,, 46	391
,, 55–61	85
,, 63	328
x. 5	,,
xiii. 22	373

2 KINGS.	
iii. 25	341

1 CHRONICLES.

	PAGE
xvi.	113
xxix. 22	333

2 CHRONICLES.

xvi. 12	4

EZRA.

ii. 2–59	478
iii. 12, 13	385
v. 1	478
viii. 1–14	,,
x. 16	480

NEHEMIAH.

ii. 14	327
iii. 15	,,
viii. 10	478
x. 1 [A.V. ix 38]	479
x. 2–28	478

ESTHER.

i. 1	329

JOB.

iii. 3	151, 158
ix. 3	203
x. 18, 19	151, 158
,, 21, 22	233
xiv. 7, ff.	273
xviii. 11	252
xix. 23–27	197
xxi. 7, ff.	253
xxxi. 30	360
xxxiii. 23	203

PSALMS.

xxvii. 2	351
xxxii. 9	167
xxxvii. 13	382
xlix. 12	348
,, 13, 21	347
,, 14, 15	191
lxxii. 16	24
lxxiii.	65
cxliv.	113

PROVERBS.

ii. 18	202
vii. 7, 10–20	11, 466
vii. 11	466

	PAGE
xv. 1	421
,, 13	234
,, 15	46
,, 24	193
xvi. 8	383
,, 32	416
xviii. 22	393
xx. 27	241
xxi. 29	395
xxii. 13	252
,, 20	103
xxv. 1	4, 440, 456
xxvi. 4, 5	205
,, 18	165
xxix. 11	377
xxx. 6	473
xxxi. 14	225

SONG OF SONGS.

i. 13	466
vi. 2	327
vii. 10	11, 465
,, 11, 12	11, 465
viii. 11	326

ISAIAH.

iii. 12	219
v. 11	,,
xiii. 10, 11	241
xiv. 18–20	373
xxiv. 2	406
xxv. 7	413
xxix. 4	248
,, 21	391
xxx. 15	352, 416
,, 26	375
xlii. 2	416
xlv. 9	378
liii.	76, 265
lxii. 14	360

JEREMIAH.

xii. 1	65
xx. 14–18	151, 158
xxii. 19	373
xxxi. 8	23
,, 29, 30	423

Index of Texts. 503

EZEKIEL.	PAGE
xvii. 23	23
xviii. 2	423
,, 32	199
xxxii. 7, 8	241

DANIEL.	
xii. 2	106

HOSEA.	
iv. 6	18
,, 11	384
xi. 2	397
xii. 2	318
,, 9	370

JOEL.	PAGE
ii. 2, 10	241

MICAH.	
iii. 3	351

HABAKKUK.	
ii. 3	309

ZECHARIAH.	
i. 4	5
iv. 2	267
xi. 16	351

MALACHI.	
i. 7	361

APOCRYPHA.

2 ESDRAS (4th Ezra).	
vii. 78 (missing fragment)	437
xiv. 44-48	465

TOBIT.	
iii. 6	201

WISDOM.	
ii.	67
,, 2	68, 347
,, 3, 4, 5	68
,, 6-10	67
,, 12	55
,, 12-20	59, 75
iii. 2, 3	71
iv. 12	377
v. 14, 15	71
,, 17-20	74
vii. 1, ff	433
,, 7	61
viii. 7	55
,, 8	339

ECCLESIASTICUS (Sirach).	
Prologue	33 ff., 39 ff.
i. 13	44
vi. 6	203
vii. 14	43, 482
,, 15	46

xii. 10	426
,, 13	41
xiii. 15	47
,, 26	45
xviii. 6	345
,, 23	43
xix. 16	42
xx. 6, 7	,,
xxi. 25, 26	,,
xxvi. 23	45
xxvii. 26	,,
,, 9	47
xxxiii. 13-15	45
xxxiv. 7	46
xxxviii. 1-15	4, 50
xl. 11	44
l. 1-4	37
,, 1-21	36
,, 27	32

1 MACCABEES.	
xiv. 28	476

2 MACCABEES.	
ii. 3, 13, 14	464

3 MACCABEES.	
ii. 1-24	36

NEW TESTAMENT.

Matthew.

	PAGE
v. 24	360
,, 38-41	385
,, 43	342
vi. 7, ff.	43, 359
,, 23	241
,, 34	238
viii. 21	356
xii. 19	416
xviii. 21	228
xxii. 31, 32	199
xxiv. 15	401
xxvii. 53	,,
xxviii. 2	233

Luke.

	PAGE
xi. 34	4
xii. 16-21	322
,, 29	377
,, 32	179
xxiv. 44	40, 461, 462

John.

	PAGE
iii. 6–8	433
,, 6	181
,, 8	231
xi. 10	334
xvii. 15	177

Acts.

	PAGE
i. 7	342

Romans.

	PAGE
i. 2, ff.	213
,, 27	170
v. 7	228
vi. 23	399
viii. 21	179
,, 22	177
,, 28	177

	PAGE
ix.	380
,, 4	9
,, 20	378
,, 20, 21	49
xi. 29	269
,, 33	404
xii. 11, 12	232
,, 16	377
,, 19, ff.	223
xiii. 1–7	218, 222, 398
,, 14	221, 234
xiv. 12	106

1 Corinthians.

	PAGE
x. 31	177
xiv. 34	209
xv.	62, 168

2 Corinthians.

	PAGE
v. 14	176

Galatians.

	PAGE
vi. 1	229
,, 7, 8	231

Ephesians.

	PAGE
vi. 13-17	74

Philippians.

	PAGE
i. 21	179
iv. 4	344

1 Timothy.

	PAGE
iv. 7, 8	177
,, 10	178
v. 23	325
vi. 9, 10	149

2 Timothy.

	PAGE
iii. 16	104

HEBREWS.

	PAGE
i. 1	200
,, 3	74
ii. 15	197
xii. 14	176

JAMES.

i. 17	104
,, 19	49
,, 21	389
iii. 2	42
iv. 23	426
v. 14, 15	4, 49
,, 20	421

2 PETER.

	PAGE
i. 21	200

1 JOHN.

v. 19	177
,, 4	403

REVELATION.

i. 20	361
ii. 1	,,
vii. 9	179
xv. 3	222
xx. 14	193

GENERAL INDEX.

*** The purely grammatical notes have not in general been indexed, nor have the names of Jewish scholars mentioned only in the extracts from the Talmud and Midrash been included in this Index. Works often referred to are noted "passim."

Ab-Beth-Din, the, 485.
Abel-beth-Maacha, deliverance of, 414, 417.
Abbott, 35.
Aboth (Massecheth), 3, 5, 10, 19, 21, 47, 239, 245, 335, 379, 386, 413, 475, 480, 486.
Aboth of R. Nathan, 11, 14, 465 ff., 489.
Æsop's fables, 204.
Æschylus, 335.
Age, the weak voice of old, 248.
Agriculture, advantage of, 364.
Akiba, Rabbi, on the Apocryphal Books, 467, 468 ; on Song of Songs, 472 ; remarkable saying on "the net spread over man," 413.
Almond tree in blossom, 257 ff.
Alphabet, ancient Hebrew, 483.
Anacreon, 431.
Anger, reproof of, 237.
Annals, blank in Jewish, 7.
Antilegomena of Old and New Testament, 6.
Apocryphal Books, see under *Extraneous, Ben Sira, Wisdom*.
Aquila, traces of, in the present text of the LXX., 51, 52, 338, 392, 406, 440.
Aristeas, 33.
Aristophanes, 310, 431.
Aristotle, 213, 388, 389.

Asher, Dr. David, *Arthur Schopenhauer*, 160.
Athbash alphabet, 127.
Atheism, Renan on, 167 ; avowed by modern Pessimists, 151 ; results of, 166.
Avicebron, see *Ibn Gabirol*.
Aurelius, Marcus, 315, 316, 342, 370, 377, 378, 391, 433.
Aurivillius, *Dissert*, 405, 475.

Bacher, 457.
Bacon, Lord, 195, 230.
Baer, *Accent.-system*, 412 ; *Metheg-Setzung*, 441.
Bagoas, 220, 372.
Baraitha explained, 451, 454.
Bauer, Ch. F., xiv. passim.
Beal, Prof. Samuel, on Nirvâna, 174.
Ben Bûta, story of, 19 ff.
Ben Laanah, the Books of, 468, 471.
Ben Satda, the Books of, 468.
Ben Sira, a Palestinian Jew, 48 ; author of the Book of Ecclesiasticus, 31 ; designations of that book, 31 ; translated from a Hebrew original, 32 ; fragments extant in Heb. and Chaldee, 32 ; its use of the LXX. transl., 33, 38 ; indications of its date, 34-38 ; reference to the Canon, 39 ; use of the Book of Koheleth, 31, 41 ; his

General Index. 507

additions to old proverbs, 46, 48; references to his work in the Talmud, etc., 46, 47, 468; referred to sometimes as canonical, 47; explanation of this fact, 48; allusions to, in the New Testament, 4, 48, 49; reference to physicians, 4; the Talmud on the Book of, 467 ff.
Ben Tiglah, Book of, 469, 471.
Beneficence, exhortations to, 226; advantages of, 228.
Bensly, R. L., *Missing Fragment of IV. Ezra*, 437, 465.
Bernard, St., *Sermones de diversis*, 230.
Bernstein, H. G., *Quæstiones*, xiv., passim, 376.
Bhagavad-Gîtâ, 162.
Biesenthal, J. H., *Trostschreiben des Apostels Paulus an die Hebräer*, 38, 421.
Bird, rising up at the voice of a, 247.
Bissell, *Comm. on Apocrypha*, 33, 34, 37, 44, 56.
Bleek, Friedr., *Einleitung in Alt. Test.*, 464.
Bloch, J. S., *Studien zur Gesch. d. Sammlung der alt-heb. Lit.*, 10, 25, 453, 457, 463, 466, 480, 482, 484; *Ursprung u. Entstehungszeit d. Kohelet*, 16, 17, 18, 20, 22, 25, 87, 92, 94, 99, 469.
Bode, C. A., 444.
Boethus ben Zonin, 462.
Boethus, founder of a sect of Sadducees, 131, 462.
Borrowing days, 271.
Böttcher, Fried., xiv., xviii., passim; *Collectanea Hebr.*, 446.
Bread cast upon the waters, 223 ff.
Brecher, Gideon, *Das transcend. Magie u. mag. Heilarten in Talmud*, 4.
Bridges, Rev. C., *Expos. of Eccl.*, xiii., 223, 229, 230, passim.
Bronze tablets at Lyons, the, 111, 112.
Buddæus, 476.
Buddhism, similarity of, to Pessimism, 158, 172, 182; superior to Pessimism as a moral system, 173; its doctrine of Nirvâna, 162, 173, 174, 182; selfish in its views, 175; practical failure of, 182; its four cardinal tenets, 182.
Bullock, Rev. W. T., *Comm. on Eccl.*, xiv., passim.
Bunyan, John, *Grace Abounding*, 48.
Butler, Bishop, *Analogy of Religion*, 177, 230.
Burial, want of, a punishment, 373.
Buxtorf, J., *Lex. Chald. and Talm.*, passim; *Tiberias*, 5, 6, 455, 476; *Florilegium Heb.*, 205; *De Abbrev. Heb.*, 443.
Byron, 152.

Caspari, C. P., *Der Syrisch.-Ephraim. Krieg*, 112.
Cassell, Dr. Paulus, 281.
Catullus, 309.
Cemeteries, name of "eternal house" given to Jewish, 201, 437, 491.
Cheerfulness, commended in youth, 234, 237; and early piety, 238.
Cheyne, Rev. T. K., *Prophecies of Isaiah*, 248, 391.
Children, the early death of, 18.
Chilon, 388.
Chiyya, story of Rabbi, 198.
Christianity, the pessimism of, 177; its optimistic side, 178; a religion suited for man, 179; charged with selfishness, 176; unselfishness of, 180.
Cicero, 68, 118, 334, 349, 350, 404.
City, going to the, 428.
Claudius, speech of the Emperor, 111.
Clericus, 431.
Cohen, David (Kahana), Heb. *Comm. on Koheleth*, 23.
"Corrections of the Scribes," the, 8.
Cox, Samuel, D.D., *The Quest of the Chief Good*, xiv., 143, 144, 229.
Cranes of Ibycus, 223.
Creation of man, Jewish opinions concerning, 374.

Dähne, *Jüdisch.-Alexandr. Religions-Philosophie*, 63.
Dale, Rev. T. P., *Comm. on Eccles.*, xiv., passim.

Davidson, Rev. Prof. A. B., *Hebrew Accentuation*, 394.
Davidson, Rev. Dr. Samuel, *Introduction to Old Test.*, 14, 49, passim.
Davids, Rhys, see under *Rhys-Davids*.
"Days of the old woman," the, 271.
Deane, W. J., *The Book of Wisdom*, 56, 58, 68, 74.
Death, man thinks little about, 370; cause of, 399; unexpected, 413; a winged Pegasus, 240; the days of, 271; Eccles. xii. supposed to be a dirge of, 239; the night of, and the terrors of the grave, 253; net spread over all people, 413.
Delitzsch, Prof. Franz, *Comm. on Koheleth*, xv. passim; mistakes of the English transl. of that comm., 119, 385, 406, 489; *Gesch. der jüdisch. Poesie*, 32, 47, 394, 396; *das Salomonisch. Spruchbuch*, 4, 58; *Comm. on Isaiah*, 391; *Comm. on Habb*. 405; *Rohling's Talmudjude beleuchtet*, 64; *Handschriftlich. Funde*, 222; *Jesus und Hillel*, 24; *Hebrew Transl. of New Test.*, 222; *Comm. on Psalms*, 412; *Comm. on Genesis*, 327; *Bibl. Psychology*, 319, 320, 420; *Talmud. Studien*, 474; *Jüdisch.-Arab. Poesien*, 493; *Amtsfrage in Mischna und Gemara*, 495.
Delitzsch, Prof. Friedr., *Wo lag das Paradies?* 128, 255, 327, 330.
Derenbourg, Joseph, *Notes détachées sur l'Ecclésiaste*, 190; *Essai sur l'Histoire et la Geogr. de la Palestine*, 440.
Diez, *Denkwürdigkeiten von Asien*, 227.
Dillmann, Prof. Dr., *Gramm. der Aethiop. Spr.*, 281.
Diodorus Siculus, 435.
Diogenes Laertius, 388.
Dods, Dr. Marcus, *Mohammed, Buddha and Christ*, 173.
Doederlein, 438, passim.
Doors shut towards the street, 245.
Dove's law of the winds, 310.
Dreams, 362, 363.
Driver, Prof. S. R., *Hebrew Tenses*, xviii., passim.

Dukes, Leopold, *Rabbinische Blumenlese*, 4, 32, 44, 50, 204, 205, 219, 381, 396, 425.
Du Meril, *Poesies Latines*, 435.
Dunash, *Sefer Teshuboth*, 433.

Ecclesiastes, see under *Koheleth*.
Ecclesiasticus, the Book of, see under *Ben Sira*.
Eichhorn, 34, 89.
Eleazar, Rabbi, on the death of children, 18.
Elster, xv., passim.
Epilogue, the, of Koheleth, 97; opinions of Krochmal and Fürst, 97; of Graetz, 98; Bloch's modification of Krochmal's view, 99; view of Renan, 100; three points of, 100; disavowal of Solomonic authorship, 102; views of Ewald and Delitzsch, 102; affirms the inspiration of the Sacred Writings, 104; gives a warning how to learn, 105; speaks of a future judgment, 106; arguments, pro and con, as to its authorship, 438.
Essen, von, Ludwig, xv., passim.
Essenes, the, 379.
Esther, reception of, into the Canon, 17, 455, 471, 473.
Eternal house, see under *Cemeteries*.
Eternity, the idea of, implanted in man's heart, 194.
Euergetes, two monarchs of that name, 34, 35.
Euripides, 434.
Evil days, Koheleth's description of the, 240; seven stanzas of Koheleth on the, 242.
Ewald, F. C. *Abodah Sarah*, 432, 467.
Ewald, Prof. H., *Dichter des alt. Bundes*, xv., passim; *Ausführl. Lehrb. der Heb. Spr.*, xviii., passim; *Gramm. Crit. Arab.*, 307; *Gesch. des Volkes Israels*, 5, 76.
Extraneous Books, the, 467, 468, 469.
Ezekiel and the Pentateuch, 457, 458.

Face, The Talmud on the expression of the, 394.

Farrar, Rev. F. W., *Life of Christ*, 24.
Fence round the Law, 10, 442, 466.
Field's edition of Origen's Hexapla, xvii., passim.
Flint, Prof., *Anti-Theistic theories*, 175.
Fools, song of, 382; the fool abroad and at home, 419.
Forgery, unjust charge of, brought against the Book of Koheleth, 111; the Book of Wisdom not guilty of, 61; forgeries of later Jewish writers, 62.
Frankel, *Vorstudien zu der LXX.*, 38.
Freedom of man, 339; controversy concerning, 379, see under *Predestination*.
Fritzsche, *Handb. z. Apokryph. d. a. T.* (on the Book of Jesus the Son of Sirach), 31, 33, 34, 35, 37, 44; *Libri Apoc. Vet. Test.*, 465.
Fürst, Prof. Julius, *Concord.*, passim; *Heb. und Chald. Wörterbuch*, passim; *Gesch. der Bibl. Lit.*, 5; *Kanon des Alt. Test.*, xv., passim.
Future beyond man, the, 387.

Gabirol, see under *Ibn Gabirol*.
Gamaliel I., his advice to the Sanhedrin, 22; supposed dialogue with St. Paul, 23, 24.
Gamaliel II., 15.
"Gaudeamus igitur," the, 435.
Geier, Martin, 224, passim.
Geiger, Dr. Abr., *Urschrift der Bibel*, 239, 348, 411, 464, 472, 482; *Jüdische Zeitschrift*, 264; *Lehrb. d. Mischnah*, 280, 328, 488.
Gemara explained, 456.
Gesenius, W., *Heb. Gram.*, edited by Kautzsch, xvii., passim; *Lehrgeb.*, xviii., passim; *Heb. u. Chald. Wörterbuch*, ed. by Mühlau u. Volck, passim; *Thes. Heb. et Chald.*, passim.
Ginsburg, Dr. C., *Hist. and Crit. Comm. on Eccl.*, xv., passim; *Levita's Massoreth ha-Massoreth*, 9, 96, 247, 475.
Given, Dr., *Truth of Scripture, etc.*, xv., 92, 120.

Goethe, *Westöstlich. Divan*, 226.
Græcus Venetus, edited by Prof. O. v. Gebhardt, 320, passim.
Graetz, Prof. H., *Koheleth erläutert*, xv., passim; *Monatsschrift*, 457, etc.; *Geschichte der Juden*, 440, 458, 467, 482, 485.
Grammar, peculiarities of, in Book of Koheleth, 121, 488.
Grimm, *Handb. z. d. Apokryphen d. alt. Test.* (on Book of Wisdom), 55, 56, 58, 59, 63.
Grotius, in *Critici Sacri*, xiv., passim; denial of the Solomonic authorship of Ecclesiastes, 81.
Gruteri, *Inscriptiones Antiquæ*, 111, 436.
Gwinner, W., *Schopenhauer's Leben*, 153, 160, 166, 173.

Hades, 193, 198.
Hagiographa, 40, 452, see *Kethubim*.
Hahn, H. A., *Comm. on Eccl.*, xv., passim; explanation of Eccl. chap. xii., 253-255.
Hamburger, *Real-Encyclopädie für Bibel u. Talmud*, 401.
Hameram or Hameras, Book of, 470, 471.
Hananya ben Hiskiya, 457.
Hands defiled by the Holy Scriptures, 16 ff., 470 ff.
Haphtarah explained, 463.
Hardy, Spence, *Legends and Theories of the Buddhists*, 173.
v. Hartmann, Eduard, *Philosophie des Unbewussten*, x., 152, 155, 156 ff., 159, 169, 170, 174, 181, 211, 212; *Phænom. des sittl. Bewusstseins*, 155, 161 ff., 207, 209, 210; *Gesch. und Begründung des Pessimismus*, 153; on women, 207; polygamy and monogamy, 212; three stages of illusion, 159; see under *Pessimism*.
Hartmann, Anton. Theod., *Verbindung des alt. Test. mit dem Neuen*, 467, 475.
Hasidim, the, 132.
Haym, 152.
Hegel, 154, 155.

Heidenheim, Dr. M., articles in *Deutsche Vierteljahrsschrift*, 478; on the seventy princes in Book of Numbers, 487.
Heine, 132, 137, 152.
Heinemann, 411.
Hengstenberg, E. W., on *Ecclesiastes*, xv., passim.
Herder, 152.
Herod the Great's interview with Ben Bûta, 19, 20.
Herodian theory of Prof. Graetz, 19.
Herodotus, 151, 347, 349.
Herzfeld, Dr. L., *Coheleth*, xv., passim; *Gesch. d. Volkes Israel*, 10, 478.
Hezekiah, his religious reforms, 3; his college of scribes, 4, 453, 455 ff., 465 ff.
Hilgenfeld's *Zeitschrift*, 354.
Hillel and Shammai, contest between the schools of, on Ecclesiastes, 14, 15, 19, 471 ff.
Hitzig, Prof. Dr. F., on Eccles., xv., passim.
Hoelemann, Prof. Dr., xv., 281, 322, 337, 342, 344, 435, 445.
Hoey, Dr. Wm., Transl. of Oldenberg's work on Buddhism, 182, 183, 184; note on Buddhism, 183, 184.
Hoffmann, Dr. David, *Der oberste Gerichtshof*, 485 ff.
Holy Scriptures defiling the hands, 16.
Holtzmann, *Die apokryph. Bücher* in *Bunsen's Bibelwerk*, 10.
Homer, 471.
Horace, 265, 324, 352, 366, 367, 375, 378, 385, 388, 431, 434, 465.
Hume, 152.
Hyrcanus, 37, 487.

Ibn Ezra, passim.
Ibn Gabirol, 160.
Ibycus, the cranes of, 223.
Illusion, v. Hartmann's three stages of, 159.

Iahaveh, Name, not used in Koheleth, 90, concealment of pronunciation of, 343, 467.

Jahn, *Einleitung*, 124.
Jamnia, First Synod of, 14, 460; Second Synod of, 15, 17, 18, 458.
Janichs, *Vers. Syr.*, xv., 431, 435.
Jerome, 306, 308, 309, 317, 335, 358, passim; on the books of Old Test., 459 ff.
Jewish division of Book of Koheleth, 282; threefold division of the Scriptures, 458 ff.
Jewish race and religion, Schopenhauer's hatred of, 160.
Joel, D., *Aberglaube u. die Stellung des Judenthums*, 4.
Joel, Dr. M., *Blicke in die Religionsgeschichte*, 458, 468.
Johnston, Rev. David, *Treatise on Authorship of Ecclesiastes*, xv., passim.
Josephus, 7, 8, 19, 37, 327, 379, 396, 429, 485; *Against Apion*, 458 ff., 461.
Joshua, Rabbi, on the early death of children, 18.
Jost, 481.
Jouy, on women, 214.
Judgments, the Divine, 399.
Justin Martyr, 315, 437.
Justinus, *de Hist. Philipp. etc.*, 372, 422.
Juvenal, 353, 367, 416, 431.

Kabus, anecdote from the, 227.
Kahana, David, *Heb. Comm. on Eccl.*, 23.
Kaiser, *Koheleth das Collect. d. Davidischen Könige*, xv. passim.
Kalisch, Dr. M. M., *Heb. Grammar*, xviii., passim; *Path and Goal*, 154, 156, 160, 162, 173, 175, 181.
Keri or K'ri explained, 482.
Kethubim explained, 452, 459, 463.
Khayyām, Omar, 168.
Kimchi, R. David, *Michlol*, ed. Fürth, 24, 258, 347, 349, 368, 404, 424, 427, 434, 441.
Kings, Koheleth on the duty of submission to, 218, 398; the oath of allegiance, 396; importance of noble birth in, 220; evil of a child king, 219 ff.; ruin caused by revelry of kings and nobles, 221; subjects not

to cast off allegiance, 222, 397 ; obedience enjoined towards, 398; patience to be exercised in case of an evil monarch, 398; curse not the king, 223.
Kirby and Spence's *Entomology*, 170.
Kleinert, Prof. Paul, *on Ecclesiastes*, xvi., passim.
Knauer, 152.
Knobel, Aug., *Comm. über Koheleth*, xvi., passim.
Koehler, Prof. Dr. Aug., *Nachexilisch. Propheten*, 332.
Koenig, Prof. F. E. *Lehrg. des Heb. Sprache*, xviii., passim.
Koeppen, 182.
Koheleth, Book of, early difficulties felt regarding, 12 ; admitted into Canon previous to the time of Hillel and Shammai, 15 ; its canonicity, 18 ; quoted as canonical at interview between Herod and Ben Bûta, 19 ; by Gamaliel, 22 ff.; prior to Herodian era, 24, 469 ; alleged contradictions in, 12 ; Book of, claimed by Pessimists, 158; Pessimism of, 141 ; name of, a title of Solomon, 82 ; its meaning, 84 ff. ; note on, 279 ff. ; Koheleth and the Koheleth, 101, 439; the Talmud on the Book of, 469.
Krochmal, Nachman, *More Neboche ha-zeman*, 8, 82, 97, 99, 467 ; Articles in *Kerem Chemed*, 477.
Kuenen, Prof., of Leyden, on the Men of the Great Synagogue, 6 ff., 476 ff.; on the Jewish Sanhedrin, 485.

de Lagarde, xvii., 127.
Lane's *Arabic English Lexicon*, 263, 271, 327, 331, 351.
Lassalle, *Arbeiterlesebuch*, 165.
Laws of Nature, uniformity of the, 229.
Leathes, Prof. Stanley, 114.
Leibnitz, 152.
Lepsius, *Königsbuch der alt. Aegypter*, 35.
Leusden, 21.

Levita, Elias, see under *Ginsburg*.
Levy, Dr. J., *Neuheb. u. Chald. Wörterbuch*, passim ; *Chald. Wörterbuch*, passim.
Levy, M.A., Article in *Zeitschrift der D.M.G.* 491.
Lewis, Prof. Tayler, xvi. passim.
Lightfoot, 97.
Literary freedom used by inspired writers, 110 ff., 453.
Liturgy, Jewish, 481, 482.
Locust, various explanations of the, 260 ff.
Long, Rev. James, *Eastern Proverbs and Emblems*, 211.
Longfellow, 91.
Louis XIV. of France, story of, 92.
Lowth, Bishop, *Hebrew Poetry*, 226.
Lucretius, 192, 269, 312.
Luthardt, Prof., *Moderne Weltanschauungen*, 166, 179.
Luther, Martin, *Table Talk*, 80, 81 ; on *Ecclesiastes*, xv. passim ; on women, 214.
Luzzatto, 121, 394, 418.
LXX. (the) version of the Book of Koheleth, 49 ff.; traces of the influence of Aquila on the present text, 50, 51, 52, 338, 392, 406, 440 ; Origen a witness for a LXX. transl. of Koheleth, 50 ; viewed sometimes as a blessing and sometimes as a misfortune, 38, 458 ; probably received sanction of Sanhedrin, 33 ; the seventy translators, 33.
Lyons, the bronze tablets at, 111, 112.

Mailänder, 161.
Maimonides, 17, 127.
Malismus or Miserabilismus, 152.
Malthusian theory, 160.
"Mammon of unrighteousness," 228.
Manilius, 315.
Marriage, see under *Women*, *Polygamy*.
Mary, the Blessed Virgin, 468.
"Masters of Collections," 103.
Megillath Taanith, 458.
Meliorism, 172.
Melito, 464.

"Men of the Great Synagogue," see under *Synagogue*.
"Men of Hezekiah," see under *Hezekiah*.
Menander, 349, 386, 431.
Mendelssohn, see under *Preston*.
Menzel, W., *Naturkunde*, 310.
Merchants recommended to engage in foreign enterprises, 224.
Messianic age, curious views concerning the, 23, 24; passages of Ecclesiastes supposed to be Messianic, 136, 357, 365.
Michaelis, J. D., 224, 236, 442, 476, 493.
Midrash, on Solomon's fall, legend of the, 123; sayings of, 81 ff.; Midrash Rabba, xix., passim.
Mill ceasing, sound of the, 241,
Milton, 343.
Mishna explained, 456.
Missions, results of Christian, 180.
Mnemonics, Masoretic, 447, 453, 282; Renan's suggestion as to, 127.
Monogamy, see under *Polygamy*.
Montfaucon, *Orig. Hexapla*, 392.
Mormonism praised by Schopenhauer, 212.
Mourners, hired, 265.
Mozley, Prof., *Sermons Parochial and Occasional*, 145.
Mühlau and Volck, *Gesenius' Heb. und Chald. Wörterbuch*, passim.
Müller, J., *Masechet Sopherim*, 38, 462, 463.

Nachtigal, 239, passim.
Name, the Sacred, concealment of, 343; not used in the Book of Koheleth, 90.
Nasi, the, 485.
Nathan, the Aboth of Rabbi, see under *Aboth*.
Nestle, E., *Vet. Test. Græci Codd.*, *etc.*, xvii., 51, 235.
Net spread over all living, 413.
Nirvâna, 173, 175, 182 ff.
Noack, *Ursprung des Christenthums*, 58, 59.

Officials, corruption of, 150, 364.
Ointment, 418.
Oldenburg, Prof. Hermann, *Buddha, sein Leben, etc.*, 182.
Olshausen, Justus, *Lehrb. der Heb. Sprache*, xviii., passim.
"One of a thousand," 203.
Onias, 36, 37, 38.
Origen, a witness to the existence of a LXX. transl. of Ecclesiastes, 50; importance of this in relation to the theory of Graetz, 51, 52; *Hexapla*, see under *Field*, *Montfaucon*.
Ovid, 309, 366, 375, 389.

"Pairs," the, 486.
Palestinian winter, the, 270,
Pandera, Son of, 468.
Paradise, the word, 327.
Paul, St., supposed discussion with Gamaliel, 22, 25; advice to Timothy, 325.
Perowne, Dean, *Comm. on the Psalms*, 113; articles *on Ecclesiastes*, xvi., passim.
Persian districts, 329.
Pessimism of the Book of Koheleth, 141; doctrines opposed to modern Pessimism, 164; Pessimism before Schopenhauer, 153; of Schopenhauer and von Hartmann, 152 ff.; Sully on unreasoned, 153; results of, according to Venetianer, 159; conduces to asceticism and suicide, 161; attempt of Taubert to deny this fact, 162 ff.; the Socialistic movement, and, 165; rapid progress of, x., 171; modern science and, 171; points of truth in, 171; resemblance to Buddhism, 172; inferiority to Buddhism as a moral system, 173; Christianity and, 177; selfishness of, 181.
Pessimist philosophers, inconsistencies of, 166.
Pharisees, on freedom and the Divine decrees, the, 379; and Sadducees, 388, 470.
Philo, 7, 56, 461, 464.

Pisistratus of Israelitish literature, the, 4.
Plato, dialogues of, 118 ; parable of the charioteer, 324.
Plautus, 351.
Plinii *Epistolæ*, 105 ; *Nat. Hist.*, 265.
Plumptre, Dean, *Comm. on Ecclesiastes*, xvi., passim ; articles on the writings of Apollos, 58 ; attack on Jewish expositors, 81 ; ideal biography of Koheleth, 133 ff. ; curious interpretation of "the grasshopper," 261.
Pluralis inhumanus, 353.
Plutarch, 263.
Polygamy and monogamy, 170, 212.
Porphyrius, 35.
Prayer on Day of Atonement, 319 ; Jewish forms of, 477, 481 ; unnecessary epithets not to be used in addressing God, 482.
Predestination and man's freedom, 339, 378, 379.
Prejevalsky's *Mongolia*, 181.
Preston, Theodore, *Mendelssohn's Comm on Ecclesiastes, transl.*, etc., xvi., passim.
Propertius, 368.
Prophecy, literal interpretations of, 24.
Prophets, former and later, 459, 464.
Proverbs, principle on which they are framed, 205 ; relating to women, 204 ff.
Psalter of Solomon, 487.
Ptolemy I., Soter, 37 ; Ptolemy II., Philadelphus, 33 ; Ptolemy III., Euergetes I., 34 ; Ptolemy IV., Philopator, 36 ; Ptolemy VI., Philometor, 35 ; Ptolemy VII., Euergetes II., or Physcon, 34, 35.
Publius Syrus, 352, 367, 431, 435.
Purim, Feast of, 473, 474, 484.
Pusey, Dr., *Daniel the Prophet*, 32, 34, 35, 38, 119.

Quarles, *Hieroglyphics of the Life of Man*, 178.

Rab, 343, 359.
Rabbinowicz, 24.

Rashi, 5, 127, 188, 196, passim.
Rau, *Diatribe de Synag. Magna*, 475.
Rawlinson, Prof. George, *Ancient Monarchies*, 150.
Rebilus, C. Caninius, 404
Remedies, Book of, 4.
Renan, Ernest, on name Koheleth, 84 ; on the Epilogue, 99 ; his new work on Ecclesiastes (*l'Ecclésiaste*), and its author, xvi., passim ; 125 ff. ; former opinion as to the date of Ecclesiastes, 117 ; on atheism, 167 ; maintains that Ecclesiastes is nowhere obscene, 265 ; *Le Cantique*, 116 ; *Histoire des Langues Sémitiques*, 117 ; *l'Antechrist*, 117.
Revue de Deux Mondes, 132.
Rhys-Davids, *Buddhism*, 173, 174 ; article in *Contemporary Review*, 175.
Robertson Smith, Prof. W., *Old Test. in the Jewish Church*, vii., 6, 18 ; on "the Men of the Great Synagogue," 5, 476 ff. ; on the Book of Ecclesiastes, 18.
Rosenmüller, *Scholia*, xvi., passim.
Row, Rev. C. A., *The Jesus of the Evangelists*, 176.

Sadducees, see under *Pharisees*.
Sallust, 112.
Samuel, Rabbi, on *Esther*, 17, 473.
Sanhedrin, institution of the, 485.
Schäfer, B., *Neue Untersuchungen über das Buch Koheleth*, xvi.
Schelling, 154, 436.
Schleusner, 68, 383.
Schmidt, Prof. Oscar, *Die Grundlagen der Philosophie des Unbewussten*, 171.
Schmidt, 239, 436, 438, 442.
Schnurrer, *Chronik der Seuchen*, 173.
Schools, see *Synagogue*.
Schopenhauer, Arthur, on Koheleth, 142, 151 ; natural temperament of 153 ; principles of his philosophy, 155 ff. ; abuse of the Jews, 160 ; recommends asceticism, 161 ; strange views of, 162 ; *Welt als Wille und Vorstellung*, 155, 158, 160, 161, 166,

167, 169, 170, 172, 178; *Parerga und Paralipomena*, 166, 169; *Leben*, by Gwinner (see under *Gwinner*); life of, 166; a misanthrope, 166; his pride, 160; inclination towards Buddhism, anecdote of, 173; on women, 207; on polygamy and monogamy, 170, 212; explanation of the passion of love, 168; apology for sodomy, 170.
Schrader, *Keilinschriften und das Alt. Test.*, 390.
Schröder, *Phœnizische Sprache*, 498.
Schürer, *Neutest. Zeitgeschichte*, 37.
Scriptures, threefold division of the Jewish, 39, 40.
Seasons, Hebrew mode of speaking of the, 242.
Seidlitz, Carl von, *Schopenhauer vom medicin. Standpunkte*, 153.
Seneca, 314, 323.
Serpents, dangers from, 422; fable about, 425.
Seven stanzas of Koheleth, the, 272.
Severus, dying words of the Emperor Septimius, 92.
Shakespeare, 68, 248, 367.
Sheol, its various meanings, 193, see *Hades*.
Silence, 342.
Silenus, 350, 381.
Simon the Just, 9, 10, 36, 475; two high priests of that name, 36, 37.
Sirach, see under *Ben Sira*.
Skopzecs, the, 161.
Smith, Eli, 493.
Smith, Dean R. Payne, *Syr. Thes.*, 443.
Smith, W., *Dict. of Greek and Roman Biography*, 223; *Dict. of Bible*, 467, see under *Plumptre*, *Westcott*.
Smith, Prof. W. Robertson, see under *Robertson Smith*.
Snake charmer, 425.
Socialistic movement, the, 165.
Solomon, buildings of, 326; vineyards and gardens of, 327; pools of, 327; attendants, 328; flocks, *id.*; legends of Targum and Talmud, 81, 91; a preacher, 85; Koheleth, a name of,

82; early doubts as to his authorship of Koheleth, 80 ff.; arguments for and against the traditional view, 81–124; no penitential confession of, in the Book of Koheleth, 124; Apocryphal Psalter of, 487.
Song of Songs defiling the hands, 471 ff.
Sophists, the three German, 154.
Sophocles, 164, 350.
Spohler, 369, etc.
Spohn, 343, 369, passim.
Stade, B., *Lehrb. der Heb. Gramm.*, xviii., passim.
Stambul, 429.
Stanley, Dean, *Jewish Church*, 35.
Stern, J., *Die Frau im Talmud*, 205.
Storm theory of Umbreit, the, 249.
Strack, Prof. H. L., article on *Hillel*, 24; *Einleitung in die kanon. Bücher*, xvi; *Kanon des alt. Test.*, 12, 41, 48, 127, 451 ff.; *Proleg. Crit. in V. T.*, 408, 482; edition of *Aboth*, 21, 245, 413.
Suicide, Pessimism conducts to, 161 ff.; prevalence of, 163; see under *Taubert*.
Sully, James, *Pessimism, a History and a Criticism*, 143, 152, 153, 156, 166.
Sun, movements of the, 21.
Sweetness of life, 232.
Swift, Dean, practice of bemoaning day of his birth, 158.
Synagogue, Men of the Great, succeeded the Men of Hezekiah, 5; work with respect to Canon, 5; doubts thrown by Kuenen and Robertson Smith on the tradition concerning, 6; 476 ff.; arguments in favour of its historical truth, 8, 478 ff.; solved difficulties with regard to Book of Ecclesiastes, 11, 13, 465; their words, 466; work as to liturgy, 481; appointed schools, 466, 480, 484; adoption of a new alphabet, 483; lectionary, 484; why no written record of their actions, 484.
Synagogue services, 357, 481.
Synonymes, Arabic and post Biblical words for, 345.

General Index.   515

Taanith, the Megillath, 458.
Tacitus, 111.
Talmud, the, tradition as to the succession of the Sacred Writings, 3; 451, 480, 486; composed of Mishna and Gemara, 456; testimony regarding the Men of the Great Synagogue, 453, 456; and the Old Test. Canon, 451 ff.; the tradition in *Baba Bathra*, 451; on the Sanhedrin, 486; legends concerning Solomon, 91; not committed at first to writing, 456, 482; see under *Ben Sira, Ben Bûta, Synagogue*.
Taubert, *Der Pessimismus und seine Gegner*, 152, 158, 163, 164, 165, 167; on the Book of Koheleth, 164; on suicide, 163; on the everlasting torture of the wicked, 179.
Taylor, Dr. C., *Sayings of the Jewish Fathers*, 9, 10, 22, 239, 245, 413, 475; *Dirge of Koheleth*, xvi., 244, 250, 251, 252, 262, 263, 267, 268.
Temple services, 357.
Tennyson, 273.
Terence, 404.
Theognis, 350, 388, 434.
Thomson, *Land and the Book*, 259.
Thorah explained, 463.
Tosafoth, the, 457.
Tripartite nature of man, 238.
Tyler, Thos., *Comm. on Ecclesiastes*, xvi., passim.

Umbreit, on *Ecclesiastes*, xvii.; storm theory of Eccl. xii., 249, 252.
Unconscious Absolute, 155.
Unconscious Will, 156; see under *Schopenhauer, v. Hartmann*.
Unreasoned Pessimism, 152.

Vaihinger, J. G., on *Ecclesiastes*, xvii., passim.
Venetianer, M., *Schopenhauer als Scholastiker*, 142, 150, 159, 170, 212.
Vineyards, 326.
Virgil, 224, 309, 314, 367, 369.
Volck, see under *Mühlau*.
Voltaire, *Précis de l' Ecclésiaste en vers*, 227.

Vows, 360, 361.

Ward, Samuel, *Life of Faith in Death*, 240.
Wardlaw, R., xiv., xvii.
Wedel, 241.
Westcott, Prof., article on *Ecclesiasticus*, 34; Westcott and Hort's *Greek Test.*, 222, 376.
de Wette, 462, 476.
Wetzstein, Consul J. G., 270, 271.
White, Henry, *Massacre of St. Bartholomew*, 219.
White and black garments, 410.
Will to live, 158, see under *Schopenhauer*; will and representation, 155; will and desire, 157.
Wilson, Andrew, *Abode of Snow*, 182.
Wine, use of, 325.
Winer, 313, *De utriusque Sirach. ætate*, 34; *Bibl. Realwörterbuch*, 35.
Winzer, *Comm. de Koh.* chap. xi. xii, xvii., passim.
Wisdom, the Book of, leaning towards Greek philosophy, 35; composed before time of Philo, 56; probably in reign of Physcon, 57; viewed as inspired, by some of the Fathers, 57; not the production of a Christian Jew, 58; views of Noack and Plumptre, 58, 59; written under name of Solomon, 60; strange denial of this by Rev. D. Johnston, 60; its author not guilty of imposture, 61; his object in assuming the mask of Solomon, 61; favourable conception of character of Solomon, 64; opposed to the freethinkers of Alexandria, 67; value of, 72, 73; allusions to its phraseology in the New Test., 74; a preparative for Christ, 76.
Witsius, 241.
Women, Koheleth's description of evil, 202; degradation of, under Persian rule, 202; a treasure or a snare, 393; Koheleth no hater of, 206; proverbs relating to, 204 ff.; women's rights, 207; low views of, held by Pessimists, 207; one-sided evidence on, 208;

Schopenhauer on women's intellectual powers, 208; on their morality, 207 ff.; von Hartmann on the want of rectitude in, 209; education of, 210; v. Hartmann on the advantage of society of, 211; Venetianer's critique of Schopenhauer's views of, 212; Pessimists on polygamy and monogamy, 170, 212; degradation of, an outcome of Atheism, 213; woman, a help-meet for man, 214.

Woodcutters, liable to dangers, 423.

Wordsworth, Bishop, xvii., passim, 237, 238.

Wright, C. H. H., *Bampton Lectures on Zechariah*, 8, 222, 267, 326, 332, 351, 391, 420, 482.

Wright, Prof. William, *Arabic Grammar*, 250, 264, 279, 281, 320, 433; *Facsimiles of Ancient MSS*, 490.

Wright, Prof. E. Perceval, *Animal Life*, 261.

Wünsche, Dr. Aug., *Die Vorstellungen vom Zustande nach dem Tode nach Apokrypha*, 73; *Bibliotheca Rabbinica*, xix., 206.

Xenophon, 366.

Young, Rev. Loyal, *Comm. on Ecclesiastes*, xvii., 142.

Zirkel, G., *Untersuchungen über den Prediger*, ix., xvii., passim.

Zöckler, Prof. Otto, *Der Prediger*, xvii., passim.

Zuckermandel, 49, 468.

THEOLOGICAL AND OTHER WORKS

BY

CHARLES H. H. WRIGHT, D.D., PH.D.

CRITICAL COMMENTARIES ON THE OLD TESTAMENT.

Zechariah and his Prophecies considered in relation to Modern Criticism, with a Grammatical and Critical Commentary and New Translation. (The Bampton Lectures for 1878.) London: Hodder & Stoughton. 1879. Second Edition. Price 14s.

"No one acquainted with Dr. Wright's earlier publications will need to be told that the Hebrew scholarship of this volume is of a high order. The admirable grammatical commentary at the end constitutes, as some will think, the chief ornament of the book."—*Rev. T. K. Cheyne, M.A., late Fellow and Hebrew Lecturer, Balliol College, Oxford, in the Academy.*

"The writer is a learned man, who has not lightly undertaken his task, and who has completed it with the most conscientious assiduity. Those who wish to be convinced of this must necessarily consult the critical and grammatical commentary, which bears witness on every page of great accuracy and extensive reading."—*Prof. Dr. A. Kuenen, of the University of Leyden, in the Theologisch Tijdschrift.—[Translated.]*

"Ich gebe Ihnen völlig recht dazu, dass Zacharia cap. 9 & sqq. nachexilisch sind ; ich habe die Aussicht der s. g. historisch-kritischen Schule stets für absurd gehalten. Ihre Belesenheit in der deutschen theologischen Literatur ist erstaunlich."—*Prof. Dr. Wellhausen, Univ. of Greifswald, now in Halle.*

"Aus der deutschen Fachliteratur kaum eine Broschüre oder Abhandlung der Zeitschriften von nur einigem Werthe sich hat entgehen lassen. . . [Der kritische und grammatische Commentar] viel schätzbares Material enthält, und den Beweis giebt, dass der Verf. ernstlich bemüht gewesen ist, seiner Arbeit eine solide sprachliche Grundlage zu sichern. . . Dieser Anhang ist reich an belehrenden Einzelheiten."—*Prof. Dr. C. Siegfried, Univ. of Jena, in the Göttingische gelehrte Anzeigen.*

"Der Commentar von Wright über denselben Propheten verräth eingehende Gelehrsamkeit und massvolles Urtheil ; in kritischer Beziehung steht der Verf. auf dem Boden des strengsten Conservativismus."—*Prof. Dr. E. Kautzsch, in Wissenschaftl. Jahresbericht über die Morgenländischen Studien (D.M.G.) im Jahre 1879.*

"We are not prepared to endorse all the conclusions at which the learned author has arrived, but we are bound to testify to the candour and impartiality, as well as to the learning and ability displayed in them. As a sample of honest and accurate criticism, of wide and varied information, of reverent and sober treatment of the divine oracles, this volume may take its stand amongst the best specimens of modern Biblical investigation."—*The Right Rev. W. Pakenham Walsh, D.D., Bishop of Ossory, in the Churchman's Shilling Magazine.*

"One of the most important contributions to the study of Scripture which has appeared in England for many years. . . . Mr. Wright is well able to hold his own against any of the German critics. His book shows wide and accurate reading in Biblical criticism. He is evidently a man of sound and independent judgment. He never substitutes vituperation for argument, or evades for one moment the difficulties he undertakes to meet. . . . After reading his book through with great care, we have scarcely found a word to which a Catholic need object."—*Rev. W. E. Addis, in the Dublin Review* [Roman Catholic].

"Characterised by sound scholarship, wide erudition, and sober judgment—qualities very necessary in handling the apocalyptic and eschatalogical visions of Zechariah. It is indispensable to the student of this obscure and difficult Prophet."—*Rev. Samuel Cox, D.D., in The Expositor.*

"The Bampton Lecturer for 1878 has produced an elaborate and learned commentary on Zechariah. There is no doubt as to his candour and erudition."—*Westminster Review.*

"By far the most instructive, critical, and most scholarly commentary yet published by any English commentator on the subject."—*English Churchman.*

"Dr. Wright has produced a very valuable and exhaustive monograph. He has furnished us with such an abundance of sound philological criticism in his noble and scholarly book, that we heartily recommend it to all earnest students of Holy Scripture."—*Ecclesiastical Gazette* (*England*).

"It is incomparably the best commentary hitherto published by an English author on Zechariah. It is the fruit of great industry and sound scholarship, of wide erudition combined with sober judgment."—*British Quarterly Review.*

"We congratulate the disestablished Church of Ireland in possessing so learned, so sober, and so acute a scholar."—*John Bull.*

"Its scholarship is of a high order, the ability manifested is most conspicuous; the research is so thorough that nothing of importance seems to have escaped the author, and the tone and temper shown throughout are such as is rarely seen in the heated atmosphere of theological warfare."—*Daily Review.*

"It is on the whole scholarly, reasonable, strong. It will quicken and guide exegetical study. It will teach men to look with boldness and composure on questions of criticism; it sets an example of respect and Christian charity towards opponents, and on all these points claims grateful acknowledgment from Biblical scholars."—*Presbyterian Review* (*New York*).

The Book of Genesis in Hebrew, with a critically-revised Text,
Various Readings, and Grammatical and Critical Notes. London and Edinburgh: Williams & Norgate. 1859. Price 5s.

"This work bears satisfactory evidence of most commendable diligence and accurate scholarship. It supplies a defect much felt in our English exegetical literature, and will prove a very useful manual, even to advanced scholars."—*English Churchman.*

"No one can fail to admit that this work is a most valuable contribution to a department of literature in which the English have not excelled. Its eminently scholarly character is sure to recommend it."—*Clerical Journal.*

"We consider the book highly creditable to the learning and the judgment of the editor, and we think he has conferred a great benefit on Hebrew students by its publication."—*Literary Churchman*

The Book of Ruth in Hebrew, with a critically-revised Text,
Various Readings, including a new collation of twenty-eight Hebrew MSS. (most of them not previously collated), and a Grammatical and Critical Commentary, to which is appended the Chaldee Targum, with various Readings, and a Chaldee Glossary. London: Williams & Norgate. Leipzig: L. Denicke. 1864. Price 7s. 6d.

"The work is full and complete. It is highly creditable to the learning, talents, and philological attainments of Mr. Wright. . . . Mr. Wright has given the Targum, with various readings, and an excellent Glossary to it, which will introduce the student to an acquaintance with Chaldee. The Critical and Grammatical Commentary on the Hebrew text is thorough and clear, omitting nothing that can throw light on the construction and meaning of the words. . . . The editor has executed his design in a manner that deserves the thanks of every student of Hebrew; and we trust that he will seen the reward of his labour in the use of his volume by junior classes in the Universities. Professors could not do better than make it a text book. It is admirably fitted for that purpose."—*Athenæum.*

"Beide Werke (Genesis und Ruth) sind die Früchte eines eisernen Fleisses und rühmliche Proben einer auf der Höhe der Wissenschaft stehenden Sprachkenntniss."—*Prof. Dr. Franz Delitzsch, University of Leipzig.*

"Mr. Wright's works on Genesis and Ruth display not only exact and extensive scholarship, but an independence and soundness of judgment eminently calculated to advance Biblical researches, and prove the author's thorough competence for the philological, historical, and critical treatment of the Scriptures."—*Dr. M. M. Kalisch, London.*

"Proben von ausgedehnter und gründlicher Kenntniss nicht nur des Hebräischen sondern auch der verwandten Sprachen und von kritischer Genauigkeit in Behandlung des Textes der heiligen Schrift."—*Prof. Dr. H. L. Fleischer, University of Leipzig.*

"In diesen beiden Schriften zeigt sich der Verfasser als ein sehr gründlicher Kenner der hebräischen Sprache und der andern semitischen Sprachen, und als ein Gelehrter der sich durch seine Akribie, Gewissenhaftigkeit, Gründlichkeit und volle Vertrautheit mit dem kritisch-exegetischen Apparat, und der neuen exeget. Literatur besonders auszeichnet."—*Prof. Dr. Chwolson, University of St. Petersburg.*

"I have already expressed my high opinion of your work on Genesis, but your recent edition of Ruth ought to go even more decidedly in your favour. It is a work of pure Hebrew scholarship, in which exact knowledge, critical acumen, and diligent research have been brought to bear upon the text of Ruth, and in which all those niceties which the commentator may pass over with a light have been carefully treated."—*The Very Rev. R. Payne Smith, D.D., Dean of Canterbury, late Regius Professor of Divinity, Oxford.*

"It displays an estimable knowledge of Hebrew and the Oriental languages, a punctilious accuracy in grammatical and critical matters, and an uncommon acquaintance with the literature of the subject, the German included."—*The late Prof. Dr. Hermann Hupfeld, University of Halle.*

"Durch diese Arbeiten [upon *Genesis* and *Ruth*] hat er nicht nur seine Gelehrsamkeit und wissenschaftliche Genauigkeit documentirt, sondern auch mit vielem Geschick die dem Standpunkte des Hebrew Student angemessene Methode befolgt."—*The late Prof. Dr. Rödiger, University of Berlin.*

The Book of Koheleth, commonly called Ecclesiastes, considered
in relation to Modern Criticism and to the Doctrines of Modern Pessimism, with a Critical and Grammatical Commentary and a Revised Translation. (The Donnellan Lectures for 1880-1.) London: Hodder and Stoughton. 1883. Price 12s.

"Ich fühle mich gedrängt Ihnen einmal in einem besonderen Schreiben auszusprechen, dass die Lektüre Ihres so gelehrten und von so gründlicher Kenntnis auch der deutschen Literatur zeugenden Buches mir von grossem Interesse ist, und dass dasselbe nach meiner Ueberzeugung bald einen geachteten Platz unter den Koheleth behandelnden Schriften einnehmen wird. Besonders gelungen erscheinen mir Ihre Erörterungen über den Unterschied des modernen und des biblischen Pessimismus."—*Prof. Dr. H. L. Strack, Univ. of Berlin.*

"Bei mancher Differenz in Einzelheiten bin ich lebhaft erfreut hinsichtlich der Hauptprobleme betreffend Gesammtauffassung, zeitliche Lage, ethischen Standpunct des Buches die Resultate Ihrer Studien so vielfach mit den meinigen convergirend zu finden. . . . Es hat mich überrascht und mit aufrichtiger Anerkennung erfüllt bei einem durch Ort und Sprache den Bewegungen der wissenschaftlichen Theologie in Deutschland so fern gerückten Gelehrten durchgängig so deutliche Specimina einer eingehenden Beschäftigung und genauen Bekanntschaft mit denselben zu finden; eine so gerechte Würdigung ihrer Erwerbungen, eine so wissenschaftlich gehaltene Ablehnung ihrer Irrthümer."—*Professor Dr. Paul Kleinert, Univ. of Berlin.*

MISCELLANEOUS WORKS.

A Grammar of the Modern Irish Language, designed for the use of the Classes in the University of Dublin. Second edition, revised and enlarged. London: Williams & Norgate. Dublin: Hodges, Foster & Figgis. 1860.

The Fatherhood of God, and its relation to the Person and Work of Christ, and the Operations of the Holy Spirit. Edinburgh: T. & T. Clark. London: Hamilton, Adams & Co. 1867. Price 5s.

"As a writer, the author is most vigorous, and as an interpreter of Scripture he is exceedingly cautious lest he should hang a false inference on any special text."—*Record*.

"A very clear and readable treatise. . . We cannot but respect the reverent, judicious, and broad spirit in which his distinctive views are put forth."—*Bibliotheca Sacra* (Boston, U.S.A.).

"Plus conciliante que polémique. M. Wright, qui s'est déjà fait connaître par les travaux d'érudition appartient dans l'Eglise anglicane au parti évangelique. . . . Sa tractation se recommande par un mérite qui lui est propre, la grande clarté exégétique qu'il met dans la discussion des points controversés."—*Bulletin Théologique* (Paris.)

Memoir of John Lovering Cooke, formerly Gunner in the Royal Artillery, and late Lay Agent of the British Sailors' Institute, Boulogne; with a Sketch of the Indian Mutiny of 1857-8, up to the final capture of Lucknow. London: James Nisbet & Co., 21, Berners Street. Second Edition, with Illustrations, 1878. Price 3s.

"This little book should be read by mothers and fathers whose sons have 'gone for soldiers.' It will show them what a private soldier can do for the honour and glory of God."—*Sunday at Home* (Article, May, 1874, p. 312).

"His memoir is interestingly written; and while no one can read his book without pleasure and advantage, it is especially suitable for barrack club-rooms, and for places where soldiers or sailors congregate."—*London Quarterly Review*.

Dublin University Reform and the Divinity School.—Four Pamphlets, with a General Preface and Appendix. Dublin: Hodges, Foster & Figgis. 1879. Cloth. Price 2s.

The Divinity School and the Divinity Degrees of the University of Dublin. Dublin: Hodges, Foster & Figgis. 1880. Price 6d.

WORKS IN PREPARATION.

The Book of Daniel, with a Commentary, Critical, Exegetical, and Homiletical, forming a volume of "The Pulpit Commentary." C. Kegan Paul & Co. London.

The Megillath Antiochos, a Jewish Apocryphon; with the Chaldee Text in both the Western and Babylonian punctuation, together with Hebrew and Arabic translations. Edited from MSS., with Various Readings, an English translation, and Critical notes.

Milton Keynes UK
Ingram Content Group UK Ltd.
UKHW040809120324
439192UK00005B/391